THE COLLECTED PAPERS

OF FREDERIC C. LANE

Frederic Chapin Lane

VENICE AND HISTORY

THE COLLECTED PAPERS
OF FREDERIC C. LANE

Edited by
A Committee of Colleagues
and Former Students

Foreword by
Fernand Braudel

THE JOHNS HOPKINS PRESS
BALTIMORE

Foreword

I T IS a pleasure, an honor, and also a quite difficult task to introduce adequately this substantial volume offered to Frederic
Chapin Lane by his friends, colleagues, students, and admirers.

It is a pleasure because Frederic Lane has always known the art
of friendship, without which, I believe, a historian is not worthy of
his name. To love the men of the past is the historian's first duty.
Our colleague has performed this with good grace, but he begins
by loving also the men of his time, including his fellow historians
who gladly reciprocate his always considerate friendliness and re-
joice in each of his successes and the honors accorded him. Show
the least courtesy to Frederic Lane; he will succeed in returning it
a hundredfold. You and he are working at the same time in the
archives of Venice, which are not always in the best of order. One
day you will receive a note from him: See in the *busta,* of such and
such number, the papers of Contarini del Zaffo, 1518–88, with
numerous freight contracts. This kind of generosity is not characteristic of all historians.

My task is also an honor because Frederic Lane is one of the best
scholars of his vast country and one of the most competent
economic historians in the world, whom, with Earl J. Hamilton
and John U. Nef, we place in top rank among the glories of
Chicago and Johns Hopkins. Indeed, apart from the bond of
friendship that links me with Frederic Lane, I find my only personal qualification to write these prefatory lines in the desire,

implicit, unless I am mistaken, in the courteous invitation of the committee of editors, to signalize the international dimensions of our colleague's thought and curiosity. He is indeed the son of New England, which he carries in his heart, with its roomy country houses, with its sweeping coastal landscapes, with its fiery autumn foliage. But he is no less at home in Paris and even more so in Venice, of which he would surely be an honorary citizen if this title were bestowed today as in the past. I think, then, that it is this international character of the work and mind of Frederic Lane that has given a French historian the honor of writing the first pages of this historical collection.

But I am left with the very difficult task of presenting appropriately the lucidity and vitality of Frederic Lane's thought, for above all that is the task, since his friends have had the excellent idea of paying him homage by collecting his scattered articles ranging from the study published in French in the *Revue historique de Bordeaux* in 1924 to his presidential address before the American Historical Association in 1965. From Bordeaux to the Italian origins of modern republicanism, from the France of Colbert to the Venice of the *Monte Vecchio:* one clearly sees that Frederic Lane belongs not only to the United States but also to the old continent facing it, from the Atlantic to the Mediterranean. These are marvelous, classic essays, which all historians will find it a pleasure to reread attentively. Certain of them are celebrated and have been read and reread. The best in my opinion is "The Mediterranean Spice Trade," published in the *American Historical Review* (1940), where one could find, long before I turned them to my own account, certain essential theses of my book of 1949 on the collective destiny of the Mediterranean after the great discoveries. No, the "Interior Sea" had not declined toward the 1560's, long after the voyage of Christopher Columbus and the circumnavigation of Africa by Vasco da Gama, for the seaport of the old commerce of the Levant remained open for profits in pepper and precious spices, and these commodities were arriving at Alexandria in Egypt by the Red Sea and overland caravans in as great, if not greater, abundance as on the wharves of Lisbon.

I

The difficulty is not to grasp the talent of Frederic Lane, easily discernible in a given page, article, or book, but to distinguish the general line that his thought has traced. Adopting this point of view one may well feel great hesitation. Take, for example, his first large book, *Venetian Ships and Shipbuilders of the Renaissance* (1934) —which is about to appear at last in a French translation after more than thirty years. This translation recently gave me occasion to reread the book, and I can state that it has retained its evident youth, without a wrinkle, though these last thirty years have counted heavily in the history of men and in historiography. The French edition will be weighted with new facts, the fruit of the author's more recent researches in Venice. But the book will not be transformed, because, I believe, there is no essential difference or contradiction between Frederic Lane's first manner of writing in 1924 or 1934 and the most recent in 1964. I am here referring to that skillful and all but cunning article (because great cunning is necessary when one is at grips with metrology) : "Tonnages, Medieval and Modern," published in the *Economic History Review* (1964).

For this continuity in Lane's work let me offer some explanations that seem plausible. First of all, I think that Frederic Lane, scrupulous, and difficult to satisfy even with his most evident successes, quickly attained his own perfection almost as soon as he began to play the game. None of us can find it hard to convince himself at once that his perfectionism is related to his training, his studies, and his mind. It is related even more closely, if I am not mistaken, to his character and to his rigorous conception of his craft and the pleasure of being a historian. Because he finds his craft a decided pleasure, he savors it as a vintage wine or a rare dish that he knows how to enjoy as a man and a citizen of the world.

He has always loved work carried on patiently and carefully controlled. He has never written until, in his judgment, his research was completely achieved or, as in the case of his valuable work *Ships for Victory* (1951), when he believed that it was his duty to bring it to an end. Given his capacity for work, he would have published two or three times as much as he has. He could also have attacked the immense subjects for which his sympathy is evident, but these big subjects he has touched in rapid and precise fashion, as if present events made it a duty or offered an opportunity to do so. In my view and without doubt in the view of many historians, the merit of the present collection will be to illuminate this second aspect of the greatness of Frederic Lane, which is much less known than the precision of his historical knowledge. See him, for example, on the grand routes of historical explanation in his brief speech before teachers of history and social science, "Why Begin at the Beginning?" (1937), or in his book *The World's History,* which he published in collaboration with Eric F. Goldman and Erling Hunt. Before December 1941, he completed an article that I find remarkable, "The Economic Meaning of War and Protection" (published in 1942), which takes us on a long voyage from the Venetian twelfth to the American nineteenth century, raising the question of the cost of protection and security in economic history and the history of economic enterprises. We applaud him for having stated his opinion, in "The Social Sciences and the Humanities" (1948), that a present-day humanism is necessary; for having opened up broader horizons with his "Force and Enterprise in the Creation of Oceanic Commerce" (1950), "Consumption and Economic Change" (1955), and "Some Heirs of Gustav von Schmoller" (1956); or, again, for showing the same desire to keep in touch with the present in his "Economic Consequences of Organized Violence" (1958). But it is necessary to have talked or engaged in discussion with him, pushing him to his last defenses, to know the real breadth of thought that he has deliberately restrained in his writings, with the love that a good workman has for perfect work. One evening, in the company of Alberto Tenenti, without really intending to do so, I obliged him to traverse immense distances. We were thinking of the dramatic situation of Islam, ever wedged betwen the diverse civilizations of the Old World, the West, Black Africa, India, and China—in a middle position that produced Islam's grandeur. At the end of the sixteenth century the hard and combative heart of Islam was embodied in Ottoman Turkey. It was engaged in struggles that extended from North Africa, the Mediterranean, and the Balkans, through Persia to the waters of the Indian Ocean and the outlet of the Red Sea. To all these scattered conflicts the immense body of Ottoman Turkey gave unity, coherence, and collective meaning. "That was the first world war in history," concluded our colleague; and surely that comparison casts a light of its own on the Turkish world whose endeavors and achievements are so often misunderstood. May I also say that in the meetings of our International Committee of Economic Historians Frederic Lane is the most skillful among us in choosing the big themes for discussion? This breadth of vision renders only more evident the firmness with which he has given his works precise limits, which he rarely permits himself to cross.

II

Ordinarily Frederic Lane does not allow himself to yield to the temptations of immense voyages. Certainly he possesses an accomplished knowledge of the methods and problems of economics, but the historian in him remains vigilant. Certainly he handles figures as does Earl J. Hamilton, but, unlike his colleague and friend, he does not besiege the entire history of the world with their crowded columns. His taste for economics and calculation is satisfied within more restricted areas, which he seeks to know in minute detail. His astonishing learning could also lead him into philosophic flights, which delight that earnest investigator John U. Nef, the more because everything in the past that Lane approaches and evokes concerns him. He puts into it his own consciousness and heart and plunges into it somewhat like a wiser, but not less restless, Michelet. I have the feeling that for Frederic Lane each thing must come in its own time and at its hour, without crowding other things, and that his real pleasure is in disentangling the problem that he has chosen, and chosen with care, then in trying to see into it clearly, even if this entails beginning the research and discussion all over again. It is a question of patience and integrity.

Everything presents itself to him as if historical truth pressed on, or pierced, a particular point of our knowledge, or rather of our ignorance—a point chosen with care and for reasons of high strategy. As for Venice, after so many years of research in an exciting field, the interest of which has yet to be fully recognized, he will be able to write (and may we hope at an early date!) an economic history of the city of the doges. Now, note his successive steps: the first (1932) concerns the manufacture of cables and ropes and the hemp trade; the second (1933), the navigation of Venetian ships; the third (1934), naval architecture at Venice. In this same year, 1934, he completed the large book on Venetian ships and shipbuilders of the Renaissance that established his reputation; but this book was also part of a concrete problem, that of the Arsenal at Venice. If the book circled the world, this was because the round ships and galleys of the *signoria* plied the Mediterranean and the northern seas and because shipbuilding was understood on the scale of a multiple Europe. Next, in 1937, deposit banks at Venice from 1496 to 1533 were investigated.

But even the very fine book on *Andrea Barbarigo, Merchant of Venice* (1944) takes off from a modest ambition. What is this small embrasure opened by the story of one individual in the commercial history of a great city? "Andrea Barbarigo," Lane writes at the beginning of his book, "was not an important figure in the history of the Venetian Republic. He had no more influence on the course of events in his time than did thousands of other Venetians." Yes, but the adventure of this man has the advantage of being known at close hand, thanks to his extensive bookkeeping, which reveals a wide experience of commercial practices. So, the "small embrasure" turns out to be excellent, and indeed, while we wait for other possible discoveries, it provides, as the late Gino Luzzatto thought, one of the best means for understanding the business life of Venice. Not Andrea Barbarigo himself, but his bookkeeping and his family are under scrutiny, and beyond that the broad landscape of the world of exchange. Nor is it from mere solicitude for erudition that the history of the merchant's descendants is followed closely. In 1496, Nicolò Barbarigo made a will in which he advised his heirs to extricate themselves from commercial affairs, which were declining, and to preserve their money by investing it in state funds and land. Actually this was bad advice, for the family lands in the area of Verona were to be confiscated by the enemy in 1516, and Venice was obliged to suspend payment of interest on its bonds.

In an article written for the studies dedicated to Gino Luzzatto in 1949, Lane returned to the business system and maneuvers of Andrea Barbarigo and several other merchants; more precisely, to the rapidity of capital turnover. What are the long and short terms—those that immobilize capital for long periods and those that restore with relative speed the sums invested and enlarged by profits? Above all, the rapid trade was in cotton, carried by the large ships of the *mude* of Syria. But this article is reprinted here where the reader can acquaint himself with it at leisure.

One can distinguish by these examples and many others the way in which Frederic Lane proceeds: establish a route of which you are sure, then advance as far as possible to discover the underlying reasons for traffic, rhythm, exchange, and the social and institutional relations involved in the life of the businessman. Nothing is spared to make the route sure and to mark it with care. This is the trait that is shown with an abundance of excellent detail in the study of "The Merchant Marine of the Venetian Republic" (1962), reproduced in the present volume. The essential in these retrospective calculations is the author's care not to be deceived by appearances or the facility of statistical abstractions. Since we are better informed about large ships, "we can be tempted to deduce that the changes intervening in the importance of this category of ships were indicative of an increase or decrease of global traffic, thus taking the part for the whole," and Frederic Lane adds, as if with a smile, "the part being better known than the whole." I like this care brought to an evaluation, and even the tabulations given and given over again in the appendix, and repeated whenever needed in the body of the text.

III

Finally, one must take into account a choice, an intellectual procedure, a style, adopted in full knowledge of what it involves. This style is explicable, as I have said, from the first within a framework of intellectual prudence that is deliberately rigorous. It is also to be explained by a curiosity about the specific that is proper to a historian, and, perhaps, in the final accounting, by a special passion for Venice, which Frederic Lane felt very early in his career. Like myself, but to a greater degree, he has found in the great city the homeland of his delights and labors: the morning spent at the Archivio dei Frari, then, as soon as possible, the afternoon at the Museo Correr or the Marciana, then the evening as well at the hospitable and tranquil Stampaglia Querini. But Venice is exacting. From the fifteenth to the sixteenth centuries its archives are not in order. Some destruction has been carried out, at times systematically. If the political papers are in place, the economic documents are incomplete. It is necessary to reconstruct them, to imagine, to stitch them together. What admirable patience of labor is required! But who would experience the least discomfort in losing himself for months at a time in these tasks and in the past and present of this unique city, far from the noises of the modern world? To be lost there!—but never for a single moment with the feeling of being imprisoned, since in Venice the smallest document from the fifteenth or sixteenth century speaks on a world scale. Venice dominated the "Interior Sea" as New York dominates the western world today.

Perhaps Venice has to some extent made Frederic Lane the historian that he is, unless he chose Venice precisely because of what he was. The fact is that since Venice was one of those points in the fifteenth and sixteenth centuries where any precise investigation is profitable, it is worth while to examine and re-examine the evidence it provides because the conclusions to be drawn are of immense significance.

The lesson that Frederic Lane teaches others, entirely by virtue of having imposed it on himself, is that of the irreplaceable value of painstaking work and of honest and exact scholarship. This is an old lesson, which of course will not surprise us since it is ever that of historical scholarship, but here it is applied to an object quite out of the ordinary. In passing from politics to include economics, history has made great progress. It has necessarily learned to transcend chronology and traditional methods of solving problems, to change its measurements, to take a different view of perspectives; but basic work on the sources remains as indispensable as in other fields, and perhaps even more so. Frederic Lane, who never ceases to ask himself questions about the useful bearing of historical perspectives on the economy of the present, is not among those who wish to burn up the road and to deliver hasty judgments. His admirable integrity guards him from this at each step of his way. Work with a magnifying glass: then it is permitted to lift up one's sight. Whenever he chooses to do this, the sympathetic and attentive eyes of Frederic Lane see far into the distance.

Fernand Braudel
Professeur au Collège de France
Président, École Pratique des Hautes Études,
Sciences Économiques et Sociales

Biographical Note

❀

FREDERIC CHAPIN LANE was born in Lansing, Michigan, in 1900, while his father, Alfred Church Lane, was State Geologist of Michigan. His father was Boston-born and a Harvard graduate; his mother, Susanne Lauriat, was daughter of the Charles E. Lauriat who made the Boston bookshop of Lauriat and Estes almost as much a literary club as it was a bookstore.

By the time that Frederic Lane was ready for grammar school the family had settled for life in Cambridge, Massachusetts. His father had become a professor at Tufts College, where he achieved a national reputation as a geologist. He had a relish for wide-ranging discussions with his students. Young Lane shared his father's delight in intellectual sparring matches, with an effect discernible in his lifelong penchant for clearly reasoned discussion.

After graduation from the Cambridge High and Latin School, Lane entered Cornell, where he received his B.A. degree in 1921. After hitch-hiking across the United States that summer, he spent a year at Tufts, where, under Professor A. I. Angers, he wrote an M.A. thesis that fixed his attention on Venice as a subject of study. Returning to Cornell in 1922 to continue postgraduate work, he undertook a study of the strikes that broke out at Lyon during the Reformation. Though he prepared this study under the direction of Preserved Smith, he also came under the intellectual influence of George Lincoln Burr, William I. Hull, Carl Becker, and—with perhaps the greatest impact on his methods and interests as a scholar—William L. Westermann.

Having won a scholarship for study abroad. Lane found himself, as much by chance as by choice, at the University of Bordeaux (1923–

24). At Bordeaux he prepared the studies published as "Colbert et le commerce de Bordeaux" and "L'Église reformée de Belges de 1660 à 1670." In the fall term of 1924 he went to Vienna and studied economic history under Alfons Dopsch.

Returning to America, he decided to seek his doctorate at Harvard, where in 1925 he was appointed assistant to Robert H. Lord. Charles Homer Haskins stands out among the teachers at Harvard whom he remembers for their influence on his thought about historiography, but his growing interest in economic history brought him under the direction of Roland P. Usher, who suggested that he investigate the diaries of Sanuto, the sixteenth-century Venetian. Interest in the commercial revolution of the fifteenth and sixteenth centuries now combined with Lane's interest in Venice to define the area of his research as an independent scholar.

In 1926 he was appointed instructor at the University of Minnesota, where he found a lifelong mentor and friend in Guy Stanton Ford. In the spring of 1927, he received an appointment from Harvard as Kirkland Fellow, and that fall he went to Venice and devoted himself to the archival researches on which he based *Venetian Ships and Ship-builders of the Renaissance*. He and his bride, Harriet Whitney Mirick, set up housekeeping under the same roof with an Italian family. Henceforth Venice was Lane's home city in Italy.

In 1928 he was appointed instructor in history at the Johns Hopkins University. Submitting the draft of his book on Venetian shipping as a dissertation, he received his Ph.D. degree from Harvard in 1930.

At Hopkins, as the one surviving member of a department of history that had been dismantled by death and retirement, he soon became a vigorously influential member of a new department. Because he was convinced that a thorough grounding in history was an essential not being provided by the undergraduate "survey" courses then in vogue, Lane at first devoted himself to a basic two-year course entitled the "History of Occidental Civilization," which became one of his notable achievements. But he was soon drawn into all the activities of a shorthanded department. Small but ambitious, it had to depend on versatility and on the opportunity that the Johns Hopkins afforded to draw on the resources of other departments. The vigor and variety of Lane's interests, in economic history, the Renaissance, the history of civilization, and historiography, made him an invaluable associate in the effort of the department to advance on a broad front, and his influence was felt in all the department's activities. The graduate students whom he chose as his assistants in the occidental civilization course regarded themselves as especially privileged not only in learning history but in receiving from Lane a thorough training in the teaching of it. His critical penetration and vigor made him a highly valued associate in the advanced seminar, into which members of other departments were drawn to assist the faculty and senior students of the department of history in developing and criticizing dissertations of candidates for the Ph.D. Through this seminar and the History of Ideas Club Lane played a leading role in the department's participation in the history of ideas movement, under Arthur O. Lovejoy's leadership, which was then running at full tide in the School of Higher Studies of the university. A literary by-product of the "History of Occidental Civilization" was *The World's History* (1947), a textbook for secondary schools, which he wrote with Erling M. Hunt and Eric F. Goldman; Lane had discovered Goldman's talent while he was an undergraduate, and he later associated with him in conducting the course.

Venetian Ships and Shipbuilders of the Renaissance was published in 1934. Returning to Venice on leave in 1939, he engaged in his researches on *Andrea Barbarigo, Merchant of Venice*. In 1946, on another leave of absence, he made an excursion into the history of the United States in World War II and wrote *Ships for Victory,* as historian of the U.S. Maritime Commission.

Lane had become associate professor at Hopkins in 1935 and professor in 1946.

In the period after World War II, his activities and appointments outside the university multiplied. For some years an active member of the Economic History Association, he was editor of its journal from 1943 to 1951, and he became a member of the Executive Committee of the International Commission of Economic History. In 1951 he accepted appointment as assistant director of the Division of Social Sciences of the Rockefeller Foundation. His work in this capacity kept him in Europe, with headquarters in Paris, from June 1951 until the summer of 1953. During this period he served as foreign correspondent of the Istituto Veneto di scienze, lettere ed arti. In the spring term of 1956 he taught at Harvard as visiting professor. In 1959 and again in 1961, during the spring terms and summer vacations, he went back to Italy on a Guggenheim fellowship to continue researches directed toward a more extensive work on the history of Venice. In 1959 he read a paper at the Colloque d'histoire maritime in Paris, and in 1961 he took part in the International Economic History Conference held at Bellagio under the auspices of the Rockefeller Foundation.

Meantime, traveling in a very different type of ship, he had retraced the Levantine voyages of the Venetian galleys.

In the period after the war honors also multiplied. In 1958 Lane became president of the Economic History Association; in 1955, he was elected to membership in the American Philosophical Society, in 1961 he was appointed honorary member of the Deputazione di Storia Patria per la Venezia and, in 1964, fellow of the Medieval Academy and a member of the Academy of Arts and Sciences. In December 1963 he was elected vice-president and in 1964 president of the American Historical Association. In 1965 he was named *Conseiller, Commission d'Histoire Maritime,* and also elected President of the International Economic History Association.

Contents

xix

SHIPS AND SHIPPING

INDUSTRY AND GOVERNMENT

Part Two: EUROPEAN COMMERCE

Part Three: THE COST OF PROTECTION

Part One

VENICE

VENICE IN THE ROUTES
OF WORLD TRADE

1

Venetian Shipping during the Commercial Revolution*

IT is generally thought that dislocation of the spice trade by the Portuguese discovery of the Cape route to India crippled Venetian commerce. A study of Venetian shipping fails to justify that notion. The effects of the Portuguese discovery upon Venetian trade have frequently been misrepresented because of a failure to distinguish between long ships and round ships. In most discussions of Venetian commerce attention has been concentrated on the merchant galleys,[1] a type of long ship built especially for the transport of spices and other precious wares. But throughout both the fifteenth and sixteenth centuries round sailing ships formed a larger part of the merchant marine. During these centuries the relative usefulness of the two types shifted, however, because of technical changes in rigging and armament. A recognition of the distinct economic functions of these different types of ships in the fifteenth century, and of their changed status in the sixteenth, is the key to the history of Venetian shipping in the period of the Commercial Revolution. When viewed as a whole the Venetian merchant marine employed in international commerce appears not to have declined, but actually to have grown in cargo-carrying capacity during the sixteenth century.

The differences between the large round ship and the long ship or galley were obvious to the eye.[2] Round ships were high and wide and

---

* From *American Historical Review*. XXXVIII (1933) , 219–39. (By permission.)

[1] For example, Alethea Wiel, *The Navy of Venice* (London, 1910), pp. 314 ff.

[2] Detailed descriptions of the variations of both types are given by Enrico Alberto d'Albertis, "Le Costruzioni Navali e l'Arte della Navigazione al Tempo di Cristoforo

dependent entirely on sails; long ships were low and narrow and equipped with oars. Round ships were built for stability and for heavy cargoes; long ships for speed and for fighting. The round ship was primarily a merchantman, the long ship was primarily a warship, and although some round ships were built especially for war, and some long ships were designed for trade, yet even so their functions were distinct in commerce and in war. The long ship designed for trade carried light precious cargoes; the round ship, heavy cargoes.

The organization of the maritime trade of Venice in the fifteenth century was based on this difference in the commercial functions of the two types. A monopoly of the transport of spices and some other light wares from the Levant to Venice had been given by law to the great galleys, a special type of long ship.[3] Voyages by these ships westward were organized for exporting spices and other precious merchandise. Besides the well-known "Flemish" galleys, which later did at least as much business in England as in Flanders and called at Lisbon and various Mediterranean ports, there were two other fleets of great merchant galleys sent westward. The galleys of Aigues-Mortes served the northern shore of the western Mediterranean, the galleys of Barbary visited its southern shore, and both fleets called at Sicilian and Spanish ports.[4]

These great galleys or merchant galleys were not particularly large

---

Colombo," in *Raccolta di Documenti e Studi pub. dalla R. Commissione Colombiana* (Rome, 1893), I., pt. 4; by John Forsyth Meigs, *The Story of the Seaman* (London, Philadelphia, 1924); and by A. Jal, *Archeologie Navale* (Paris, 1840).

[3] Archivio di Stato di Venezia (cited hereafter as A. S. V.), Ufficiali al Cattaver, busta 1, cap. 1, ff. 65–72. These regulations proceeded from the principle that "light goods" could be brought to Venice from the Levant only by "armed ships," later interpreted to mean the great galleys, the merchant galleys of the state. Exemptions were then made for specific wares and specific times although many wares permitted to come on "unarmed ships" (round ships) were obliged to pay freight to the galleys. But spices, even if loaded in the Levant by other ships, could not complete the transit to Venice, between 1435 and 1514, except in the merchant galleys, or, if the galleys were filled, in a selected ship which traveled with the galleys under the same command to carry the surplus. Such ships, when their cargo is mentioned, carried but a negligible amount. See references below on spice imports, and A. S. V., Senato Misti, reg. 47, ff. 19, 128; reg. 48, ff. 12–13; reg. 52, f. 14; reg. 57, f. 134; Ufficiali al Cattaver, busta 2, cap. 4, f. 25; A. S .V., Senato Mar., reg. 18, f. 29; Arsenale, busta 8, ff. 2–3; Marino Sanuto, *I Diarii* (Venice, 1879–1903), XVIII., col. 178; XXXVI., col. 382.

[4] The westbound galleys were obliged to load all the spices and other light goods offered before they could load heavy goods such as wine. See Senato Misti, reg. 47, f. 106; reg. 49, ff. 81–84, 86, 91; reg. 54, ff. 68–69.

vessels compared to many of the Venetian round ships of the time. They carried between 140 and 250 dead-weight tons of cargo below deck.[5] Though smaller they were considered safer than the round ships because in addition to the sails on which they relied during most of the voyage the galleys had oars to use in entering and leaving ports. Moreover they were warships with crews of over 200 men armed as the *signoria* might direct and commanded by a noble whom it selected.[6]

But the bulk of the Venetian merchant marine was composed of round ships. In the proverbial golden age of Venice, roughly from 1420 to 1450, she had 300 such ships of 100 dead-weight tons or more.[7] Most of these 300 were probably used for fishing or for carrying about the Adriatic such humble cargoes as grain, oil, wood, and stone and did not figure as long-distance carriers on the great routes of interregional trade. But it may be estimated that at least thirty to thirty-five of them were ships of 240 tons or more and were habitually used on voyages beyond the Adriatic, mainly on the longest well-established voyages,

[5] In 1440 the galleys of the measure of Flanders, those used on most of the voyages, were forbidden to be over 440 *milliarii*. Senato Misti, reg. 60, f. 249. One *milliarius* = 0.47 dead-weight tons. In 1481 they were forbidden to be over 450 *milliarii*. A. S. V., Senato Terra, reg. 8, f. 114. These limitations were fixed in order to check the tendency of the shipwrights to enlarge the galleys up to 500 or 600 *milliarii*. A computation at the bottom of the page, Senato Terra, reg. 3, f. 75, in 1452, shows that at that time the merchant who rented the galley from the state for the voyage was expected to collect freight on 430 *milliarii*. The galleys of the measure of Romania were legally of but 140 to 165 tons burden. Senato Mar, reg. 1, f. 13.

[6] For the large crew, see Senato Misti, reg. 49, ff. 114–15. Details of the armament, the military command, the ports of call, the freight rates, etc., were determined for each voyage by the terms of the resolutions under which the galleys were auctioned. For the years before 1440 these resolutions are contained in the series Senato Misti, for 1440–69 in Senato Mar, and after 1469 in a special series called Senato, Deliberazione, Incanti Galere, which comes down to 1569. In this last series the years 1499–1519 are missing, but the diary of Marino Sanuto does much to fill the gap.

[7] This figure is given both in Senato Mar., reg. 15, f. 145 (1502), where the records of the Consoli dei Mercanti are referred to as the source of information, and in the "Deathbed Oration" of Doge Tommaso Mocenigo, of which the most convenient edition is in Heinrich Kretschmayr, *Geschichte von Venedig* (Gotha, 1905, 1920), II, 617. The figures in Mocenigo's oration are the subject of some dispute, but the plausibility of those concerning shipping may be independently established, if not as in this case confirmed, and the financial figures have been supported by independent evidence by Gino Luzzatto, "Sull'Attendibilità di alcune Statistiche Economiche Medievale," *Giornale degli Economisti*, XLIV (no. 3), 126. For the ratios of conversion of weights and measures used here, see the dissertation by the author, "Venetian Ships and Shipbuilders of the Fifteenth and Sixteenth Centuries" (Harvard College Library). [Ed. note: and see below, chap. 21.]

such as those to England, Syria, and the Crimea.[8] They were the great merchantmen of their day, distinct in rigging and in structure from the coasting vessels.[9] They traveled much the same routes as the merchant galleys but with different cargoes—cotton and alum from Syria, wine from Crete to England, slaves and foodstuffs from the Black Sea, and grain, oil, and salt between various Mediterranean ports.[10]

[8] The estimate "thirty to thirty-five" is obtained by extension of the ratio found to exist in Table I below. Table II gives a comparison of the number of ships employed on three fairly representative voyages about 1448–49 and in 1558–60. The total numbers employed on the three voyages were eighteen at the earlier date and twenty at the later date. The total number of ships of the type here considered was at the later date forty (see below). The assumption is that, if x equals the number of such ships about 1448–49, then 18:20 as x:40. The result, thirty-six, has been modified in consideration of the probably greater importation of grain at the later date in view of the increase in the population of Venice. Giulio Beloch, "La Popolazione di Venezia nei Secoli XVI. e XVII.," *Nuovo Archivio Veneto* (n. ser., anno II, t. III), 1–49.

[9] Albertis, *op. cit.* (n. 2). Throughout the following discussion of round ships and their voyages the assumption is made that ships of 240 tons, or more, predominated in the Venetian carrying trade outside the Adriatic, and that the number of such ships—in the whole merchant marine or employed on a particular voyage discussed —is an index of the volume of trade. The exact figure, 240 tons, is dictated by the sources, especially the ship lists of 1558–60 cited below, and the assumption implies a more common use of large ships at that time than might be expected. But in the case of Venice some distinction is necessary between local and international shipping, and the following considerations support the assumption. The size of ship profitable on a particular voyage depends upon the length of the voyage and the volume of goods moved in that trade. Besides the specialization in rigging and shape which then existed in the Mediterranean between merchantmen for long voyages and for coasting voyages, specialization in size is to be expected. Such specialization was encouraged if not dictated by the Venetian government. It forbade ships of less than 240 tons to load salt at Cyprus (Senato Mar, reg. 13, f. 24; reg. 15, f. 145). When ships of the Adriatic or coasting type began to trade beyond the Adriatic they were forbidden to do so. Senato Mar, reg. 9, f. 19; law of August 13, 1602, printed in *Parti prese nell'Eccellentissimo Conseglio di Pregadi; con diversi Leggi cavate dal Statuto in Materia de Navi e sua Navigatione* (Venice, n. d.). That such specialization existed in practice appears from the fact that out of 135 ships mentioned in ship lists in the Notatorio di Collegio (A. S. V.) nos. 5–11, 1384–1457, as going or intending to go from Venice to Syria, the Crimea, or Alexandria, 129 were of 240 tons, or more, four have no sizes given, and only two, and two that did not go, are given as less than 240 tons. To be sure, out of the 135 ships, 100 were applicants for the Syrian voyage. Concerning the voyage to England, it is clear that ships well over 240 tons were considered necessary for the voyage. Senato Mar, reg. 9, f. 162; reg. 12, ff. 156–57; reg. 13, f. 27.

[10] Cotton and alum, Senato Misti, reg. 55, f. 181. Oil, fruit, soap, *ibid.*, reg. 57, f. 244; Senato Terra, reg. 10, f. 170. Wine, Senato Mar, reg. 9, f. 162 and below. Grain, Senato Misti, reg. 55, f. 184; Senato Mar, reg. 4, f. 19. Salt, Senato Misti, reg. 54, f. 37;

In the volume of cargo they carried, the thirty to thirty-five great round ships were a much more important part of the merchant marine in the fifteenth century than were the eighteen or twenty merchant galleys which annually sailed at that time. Thirty-five round ships would have carried about 15,000 tons of cargo[11] and twenty merchant galleys about 4500 tons. Such a comparison serves the purpose of placing the merchant galley fleets in proper perspective as but a small part of the fleets of Venice trading outside the Adriatic. In the shipping industry the galleys were of secondary importance. But they were of primary importance in the maintenance of Venice as the leading "world market" of the fifteenth century. They consistently carried more precious cargoes than other ships so that a comparison on the basis of value instead of capacity would yield quite different results. Moreover, their average total burden was well over 250 tons, since besides the cargo in the hold they carried on deck a very large crew[12] and a number of passengers. Both crew and passengers were allowed to keep with them some personal possessions among which they found place for a certain amount of salable wares, so that the total weight of persons, equipment, and goods carried on deck was probably as great as that below deck.[13]

These two distinct types of Venetian merchantmen, great galleys and round ships, were products of distinct branches of the shipbuilding

---

Senato Mar, reg. 6, f. 27. Black Sea trade, Senato Misti, reg. 54, f. 102. The transport of slaves on merchant galleys was forbidden, *ibid.*, reg. 49, f. 114.

[11] If the estimate of the capacity of the round ships was made on the same basis as was the estimate of their number the result would be about 14,000 tons. But another method is available, for in ship lists in the Notatorio di Collegio, no. 10, between Jan. 1449, and April 1450 inclusive, there is mention of twenty-one different ships with a total capacity of 10,153 tons. The lists in the Notatorio do not include all ships of any given class, but are merely lists of ships applying to serve against pirates or to take part in the Syrian voyage. The figure twenty-one does not, therefore, indicate the full number of ships of 240 tons or more. Instead, the number of such ships is better estimated at thirty to thirty-five, as explained above. Hence the total capacity may be calculated by adding to the known capacity of the twenty-one ships that of nine to fourteen additional ships, estimated, on the basis of those known and with due allowances, as 360 tons each. The result is 13,393 to 15,193 tons.

[12] In 1412 the size of the crew from commander to cook was legally fixed as 212. Senato Misti, reg. 49, ff. 114–15.

[13] The resolutions for auctioning the galleys are full of rules to stop overloading on deck. A description of the great galleys in 1501, quoted by Jal, I, 384–87, said that they carried 500 *milliarii* below deck and 500 *milliarii* on deck. The average size of the galleys increased somewhat during the fifteenth century because the smaller type gradually went out of use.

industry. The great galleys were built by the state in the arsenal. The round ships of commerce were built by private enterprise in private shipyards. When at the end of the fifteenth century the state felt it necessary to build round ships the government resorted to private shipyards. But in the main the production of round ships is synonymous with private shipbuilding.

After 1460 the two parts of the shipbuilding industry and of the merchant marine thus distinguished had different and frequently contrasting histories. The latter part of the fifteenth century was the period when the galley voyages were most numerous and regular and when this branch of the Venetian merchant marine was at the height of its fame. During that same period the fleet of large round ships was reduced to half its former size. In the first half of the sixteenth century, on the other hand, the merchant galley fleets dwindled and almost disappeared, but the large round ships increased in number so that in 1560 they were certainly larger and probably more numerous than they had ever been.

The decline of private shipbuilding at Venice was most severe between 1463 and 1488. By 1487 building was completely at a standstill.[14] The mental habits of the political historian may lead him to associate this decline with the naval advance of the Ottoman Turks, but the Venetians themselves, much as they were impressed with the political and military importance of that new danger in the East, did not consider it the cause of the weakening of their merchant marine. Instead they blamed nearby competitors better supplied with materials.

The building of smaller craft was the first part of the industry affected. River barges and small boats were built in Venetian possessions in Italy and brought to Venice for sale.[15] As the forests which had once surrounded the lagoons disappeared, the barge builders pursued them back toward the mountains.

The major role in this sudden depression of the Venetian industry was played by the eastern shore of the Adriatic. The great outcry against competing ships in the years 1467 and 1469 was directed against a particular type called *marani*, most of which were built in Istria. They had become so numerous that it was impracticable for the state to dispense at once with the use of such ships in sending supplies, but they disposed of the competition of Istria in the future by forbidding the

[14] Senato Mar, reg. 9, f. 19; reg. 12, ff. 125, 187.

[15] Senato Misti, reg. 47, f. 151; reg. 54, f. 5; reg. 59, f. 134; Arsenale, busta 6, ff. 13–15.

building of any ship of sixty tons or more between Venice and the Gulf of Quarnero.[16]

The center of competition then moved down the Adriatic. The bitterest protests were raised against the Ragusans who were at that time gaining a leading place in the Mediterranean carrying trade. The multiplication of Ragusan ships was attributed by the Venetians to the plentiful supply of wood, iron, and sailors available at Ragusa. To meet the situation the senate levied an anchorage tax of 100 ducats on Ragusan ships visiting any port under Venetian dominion. Well might the chronicler Malipiero say that Ragusan ships had been banned from Venice.[17] Later exemption was made of grain ships since the need for food was paramount.[18] But the exclusion from Venetian trade of ships flying the Ragusan flag, even if it could be achieved, would not revive the home industry. The advantages of building in Dalmatia were the root of the trouble. Venetians brought Ragusan ships and built their own ships there or in the Venetian possessions in Dalmatia. By various subterfuges Ragusans acquired citizenship in the Venetian cities of Dalmatia and kept up business under the flag of San Marco. Between 1487 and 1490 the senate was actively putting teeth in old laws forbidding such practices and passing new measures to meet the wiles of the Ragusans. The senate even went so far as to forbid the building of any ship of thirty tons or more in Venetian Dalmatia, but the protests of their Dalmatian subjects secured the modification of this provision. In their final form these regulations were designed to permit the Dalmatians to continue to build the ships they needed for their Adriatic voyages, but to sever the Dalmatian industry from any connection with Venetian capital, and to cut it off entirely from any association with the Ragusans.[19]

Besides the competition of the inland barge builders and that of the Istrian and Dalmatian coasts, the Venetian shipbuilders suffered from the rivalry of more distant regions. Ships from Genoa, Portugal, the Basque country, and even England were competing with theirs on the long voyages which had been the chief support of the very largest Venetian ships, those of from 600 to 700 tons. Ships of that size were of special importance to the state because of their utility as naval auxiliaries and supply ships, and the rise of the Ottoman navy made the need

[16] Senato Mar, reg. 8, f. 144; reg. 9, ff. 19, 21, 136, 146, 157, 170.

[17] *Ibid.*, reg. 12, f. 21. Domenico Malipiero, "Annali Veneti," *Archivio Storico Italiano,* VII, ser. 1, pt. 2 (1843), 620.

[18] Senato Mar, reg. 16, f. 57.

[19] *Ibid.*, reg. 12, ff. 125, 148, 187; reg. 13, ff. 3–7, 15.

of them all the more acute. Consequently, when offers of loans and increased freight rates failed to induce private citizens to build ships of the desired size, the *signoria* was forced to build its own.[20] Between 1475 and 1488 the state built four ships ranging from 600 to 2400 tons, and between 1488 and 1498 ordered six, of which at least five were built, most of them of 1200 tons.[21] Thus the state obtained the large ships needed to strengthen her war fleet, hunt pirates, send supplies, and, if necessary, import grain and salt.

Meanwhile desperate efforts had been made to recapture from the competitors of Venice the transport of wine from Crete to England, and since 1488 there had been some increase in the number of large private ships.[22] Ship lists of 1499 suggest that the fleet of private ships of 240 tons or more then totaled about 10,000 tons in twenty-five ships.[23] The four round ships of the state afloat in 1499 had a total capacity of 5100 tons. But these state ships only occasionally acted as merchantmen. Moreover it was only an extraordinary effort which kept so much shipping afloat that year. During the war with Turkey from 1499 to 1502 the attempt to control the Cretan wine trade had to be abandoned. In 1502 it was reported that there were but sixteen Venetian ships of the type used on long voyages, namely, of 240 tons or more.[24]

The second half of the fifteenth century, considered as a whole, was, accordingly, a period of decline in Venetian shipping. At this time

[20] *Ibid.*, reg. 9, ff. 20, 99, 120–21, 162; Arsenale, busta 6, f. 10. There were no private Venetian ships of 600 tons or more in 1486 and 1488. Senato Mar, reg. 12, ff. 87, 157.

[21] Senato Terra, reg. 7, ff. 98–100, 139–40, 145, 157, 161, 177, 179, 192; reg. 8, f. 74; Senato Mar, reg. 10, ff. 155, 189; reg. 11, f. 103; reg. 12, ff. 123, 153; reg. 13, ff. 50, 90; reg. 14, f. 141; Malipiero, p. 645; Sanuto, I, 849–50; II, 1241–49; IV, 51.

[22] On the Anglo-Venetian quarrel over the Cretan wine trade, see *Calendar of State Papers, Venetian*, ed. by Rawdon Brown (London, 1864), I, 175 ff., and Georg von Schanz, *Englische Handelspolitik gegen Ende des Mittelalters* (Leipzig, 1881), I, 130–42. A Venetian tax on foreigners exporting wine from Crete was to some extent successful in stimulating the building of large ships. There is mention of six ships of 600 tons or more between 1488 and 1497 in Sanuto, I, 81, 504, and Senato Mar, reg. 12, 13, and 14.

[23] Lists in Sanuto, II, 1080–81, 1242–49, and in the manuscript copy of the *Diarii* in the Biblioteca Marciana, Venice, MSS. It., Cl. VII. 230, ff. 418, 481–83. There are two mistakes in the printing. The comprehensiveness of the lists is indicated by records concerning the mobilization of the merchant fleet, Sanuto, I, 780, 923; II, 629, 784, 919; Senato Mar, reg. 14, f. 196. The lists present difficulties of interpretation, but the results may be taken in conjunction with the general statement of the time, like those quoted in the text and that in Sanuto, II, 225, that in 1498 there were but twelve Venetian ships of 300 tons or more.

[24] Senato Mar, reg. 14, f. 181; reg. 15, f. 145.

when the wealth of Venice was the envy of all Christendom there was a weakening of the maritime activity by which the republic had risen to splendor. The brief revival of shipbuilding in the years just before 1499 was of an artificial character. The years 1488 and 1502 represented the double bottom of a prolonged depression. The stagnation of building was such that during those years, both in number and in capacity, the Venetian round ships adapted to trade beyond the Adriatic were not more than half what they had been in the middle of the century. The loss of smaller ships was likewise severe.[25] The merchant galleys sailed their yearly rounds with admired regularity, but there was no increase in their number to compensate for the losses elsewhere.

The turn of the tide came in 1502. Then occurred the most thoroughgoing and most successful of the many attempts to aid the shipbuilders. The shipowners' own views of their troubles were set forth at length in the preamble to the remedial law of 1502. They complained of the low freight rates secured by shippers, the innumerable dues and obligations laid on the ships by the state, the loss of the western trade because of the permission given to foreigners to load in Crete, the restrictions on carrying salt and grain between different ports in the western Mediterranean, and the competition of the Basque, Portuguese, and Spanish, who, they said, had earlier never come within the Straits of Gibraltar. The situation was met by restoring to private ships complete freedom to load all cargoes including salt and grain but excluding three special classes—goods forbidden by the Church, goods reserved for the galleys, and Moorish merchants and their wares. The dues laid upon the ships by the state were lessened. The senate approved a schedule of minimum freight rates, made provision for their prompt payment, and offered generous bounties to builders of new ships.[26]

So great was the revival in the building of round ships following the passage of this law that in 1507 the bounties were suspended as no longer necessary and too great a burden on the finances of the state.[27] Not only were a good number of large ships being built, but half of the seven in process of construction were of the very biggest type in commercial use.[28]

---

[25] *Ibid.*, reg. 12, f. 125; reg. 15, f. 145; A. S. V., Cinque Savii alla Mercanzia, ser. 1, busta 135, ff. 99–100.

[26] Senato Mar, reg. 15, f. 145.

[27] *Ibid.*, reg. 16, f. 152. A list of the large ships built or being built in 1504 is given in Sanuto, V, 1000.

[28] List given in A. S. V., Notatorio di Collegio, no. 27, under date July 5, 1507.

These years of prosperity for the private shipbuilders (1502-7) were precisely the years when the discovery of the route to India around the Cape of Good Hope was having its effect on the Levant trade of Venice. But that discovery affected only the cargoes of the galleys, not those of the round ships. It is even likely that the discovery of new routes to the East and West Indies was a distinct help to the private shipbuilders of Venice. The Portuguese and Spanish ships had been entering the Mediterranean and taking cargoes away from the Venetians. Now they had new seas to sail. Therefore, from the point of view of the largest part of the Venetian merchant marine, the round ship, the years following the great discoveries were years of expansion. To be sure, this prosperity was not maintained without interruption. Complaints of the lack of a sufficient number of ships occur from time to time and between 1534 and 1540 the freight rates on salt were raised and offers of loans were made to encourage building.[29] But in the years 1540 to 1570 there is no sign of depression, but instead positive evidence that the number of large round ships had doubled since the beginning of the century. Only the other branch of the merchant marine, the great galley fleets, can then have been adversely affected by the discovery of the new sailing routes.

In the detailed story of the disruption and practical disappearance of the voyages of the merchant galleys, quarrels with the sultan of Egypt and diplomatic and naval difficulties elsewhere bulk large,[30] but it is generally agreed that these were but incidental circumstances and that the determining factors lay deeper. Three such determining factors may be mentioned—the revolutionary improvements in the rigging of the round ship, the development of guns, and the discovery of the Cape route to India. Of these three only the last has usually been emphasized, to the complete neglect of the others.

The nature and extent of the influence of the Portuguese route are shown by the rough statistics of the spice trade contained in the diaries of the Venetians Sanuto and Priuli and in the reports of Ca' Masser, the secret observer of the *signoria* in Portugal. Before the discoveries, about half of the galleys which left Venice each year went to the Levant. In the return cargo of these nine or ten galleys spices formed the largest item, and in the last years of the fifteenth century they brought back

[29] Gino Luzzatto, "Per la Storia delle Costruzioni Navali a Venezia nei Secoli XV. e XVI," in *Scritti Storici in Onore di Camillo Manfroni* (Padua, 1925), pp. 381-401.

[30] Wilhelm von Heyd, *Histoire du commerce du Levant au moyen âge* (Leipzig, 1885-86), II, 508-52, and innumerable references in Sanuto, *Diarii*.

about 3,500,000 English pounds of spices a year, of which about
2,500,000 pounds came from Alexandria, and of which 40 to 50 per cent
was pepper.[31] The commercial effects of the discovery of the Cape route
to India were first felt in the Levant in 1502. In the four years 1502 to
1505 the Venetians imported on an average not more than 1,000,000
pounds of spices a year.[32] The first large cargoes arrived in Portugal in
1503, and in the four years 1503 to 1506 the Portuguese imported an
average of about 2,300,000 pounds a year of which 88 per cent was
pepper.[33] The average yearly import of the two countries combined was
at this time, therefore, a little less than the total Venetian imports
before the discoveries—a comparison which suggests that for the first
few years at least the Portuguese were more successful in disorganizing
the Alexandrian spice market than in supplying the needs of Europe.
In 1505 a dispute between the Venetians and the sultan of Egypt over
the price of pepper led to the astounding escape of the Venetian galleys
under the fire of the forts of Alexandria and the severance of relations
for some years. From the resumption of trade in 1508 until 1514 the
Venetian spice imports from Alexandria remained only a quarter of
what they had been and pepper became a distinctly minor item in the

[31] Estimate based on the following figures from Sanuto, II, 112, 128, 165, 172; IV,
38–39, 47; *I Diarii di Girolamo Priuli, 1494–1512,* published in *Rerum Italicarum
Scriptores* (2d ed., vol. XXIV, pt. 3; Città di Castello, 1911) , I, 73, 109:

1497 galleys of Beirut	spice cargo	2639 *colli*
galleys of Alexandria	spice cargo	2320 *colli,* corrected from 4320
galleys of Alexandria	pepper	1250 *colli*
1498 galleys of Beirut	spice cargo	3000 *colli*
galleys of Alexandria	spice cargo	2155 *colli*
galleys of Alexandria	pepper	933 *colli*
1501 galleys of Beirut	spice cargo	3200 *colli*
galleys of Alexandria	spice cargo	2570 *colli*
galleys of Alexandria	pepper	950 *colli*

The war with Turkey prevented galleys from completing voyages in 1499 and 1501,
and during those years non-Venetians exported more spices than usual from Egypt,
Sanuto, III, 37, 942; IV, 6–10.

The *collo* of Alexandria equaled about 1120 lb. (*ibid.,* XVII, 191) . For the bales
on the Beirut galleys *colli* and *sacho* are used interchangeably by Priuli. See Rinaldo
Fulin, *Diarii e Diaristi Veneziani* (Venice, 1881) , p. 247. This bale has been considered equal to 290 lb., although some may have been larger. Sanuto, *loc. cit.;* Senato
Mar, reg. 12, f. 136; reg. 56, f. 109.

[32] Sanuto, IV, 260–65; V, 78, 826–28, 902; VI, 129; Fulin, pp. 165–82.

[33] Leonardo da Ca' Masser, "Relazione sopra il Commercio dei Portoghesi nell'
India, 1497–1506," *Archivio Storico Italiano,* II (1845) , app., 13 ff. Previous Portuguese imports had been only 224,000 lb. in 1501, and 173,000 lb. in 1502.

cargo lists.[34] Trade with Beirut was less interrupted, according to Sanuto, but was likewise below its former volume.

After 1514 the records of the galley voyages no longer give accurate indexes of the amount of spices reaching Venice, for in that year the galleys lost their monopoly of the transport of spices. The round ships were then permitted to load spices in Alexandria for Venice, and when, in 1524, the galleys brought back no spices it was because the round ship *Cornera* had taken them all, and the galleys loaded linen and wheat instead, wares usually carried by round ships. After 1514 Venetian policy wavered. Some spices were brought by round ships, and galleys were sometimes sent instead, or in addition, until 1570.[35] A surprising index of the size of the spice trade at Alexandria in these years is contained in a loose sheet in the archives of the Donà dalle Rose family. This document purports to be a copy from the books of the Venetian colony in Alexandria of the amount of pepper sent from Alexandria in the years 1560 to 1564, inclusively. It shows an annual export of 1,310,454 pounds of pepper from Alexandria alone, or fully as much pepper as in the period before the Portuguese had entered the spice trade.[36] Uncorroborated this one document may not be considered conclusive, but it suggests the possibility of a revision of ideas concerning the later sixteenth-century Levant trade.[37]

[34] Sanuto, VI, 156–57, 170, 199–207. Cargoes reaching Venice from Alexandria are recorded as follows:

1508, 1100 *colli* (*ibid.,* VII, 591, 597).

1509, none returned.

1510, 1000 *colli* (*ibid.,* X, 799, XI, 57, 69; Fulin, p. 209).

1511, none returned.

1512, 1180 *colli* (Sanuto, XIV, 25–26).

1513, 300 *colli* (*ibid.,* XVI, 177, 209).

[35] Sanuto, XVIII, 178; XXXV, 254, 332, 337; XXXVI, 382; Senato Mar, reg. 18, f. 29; Arsenale, busta 8, ff. 2–3, busta 9, f. 37; Senato Deliberazione, Incanti Galere, reg. 2, libri iv and v.

[36] Museo Civico, Venice, Archivio Donà dalle Rose, busta 217, f. 276. The authenticity of documents in this bundle is discussed in the note to Table I. The figures are given first in *colli e nichesse* and then in cantara. The figure given above is computed from the number of cantara, assuming they were the *cantara forfori*, the measure used at Alexandria in selling pepper, equal to 94 lb. See Bartholomeo de Paxi, *Tariffa de Pexi e Mesure* (Venice, 1503), no paging, and Adolf Schaube, *Handelsgeschichte der Romanischen Völker des Mittelmeergebiets bis zum Ende der Kreuzzüge* (Munich, Berlin, 1960), p. 814. Had the computation been made by assuming that *nichesse* like *colli* contained 1120 lb., the result would have been 1,668,800 lb.

[37] Contrast the statement by J. A. Goris, *Étude sur les Colonies Marchandes Méridionales à Anvers de 1488 à 1567* (Louvain, 1925), p. 195. See also the discussion by

It is true, however, that in the opening years of the sixteenth century the Venetian supply of spices, especially of pepper, was considerably less than it had been, and that throughout the century Venetian traders in the West met competition from Portuguese sources. This may be counted one reason why between 1509 and 1535 all the voyages of the Venetian merchant galleys westward were discontinued. Aside from the risks resulting from the wars of the early sixteenth century, there was far less prospect of profit to warrant sending west to Spain, Portugal, England, or Flanders the expensive great galleys whose sole justification had been their adaptability to precious cargoes.

Lack of spices was not the only reason why the galley voyages were so largely discontinued. Even before the Portuguese discovery the Venetian state had been forced to offer bounties with the galleys to persuade anyone to rent them for the western voyages. Whereas in the period 1418 to 1427 the English and Flemish galleys were auctioned for prices which brought the state an average of about 5400 ducats for the fleet each year,[38] in the period 1480 to 1489 a subsidy of 1000 to 5000 ducats was offered with each galley auctioned and the amounts bid were far less than these subsidies. For all three of the western voyages the state was practically giving the use of the galley and something besides in order that wares be safely moved and the position of Venice as world market be maintained.[39] To raise freight rates presumably would have handicapped Venetian traders using the galleys, but only in case there were other ships able to offer better service in proportion to what they charged.

Such a ship had been created by the transformation which took place in the rigging of round ships during the fifteenth century and by the development of firearms. The transformation of the one-masted cog into a full-rigged, three-masted ship possessed of spritsail, topsail, and mizzen lateen sail occurred about the middle of that century. The importance of the change is stressed by specialists on early shipping.

A. H. Lybyer, "The Ottoman Turks and the Routes of Oriental Trade," *Eng. Hist. Rev.*, XXX, 577, and "The Influence of the Rise of the Turks upon the Routes of Oriental Trade," Amer. Hist. Assn., *Annual Report,* I (1914) , 125.

[38] The amount received for the galleys is recorded in the registers of the senate after the resolutions for auctioning them. These resolutions occur at about the same time each year, those for the Flemish galleys in January or February. Galleys also went at this time to Aigues-Mortes, usually auctioned in January and yielded an average yearly profit of about 1850 ducats.

[39] The three voyages operated at a loss to the state were those to Flanders, Aigues-Mortes, and Barbary. The Levant galleys, protected by their monopoly of the spice transport, continued to yield a profit as in the earlier period.

For example, Oppenheim says that the sailing ships of 1485 differed less in appearance from sailing ships of 1785 than they did from those of 1425.[40] These changes in rigging may not have materially increased the speed of the ship, but they made her much more manageable. From the point of view of safety the advantages which the oars had given to the great galley were thus largely counterbalanced by the new rig of the round ship.

Equally important in robbing the merchant galley of the special security which had alone justified its existence was the increase in the use of guns in naval warfare. A high round ship well furnished with cannon and properly manned could provide as good protection from attack as a low galley whose crews were comparatively unprotected from gunshot. The light galley long remained important in Mediterranean war fleets because galleys were needed to chase galleys. But merchantmen required not offensive but defensive strength. The great galley had always been so expensive a vessel that its freight rates had been double those of the round ships. As long as the galleys were so much safer that it was considered unnecessary to insure the wares they carried, they could maintain their position. But when better rigging and the use of muskets and cannon deprived the merchant galley of its superior safety, it could no longer compete with the cheaper type of shipping.

Certainly the decline of the merchant galley fleets of Venice was out of all proportion to the decline of her trade. To some extent what had before 1535 been carried by the galleys was thereafter carried by round ships,[41] and this may be one explanation of the renewed prosperity of private shipping at Venice after the discontinuance of most of the galley voyages.

The mid-sixteenth century was probably the period when the Venetian-built fleet of ships designed for trade beyond the Adriatic, namely, those of 240 tons or more, was the largest in its history. Certainly the number and capacity of such round ships in private hands

---

[40] M. Oppenheim, *A History of the Administration of the Royal Navy and of Merchant Shipping in Relation to the Navy* (London, New York, 1896), p. 40. See also A. Anthiaume, *Le Navire et sa Construction en France et principalement chez les Normands* (Paris, 1922), pp. 57, 64, 127; Bernhard Hagedorn, *Die Entwicklung der Wichtigsten Schiffstypen bis ins 19. Jahrhundert* (Berlin, 1914), pp. 54–64; and Romola and R. C. Anderson, *The Sailing Ship* (London, 1926), ch. VII.

[41] The ship lists of 1558–60 cited below do not show, however, any voyages by round ships to the North African ports which the galleys had visited. The rise of the pirate states is the probable explanation of the loss of this trade.

had doubled since the beginning of the century, a gain which far more than counterbalanced the decline of the merchant galley fleets. In 1558 and 1559 the Venetian merchant marine included forty round ships of 240 tons or more having a total capacity of 18,000 tons.[42] The principal voyages on which the ships were employed are shown in the accompanying table (Table I). A comparison between the voyages at that date and at a date in the previous period of prosperity well before the discovery of new trade routes has been made in Table II, so far as information from the earlier period permits. Except that no figures have been found at the earlier date for the grain trade or for the relatively short voyages, the trades compared may be considered fairly representative. They suggest comparative stabilization. There is a local shift in trade center from Syria to Cyprus, for in 1558 to 1560 there were almost no clearances for Syria, whereas in 1450 Cyprus had been of secondary importance. Apparently cotton, which in the fifteenth century furnished the bulk of the cargo of the ships from Syria, was in the sixteenth century produced in Cyprus, whose sugar plantations, famous in the fifteenth century, had meanwhile been ruined by the competition of the new Portuguese possessions in the West.[43] While, however, Cyprus furnished the bulk of the freight in the sixteenth century, Venetians were still active in Syria, and some part of the ship cargoes may have come directly or indirectly from the mainland. Another slight change between the two dates is the increase in the size of ships used. Ships of 600 tons were numerous in Venice in the mid-sixteenth century not only because Venetians had, by means of them, regained at least in part the carrying trade between the Mediterranean and the English Channel, but also because such ships were more largely employed on purely Mediterranean voyages. That does not suggest that the volume of trade had been decreased by the Portuguese discoveries.

A definite break in this maritime prosperity of Venice appears in 1570 to 1577 with the short but expensive war with Turkey, the loss of Cyprus, and the plague which killed a quarter to a third of her population. The notable fact in the resultant crisis is not the blow dealt by such a disastrous conjunction of calamities, though this was adequate cause for an interruption of activity, but the lack of resilience

[42] Only about 4000 tons of active shipping was lost by the stoppage of galley voyages, a fall from 5000 to 1000 tons, between 1501 and 1540. A list of the names and sizes of all Venetian ships of 240 tons or more in 1557–60, in addition to the record of voyages, is given in Museo Civico, Venice, Archivio Donà dalle Rose, busta 217.

[43] Sanuto, I, 270–71; *The Travels of Pedro Teixeira* (Hakluyt Society; London, 1902), p. 134.

which prevented Venice from again establishing her merchant marine on its former basis. This incapacity to come back and regain her former position was not due to a decline of Mediterranean trade, or to a decrease in the volume of goods to be moved between her ports, but to the unstable basis of her shipbuilding industry.

The period before 1570 had been a time of prosperity only for the builders of large ships. The smaller vessels employed in bringing grain, wine, oil, and cheese to Venice had not been made in the city but had been bought abroad, for there were no Venetian ships of their size to go on the voyages which these smaller, foreign-built ships undertook. Such was the testimony of the Venetian board of trade.[44] Thus it appears that although the builders of large ships had definitely recovered during the sixteenth century from the depression which occurred in the late fifteenth century, the part of the shipbuilding industry devoted to supplying the more numerous small ships for the Adriatic trade had been definitely lost.

And the building of large ships had been kept at Venice chiefly by the presence there of skilled artisans and the advantages which were enjoyed by ships entitled to fly the banner of San Marco. Otherwise they, too, might have been purchased from foreigners. In 1531 complaints of the number of large foreign-built vessels which were being purchased by Venetians and even granted the right to sail as Venetian led to the reenactment of the laws which forbade such practices.[45] But the laws could not be strictly enforced. In times of famine whoever brought grain to Venice was sure of good will, and if he bought a foreign ship in order to bring the grain it was with the hope that the ship would be given the privileges of Venetian registry. Thus, in 1542 and 1543 five foreign ships were granted the right to fly the Venetian flag. Four had been bought at Constantinople and sent to Venice with grain, and the other was a Basque ship which had been in the service of the state.[46]

Another way to evade the law was to refit or finish at Venice a ship originally built elsewhere. The petition of Giovanni Morello, for example, explained that he and his associates had begun a ship in the Po river solely because of the supply there of wood which could not be had at Venice without great damage to the arsenal. Or again, the Querini brothers recounted how they had lost a 720-ton ship from

---

[44] Cinque Savii, ser. 1, busta 135, ff. 99–100.

[45] Senato Mar, reg. 22, f. 85.

[46] *Ibid.,* reg. 26, ff. 72, 98, 99, 107; reg. 27, f. 30. That was an unusually large number for so short a space of time and was occasioned by a particular grain shortage.

which they had salvaged rigging and artillery. They wished to build another but found difficulty in getting the necessary wood and so bought and refitted a Basque ship. Another instructive petition explained that only the body of the ship had been made away from Venice while the decks and castles had been added at Venice.[47] The large number of such petitions creates the suspicion that although pine and larch for superstructures could be had at Venice, the oak essential for body timbers had become dear and very hard to find there.

This impression is strengthened by an examination of the shipbuilding industry in the Dalmatian city of Curzola in the sixteenth century. In favor of Curzola an exemption had been made to the general rule that large ships should not be built in Dalmatia by Venetian capital, and Venetians were building there ships of 300 to 600 tons. They were aided by licenses to export the materials needed to finish their ships free of duties. The list of what they exported may make one wonder why they chose to build away from Venice since it included pine and larch planks, masts and spars, iron, pitch, and cordage. But Curzola is conveniently placed across the Adriatic from the forests of Monte San Angelo in Apulia, the source of the timbers used in the celebrated Ragusan ships.[48]

Certainly the oaks grown in the Venetian dominions did not suffice for both the demands of the arsenal and those of the private builders, and despite the constant effort of the state to preserve the oak woods, ship timbers were harder and harder to find. In 1546 when a tax was proposed on licenses to cut oak, it was asserted that it would not greatly affect the builders of large ships since they did not cut in Venetian territory one third of the oak logs they used. Whether that statement is accurate or not, the cutting of oak for private builders was sufficient to cause the arsenal alarm for its own supply. Accordingly, the senate in 1559 provided that thereafter all those receiving state loans to help them build their ships must agree to cut no oak in the dominions of the *signoria*.[49] There was no complaint of immediate depression because of the necessity of seeking lumber abroad. Yet from buying abroad the essential timbers to buying abroad the ship itself was only a step.

---

[47] *Ibid.*, reg. 28, ff. 85, 92; reg. 36, f. 115; files, Sept. and Oct. 1545, Feb. 25, 1564. The Querini brothers stated that twenty-five others, of whom they named fourteen, had been granted the favor they sought, namely, Venetian registry.

[48] Senato Mar, reg. 21, ff. 61, 85; reg. 22, f. 13; reg. 29, f. 168; Cinque Savii, ser. 1, busta 135, ff. 65, 83. Bartolomeo Crescentio, *Nautica Mediterranea* (Rome, 1607), pp. 3–5; Pantero Pantera, *L'Armata Navale* (Rome, 1614), p. 67.

[49] Senato Mar, files, Dec. 28, 1546; reg. 34, f. 57.

That step was taken about 1590 after the offer of bounties had failed to revive Venetian shipbuilding to its former levels. The law against granting Venetian registry to foreign-built ships was repealed and between 1590 and 1599 the records of the board of trade mention fifteen such large ships for which Venetian registry was sought. During that same period eight large ships were built in Venice, and thirteen in Venetian possessions.[50] The Venetians bought most ships from Holland although they found some in the island of Patmos and some in the Black Sea. The activities of Francesco Morosini are significant for the international shipbuilding situation of the time. He was interested in the business of transporting wine from Crete to the West, but preferred to build his ships in Holland instead of Venice. After beginning one 720-ton ship in Holland he promised to build four more if he was granted bounties for them and Venetian registry. Although his ships were not granted bounties they were given Venetian registry and five were built.[51]

Some years later, however, in 1627, even those buying approved foreign-built ships were offered bounties.[52] But before such extreme measures were taken, the favors shown to purchasers of foreign ships had enabled the Venetian marine to make a tardy and partial recovery from the slump which had followed 1577. The number of ships of 360 tons or more in the fleet in 1606 compares not unfavorably with similar figures for 1558 to 1559:

1558–59 27 ships, total tonnage 14,850 tons.
1606   27 ships, total tonnage 11,460 tons.

But more than half of the fleet, fourteen ships, were in 1606 of foreign build.[53] The continually increasing dependence on foreign-built ships

[50] Cinque Savii, ser. 1, busta 25, ff. 71–75, 101, 112, 124; busta 26, ff. 35, 110, 117, 181, 182, 193, 195; busta 27, f. 12; busta 138, ff. 160, 169; busta 139, ff. 5, 9, 70, 73, 135, 167; busta 140, f. 61.

[51] *Ibid.*, busta 27, f. 37; busta 139, f. 167; busta 141, f. 124; Senato Mar, files, Mar. 29, 1597.

[52] *Parti Prese . . . in Materia de Navi e sua Navigatione*, pp. 32–33. Three ships were immediately bought with the aid of the loans, the bounties taking that form, and all three were *Fiamengo*, i.e., Dutch. Cinque Savii, ser. 1, busta 147, ff. 113, 126, 186.

[53] Museo Civico, Venice, Archivio Donà dalle Rose, busta 217, f. 46, an abstract of a report of the board of trade which is referred to in their archive, Cinque Savii, ser. 1, busta 141, f. 128, although it is there stated that there were twenty-six such ships in all, twelve Venetian and fourteen foreign-built.

is emphasized by an enumeration of the merchant fleet in 1693 which gives the following figures:[54]

Four-masted ships
    Made in Venice............................ 9
    Of foreign make bought by Venetians........... 35
    On the shipyards........................... 5
    On voyage for Hebrews...................... 6
Marciliane, smaller ships used in the Adriatic...... 68

The decline in Venetian shipbuilding was therefore obviously far greater than any decline in Venetian commerce. The papers of the board of trade give vividly the impression that in the early seventeenth century there was plenty of trade in the Mediterranean and that Venetian-built ships were not numerous enough to carry even the business that was in Venetian hands. Neither the advance of the Turk, nor the supposed exhaustion of Venice in the Italian wars, nor the reputed loss of the spice trade to the Portuguese can be said to have ruined her commerce. The passing of the maritime glory of Venice was primarily a failure to keep up with other seagoing peoples who expanded more rapidly. A basic reason for this failure was the exhaustion of one of the most vital of her natural resources, ship timber.

When this depletion of the oak woods[55] was first clearly recognized—in the last half of the fifteenth century—the shortage seems to have been peculiar to Venice. At least the Ragusans and Basques had a sufficiently plentiful supply so that their competition was severely felt. At the end of the sixteenth century the scarcity of oak timber appears to have been general throughout Mediterranean countries.[56] In the seventeenth century, maritime supremacy was definitely in the hands of that people who controlled the lumber resources of the Baltic, the Dutch.[57]

---

[54] Cinque Savii, ser. 3, busta 97.

[55] For specific statements of the concern of the government with the harm done to private shipbuilding by the lack of oak timber, see Arsenale, busta 6, f. 16, and busta 8, ff. 73–75; Senato Mar, reg. 19, f. 120. For the elaborate conservation policy then developed, see Adolfo di Berenger, *Saggio Storico della Legislazione Veneta Forestale dal Sec. VII. al XIX.* (Venice, 1863).

[56] The exhaustion of Spanish supplies is indicated by C. H. Haring, *Trade and Navigation between Spain and the Indies in the Time of the Hapsburgs* (Cambridge, 1918), pp. 259–61, and Julius Klein, *The Mesta: A Study in Spanish Economic History, 1273–1836* (Cambridge, 1920), pp. 320–21.

[57] Violet Barbour, "Dutch and English Merchant Shipping in the Seventeenth Century," *Ec. Hist Rev.,* II, 261 ff. Miss Barbour emphasizes the extent to which the su-

It is not intended here to deny that the opening of the oceanic trades placed Venice under other handicaps. Her naval and military resources were so thoroughly committed to defending her position against the Turk that she could not have given political backing to merchants adventuring to the Indies. Her rigid commercial policy had been shaped with the one thought of drawing the maximum advantage from her strategic location on the route between Europe and the Near East. Such of her nobles as remained merchants were bound both by capital investments and commercial habits to the long-exploited and still profitable Levant trade. The peoples of western Europe, unhampered by such heavy fetters of past greatness, and bred to the navigation of the open ocean, could more readily profit from the new opportunities. But Venice faced the additional and, it would seem, decisive disadvantage that she depended upon her competitors for the essential instruments of commerce, ships.

The need for ships was enormously increased in the sixteenth century by the development of the transoceanic trades. This new demand could not be met by the old shipbuilding centers in Italy. An attempt to meet it was made by the Iberian ports, but before the end of the century their supplies were giving out. The carrying trade of both the Indies and even that of the Mediterranean then passed in very large measure to the countries of northwest Europe able to draw upon the still unexhausted forests of that region. In analyzing the shift of economic leadership from the Mediterranean to northwest Europe one should consider not only the migration of technique, the shifts in trade routes and trade centers, and the relative effectiveness of political organization, but also the depletion of the natural resources of the Mediterranean regions.

premacy of Dutch shipping during the seventeenth century is bound up with the Dutch control of the Baltic timber trade. On Baltic supplies and English oak, see R. G. Albion, *Forests and Sea Power* (Cambridge, 1926), ch. III and IV.

TABLE I

Number and capacity of ships of 240 tons or more employed on different voyages from Venice, 1558-60 *

Voyage	Number and Capacity of Ships Cleared, by Periods							
	Average 1558 and 1559		Full year 1558		Full year 1559		First six months 1560	
	No. ships	Capacity (tons)	No. ships	Capacity (tons)	No. ships	Capacity (tons)	No. ships	Capacity (tons)
All voyages	44–45	20,400	41	20,040	48	20,760	27	12,840
Cyprus and Syria	13	7,170	11	6,060	15	8,280	10	5,640
Grain	11	4,920	13	6,120	9	3,720	5	2,580
England and West	3	1,830	4	2,640	2	1,020	3	1,380
Constantinople	3–4	1,680	4	1,620	3	1,740	1	600
Corfu and Zante	2–3	1,050	1	540	4	1,560	2	720
Alexandria	2	810	1	540	3	1,080	2	840
Others	9–10	2,940	7	2,520	12	3,360	4	1,080

* The table is based on a document in the Museo Civico, Venice, Archivio Donà dalle Rose, busta 217, entitled "Navi Grosse de Venetia, loro Viaggi e loro Patroni." The bundle contains, besides other documents referred to in the present article, a copy of a treaty made in 1442 through Andrea Donà and various papers recognized by the archivists as in the handwriting of Leonardo Donà, doge of Venice, 1606–12. Apparently they are all papers accumulated by the Donà family during the fifteenth, sixteenth, and seventeenth centuries. There is therefore no obvious reason to doubt the authenticity of these ship lists. The list of voyages gives the exact day of the departure and of the arrival in Istria and in the port of Malamocco, except that there is no mention of the return of most of the ships sailing in 1560. The earliest entry on this list is of Oct. 19, 1557, and the latest July 6, 1560, so that the lack of mention of the return of ships sailing in 1560 suggests that the list is contemporaneous with the voyages.

Although some of the ships recorded as clearing for Cyprus almost certainly loaded grain also, voyages for grain are entered as a separate item because some ships are mentioned as clearing for a grain voyage without any more precise designation. This is to be accounted for by the fact that the *signoria* arranged with ship captains to sail over a general area and collect what grain they could find. Of the total of twenty-seven ships clearing in the two and a half years for grain, sixteen are recorded without further indication, four sailed for Volo, three for "the Archipelago," two for Sicily, one for La Cavalla, and one for Cyprus. It is to be noted that the years in question were as a whole years of bad crops on the mainland and country people came to Venice to buy. Agostino Agostini, *Istoria Veneziano*, ff. 251–62, in Bibl. Querini Stampalia, Venice, MSS. Cl. IV., cod. 16.

If averages for the three years were taken, constructing figures for the full year 1560 from those for the first six months, on the assumption that the total clearances for that

Note to Table I continued
year were in the same proportion to those for its first half as the totals for 1558 and 1559 were to the first halves of those years, the averages so obtained would not differ from those given by as much as two ships except in the case of grain. About 70 per cent of the grain clearances were in August, and since grain imports varied seasonally the clearances for the first six months are not adequate evidence of the clearances for the whole year.

TABLE II

Comparison of the number and capacity of ships clearing annually
for selected voyages about 1448–49 and in 1558–59*

	Number and Capacity of Ships Cleared, by Periods			
	Number of ships		Capacity in tons	
Voyage	1448–49	1558–59	1448–49	1558–59
Syria and/or Cyprus	12	13	5,400	7,170
English Channel and the West	3	3	1,800	1,830
Constantinople and/or Black Sea	3	3–4	1,300	1,680

* The figures for the later period are taken from Table I. The figures for the earlier period are estimates obtained as follows:

The estimates for the voyage to Syria and Cyprus are based on statements of the number and capacity of the ships going in the spring *muda* 1418, the spring and fall *mude* 1426, spring and fall 1427, spring 1428, spring and fall 1431, fall 1433, and fall 1449. See Senato Misti, reg. 52, f. 66; reg. 55, ff. 181–91; reg. 56, ff. 16, 25, 56, 71, 75, 104, 114, 152–56; reg. 58, ff. 19, 22, 26, 46, 53, 60, 62, 73, 190, 213; Notatorio di Collegio, nos. 7–10.

The estimate of the number going to England and the West, which is taken to mean beyond the Straits of Gibraltar, is based on mention of ships in 1446, 1448, 1449. Senato Mar., reg. 2, f. 156; reg. 3, ff. 43, 48–49, 70, 121, 135. The estimate of capacity is based on mention of the size of some of the ships in lists in the Notatorio, and on the considerations that the largest ships were used on the voyage and that there were at least six Venetian ships of 600 tons or more at the time. Notatorio, nos. 10 and 12, f. 98.

The estimates for Constantinople and the Black Sea are based on the mention of ships on that voyage in 1446–48 (Senato Mar., reg. 2, f. 134; reg. 3, ff. 48, 53, 58), and the statements of the number and size going at the beginning of the century, 1398, 1400–02 (Notatorio, no. 5). The number of ships was the same at the beginning and middle of the century.

2

The Mediterranean Spice Trade: Its Revival in the Sixteenth Century*

THE Portuguese did not reduce the Levantine spice trade to permanent insignificance. Although the flow of spice through the traditional routes of the Levant was severely checked during the first decades of the sixteenth century, it later found its way through the obstacles raised by the Portuguese. Even pepper again came through the Red Sea in approximately the volume of the years before the Portuguese opened their new route to India. This thesis was suggested by the following figures[1] for the Venetian pepper exports from Alexandria:

Yearly average, before Portuguese
interference was felt.........about 1,150,000 lb. Eng.
Yearly average, 1560–64, inclusively...1,310,454 lb. Eng.

The source of the figures for 1560 to 1564 and their isolated character make it desirable to present corroboratory evidence of the revival of the Levantine spice trade.

The travel diary of a young Venetian nobleman, Alessandro Magno, furnishes a picture of the trade in Egypt in the middle of the century.[2]

* From *American Historical Review*, XLV (1940), 581–90. (By permission.)

[1] See above pp. 12–14, "Venetian Shipping during the Commercial Revolution." The source for the later figure is an isolated sheet in the Donà dalle Rose family papers, busta 217, Museo Civico, Venice. The figures given are there said to be copied from the records of the Venetian consulate in Alexandria.

[2] Folger Shakespeare Library, Washington, D.C., MS. 1317.1, no paging, third voyage. I am indebted to Professor Kent Roberts Greenfield for calling this manuscript to my attention and to Dr. J. Q. Adams, the director of the library, for permission to quote from it.

On April 4, 1561, Alessandro sailed for Alexandria in the *Crose,* a round ship of about 540 tons.[3] Such ships had very largely taken the place of the merchant galleys which in the previous century monopolized the shipping of the more precious types of merchandise.[4] Copper and woolen cloth, which had been among the chief items in the cargo lists of the galleys, bulked large among the wares carried by the *Crose.*[5] As his own venture, Magno took along some silk cloth and two thousand ducats.

As soon as he reached Alexandria, on May 2, he presented his letters of recommendation to the resident Venetian merchants and was assigned a room in one of the houses or *fondachi* belonging to the Venetian colony. The Venetians had two such *fondachi* at Alexandria, the other "nations," the Genoese, Ragusans, and French, who were less numerous, each having one. Venetians were settled at Cairo also, for in 1552 they had obtained permission to trade in that city.[6] Young

---

[3] The description of this ship in Magno's diary agrees with that in the ship lists from the Donà dalle Rose papers (see p. 23, Table I, n.).

[4] See p. 8. The galleys auctioned for the voyage to Alexandria after 1536 were as follows: 2 in 1549, 2 in 1550, 2 in 1554, 2 in 1555, 2 in 1557, 3 in 1563, 3 in 1564—Archivio di Stato di Venezia (cited hereinafter as A.S.V.), Senato, Terminazione, Incanti Galere, reg. 2, lib. 4 and 5.

[5] Alessandro Magno gives the complete cargo of the *Crose* as follows: *rami lavoradi* (manufactured copper), *balle* 250; *rami in verga* (copper in bars), *cassette* 85; *pani de lana* (woolen cloth), *balle* 129; *pani de seda* (silk cloth), *cassette* 21; *carisee* (kerseys), *balle* 28; *barette* (caps), *casse* 35; *coralli* (coral), *casse* 23; *ambre* (amber), *casse* 1; *coralli e ambre* (coral and amber), *casse* 12; *sbiacche* (white lead), *barili* 100; *jrios* (Florentine iris, a dye?), *caratelli* 15; *banda raspa* (tin plate, filed down), *barili* 22; *Pater nostri de vedro* (glass rosaries), *casse* 7; *Pater nostri e barrette* (rosaries and caps), *casse* 3; *merce* (merchandise), *cai* 11; *carta* (paper), *balle* 30; *assafetida* (assafetida), *fagoti* 2; *tabini* (a kind of fine cloth?), *ligacetto* 1; *contadi* (cash), ducati—. Alessandro gives also the cargo for Zante and says the total freight paid by shippers was eighteen hundred ducats. Cargo lists of galleys may be found for comparison in Marino Sanuto, *I Diarii* (Venice, 1879–1903), III, 1187–88 (for 1500); IX, 536 (for 1510); XII, 77–78 (for 1511); and XXXX, 175–76 (for 1525).

[6] [Friedrich] Wilken, "Über die Venetianischen Consuln zu Alexandrien im 15ten und 16ten Jahrhunderte," K. Akademie der Wissenschaften zu Berlin, *Abhandlungen aus dem Jahre 1831* (Berlin, 1832), Historisch-philologische Klasse, p. 44. The restriction of Venetian traders to Alexandria had become galling to Venetians in the middle of the sixteenth century because Jews and others interjected themselves between the Arabs in Cairo and the Venetians in Alexandria. These intermediaries not only took a middleman's profit in the trade in grain and spices but even succeeded in loading their own spices and other wares on Venetian ships. To meet this competition the Venetians requested that they be allowed to trade at Cairo. A.S.V., Senato Mar, reg. 32, ff. 35–36.

Alessandro soon moved there and spent a good part of his time there seeing the sights and taking a trip to the pyramids. When at Alexandria he had bartered some of his silk cloth for pepper and had used some of his cash to buy more pepper. Before making the rest of his purchases he meant to await the arrival of a caravan which was expected from Tor, the Red Sea terminus of the ships bringing wares from India. After about a month of sight-seeing around Cairo he returned to Alexandria and then wrote instructing a relative in Cairo to invest the rest of his funds in pepper as soon as the new merchandise arrived from Tor. These plans were upset by the decision of the captain of the *Crose* not to wait any longer. As soon as it was known that the ship was leaving, "everyone began to buy furiously. Pepper, which before had been worth twenty ducats a cantar went to twenty-two, and could not be had, and everything else similarly." Alarmed by the sudden rise in prices, Alessandro canceled his orders to buy pepper in Cairo and put the rest of his money into cloves and ginger, which he bought in Alexandria. The *Crose* weighed anchor on October 19, before the arrival of the autumn caravan from Tor,[7] yet it carried more than a half million pounds of spices including a little more than 400,000 lb. Eng. of pepper.[8] Alessandro was back in Venice on November 18 and soon sold

[7] Because of the monsoons, wares from India reached Egypt mainly in the fall. Wilhelm von Heyd, *Histoire du commerce du Levant au moyen âge* (Leipzig, 1885–86), II, 446–47, 500.

[8] In his travel diary Magno gives two lists of the cargo of the ship, one from the record of the Venetian consulate, one from the ship's manifest. The largest items among the spices were entered on the ship's manifest in *colli,* and the total number of *colli* is 478, which, at 1120 lb. Eng. per *collo,* is 525,360 lb. Other items are given in *nichesse, fardi, casse,* etc., the weights of which are unknown to me. Besides spices and drugs the ship carried a few bales of cotton, linen, and carpets, some hides, and 800 *ribebe* of broad beans. The following cargo of spices and drugs is given from the records of the consulate in cantara (presumably cantara of different weights since the units used in measuring were different for different spices), except in the case of indigo: *piper* (pepper), cantara 4452; *zenzeri buli* (dressed or coated [?] ginger), 266; *belledi* (ginger native to west coast of India), 828; *sorati* (ginger from Surat), 554; *mordassi* (ginger with biting taste [?]), 96; *mechini* (ginger from near Mecca), 45½; *Zedoaria* (zedoary), 35½; *canelle* (cinnamon), 32½; *nose* (nutmeg), 61; *garoffoli affus de* (cloves), 26; *spigo nardo* (spikenard), 6½; *macis* (mace), 32½; *galanga* (galingale), 18¼; *boraso pate* (borax cakes), 4; *zucari* (sugar), 66; *sandoli rossi* (red sanderswood), 24; *nose condite pate* (candied nutmeg cakes), 4; *porcelette* (purslane or pursley [?]), 4; *assafetida* (assafetida), 2; *aloe patico* (hepatic aloes), 138; *salarmoniago* (salammoniac), 3½; *turbiti* (turpeth), 7½; *cocole* (kermes dye), 72; *mira* (myrrh), 50; *incenso* (frankincense), 178; *penacchi* (plumes), 34; *goma arabica* (gum Arabic), 97; *endeghi* (indigo); . . . *zurli* (bundles wrapped in cowhide), 43; *mirabolani* (myrobalans), 50; *tamarindi* (tamarind), 91; *cassia* (cassia),

at 97 ducats a *cargo* the pepper he had bought at the equivalent of a fraction more than 56 ducats a *cargo*. He figured his profits as 266 ducats, 18 denarii, and 22 piccoli.

Syria as well as Egypt had been a center for spice exports to the West in the fifteenth century, and Syria shared the revival in the mid-sixteenth century. Here also the Venetians moved their chief colony farther into the interior and transferred their consulate from Damascus to Aleppo, which was nearer the route to Bagdad and Basra. This route gave access to the wares of India, whence, says a *relazione* of 1553, "come all the spices, which are one of the primary foundations of the trade of our colony."[9] The arrivals at both Aleppo and Damascus of caravans with spices are described in the dispatches of the Venetian consuls, Giovanni Battista Basadona (1556–57) and Andrea Malipiero (1563–64).[10] From 1560 to 1563, however, during the Turkish-Portuguese hostilities, the caravans from Basra were very small, and while the Venetian trade at Alexandria prospered, that at Aleppo languished.[11]

On the volume of the spices moving through the Levant in the mid-sixteenth century much can be learned from Portuguese sources. The Portuguese embassy in Rome assembled what news it could collect from the Levant in order to warn its royal master of the preparation of

---

47; *curcuma* (turmeric), 20; *piper longo salvadego* (long pepper, wild), 23; *siena* (senna), 100; *zenzeri verdi* (green ginger), 4. Cargo lists of galleys may be found for comparison in *I Diarii di Girolamo Priuli*, published in *Rerum Italicarum Scriptores* (2d ed., vol. XXIV, pt. 3; Città di Castello, 1911), I, 73 (for 1497), and in Sanuto, XIV, 25–26 (for 1512).

The equivalence, 1 *collo* = 1120 lb. Eng. is based on Sanuto, XVII, 191, and is presumably a rough general average. Copies of invoices giving individually the weights of 59 *colli* shipped from Alexandria in 1497 show that their weights varied between 968 and 1222 lb. Eng. The average for the 59 bales or *colli* was 1083 lb. Eng. per *collo*. A.S.V., Misc. Gregolin, busta 10, Lettere commerciali, fragment of a letter book of Michele da Lezze.

[9] Eugenio Albèri, *Relazioni degli ambasciatori veneti al Senato* (Florence, 1840), III, 223, "Relazione anonima della guerra di Persia." See also the *relazione* of Marino Cavalli in 1560 (*ibid.*, III, 283–84), that of Daniele Barbarigo in 1564 (*ibid.*, VI, 3–10), and Guglielmo Berchet, *Relazioni dei consoli veneti nella Siria* (Turin, 1866), introduction.

[10] A.S.V., Relazioni (Collegio, Secreta), Consoli, busta 31. I am indebted to the Social Science Research Council for a grant-in-aid which made it possible to consult these and the later-cited reports of Venetian consuls.

[11] *Ibid.*, letter from Lorenzo Tiepolo, May, 1563; Museo Civico Correr, Venice, Cod. Cicogna, busta 3154, *relazione* of Lorenzo Tiepolo, published by Sacerdote Daniele Canal, *Per Nozze Passi-Valier Tiepolo* (Venice, 1857), p. 40; A.S.V., Senato Mar, reg. 35, ff. 29, 164.

Turkish war fleets in the Red Sea or Persian Gulf.[12] In 1559 Lourenço
Pires de Távora became Portuguese ambassador to the papal court,[13]
and he at once set to work to improve the Portuguese news service in
the Levant. He engaged the services of two Jews, Isaac Becudo and
Mathew Becudo, who possessed the friendships or connections necessary for gathering information and for sending secret dispatches to the
Portuguese consul in Venice. Isaac posted himself at Aleppo, Mathew
at Cairo,[14] and their letters were forwarded from Venice to Rome and
from Rome to Lisbon.[15] Those of Mathew, at least, described not only
the naval activity but also the spice trade, and Pires interested himself
in this trade. His career before coming to Rome had given him occasion
to be informed about it. He had sailed to India as admiral of a spice
fleet in 1546.[16] Later, when he was the Portuguese ambassador to
Emperor Charles V, King John III acted on his advice in closing the
royal spice-selling agency in Antwerp.[17] At Rome Pires supplemented
the information furnished by the Jews already mentioned with reports
from Venetians, Genoese, and Ragusans,[18] and above all from Antonio
Pinto, a Portuguese, who became Pires's secretary. Pinto had been at
Cairo as a captive of the Moslems and after his release returned there to
negotiate the ransom of other prisoners.[19]

After Pinto's return from this trip, Pires wrote in November, 1560, as
follows: "From this Antonio Pinto of Cairo and also from important
persons of Venice and Ragusa with whom I have spoken, I understand
that there come to Alexandria each year 40,000 quintals [4,480,000 lb.]
of spices, being pepper for the principal part." Pires then described in
detail the routes by which the spices came from India and concluded,
"there being so much which comes to the dominion of the Turks, it is
no wonder that so little comes to Lisbon."[20]

So seriously did Pires consider the competition of the routes through
the Red Sea and Persian Gulf that he advised arranging a contract to

[12] *Corpo Diplomatico Portuguez*, published by the Academia Real das' Sciencias de
Lisboa, ed. by L. A. Rebello da Silva and others (Lisbon, 1862–1910), III, 396–97;
IV, 14–15; VII, 35, 153, 201, 434; VIII, 115, 364.

[13] *Ibid.*, VIII, 148.

[14] *Ibid.*, pp. 171–75, 396; IX, 13, 108, 489.

[15] *Ibid.*, VIII, 236, 250, 354; IX, 108, 251.

[16] Fortunato de Almeida, *História de Portugal* (Coimbra, 1922–29), III, 435 n.

[17] Fr. Luiz de Sousa, *Annaes de elrei Dom João Terceiro*, ed. by A. Herculano
(Lisbon, 1844), pp. 420–23.

[18] *Corpo Dipl. Port.*, IX, 110, 134–35, 303.

[19] *Ibid.*, VIII, 154, 174, 295, 415; IX, 89–90, 109, 485.

[20] *Ibid.*, IX, 110–11. This passage is mentioned by Almeida, III, 562.

have the spices for the king of Portugal brought through the Levant in case peace could be arranged with the Turks. The chances of peace seemed to him slight in 1560 because of the "insolence" of the Turks,[21] but the possibility of such an arrangement between the Portuguese and the sultan was worrying Venetian statesmen four years later.[22]

Large quantities of spices continued to reach Alexandria for some years after 1560. In 1561 spices were so abundant in Egypt as to encourage a rumor at Venice and Florence that the Portuguese viceroy of India was in revolt and therefore had sent the spices to Alexandria instead of to Lisbon. Not crediting this wild rumor, Pires sought some other explanation of the "disorder in the guarding of pepper." For that year, at least, it seemed that the Levantine supply of spices would dominate the European market, for the Portuguese fleet to India had missed the monsoons. The Venetians and Germans were counting on the scarcity of spices in Lisbon and were pushing up the price in Venice. The whole situation, said Pires, was a clear demonstration of how much damage the Portuguese king suffered from the competition of the Red Sea route.[23]

Since Lourenço Pires left the Portuguese embassy in Rome early in the spring of 1562, we have no more of his illuminating reports.[24] The spy in Cairo, Mathew Becudo, was caught, imprisoned, and sentenced to death. His friends and his money secured his release, however, and he was able to send further reports, at least on spices, to the Portuguese consul in Venice. In October 1564, Mathew recorded the capture by the Portuguese fleet of four Moslem merchant ships near Mecca, yet, in the same letter, he estimated that 30,000 quintals of pepper would enter the Red Sea that year and said that Venetian sources estimated the pepper available at 25,000 quintals (2,800,000 lb. Eng.).[25]

Large quantities also arrived during the next two years, according to the letters from the Venetian consul at Cairo. In August, 1565, he wrote that messengers from Mecca reported the arrival at Jiddah with spices of the following ships: one from Daibul, four from Gujarat, two from Surat, eight from Baticalà, three from Calicut, two from Mordassi (?), and three from Assi (a kingdom in the island of Sumatra). Two others

[21] *Corpo Dipl. Port.*, IX, 134–36, 251–52.

[22] Albèri, VI, p. 6, *relazione* of Daniele Barbarigo.

[23] *Corpo Dipl. Port.*, IX, 251, 261, 271, 277, 303–304.

[24] *Ibid.*, IX, 508.

[25] *Ibid.*, IX, 472; X, 186. That the amount reaching Egypt may have been twice the amount reaching Venice is understandable in view of the consumption of the Levantine countries and the imports of Ragusa and other rivals of Venice.

from Assi were expected. Next year, in May, 1566, he reported that five ships from Assi and three from Baticalà had already reached Jiddah with 15,000 *boara,* about 24,000 cantara of pepper (2,256,000 lb. Eng.). Even if the additional ships expected from Gujarat, Calicut, and elsewhere did not arrive, he wrote, an excellent supply of spices was assured for that fall.[26]

These figures, from both Portuguese and Venetian sources, indicate that the importation of spices from Alexandria to Europe about 1560 was as large or larger than it had been in the late fifteenth century. They suggest that shipments from the Indian Ocean to the Red Sea roughly equaled or occasionally exceeded the Portuguese imports.[27] Evidently the consumption of spices, or at least of pepper, increased greatly in Europe during the sixteenth century.[28]

Shipment from Alexandria westward went principally to Ragusa,

[26] A.S.V., Dispacci, Consoli, busta 20. I assume that the cantar referred to by the consul was the Alexandrian *cantar forfori* of about 94 lb.

[27] Heyd (II, 533), estimated Portuguese imports at 25,000 to 35,000 quintals, but the amount actually received, 1503–6, was less. Leonardo da Ca' Masser, "Relazione sopra il commercio dei Portoghesi nell'India, 1497–1506," *Archivio Storico Italiano,* II (1845), app., 13 ff. Some later records of cargoes of Portuguese fleets are: 1518, 48,097 cantara, Sanuto, *Diarii,* XXV, 594–95; 1519, 37,530 cantara, *ibid.,* XXVII, 641; 1530, 18,164 cantara, *ibid.,* LIV, 131; 1531, 20,586 cantara, *ibid.,* LV, 63. A falling off in Portuguese imports in the middle of the century is suggested by the tenor of Pires's remarks. Estimates of the volume of the annual Portuguese imports at the end of the sixteenth century vary from 40,000 quintals of pepper alone to 20,000 quintals of pepper and 10,000 quintals of other spices. Bal Krishna, *Commercial Relations between India and England* (London, 1924), pp. 45–46. Bal Krishna's apparent source for the higher figure—*The Voyage of John Huyghen van Linschoten to the East Indies* (Hakluyt Society; London, 1885), II, 220–22—does not seem to me to justify this figure but rather to support other indications that 30,000 quintals of pepper was the amount which the Portuguese *hoped* to load in India each year. The standard of 30,000 quintals of pepper is given in Charles de Lannoy and Herman vander Linden, *Histoire de l'expansion coloniale des peuples européens: Portugal et Espagne* (Brussels, 1907), I, 199, and M. A. Hedwig Fitzler, "Der Anteil der Deutschen an der Kolonialpolitik Philipps II. von Spanien in Asien," *Vierteljahrschrift für Sozial- und Wirtschaftsgeschichte,* XXVIII (1935), 249. The cantar used in the above-cited passages in Sanuto is clearly the Portuguese quintal equaling about 112 lb. Eng. I assume that the quintal used in the Portuguese reports to the Portuguese court was also the Portuguese quintal, not the Alexandrian *cantar forfori* of about 94 lb., and that the Portuguese quintal is also that meant in other works cited in this note.

[28] A numerical statement must contain a large element of conjecture, especially so because the figures for imports through Syria are not satisfactory for any part of the century. My guess would be: annual pepper imports of western Europe about 1500, 1½ to 2 million lb.; about 1560, over 3 million lb.

Messina, and Venice. From these three *scalas,* said Pires, spices were sent to all Italy and Germany.[29] Venice was still the leader in the Levant trade, according to her own reports and those of the Portuguese, and Venetian trade with Germany was "in full bloom."[30] Some of the German merchants, however, had begun to do business through Ragusa, for the Venetian-Turkish War (1537–40) had enabled the Ragusans to take a larger part in the Levant trade.[31] At Venice Germans were prevented from buying directly in the East. By trading through Ragusa they could send their own agents to the Levant.

The switch of Portugal's German customers to the Alexandrian spice market seemed to Pires a particularly alarming aspect of the situation, which he thus described in 1560:

> The Fuggers of Augsburg sent the last year one of their factors to buy pepper in Alexandria to try out that route. Beginning with only 10,000 crusados he bought a quantity which they loaded in a Ragusan ship and from there in long boats to a place belonging to the emperor which is called Fiume. He returned this September with a larger sum [and] ought to buy advantageously [by] this route, and it would be very bad to have this buyer or bidder absent from the contracts and purchases in Portugal, but this business of the Fuggers being to the disadvantage of the export of the Venetians and passing by a route through their sea, I believe they will arrange to stop it.[32]

The use by the great German merchant houses of Ragusa as a way station may be the explanation also of the agents posted in Cairo and Alexandria by the firm of Ulstetter.[33]

Although Pires did not mention French merchants, Marseilles also imported spices from Alexandria. The diplomatic alliance of France and Turkey was supplemented in 1535 by commercial treaties which gave the French a legal standing on which to base competition with the

[29] *Corpo Dipl. Port.,* IX, 111.

[30] J. Falke, "Oberdeutschlands Handelsbeziehungen zu Südeuropa im Anfang des 16 Jahrhunderts," *Zeitschrift für deutsche Kulturgeschichte,* IV (1859), 610, 615, 625; Henry Simonsfeld, *Der Fondaco dei Tedeschi in Venedig und die deutsch-venetianischen Handelsbeziehungen* (Stuttgart, 1887), II, 123–25.

[31] A.S.V., Senato Mar, reg. 24, ff. 80, 149; reg. 25, f. 55.

[32] *Corpo Dipl. Port.,* IX, 111–12.

[33] Falke, p. 611. Because of the Venetian restriction on the trade of German residents in Venice, André-E. Sayous expresses doubt of Falke's assertion in "Le commerce de Melchior Manlich et Cie d'Augsburg à Marseille et dans toute la Méditerranée entre 1571 et 1574," *Revue historique,* CLXXVI (1935), 396, but the existence of a route around Venice through Fiume and Ragusa renders it quite credible.

Venetians in the Ottoman Empire.[34] The Marseilles merchants whose company received the rights to coral fishing off Tunis were pushed into the Levant trade because most of the coral had to be marketed in Alexandria. From the papers of this *Compagnie du corail* we learn that in 1565 its ships came from Alexandria full of spices and these spices from the Levant were sent to Lyons, Paris, and even to Rouen. They competed in Toulouse with the spices brought through Bordeaux from Lisbon.[35]

Why could so much spice be shipped to Europe through the Levant in spite of Portuguese control of the route around Africa? Although an answer to that question cannot be fully given and demonstrated within the limits of this note, a suggestion may not be out of order. Portuguese policy was dominated by the desire for high prices, and the Portuguese "monopoly" depended upon interfering with the Red Sea trade. The prices charged by the Portuguese at Lisbon or Antwerp were so high that the Levantine spice trade could be revived whenever Portuguese interference could be overcome. For some decades after 1500 the Portuguese put serious obstacles in the way of the Red Sea trade and forced the prices of spices at Alexandria up above their fifteenth-century level. Later the Portuguese officials in India became so inefficient, or so easily corrupted, that they no longer placed costly obstacles in the way of trade through the Red Sea and the Persian Gulf. A Venetian consul reported that the spices which came to Cairo were "allowed to pass by the Portuguese soldiers who govern India in the Red Sea, for their profit against the commands of their king, for they can make a living in that region only by selling cinnamon, cloves, nutmeg, mace, ginger, pepper, and other drugs."[36]

The years 1560 to 1566, for which the evidence presented is most detailed, may have been the peak of the revival, but spices from the Levant were already affecting Antwerp prices in 1540.[37] Alexandria and

[34] Paul Masson, *Histoire du commerce français dans le Levant au xviie siècle* (Paris, 1896), pp. xii–xiv.

[35] Paul Masson, *Compagnies du corail* (Paris, 1908), pp. 123–25. See also Masson, *Histoire du commerce*, pp. xv–xvi, and Sayous, p. 406.

[36] Museo Civico-Correr, Venice, Cod. Cicogna, busta 3154, *relazione* of Lorenzo Tiepolo in 1556 (in Canal). See the *relazione* of Antonio Tiepolo in 1572 (Albèri, XIII, 204), which says that the "robbery" of the Portuguese officials in India allowed Alexandria to participate in the spice trade, "perhaps for the greater part."

[37] Florence Edler de Roover, "The Market for Spices in Antwerp, 1538–1544," *Revue belge de philologie et d'histoire*, XVII (1938), 215–18. The imports of Venice from Alexandria picked up enormously, and from a low level, between 1550 and 1554. Museo Civico-Correr, Venice, Cod. Cicogna, busta 3154, *relazione* of Daniele Barbarigo.

Aleppo remained sources of spice shipments to Europe during the rest of the century. When Philïp II of Spain became king of Portugal he tried to put new energy into cutting the Red Sea route,[38] but spice cargoes were still coming to the Levant when the Dutch ships reached India.[39] For the Venetians as well as the Portuguese the arrival of the Dutch in the Indian Ocean was counted a catastrophe.[40] Again Venetian consuls in the Levant, like those of a hundred years before, lamented the decline of the caravans which used to arrive from India rich with spices.[41]

The evidence here presented indicates that the Mediterranean cities had a prominent part in the spice trade during certain years in the later sixteenth century. How far that affected their general importance as commercial centers is a different question and one which cannot be answered without taking into consideration a great many other factors. The answer might involve the conclusion that spices were a relatively minor element in the shift of the commercial center of Europe from the Mediterranean to the North Sea. The spectacular vicissitudes of the spice trade have attracted so much attention that there is real danger of overemphasizing their influence.

[38] Fitzler, pp. 248 ff.; *Fugger News-Letters*, ser. 2, ed. by Victor von Klarwill, trans. by L. S. R. Byrne (London, 1926) , pp. 109, 111; Albèri, IX, 309, and XIII, 396.

[39] Berchet, pp. 80, 102–3.

[40] *Fugger News-Letters*, ser. 1, ed. by Klarwill (New York, 1924) , no. 201: "in time great harm will befall the kingdom of Portugal *and the Venetians*" (italics mine) .

[41] The *relazione* of 1625 by Antonio Capello, says: "Questi [i.e., Venetians in Egypt] da certo tempo in quà sono diminuti et semati assai di numero et di conditione per il mancamento delle specie dell'Indie, che per la nuova navigazione ritrovata da fiamenghi hanno preso altro corso ne capitano più nel Cairo o in poco quantita; in particolar il garofalo veniva tutto da quelle parti et hora non se ne vede, et bisogna a chi ne vuole farlo venire di qua." Museo Civico-Correr, MS., P. D. 306c II and MS. Wcovich-Lazzari, busta 20. The *relazione* of Gerolamo Foscarini, 1628, says: "Diverse sono le cause, per le quali, da molti anni in qua, il negotio di tutto il Levante e quello d'Alessandria in particolar è grandemente decaduto. La prima, senza dubbio fu, la navigation ritrovata da Fiamenghi." A.S.V., Relazione (Collegio, Secreta) , Consoli, busta 31. Earlier *relazioni* of 1597, 1602, and 1615, in the same *busta*, make no mention of the Dutch. For *relazioni* from Syria in these years see Berchet.

BUSINESS AND FINANCE

3

Family Partnerships and Joint Ventures*

I

CORPORATIONS have been the big basic units of recent American business; in the Venetian Republic the basic units of business life were family partnerships. To be sure, since a Venetian family partnership was not an organization formed only for business purposes, it did not correspond exactly to a corporation. There were in the Venetian economy during the later Middle Ages some enterprises which required the use of so much capital that normally several families banded together to spread the risks and for such occasions they formed joint ventures. From some points of view these joint ventures, rather than the family partnerships, corresponded in Venetian economy to the corporation in modern economy; for they were organized for strictly business purposes, they involved large capital, and their ownership was divided into shares. But the joint ventures lacked the permanence of the modern corporation and they had quite limited objectives. They lasted only for the duration of a voyage or until a cargo had been sold. Moreover, they did not have such large capital funds as did the family partnerships which created them. Venetian business enterprise, having been fathered by the state and mothered by the family, remained subordinated to these older and stronger institutions. This fact is not surprising, for when viewed in historical perspective the modern corporation appears a parvenu of uncertain future. In most societies, at

* From *Journal of Economic History*, IV (1944), 178–96. (By permission.)

A grant-in-aid from the Social Science Research Council made possible the collection and photofilming in Venice in the spring of 1939 of the main materials used in this study. I wish to express my appreciation for this aid and also for a grant by the American Philosophical Society out of the Penrose fund which in 1943 supplied me with the assistance of Dr. Helen Wieruszowski as a research assistant.

most times, it has been the great family which by its wealth, power, prestige, and presumption of permanence has been the outstanding institution in private economic enterprise.

As late as the sixteenth century Venice presented a fine example of family capitalism in the *fraterna* or the family partnership. Originally *fraterne* derived their existence from the physical fact that brothers often lived together in the same house, shared the same board, and consumed together the products of their country estates. Under Venetian law members of a family thus living together and doing business as a unit automatically became full partners without any formal contract.[1] Even after the family partnership became the dominant form of business organization in Venice, it continued to be more than a mere business partnership. All the property inherited from the father—houses, land, furniture, and jewelry as well as ships and merchandise—was entered on the books of the *fraterna* unless withdrawn from it by special agreement. Expenditures for food and household furnishings, as well as business expenses, were recorded in its ledgers along with the big sales and purchases which kept merchandise moving through Venice.

Many men prominent in Venetian politics belonged to family partnerships which were the leading business firms of the city. One example mentioned by chroniclers is the Doge Andrea Vendramin, elected in 1476. In describing him at the time of his election, Malipiero says he was very rich, worth 160,000 ducats.[2] This may have been but the fragment of his fortune left him in his old age after he had spent very liberally on his political career. Especially noteworthy among his political expenses were the dowries of 5,000 to 7,000 ducats which he had given with each of his six daughters in order to have influential sons-in-law. In his youth, continues Malipiero, "he was a great mer-

---

[1] Pompeo Molmenti, *La storia di Venezia nella vita privata* (7th ed.; Bergamo, 1927), I, 456; Antonio Pertile, *Storia del diritto italiano* (2d ed.; Turin, 1894), III, 282.

[2] The fortune of Cosimo de' Medici and his brother in 1440 was 235,137 florins and rose, according to Sieveking's estimate, to 400,000 florins in 1460. Heinrich Sieveking, "Die Handlungsbücher der Medici," *Sitzungsberichte der Philosophisch-Historischen Klasse der Kaiserlichen Akademie der Wissenschaften* (Vienna), CLI (1905), Abh. V, 4, 11–12. Both the florin and the ducat contained about 3.5 grams of gold. The relative value of money is somewhat indicated by the fact that the salary authorized for a skilled worker to supervise the repairs on the ducal palace in 1483 was 100 ducats a year. Dominico Malipiero, *Annali veneti dell'anno 1457 al 1500*, ed. by Tommaso Gar and Augustino Sagredo, *Archivio Storico Italiano*, ser. i, VII (1843), 674.

chant and when in *fraterna* with his brother Luca they used to ship enough merchandise from Alexandria to load one and a half or two galleys, and he had many factors who have grown rich managing his affairs.[3]

As late as the sixteenth century, leadership in government and in business was combined. An active politician and the leading banker of Venice between 1509 and 1528 was Alvise Pisani. He survived a number of runs on his bank, saving the situation during the most serious run in 1499 by a skillful personal appeal to the crowd on the Rialto, and at one time he concentrated in his hands nearly all the banking business of the state.[4] When the bank of Lorenzo di Tassis in Rome failed in 1518, Alvise Pisani learned of it earlier than did Lorenzo's brother Andrea, who was in Venice at the time. Consequently Pisani was able to make good his claim against Andrea di Tassis before the latter could get away. The Florentines and Genoese lost heavily, but the Venetians did not.[5]

Like Doge Andrea Vendramin, Alvise Pisani spent freely for political advantage. He, too, married his daughters (he had five) to members of families of political influence, and it cost him 40,000 ducats in dowries. One of his sons was a wealthy cardinal. He himself was frequently a member of the highest councils of the Republic, and although he did not attain the highest office, the dogeship, he received a number of votes in one ducal election. Even his death was in a sense a success, for he died in the service of his fatherland when the army with which Venice and her allies were besieging Naples was decimated by the plague. The solvency of his bank was celebrated four months later when his son, dressed in black and surrounded by many of the highest dignitaries of the state, came forth from the celebration of Mass in the church on the Rialto, signaled for the sounding of trumpets and fifes, and ordered the scarlet-clad public crier to proclaim that the bank was to be liquidated and that all who wished might come and receive their money.[6]

Alvise's mercantile operations were carried on in co-operation with his brothers, Lorenzo and Almorò. They died about 1528 also and some account books of the executors and heirs of Almorò survive in the Frari

---

[3] *Ibid.*, 666, and cf. 661.

[4] See pp. 80–86.

[5] MS, Diario di Marcantonio Michiel, Museo Civico-Correr, Venice, MS Cicogna 2848 (MI, 469), ff. 288 v°–289 r°.

[6] Marino Sanuto, *I diarii* (Venice, 1879–1903), XXXV, 376; XXXVI, 410; XXXVII, 40; XLVIII, 137, 237; XLIX, 124–25, 240; LII, 79, 82.

at Venice.[7] Although Venetian sources constantly refer to such *fraterne* as those of Vendramin or Pisani, no ledger of an equally rich *fraterna* or individual has been found among surviving account books.[8] Consequently the Pisani books come as near as any that have survived to affording a glance into the organization of big business in Venice.

Another glance, from a different angle, is offered by the journal of Lorenzo Priuli, also a holder of the highest offices beneath the dogeship and father of the well-known banker and diarist, Girolamo Priuli. The Pisani and Priuli families were connected through Vincenzo Priuli's marriage to a daughter of Alvise Pisani. Besides being an active naval officer, at one time commanding the merchant galleys of Beirut, Vincenzo was active in the business of importing wool from England. Girolamo Priuli kept his bank in his own name, but Vincenzo's operations in wool and many other transactions handled by him, by

[7] Archivio di Stato di Venezia (cited hereafter as A.S.V.) , Registri Privati, Raccolta Barbarigo-Grimani, registri contabili, reg. 19–24. The most informative is reg. 21, a ledger compiled for the executors by copying balances from other books, mainly from a book referred to as "Libro B." The nature of these entries shows that Libro B must have been the ledger of a Pisani *fraterna*. Perhaps it included all three brothers but the weight of evidence is to the effect that the *fraterna* included only Almorò and Lorenzo. The will of Lorenzo Pisani (A.S.V., Archivio notarile, notaio Gerolamo di Bossis, Testamenti, III, no. 33) , drawn up in 1511, refers to the "dittam nostram vocatam Lorenzo et Almorò Pisani" and makes provisions in case Almorò does or does not wish to continue "dictam dittam." Besides being an interesting early example of Venetian use of *ditta,* the passage implies that already in 1511 Alvise had withdrawn from the family partnership, at least in name. Since Alvise was then already a banker he may have wished to separate his brothers' obligations from those which he, as banker, had to assume. To be sure, one of the accounts carried over from Libro B is that of "Alvise Pisani e fradelli." But the balance is much smaller than would be expected if this were really the capital account of Libro B, and the account of "Alvise Pisani e fradelli" may concern only tax levies which were still levied or recorded jointly. I cannot identify any entry in the surviving books as the balance of the account which had, in Libro B, served a capital account. Perhaps that account did not interest the executors who, in a new book (reg. 19) , opened a new capital account for the estate of Almorò. On the other hand, the practical cooperation between Alvise and his brothers and the identification of Alvise with the *fraterna* in common opinion appears in connection with the voyage of the galleys of Barbary of 1519. Marino Sanuto, the well-informed diarist of the time, says that Alvise Pisani had forty-six of the forty-eight shares of the two galleys. *Diarii,* XXX, 103, 109. Libro B of the Pisani showed ownership of some of these shares, so that either Sanuto was mistaken or Alvise had some share in the *fraterna* of which Libro B was the record.

[8] On surviving Venetian account books, see my *Andrea Barbarigo, Merchant of Venice, 1418–1449* (Baltimore: The Johns Hopkins Press, 1944) , pp. 137–50.

Girolamo, and by a third son, Francesco, are described in Lorenzo's book. It is the central record (1505–35) of the management of another large family fortune.[9]

A third glimpse into big business comes from the letter book of Michele da Lezze.[10] He was named, together with Alvise Pisani, as one of the ten richest men in Venice,[11] but the operations recorded in his letters are disappointingly small and surprisingly simple. His letters and the Priuli journal have the advantage of being a moving record and therefore of telling more about the methods of business operations than do the surviving Pisani books, although neither opens with any sort of inventory. They do not give an over-all view of a family fortune as do the Pisani ledgers.

II

The wealth of the three Pisani brothers once totaled close to 250,000 ducats and possibly more, for Alvise's wealth may have exceeded greatly that of the other brothers.[12] The surviving books certainly fail to give a full indication of Alvise's property. By some earlier division of the family inheritance he had acquired title to the family palace on the Canal Grande at Santa Maria Zobenigo. This is commonly called the Palazzo Pisani-Gritti, recently made into a modern hotel. Alvise's ownership is revealed incidentally through the fact that the other brothers paid him rent for an upper floor. How much else Alvise owned personally, either in real estate or in liquid funds, and how much claim if any he had on the possessions of the family partnership are not clear. Probably he had withdrawn earlier from the family estate as his share a sum at least as large as that which remained for the other, less prominent brothers.

[9] MS, Museo Civico-Correr, Venice, Archivio Tron Donà, uncatalogued, but brought to my attention by a hint from Mr. and Mrs. de Roover and by the kindness of the librarian, Signore M. Brunetti. Studied on photofilms in my possession. It is cited hereafter as Priuli journal. On the family, see Rinaldo Fulin, "Girolamo Priuli e i suoi diarii," *Archivio Veneto,* XXII (1881), 137–54.

[10] A.S.V., Miscellanea Gregolin, busta 10, Lettere commerciali, 1482–99, and some detached sheets in buste 12 bis. Studied on photofilms in my possession.

[11] Sanuto, *Diarii,* XXXV, 389.

[12] The figure 250,000 ducats is reached by assuming that Alvise's wealth was, like that of the other brothers, about 85,000 ducats, the sum debited to their accounts in the liquidation. A.S.V., Raccolta Barbarigo-Grimani as cited, reg. 21, k. 105, 123. This checks approximately with the credits to the new capital account of the Almorò estate in *ibid.,* reg. 19.

The investment of the Pisani family wealth was widely diversified and shows the forms of investment then available to men with capital. A very sizable amount was in real estate on the mainland. At Boara near Rovigo a factor named Paul the Winehead ("Paolo Capo di vin") collected rents for them from an estate valued at 20,000 ducats. At Treviso the Pisani owned the mills which stood then, as mills do today, above the streams flowing through that city. The holdings in government bonds reached an impressive total on their books. The market value of these government bonds was much less than their book value; just how much less varied greatly from year to year with the fortunes of war. Of the commercial assets taken over by the executors when the brothers died in 1528, the biggest was a shipment worth 5,378 ducats sent to Constantinople, but there were many worth between 2,000 and 4,000 ducats. Another part of the *fraterna* capital was in merchandise *in monte,* that is, wares being held in Venice in the basement of the family palace or in warehouses. Very little was being held in bills of exchange, but this may well have been because exchange operations were left to Alvise's bank, in which the *fraterna* had a tidy balance. Perhaps the Pisani made some restrictions about what wares they would handle, but no sign of it appears. Their funds moved a heterogeneous collection of commodities—cloth, wool, tin, salt, grain, spices, bowwood, and many others.

In addition to moving wares in international commerce, the Pisani *fraterna* sold a great deal to retailers and manufacturers in Venice. They helped finance the local woolen industry, not by going into partnership with the cloth manufacturers but by supplying them with their materials. When the executors took over the *fraterna* affairs, 5,000 to 6,000 ducats were invested in wool which was being made into cloth or was already in cloth in the finishing processes. The Pisani partnership gave out the raw materials and received in return the finished products. Yet the individuals in the woolen trade with whom the Pisani dealt were not craftsmen but gentlemen with *Ser* before their names. Perhaps there was a sort of double putting-out system in Venice. The Pisani, and other merchants who imported wool and cloth, "put it out" to merchant employers who, in turn, "put it out" to the craftsmen. But the Pisani could and did supply from their warehouses the needed dyestuffs as well as the wool or cloth.

Diversification was also evident in the investments of the Priuli family. They received rents from real estate in Venice and grain for their household from their country place. The sons traded with family funds in spices, silver, cloth, and a variety of government obligations as well as in wool. Vincenzo sold the imported wool to the *drapieri* of Venice on two or three years' credit. A balance sheet for any year from 1505 to 1510 would probably have shown a substantial portion of the Priuli's assets in this sort of commercial accounts receivable. Michele da Lezze similarly traded in spices from Egypt, wool from England, gold from Barbary, and so on.

The commercial investments of a family partnership could be supplemented by those made by brothers individually and this was done by the Pisani. While the *fraterna* owned some property and carried on some commercial operations, each of the Pisani brothers also held property in his own name and engaged in business activities on his own account. In case of bankruptcy it might have been difficult for one brother to avoid liability for the debts of the others, but the separate accounts of the brothers could certainly affect the way they assigned profits among themselves.

The money which a brother invested in his own name might be obtained from his wife's dowry or from a separate legacy.[13] It could also be had in great amount by borrowing from the partnership. Both Almorò and Lorenzo were in debt to the Pisani *fraterna* for about 43,000 ducats when they died. Alvise Pisani and his son Giovanni together owed the family partnership about 10,000 ducats. Some of the sums thus drawn from the *fraterna* may have been used for personal expenses and have ceased to exist as capital. A good deal of it, however, was certainly used in commercial operations distinct from and yet somehow connected with those of the *fraterna*. This connection is evident in many partnerships which may in a certain sense be considered subsidiaries of the family partnership.

The clearest examples of such affiliated partnerships are the "Western" or London Company and the Syrian Company. "The London Company," as I shall call it, was a partnership among Lorenzo Pisani, Almorò Pisani, and Nicolò Duodo. Since this company was also referred to as "Nicolò Duodo e Cia," Duodo appears to have been the active partner. How much of the capital he contributed, if any, cannot be determined. The sum due Lorenzo and Almorò when the executors took over appeared on the books at a book value of 8,248 ducats. The assets actually consisted entirely in bills payable, presumably credit balances which were left over from many years of operation and which included many bad debts. The heirs or executors were willing to release all their claims in favor of Nicolò Duodo if he would pay them half that

[13] Pertile, *Storia del diritto italiano,* III, 282.

sum. Besides the amount which Nicolò Duodo, as manager or survivor of the London Company, owed to his partners Lorenzo and Almorò, the London Company as a whole owed to the Pisani *fraterna* 5,500 ducats. This debt did not represent the unsettled balance due on shipments from Venice to London. It was called "per conto a parte," that is, it was a special credit extended by one of the partnerships to the other. At the same time, as has been said, Almorò and Lorenzo were debtors on the books of the *fraterna* of which they were members. In brief, the situation at the liquidation of the partnership was as follows: Nicolò Duodo owed money to Lorenzo and Almorò, his partners in the London Company; these brothers owed money to their family partnership; and the London Company also was in debt to the Pisani family partnership. This network of debts justifies calling the London Company an affiliate and the Pisani *fraterna* the major company.

The affairs of the London Company show how the sums withdrawn by the brothers from the family partnership could be used to set up a branch company to act as their agent. A similar subsidiary company devoted to the Syrian voyage was managed for the Pisani by Giovanni della Riva. The subordinate position of the company is clearly implied by della Riva's previous career. From 1507 to 1516 he was the salaried agent of the family in Syria, first at 120 ducats a year as a mere factor, and later at 250 ducats a year as branch manager in charge of the warehouse or workshop which he had built for the Pisani at Aleppo. Finally he was made a partner in the Syrian Company.

The three companies named—the parent *fraterna,* the London Company, and the Syrian Company—acted as agents for each other in buying and shipping or in receiving and selling. As we do not have the ledger of the *fraterna* itself, but merely excerpts carried from it into the executors' books, we have very few examples of how this worked in practice. One interesting entry does show, however, that the Syrian Company shipped cotton to the London Company. This probably does not imply any direct voyage from Syria to London, but it does mean that the cotton was consigned by the Syrian Company directly to the order of the London Company. When the cotton was lost by shipwreck, the London Company bore the loss.

While the relation to the *fraterna* of these two affiliates is fairly clear, a number of other associations illustrating the many ramifications of the Pisani business are mentioned without enough detail to define their position. Spanish associates were referred to cryptically in the will of Lorenzo Pisani. Giovanni Francesco Pisani e Cia in the "West" and Vincenzo Pisani in Syria appear to have been minor subsidiaries designed to give young men of the family a chance to try their skill. Of salaried factors in foreign market places there is no mention except for Giovanni della Riva who was ultimately taken into partnership. Consequently we are left to assume that these partnerships were enough to supply at key places the loyal agents needed for extensive international operations. Elsewhere ordinary commission houses may have given adequate service.

A very special affiliate of the family was the bank of Alvise Pisani. The bank had been inherited as a going concern from the father, Giovanni, who had run it with his brother Francesco. It was clearly a separate firm.[14] The deposit of the *fraterna* in the bank was about 2,500 ducats and those of Almorò personally were considerably larger, but since the total deposits in Alvise's bank were probably over 250,000 ducats, its debts to the Pisani family do not seem sufficiently large to place the bank in a dependent position.[15] There is no reason to think that the bank paid any interest on these deposits or that the brothers shared in any way in the profits Alvise may have made from his bank. If there was a mutually profitable relation between the *fraterna* and the bank, it was probably connected with the buying and selling of bills of exchange.

III

Besides acting through relatively permanent subsidiaries, the Pisani *fraterna* conducted its affairs through a number of strictly temporary partnerships formed for a particular purchase or a particular voyage. These temporary associations of capital were of great importance to Venetian economy. In a strict legal sense, at least in Venetian eyes, they may not have been true partnerships at all but arrangements for joint ownership and for conferring power on a common agent.[16] In regard to joint ownership, the object owned could often be physically divided among the owners. This actually might have been done in the case, for example, of a cargo of salt which the Pisani *fraterna* and two or three other merchants jointly imported and sold to the Salt Office. In practice

[14] It is referred to by Sanuto and the Priuli journal simply as the bank of Alvise Pisani, and its accounts were not carried into reg. 21 (Raccolta Barbarigo-Grimani) as accounts of the *fraterna*.

[15] On the number and size of Venetian banks of the time, see my figures in "Venetian Bankers, 1496–1533," pp. 69–86, below.

[16] This interpretation was suggested to me by Roberto Cessi, *Note per la storia delle società di commercio nel Medio Evo in Italia* (Rome, 1917), reprinted from *Rivista italiana per le scienze giuridiche* (March 1917), 3–5; and "Studi sulle 'Maone' medioevali," *Archivio storico Italiano*, LXXVII, ser. 6 (1919), 6–7.

the cargo jointly owned was not usually divided but was sold by one of the joint owners who acted as agent for the others.

By extension, joint ownership was applied to objects which could not in a physical sense be divided. If the cost of an operation was high enough to place a strain on any single family fortune, the liability could through a temporary partnership or joint venture be divided among a number of distinct investors. The farm of the wine tax for a year usually ran to about 70,000 ducats. By holding some shares in the farm, the Pisani assumed less risk than if they had put the whole 70,000 ducats, something like a fourth of their wealth, into that one venture.[17]

Among these temporary partnerships, or agreements for joint ownership and agency, the associations of capitalists to finance the voyages of the merchant galleys are of special interest. More capital was involved in these voyages than in any other type of enterprise in the Venetian economy. A fleet of three or four galleys employed a crew of 600 to 800 men and the voyage to Flanders took at least a year, often nearer two years. The cargo carried by a fleet of the Flemish galleys was worth about 250,000 ducats. The relatively short voyage to Alexandria required only three to six months, but the cargoes were often valued at half a million ducats.[18] The cost of these galleys, of their fittings, of food and wages for the crews, and especially of the cargoes exceeded the resources of even as rich a family as the Pisani.

By a system of renting galleys, the state supplied an important part of the needed capital. Ever since the middle of the fourteenth century, great merchant galleys had been built almost exclusively by the Arsenal of the Republic. When the senators decided that a fleet of galleys should sail, they stipulated the route, the size of the crew, and many of the freight rates. Sometimes the senate offered a subsidy with the galleys. Then the galleys were put up at auction and the operation of the galleys for a specified voyage was awarded to the highest bidder, provided the successful bidder was subsequently approved by the senate as a capable person of proper age with reliable financial backers. If approved he became galley master, the *patron*.[19]

Because galleys were leased by the state, wealthy families such as the

---

[17] Sanuto, *Diarii*, II, 27, 1335; III, 733; LIII, 509. For Pisani's shares in the wine tax and for all the foregoing description of Pisani assets, see A.S.V., Raccolta Barbarigo-Grimani as cited, reg. 21 *passim*.

[18] Frederic C. Lane, *Venetian Ships and Shipbuilders of the Renaissance* (Baltimore: The Johns Hopkins Press, 1934), pp. 24–26; Jules Sottas, *Les Messageries maritimes de Venise aux xiv & xv siècles* (Paris, 1938), pp. 106–36; Sanuto, *Diarii*, VIII, 474.

[19] Sottas, pp. 71, 89, 90, 94.

Pisani and the Priuli had less incentive to own ships. Without this action of the state, they would have needed galleys of their own in order to make sure of being able to send their wares. An investment in merchant galleys might have led to the maintenance of a small private replica of the Arsenal or to the financing of various shipbuilding and shipowning partnerships as relatively permanent subsidiaries. Of course, if the Pisani partnership had been interested in routes or commodities not served by the merchant galleys, especially if they had been pioneering the exploitation of a new route, then they would have needed their own ships. Since there is no mention of shipowning or shipbuilding partnerships in either the Pisani or the Priuli books, it appears that they were content to operate in well-tested branches of trade and mainly in the types of merchandise carried by galleys. Consequently they did not need to worry about the long-run overhead costs of a merchant fleet. They could rent a galley for one voyage, assume the overhead only of that voyage, and then turn the galley back to the Arsenal, on which fell all the problems of overhead costs.

Although the state, by keeping galleys for rent, supplied part of the capital engaged in the voyages, most of it was private capital and was supplied by *fraterne*. One of these family partnerships might have borne practically the whole cost and risk of a galley or two, but generally costs and risks were shared among a number of *fraterne* which entered into temporary partnerships with each other or with persons of wealth. Some of these partnerships were galley partnerships, others were called *maone,* partnerships of the whole fleet.

The galley company which put up the money to rent and outfit the ship was the most basic of the partnerships centering around the individual galley. This "company of the galley" was divided into twenty-four shares *(carati)* on the model furnished by shipowning partnerships. The shareholders were commonly called *parcenevoli*[20] and might own so much that the *patron* was really their employee.[21] Although the surviving records of the Pisani are only excerpts from the *fraterna* books, they show that the Pisani invested at least three times in Barbary galleys, at least once in a Beirut galley, and twice in Flemish galleys.

How much outlay of capital was involved in such investments? The ideal sources from which to answer this question would be the accounts of the galley kept by the *patron* or by the official clerk, the *scrivan*. The

[20] This is the more common term, and that given by Giuseppe Boerio, *Dizionario del dialetto veneziano* (Venice, 1867) , s.v., but *caratadori* was also used.

[21] Cf. the Barbary galleys mentioned above in n. 7.

Pisani books and the entries in the Priuli journal supply only tantaliz-ingly incomplete clues. Lorenzo Priuli and Sons owned eight *carati*, that is, one third, of the galley company of which Federigo Morosini was *patron*. Their galley was one of the three "Flemish" galleys which made a quick voyage, leaving Venice in September 1504 for England and returning in October 1505 with a full cargo.[22] The *patron* reported to Lorenzo Priuli and Sons in April 1507 that the total "cost" of the galley amounted to 7,503 ducats and 7 grossi. But just what "cost" this figure represents is very hard to say. It is probably a sort of net cost in the "West," figured by the *patron* by deducting from his total expenses in England the amount of freights he had collected there.[23] (Some freights were payable in England, others in Venice.) Figures of the same order of magnitude occur in the balances of the galley accounts in the Pisani books. Their twelve shares of a galley of Flanders in the fleet which sailed early in 1518 was debited for 4,220 ducats, and their shares in the galleys of Barbary of 1519 to 1521 were carried at just about the same amount.[24] These balances appear also to represent the amounts spent on the galley in excess of the receipts collected by the *patron* from shippers during the voyage. The cost above receipts of each galley had to be advanced by its *parcenevoli*.[25] It was paid back to them by assigning them their shares of the galley's

[22] Sanuto, *Diarii*, VI, 45, 67, 209, 249. The fleet commander *(capitanio)* wrote from Southampton that they would have 17,000 ducats of freight, presumably on the return voyage.

[23] For the account of the *patron* had been kept in sterling. The entry reads: "Per Galia de Fiandre pattrono Federigo Morexini, Capettanio Ser Marco Antonio Con-tarini // A ser Federigo Morexini come patrono per tanti ne asegna per suo conto montar dita galia ducati 7503 grossi 7, che tocha a noi per karatti 8 ducati 2501, grossi 2, computando i danari ave de Vincenzo a sterlina 54 per ducato, val L. 250, s. 2, d. 2 p.–." Priuli journal, k. 19.

[24] Raccolta Barbarigo-Grimani as cited, reg. 21, k. 12, 13, 76, 77, 103, 138.

[25] Otherwise the *patron* would have had to put up the money. Full record of the payments made by the Priuli as *parcenevoli* to their *patron* is not available since their journal begins when the galleys were already in the West and some payments were presumably made earlier. But an entry of September 30, 1505 (k. 5), records the payment to the *patron* by Vincenzo of £264 13s. 6d. sterling or 1,323 ducats (at 48 ducats per £ st.), and the following entry April 28, 1507 (k. 19), if completed, would apparently have balanced the account of "Morexini come patron": "Per Ser Federigo Morexini come patron // A Ser Vincenzo mio fiol per conto da viazo [?] per tanti dito Ferigo li fa boni come per suo conto apar per quelo dice dover aver da noi per il resto de la galea [for the amount said Federigo shows by his account he has credited to him (Vincenzo) against what he (Federigo) says he should have from us for the balance of the galley account] ducati 96, grossi 8. Non li trazi fuori perche ne he eror in dito conto che Ser Federigo Morexini mete aver auto dal Vincenzo

accounts receivable, namely, their shares of the freights payable in Venice after the galley's return and, in some cases, their shares of the subsidy which the senate had offered with the galley.[26] Consequently these "costs" are some indication of the amount of capital advanced for the voyage, but the total required from *parcenevoli* before and during the voyage may have been much larger. Perhaps the figures of 7,500 ducats or 8,000 ducats should be doubled or tripled to represent the full amount of the outlay above receipts which had to be paid out during the voyage of a Flemish galley. Even so, the sums involved were small compared to the wealth of a family such as the Pisani.

If the Flemish voyage had involved only the cost of operating galleys, there would hardly have been need of share-owning partnerships to spread the risk among several families. But the *parcenevoli* had other and heavier commitments at the same time. The big investment was in the cargoes. Of course, the cargo worth a quarter of a million ducats brought by a fleet of three of the Flemish galleys was made up of wares owned by a great number of different shippers who had no partnership among themselves and who did not need any such association in order to ship. The galleys were regulated by the senate as if they were public carriers and they were obliged to load the most important items in their cargoes at rates fixed by law. But the *patroni* and *parcenevoli* of the galleys could expect some favor in the loading of their wares. At least they had assurance that their wares would not be those left behind if the galleys were crowded and would not be put where they were most likely to be wetted by the sea. If merchants were going to invest in the operation of a galley, they had incentive to invest also in its cargo.

---

in ponente £257 17s. 5d. de sterlina et Vincenzo mi asegna averli dato £264 13s. 6d. de sterlina. Et perho questo partida stara sospexa fina sia dechiarita."

[26] A number of assignments to the Priuli of their share of the subsidy are under October 1, 1506 (k. xv), and December 30, 1506 (k. xvi). For example, the first reads: "Per Hoffitio di governadori del Intrade per conto de Cresiamenti // A Galia de Fiandra, patron Federigo Morexini, Capitanio Ser Marco Antonio Contarini, in la qual participo in ⅓, per tanti dito Ser Federigo ne scripsse questo giorno per parte del don de dita galea, deli carati 8 me aspeta—L.32, s.–, d.–, p.–." What appears to be the settlement for freights reads (k. 21): "Per Francesco Foscari e fradelli fo de Ser Nicolò // A galia de Fiandre patronizata per Ser Federigo Morexini, Capitanio Ser Marco Antonio Contarini, che mi tocho i ditti per debitori per la nostra parte di ducati 600 el he sta conza la loro partida, come apar per poliza de Santo de Caxa [scrivan]." The collection of freights was complicated by the fact that many freights were paid to the Arsenal, in this instance as a penalty for overloading. Both Priuli and Pisani settled the payment of some freight on the wares they shipped on their galleys by crediting their galley account. Priuli journal, k. xxiii; Raccolta Barbarigo-Grimani, reg. 21, k. 76.

Moreover, they might need to do so to make sure that there was enough cargo and that their galley did not sail half empty. In practice, the same persons or families that financed the operation of a galley for a voyage financed also a good part of its cargo.

The investment of the Priuli in the Flemish galleys of 1504 consisted not only in their share in the galley company but also in the use of family funds to buy cargo. They purchased in three ways—individually, jointly with other members of the galley company, and jointly with all the shareholders of all the galleys of the fleet. By far the largest outlay was made directly by the family through the purchase for its account of wool, cloth, and oxhides worth about 10,000 ducats.[27] This may be considered the center of the whole venture from the point of view of the Priuli. Collections from the sales of the wool were to be a main income of the family for some time. Their investment in the galley company was very probably a subordinate investment made for the purpose of being sure of getting the wool.

Just as desire to obtain wool led to joining in a galley company so that the galleys would sail, the ownership of shares in the galley company led in turn to other purchases. Some were for the purpose of assuring an adequate cargo. The Priuli joined for one third, the amount of their share in the galley, in the purchase of 200 *botti* of Cretan wine, *malvasia,* bought by the *patron* Ser Federigo Morosini.[28] Had there been enough spices to fill the outgoing galleys, there would have been no occasion to buy wine. Indeed, wine could not be loaded on the galleys until all spices that were offered had been loaded. Consequently the Cretan wine was usually sent to England by the large high "round ships." But, as Girolamo laments in his diary with all the more vehemence because his family was involved, spices were not being shipped to the West from Venice in 1504 because spices were arriving from India in Portugal.[29] The *patroni* had to buy wine to fill their vessels.

While some joint purchases were made by the *patroni* and *parcenevoli* of a single galley, others were made jointly by all the *patroni* and *parcenevoli* of the fleet. The purchase of wine to complete the cargo for the outward voyage was arranged separately for the Morosini galley, but a purchase of lead for the return trip was made jointly for all the

[27] Priuli journal, k. 5, v (left-hand pages are numbered in Arabic, right-hand pages in Roman).

[28] *Ibid.,* k. 19. The total cost of their share of the wine was about 750 ducats.

[29] Girolamo Priuli, *I diarii,* ed. by Roberto Cessi, in *Rerum Italicarum Scriptores* (2d ed., vol. 24, pt. III; Bologna. 1933–37), II, 352–56, and earlier, p. 168.

galleys. Such a union of all the shareholders in the ships of the fleet, of all the *patroni* and *parcenevoli* of all the galleys, was called a *maona*.[30] Joint activity by this whole group has been little noted, and historians of Venice have seemed unaware of the existence there of any business organization called a *maona*. In truth, the Venetian *maona* may be considered more important because of its potentialities than because of what it actually was. It is an instructive case of what proved in the end to be arrested development.

A number of purposes might lead to the formation of a *maona*. Sometimes the senatorial regulation of the voyage stipulated that the freights of all the galleys in the fleet be pooled in one fund, and in that case the *patroni* were almost compelled to make some supplementary agreement for the administration of that fund.[31] Even when the senate made no such rule, the *patroni* had a common interest in seeing that there was adequate cargo for the fleet as a whole. It was the common practice of merchants to split up their shipments and load part of their wares on each galley so as to lessen the danger of loss from shipwreck. Consequently no one galley could expect to go full while the others went empty, and to a certain extent good cargo for one meant good cargo for all. A way of trying to assure good cargo for all was for the *maona* to agree to joint purchases that would help to fill the galleys. The lead bought for the account of the *maona* to which Lorenzo Priuli belonged was quite possibly bought jointly to ensure that each galley had enough ballast.

Assurance of adequate cargo for the whole fleet was indubitably the purpose of a *maona* contract referred to by Michele da Lezze, the wealthy contemporary of Alvise Pisani and Lorenzo Priuli. Michele da Lezze owned a third of one of the Barbary galleys of the fleet of 1506. Writing to his son Luca who was going on the voyage as a *patron,* Michele refers more than once to the *maona* formed by the *patroni.*

[30] Priuli journal, k. 9 (February 28, 1505 Venetian style, 1506 new style) "Per piombi pezi 54 comprati per Maona di Caratadori dele galie Capitanio Ser Marco Antonio Contarini." I have not found the word *maona* in the official records (for example in Senato, Mar) and it is not given in Boerio, *Dizionario,* so it is surprising to find it used in the Priuli journal and in the da Lezze letter cited below, in exactly the sense in which it was used more than a hundred years earlier at Genoa, according to Roberto Cessi, "Studi sulle 'Maone' medioevali," *Archivio storico italiano,* LXXVII, ser. 6 (1919), 5–9, 15–22. The Venetian use confirms Cessi's demonstration that the *maone* were not, strictly speaking, associations of bondholders, but associations of the owners or shareholders of a fleet.

[31] Such an agreement among the *patroni* for the administration of all freights as one *corpo* is attached to the commission of the *capitanio* of the galleys *al trafego* of 1486, MS, Museo Civico-Correr, Venice, MS III, 1057, ff. 19–21. Studied on microfilm.

They had agreed, in order to have a satisfactory loading of wool in Valencia, that each of them would buy his share up to the amount of 500 sacks if that were necessary to bring the total cargo of wool up to 2,000 sacks. Although this did not necessitate joint action, it gave occasion for it, and in fact the *patroni* agreed to handle the wool as a unit.[32]

The need of the individual galley for funds to cover operating expenses and the need of the whole fleet for cargo induced some agreements for joint action on the part of the galley company in the one case and of the *maona* in the other. Joint action was also stimulated by the desire for monopoly or for a favorable bargaining position. Merchants generally were on the lookout for ways of making agreements to effect some temporary monopoly or near monopoly. Groups that had learned to act together as a galley company or as a *maona* seeking cargo could the more easily act together to prevent competition.

Desire to avoid competitive bidding may have been one motive for making jointly the purchases of wine and of lead in which the Priuli shared, and it may have been behind the handling as a joint account of the wool bought by the *maona* to which Michele da Lezze belonged, although only as a secondary motive. It was plainly an important consideration in a contract among *patroni* and *parcenevoli* of the Flemish galleys of 1487 which provided for joint action on behalf of the *patroni* in the sale of soap in London or at ports along the way. In addition to arranging to avoid competition in the sale of soap in London, these *patroni* of the *maona* of 1487 agreed that fifty to sixty thousandweights of gallnuts should be bought jointly by a single agent in Venice and should be sold, similarly, all on a joint account, by one of the *patroni*.[33] These agreements gave no assurance of complete monop-

---

[32] "Et perche chomo tu sai ditti pattroni siano convenutti insieme fra loro che in chaxo ch'el manchasse lana per el chargo di ditte galie ogniuno deno far per la sua ratta sacchi 500 de lana fino a la summa di sacchi 2000. . . . I sachi di lana farai per conto di la maona, quelli se convegniera chargar e vegnir in questa terra in nome di patroni per uno montte." A.S.V., Miscellanea Gregolin, busta 10, Lettere commerciali, 1482–99. Copialettere of Michele da Lezze filed under the year 1497, f. 38 verso.

[33] Since the purchase of the soap and the amount to be bought were left to the discretion of the individual *patroni*, the contract did not create any obligation to load soap so as to assure a full cargo. On the other hand, the contract did stipulate in regard to both the soap and the gallnuts that if one of the galleys lacked space to load its share of these wares because of the obligation on the galleys to load spices in preference to other merchandise, the other galleys would take all they could up to the amounts specified in the contract. A.S.V., Miscellanea Gregolin, Lettere commerciali, busta 10, filed under year 1487. In the same busta, under 1487 and 1491, are papers about a lawsuit over some other soap loaded on these galleys which the

oly, but their signers at least renounced competitive bidding among themselves.

Altogether, there were substantial motives pushing the *patroni* and *parcenevoli* of each fleet into associations and partnerships of various kinds. Desire to suppress competition among themselves gave an impetus to general merchandising agreements, but more insistent were the needs for pooling operating expenses and for making sure of full cargoes. These motives arose from the very nature of the enterprises in which the merchants were engaged, just as, in later times, trading between England and India or the building of railroads created, from the nature of those enterprises, motives for large-scale business organization.

Had the Venetian government kept its hands off the merchant marine, there would have been real need in Venice for turning the *maone* into better organized and more permanent institutions. If the state had not supplied the galleys, private merchants would have had to tie up their funds in galleys and in ships' stores. Possession of this enduring physical equipment would have given the *patroni* and *parcenevoli* reason for making more permanent combinations to assure profit on the future use of their investment. As it was, the state intervened; it supplied the galleys, determined the basic freight rates, and appointed the fleet commander needed for common protection. Thus the galley company and the agreements of the *maona* were encouraged to remain only temporary joint ventures because the government required merchant operators to charter the merchant galleys anew for each voyage. Since the state did so much, the famed Venetian galley voyages created no need for any private business institution having either the longevity of the corporation or the large capital and the large powers of command which are organized in the corporation. A variety of agreements, each temporary and each providing for only a relatively small part of the needed capital investment, sufficed to finance the voyages of the merchant galleys.

IV

Senatorial initiative and regulation, changing slightly from year to year, rich family partnerships of relative permanence, and joint ven-

---

owner thought should have been sold by the *patron* acting for the *maona* along with the soap of the *maona*, but which was not so sold. At least one competitor felt he had been kept off the market by unfair practice. Although the contract concerns a *maona* it does not use the word.

tures of a few years' duration—all three together formed the structure of Venetian business. It was a very flexible structure. Under it, Venetian mercantile capital was kept liquid and could be moved rapidly from one branch of trade to another. The family firms could invest one year in the Barbary voyage or in wool imports from England. Another year, if the trip to Barbary was too dangerous or if the Venetian market was overstocked with English wool, the funds of the great families could be used to import spices from Egypt or Syria. Under senatorial direction the same galleys went first on one voyage, then on another; similarly, through the medium of joint ventures, investments went first into one field of trade, then into another. Neither a galley company nor a *maona* created any vested interest in a particular voyage. Each had a minimum of overhead and was dissolved as soon as it had served the special purpose for which it was created. Investment in such companies was in harmony with the efforts of the rich family partnerships to spread their risks, and their policy of diversification helped in turn to keep fluid Venetian mercantile wealth as a whole.

Diversification and flexibility were generally desiderata in the affairs of the resident merchants who were the typical capitalists of the later Middle Ages.[34] But these qualities were even more emphasized in Venice than in most commercial centers. This emphasis explains why Venice appears in certain respects old-fashioned in the age of the Fuggers. Although she was then a leader of Europe in many aspects of capitalistic business practice, Venice lagged behind in the development of the joint-stock company, which began to appear elsewhere in the fifteenth century, and in the sixteenth became a regular feature of the mining industry, oceanic commerce, and colonization.[35] Compared to Florence or Genoa, Venice was behind also in the development of

[34] N. S. B. Gras, *Business and Capitalism: An Introduction to Business History* (New York; F. S. Crofts and Company, 1939) , p. 67.

[35] The Casa di San Giorgio of Genoa was a great many things at once and had some of the features of a chartered joint-stock company, although, to be sure, these were overshadowed by other features of that many-sided institution. Heinrich Sieveking, *Genueser Finanzwesen*, vol. II: *Die Casa di S. Giorgio*, in *Abhandlungen der badischen Hochschulen*, III (Freiburg, 1899) . Cf. the judgment of Alfred Doren, *Storia economica dell'Italia nel Medio Evo*, trans. by G. Luzzatto (Padua, 1937) , pp. 423–24. On the other hand, clear cases of fifteenth-century Portuguese joint-stock companies are described in Hedwig M. A. Fitzler, "Portugiesische Handelsgesellschaften des 15. und beginnenden 16. Jahrhunderts," *Vierteljahrschrift für Sozial- und Wirtschaftsgeschichte*, XXV (1932) , 209–49. On the sixteenth century, see Jakob Strieder, *Studien zur Geschichte kapitalistischer Organisationsformen* (2d ed.; Munich and Leipzig, 1925) , and William Robert Scott, *Constitution and Finance of English, Scottish and Irish Joint-Stock Companies to 1720* (3 vols.; Cambridge, 1910–12) .

general business partnerships designed to live for many years independent of family ties and to earn profits on a definite fund of commercial capital.[36] While the use of general business partnerships and embryonic forms of chartered joint-stock companies was spreading elsewhere, family partnerships continued to dominate in Venice, supplemented by short-lived joint ventures. This "backwardness" of Venice in business organization should not be considered a sign of stupid traditionalism, however; a tendency for the Venetian galley companies or the *maone* to develop into joint-stock companies of some permanence, with policy and personnel of their own, was checked by the fact that this would have introduced into the Venetian economy undesirable elements of rigidity.

Reasons why the Venetians especially should fear rigidity in business organization are not hard to find. To the best of her ability Venice made herself the universal middleman. Some cities were relatively specialized: cloth trades were the main basis of Florentine prosperity; Ulm depended largely on a particular kind of cloth, fustian; and Augsburg merchants combined the cotton and fustian trade with financing princes and handling the overland exchange between Italy and the North. In comparison, Venetian merchants had open to them an unusually wide range of commercial opportunities—in Constantinople, Syria, Spain, England, and many other regions, and in spices, cotton, wool, and many other commodities—but their group of opportunities was continually changing. While all international commerce of the time was subject to violent interruptions, the commerce of Venice was especially full of sudden vicissitudes because her geographic position had been exploited to make Venice a "world market." Consequently Venetian merchants needed flexibility.

Geography is only a permissive factor, however, not a compelling factor in history. The respect for the integrity of state power which distinguished Venice from the other medieval Italian cities was a vital element in the development of senatorial control over navigation. Venice was also noted among the Italian cities for her patriarchal character; the family was exceptionally important in her government and society as well as in her economy. These traditions were in constant interaction with the social and geographic environment of the Venetians. Faced with an economic situation which called for business forms

[36] Cessi, *Note per la storia delle società,* pp. 50–58; Doren, *Storia economica,* pp. 420–22.

of great flexibility, the Venetians found in the supervisory role of the senate, in the great family partnerships, and in short-lived joint ventures institutions that met the economic need and also were in harmony with their inherited ideals of state leadership and family solidarity.

4

*Investment and Usury**

THE recent economic pre-eminence of the West was obviously connected with the high position that businessmen held in western
civilization in the nineteenth century, and the priority of the West in
economic development was linked to their earlier role. This role
depended in very large measure on their command of credit, that is, it
depended on the ability of businessmen to invest in trade and industry
more than their own personal funds. Like many other fundamental
features of western civilization, the practice of doing business with
borrowed money took root in the Middle Ages. In the period when the
Christian church was at the peak of its power as an institution, when
canon lawyers, theologians, and popes were condemning interest as
usury, organizations for conducting business with other people's money
became a basic part of western economic life.

This apparent paradox is partly removed, but only partly, by an
explanation of the rather ambiguous terms "borrowing" and "usury."
A man who is out to produce some goods or services with an eye to his
own profit and who lacks for his purpose sufficient money of his own
can use a variety of legal forms in inducing others to give him the use of
their funds. Waiving legal technicalities, I have referred to his "borrowing." But the managers of a modern corporation who want more money
for their schemes and who obtain it by selling stock are not in a legal
sense borrowers. Similarly, a thirteenth-century businessman seeking
the use of other people's funds could do so by various means. Whether
the relationship created by a particular contract was a loan or a
partnership could be a difficult legal and moral question. If it was what

* From *Explorations in Entrepreneurial History,* II, ser. 2 (1964), 3–15. (By permission.)

they would call a loan, a *mutuum,* and if he paid interest on it, in our
sense of the word "interest," it was in principle sinful in the eyes of the
church, being usury even if the rate of interest was extremely moderate.
But there were contracts that were morally approved, perhaps because
they were called partnerships, which permitted a businessman to
mobilize under his command other people's resources. I will use the
word "investment" to avoid the legal problem raised by either "loan"
or "partnership."

Among all the cities of medieval Europe, Venice was the first to
become capitalistic in the sense that its ruling class made their livelihood by employing wealth in the form of commercial capital—cash,
ships, and commodities—and used their control of government to
increase their profits.[1] How did commercial investment develop at
Venice? How was it affected by the condemnation of usury? I shall
consider first the kinds of contracts used in commercial investment and
how they changed, and then the reasons for these changes.

The early commercial documents show the use at Venice on the one
hand of the kind of ordinary loans on security which the church fathers
censored as usurious and on the other hand of real partnerships,[2] a form
of contract which was never condemned. Approval of partnerships was
a matter of course and was so assumed by Pope Innocent III about 1200
when he recommended that a dowry be committed to some merchant in
order that from the honest gain so won the husband might better
support the burdens of matrimony.[3] Full partnership had the disadvantage, however, that it involved the investor in liabilities that were
theoretically unlimited and of which the practical range was difficult to
foresee. Neither the ordinary loan nor the ordinary partnership was as

[1] This sensible definition is that used in Oliver C. Cox, *The Foundations of
Capitalism* (New York, 1959) , ch. I–VI.

[2] *Documenti del Commercio Veneziano nei secoli xi–xiii,* ed. by R. Morozzo della
Rocca and A. Lombardo. 2 vols. (Documenti e Studi per la storia del commercio e
del diritto commerciale italiano pubblicati sotto la direzione de Federico Patetta di
Mario Chiaudano, XIX and XX; Turin, 1940) , cited hereafter as *Documenti,* Doc.
14 and 16; Gino Luzzatto, *Studi di storia economica veneziana* (Padua, 1954) , p. 106;
and *Storia economica di Venezia dall' XI al XVI secolo* (Venice, 1961) , pp. 81–89.

[3] Gabriel Le Bras, s.v. *Usure. Dictionnaire de Théologie Catholique,* p. 2361, See
also John T. Noonan, Jr., *The Scholastic Analysis of Usury* (Cambridge, Mass.,
1957) , p. 137, and W. Enderman, *Studien in der romanisch-kanonistischen Wirt-
schafts- und Rechtslehre* (2 vols.; Berlin, 1874–83) , I, 343–36. In general on medieval
economic teachings, see Raymond de Roover, "The Scholastic Attitude Towards
Trade and Entrepreneurship," *Explorations in Entrepreneurial History,* I, ser. 2
(1963) , 76–87, and Gabriel Le Bras's chapter in *The Cambridge Economic History*
(Cambridge, 1963) , and his bibliography, pp. 671–74.

popular in twelfth-century Venice as was a third form provided for in Roman law, namely the sea loan. This was distinguished from the ordinary loan by the fact that the lender took the risks of shipwreck or piracy and was allowed therefore a higher rate of return.

Another form of credit unknown to Roman lawyers but in use since the tenth century was what the Venetians called a *colleganza*. It was a kind of profit-sharing sea loan or agency having some of the features of a partnership. Of the two parties to the contract, one, the *tractans* or *procertans,* undertook to travel and trade with the fund which was the subject of the contract. He may be called the active or traveling merchant. The other, who is often referred to as the *stans* or stay-at-home, I think it generally best to call the investor, for whether he moved about or stayed put was not essential to the contract. The essential was that he put up funds on which he took the risk of loss by shipwreck or piracy and on which he received a return that depended on profitable trading conducted by someone else. If there was profit, he received three fourths of it, the other fourth going to the traveling merchant.

These were the essential features of what at Venice and Ragusa was called a *colleganza* and was elsewhere, as at Genoa, called a *commenda.*[4] It appears in most general discussions under the name *commenda,* but in speaking exclusively of Venice it seems best to use the Venetian name, *colleganza.* The *colleganza* may be thought of as developing out of the sea loan when investors agreed to accept a percentage of the profit instead of requiring a fixed sum or a stated percentage on this loan. Other features distinguishing the *colleganza* then followed logically, for once the investor's gain depended on the amount of profit, he was interested in requiring an accounting of all pertinent expenses and receipts. Venetian laws required an accounting within thirty days after return to Venice and stipulated how much of his personal as well as traveling expenses the traveling merchant could charge as costs against the return on that investment.[5]

[4] The *commenda* or *colleganza* and related contrasts are well illustrated and explained by Robert S. Lopez and Irving W. Raymond, *Medieval Trade in the Mediterranean World* (Records of Civilization, Sources and Studies, LII; New York, 1955). Guido Bonolis, *Diritto marittimo medievale dell' Adriatico* (Pisa, 1921), describes the *colleganza* not only at Venice but also elsewhere in the Adriatic.

[5] *Gli Statuti Maritimi Veneziani fino al 1255,* ed. by R. Predelli and Adolfo Sacerdoti (Venice, 1903), "Statuti di Zeno," ch. CXII; also in *Archivio Veneto* (1903). Florence Edler de Roover, "Partnership Accounts in Twelfth Century Genoa," *Bulletin of the Business Historical Society,* XV (1941), 92, describes the only known record of such an accounting: "Once the aggregate proceeds of the venture had been determined, the expenses of the traveling partner were deducted."

In the earliest *colleganza* contracts the traveling merchant supplied one third of the trading fund, the investor supplied two thirds. The profits were then divided equally. This is called the two-sided *collegantia*, or *societas maris*. In such an arrangement the investor was receiving exactly the same amount he would have received if the contract had provided that he get three fourths of the profit on his two thirds (since ¾ times ⅔ is %₁₂). The two-sided *colleganza* thus gave exactly the same claim on profits as a one-sided. In the two-sided form, the traveling merchant contracted to administer as a unit a fund to which he contributed one third and to account for it as a unit. He had to commit some of his own funds to the same purchases or ventures and to charge expenses to the combined account.

Surviving contracts indicate that the one-sided *colleganza* almost completely displaced both the sea loan and the two-sided *colleganza* early in the thirteenth century.[6] Venetian legislation clearly indicates that the unilateral *colleganza* became the form which merchants seeking funds to take overseas were expected to use. Conversely, it was the form most used by those who had money available for investment. Indeed, since opportunities to invest in land were restricted in Venice, *colleganze* and government loans were almost the only means by which widows or pious foundations or wealthy merchants on their retirement could obtain an income on their funds; and the Venetian equivalent of government bonds—namely forced loans which the lenders could sell—did not become available in much quantity until very late in the century.[7]

The amount of commercial credit embodied in *colleganze* became so large that it disquieted the governing councils of Venice. In 1324 they forbade anyone to send or carry overseas in *colleganza* a sum greater than the amount for which he was assessed in the government's levying of forced loans. After being periodically thus restricted, *colleganze* gradually ceased to be important in financing the Levantine trade.

[6] Besides the *Documenti* cited in n. 2 the following contain commercial contracts: *Nuovi documenti del commercio veneto dei secoli xi–xiii*, ed. by A. Lombardo and R. Morozzo della Rocca, in *Monumenti storici*, n.s., vol. VII (Deputazione di Storia Patria per la Venezia; Venice, 1953) ; *Documenti della colonia veneziana di Creta: I. Imbreviature di Pietro Scardon*, ed. by A. Lombardo (Documenti e studi per la storia del commercio e del diritto commerciale italiano pubblicati sotto la direzione di Federico Patetta e Mario Chiaudano, XXI; Turin, 1942) ; *Famiglia Zusto*, ed. by L. Lanfranchi (Fonti per la storia di Venezia, sez. IV, Archivi privati; Venice, 1955) .

In vol. II of the *Documenti* cited above, covering 1204–61, and in the *Nuovi documenti* there are hundreds of *colleganze* but only nineteen contracts that can be considered sea loans, even including doubtful cases.

[7] Luzzatto, *Storia economica*, pp. 84–90, 108–9.

Commission agents were used instead. Merchants no longer made a practice of traveling out and back with the same fleet; the commission merchant resided in an overseas port for several years. He accepted goods or cash on consignment, sold and bought as ordered, and charged for his services a small percentage of the total value of the turnover. Larger and more permanent associations of capital were arranged through full partnerships.[8]

Having been ousted from its great role in international trade, the *colleganza* continued in three forms. For trading voyages into little known territory, such as that of Alberto Loredano to Delhi, India in 1338, it was used in its old form.[9] At Chioggia it was slightly modified to allow for the ownership by the active merchant of the vessels used for trade, probably in nearby markets.[10] But most contracts of *colleganze* in the fourteenth century were loans to shopkeepers and craftsmen or to banks for use "in Rialto," as the expression went. This form, called the local *colleganza*, involved no sea risk. The loaner often took the risks of thievery and fire, and did not specify the return exactly. In practice the loans were generally renewed at some standard rate, 8 per cent in 1330 and 5 per cent after 1340.[11]

What relation does all this have to the teachings about usury, this development from sea loan to two-sided *colleganza*, then to one-sided *colleganza* so extensively used that it crowded out even the sea loan, and then to the use of commission agents in overseas trade, and within Venice to a kind of *colleganza* that provided capital for local trade and banking? Not as much as is commonly supposed. The changes can just as well be interpreted as adjustments of commercial customs to changing economic needs. There has been a tendency to attribute to the

---

[8] Roberto Cessi, "L'Officium de Navigantibus e i sistemi della politica commerciale Veneziana nel sec. xiv," *Nuovo Archivio Veneto*, n.s., XXXII (1916); reprinted in his *Politica ed economia di Venezia nel trecento* (Rome, 1952), pp. 23–61. See also Luzzatto, *Studi*, pp. 73–78, and *Storia economica*, pp. 90–93, 123–24. For later practice, see Frederic C. Lane, *Andrea Barbarigo, Merchant of Venice* (Baltimore, 1944), pp. 93–96.

[9] Robert S. Lopez, "Venezia e le grandi linee dell'espansione commerciale nel secolo xiii," in *Civiltà veneziana del secolo di Marco Polo* (Centro di Cultura e civiltà della Fondazione Giorgio Cini; Venice, 1955), pp. 55, 63 ff., where his other studies of the same documents are cited.

[10] Roberto Cessi, *Note per la storia delle società di commercio nel Medio Evo in Italia* (Rome, 1917), reprinted from *Rivista italiana per le scienze giuridiche* (March, 1917), 48–49, citing the "atti del notaio Susinello Marin," 1348–54.

[11] A. Arcangeli, "La commenda a Venezia specialmente nel secolo xiv," *Rivista italiana per le scienze giuridiche*, XXXIII (1902), 107–64; Luzzatto, *Studi*, pp. 74–78, 98–99, and *Storia economica*, pp. 88–90, 104–5.

usury laws every departure from what seems natural to us in the light of modern practice,[12] even when the forms used can be satisfactorily explained by their suitability to the economic conditions of the times.[13]

A reasonable explanation of the changes in the forms of investment can be found primarily in the larger supply of funds seeking commercial investment. Evidence that the flow of capital into the Levant trade was excessive in the eyes of contemporaries is strongest in the early fourteenth century, but when one considers the general increase of wealth in the cities of Italy and particularly in Venice, it seems reasonable to suppose that the same factor—the funds accumulating in the hands of pious foundations and of old families—was operating throughout the centuries between 1000 and 1300. References to a standard interest rate of 20 per cent in the twelfth century and 5 per cent in the thirteenth is some indication of such a change.[14]

Consider first the change from sea loan to *colleganza*. It substituted for a fixed obligation an obligation to share profits. To that extent it was like issuing common stock to finance an expansion of business, instead of selling bonds. It placed more of the risks on the investors.

The fact that early *colleganze* were two-sided may be considered a concession to investors that was necessary when the supply of capital was still relatively small. In order to persuade investors to take some of the commercial risk, the managing merchants had for a time to commit part of their own capital to the same ventures. In the thirteenth century, investors became so eager that this was no longer necessary.

When commercial practices were then made the subject of legislation in Venice, the sea loan and the two-sided *collegantia* were passed over as obsolete. The one-sided *collegantia* was being used by men and women of widely diverse occupations and conditions to participate in maritime trade. A very wide popular participation in overseas commerce occurred and can be even more thoroughly demonstrated at Genoa at

[12] Endemann's basic study (cited in n. 3) expresses this tendency because Endemann took as his theme the influence of the canon law on the Roman law. F. Salvioli, "La dottrina dell'usura secondo i canonisti e i civilisti italiani dei sec. xiii, xiv," in *Studi giuridici in onore di Carlo Fadda* (1906) , vol. II, argued that Endemann exaggerated the extent that the civilists accepted canon law. But all studies that focus on "usury doctrine" and then refer incidentally to the forms of commercial contracts give the impression that the doctrine was the important causal factor, even if that is not their intention. For example, Noonan, pp. 136–53.

[13] Such explanations are well used in the broad survey by M. M. Postan, "Credit in Medieval Trade," *Economic History Review,* I (1928) , 246, 249.

[14] Although of course the kinds of loans may not have been exactly comparable. Luzzatto, *Studi,* pp. 73–79, 98.

the beginning of the thirteenth century; the prevalence there of one-sided *commenda* contracts rose from 22 per cent of all contracts in the mid-twelfth century to 91 per cent in the early thirteenth.[15] With a large number of relatively uninformed investors eager to place funds, a managing merchant could take advantage of the situation, pad his expense accounts, charge more expenses to one investor than to another, consign to other agents funds or goods he had contracted to handle himself, and delay making his report, even after coming back to Venice. Venetian lawmakers were concerned to prevent such practices, in short, to protect investors who were no longer in a sufficiently good bargaining position to protect themselves.[16]

The ever-expanding volume of funds seeking investment played a role also in the next step, the use of commission agents instead of *colleganze* in overseas trade. Many changes in commercial technique contributed to this change—quicker, more regular voyages, bills of lading, better bookkeeping, etc.—but for Venice, at least, Professors Luzzatto and Cessi, who have studied in detail the disuse of the maritime *colleganza* ascribe much importance to alarm at the volume of capital being invested in the Levant.[17]

Although the shift from one form of contract to another is not, in my judgment, to be attributed to the ecclesiastical prohibition of usury, the church doctrine may perhaps explain why a rate of return was not specified in the local *colleganze*. By leaving the amount of interest dependent on what certain banks would pay, these contracts introduced an element of risk or at least uncertainty. Possibly a canonist favorable to the Venetians would have argued that these deposits at interest were legal because the return was uncertain.[18] Such a crack in

---

[15] Hilmar C. Krueger, "Genoese Merchants, Their Associations and Investments, 1155 to 1230," in *Studi in onore di Amintore Fanfani* (Milan, 1962), I, 423–26.

[16] R. Cessi, ed., *Deliberazioni del Maggior Consiglio*, II, 109–12, 226; II, 357–58.

[17] See n. 8 above.

[18] Professor Le Bras makes a distinction between risk and uncertainty not made by Noonan. After explaining Pope Gregory IX's exclusion of *periculum sortis* as a justification for usury, Le Bras admits *ratio incertitudinis*, saying "Quand l'issue d'une opération est incertaine, que l'on ne sait si elle sera finalement courteuse ou profitable, la doctrine tend à éscarter le soupçon d'usure." *Dictionnaire de Théologie Catholique*, s.v. *Usure*, p. 2363.

Pope Gregory IX's decretal *Naviganti* was generally interpreted as meaning that risk did not in itself justify the receipt of interest or profit, but St. Thomas Aquinas, St. Bernardine of Siena, and St. Antoninus maintained that risk was a sign of ownership and that ownership justified a return. To many laymen indifferent to legal distinctions this may have seemed to amount to the same thing. Noonan, pp. 137–38, 143–44, 150–51.

the doctrine, if widely accepted, would have burst the dam and swept away the whole usury doctrine or made it an anachronism. In fact, the rate of return on local *colleganze* seems often to have been well understood in advance, and courts enforced on recalcitrant debtors rates varying from 5 to 12 per cent.[19]

One reason for not attributing to the usury doctrine such a change as that by which the *colleganze* displaced the sea loans is the use even at the time when this change was going on of many contracts that were clearly usurious according to the teachings of the church. Loans at 20 per cent with land pledged as security were made by Pietro Ziani, who was doge from 1205 to 1229, and by his father Sebastian Ziani, who was doge from 1172 to 1178 and in the latter year entertained most magnificently Emperor Frederick I and Pope Alexander III.[20] Another contract which would seem also to have been clearly usurious according to the teachings of the churchman was that by which a son in 1213 promised his widowed mother, Agnese Gradenigo, 10 per cent a year on her money and he took all the risks.[21]

The reasons for using one form of contract instead of another can hardly ever be determined in an individual case. A few years after 1213, Domenico Gradenigo promised his mother three fourths of the profits on her money and she took the sea risk.[22] Had Agnese Gradenigo felt guilty of exacting usury from her son? Or was the mother at the later date less concerned with an assured income? Or hoping for a higher return? If the only concern had been the illegality of usury, an agreement between mother and son for a fixed interest could easily have been hidden under a contract for a free loan. There are many examples of such loans *pro amore*.[23] Some of these free loans probably hide the payment of usury; some were probably really accommodation loans such as businessmen have used during the centuries.[24] When there is no evidence of the circumstances, there is little reason to jump to either conclusion about the individual case.

In regard to the general change, there is evidence on at least one point. The disappearance of the sea loan used to be ascribed to the

---

[19] Luzzatto, *Studi*, pp. 78–79; and "Tasso d'interesse e usura a Venezia nei secoli xiii–xiv," in *Miscellanea in onore di Roberto Cessi* (Rome, 1958), I, pp. 194, 201.

[20] *Documenti*, 220, 463; Luzzatto, *Storia economica*, pp. 25–26.

[21] *Documenti*, II, 549.

[22] *Ibid.*, no. 588.

[23] *Ibid.*, no. 536; cf. 534.

[24] For examples, see Stuart Bruchey, *Robert Oliver, Merchant of Baltimore, 1783–1819* (Baltimore, 1956), pp. 122–23.

decretal *Naviganti* of Pope Gregory IX of 1234.[25] But at Venice the sea loan had gone out of use before 1234 so that its disappearance cannot be attributed to that specific decree.[26]

Although the usury doctrine has been appealed to more often than necessary to explain features of medieval business practice, its general, long-run influence on economic life is not of course to be ignored. Its greatest importance was its moral influence. One could argue that the Venetians were at first quite unconcerned about the sin of usury and gradually became so as churchmen became more vehement and specific on the subject. The Ziani were following old Venetian customs in collecting 20 per cent, as they did even on well-secured loans, and they probably felt no sense of sin. Church doctrine was given more teeth during their lifetime, however, by the Third Lateran Councils of 1179, and was then energetically disseminated by the preaching friars.[27] During the thirteenth century, Venetians certainly expressed a detestation of usury. In 1254 they began passing laws against it,[28] and Da Canale's thirteenth-century chronicle lumps together heretics, usurers, murderers, and thieves—boasting that none of these dared live in Venice.[29]

When the Venetians did become concerned about usury, they developed a standard different from that of the ecclesiastical authorities—what might be called a businessman's standard. Indeed, in the fourteenth century the Venetians applied a conception of usury much like that current today. It approved as nonusurious the payment on investment of a rate of return determined at least in theory by market conditions. Accordingly it approved as perfectly legal, in spite of the law against usury, the contracts described above as "local *colleganze.*" Such a contract was considered usurious only if the borrower was charged an unusually high rate or taken advantage of in some way, such as being made to give unusual security.[30]

[25] Arcangeli, pp. 132–33; Bonolis, p. 473; Raymond de Roover, in *The Cambridge Economic History* (Cambridge, 1963), III, 55.

[26] See above, n. 6.

[27] Noonan, pp. 19–20.

[28] Cessi, *Deliberazioni*, II, 222; A. Roberti, *Le Magistrature guidiziarie veneziane*, I, 204.

[29] Martino da Canale, *Cronaca veneta*, ed. by Polidori and Galvani, *Archivio Storico Italiano*, VIII (1845), 270.

[30] Gino Luzzatto, "Tasso d'interesse e usura a Venezia nei secoli xiii–xiv," in *Miscellanea in onore di Roberto Cessi* (Rome, 1958), I, 195–202. On conflicts at Florence at this time over usury, see Marvin B. Becker, "Florentine Politics and the Diffusion of Heresy in the Trecento: A Socio-Economic Inquiry," *Speculum*, XXXIV (1959), 60–75.

A legal basis for these interest-paying deposits was laid in 1301 when a commission drew up regulations to prevent four kinds of illicit deals in money: in selling exchange, in buying or selling goods on credit, in dealing in futures, and in placing money at interest (*ad presam*).[31] In all four cases the exceptions were important, but the last is our concern here. Money could be placed at interest only with a bank, or other establishment which was well known as generally accepting money at interest. The establishment was not to pay a particular investor other than the same rate it was paying to other depositors. If it had no other money on deposit, it could not pay the depositor (or lender) more than one half of the profit that the establishment itself had made with the money placed with it. This last is in accord with the provision in the earliest example of *colleganza* for trade on the Rialto, which provided that each party receive one half of the profits.

No doubt these rules only sanctioned and perhaps restricted practices already current in the thirteenth century. Many contracts and court records show that these practices continued in the next century. Particularly significant is a petition asking for a pardon in 1339.[32] Its significance does not lie in the fact that the pardon was granted to a certain Vitale Dente convicted of usury, nor even in the particular act for which he felt he had been unfairly condemned. Its significance lies in what he assumes to be a perfectly innocent practice; namely, that he had loaned 2,500 ducats with the provision that he would be repaid the capital and such profit or loss as was paid by stipulated banks, but not more than 14 per cent. What caused his condemnation by the magistrates for usury was a clause inserted in the contract saying that his word was to be taken concerning the profit or loss ("credi debeat suo verbo tam de prode quam de danno"). He maintained that he had regarded these words as meaningless notarial jargon. The magistrates said they had inquired of the bankers as to whether Vitale had ever asked them how much they were paying and the bankers said no. Hence, following the law, the magistrates said they condemned Vitale, but they made no protest against his pardon. Whether they or the nobles voting for pardon were moved by Vitale's arguments, or general good reputation, or by entirely different motives does not much matter. The standard of fair practice is evident in the general assumption that he would never even have been accused if his contract had called simply for collecting the going rate of interest actually being paid by bankers.

It has been asserted that the prohibitions of usury prevented the

[31] Archivio di Stato di Venezia, Commemoriali, reg. 1, f. 16.
[32] Archivio di Stato di Venezia, Grazie, reg. 8, f. 36t.

development of the concept of interest.[33] Although it is true that Venetian businessmen did not distinguish clearly between interest and profit, certainly not in their language, they did conceive of interest rates as prices paid for the use of funds. They applied this concept also in setting prices on wares sold for delayed payment. For example, Andrea Barbarigo wrote to the agent who was selling his cloth in 1440, "I think they [some cloths he had shipped] will bring 30 ducats if sold for payment in six months and 28 ducats if sold for cash. If you cannot sell them for cash at 2 ducats less than the term price, I even prefer that you sell for cash at 3 ducats less, because one knows how to gain more than 12 per cent a year on one's money."[34] And they were accustomed to figuring how sums grew at various rates of compound interest.[35]

Venetian businessmen and the Venetian courts regarded usury as an abuse of practices which were normally used legitimately to collect a going rate of return. This conception may be regarded as a joint product of the church's teaching and of other factors bearing on economic life. The importance in this connection of the church's teachings does not lie chiefly in their effect on legal forms, since the changes in the forms of commercial credit are best explained by other economic conditions. But among these other economic conditions one of the most influential was the increasing volume of funds seeking investment in commerce, and this demand for commercial investment is itself to be explained in part by the condemnation of usury. The usury doctrine's chief influence was thus indirect.

As soon as any appreciable amount of liquid capital was accumulated in the hands of retired merchants, widows, or institutions, they sought ways of making their wealth yield income. In such cities as Venice, where investment in land had limited possibilities, they put their money with someone who could promise a return. Practical necessities of commerce and the traditions rooted in Roman law shaped the forms of contracts. When the moralists and the canon lawyers examined their contracts they denounced as usurious all loans bearing a fixed interest even if the interest charge was very moderate and even if contracted between businessmen as commercial investments. But if there was risk

[33] Selma Hagenauer, "Das *justum pretium* bei Thomas von Aquina," *Vierteljahrsschrift fur Sozial- und Wirtschaftsgeschichte,* suppl. XXIV (1931), 112.

[34] See below, p. 126.

[35] A commercial arithmetic of about 1400 (Biblioteca Nazionale Marciana, Mss, It. Cl. IV, cid. 497, f. 43) contains such problems as how much a man must deposit at a bank at 10 per cent "di pro al anno" in order to have £1,000 in 15 years to dower his daughter.

and uncertainty about the return, the transaction would probably be approved as a partnership. In practice, loans to consumers were at a fixed rate and secured by collateral. Businessmen were better able to obtain funds without pledging specific security and without specifying the yearly return. Therefore loans to businessmen more generally escaped being obviously usurious. A distinction between productive loans and those that were merely exploiting consumers was recognized in the fourteenth century by the merchant nobles of Venice and by some Roman lawyers.[36] It is hinted at by some moralists in the fifteenth century, openly championed in the sixteenth, and practically recognized in the church's teaching generally in the seventeenth century.[37]

In so far then as rich persons paid any attention to the teachings of the church and at the same time sought some returns on their wealth they were under pressure to seek land or commercial investments. The Venetians assumed that a man had as much right to income from commercial property as from landed property. As long as he invested in commerce through some contract by which he took a measure of the risk and the return was uncertain, he regarded his return as legitimate. If he was concerned about usury the effect would be to turn him from mere moneylending to commercial investment.

So far as this was true generally the practical effect of the usury doctrine was to increase the funds placed at the disposal of the businessman and thus to encourage economic growth. Consider from the point of view of growth the alternatives open to a person of wealth. If he spent it improving land that he owned, that of course contributed to economic growth, but merely buying land by itself did not. His purchase merely transferred his liquid wealth to other persons. If they consumed it, the wealth never became capital from a social point of view; it contributed nothing to economic growth. Similarly, the manifest usurer making consumption loans from his pawnshop added to his personal fortune but did not add to the aggregate wealth of the society.

In contrast, commercial investments—whether through sea loans, or *colleganze* of various kinds, or full partnerships—did on the whole contribute to economic growth. They built up a network of trade and transportation, a system of regional specialization, and a diffusion of technical skills.

When we inquire concerning the effect of the usury doctrine on

[36] By Bartolus and Baldus according to F. Salviolo, "La dottrina," *Studi Fadda,* II, 273–74.

[37] On similar ideas in St. Bernardine, see Raymond de Roover, "The Scholastic Attitude," p. 83; and on latter teachings, Noonan, pp. 252–5, 259–66, 361.

economic growth, the most important question is whether it discouraged the kind of loans to consumers which were unproductive socially. To the extent that it did so, the doctrine created pressure on men possessed of liquid wealth to find some other way in which to make their wealth yield income. It thus encouraged the flow of capital into commerce. It is logical to conclude then that the usury doctrine in so far as it was effective stimulated economic growth. But whether or not it really did have that general effect is difficult to prove.

5

Venetian Bankers, 1496–1533*

THE development of negotiable commercial paper in the seventeenth century marks the end of the "primitive" stage of deposit banking. Earlier bankers, unable to discount bills so as to spread the risk of their loans over a multitude of mercantile operations, were lured into overambitious ventures. They held a volume of deposits which enabled them, in ordinary times, to satisfy their depositors without keeping all their funds on hand in cash. But their efforts to draw profits from the money entrusted to them led to direct participation in commercial undertakings and loans to princes. Such firms as the Bardi of Florence or the Welsers of Augsburg touched dazzling profits, grew bolder, and, engaging their depositors' funds yet more deeply in government loans or speculations in commodities, ended in sensational failures. The well-known stories of such international bankers leave the impression that the great dangers of bank failure in that early stage of deposit banking came from the two sources named—commercial speculation and loans to princes.

The international bankers supplied the needs of some centers; those of other cities were met by local banks. The latter were sometimes profit-seeking ventures of private bankers, sometimes public institutions subject to the city government. Although the municipal banks of Barcelona (1401) and Valencia (1407) have sometimes been confused with *giro* banks, on the assumption that they merely transferred payments on their books and did not make loans, this is a mistake. *Giro* banks did not come into existence until the late sixteenth century, at Venice in 1584 and at Amsterdam in 1609. It is true, however, that the chief function assumed later by the *giro* banks had been performed earlier by the public or private local banks. Through the transfers of

* From *Journal of Political Economy*, XLV (1937), 187–206. (By permission.)

deposits from one account to another, they furnished a method of making payment which was easier than handling coins.[1]

Venetian banks about 1500 were primarily local banks. They have been studied hitherto almost entirely from a single type of source, namely, official enactments.[2] The difficulty with this source is that the texts of laws tell little concerning their enforcement. A fuller picture of the activities of the Venetian banks may be gained from contemporary chronicles and diaries.[3] The diary of Marino Sanuto has almost the reportorial scope of a newspaper, and permits piecing together a picture of the opportunities and dangers facing the Venetian bankers during the years 1496 to 1533.

Like international banking firms, the Venetian bankers indulged in risky ventures in trade and government finance. But two other factors also threatened their solvency. One was connected with the tight-money crises produced by the Venetian system of war finance, the other with the temptations arising from coinage difficulties and from the fluctuation of the market ratio of gold and silver. Judged by the history of the Venetian banks from 1496 to 1533, these two factors were more responsible for banking difficulties than were short-term loans to the government or excessively ambitious commercial enterprises.

Sanuto describes the fortunes of the ten banks of his time. These were: (1) the Garzoni; founded in 1430 by Messer Nicolò di Bernardo "e compagni"; passed under direction of Andrea Garzoni; failed in 1499; reopened and failed again in 1500;[4] (2) the Lippomani; founded

---

[1] Abbott Payson Usher, "The Origins of Banking: The Primitive Bank of Deposit, 1200–1600," *Economic History Review*, IV (1932–34), 401, 406–9; Armando Sapori, *La crisi delle compagnie mercantili dei Bardi e dei Peruzzi* (Florence, 1926); Richard Ehrenberg, *Das Zeitalter der Fugger* (Jena, 1912), I, 193–211.

[2] E. Lattes, *La libertà delle banche a Venezia dal secolo XIII al XVII* (Milan, 1869); Fr. Ferrara, "Documenti per servire alla storia dei banchi veneziani," *Archivio Veneto*, I (1871), 107–55, 332–63; and "Gli antichi banchi di Venezia," *Nuova Antologia*, XVI (1871), 177–213, 435–66. The documents published by Lattes and Ferrara were the basis, as far as the period here considered was concerned, of the studies of Charles F. Dunbar, "The Bank of Venice," *Quarterly Journal of Economics*, VI (1892), 308–35, and of E. Nasse, "Das venetianische Bankwesen in 14, 15, u. 16 Jahrhundert," Conrad's *Jahrbücher für Nat. Ok. u. Statistik*, XXXIV (1879), 329–58. Ferrara referred to material collected from private sources, but all that appeared in the *Archivio Veneto* were official acts.

[3] Marino Sanuto, *I diarii* (58 vols.; Venice, 1879–1903); Domenico Malipiero, "Annali veneti dell'anno 1457 al 1500," *Archivio Storico Italiano*, VII, ser. 1 (Florence, 1843); Girolamo Priuli, *I diarii*, in *Rerum Italicarum Scriptores* (2d ed.; Città di Castello, 1911), vol. XXIV, pt. III.

[4] Sanuto, II, 391; Malipiero, p. 531.

in 1480 by partnership of Tommaso Lippomano and Andrea Capello; managed in 1499 by Girolamo Lippomano; failed in 1499;[5] (3) the Pisani; founded in 1475; liquidated paying in full in 1500; reopened in 1504; liquidated paying in full in 1528, after the death of Alvise Pisani who had managed it;[6] (4) Matteo Agostini; survived the crisis of 1499 but failed in 1508;[7] (5) Girolamo di Priuli; founded in 1507; forced to liquidate in 1513;[8] (6) the Capelli; founded in 1507 by Antonio, Silvan, and Vettor Capello and Luca Vendramin; continued after 1528 by Silvan Capello and sons;[9] (7) Matteo Bernardo; founded in 1521; liquidated, paying in full, in 1524; reopened in 1529;[10] (8) Antonio di Priuli; founded in 1522 in close alliance with the Pisani bank and continued until 1551;[11] (9) Andrea e Piero da Molin; founded in 1523; forced to liquidate in 1526;[12] and (10) Andrea Arimondo; founded in 1524; failed in 1526.[13]

These were probably all the banks existent in Venice between the triumphant liquidation of Pietro Soranzo in 1491 and the opening of a new group of banks about the middle of the sixteenth century.[14] The list does not include mere money-changers,[15] nor does it include the Jewish banker Anselm, who during this interval performed many of the functions of contemporary Christian bankers.[16] The ten firms named were the *banchi di scritta,* those which did business by writing transfers of deposits from one account to another. Payments from one merchant to another were made by the two parties appearing before the banker and personally ordering the transfer made on his books. This was a great convenience both because it avoided the slow counting out of

[5] Malipiero, p. 671; Sanuto, II, 723.

[6] Ferrara, *Nuova Antologia,* XVI, 198; Sanuto, III, 158; V, 942; XLIX, 124, 240.

[7] Malipiero, p. 716; Sanuto, VII, 283.

[8] Sanuto, VII, 30; XVII, 328, 354, 360.

[9] Sanuto, VII, 81; XLIX, 7.

[10] Sanuto, XXXI, 182; XXXVI, 484; LI, 132–33.

[11] Sanuto, XXXIII, 545–46; Ferrara, *Nuova Antologia,* p. 438.

[12] Sanuto, XXXIV, 279; XLIII, 376, 388.

[13] Sanuto, XXXVI, 203; XLIII, 57, 80.

[14] Ferrara, *Nuova Antologia,* XVI, 185–207, 434–51, gives the same names for the bankers of these years, but is not in all cases informed concerning the years in which they operated.

[15] Mentioned as a quite distinct business, but as being in debt to the banker (Sanuto, III, 1040; Priuli, I, 112). The law of 1528 (Lattes, p. 95; Sanuto, XLIX, 89) said they had begun to accept coin on deposit at illegal rates and forbade it, but it is unlikely that they had become a means of avoiding the bank laws to any great extent or there would have been more comment in Sanuto.

[16] Sanuto, XXIII, 182, 407. The Jews had a different legal status.

imperfect coins and because the entry on the banker's book was an
official record of the whole transaction, which made unnecessary any
other legal papers.[17]

These *banchi di scritta* were essential to the economic life of the city.
The total deposits of the four banks doing business in 1498 were
something over one million ducats.[18] The number of depositors of the
Lippomano bank at the time it defaulted was 1,248, of whom 700 were
Venetian nobles. If it were assumed that the other two large banks of
the time had a similar number, and if no allowances were made, on the
one hand, for those having accounts in more than one bank or, on the
other hand, for those who got out before the crash, the figure for the
total number of bank depositors would be about 4,000. This would
mean that one out of every thirty of the population of Venice had a
bank account. When Lippomano closed down, more than 600 of his
depositors had accounts of less than twenty ducats. His enemies reviled
him for the loss of the dowries of young maidens, of savings which had
been put aside in presumed safety by citizens and nobles for the
payment of taxes, and of the deposits of monasteries and hospitals.
Obviously, besides the big accounts of merchants, the bankers carried
many small accounts and many not mercantile.[19]

Some of the funds in the bankers' hands were what may be called
"conditioned deposits," deposits earmarked for specified future payments under certain conditions. The many deposits which were intended for dowries may be considered in this class.[20] The guaranties
which the renters of the state merchant galleys gave to the state might

[17] Dunbar, pp. 311–14; Lattes, p. 125.

[18] The Garzoni failed in February, owing between 96,000 and 250,000 ducats, and
said they had paid out 128,000 ducats since Christmas (Sanuto, II, 391, 401). The
Lippomani owed about 120,000 ducats, and it was said they had paid out 300,000
ducats (Malipiero, p. 715; Sanuto, II, 731). The Pisani, after two severe runs on their
bank, had more than 95,000 ducats in deposits left (Sanuto, III, 158–59). They had
stopped one of the runs by raising a guaranty fund of 320,000 ducats, besides a previous reserve of 100,000 ducats in government bonds (Priuli, I, 124). The Agostini
deposits were at that time less (Malipiero, p. 716). Any exaggeration by the bankers
of the withdrawals immediately before the failures is probably more than offset by
the previous slow drain of deposits. The Banco di Rialto had liabilities in 1588 of
546,082 ducats, in 1594 of 705,889 ducats (Lattes, pp. 163–64).

[19] Sanuto, IV, 244–45; V, 654–55, 1056–57. The second Garzoni bank had only 518
creditors when it failed in March, 1500 (Sanuto, V, 707) but this was the bank
opened within a year after its failure in 1499. To it were transferred the accounts
of those large creditors, from 20 lire up, who agreed to wait for this money. To the
others the Garzoni offered their money at once (Sanuto, III, 96–98; Priuli, I, 260–61).

[20] Usher, pp. 413–14; Sanuto, II, 425–26; IV, 245.

be in the form of deposits made by the guarantors in the banks.[21] Tax collectors had on deposit in the banks funds which could be seized in case they did not fulfill their commitments.[22] On some occasions the bankers may have guaranteed future payments without requiring a deposit. References in the diary to payments guaranteed by a banker frequently do not make clear whether the banker had received a deposit to be used for the purpose.[23]

Of the ten banks listed, only four ended definitely insolvent—not as bad a record as is usually implied.[24] In all four failures, those of the Garzoni, Lippomani, Agostini, and Arimondo, a statement of the resources remaining after the bank had failed was attempted by Sanuto. These figures include, besides the assets of the bank, all the available possessions of the banker:

LIPPOMANI[25]

	Ducats
Liabilities	*ca.* 120,000
Assets	
Private loans	18,000
Jewels	14,000
Real estate	12,900–27,500
Cash	10,000
Government bonds and interest	34,000–41,000
Credits against Salt Office	18,000
Advances to the government, unsecured	8,000
	114,900–136,500[26]

GARZONI[27]

	Ducats
Liabilities	96,000 to 200,000
Assets	
Total loans	55,000 or 85,000
Less bad loans	10,000

---

[21] Sanuto, II, 732.

[22] Sanuto, II, 120.

[23] Sanuto, II, 452; III, 112.

[24] Ferrara, *Nuova Antologia*, XVI, 442, 459–60; P. Molmenti, *Storia di Venezia nella vita privata* (Bergamo, 1925), II, 38–40. With more reserve, Dunbar, p. 319; Roberto Cessi and Annibale Alberti, *Rialto* (Bologna, 1934), pp. 300–1.

[25] An attempt to combine and reconcile data from Sanuto, II, 731, 738–39; III, 1066; V, 1056–57; Priuli, I, 122–23; Malipiero, p. 717.

[26] Plus personal debtors for unknown sums.

[27] Sanuto, II, 391, 401; Malipiero, p. 531.

Net loans. . . . . .45,000 or 75,000
Jewels and silver. 15,000
Government bonds and interest. 20,000
Real estate. 45,000
                                         ――――――――――
                                         125,000 or 155,000

AGOSTINI[28]

Ducats

Liabilities. 110,000

Assets

Good private loans. 10,000
Jewels. 25,000
Real estate. . . . . Undetermined
Cash
　　At state treasurers. 3,000
　　At mint. 6,000
                         ――――――
　　　Net cash. 9,000
Government bonds. . . . . Undetermined

ARIMONDO[29]

Ducats

Liabilities
　Total debts. 27,000
　Less insured debts[30]. 16,000
                              ――――――
　　Net debts. .11,000

Assets
　Merchandise
　　On ships. . . . . .Undetermined
　　Alum or potash in warehouse. 1,500
　Government bonds. 1,500
　Real estate ⎫. .Value not stated,
　Jewels　　　⎭　　　　　　　　　　　　　　but believed suf-
　　　　　　　　　　　　　　　　　　　　　ficient to cover
　　　　　　　　　　　　　　　　　　　　　the balance by
　　　　　　　　　　　　　　　　　　　　　more than 6,000
　　　　　　　　　　　　　　　　　　　　　ducats

―――――――――

[28] Sanuto, VII, 283, 298, 307. An arrangement for payment over two years was approved (Sanuto, VII, 722).

[29] Sanuto, XLIII, 80, 144.

[30] This passage reads: "Il debito è ducati 27 milia, et asegura di questa per ducati 16 milia." In the report of the run on the Molin bank in 1526 it was said: "Voleno asegurar et pagar tutti" (Sanuto, XLIII, 376). When news of riots in Alexandria

These figures are probably not often accurate, for they were gathered from common rumor, or the avowals of the defaulting banker, or the impressions of the receivers when they first took over the closed banks. They are nevertheless valuable, for Sanuto's repeated references to the same categories of assets, even when he was unable to state the amounts, reveal the accepted categories of bankers' resources. These were long-term government bonds, short-term credits secured by assignments of income to be received from governmental bureaus, personal loans, jewels, real estate, cash or bullion, and merchandise.

In these financial statements no distinction has been made between the personal resources of the bankers and those of the banking enterprises. Even though such a distinction was made in the account books, it was of little legal importance, for the banker was fully liable for the debts of the bank.[31] Only in the case of the Lippomani is there given an accounting in which any distinction is drawn between the assets of the bank and those of the bankers:[32]

LIPPOMANI BANK

	Ducats
Liabilities	ca. 120,000
Assets	
Loans, good	18,000
Loans, bad	4,000
Due from Soranzo, silversmith for the bank	20,000
Due from good debtors of Soranzo	18,000
Due from the Capelli, former partners	13,000
Due from the Lippomani personally	17,000
Cash	10,000
Unsecured advances to the state	8,000
	108,000

reached Venice in 1524, the credit of Matteo Bernardo suffered, and he sought insurance (Sanuto, XXXVI, 146, 149). There are no similar references to insurance during the crisis of 1499.

[31] Even the heirs of Nicolò Bernardo were held as principals to pay the debts of Garzoni's first bank, although they claimed that for years they had had nothing to do with the bank except as guarantors of 2,000 ducats each. But because their names still appeared in the firm and they shared in profits, they were sentenced to pay (Sanuto, IV, 304).

[32] Sanuto, II, 738–39. From Lippomano's own account, but he gives the total assets as 98,000 ducats, apparently allowing for some duplication in the accounts with Soranzo. Soranzo's debt is elsewhere put as high as 40,000 ducats (Sanuto, III, 1017. 1066).

Most of the assets of the Lippomani bank, at the time of its failure, were loans due from the Lippomani personally or their business associates. Similarly in Agostini's failure, the Agostini were the chief debtors of their bank. Perhaps other and sounder bankers financed their mercantile ventures largely out of their own capital and borrowed less from their banks. Agostini and Lippomano were the two bankers most blamed for dishonest banking. This may have been more because of their attempts to avoid the liquidation of all their personal possessions to pay the debts of the bank[33] than because of their excessive borrowing from their banks. But the combination was certainly damning. Practically, the resources of the bank and of the banker were considered the same, and he was counted the dishonest banker who tried to keep his own wealth after he had taken that of his depositors.

Which types of investment were made in the name of the bank, and which in the name of the banker, or that of his son or of a business associate, are questions of bookkeeping which from the diarist sources can be answered only tentatively. Long-term government bonds, merchandise, and real estate generally appear to have been assets of the banker, not assets entered on the books of the bank. Mercantile ventures were probably not made in the name of the bank although they were financed by loans from the bank to the banker and his associates.[34] On the other hand, personal loans, loans on jewels, and short-term credits to the government were, quite clearly, investments made in the name of the bank.

The distinction was of little importance to depositors so long as all the banker's resources were fully liable for the debts of the bank and the banker used the resources of the bank for his trading ventures. Contemporary references, including those of Girolamo Priuli, a merchant and banker himself, make practically no distinction between the affairs of the bank and those of the banker. When there was a run on the bank the important question was how much cash could the banker and his family realize from all their resources. In sixteenth-century Venice, banking was not a specialized business; it was a part of the larger operations of merchant nobles.

The purchase of silver bullion from German importers was an important function of the banks.[35] When the Garzoni failed they were found to have suffered heavy losses from buying silver at a price above

---

[33] Sanuto, VII, 307; II, 731.

[34] Alvise Pisani acting in the names of his son and others (Sanuto, XXVI, 48, 495; XXVII, 219).

[35] Despite the laws (Lattes, pp. 34, 55, 70).

the mint ratio in order to increase their specie reserves.[36] The Lippomani not only financed the silversmith Soranzo, but also bought silver
themselves by giving credit for it on their books.[37] The Pisani are
pictured as one of the chief silver customers of the Fuggers.[38] When in
the autumn of 1500 there was no bank left at Venice save that which
had been the smallest, that of the Agostini, the German merchants
complained before the doge that they had no satisfactory market for
their silver. Agostini would buy only on his own terms. Therefore the
bullion was not finding its way to the mint.[39]

Jewels played a consistent part in the bankers' reserves, for they were
extensively used as securities for loans. The Venetian bankers were
pawnbrokers not only for princes but for men of lower station.
Bernardo lent on jewels to the pope, Garzoni to the Marquis of
Mantua, Agostini to an army captain who had pawned his wife's
wedding ring.[40] These firms combined the now distinct businesses of
pawnbroking and commercial banking.

Merchandise and shipping occupied a larger part of the bankers'
funds than is suggested by the statements of the assets left in the
defaulting banks. During the crisis of 1499 the Pisani had about 40,000
ducats invested in the "western voyage," in wool and in cloth, and they
had recently purchased a large ship.[41] During the winter of 1518 to 1519
a combine headed by the Pisani bank financed the voyages of the
merchant galleys of Flanders and Barbary.[42] The Molin bank had much
of its resources in merchandise.[43] The bankers Antonio di Priuli and
Matteo Bernardo were counted among the four leading merchants of
Alexandria,[44] and in 1533 Bernardo was accused of seeking to monopolize the export of English wool to Venice.[45]

The loans of the banks, both to private individuals and to the state,
were more voluminous than shown by the statements of the defaulters.
Loans to merchants were in the form of overdrafts, sometimes for

---

[36] Sanuto, II, 391; Malipiero, p. 531.

[37] Sanuto, II, 736.

[38] Alfred Weitnauer, "Venezianischer Handel der Fugger," *Studien zur Fugger-
Geschichte,* IX, 96, 171.

[39] Sanuto, III, 1091; cf. II, 736, 930.

[40] Sanuto, LV, 79; II, 736; III, 862.

[41] Sanuto, I, 780, 935; Malipiero, p. 551; Priuli, I, 124.

[42] Sanuto, XXVI, 48, 495.

[43] Sanuto, XXXVI, 146, in 1524.

[44] Sanuto, XLIII, 394.

[45] Sanuto, LVIII, 249, 257.

hundreds of ducats, sometimes for thousands.[46] Very large credits were extended to the state, but the dangers to the banks of these advances have been overemphasized.[47] The defaulting bankers did not have any large percentage of their funds in short-term loans to the government.

The bankruptcies which occurred between 1496 and 1533 cannot be ascribed to the failure of the government to repay loans from the banks. In the first part of this period, however, the bankers suffered from dangers arising in connection with the funded debt and the system of war finance. The financial panic of 1499 to 1500, in which the Garzoni and Lippomani failed and the Pisani, although hard pressed, paid 100 per cent, came during a political crisis. In 1499 Venice was involved in war on two fronts and was obliged to maintain an army in Lombardy at the same time that it armed its navy to match the fleet which the Great Turk was preparing at Constantinople. Although wars were a constantly recurring feature of Venetian life, they were all treated financially as if they were unusual emergencies. They were financed by forced loans levied upon all the well-to-do in proportion to their wealth. In return for the payment of a fraction of his wealth the investor, for so we may here call the taxpayer, received a government obligation. Since interest was paid at 4 or 5 per cent, these government bonds would have been possessions welcome to the taxpayers had they not been issued in excessive amounts. When they were forced out too rapidly, however, some people did not have enough ready money to pay for their new allotments. Since the bonds formed a forced loan to which the taxpayers had to subscribe, many taxpayers were forced to sell the government bonds they already possessed in order to pay for their share of the new issue. These sales drove down the price of the bonds. When the government then proceeded to demand more loans, the low price of his old bonds increased the difficulties of the taxpayer in finding the funds needed to buy the new bonds. Collection of the loan became extremely difficult, despite the seizure of the property of those who failed to subscribe. Rendered desperate by mounting war expenses and difficulties of collection, the government issued yet more bonds and these forced the price even lower. The first series of government bonds

[46] Sanuto, II, 391, 487. Cf. the apparent prohibition in 1467 of any large loan on one signature (Lattes, pp. 72–73). Cf. Dunbar, p. 315. But could not this be interpreted as limiting only the loans made by a single member of the banking firm?

[47] Ferrara, *Nuova Antologia*, XVI, 204–13, 459–60; Molmenti, II, 38–40; Enrico Magatii, "Il mercato monetario veneziano alla fine del secolo xvi," *Nuovo Archivio Veneto,* XXVII (n.s., 1914), 245.

of this type, the *Monte Vecchio*, became so depreciated that they were abandoned and in 1482 a new series started called the *Monte Nuovo*.[48] But these also were issued in excessive amounts. From eighty in 1497 their price dropped to fifty-two in 1500.[49] Property to the value of more than 300,000 ducats was in default for tax payments, but no one would buy.[50] This "tightness" of money produced by excessive demands on the taxpayers and the great military expenditures were the chief explanations of the 1499 failures offered by contemporaries.[51]

It is easy to imagine how these excessive issues of government bonds reacted unfavorably on the banks. Clients withdrew funds to pay for the government loans.[52] A good part of the bankers' personal wealth as well as that of their friends and relatives was likewise absorbed by the government bonds, and the guaranty funds, which the state required from all the bankers, were, at that time, composed of such bonds.[53] These securities diminished in value on the very occasions when they were most needed because the banks were endangered by the withdrawal of funds by depositors. It was the general dependence on the money market, which in turn depended on the volume of government borrowing and taxation, which placed the bankers in jeopardy, not demands for loans made on the banks by the government. When Andrea Garzoni revealed his embarrassment, the state repaid what it owed to his bank.[54] The failure to settle promptly with Girolamo Lippomano was not the reflection of a general situation but the result of personal attacks on Girolamo.[55]

The depression of 1499 was short-lived. By December, 1502, govern-

---

[48] Gino Luzzatto, *I prestiti della Repubblica di Venezia* (Doc. finan. dᵔlla Rep. di Venezia, ser. 3, R. Accademia dei Lincei, Padua, 1929, vol. I, pt. I) , carries the story of these loans to 1482.

[49] Priuli, I, 71, 141, 321; II, 7, 27; Sanuto, I, 575.

[50] Sanuto, II, 1121–22; Priuli, II, 61, 64; Malipiero, p. 532.

[51] Sanuto, II, 391–92; Malipiero, p. 532; Priuli, I, 290–91. I presume that most of the funds borrowed were disbursed outside Venice—e.g., to the army in Lombardy, to merchants bringing wood, iron, and copper from Germany, and to the fleet at Corfu.

[52] Sanuto, II, 391.

[53] Sanuto, II, 726; Priuli, I, 124; Lattes, pp. 71, 81–82. The investments in government bonds were not made by bankers as bankers but as individuals and as taxpayers. There is no evidence that the government demanded or even urged on the bankers the purchase of these government bonds.

[54] Sanuto, II, 332, 377. Malipiero (p. 531) says he was offered a loan of 30,000 ducats to tide him over and he refused, saying his debts were too great.

[55] Sanuto, III, 319, 324, 422, 423, 429, 1066.

ment bonds, *Monte Nuovo,* were again selling at seventy-five.[56] The failure of the Agostini in 1508 was attributed to no other cause than their own incapacity or dishonesty. Agostini owed his bank 65,000 ducats out of the 110,000 due, and had sent his wife, sons, and personal wealth off to Mantua a month before, "so that one may say he wished to fail with the money of others."[57]

Another crisis similar to that of 1499 came in 1509 when all the great powers of western Europe were leagued against Venice. In that emergency interest payments on the *Monte Nuovo* were suspended. There was a run on the Pisani bank. Pisani went to the government for help, received 15,000 ducats in cash, and with the aid furnished by his wealthy relatives outlasted the panic.[58] No banks failed that year, yet Girolamo Priuli may be considered a victim, indirectly, of the crisis of 1509. He was forced out of business in 1513. His extension of credits to the government was a factor in his closing, but the basic element in his misfortune was his personal loss of 10,000 ducats by the suspension of payments on the *Monte Nuovo* in 1509. He did not fail, technically speaking, for many of his creditors accepted payments in credits on the government and his bank was not placed in the hands of receivers.[59]

There remained, from 1513 to 1521, the great bank of Alvise Pisani and the more modest firm of Capello and Vendramin. During this interval confusion of the coinage brought the bankers new difficulties and opportunities. By 1522 there was created a situation in which the banks could continue to do business although they did not pay cash on demand. Sanuto described the banking situation in December, 1522, thus:

> . . . These [the banks] do business by transfers on their books [*fanno facende di partide*] but there is little cash in circulation, nor do they any longer keep money in the bank as they used to do, but, after a deposit is credited [*fata la partide*], if the depositor wishes to draw his money, even if not a large sum, they send above to get it. And this is because of the great variety of coins current in this country.[60]

[56] Sanuto, IV, 580.
[57] Sanuto, VII, 283, 298, 307, 722.
[58] Sanuto, VIII, 296–98.
[59] R. Fulin, "Girolamo Priuli e i suoi Diarii," *Archivio Veneto,* XXII (1881), 140–43; Sanuto, XVII, 328, 354, 369, 405. Priuli was imprisoned for debt in 1517, but that was for overdrawing the state treasury (Sanuto, XXIV, 492).
[60] Sanuto, XXXIII, 545–46.

Again in June, 1523, he commented: "The banks are in bad shape. They do not keep money in the bank nor can one withdraw without a loss . . . and they are banks, one may say, for transfer only [*solum di scritura*]."[61]

The slowness of the banks in paying cash was explained by the lack of good coins with which to pay. Especially scarce were good Venetian silver coins, for German silver which had formerly come to Venice to be minted and exported to the Levant went elsewhere when the pepper trade was diverted by the Portuguese. Furthermore, the market ratios between gold coins and silver coins frequently diverged from the legal ratios.[62] Difficulties over the ratios between the two precious metals were inherent in the bimetallic system. The "bank of St. George" at Genoa had given up its banking business in 1444 rather than obligate itself to maintain the gold-silver ratio at the point fixed by the state. When it resumed its general banking business more than a hundred years later at the end of the sixteenth century, it opened quite separate accounts for different coins.[63] The private bankers of Venice had met these difficulties about 1520 with the same method later used by the Venetian state bank.[64] They permitted bank money, the bank ducat, to become a unit of value and means of exchange which was distinct from any unit of coinage, and was bought and sold in the money market at a price of its own. Such a divorce between the bank money and the coined money was, strictly speaking, illegal, but was made possible by the recognized shortage of good coins.

The divorce between bank money and coined money arising from the shortage of full-weight coins offered tempting but dangerous opportunities to the bankers. Since they could stall off depositors seeking cash, they could increase their loans, by writing new deposits to the credit of the borrowers, with relative impunity. Even though bank money sold at a discount the banker could hope that, by the time a shift in the international movement of specie made good coins plentiful, he would be able to pay in full. Meanwhile he could pocket the profits from his loans.

As early as 1520 the bank money had depreciated in terms of full-weight specie. Its depreciation was accounted for by Sanuto entirely in

[61] Sanuto, XXXIV, 237.

[62] Sanuto, XX, 155; XXXIII, 546; also Nicolò Papadopoli-Aldabrandini, *Le Monete di Venezia* (Venice, 1893–1907), I, 100–45.

[63] H. Sieveking, "Die Casa di S. Giorgio," in *VWS Abhand. der Badischen Hochschulen,* III, 73, 200–1.

[64] Dunbar, pp. 330–32, on "ducat" of the *bancogiro*.

terms of the many bad coins in circulation, but one may suspect that an expansion of bank credit was partly responsible. Such an expansion is understandable in light of the large activities of the Pisani bank. Alvise Pisani was in full stride on a political career which made him one of the chiefs of the Council of Ten at forty-six, which was then considered a youthful age for such a post. He placed his bank at the service of the state to such an extent that in 1519 he had the government in his debt to the amount of 150,000 ducats. At the same time he was deeply involved in mercantile ventures.[65]

The ways in which the banker lent to the state were various. He sent cash to the camp to pay troops,[66] furnished a letter of credit to an ambassador, drew a bill of exchange for the payment of a subsidy or tribute,[67] or met the expenses of galley commanders.[68] But Pisani had performed more than these ordinary services. Since the system of forced loans had broken down, the Venetian Republic had been making more use of voluntary loans, and in 1516 it was provided that such a loan should be repaid in credits on the books of Pisani's bank, which thus underwrote the loan.[69]

In return for the cash he had furnished, or for the obligations to pay at a future date which he had assumed, the banker was assigned certain revenues to be paid to him as collected.[70] Most of the banker's loans to the state did not involve an immediate outlay of cash; they usually resulted merely in creation of deposits on the banker's books. The holders of these deposits would not in all cases wish at once to draw out the cash. Their deposits were probably used as were the others recorded on the banker's books. The holders of these deposits could and probably would use them to settle many of their debts, and this would frequently have no other result for the banker than a transfer of credit on his books from one account to another. There was, therefore, a

---

[65] Sanuto, XVIII, 173, 250; XXI, 465–67; XXVI, 48, 495; XXVII, 219, 526–27. When in 1520 the Council of Ten found it necessary to reaffirm the legal ratio at which the banks must pay in gold, Pisani seemed to take it personally (Sanuto, XXIV, 414–15).

[66] Sanuto, XXI, 503.

[67] Sanuto, XXIII, 426, 563, and "lettere di cambio . . . et lettere di credito," XXIX, 584.

[68] Sanuto, XX, 92, 225.

[69] Text of the decree authorizing the loan (Sanuto, XXII, 508–9).

[70] Usually the revenues assigned were not paid to the banker until after the obligation he had assumed for the state had become due. When Antonio di Priuli collected from taxes assigned him 6,000 ducats out of the 14,000 owed him for a bill of exchange on Lyons before the bill was due, he was compelled to surrender the 6,000 ducats and accept assignment on other taxes (Sanuto, XLVIII, 398, 406–8, 438).

reasonable chance that the credits created on the banker's books would not be drawn out until after he had collected the revenues assigned. Meanwhile the amount of bank credit circulating as a medium of exchange would have increased. Any loans to the government which the banker could manage simply by crediting additional deposits on his books would produce a certain inflation. The dominance of Pisani's bank between 1513 and 1521 would have made it easier to engineer and control such an inflation.

The situation in 1521 and 1522 may be summarized thus: There had been a depreciation of bank money in terms of specie. Sanuto looked to the confusion of the coinage as the explanation of this depreciation. Ordinarily we would look to an expansion in the volume of the money. The evil state of the coinage really explains only the capacity of the bankers to avoid the law requiring them to pay on demand in full-weight coins. A considerable increase in the quantity of bank money is suggested by the large credit operations of Alvise Pisani as well as by the depreciation of bank money.

The resulting situation certainly offered dangerous temptations. The immunity of the banks from the necessity of meeting their current obligations in full made banking appear a very attractive enterprise, and the number of banks increased from two to six within two years. The great merchant Matteo Bernardo opened a bank in 1521.[71] Antonio di Priuli entered the business in 1522 to supplement, strengthen, and ultimately take over the business of his father-in-law, Alvise Pisani.[72] In June, 1523, there were three or four other firms planning to open banks, and two of these projects, those of the Molini and the Arimondi, materialized within the next year.[73]

In the midst of this sprouting of new banks came new banking laws—those of 1523, 1524, and 1526. The existent situation was thought to be dangerous and two basic changes were proposed to render the banks sound. The easiest to enforce was the change in the bonds which each banker had to post before he could enter the business. Surety could no longer be posted in government bonds.[74]

The second essential change ordered was a resumption of cash

---

[71] Sanuto, XXXI, 182.

[72] Sanuto, XXXIII, 545–46.

[73] Sanuto, XXXIV, 237, 283; XXXVI, 203.

[74] Lattes, pp. 81–94; Sanuto also gives the text of the laws of 1523 in XXXIV, 251; mentions that of 1524 in XXXVI, 382; and gives full lists of the bondsmen and the sums for which they were guarantors in XXXV, 467–72; XXXVI, 33–35, 348–51; LI, 83–84.

payments at the full legal rate. This was harder to enforce. The section of the law of 1523 ordering the bankers to pay in full-weight gold coins at the legal ratio remained a dead letter. Bank money continued to sell at a discount.[75] In June, 1524, a means of enforcement was provided in three bank commissioners with offices in the Rialto and with adequate clerical assistance. Every banker was required to deposit 500 ducats in the hands of the commissioners, and, if the depositor could not get his money from the banker at the legal rate, the commissioners were to pay it to him and collect from the banker so that there would always be 500 ducats for each bank in the hands of the commissioners. Eleven days after this law was passed the commissioners opened their offices and two days later they had received the deposits of 500 ducats from the Pisani, Priuli, Molin, and Arimondo banks. In the money brought by the cashier of the Pisani bank were some forbidden German coins, and that bank was accordingly fined 50 ducats. The next day the commissioners demanded the 500 ducats from Bernardo but he excused himself, saying he was liquidating. A week later he had settled with his depositors and closed his bank.[76]

Thus for a year or so the law was enforced and the banks paid without discount. But by the spring of 1526 the two retiring bank commissioners reported that bank money was at a discount of 6 per cent or more. They suggested liquidating all the banks within the next eighteen months, because they feared the demand for a renewal of the surety bonds, as required by law, would cause some to fail. It was tacitly understood that the Molin and Arimondo banks were meant. Nothing was done, however, nor were new bank commissioners elected.[77] In July bank money was at a discount of 14 per cent.[78] In October Andrea Arimondo died "from melancholia of the bank" because he could not pay.[79] On November 6 the senate finally acted. The prohibitions against in any way selling bank money at a discount were reiterated and elaborated, the order to pay in coin reaffirmed, and, what was more to the point, bank commissioners were again elected, one for each of the four banks.[80] The feared run on the Molin bank promptly materialized and by December 5 the Molini partners had to appeal to the chiefs of the Ten to come to the Rialto and by their authority restore some order

[75] Sanuto, XXXVI, 203, 355.
[76] Sanuto, XXXVI, 382, 395, 398, 399–400, 401, 484.
[77] Sanuto, XLI, 141–42.
[78] Sanuto, XLII, 181, "especially that of Molin and Arimondo."
[79] Sanuto, XLIII, 57.
[80] Sanuto, XLIII, 173, 187–93, 232.

among the crush of depositors seeking funds. The Molini doubled the guaranty fund pledged by their friends. At the ducal palace their capacity ultimately to pay in full was assumed. Their obligations were only 35,000 ducats, a small sum compared to the debts of the Garzoni, Lippomani, and Pisani in 1499. On December 7 the senate approved and so imposed a program of liquidation over the term of a year. Thus by the end of 1526 practically all the mushroom banks which had sprung up since 1521 had been liquidated without serious loss.[81]

An incidental feature of the banking law of 1526 was the prohibition of the use of checks. While checks were beginning to be used in other cities, Venice clung to the old-fashioned system requiring the depositors to appear personally at the bank when they wished to withdraw or transfer funds from their accounts. In this respect Venice was especially conservative,[82] yet, in view of the way bank deposits had developed at Venice into a form of money the value of which relative to specie rose and fell according to financial conditions, it is easy to understand the opposition of the Venetian government to the circulation of checks. Checks made easier speculations which accentuated the fluctuations of bank money.

Although Venice lagged behind other banking centers in developing the use of checks, banking practice was not stagnant at Venice. On the contrary, under the leadership of Alvise Pisani, steps were taken toward the successful use of an expansion of bank money to finance government expenditures. In the seventeenth century, through the facilities offered by the concentration of deposits in the state bank, the Banco del Giro, Venice used bank money extensively to finance war. Not only did the state then spend the specie reserve of the bank; it even paid for war expenses in bank money, i.e., by giving the sellers credits on the books of the bank. Since this bank money circulated as legal tender, the effect was much the same as if Venice had paid for war supplies with an issue of paper money. There was an inflation of the medium of exchange.[83]

Earlier, in 1499 for example, war expenses had produced a contraction of the medium of exchange. The heavy wartime issues of forced loans were accompanied by a sharp drop in the value of government bonds, a piling up of property condemned for nonpayment of taxes, and a general "tightness" of money. Specie became extremely scarce and the volume of bank money contracted sharply. This sort of a crisis

---

[81] Sanuto, XLIII, 376, 388, 394, 396.

[82] Usher, p. 426.

[83] Giuseppe Siboni, "Il banco giro di Venezia," *Giornale degli economisti*, V (ser. 2, 1892), 289–93; Dunbar, pp. 327–28, 332.

had been characteristic during earlier wars: before the War of Chioggia (1378–81) government bonds had sold at 99½; toward the end of the war (March, 1381) they sold at 18.[84]

The operations of the sixteenth-century bankers, especially those of Alvise Pisani, bring us much nearer to the seventeenth-century system. The "bank ducat" was treated as a distinct monetary unit with a value different from the specie ducat. Even when not readily convertible into specie, the bank ducat continued to serve as a medium of exchange within the city. The way Pisani helped finance the government had the effect of increasing the volume of his deposits and so the volume of bank money. The effect was like that of an inflation of paper currency in that the inflated medium of exchange depreciated. Thus many features associated with the operations of the later state bank are clearly forecast in the operations of sixteenth-century private banking.

[84] Luzzatto, *I prestiti*, I, cxxix, cclxxiv.

6

The Funded Debt of The Venetian Republic, 1262–1482*

IN Venice the long-term government obligations, which were called *prestiti* or *imprestiti*, were forced loans. Subscription to these loans was obligatory for all Venetians of wealth in an amount proportionate to their wealth, and an assessment of the property of all those who had more than a certain minimum determined how much each Venetian had to lend when a levy was ordered. This assessment was called the *estimo*. Before 1262 the loans were considered temporary; payments on them were considered repayments of principal. In 1262 outstanding loans were consolidated into one fund, later known as the *Monte Vecchio,* and payment of 5 per cent annually of the face value of the loan was assured. Thereafter new levies generally exceeded repayments, although an effort at repaying subscribers was kept up until 1363, and in 1375 a sinking fund was established to buy in bonds at market prices. The interest was paid regularly at 5 per cent each year until the crisis of the War of Chioggia in 1379. It was resumed in 1382 but made subject to withholding taxes that gave 4 per cent to some categories of taxpayers and 3 per cent to others. We may call these *prestiti* government bonds, in spite of the fact that no certificates of indebtedness were given to the bondholders, whose only evidence of claim was in the records kept by the Bond Office, the Camera degli Imprestiti. The bonds were readily transferable and became a popular form of invest-

* Translation of "Sull 'ammontare del 'Monte Vecchio' di Venezia," in *Il debito pubblico della Repubblica di Venezia,* by G. Luzzatto (Milan: Cisalpino, 1963), pp. 275–92. (Translation by permission.)

ment, at least by 1320 and probably before. After a new series was begun in 1482, the old series was known as the *Monte Vecchio*.[1]

The size of the *Monte Vecchio* can be calculated for some years by what I shall call direct methods, that is, either from an explicit statement of the total amount outstanding or from a statement of the amount of interest paid annually. Figures from these sources are indicated in Table I as those obtained by Method A.

For other years the total debt can be estimated only by indirect methods. These indirect methods involve large risks of error but seem

[1] Gino Luzzatto, *I prestiti della Repubblica di Venezia (sec. xiii–xv)* (Documenti finanziari della Repubblica di Venezia, ser. 3, R. Accademia dei Lincei, vol. I, pt. I; Padua, 1929), intro.

TABLE I

ESTIMATES OF THE SIZE OF THE FUNDED DEBT, MONTE VECCHIO.[a]

Year (end of)	Preferred Estimate (rounded off)	Estimate Method A[b]	Estimate Method B[c]	Estimate Method C[d]
1255	15,000			15,000
1279	400,000	408,000		
1291	900,000		879,700	
1299	1,500,000		1,467,000	
1313	2,800,000		2,785,000	
1334	1,800,000		1,806,300	
1343	1,100,000		1,066,300	
1353	3,100,000		3,015,700	
1363	3,700,000		3,460,700	3,961,880
1373	6,000,000		5,605,700	6,106,880
1379	8,500,000		8,150,700	8,651,880
1381	12,300,000		12,216,700	12,377,880
1386	12,800,000	12,827,880	12,683,700	12,827,880
1390	11,000,000	10,996,960		
1393	12,500,000	12,541,880		
1395	10,000,000	10,140,000		
1402	9,500,000			11,850,000
1404	14,000,000			15,450,000
1413	23,000,000		21,700,000	24,000,000
1423	15,600,000	15,600,000		
1438	16,500,000	16,500,000		
1482	21,500,000	21,461,123		
1521	21,500,000	21,461,123		
1620	0	0		

[a] Par values in lire a grossi; after 1328, 1 ducat = 2.6 lire a grossi.

[b] *Method A.* For 1279 estimates, calculated from the amount of interest, see Luzzatto, *Prestiti*, doc. 25 and p. xxxiii. The figures for 1386–95 similarly are calculated from the record of interest in the *Cronaca Alberegna* (*ibid.*, pp. cxcvii–cxcix). For 1423 the figure is from the political testament of Doge Mocenigo (*ibid.*, p. ccxiii). For 1438 it is from the statement about interest payments in a document of January, 1439 (*ibid.*, p. ccxxxii, n. 1). For 1482–86, there are two records of interest (*ibid.*, p. cclxvii, n. 2) which are

Notes to Table I continued

close to agreement, one of which explains how many loans were at 4 per cent, how many at 2 or 3 per cent. The total amount of interest is approximately the same as that indicated by a document of 1520 which gives more detail *sestiere* by *sestiere* of the different rates of interest (*Bilanci Generali*, I, 1, doc. 153). Assuming that the rates of interest were the same in 1482 as in 1520, I have used the 1520 figures for 1482. Since there were no issues to increase the debt in the meantime, we may interpret doc. 127 in *Bilanci Generali* (I, 1) as giving net payments, after the withholding taxes, although Luzzatto seems to interpret it otherwise in *Prestiti*, p. cclxvii, n.

c *Method B.* Starting with the figure for 1279, I have for the successive dates added the intervening levies and subtracted the repayments made in the meantime. Levies and repayments were estimated in connection with the *estimo* as described in the notes to Table II. Estimates after 1386 involve widening margins of error because of uncertainty concerning the size of the *estimo* after the reassessment of 1404.

The figure for 1413 was calculated by starting with the well-documented estimate that the debt was just about 10,000,000 in 1396. Between 1395 and 1404 the only levies were in 1403 and 1404. They totaled about 60 per cent. Assuming the *estimo* had been raised in the general prosperity of the period to a level almost as high as it was in 1379, I estimate it as 6,000,000, of which 60 per cent is 3,600,000. Levies in 1405–13 total about 90 per cent. If the new assessments totaled 9,000,000 lire, as concluded below in Method C, these levies added 8,100,000 lire to the debt. The total debt in 1413 was then:

Debt of 1396	10.0 million
Added, 1403–4	3.6
Added, 1405–15	8.1
	21.7 million

d *Method C.* For the years before 1386 I have started with the figure for 1386 reached by Method A, and for each preceding date have subtracted the levies issued in the meantime, after allowing for retirement of debt by the sinking fund. The sinking fund was estimated at 260,000 lire in deriving the figure for 1373 from that for 1379.

Starting again from the figure for 1423 given by Doge Mocenigo, namely 15.6 million lire (6 million ducats), one can work back by using his earlier statement that in his time they had canceled 10.6 million lire (4 million ducats): "nel tempo nostro [i.e., during his dogeship] havemo diffalchado 4 millioni" (Luzzatto, *ibid.*, p. ccxiii). But we cannot take the sum of Mocenigo's two figures, namely 26.2 million lire, as the total debt in 1413, for while 10.6 million were being paid off during his time by the sinking fund, new levies of about 25 per cent during the years 1414–23, inclusively, were adding to the debt. How much they added depended on how high the assessments were after the revisions of 1405 and later years. To have figures somewhat in line with the others I have estimated the assessment at 9 million lire. Subtracting 25 per cent thereof, namely 2.25 million from 26.2, gives the estimate of 24 million entered in the table.

In the nine years between 1404 and 1414, levies were 95 per cent. Accordingly I have deducted 8,550,000 to arrive at the estimate for 1404.

In the two years 1403 and 1404, levies were about 60 per cent and based on the old *estimo*, which had not been systematically revised but which I estimate would have risen to 6 million, given the general prosperity of the two previous decades. Hence I deducted 3.6 million to arrive at my estimate for 1402.

If I had allowed for the operation of the sinking fund between 1402 and 1414, the figures for 1402 and 1404 would be higher. They seem too high already when compared to the figure for 1396, for there was probably some reduction of the debt through the operation of the sinking fund between 1396 and 1402. The market price rose from 56–61 in 1395–96 to 66 in 1402.

worthwhile, especially to fill the gap between 1279 and 1386, and in view of the relative consistency of the results.

The indirect method uses two elements: (1) the assessed valuation, called the *estimo,* and (2) the amount of levies and repayments. When these levies and repayments were ordered by the government, they were stated as a percentage of the *estimo.*

Let us assume that the *estimo* is known—I shall discuss later how figures for the *estimo* may be found. Knowing the *estimo* and the percentages thereof levied during any period of time, we can calculate how much was added to the debt. Allowance must then be made for repayments in the same period. The net increase in the debt can be added to the figure for the size of the debt obtained by Method A and we thus obtain the figures listed in Table I as those obtained by Method B. Starting at the other end, by what I have called Method C, one deducts the net increase during each period. The gap between the figures reached by these two methods represents a margin of error of at least 10 per cent and in some years of as high as 30 per cent. Even so the figures are useful.

In allowing for repayments in pertinent periods, I have considered these repayments to have been percentages, not of the assessment at the time of repayment, but of the assessment at the time that the loan was made.[2]

Estimates of the total assessments, the *estimo,* are presented in column 5 of Table II. The figure for 1380 is based on the one complete assessment list which has survived, that drawn up in 1379 and put into effect the following year. For other years, two methods of estimating have been used.

The first of these methods depends on having independent evidence

---

[2] In one of the journals of the administration of estates kept by the *Procuratori* of San Marco, one reads: "recipimus libras 50 de capitale pro una pro centenario" (Luzzato, *Prestiti,* p. xxxii, n. 2) . Clearly, the 50 lire were a repayment on principal of a forced loan at the rate of 1 per cent. But 1 per cent of what? That it must have been 1 per cent of the *estimo* at the time when the loan was subscribed to, not at the time of repayment, is shown by the records of the estate of Marco Querini (*ibid.,* pp. xxxi–xxxiii) and by a decree of March 28, 1258, recorded in *Deliberazioni del Maggior Consiglio di Venezia,* ed. by Roberto Cessi (Bologna, 1931) , II, 273. Any other practice would have been quite unreasonable, for after reassessments such as those of 1291 and 1312, it would have been manifestly unjust to give a "repayment" of 1 per cent of the new assessments to men who might have lent nothing twenty years earlier when the loans being repaid had been issued.

Repayments were numbered, and some effort was made to enter their numbers in the books of the Camera degli Imprestiti (Luzzatto, *Prestiti,* pp. xxxi, cxxvii) .

TABLE II

Levies (issues) of the Monte Vecchio and their Repayment, 1255–1385.[a]

Levies	Repayment	Amount Percentage of *estimo*	Amount Estimated lire a grossi	*Estimo*
1255–62	1269–78	12.56		
1262–69		0.0		
1270–79[b]	1281–1303	12.25	408,000	3,300,000
1280–86	1304–6	3.87		
1287–91[c]	1306–19	16.6	500,000	3,300,000
1292–93[c]		0.0		
1294–99[c]	1320–32	19.5	770,000	3,900,000
1300–7[d]	1332–34	5.67	200,000	4,000,000
1308 (to June 12)[d]	1334–40	19.7	800,000	
1312 (June to 1313)[d]	1341–43	13.55	750,000	5,000,000
1314–23[e]	1343–53	5.5	275,000	
1324–34[e]	⎫	1	50,000	
1335–38[e]	⎪	14	700,000	
1339–44[e]	⎪	0.0	0	
1345–48[e]	⎪	14	700,000	
1350–53[e]	Sinking fund	31	1,550,000	
1354–63[e]	purchases	19	1,045,000	
1364–76[f]	⎪	45	2,475,000	5,500,000
1377–79[f]	⎪	45	2,475,000	
1380–81.	⎪	62	3,902,280	6,294,000
1382–85.	⎭	9	450,000	5,000,000

[a] Percentages levied and repaid were compiled from the lists in Luzzatto, *Prestiti*, pp. cxvii–cxxix, cclxix. The first repayment recorded is that of September, 1260. It was 0.5 per cent, just enough to repay what was outstanding in 1255, according to my estimate (see notes to text). Other repayments began in November, 1269, and by the end of 1278 they totaled 12.5 per cent. That was just about enough to repay the borrowing of 1255–62.

Meanwhile there had been new levies in the decade 1270–79. The first repayment which could be used to retire those levies was in 1281. (In 1279 and 1280 no repayments are recorded.) Beginning with 1281 and adding subsequent repayments, we do not reach the total of 12.25 until the repayments of 1303 are included.

The dates of retirement of subsequent issues have been determined by the same method. The figures in lire for the amount of the levies in various periods have been derived from those for the *estimo* and for levies given in percentages, and in view of the margin of error they have been rounded off. The *estimo*, i.e., the total assessments for the period indicated in column 1, was estimated as indicated below.

[b] The appropriation in 1279 to pay the interest was 20,400 lire a year, which is 5 per cent on 408,000 lire (*ibid.*, doc. 25). Since all loans issued before 1270 had been repaid just before 1279 (see col. 2) the debt of 408,000 lire must have been created by the loans issued (i.e., levied) in 1270–79. Since they were 12.25 per cent of the *estimo*, the *estimo* was close to 3.3 million.

[c] A revision of assessments by the heads of parishes (*capi contradi*) was ordered in 1287 in order to raise assessments. In January, 1291, the *capi* were threatened with penalties if they did not do their duty, but in May, 1291, with a war threatening Istria, the task of upping the assessments was given to a special commission of six nobles.

Notes to Table II continued

After this reassessment, no loans were issued until 1294. The heavy loans issued in 1294–99, however, were probably based on assessments substantially higher than those in use earlier (*ibid.*, xxxv–xxxvi). A rise was to be expected because of extensive new building, and because more vigorous enforcement of taxation on the property of churches and monasteries is evident in this period. Such property had originally been exempt, but any property acquired by the church or clergy after 1258 was held to be subject to the obligation to make forced loans (*ibid.*, p. xxi), and in 1296 an effort was made to force such payment not only of current loans but of past loans (*ibid.*, pp. xxxvii–xxxix).

The *estimo* just before 1291 is estimated from the retirement appropriation of 5,000 lire a month voted in 1314–18, the latter part of the period in which the loans levied in 1287–91 were being retired (*Doc. Finan.*, ser. I, *reg.* 1, doc. 6, 85). In the four years 1315–18 repayments totaled 7.15 per cent (*Prestiti*, p. cxxvi). The relation between appropriations and repayments was very far from precise for two reasons. On the one hand, more might be repaid since it was a standing rule that any general surplus in the income of the state should be used to repay the debt; on the other hand, funds allotted to repaying *prestiti* were frequently diverted to other uses. Consequently it seems well to consider the apparent intent of the appropriations as well as the actual result. It appears that the appropriation was intended to repay 2 per cent a year. The total appropriation over the four years was 240,000 lire. If this was enough to pay only about 7.15 per cent, the total of assessed valuations must have been 3,350,000 lire. If instead it was enough to pay 8 per cent, the assessed valuation, namely that of 1287–91, was 3,000,000 lire. I have entered 3,300,000 in Table II.

The large issues of forced loans made for the Second Genoese War, based on new assessments made in 1291, were not repaid before 1319. In 1319 the appropriation for repaying *prestiti* was raised to 6,500 lire a month, enough to yield 312,000 lire in four years (*reg.* 1, doc. 85, 101, 107, 121). During the next four years, repayments totaled 10 per cent (*Prestiti*, p. cxxvi), so that the indication of these figures is an assessment in 1294–99 of 3,120,000 lire, although that does not allow for the fact that some surplus as well as the appropriation may in those years have been used for making repayments. If so, then the assessment should be estimated at a higher figure.

In 1324 the appropriation was raised to 7,000 lire a month and in 1325 it was reduced again to 6,500 (*ibid.*, p. lxxii). During the thirteen-year period 1320–32 the total amount from these special appropriations should have come to 1,020,000 lire. The repayments amount to 19.5 per cent, enough to repay the levies of 1294–99. If the whole appropriation of 1,020,000 lire was really used in making these repayments, then the assessed valuation in 1294–99 must have been about 5,000,000 lire. But it seems almost certain that some were diverted to other uses since no repayments at all are recorded for 1325–29. The evidence regarding the *estimo* of 1294–99 thus permits the estimate to range from about 3 to about 5 million. Assuming that the appropriation of 6,500 lire a month was intended to restore 2 per cent a year, I estimate that *estimo* as 3,900,000 lire.

ᵈ A reassessment was made in June, 1312, during the War of Ferrara. It would be particularly desirable to have a good basis for estimating the total assessed valuation just before and after this revision of the *estimo*. The heavy loans issued during the War of Ferrara were being repaid between 1335 and 1343, but the nature of the records does not permit us to distinguish effectively between the amount required for a given rate of repayment of the issues before June, 1312, and the amount required for the same rate of repayment on issues levied after that date.

Gino Luzzatto calculated the total repayments of the years 1339–42 as 25 per cent. He calculated the appropriation for those years as totaling 1,116,000 lire, because the fund for repaying the debt had been raised in 1339 to 25,000 lire a month and set in 1340–42 at 22,500 lire a month (*Prestiti*, p. lxxxvii). Accordingly he estimated the total assessed valuation at about 4,500,000 lire. That must be some kind of an average of valuations before and after the reassessments of 1312.

Notes to Table II continued

To break down the figures for 1339–42 so as to show which issues were being re-funded is difficult. In 1339 a total of 9 per cent was restored, an extraordinary amount for one year. In 1340 a single payment of 5 per cent, also unusually large, retired not only all issues prior to June, 1312, but also about 1 per cent of the issues after that date, according to my calculations. In 1341 and 1342 there were repayments which applied entirely to retiring levies based on the new assessment of 1312. The amount restored in those two years was only 10.5 per cent. The appropriation for the purpose was 22,500 lire a month so that the total in the two years was 540,000 lire, which is 10.5 per cent of 5,144,276 lire. On the other hand, if the 9 per cent paid in 1339 came entirely from the appropriation, which was then 300,000 lire a year, the *estimo* shortly before 1312 was only 3,333,333 lire. But estimates based on just one or two years are not very convincing. I estimate the *estimo* at about 4 million prior to 1312 and after 1312 at about 5 million. The latter figure appears the more credible when one takes into consideration the figures for later years of the century.

Another way to try to estimate the *estimo* at the time of the War of Ferrara is to start from the amount of levy that appeared to be necessary to raise a given sum. A number of the loans levied in 1311–13 are said to be for the purpose of paying the indemnity to the pope. These loans total 9.5 per cent. Professor Luzzatto (*Prestiti*, p. xlii) remarks that this might lead to the improbable conclusion that the total assessment was hardly more than 1,000,000 lire. I not only agree that such a figure is improbable, but believe it the result of a miscalculation. Luzzatto figured that the indemnity was only 50,000 florins, but the authority on the War of Ferrara whom he cites, although able to find documentary authority for only the 50,000 florins paid after the interdict was lifted, accepts the statements of contemporaries that 100,000 florins had been paid in all (G. Soranzo, *La guerra fra Venezia e la Santa Sede per il dominio di Ferrara* [Città di Castello, 1905], p. 226 n.) The dating of the levies supports this conclusion. Levies in March, 1311, and September, 1312, totaled 5 per cent of the assessment. Florentine bankers were pressured in October, 1312, into arranging payments to the pope, the Peruzzi providing 30,000 florins. The lifting of the ban was then published, in January, 1313. Levies of 3 per cent and 1.5 per cent were made in July and December, 1313, and then 50,000 florins more were paid the pope, according to the published agreement, in two installments, one in September, 1313, and the other in March, 1314 (*ibid.*, pp. 221–32; Luzzatto, *Prestiti*, p. xlii).

At that time 100,000 florins were equal to 260,000 lire a grossi, for the rise of the florin from 18 to 24 occurred before 1310. See K. H. Schäfer, *Die Ausgaben der Aposto-lischen Kammer unter Johann XXII nebst den Jahresbilanzen von 1316–75*, vol. II of *Vatican-ische Quelle zur Geschichte der Päpstlichen Hof- und Finanzverwalting* (Paderborn, 1911), pp. 126–27. If, in order to end with a round figure, we consider that the bankers received a commission which raised the total cost to 285,000 lire, which is 9.5 per cent of 3,000,000 lire, we have a more reasonable figure. But the delays and difficulties of collection were so great, as Luzzatto emphasizes, that it is also reasonable to believe that only three fourths, or even three fifths, of what was due could be immediately collected and that the total assessments in the period varied from about 4,000,000 to 5,000,000 lire a grossi.

ᵉ After 1314, there must have been some reduction in the *estimo* in 1325 as a result of exempting from the levies persons with less than 100 lire of wealth (doc. 120) and then at some later date, but perhaps only for the *estimo* of 1379, those of less than 300 lire (*ibid.*, p. xxi). On the other hand, the postwar return of prosperity in 1314–25 may well have balanced this reduction (*ibid.*, p. lxxix and n.); it seems unlikely that the government would have exempted those of small wealth unless an increase in assessments enabled them to maintain the total. For that reason and because there is no basis for any other estimate, I have treated the total assessed valuation estimated for 1314 as applicable to the following thirty or forty years.

A considerable change in the total assessments must have resulted from the Black Death, from the rapid subsequent recovery, and from the rise in general values reported

Notes to Table II continued

during the 1350's (*ibid.*, pp. c–ci). I have chosen the figure 5,500,000 lire because it works out fairly well with other figures in the series. Although the figure 6,000,000 lire would have served better to bring the figures in Table II into agreement, it seems too big a jump from the figures for 1309–14.

In 1354–63, there are records of six payments but not their amounts. I have estimated them as 2 per cent each, giving a total of 12 per cent, although a total of anywhere between 6 and 24 per cent seems perfectly likely.

In 1375 repurchase through a sinking fund was ordered and an appropriation equal to 50,000 ducats provided (*ibid.*, pp. cxiii–cxiv). There is no telling how long these funds were received and used for the purpose, but the heavy financial pressure of 1377 makes it seem unlikely that they were used for more than two years at most. I have allowed 100,000 ducats for repurchase through this fund, i.e., 260,000 lire a grossi.

ᶠ The *estimo* compiled at the end of 1379 and put into force in 1380 is published complete in Luzzatto, *Prestiti*, doc. 165 (cf. pp. cxliii–cxlv). Holdings of *prestiti* were not assessed (*ibid.*, pp. lxviii–lxvix, cxlvii). A reduction in these assessments to allow for the loss of wealth during the war was authorized in May, 1381, but the reduction was limited to 1.5 million lire (*ibid.*, p. clxxv). Therefore I have estimated the assessments for 1382–85 as 5 million. This lower assessment was probably used for the 10 per cent collected in December, 1381. The *estimo* was then lowered further. One bit of evidence indicates it was down to 3,333,333 lire in 1386, but I agree with Professor Luzzatto that that figure is excessively low. He gives 4 million for 1386 and in another place uses 4.5 million as a sort of average for the period 1382–90 (*ibid.*, pp. clxxxviii, ccxiii).

An entirely new *estimo* made with new rules went into effect in 1405 and was frequently revised thereafter (*ibid.*, pp. ccvii, ccxiv–ccxxix, ccxxxv–ccxxxvi, ccxlix). No effort has been made to extend this table beyond 1385 because the margin of error is widened by the creation of the sinking fund in 1375, by conversions of short-term obligations into *prestiti* to an unknown extent after the War of Chioggia (*ibid.*, pp. clxxxvi–clxxxvii), and by the lack of any good direct evidence in the fifteenth century of the size of the *estimo*, except for one from none too good a source, showing that the *estimo* in 1426 was 4,364,200 lire a grossi (*ibid.*, p. ccxl, n.).

---

of the size of the debt for the pertinent period. Knowing the levies that produced that debt, and what percentage of the *estimo* they were, we can calculate the total *estimo*. For example, the amount of interest appropriated shows that the debt in 1279 was 408,000 lire a grossi (Table I). The levies during the period from 1270 to 1279 were 12.25 per cent. Since there is reason to believe that those levies of 12.25 per cent created the debt of 408,000 lire, as will be explained shortly, I calculate that the *estimo* during the period before 1279 was about 3.3 million lire.

The second method of estimating the *estimo* is offered by appropriations of specified sums for retiring the debt. These sums can be compared with the percentage actually retired during the period in question or with the percentage which was expected to be retired according to the law making the appropriation. For example, the *estimo* of 1287 to 1291 can be estimated from the appropriation of 60,000 a year during the four years 1315 to 1318. Those were years in which the loans made in 1287 to 1291 were being repaid (see Table II). If the appropriation of 60,000 a year could repay 2 per cent a year, as it probably was supposed to do, the *estimo* for 1287 to 1291 was 3 million lire (a grossi). Actual repayments during the four years totaled only 7.15 per cent, instead of 8 per cent, indicating that the *estimo* was 3,350,000 lire. The 3.3 million entered in Table II is a compromise.

These methods require knowing in what years the levies that created a given addition to the debt were collected and when the collections of those years were repaid. This can be calculated with assurance from the list of levies and repayments, provided that the list is complete and that we know the amount of debt outstanding in 1255. Although Luzzatto's list of levies and repayments is not entirely complete, it seems sufficiently so to make this calculation worth while.[3] As to finding a

---

[3] I have for the sake of consistency compiled Table II from the lists of levies and repayments given by Luzzatto (*Prestiti*, at the end of his introductory chapters). Small additions or corrections could be made in the list as printed but they would not make a significant difference in the tables.

In making his list, Professor Luzzatto chiefly relied on the records of the estates administered by the *Procuratori* of San Marco. After 1270 their records of levies and repayments are, he says, "quasi-complete" (pp. cxxv–cxxvii), and after 1335 they are confirmed by other lists. Repayments before 1270 also are revealed by the records of the *Procuratori*, but the record of levies comes mainly from a list found in the *capitolare* of the Ufficiali degli Imprestiti. It is full of gaps, and yet the figures for 1255 to 1259 seem to Luzzatto very high. But the amount it records per year is not out of proportion to later yearly levies, except in the year 1256. The outbreak of the Genoese War in that year suggests an explanation. One wonders whether levies for a single purpose were lumped together in this record even if in fact they were spread out over several years. This might account for the fact that a 3 per cent levy in 1262 does not appear in Luzzatto's list. It is recorded in the early version of the law of March 12, 1262, establishing the 5 per cent interest. This version is preserved in the Archivio di Stato di Venezia in Miscellanea Codici 133, which differs from the version printed in the *Documenti Finanziari* cited, above, ser. I, *Regolazione dell'entrata e delle spese*, vol. I, doc. 1, which is almost certainly a shortened version (see Cessi's introduction to *Deliberazioni del Maggior Consiglio de Venezia*, II, viii–xi). In compiling Table II, I have not added this 3 per cent to the levies recorded by Luzzatto. He considers the figures before 1262 already suspiciously high.

Two special cases of conflicting evidence which caused Luzzatto to question the value of his list should perhaps be mentioned:

(1) In April, 1296, the *Procuratori* were protesting their being ordered to lend the state 47 per cent of the value of the ecclesiastical properties, funds which had hitherto secured exemption. This might be considered a confirmation of the completeness of the list, for the loan imposed on ecclesiastical properties is within 1 per cent of the total of all loans on the list since 1262, and the repeal of the ecclesiastical exemption had been made only in 1258 and hardly applied to earlier loans, except that it puts the state in the utterly unreasonable position of demanding subscription to loans that had already been retired. That is what a literal reading of the decree required, however (Luzzatto, *Prestiti*, doc. 67), and the demand was recognized as excessive and was modified in the same decree that gives the figure as 47 per cent (*ibid.*, doc. 68).

starting point, there is, fortunately, evidence indicating that the *prestiti* outstanding in 1255 were small, about 0.5 per cent.

One item of evidence is in the *capitolare* of the Ufficiali degli Imprestiti. Taken as a whole these regulations setting up the Loan Office contain few or no provisions regarding the problems that would have arisen if the Camera degli Imprestiti were being called on to administer loans that had been made twenty to thirty years before on the basis of assessments then valid but no longer applicable in calculating obligations to subscribe to new loans. There is one provision concerning loans made before 1255, however. It is in the paragraph authorizing the Ufficiali to hear all the claims of those who assert that they should receive interest and requiring them to apply to such claimants all previously passed regulations. Among these regulations, there is mention of one passed August 1, 1255, ordering that "whosoever did not make the loans previously ordered at the time they were imposed" should pay 25 soldi instead of 20 soldi as a forced loan that year.[4] This indicates that the loans outstanding were only about 0.25

---

(2) In March, 1335, a decree ordering consolidation of records referred to twenty-eight *poste*. From the context, *poste* seems to mean unpaid levies (doc. 130 and p. lxxxiii, n.). Luzzatto's list records twenty-eight levies between March, 1310, and March, 1335. If only those twenty-eight remained unpaid in 1335, then the total debt in 1335 was only 1.5 million instead of 1.8 million and other figures should be lowered accordingly. My calculation, however, indicates that all the levies made since May, 1309, were still unpaid in 1335, namely those of twenty-eight years (counting the years at both ends). I suggest that *poste* referred to all the loans of a single year.

[4] Luzzatto, *Prestiti*, p. 40. Clearly, citizens who had not subscribed to earlier forced loans at the time of issue were ordered to pay "soldos quinque pro libra," that is 25 per cent, before they could receive any of the 5 per cent interest. But 25 per cent of what? Three possibilities seem worth considering:

(1) 25 per cent of the assessment. This would imply that the outstanding *prestiti* were already 25 per cent of the *estimo*. This seems improbably high in view of the levies in the next decades, the previous practice of repaying the capital of loans in about a dozen years, and the sums regarded as necessary for a specified amount of repayment in 1319. (See below in notes to Table II.)

(2) 25 per cent of each unpaid levy as an additional loan or as pure penalty. The use of the phrase "sub soldis quinque pro libra" (*ibid.*, doc. 68) in the Great Council termination of April 2, 1297, suggests this possibility, but it is by no means clear. The 25 per cent is not called a penalty and would have been an extremely heavy penalty.

(3) 25 per cent of the 1 per cent which was being levied in 1255. In this case the meaning of the law is that those who have avoided subscription to previous issues of forced loans were to pay an additional 0.25 per cent on top of the 1 per cent which was being collected from all citizens. This would seem entirely reasonable if the

per cent of the *estimo*. A slightly higher percentage is indicated by the record of the estate of Marco Querini, namely 0.5 per cent.[5]

The composition of the estate left by Doge Rainieri Zeno in 1266 also indicates that the debt was small in 1255. He had about 6,000 lire in *imprestiti* out of an estate of about 50,000, almost exactly the same as the 12.5 per cent levied from 1255 to 1266 (see Table II). Of course assessment was less than real wealth even for a doge, but Ranieri Zeno's *imprestiti* included not only his own and those of his father but also those he had purchased from a certain Ottobelini.[6] That the debt was small in 1255 is not surprising in view of the relatively peaceful decades that Venice enjoyed before the first war with Genoa and the general practice of repaying without interest in eleven to thirteen years. That there were some forced loans outstanding is shown by records of 1252

---

total of old loans outstanding was only about 0.25 per cent of the *estimo* in use in 1255.

[5] During the period 1276–87, Marco Querini's estate was one of those which was no longer obligated to make loans (presumably because the other property had been transferred to his heirs) but it was receiving sizable repayments of principal as well as of the interest on loans made in the past (*ibid.*, p. xx and doc. 17). Since it was receiving repayment of the loans made before 1276, the amount of these repayments shows how many *prestiti* Querini held in 1276.

He received 8 lire, 7 soldi, 6 denarii per 100 lire of assessment, and in addition a final payment in 1287 to liquidate his account. This final payment was in accord with an order given the Camera degli Imprestiti in November, 1286, to liquidate the accounts of 255 citizens who were no longer subject to the levy and whose names could be cleared from the books by using 918 lire to liquidate their accounts (*ibid.*, doc. 46). Using this special payment to round off our figures, we can conclude that the amount of *imprestiti* with which Querini was credited in 1276 was about 8.5 per cent of his assessment.

Let us consider how Marco Querini would have acquired these *prestiti*. The total of all the levies recorded between 1255 and 1275 is 19 lire and 7 denarii per 100 lire of assessment; the repayments recorded in the same period total 11 lire per 100, leaving Querini a balance of 8 lire, 7 denarii per 100 lire of assessed wealth. If Querini had started with no *imprestiti* in 1255, he would have accumulated, by 1275, *prestiti* to the value of 8.06 per cent of his assessment. Since the account was settled by paying him 8.5 per cent, approximately 0.5 per cent has to be accounted for by the fact that he already had some *prestiti* in 1255.

Of course it is possible that Marco Querini added to his wealth and to the amount for which he was assessed sometime about 1255 and that other men had been forced to subscribe to earlier loans from which he was free. But if there had been outstanding in the hands of others large amounts of *prestiti* issued before 1255, the repayments would have gone to them and would not have been available to repay his loans. The fact that loans he had accumulated in 1255–75 were repaid in 1276–87 indicates that all loans made before 1255, except about 0.5 per cent, had already been repaid at that date.

[6] Gino Luzzatto, *Studi di storia economica veneziana* (Padua, 1954), pp. 83–85.

and 1253 concerning the claims of heirs to *prestiti* registered in the names of their deceased relatives.[7] With all these considerations in mind I have taken as a starting point the assumption that the debt outstanding in 1255 was 0.5 per cent of the *estimo*.

If this estimate is too low, one cannot say that repayments were surely made at the dates indicated in Table II, but one can say that they were surely not repaid earlier than the dates indicated, provided the record of repayments is complete. The chance of error from having too low an estimate of the debt in 1255 and the chance of error from gaps in the record of all levies balance each other to some extent and give more credibility to the figures presented.

Another problem in constructing a cumulative series is that the amount of the *estimo* varied from year to year. Although general reassessments were few and far between, the total valuation must have changed by reassessment of individuals as deaths, marriage dowries, and such displays of wealth as the building of new palaces made it obvious that the assessment rolls, which were kept by the Camera degli Imprestiti for each *sestiere* and parish, needed modification. Men who had lost their wealth could and would claim to be relieved somewhat of their obligation to make forced loans. Men who had received rich legacies or added obviously to their wealth in other ways would have their assessments raised. The *estimo* would go up somewhat in prosperous years and especially in a building boom, even if it did not keep up with rising wealth, and after some years there would be a demand for a general reassessment, perhaps under new rules.[8] In Table II, levies are grouped so as to lump together years in which there was probably no general revision of assessments and in which the total would not change much.

In order to allow as far as possible for changes in the *estimo*, I have used short periods and dated them so that general revisions of the *estimo* occurred at dividing dates. I have also separated the periods of heavy borrowing from those when borrowing was light. Some periods of heavy borrowing have been divided because of revisions of the *estimo*, e.g., in 1312, 1379, and 1404. The individual periods are consequently of unequal length, from two to ten years.

---

[7] Luzzatto, *Prestiti*, p. xxi, doc. 9–12. Since these all appear to be cases in which the title was in dispute, repayment may have been withheld beyond the normal period for those individuals.

[8] *Ibid.*, pp. xix–xxiv, ccxx; see the notes to Table II concerning particular reassessments.

7

Venture Accounting in
Medieval Business Management*

F ROM its beginning, accounting has been shaped by the needs of
the businessman and has in turn affected the handling of business
problems. A clear illustration of this is the contrast between the system
of accounts found in the ledgers of Florentine cloth manufacturers and
the system of accounts found in the ledgers of Venetian merchants of
the fifteenth and sixteenth centuries.[1] Cloth manufacturers such as the
younger branch of the Medici arranged their entries under a wage
account, a wool account, a cloth sales account, and so on, because their
main concern was to keep track of these materials or obligations. The
Venetians, being mainly exporters and importers, were concerned
chiefly with keeping track of wares shipped, wares received, and
amounts owed by or to agents. Accordingly, the distinctive key accounts
in Venetian books are (a) the accounts opened for each kind or lot of
merchandise received and (b) the accounts debited when wares were
shipped. The latter are best called shipment, or venture, accounts. For
example, when a Venetian merchant bought Florentine cloth to ship it
to Constantinople, he opened a Florentine cloth account in which he
entered as debits all the costs of the cloth including the cost of packing
it for shipment. When he sent the cloth to his agent in Constantinople,

* From *Bulletin of the Business Historical Society*, XIX (1945), 164–72. (By permission.)
[1] On Florentine industrial accounting, see Raymond de Roover, "A Florentine
Firm of Cloth Manufacturers," *Speculum*, XVI (1941), 3–33; on the Venetian books
discussed below, see Frederic C. Lane, *Andrea Barbarigo, Merchant of Venice, 1418–
1449* (Baltimore, 1944), pp. 140–81.

he closed the Florentine cloth account by transferring the balance to the debit side of an account called shipment (*viazo*) to Constantinople entrusted to Carlo Cappello (or whatever was the name of the agent). To such a shipment, or venture, account he debited all goods sent to a particular agent at a particular place, or at least all so shipped by a particular fleet. Since the ledgers were indexed, reference to *viazo* in his index quickly gave a Venetian merchant a full record of his shipments.

Besides the shipment account, there was the account of the overseas agent—for example, one entitled Carlo Cappello for the Constantinople agency. But the shipment account made it unnecessary to debit the agent's account every time wares were shipped. Use of the two accounts, the shipment account and the agent's account, served to separate the record of the agent's obligations from the record of shipments.

Similarly, the Venetians effected a separation between the record of the credits due the agent and the record of the arrival of his shipments, but they needed no special account for this purpose. When an agent shipped wares from Constantinople to Venice, the first indication of it in the books of the consignee was the opening of an account for the merchandise received—for example, an account for silk from Constantinople—and usually the first entry on this silk account was a debit recording payments made to remove the wares from the customhouse. This entry described the wares fully, reproducing the invoice and noting any mistakes therein. Then followed debits for freights paid and other expenses, and credits to the account for the sale of the merchandise. Later, when a report arrived from the agent telling precisely how much the wares cost, that sum was debited to the silk account and credited to the agent's account. The account of the agent was thus based entirely upon records which he himself furnished and was completely independent of the records of the shipments to or from him.

Consequently Venetian merchants kept track of their exports and imports through a cycle of accounts such as is set forth in Figures 1, 2, and 3. Each arrow indicates a debit to the ensuing account and a credit to the preceding account. If by "banks," bank deposits are understood, and by "personal accounts," accounts payable, the diagrams can be read as representing not only cycles of accounts but also successive transformations in the form of the merchant's capital. This succession was not exactly in the order pictured unless the merchant in buying always paid cash before delivery and in selling always gave credit. Although in fact he generally both gave and received some time in which to pay for purchases, the diagrams do roughly picture cycles of investment as well as represent accurately the cycle of accounts.

In many cases when the wares received from an agent in the Levant were not sold in Venice but sent to an agent in the West, or vice versa, the cycle was as indicated in Figure 2.

Sometimes a new cycle was begun, without passing through the bankers' accounts, as in Figure 3, when wares imported were bartered for wares to be exported. For example, cotton received from Syria

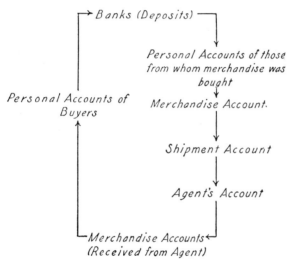

Fig. 1. Cycle of accounts recording purchase, export, import, sale, and receipt of payment.

was sometimes sold to a German who paid in copper which was sent back to Syria for sale.

Although the original purpose of setting up the shipment accounts may have been only to separate the records of merchandise from the records of agents' obligations and thus enable a merchant to be sure of what he owed and was owed, once the accounts had been set up, their existence dominated the methods used to determine profit or loss. The Venetians did not figure profits by yearly balancing of the books or by any form of consolidation surveying the business as a whole at regular intervals. They used a relatively easy method of finding profits, which was a result of having these shipment and merchandise accounts. On the cycles pictured, the personal accounts and bank accounts would all

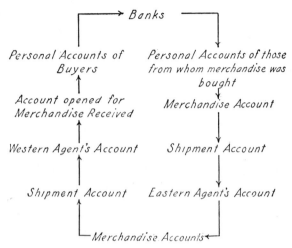

Fig. 2. Cycle of accounts recording purchase, export, import, re-export, import, sale, and receipt of payment.

balance, if there were no bad debts, as soon as the movement of capital was completed. The shipment and merchandise accounts, on the other hand, would not be balanced even when the cycle of investment was entirely completed, and they were the accounts the merchant worked with in finding whether the investment had been profitable. He did so,

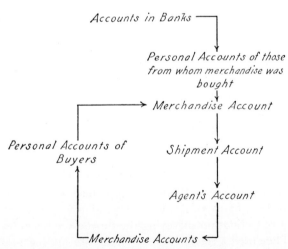

Fig. 3. Cycle of accounts recording purchase, export, import, barter, and re-export.

as soon as the business operation was completed, by carrying to a profit and loss account the difference between the two sides of the unbalanced shipment and merchandise accounts.

Very different was the Florentine method of calculating profits. Florentine merchants did balance their books at fairly regular intervals and calculated the returns earned on the business as a whole. To do this, they closed one account into another. In the Medici industrial accounting, the wages account was closed into manufacturing expenses and manufacturing expenses into cloth sales. The business of the Florentine cloth manufacturers was in a real sense all one venture and for that reason their finished cloth account could be used to sum up all the others.

The business of most Venetian merchants involved a series of separate ventures, the success of a shipment to Constantinople and that of a shipment to Alexandria being generally independent of one other. Consequently, as a rule each of the shipment accounts and each of the accounts opened for merchandise received were independently closed into profit and loss. This system is appropriately called venture accounting, for by it the merchants' operations were divided into ventures, and in computing profit or loss each venture was treated as an independent unit.

Besides the many shipment and merchandise accounts, the Venetians used a number of other kinds of accounts which had to be closed through profit and loss. There were separate accounts in the ledger for investments in trading partnerships, in shops, in shares of ships (*carati* accounts) or of companies operating merchant galleys. In recording dealings with bills of exchange, exchange bought or exchange sold accounts were sometimes used to prevent confusion between the obligations of agents and the gains or losses which might come either from fluctuations in exchange rates or from the use of bills of exchange to borrow or lend money.

The main characteristics of the venture system are found in all the surviving Venetian account books and in those of Ragusa (on the eastern coast of the Adriatic), but, naturally, different merchants, according to their capacities and to the various problems encountered, handled the system differently. The oldest Venetian mercantile account books (1406–36) are those of the Soranzo family, four brothers who were primarily cotton importers and who took turns going to Syria to buy cotton. The brother in Syria acted while there as commission agent for other Venetian merchants as well as for his partnership. Accordingly the Soranzo brothers faced at least two main accounting problems: how to co-ordinate the activities of the brothers; and how to record the profits and losses on the importation and sale of cotton. The first problem, that of putting together into a single record the activities of various partners at various places, was not well handled. The Soranzo family seems to have gone to extremes in the number of their books of primary entry and in ledgers left unbalanced during a period of thirty years. But the record of cotton imports was carefully kept in a successful adaptation of the venture system to their specific problem. Since they were importing the same commodity for years on end from the same agent, if they had entered the receipts on the same cotton account they would not have had a way of telling as they went along the amount of their profit on cotton sales except by taking inventories. The uncertain valuations and the bother involved in taking inventory were avoided by opening a new merchandise account for each season's imports. There were distinct accounts for "Cotton received by the fleet of March, 1419," "Cotton received by the fleet of September, 1419," and so on. Each such account could be closed through profit and loss as soon as that season's receipts were sold.

One of the stay-at-home Venetian merchants who employed the Soranzo brothers as his agents in Syria was Andrea Barbarigo, whose account books (1431–49) are the most complete and informative of those extant. Andrea Barbarigo entered on the same cotton account all shipments of cotton from the same agent even if they were spread over several years, but he did not import cotton long enough from the same agent to cause himself any serious difficulty in finding his profits. For his most constant importations, those of English cloth, he opened new accounts for each lot received, and accordingly he also had no need of an inventory for figuring his profits, since he could close each account when that lot had been sold.

Andrea Barbarigo's ledger illustrates fully the whole system of venture accounting which has here been described. Another view of the practice in the same period and from another angle is the ledger kept by Jacomo Badoer while he was commission agent at Constantinople (1436–40). Notable in both these merchants' methods is their use of a merchandising expense account especially adapted to venture account-ing. The merchandise expense account of the Medici consisted almost entirely of debits and was balanced by transferring its total to some other accounts, such as cloth sales. If the Venetians had used this type of merchandise expense account it would have interfered with calculating separately the profits on each venture. Instead, the merchandise ex-pense accounts of Andrea Barbarigo and of Badoer consisted almost entirely of credits. Expenses incurred in shipping or receiving wares were debited to the appropriate venture or merchandise account at the time when the expense was incurred or reported. When the expense was paid, the expense account was debited and the corresponding credit was recorded to cash or to a person, perhaps a banker who made the payment.[2]

This type of expense account did not interfere with calculating separately the profits on each venture. But why was it used at all? Its function seems to have been to keep a record of expenses payable, regardless of just what had actually been paid or in what form. Badoer, being a commission agent managing the receipt and shipment of wares for many merchants, may have found it convenient to set forth very clearly the record of all such handling charges, which he was charging to the accounts of his correspondents, without stating in the same entries just how he paid them.

Besides the general accrued expense accounts of this type, two other special accrued expense accounts appear in some of the fragmentary Venetian ledgers: one for a certain type of tax and the other for freights paid. These accounts, similarly, were credited when the tax or freight was incurred and were debited to record its payment. Accounts of this sort were useful to big companies, like the great Pisani firm of the early sixteenth century, which had many dealings with the government and which both shipped much merchandise by the merchant galleys and frequently operated such galleys. Sometimes the Pisani paid freight and taxes, sometimes they were collecting them under contract with the government, and they could cancel debts against collections. Consequently they found it useful to have a separate record of expenses of this kind.

The way the system of venture accounting might be adapted to the special needs of a particular firm is illustrated on one special point by the practices of Nicolò and Alvise Barbarigo from about 1463 to 1473. For that decade these two brothers limited their commercial operations to exporting wares and especially silver from Venice to North Africa and exchanging most of it there for gold. According to the usual practice outlined above, they opened each year a silver account, a shipment or venture account, an account for Alvise as agent—since he was usually the brother who sailed on the Barbary galleys and handled

---

[2] Although not distinguished in any way by their titles from asset expense accounts, these "expense accounts" were essentially records of liabilities, rather than of expenditures, and are similar to our expenses accrued or payable accounts.

the wares—and a gold received account. But not only did the silver account close into the venture account, the balance from the gold account and any balance in Alvise's account, because of expenses which he could charge to the family partnership, were also carried to the venture account. In the books of Nicolò and Alvise Barbarigo, the *viazo* account is not merely a "shipment" account but is better called a "venture" account, for it came close to giving the net result of the year's operations, the result of the Barbary voyage as a whole.

Such consolidation was relatively easy for Nicolò and Alvise Barbarigo, who hardly ever shipped on more than one voyage at a time. In contrast, their father, Andrea Barbarigo, had kept wares going in all directions at once and he would have found it very difficult in many cases to say where one venture ended and another began. But there may have been many merchants who found it practical to use the *viazo* account as did Nicolò and Alvise Barbarigo to close some of the merchandise accounts in ways which would sum up connected mercantile operations.

Manufacturing as well as commerce was of importance at Venice, although of secondary importance, and consequently Venetian merchants needed to adapt their system of venture accounting to record industrial operations. Andrea Barbarigo, who put out to be dyed in Venice part of the cloth he imported from England, handled the accounting by recording all the cost of industrial operations on the appropriate cloth accounts. This method had the disadvantage of confusing profits and expenses of importation with the profits and expenses of manufacturing, but since manufacturing was a definitely subordinate part of Andrea Barbarigo's activity, being only incidental to merchandising, the disadvantages may not have appeared serious.

Another method by which the Venetians fitted industrial accounting into venture accounting was to set up a goods-in-process account. In the books of the big sixteenth-century Pisani partnership there were accounts called "wool given to be worked on" and "cloth given to be worked on." The same practice had probably been used for a hundred years by those Venetian firms whose operations were such as to give them need for accounts of this type, since in Ragusa, where accounting practices were almost the same as at Venice, similar accounts were used in 1438 to record wax manufacture. But the use of a goods-in-process account necessitated some departure from the usual pattern of venture accounting. Perhaps the goods-in-process account was closed, as was the similar account in the Venetian-style ledger of an Antwerp printer about 1565, by transfers to a goods-in-stock account, and the goods-in-stock account was adjusted by an inventory in order to discover the profit. But the use of an inventory involved a substantial departure from the usual practices of venture accounting. One of its great advantages was that it avoided the need for an inventory.

Basically connected with the lack in the surviving Venetian books of any references to inventories is the very infrequent and imperfect closing of the Venetian ledgers. The best practice surviving is that of Andrea Barbarigo who drew up trial balances of a sort in 1431, 1435, 1440, and then let his accounts run on unbalanced until his death. But his son went twenty years without making any kind of a balance sheet. Our picture of Venetian practice may be lopsided because none of the surviving account books belonged to short-term partnerships; all are books of personal proprietors or of family partnerships; but while there were at Venice some of the short-term partnerships which the Medici books indicate were the usual rule at Florence, precisely the dominance of family partnerships is characteristic of Venice. Judged by the surviving samples, these family firms appear to have been content to go for decades without attempting a balance sheet. Most rich families owned substantial amounts of government bonds and some real estate in the city, the countryside, or the colonies; trade was not their only means of livelihood. Their possession of other sources of steady income may explain their apparent indifference to periodically summing up their commercial gains or losses as a whole. And it must be recognized that for merchants, much of whose wealth was at any one moment overseas, no over-all estimate could be made with accuracy.

If we judge an accounting system by its success in achieving the end now generally accepted—namely, the determination regularly and periodically of the rate of return on the capital invested—Venetian accounting about 1500 appears definitely inferior to the Florentine. If we look back to the first formulation of double entry about 1320 we must, on the evidence now available, award the palm to Genoa, since there is no evidence concerning the use of double entry at Venice as early as at Genoa. Yet Venice had a greater reputation than either Genoa or Florence as Europe's schoolmaster in bookkeeping and accounting. Two reasons for that reputation are well known. At Venice the professional teachers of bookkeeping refined to a high degree the stylizing of entries and their arrangement in ways conducive to clarity, cross reference, and ease in arithmetical calculation. At Venice the first books on bookkeeping were published, a testimonial, however, to the importance of Venice in the book trade as well as to the fame of her merchants. To these reasons for the popularity of "the Venetian method" may be added a third. The venture system of accounting used at Venice was the most practical form for merchants much of whose wealth was coming and going on the seas. It could be varied to suit many situations as is shown by the extant Venetian account books, few as they are. It was a flexible system which enabled a merchant, while keeping a clear and accurate record of his obligation and his debtors, to calculate not regularly but easily and realistically his profits and losses.

8

Rhythm and Rapidity of Turnover in Venetian Trade of the Fifteenth Century*

ONE approach to the study of rapidity of turnover in medieval business is through examination of the speed of the mail service and of transportation.[1] For Venice, knowledge of the transportation facilities, even if only rough knowledge, does indeed furnish starting points for an estimate of the speed of its international trade. The regularly scheduled sailing of the merchant galleys and of some groups of unarmed sailing vessels created a well-defined pattern of commercial movement. Rhythm in the transportation system gave rhythm to the whole commercial life of the city. Although Venice could be called a city of perpetual fairs, as Antwerp was later, in the sense that both trade and the clearance of payments were possible throughout the year, yet the intensity of trade varied. The arrival and departure of ships were concentrated in certain seasons. The intervals between those seasons were the periods when trade was most brisk; and, using "fair" in a general sense, we may call these periods "fairs."

I

There were two main fairs in this sense. To be sure, a treatise on trade written in the early fifteenth century mentions three. It says

---

* Translation of "Ritmo e rapidità di giro d'affari nel commercio veneziano del quattrocento," in *Studi in onore di Gino Luzzatto*. 4 vols. (Milan: Dott. A. Giuffre, 1949) , I, 254–73. (Translation by permission.)

[1] Gino Luzzatto, *Storia economica dell'età moderna e contemporanea*, pt. I (Padua, 1932) , pp. 36–51; Armando Sapori, *Studi di storia economica medievale* (ed. 2; Biblioteca storica Sansoni, n.s., V; Florence, 1946) , pp. 685–87.

money was dear at Venice because there was so much buying, including buying on credit, at three periods. The first was from the middle of January to February 10, when wares were being purchased to be sent on the ships which left in February for Syria. The second, of minor importance, was in April, when purchases were made for shipment on the galleys going to Flanders. The third and main period in which money was tight was from July to September because of the wares bought for shipment on the merchant galleys going to Syria and Alexandria. The second of these periods is not presented as of importance equal to the other two.[2] It was changed, later in the century, and merged more or less with the summer period, when the departure of the Flemish galleys was fixed at July 15. The official sailing schedule, from which there were of course many departures in practice, was then roughly as follows:[3]

Feb. 10–15	Unarmed sailing ships to Syria.
Mar. 1–15	Galleys *al trafego* to Tunis and Tripoli.
Apr. 22 to May 8	Galleys of Barbary and Acqua Morte.
July 15	Galleys of Flanders.
July 25	Galleys of Romania.
July and early Aug.	Unarmed sailing ships to Syria.
Aug. 24	Galleys to Beirut.
Aug. 30	Galleys to Alexandria.

Some purchasing for export by sea was thus spread out through the spring, as was also the very important purchasing by the Germans for export over the Alps as soon as the passes ceased to be blocked by blizzards. But two main periods of trade are still to be distinguished: a winter period, terminated by the departure in February of the spring fleet for Syria, and a summer period, terminated by the departure of both unarmed ships and merchant galleys for both the Levant and the Channel in July and August.

[2] *El libro di mercantantie et usanze di paesi,* ed. by Franco Borlandi (Documenti e studi per la storia del commercio e del diritto commerciale italiano, VII; Turin, 1936) , p. 167.

[3] For the galleys, this timetable is based on Senato, Incanti Galere, reg. 1, 1480–89; for the round ships, on many references in Archivio di Stato di Venezia, Senato Mar, reg. 16, 17. See also my *Venetian Ships and Shipbuilders of the Renaissance* (Baltimore: The Johns Hopkins Press, 1934) , pp. 46, 136. This timetable is not substantially different, except that the time of departure fixed for the galleys of Flanders varied from March 15 to June 25, from the schedules for the years 1441–50 compiled in the *tesi di laurea* of Gino Giomini (R. Istituto Superiore di Scienze Economiche e Commerciali, 1934) ; through the courtesy and helpfulness of Gino Luzzatto, I was able to consult this thesis.

The distinction between the winter and the summer periods of intense trade is yet more apparent when these periods are defined with reference to the arrival of fleets at Venice. The winter period was opened by the return of the three galley fleets that had gone to the Levant in the fall, of the cogs or caracks which had sailed for Syria in midsummer, and of the galleys *al trafego* of Barbary and of Acqua Morte from their year's cruises around the Mediterranean. In the fourteenth century, when the galleys of Flanders left in March, they too were supposed to be back before the end of that year; in the mid-fifteenth century, however, they did not usually come back until spring or later in the next year. On the other hand, many ships which left Venice in the spring for Spain or for the Black Sea came home in the fall, so that the winter trade season was fed with supplies from many sources. Its main feature, of course, was the presence of the spices and other precious cargoes brought back at the beginning of winter from the Levant, and it was a particular concern of the Venetian senate that these fleets should be back on time for "the fair." The period which may be called the winter fair was between the arrival of galleys and ships in early winter and the departure of ships again in February.[4] Even though its boundaries were not rigidly defined by law, it was a period when exchange of wares and clearance of payments were intense.

To define the summer period in terms of arrivals we must ask when galleys of Flanders arrived and when the ships which had been to Syria in the spring were expected back. In both cases the end of May was the date at which they were hoped for, even if actual arrival was often later.[5] Consequently, June, July, and August formed the period of intense exchange which might be called the summer fair.

The timing of the voyages so as to concentrate trade in these two periods made possible a relatively rapid turnover of some key commodities. Two investments in cotton, for example, could be made within one year. Cotton brought from Syria by ships arriving at Venice in June or July could be sold for silver coin or for cloth which could be exported on the ships leaving in July or August. When they returned in December the cotton they then brought could again be sold and a new shipment east made in the following spring. In short, the voyages

---

[4] "Fairs" are referred to in the resolutions of the senate regulating the voyages (Archivio di Stato di Venezia, Senato Mar, reg. 11, f. 129; reg. 16, f. 1).

[5] These rough generalizations are based on the many references to arrivals in various chronicles and diaries, especially in the *Diarii* of Marino Sanuto. See also my *Venetian Ships and Shipbuilders of the Renaissance*, p. 46.

allowed a merchant to turn over his capital twice a year in the cotton trade.

In the spice trade the rhythm of the voyages provided for only one turnover a year, but that could be completed in less than half a year by investing in silver in August just before the galleys left for Alexandria and then selling the spices in January just after the galleys returned to Venice. Exchanging the wares of Alexandria with those of London could be done in two years according to the following sailing schedule:

Jan. (1st yr.)	Arrival at Venice with spices.
July (1st yr.)	Departure to London with spices.
May (2d yr.)	Return from London with tin or other cargo.
Aug. (2d yr.)	Departure to Alexandria with tin.
Jan. (3d yr.)	Arrival at Venice with spices.

Thus investment by a merchant in the complete cycle of exchange between Alexandria and London meant engaging his capital for a two-year period.

The decrees with which the Venetian senate set up this schedule of voyages and made exceptions and modifications according to circumstances are evidence that the senate believed regular and rapid turnover an essential element in the city's prosperity. The institution of the *muda*[6] was not based on the greater safety enjoyed by ships traveling in convoy, for only occasionally were the ships of the same *muda* required to travel together. It was administered with the objective of bringing to Venice as soon as possible all the commodities which were ready in Levantine *scale* at the stipulated date. The institution of regular loading periods was, I believe, aimed against the tendency of ship captains to delay their sailings in the hope of completing their cargoes and against the desire of merchants to delay their purchases to the last moments in the hope that prices would fall. The senate did not intend to allow these individual interests to interfere with the benefit which the mercantile community as a whole would derive from having the voyages move on schedule.[7] By maintaining the *muda,* the Venetian

---

[6] For a discussion of the special meaning of *muda* in medieval Venice, see pp. 128–41.

[7] A senatorial resolution of June 1, 1420 reads in part: "niun altra cossa e de plui utilitade alla marcadantia che conservar le mude, per quelle e sustimento de la marcadantia" (Senato Misti, reg. 53 (doppio), ff. 115–16). Cf. Senato Mar, reg. 11, f. 129 (1492), and reg. 16, f. 1 (1503). Modifications of the usual rules about *mude* which show that the objective was the regular movement of wares to the Venetian market, not travel in convoy, are Senato Misti, reg. 57, f. 86 (March 29, 1429); reg. 47, ff. 63, 64, 74 (July and August, 1406).

senate showed its awareness of the importance of keeping capital moving. In that sense it showed appreciation of the famous capitalistic aphorism of Benjamin Franklin, "Time is money."

II

But did wares really flow through Venice with the maximum speed permitted by the timing of the voyages? Were the merchants sufficiently eager to turn time into money? And was the market sufficiently fast so that they could sell promptly and yet profitably? Some partial answers to these questions can be found in merchants' account books.

Some merchants turned over part of their capital according to the schedule of the transportation system. A relatively simple illustration in the cotton trade is provided by the account book of Nicolò Barbarigo. A Venetian noble, Barbarigo engaged but little in trade, so that it is easy to keep each of his investments separate. In January, 1472, he sent 600 ducats in coin to Syria, received back that same summer fifteen sacks of cotton, promptly disposed of eleven sacks of these, and obtained in return about 500 ducats worth of coin and cloth which he sent back to Syria by the ships leaving in August.

A clear-cut case in which the complete cycle of two turnovers in cotton within twelve months was effected is harder to find. Something always seemed to come up to prevent it. After Nicolò Barbarigo sent out his second investment in August of 1472 the ships sailing to and from Syria fell behind their schedules. None of the capital he sent out in August came back in the form of cotton until the following March. This cotton was not all sold until November. Thus the second turnover of 600 ducats of capital took about sixteen months. Moreover, in August, Nicolò had doubled his investment by sending a second 600 ducats, approximately. He did not realize on this sum by selling the return cotton until February, 1474, and since he sold giving credit for a year's term, he did not get cash available for a new shipment to Syria until February, 1475—three years after his investment.[8]

More significant indication of the speed of turnover in the wholesale cotton trade can be gained from the ledger of Lorenzo Soranzo and Brothers, for they imported cotton regularly over a period of about thirty years. In their ledger they set up a separate account for the cotton

---

[8] A.S.V., Registri privati, Registri Barbarigo, reg. 6, k. 122, 125, 132, 141, 152. He seems then still to have had some cotton left and to have reinvested a little, with extremely slow turnover.

of each season or *muda*. For example, an account of the cotton of the *muda* of March, 1416, recorded cotton received by ships which left Syria in March of 1416 and reached Venice before June 12, 1416. By extension the word *muda* was often applied to the fleet, but in legal language it meant the period of time during which loading was permitted in designated Levantine ports. As a general rule the *mude* for Syrian ports were March and September, but when sailings were delayed by war or weather, a special vote of the senate could change the *mude* for that particular year. Consequently, when the Soranzo book-keeper designated some cotton as being "of the *muda* of March, 1418," some doubt yet remains as to just when the cotton was really loaded, or when it reached Venice. Only a close comparative study of the decrees of the senate, of contemporary chronicles, and of the bookkeeping entries concerning payments for withdrawal from customs would date fully the real movement of each shipment of cotton. But for our general purpose of gaining a preliminary estimate of the rhythm of trade and turnover at Venice, it is significant to compare the dates of sale of the cotton with the dates at which that cotton was supposed to be loaded in Syria according to the regular system of voyages. For the six years 1416 to 1421, this is shown in Table I. In 1416 and 1417, a substantial part of the cotton which the Soranzo brothers imported was sold in the summer or winter "fair" immediately after its receipt. Sale was quick enough in 1417 so that two thirds of the cotton imported by the March fleet was sold before ships left again to load more cotton in September, and almost all which came back in the fall was sold during the winter. Accordingly, the Soranzo brothers could turn over that part of their capital twice in one year. Moreover, during 1416 and 1417 no cotton was kept in stock for more than a year. Those years demonstrate, as did Nicolò Barbarigo's first investment in 1472, that two turnovers in one year were not a pure mirage. Sometimes merchants did move a large part of their wares just as fast as was provided for by the regular schedule of voyages.

In 1418 the turnover of the Soranzo brothers slowed down; the pattern shown by Table I changes abruptly. The reason for this was that the trade war which Emperor Sigismund, king of Hungary, was waging against Venice became most nearly effective in 1418 to 1422.[9] The chief part of the cotton market was normally formed by the Germans who came to buy at the Fondaco dei Tedeschi, or, as the

---

[9] Henry Simonsfeld, *Der Fondaco dei Tedeschi in Venedig und die deutsch-venetianischen Handelsbeziehungen* (Stuttgart, 1887), II, 45.

TABLE I

COTTON SALES (IN SACKS) BY SORANZO BROTHERS;
PERIOD OF LOADING COMPARED TO PERIOD OF SALE.[a]

Period of Loading in Syria		Period of Sale[b]							
Year	*Muda*	Summer	Fall	Winter	Spring	Summer	Fall	Winter	Later
1416	Mar.	18	6	37	5	0	0	0	0
	Sept.	–	–	0	31	0	0	0	0
1417	Mar.	48	0	24	0	0	0	0	0
	Sept.	–	–	57	3	0	0	0	0
1418	Mar.	0	0	39	90	0	0	0	0
	Sept.	–	–	0	27	1	30	45	0
1419	Mar.	0	0	21	1	0	0	2	45
	Sept.	–	–	24	0	0	0	0	48
1420	Mar.	0	0	5	4	27	9	1	31
	Sept.	–	–	no imports	.	.	.	.	.	.
1421	Mar.	0	0	0	0	0	9	0	0
	Sept.	–	–	0	0	0	4	2	2

[a] Compiled from photofilm of the pertinent cotton accounts in Soranzo libro reale nuovo, in A.S.V., Miscellanea Gregolin, busta 14, registri commerciali. A more complete study of the whole of the affairs of the Soranzo brothers would be valuable. Cf. my *Andrea Barbarigo, Merchant of Venice, 1418–1449* (Baltimore: The Johns Hopkins Press, 1944), pp. 145–46.

[b] Three-month period, i.e., winter (Dec., Jan., Feb.), spring (Mar., Apr., May), etc.

Venetians then said, at the *fontego*. But in July, 1418, the Soranzo firm wrote to one of its agents, "The last ships which arrived from Syria have brought 5,400 sacks, and there are more than 1,500 sacks left over [from cargoes of previous fleets] so that altogether there are 6,900 sacks here, which is a very great amount. And no business has been done because there are no merchants in the *fontego,* but only in the Rialto"; and to another, "Until now nothing of any sort has been done in cotton because no merchants have arrived at the *fontego* because the routes are not secure in view of the interference from Hungary."[10] So the cotton of

[10] A.S.V., Miscellanea Gregolin, busta 13, Soranzo letter book, in letters to L. Bembo and to Piero Soranzo.

the Soranzo brothers piled up until 1422, when buyers must have appeared, for they sold 140 sacks in that year.

A similar contrast between rapid and slow turnover also appears in the affairs of Andrea Barbarigo (father of the Nicolò just mentioned), a merchant of varied affairs and a contemporary of the Soranzo brothers. His first investments in cotton, in 1431 to 1433, were very slow in coming back. In this case a war with Genoa unset the ideal rhythm.[11] On the other hand, Andrea Barbarigo received in June, 1435, and sold in the next two months twenty-five sacks of cotton which were the return on an investment some of which he had sent to Syria in the winter of that same year. He consigned more wares to Syria by the ships leaving in August, 1435, and received more cotton on ships arriving in January, 1436.[12] But Andrea Barbarigo's many affairs are so interlaced that I hesitate to say that the two shipments and sales represented the same capital.

The instances which have been considered, drawn from the affairs of three different merchants, indicate that there was a real and positive correlation between the regularity of the voyages and the rapidity of turnover of capital. To be sure, transportation facilities were every now and then interrupted so that goods had to be held two or three years. If there were no such interruptions and if weather conditions were normal, turnover twice a year was possible, but on an average a wholesale cotton merchant's turnover would not have been made twice a year. Some carry-over of cotton from one season to another was normal. The instances examined indicate that a part of the capital invested in the cotton trade—perhaps a half or a quarter—was turned over no faster than once a year even in "normal" times. Yet turnover of capital twice a year happened often enough to enough investors so that it could seem worth striving for; and both the senate in its regulation of voyages and the individual merchant in the merchandising could view it as a goal both profitable and practical.

If the same questions were asked of the account books in regard to other main branches of Venetian wholesale trade—spices, wool, copper, and so on—somewhat different answers might be obtained for various commodities. But the conclusions would hardly be any more definite. Examples can be found of pepper's being sold for cash at the "winter" fair immediately after the return of the galleys, and examples also of

<hr>

[11] See my *Andrea Barbarigo,* pp. 61–75.

[12] A.S.V. Registri privati contabili, Registri Barbarigo-Grimani (cited hereafter as Registri Barbarigo), reg. 2 (Ledger A), k. 194, 199, and the letters in reg. 1 (Journal A), letter to Lorenzo Soranzo, August 2, 1435. Cf. my *Andrea Barbarigo,* p. 112 n.

one year's import which was sold gradually over several years. The most that can be proved by these examples is that turnover was less rapid when the regular voyages were interrupted. When the voyages went on schedule, some merchants sometimes turned over some of their capital at the maximum rapidity provided by the schedule of voyages; others did not. But the account books provide no statistical base for estimating the average rapidity of turnover for a particular commodity. To estimate such an average it would be better to collect from merchants' letters many estimates as to the size of the carry-over from year to year.

III

Another way of approaching the problem suggests itself. Did not some merchants mix retail trade with wholesale? Did noble merchants deliberately keep a carry-over of wares in the storerooms of their palaces because they liked to have reserves in that form? Was not diversification the general rule? And how did an individual merchant combine in his operations the many rhythms of turnover of the various commodities in which he traded? In short, what would be the total picture of turnover as seen from the inside of a particular business?

The ways in which we can attempt to answer that question are determined by the nature of the sources, particularly the account books. An inquiry into the rapidity of turnover in modern business might begin by seeking to compare the working capital of a firm or group of firms with the total volume of a year's business. Dividing the volume of business by the capital so used would give a statement of the speed of turnover. A modern business has accounts which make such calculation possible. The accounting of short-term Florentine partnerships was also of a kind to suggest the possibility of applying the same method in the study of their affairs. But the ways Venetian merchants totaled up their accounts do not give any figures concerning the total purchases or sales by year or any other period of time. Even a determination of the total capital invested in merchandising is difficult. The venture form of accounting used at Venice reveals rapidity of turnover only if we can follow the outcome of a venture, or group of investments, which represents the bulk of the merchant's business.[13]

An analysis of this sort is possible in the affairs of one merchant,

---

[13] For a general view of the history of accounting, see the article "Ragioneria," the first part by Gino Luzzatto, in the *Enciclopedia italiana*. My analysis of Venetian accounting is in my *Andrea Barbarigo*, pp. 153–80; see also pp. 99–108.

Andrea Barbarigo. He may be considered typical perhaps of those nobles who put practically all they had into commerce, devoted themselves assiduously to the affairs of the Rialto, and in that way succeeded in accumulating considerable capital. He was not a rich man in comparison with many other Venetian nobles, but he had begun with next to nothing and in 1440 disposed of a capital of about 10,000 ducats.[14] Almost all of this was in commerce, practically none in government bonds or real estate. He was a merchant who diversified his commercial investments very widely, traded in many wares and to many countries, and sold both by wholesale and, through agents, at retail. The branch of his affairs to which he gave most personal attention, aside from bills of exchange, was the import and resale of English cloth.

A good starting point for studying his turnover is the arrival at Venice at the end of May, 1441, of a consignment of English wares worth about 5,500 ducats. The wares and their costs until loaded on the galleys in England were as follows:[15]

Panni mostovalieri, pezze 16 [cloth]	730	ducats
Panni bastardi, pezze 100 [cloth]	1,335	
Panni loesti, dozene 500 [cloth]	2,030	
Panni carisee, pezze 50 [cloth, kerseys]	339	
Stagno, pezze 67, l. 18,489 [tin]	986	
Total	5,420	ducats

By the time they reached Venice these wares had been almost completely paid for. In addition to this sizable investment, almost two thirds of his capital, Barbarigo had about 3,000 ducats more invested in "western wares," namely, in English cloth received earlier and in Spanish oil and wool.[16]

To simplify the exposition let us consider only the capital represented by the wares which Andrea received from London in 1441 and began to draw from the customhouse in the last days of May. How long would it take him to sell or reship the merchandise? When would he be able to have the returns in liquid form or in wares to be shipped to the West so as to secure another consignment of equal size?

---

[14] *Andrea Barbarigo,* pp. 184–85.

[15] Registri Barbarigo, reg. 4 (Ledger B), k. 28. From this starting point, the data on which the subsequent analysis is based were found by following the cross references accompanying each entry in the ledger.

[16] Estimated from the *conto saldo* opening Ledger B and from an examination of many of these accounts.

Sales and reshipments were rapid. Within three months Barbarigo disposed of two thirds of the consignment (see Table II). Those months formed precisely the period extending from the return of the Flemish galleys and of the spring Levantine ships to the departure of galleys and ships for the fall Levantine voyage—in short, the period called the "midsummer fair." In this fair, before August 6 in fact, Andrea sold his *loesti* cloths and most of his kerseys and shipped a part of his tin to Alexandria, a part of the bastard cloths to Constantinople,

TABLE II

SALES OR RESHIPMENTS BY ANDREA BARBARIGO OF WARES RECEIVED ON THE GALLEYS OF FLANDERS IN MAY, 1441, AND COLLECTION OF PAYMENTS THEREON.

Period	Value[a]							
	Sales or Reshipments[b]				Payments Collected[b]			
	L.	s.	d.	p.	L.	s.	d.	p.
Before Sept. 1, 1441	571	13	1	13	26	16	–	–
Sept. 1, 1441 to Feb. 28, 1442	21	4	11	20	38	–	–	–
March 1, to Sept. 1, 1442	21	13	3	–	58	17	10	19
Sept. 1, 1442 to Feb. 28, 1443	212	4	9	16	379	19	3	29
March 1, to Sept. 1, 1443	60	9	4	14	199	1	11	26
Later					164	14	2	0
Total	887	5	5	31	867	9	4	10

[a] In lire di grossi; 1 lira = 10 ducats.
[b] Lire, soldi, denari, piccoli.

and another part of the bastard cloths to an agent at Fermo in the Marches. If Barbarigo's activity was characteristic, then those were certainly months of intense commercial activity; the turnover of wares was almost as fast as that indicated by the timetable of the galleys.

Most of what Barbarigo did not sell during the summer fair was intended for local and piecemeal distribution. The one exception is formed by twenty pieces of kerseys which were sold to Piero and Lorenzo Soranzo in January, 1442, just in time to go by the spring ships of that year. Barbarigo had held them over for six months, perhaps because he could not find a satisfactory buyer during his rush of summer business, perhaps because he expected higher prices at the winter fair, or perhaps because he had at first planned to send them to some other *scale*. But of the imported wares destined for Levantine markets, only about 4 per cent by value was held by Barbarigo so as to miss the fall fleets, and even that 4 per cent was on its way eastward the following winter, before another Flanders fleet arrived with a new supply.

The slow-moving part of Barbarigo's imports was the more expensive types of cloth and that part of the tin which he undertook to sell in Venice. He sold to tinsmiths about 12,000 lb. in lots of from 200 to 3,600 lb. This type of sale to the local industry might be expected to require more time than the deals of international commerce, but at least Barbarigo secured better prices by these delayed sales. The tin which he sent to Alexandria in August, 1441, was valued at only 90 ducats a thousandweight. For what he sold from January to May, 1443, Barbarigo received 100 ducats a thousandweight.[17]

The more expensive types of cloth were sold not by Andrea himself but by a "draper," Alvise di Stropi, and Andrea did not record the sales until Stropi had rendered an account. In this case therefore the figures in Table II are misleading. Half the figure there entered as sales (Sept. 1, 1442 to Feb. 28, 1443) refers to cloth sales by Stropi which were recorded at those dates. But since he began payments earlier, Stropi presumably had sold most of the cloth sometime before he rendered the accounts. It is probable that almost as soon as they were received in the summer of 1441 these cloths were consigned to Stropi for dyeing, finishing, and sale in small lots, but their sale by Stropi was spread out over the next two years.[18]

To summarize the movement of wares, those destined for reshipment in large lots from Venice to other markets, about two thirds of the consignment, were moved rapidly. They were nearly all reshipped by Barbarigo himself or sold to others in time for reshipment within three months. The other third of the consignment, the part destined for sale in small lots in Venice, moved much more slowly.

When we turn from the movement of the merchandise to study the movement of Barbarigo's capital, we face the question of the time

---

[17] The tin account in Barbarigo's Ledger B, k. 45.

[18] Registri Barbarigo, reg. 4 (Ledger B), the Alvise di Stropi accounts which begin on k. 33. I compiled from these accounts the amounts paid to Andrea Barbarigo on account of cloth which he had left with Stropi for sale. The cloth which Andrea received in 1441 concluded the first lots which Stropi handled for him. On later lots Andrea received payments more and more slowly, but it is impossible to tell from Andrea's accounts whether this was because the sales were slow or merely because Stropi was becoming heavily in debt to Andrea Barbarigo.

required to collect payment. In compiling Table II, I have counted as "payments collected" those transactions recorded on Andrea's books by debits to cash, to banks, and to personal accounts previously having a credit balance. The last are a very small part of the total. The most common form of payment, even by the tinsmiths, was credit at one of the four Venetian banks of the time—those of Nicolò Bernardo, Luca di Soranzo, Bernardo Ciera, and Francesco and Bernardo Balbi.

The slowness with which Andrea collected payment contrasts sharply with the speed with which he had moved merchandise during the summer of 1441. Out of the 5,717 ducats' worth immediately disposed of, 3,389 ducats' worth was sold, the rest shipped. From the 3,389 ducats' worth sold at that time, Barbarigo collected in the same period only 268 ducats, of which only 110 ducats were cash, the rest being payments of his obligations. During all the ensuing twelve months his collections continued small and consisted mainly of what Stropi was turning over for the cloth consigned to him. In May, 1442, Barbarigo realized a little also on his shipment a year earlier to Alexandria. For the tin which he had sent to that port he received a consignment of ginger and cinnamon. When he sold part of this, he collected payment promptly. But after fifteen months the total of his collections was only about 20 per cent of the capital invested in the consignment received in May, 1441.

He collected a far larger amount during the next six months, mainly in the months of January and February, 1443. The western cloths which he had sold so promptly in the summer of 1441 had been sold on credit for a long term, until the "ships of January, 1443." Actually he received payment on most of these accounts between January 12 and the middle of February, although a few payments were not made until March, 1443.[19] In the spring of 1443 Barbarigo received also the final payments from the sale in small lots of tin and cloth and cashed in also on another part of the cinnamon received from Alexandria. Altogether the collections effected by September 1, 1443, were substantially larger than the total cost of the shipment received in the spring of 1441. It was not only larger than the initial cost but also was large enough to cover all the incidental expenses incurred in the meantime in connection with those wares. What remained to be collected, more than two years after the arrival of the wares, was 18 to 19 per cent of his total receipts from this cycle of affairs, and it was all part of the profit (see Table III).

A part of what remained to be liquidated was a little cinnamon

---

[19] Registri Barbarigo, reg. 4 (Ledger B), k. 46, 44, 47.

TABLE III

PROFITS AND LOSSES DIRECTLY CONNECTED WITH ANDREA BARBARIGO'S IMPORTS FROM LONDON IN 1441 AND THE RETURN OF THE FUNDS TO LONDON.[a]

Merchandise of Shipment Account	Profits[b]				Losses[b]			
	L.	s.	d.	p.	L.	s.	d.	p.
Cloth *bastardi*	30	18	6	27				
Tin	54	13	2	19				
Cloth *loesti*	71	1	5	16				
Shipment of tin to Alexandria					4	6	7	25
Ginger	9	18	8	2				
Cinnamon, long		17	2	11				
Cinnamon, thick							7	11
Shipment to London	1	13	11	6				
Cloth, *mostovalieri*[c]	20							
Cloth, kerseys[c]	18							
Shipment of cinnamon to London[c]					4			
Shipment of bastard cloths to Constantinople[c]	31	10	8	11				
Shipment to Fermo[d]	16							
Bad debt from sale at Constantinople					48	18	10	22
Total	254	13	8	28	57	6	1	28
Net profit[e]	197	7	7	0				

[a] Some of these profits and losses illustrate the need for reviewing a whole cycle of operations in order to calculate the profit on an investment. Part of the profit on the tin results from evaluating the tin at 90 ducats a thousandweight when charging it to the voyage of Alexandria. Its initial cost was only about 54 ducats a thousandweight. Whether this evaluation was the current market quotation in Venice at the time cannot be determined. Anyhow it was so high a valuation that the tin could not, on that basis, be sold at a profit at Alexandria. Hence Barbarigo's books show more profit on the tin, but a loss on the voyage of Alexandria. There are other cases in his books when wares imported from one *scala* were valued at cost when exported to another *scala* (e.g., Ledger A, k. 92). In that case there was no profit on the merchandise account but a good profit on the voyage account. Thus mere bookkeeping valuations determined which step in his operations showed a profit. Only by following all or nearly all of a whole cycle of investment can the sources of his profits be properly estimated.

[b] In lire di grossi; 1 lira = 10 ducats.

[c] Unclosed accounts, but the profit or loss is clearly, even if not precisely, indicated by the entries already made to the account.

[d] A rough estimate (see text, pp. 123–24).

[e] The difference between the initial cost of the shipment, 5,420 ducats, and the total sales prices, 8,873 ducats, as in Table II, was only in part due to profits; another part was merchandising expense. Counting all this merchandising expense as part of the investment would give a total investment of 6,999 ducats. But only a fraction of the merchandising expense was invested for anywhere near two years. Consequently I consider that a round figure of 6,000 ducats represents roughly the investment on which Andrea Barbarigo earned, in round figures, 2,000 ducats.

which had been shipped to his London agents but not yet sold by them and two other investments which require some explanation. One concerns the "Voyage of Constantinople," the other, the "Voyage of Fermo." Both illustrate the extreme complexity of Andrea Barbarigo's commercial activity and the difficulty of saying just when an investment had been liquidated and a turnover completed.

The agent at Constantinople, Carlo Cappello, to whom Barbarigo had shipped some of the English bastard cloth, was able to sell the wares, but instead of collecting all payments for them himself, he transferred back to Barbarigo the task of collecting at Venice from the chief customer. Barbarigo succeeded in collecting only in October, 1445, and then only about half of this debt, i.e., 400 ducats. He wrote off the rest as a loss. Besides this assignment on a customer who proved a poor credit risk, Barbarigo received from Carlo Cappello in the spring of 1443 a consignment of pepper, silk, and Hungarian florins. These wares represented in part the rest of the return on Barbarigo's English cloth and in part the return on other merchandise, particularly on oil which had been shipped in Barbarigo's name from Valencia to Constantinople. Consequently it is impossible to determine with any mathematical exactitude what part of this consignment was a return on the English cloth, what part a return on Valencian oil, and so on. Yet, since Andrea immediately turned the pepper and the florins into 700 ducats of bank money and since only 260 ducats were then due from Constantinople on account of the bastard cloths, the latter sum has been included among the payments received in the spring and summer of 1443.

From the English cloth sent to Fermo, Andrea received no prompt payment because of the death of his agent there, Troilo Pacaron. This agent was a trusted business associate who had long been arranging deals for Barbarigo in the Marches while Barbarigo looked after his affairs in Venice. At Pacaron's death their affairs were closely entangled, and Barbarigo had to sue Pacaron's heirs to obtain a settlement. The court allowed Barbarigo's claims, and consequently he registered in his ledger in 1448 a substantial profit on his shipments to Pacaron, but it is impossible to determine exactly how much of it resulted from the cloth sent in the summer of 1441 and how much from other shipments.[20]

[20] On the complexity of Pacaron's accounts, see my *Andrea Barbarigo,* p. 167 n. Following up Andrea's collections required in the case of most merchants the consultation of many accounts in Ledger B by means of the cross references and of the index.

Because of these difficulties, inherent in the nature of Barbarigo's accounts, the figure in Table II relating to payments received after September, 1443, is necessarily only a loose approximation. It serves to indicate correctly, however, that a significant part of the collections from the cargo received from England in the spring of 1441 was not liquidated until four, five, or perhaps seven years later. The sum thus tied up was a small percentage of the capital involved, but was more than three fourths of the profit Barbarigo was making on that consignment.

Although his profits were in the form of slow-paying accounts receivable, in two years Andrea had at least liquidated enough of the consignment so that he was able to pay for another equally large. And, in fact, the galleys which reached Venice from the West in the summer of 1443 brought him a new consignment of English wares to the value of 5,460 ducats, approximately the same value as that of the shipment he had received two years before.[21]

The arrival of this large new shipment is a superficial indication that Barbarigo's cycle of investment was completed, that he had turned over his capital in the two years. To make sure, it would be desirable to trace the flow of funds to London to pay for the shipment. This can easily be done only in so far as Andrea built up a balance in London by shipping merchandise. He did send to London by the galleys leaving Venice in 1442 some of the cinnamon received from Alexandria in exchange for part of the tin contained in the consignment of 1441.[22] If Barbarigo had similarly exchanged all the consignment of 1441 for wares which he shipped back to the West, then, but only then, would his accounts directly indicate that the consignment of 1443 was paid for with the return on the cargo of 1441. In fact, however, nearly all the returns on the cargo of 1441 passed sooner or later into Barbarigo's bank accounts. The funds were sent to London mainly through bills of exchange and it is difficult to tell whether they represent precisely the same funds previously tied up in the consignment of 1441. But a strong presumption to that effect arises from two considerations. First, there was a close correlation between the amount of these funds collected between September, 1442, and September, 1443, and the size of the remittances to London in the same period. Secondly, an examination of Barbarigo's other ventures in the two years under consideration indicates that his

---

[21] Registri Barbarigo, reg. 4 (Ledger B), k. 104. Andrea received the goods from customs July 9, 1443. See his journal (reg. 3) on that date.

[22] Registri Barbarigo, reg. 4 (Ledger B), k. 28, 63, 64.

other funds were employed in other investments as much in the summer of 1443 as in the summer of 1441. They could not therefore have been used to pay for the cargo arriving in the summer of 1443. The obscure element in the situation is the extent to which Andrea Barbarigo was receiving credit from or giving credit to his London agents.[23]

The conclusion from this trial run over a section of Andrea Barbarigo's affairs is that he turned over his capital in about two years. He had liquidated for reinvestment in 1443 the sum received in western wares in 1441, although the profits earned on the investment were still tied up, not necessarily unproductively, in the form of unpaid debts or slow-moving goods acquired in the process of disposing of the wares. As a whole, however, these conclusions concerning Andrea Barbarigo's collections of debts seem to me much less soundly based and much less significant than the statement in Table II concerning the speed with which he disposed of the merchandise.

IV

How much can be generalized from this particular instance? First, in regard to this particular merchant, Andrea Barbarigo, the years 1441 to 1443 must be considered as more or less characteristic of his whole style of business. The general history of his dealing with agents in the earlier period of 1430 to 1440 shows a somewhat similar rhythm of about two years to liquidate one commitment of capital and to be ready for free choice of a new investment.[24]

But in any complicated set of accounts it is hard to be sure just how much the merchant is in debt or how much he is being financed by others. It was possible for a merchant with the right connections and reputation to operate largely with borrowed money, as Andrea did on some occasions. When in 1433 he instructed his agents in London to buy cloth for him Andrea wrote: "I advise you that I do not expect to have the money so that it will be necessary to pay out of the returns [from the sale] of the same or make some deal [in exchange]. After September I think Messer Francesco [Balbi] will give me credit until Christmas."[25]

---

[23] See the various accounts of Ledger B of "Zuane e Lorenzo di Marchanovo," "per conto proprio," "per conto de danar d'imprestidi," etc.

[24] See my *Andrea Barbarigo*, esp. ch. III.

[25] Registri Barbarigo, reg. 1 (Journal A), copialettere, letter of Feb. 17, 1432 (old style) to Vettor Cappello and Brothers, the longer letter: "Avixandovi non credo

It would be nice to avoid the complications which enter when we take into account buying on credit, giving of credit when selling, and other forms of borrowing and lending. But they have to be considered if we wish to calculate the merchant's profits and compare one merchant's success with another. An attempt to discover the amount of profit made by Andrea Barbarigo in the two-year turnover just described is presented in Table III. The conclusion is that he made a profit of nearly 2,000 ducats by investing about 6,000 ducats for those two years, that is, a little over 15 per cent a year. This is not far from the average rate at which Andrea won earnings on his capital during the whole period of 1431 to 1445.[26]

It would be dangerous, however, to jump to any conclusions about what rate of profit might be considered usual in fifteenth-century Venice on the basis of an analysis of the affairs of one individual or of a few transactions. Of more general significance, I believe, is the casual statement Andrea Barbarigo made to one of his most important agents, that one could readily make 12 per cent a year on one's money. The estimate is in a letter in which he is comparing the advantages of selling for cash or for delayed payment with little or no risk. He wrote: "I think they [some cloths he had shipped] will bring 30 ducats if sold for payment in six months and 28 ducats if sold for cash. If you cannot sell them for cash at 2 ducats less than the term price, I even prefer that you sell for cash at 3 ducats less, because one knows how to gain more than 12 per cent a year on one's money."[27] The figure 12 per cent seems surprisingly low, especially since it seems to include recompense for the time and talents of the merchant as well as what we would call interest on his capital. Some modern writers speak of higher profits as usual, even as much as 50 per cent. But they seldom inquire closely into how long a period of investment was necessary to win that amount of profit. The letter of Andrea Barbarigo just cited proves more clearly than anything in his accounts that he thought in terms of profit per year, for he says "gain more than 12 per cent a year."

---

trovarme su denari, e diti pani me convira pagar del trato de si over far qualche torno. Pasando setembre penso Messer Francesco me servira fino a Nadal." In fact Andrea did overdraw his account at the Balbi bank by 400 to 600 ducats from October, 1433, to January, 1434. See my *Andrea Barbarigo,* p. 25 and n.; cf. pp. 73–76.

[26] *Ibid.,* pp. 183–86.

[27] Registri Barbarigo, reg. 1 (Ledger A) copialettere, 1440, Aug., to Pacaron: "crede valera al tempo de 6 mexi duchati 30 e a contadi 28, e quando non li podesti vender per duchati 2 de men a contadi che al termene anche me piaxeria avanti i vendesti a danari per duchati 3 men del uno che a termene, perche di danari ne saperia avadagnar al ano piu di 12 per cento."

My conclusion, then, from this attempt to use account books to study rapidity of turnover in fifteenth-century Venice is that they must be studied together with contemporary merchants' letters and records of the voyages of the main merchant fleets. Statements in which merchants generalized their experience as to what was a reasonable profit are worth more than figures arrived at with difficulty from the accounts concerning the profits on particular transactions. Statements in which merchants sum up what they have learned on the Rialto concerning the size of the usual year's import and of the carry-over from year to year are a better basis for estimating the average turnover of merchandise in wholesale trade. The account books have mainly an auxiliary use in showing that the statements in merchants' letters and in the senatorial regulation referring to rapid turnover as an attainable goal are to be taken seriously. The movement on schedule of the merchant galleys and the "ships of Syria" was indeed an aid to the rapid movement of investments. And since both letters and accounts support the thesis that the merchants of Venice realized the importance of rapid turnover, it is reasonable to believe that similar considerations influenced the senate when it declared, as it did repeatedly, that the observation of the *mude* and the regular arrival of ships in time for the fairs were of the greatest importance to the city's prosperity.

9

Fleets and Fairs*

I

THE way the word *muda* is used in Venetian commercial regulation raises a number of questions that have far-reaching importance
for the understanding of Venetian commercial policy and have general
significance in appreciating the degree of rapidity and the element of
periodicity in medieval trade. It seems worth while to make clear the
nature of these questions, even though much more archival research
will be necessary before definite answers can be given to most of
them.

There are two meanings of *muda* with which I am here concerned.[1]
Muda meant a fleet or convoy of ships, and it also meant a period of
time during which ships were loaded.

That *mudua, muda,* or *muta* meant a fleet of ships sailing together
for mutual protection with or without the escort of warships is well
known. That is the meaning given by Du Cange,[2] Ashburner,[3] and
Schaube,[4] and in F. Elder's *Glossary.*[5] It is the meaning referred to in

---

* From *Studi in onore di Armando Sapori.* 2 vols. (Milan: Cisalpino, 1957) , I, 651–
63. (By permission.)

[1] Other meanings, such as the tax of that name or a change of offices, are irrelevant
here. See G. Boerio, *Dizionario del dialetto veneziano* (2d ed.; Venice, 1856) , s.v.
muda, mua.

[2] C. Du Cange, *Glossarium mediae et infimae latinitatis* (Niort, 1885) .

[3] W. Ashburner, *The Rhodian Sea-Law* (Oxford, 1909) , p. cxlviii.

[4] A. Schaube, *Handelsgeschichte der romanischen Völker des Mittelmeergebiets
bis zum Ende der Kreuzzüge* (Munich and Berlin, 1906) , pp. 153, 166, 169, 193, and
in all the other references in the index.

[5] F. Edler (de Roover) , *Glossary of Medieval Terms of Business* (Italian Series,
1200–1600; Cambridge, Mass., 1934) .

Kretschmayr's *Geschichte von Venedig*[6] and in Luzzatto's *Storia economica d'Italia*.[7] Certainly *muda* was used to refer to a fleet of ships, and perhaps that was its only meaning in the thirteenth century. But *mudua* or *muda* was also used to denote the time during which specified goods might legally be loaded in specified places by a specified class of ships for transport to Venice. Although this usage and its implications have received very little attention,[8] it is the more common meaning of *muda* in Venetian commercial regulation in the fifteenth century.

Failure to recognize this second meaning can lead to misunderstandings concerning Venetian shipping practices. For example, "navi della muda di Marzo" does not always mean ships of a convoy sailing in March. In the fifteenth century it is more likely to mean ships which loaded in the East during March. It does not mean necessarily that they sailed in convoy. Neglect of the second meaning of *muda* has led to exaggeration of the extent to which Venetian ships commonly traveled in convoys or "caravans." As a general rule the merchant galleys sailed together as a convoy, but the round ships (*navi* or *coche*) commonly sailed separately in time of peace and were gathered into convoys only when danger threatened.[9]

A clear example of the use of *muda* to mean a period of time is the following special provision recorded in Sanuto's diary, Sept. 26, 1511: "Fu posto, per savii ai ordini, che la nave Nicolosa, qual [è] sorapporto e va in Soria, habi zorni 8 di muda poi zonta a Baruto. Sier Batista Marexini, consier, messe XV, e cussi andò la parte di XV, et fu presa."[10] An earlier example is in a decree of 1406 concerning cotton and some other wares to be imported from Greece that fall. The general rule was

[6] H. Kretschmayr, *Geschichte von Venedig*, I (Gotha, 1905), 358, II (1920), 148, 222, 293–95, 458.

[7] G. Luzzatto, *Storia economica d'Italia* (Rome, 1949), I, 313–14.

[8] W. Heyd, *Histoire du commerce du levant au moyen âge* (Leipzig, 1886), II, 453, recognized the *muda* as a period of exchange after the arrival of the galleys at Alexandria, but seemed to regard it as a peculiarity of Alexandria. J. Sottas, *Les messageries maritimes de Venise* (Paris, 1938), p. 105, recognized the *mude* as periods of loading for the ships in Syria, but did not note its application in this sense to Greece and the Levant generally.

[9] A.S.V., Senato Mar, reg. 11, 146, July 18, 1482. After noting the threat of war, the preamble to this decree says: "Et navigantibus navibus nostris divisis a separatis prout tempore pacis facere solebat, de facili illis sequi possit aliquod sinistrum et periculum."

[10] M. Sanuto, *I diarii* (Venice, 1879–1903), XII, 587.

that this cotton must be loaded before the end of September. Since ships were not available to load at that time, the senate provided that cotton which had been registered with the Venetian officials in the Levantine ports before the end of September could be loaded until the end of October: "dicta muda ex nunc intelligatur elongari usque diem medium mensem octobris proximis."[11]

In this case and in many others *muda* is used as the equivalent of *terminus*. Consequently, *muda gothonorum*[12] means "period of cotton loading" and not "cotton fleet." Admittedly there are instances in which we cannot be sure whether *muda* referred to the loading period or to the fleet, because the meaning was substantially the same in either case. Illustrations are the references in account books to "cotton of the *muda* of March, 1418."[13] Similarly, reports that an agent had shipped "per le navi de la muda pasada" can be read as "ships of the last fleet sailing" or as "ships loading the last loading period."[14] But such references occurring in years when the chronicles and the senatorial regulations indicate that the ships were not sailing in convoy are to be translated as "ships of the last loading period" or "of the last season," and there are many uses when the only sensible translation for *muda* is "period in which to load."

II

Once it is recognized that *muda* meant "the period prescribed for loading," the question arises: What was the purpose of these loading periods? How did they originate? In exploring these questions, I will use the word *muda* always in the sense of a loading period.

The *mude* varied according to the kind of ship, the kind of goods, and the place of export. For present purposes, the ships of the Venetian merchant marine can be divided into three classes: merchant galleys, large round ships sailing under specified conditions, and other vessels. The merchandise transported can also be divided into three classes: one category of "light goods" (*havere subtile*) which were as a general rule

---

[11] Senato Misti, reg. 47, ff. 63, 74.

[12] Senato Misti, reg. 47, f. 17. For *terminus*, see f. 1.

[13] See p. 114.

[14] A.S.V., Miscellanea Gregolin, Lettere commerciali, busta 13, carteggio del Soranzo, e.g., to Piero, July 10, 1418.

The passages from the Datini agent in Venice that are quoted in F. Edler, *Glossary of Medieval Terms of Business*, s.v. *muta*, can also be read as meaning either "cotton of this fleet" or "cotton of this loading period."

to be carried only by the great galleys (spices, silks, etc.), another category of "light goods" which could be brought to Venice by round ships but the loading of which was restricted to specified periods (the *mude*), and heavy goods, such as grain and salt. These last could be loaded at any time and by any type of vessel for import to Venice; the first two categories are those whose loading was restricted to the *mude*.

The dates of the *mude* for ships coming from the Byzantine area (Romania) were set in 1328 as follows:

From Constantinople	Mar. 15 to Apr. 15	Sept. 15 to Oct. 31
From Romania Bassa	Apr. 15–30	Sept. 15 to Oct. 31
(up to and including Crete and Negroponte)		

In 1360 the *mude* of ships from Cyprus were fixed as March 15 to 31 and September 13 to 30. These dates were changed from time to time during the next two centuries, but they indicate roughly the general pattern.[15] The *mude* of the merchant galleys corresponded roughly with the fall *mude* of the round ships (*navi* or *coche*). The *muda* of each voyage was reconsidered each year at the time the galleys were auctioned and frequently was set as a stipulated number of days after the arrival of the galleys at the Levantine end of their journey.

The general system above outlined—dividing all merchandise into three categories and stipulating for the first two categories the dates at which they might be loaded and the kind of ships on which they might be brought to Venice—was subject to much modification year by year. Special arrangements to meet particular situations were the rule. Almost any generalization stating that only a specific class of ships was permitted to load a particular commodity such as cotton, and only at dates specified, will be found inapplicable in some years. In spite of all the exceptions, a general pattern can be found in Venice's Levantine trade. Wares of relatively small value compared to their bulk moved in all seasons on all kinds of round ships—sailing vessels able to offer the cheap transportation appropriate for such wares. The most precious wares, spices and fine silks and dyes, came on merchant galleys, both because the law generally forbade their import on other ships, or required them to pay the freight to the galleys even if they came on other vessels, and because the security and speed of the galleys made

---

[15] A.S.V., *Ufficiali al Cattever*, busta I, ff. 65–72. In addition to the regulations there collected, many more are to be found in Senato Misti and Senato Mar. On the general system of Venetian voyages, see pp. 110, 112, and the works there cited.

them the best suited for this kind of cargo. Less precious wares (as we might call the other "light goods" such as cotton) came on relatively large round ships that loaded in the Levant in fall and spring at the dates specified for their *mude*. Examination of some of the exceptions or special arrangements throws some light on the purposes of the whole system. But before examining particular cases, let us consider the general possibilities.

III

What was the purpose of restricting the time of loading of the ships? Even a fragmentary examination of the evidence suggests that at least seven possibilities must be kept in mind.

1. Avoiding bad weather is mentioned as one advantage in having the galleys leave as early as possible for their fall voyage back to Venice.[16] Especially feared was the voyage up the Adriatic in January or February. The wintry north wind made it desirable that ships return in November, but in fact they returned throughout the winter, even in January and February.[17] Voyages down the Adriatic were regularly made in January or February, as is shown by references to the "navi del gennaio"[18] and by senatorial orders to fleets about to leave in January or February.[19] Diarists such as Antonio Morosini, Girolamo Priuli, and Marino Sanuto mention ships at sea throughout the year. As a practical matter, there was not in effect any "closing of the sea" during the winter.[20] Nevertheless there was a desire to avoid sailing in certain waters at the seasons when those waters were particularly dangerous.

2. Restriction on the time of loading may, at least at one time, have been merely a measure to facilitate the organization of convoys. When many ships had to sail together for mutual protection, some means had to be found to get all of them ready to sail at the same time. If ship captains claimed that they had not yet loaded their cargo either the whole convoy was delayed or the unloaded ships had to be left behind, and neither alternative was beneficial to the Venetian market place or

[16] Senato Mar, reg. 11, f. 129; reg. 14, f. 31; Senato Misti, reg. 53 (doppio), ff. 115–16.

[17] G. Luzzatto, "Vi furono fiere a Venezia?" in *Studi di storia economica veneziana* (Padua, 1954), p. 206.

[18] See p. 121.

[19] Sanuto, *Diarii*, VI, 296, 554; VII, 250, 755; Senato Misti, reg. 47, f. 91 (1407), Notatorio di Collegio, reg. 7, f. 88.

[20] On "the closing of the sea in winter," see W. Ashburner, *The Rhodian Sea-Law*, pp. cxlii–cxliii, and below.

the fiscal interests of the Venetian government. A system of restricted loading periods may have been instituted to facilitate the better protection of shipping through convoys. In periods when no hostile fleets made protection in convoys necessary, ships were left free to sail individually, but there was no telling how long the seas would be secure. It might be necessary again and at short notice to organize the shipping into convoys. This could be done much more quickly and easily if the *mude* were maintained even while ships sailed unaccompanied. Since they would be returning to Venice and departing from Venice at approximately the same time twice a year, there was little difficulty in reinstituting the convoy system whenever hostile fleets appeared.

3. The *mude* encouraged a more efficient use of ships. It shortened the amount of time they had to spend in Levantine ports waiting for cargo and thus enabled them to make a quicker round trip between Venice and the Levant. The round ships that went to Greece, Cyprus, and Syria often made two round trips a year in the fifteenth century. This either benefited the shipowners by enabling them to collect more freight or benefited the shippers by lowering freight rates.

If cargo was already at hand and waiting when a ship reached a Levantine port, five to eight days would suffice to unload and take aboard the new cargo.[21] Very much longer was needed if the arrival of the ship was unexpected. No doubt there had been a time when Venetian fleets carried out a swarm of traveling merchants who stayed two or three months in the Levant selling the wares they had brought with them and finding new merchandise in which to invest for the return voyage. By the fifteenth century, indeed long before, merchants in Venice had factors overseas who resided in the Levant and bought in anticipation of the arrival of the ships. But many purchases were made only after ships came in with more wares and cash. There was always the temptation to delay purchase in the hope of a better price or to threaten not to buy at all, right down to the eve of a well-reported sailing date in the hope of beating down the price, or then, if that did not work and the agent faced the prospect of sending nothing back to his principal in Venice, to try to delay the sailing in order to make some purchases at the very last minute. While some merchants were eager for a quick sailing, others would wish to delay; and the ship captain would

---

[21] This is the minimum allowed for the *muda* when it is fixed as a stipulated number of days after the arrival of the ships. Senato Mar, reg. 16, ff. 98, 172; reg. 17, f. 60 (1506–9).

be torn between the desire for a quick turn around and that for a full cargo. A terminal loading date fixed by the senate forced the merchants to end their haggling and kept the ships moving.

4. A quicker turn around meant not only more efficient use of shipping but also more efficient use of the merchants' capital. The shipper benefited not only from cheaper freight rates but from quicker turnover of his mercantile investment.

5. The *mude* maintained the activity and prestige of the fairs of Venice. Since the fairs added to the wealth of the Venetians by speeding their turnover in commercial enterprises, this advantage in the maintenance of the *mude* is almost indistinguishable from that just mentioned. But the concentration of goods in Venice at the time of the fairs was also important in giving Venice the reputation of a world market, a place where everything could be had in large quantity. It thus attracted merchants from all sides and helped to make the reputation valid.

To be sure, there is reason to question what is meant by a reference to the fairs at Venice. Venice had no period of fair in the sense of a period during which special rights or liberties were offered foreign merchants who were thus attracted from near and far. One fair, and only one, was an important local festivity, the fair of the Ascension, which lasted fifteen days. For this fair, booths were built in the Piazza San Marco, and the craftsmen of Venice there made display of their choicest products. The foreigners who came to sell at this fair in the Piazza were from nearby cities of the Veneto.[22] The timing of this fair did not fit in very well with the movements of interregional trade through Venice. The ships of the spring *muda,* leaving the ports of the Levant in March or early April, would in some years reach Venice at the time of the fair of the Ascension in May, but their arrival could not be counted on as a general rule.

A second fair, for which the *mude* were more important, was that of the Christmas season. A decision to fix the *mude* of the galleys of Beirut and Alexandria so that they would terminate at the end of October was made in 1483, with the argument that it was important to have the galleys return in time for the fair, when the Germans were accustomed to buy spices.[23]

---

[22] G. Luzzatto, "Vi furono fiere a Venezia?" pp. 202–5; M. Sanuto, *Diarii,* IV, 37; XXXVIII, 346.

[23] Senato Mar, reg. 11, f. 129. The change is reflected in the galley auctions for 1482 and 1483; see Senato, Incanti galere. In 1494 the *muda* was moved up again to mid-October (Senato Mar, reg. 14, f. 31), and in 1496 the galleys of Beirut and Alexandria returned Nov. 11 (Sanuto, *Diarii,* I, 379, 380).

A third fair is referred to by Girolamo Priuli. In giving a list of the spices exported through the *fontego,* or Fondaco dei Tedeschi, from July 1 to August 7, 1506, he referred to "questa fiera di luio," and in July, 1505, he referred to "La fiera consuetta deli *(sic)* Todeschi di San Jacomo."[24] Four fairs as periods of settlement are named by a late sixteenth-century analyst of Venetian banking problems: "da i Re, della Pentecoste, d'Agosto, da tutti i Santi."[25]

Although it is difficult to find a consistent explanation of all the various casual references to fairs, it is clear that there were normally two periods in which business was most active. One was in midwinter, between the return of galleys and ships of the fall *muda* and the departure of the ships of the spring *muda,* roughly December and January. The second was between the return of the ships of the spring *muda* (and the return from the West of galleys or ships which had wintered in the English Channel and returned in the spring) and the departure of ships and galleys for the fall *muda,* roughly June, July, and August. Some more precise combination of *mude* overseas and fairs in Venice may have been envisaged by Venetian merchants and legislators, but the vicissitudes of weather and of politics prevent its being discernible in the records of the voyages, and it seems most reasonable to interpret mention of the fair as referring not to precise dates but to the period of lively business between the return of one group of ships and the departure of another. Using fair in this broad sense, we may say that the *mude* maintained the fairs of Venice.

6. In a certain sense the *mude* also created fairs in the Levantine ports where the ships called for cargo. They did so by creating in those ports a preannounced period of intensive trade terminating on a specified day. All goods to be shipped that season had to be bought and presented for loading before the end of the *muda.* The *muda* was like a fair in forcing buyers and sellers to come to agreement within a stipulated period and in creating conditions such that the full extent of demand and supply became more visible during that period than during the rest of the year.

This function of the *muda* is clearly apparent in reports of the Venetian trade at Alexandria. The captain of the merchant galleys that returned from Alexandria in December, 1498, reported that prices had been high and that agreement on prices had been reached only at the

[24] G. Priuli, *I Diarii* (2d ed.; Rerum Italicarum Scriptores, XXIV, III; Bologna, 1933–37, II, 382, 431.

[25] E. Lattes, *La libertà delle banche a Venezia dal secolo XIII al XVII* (Milan, 1869), p. 129.

last moment, so that out of the total cargo of 2,125 *colli,* 1,400 *colli* had been "made" (bought and loaded) in one day and one night. The consul, who had returned with the galleys, recommended that all contracts be made five days before the end of the *muda,* so that the errors and high prices of the last-minute rush might be avoided.[26] When a new commercial treaty was made with the sultan of Egypt in 1507 it provided for six to eight days after the *muda* as a period for settling accounts ("azio le merchadanti possino far le sui pagamenti et consegner le sue merze").[27] The tendency to postpone agreement on prices until the very end of the loading period was operative also in 1510. Perhaps agreement was especially difficult that year because some French ships were leaving very well loaded about the time the Venetian galleys arrived. After being in the port of Alexandria for seventeen days, the captain wrote home that no prices had been agreed on. Fearing his fleet would have no cargo, he sent a letter to the Venetian consul warning that he meant to obey the law and would not permit any loading after the *muda.* That broke the deadlock, prices were agreed to, and they loaded all night and all the next day. The *muda* as a loading period was observed, but it was twenty days after the *muda* before he obtained clearance from the port authorities and was able to set sail.[28]

The spice trade was of course subject to special influences, such as the sultan's financial interest, but it seems likely that the *mude* for cotton, sugar, and other products may have created trading periods somewhat equivalent to produce fairs. The *mude,* like the fairs, tended to regulate the marketing system of specified products in the areas dominated by Venetian shipping. But from the Venetian point of view this may have been merely incidental to the regulation of Venetian shipping and the Venetian market.

7. The *mude* regulated not only the time of the arrival of goods on the Venetian market place but also the quantity. At least it made the flow regular and relatively foreseeable. A glut of eastern wares was frequently complained of. Sometimes this was a chronic condition due to causes operating over decades. But there were dangers also of temporary oversupply of eastern wares when the ships had in one year

[26] Sanuto, *Diarii,* II, 171–72.

[27] *Ibid.,* VII, 221. Cf. C. A. Marin, *Storia civile e politica del commercio de'Veneziani* (Venice, 1800), V, 291, 302, 304, 308.

[28] Sanuto, *Diarii,* XI, 56–58, 64, 69, The word *muda* has a very flexible meaning in those passages. Often it means the end of the loading period, but in one case, "rota muda," like "rota il precio" in other passages, must mean "agreed to a price."

brought back extra-large cargoes from the East. The situation would then be all the worse if there were rumor of more wares likely to arrive any day on ships that had not yet returned. Restriction of the times of loading prevented such exaggerated swings in the market situation. At the termination of the *muda,* the supply for the next six months, or for the next year in the case of spices and similar wares brought only by the galleys, was known. Either it was recorded on the ships' manifests or it was registered with the local Venetian consul or customs officer. Report of the supply of each of these regulated commodities often reached Venice by sloops or dispatch boats of some kind before the galleys or ships of the *mude* arrived, and prices rose or fell according to the news received. Until the time of the next *muda* the supply was known. Investments for the next voyage could be made accordingly.

IV

Which of these seven functions of the *mude* were most important to the Venetian legislators? How far were they aware of them all? Which were of primary and which of secondary importance?

To answer these questions would require a more thorough examination of the Venetian archives than I have been able to make. I can consider only a few decrees that show the nature of the problem.

First, let us consider some decisions advancing or postponing the dates of the *muda*. Permission to postpone the end of the *muda* required some special justification, some mishap such as the breaking of a mast which made it impossible to complete the voyage on time. Faced with the alternative of getting no cargo back or permitting late loading, the senate was likely to prolong the *muda,* especially that of the merchant galleys at Alexandria. It stated its reasons thus in 1527: "se vede manifestemente il danno de nostri mercadanti e dal cavedal nostro, et ex consequenti di datii nostri, imperocchè intendendo forestieri che da nostri no possino esser levate mercantie, i mandarono a levarle, et cosi quelle diveniriano altrove, oltra che le robe de nostri conveniriano restar di li."[29] There was strong pressure in each particular case to prolong the *muda* as long as necessary to have cargo. But general policy was against all these exceptions. The general principles involved were always in favor of enforcing the limits of *mude*. In 1503 storms prevented the ships for the spring *muda* from sailing from Venice as early as usual. Therefore they were permitted to have *muda*

---

[29] Senato Mar, reg. 21, f. 58.

until April 15. Recognizing that it had made a dangerous exception to the general rule, the senate placed obstacles in the way of making such exceptions in the future, proclaiming "la grandissima importantia de le mude de le nave: le quale per le lezze nostre, non senza causa, sono sta limitade al Marzo et Septembrio, si per utile de i viazi et mercadanti nostri, come per li tempi de le fiere."[30] Another example of lip service to the importance of preserving the regular *mude* is in a resolution introduced in 1420: "perche niuna altra cosa è de plui utilitade alla marcadantia de conservar le mude, perche quelle è sustimento de la mercadantia."[31] There are many such references to the welfare of trade and one would wish to find some that were more explicit.

That considerations other than the weather, safety, and arrival prior to the fairs were important is suggested by the many provisions concerning wares which had reached the Levantine ports in time for the *muda* but for some such reason as the lack of sufficient space had not been loaded on the ships or galleys making the voyage that year. In the auctions of the galleys of Beirut and Alexandria mention is regularly made of the means by which the *rata* (the wares for which the galleys did not have space) might be sent to Venice by a round ship (*cocha* or *nave*) or by a pilgrim galley. To ensure that these vessels brought only the *rata* and not spices that had arrived at the *scale* after the *muda,* the consuls in the *scale* were ordered to make a list immediately after the departure of the galleys of all the *rata* and to place these goods under lock and key.[32] Frequently when the *muda* of cotton of Greece was extended, it was provided that the cotton loaded late must have been presented to the Venetian rectors in the port during the regular period of the *muda.*[33] In 1417, fears of Catalan pirates prevented the silks and dyestuffs from Morea from reaching the *scale* where the galleys called in time to be brought by them to Venice. Accordingly the senate provided that all silk which reached Corfu by December 10 might be brought to Venice by any ship. The carrier must be able to show a certificate from the officials in Corfu declaring that the silk he had loaded had arrived there by December 10.[34] It was usual that merchandise which was obligated to the galleys and which had accumulated at Modon or Corfu

---

[30] Senato Mar, reg. 16, f. 1. Cf. Sanuto, *Diarii,* IV, 773.

[31] Senato Misti, reg. 53 (doppio) , ff. 115–16.

[32] Galley auctions in Senato, Incanti galere; cf. Ufficiali al Cattaver, reg. 1, f. 74 (1371) .

[33] Senato Misti, reg. 47, ff. 63, 74.

[34] *Ibid.,* reg. 52, f. 67.

in time for those galleys but could not be loaded for lack of space could be brought to Venice by any ship or galley.[35]

All these provisions placed a premium on getting the wares to the *scale* ready for loading at the traditional times. They suggest regulation of the eastern markets, possibly for the purpose of making the supply visible by a determined date, probably for the purpose of having cargoes ready so that there would be a quick turn around of ships and a quick turnover of the merchants' capital.

On the other hand, there were many provisions for loading before the *mude*, although this was permitted only on condition that the goods so loaded were not released to their owners in Venice until after the arrival of the ships or galleys of the next *muda*. Spices, silks, and dyes might be loaded in the East at any time and brought to Modon, there to await the galleys, which were supposed to load them there for transport to Venice.[36] The dyestuff *grana* and other "light goods" of Crete which had been obligated to come to Venice by galley were allowed to come by other vessels, but with the proviso that they must be placed under lock and key in the customhouse until the galleys of Alexandria had arrived.[37] When a galley was sent to Trebizond at an unusual time of year to load silk waiting there it was ordered to keep separate two categories of silk, that which had arrived at Trebizond prior to or during the usual fall *muda* and that which had arrived after the end of that loading period. On arrival at Venice the latter silk was to be placed under lock and key in the customhouse and not released until the arrival of the next galley sent to Trebizond.[38] Sugar and cotton loaded after the *muda* in Syria in the summer of 1429 were similarly treated.[39] These provisions and most other measures providing for the loading in eastern *scale* of wares that had arrived too late for the *muda* are perhaps to be explained by a desire to move Venetian wares from dangerous places. They assured the safety of the goods but prevented their being fully available in Venice until the date they would have reached that market had the *muda* been strictly enforced.

Once the system of the *mude* was established, the maintenance of the system became in itself the end referred to in most of the decrees adjusting the system to the extraordinary circumstances which were

[35] Sanuto, *Diarii,* XVIII, 10.
[36] Senato Misti, reg. 49, f. 30.
[37] *Ibid.*, reg. 47, ff. 61, 128.
[38] *Ibid.*, reg. 47, f. 85 (1406–7).
[39] *Ibid.*, reg. 57, ff. 86, 147.

constantly arising and giving occasion for temporary modifications. Provisions such as those cited in the previous paragraph show a concern with preventing merchants who did not observe the *muda* from profiting at the expense of those who did. To do otherwise once the system was established would seem manifestly unjust. And the system of the *mude* is often referred to as almost an end in itself, without any clear statement of its purpose.

V

Concerning the origin of the *mude* much more research is necessary before speculation at any length is profitable. There are some indications that the regulation of the periods of loading in the Levant was an application overseas of a system which had first been put into effect in Venice itself and that in both cases it was instituted to facilitate the organization of convoys that would permit Venetian fleets to move in more safety during the Genoese wars of the thirteenth century. The maritime statutes of Rainier Zeno refer to a "muduam Augusti" in such a context that they clearly mean a fleet leaving Venice in August. They provide that the ship captains must make their contracts with shippers and seamen before the end of July.[40] Specified periods of departure are mentioned in the *rubiche* of the senate in the early fourteenth century.[41] Together with the collection of regulations concerning the *muda* in the *capitolare* of the Ufficiali al Cattaver, they show the essentials of the system in operation in 1328, permitting two voyages a year to the Levant.

While tempted to believe that the regulation of period of loading was a result of organizing shipping into convoys, I do not feel sure of it. The changes that took place in Venetian shipping between 1280 and 1328, the period during which the cog and the great galleys came into use, are not sufficiently well known. And the word *muda* raises doubts. If it meant "convoy" before it meant "period of loading," that would accord perfectly with the theory that the restrictions on loading developed first to facilitate convoys and that after the use of convoys for cogs was abandoned the *mude* were preserved for the multiple purpose of making it easy to return to a convoy system and of giving a quick turn

---

[40] "Gli Statuti marittimi veneziani fino al 1255," ed. by A. Sacerdoti and R. Predelli, *Nuovo Archivio Veneto*, n. s. V (1903) , 237.

[41] G. Giomo. "Le rubriche dei Libri Misti del Senato perduti," *Archivio Veneto*, XIX (1880) , 109.

around for the ships, a quick turnover on capital, and full supplies for the fairs of Venice. But the word, as a word, seems more associated with exchange than with ships.[42] How did *muda* or *muta* or *mudua* come to mean a fleet? Is it not possible that it first meant exchange, then a period of exchange, then the ships that produced by their arrival or departure the period of exchange? If such were the history of the word, then perhaps the restrictions on loading preceded the organization of convoys, and the origin of these restricted periods of loading is to be sought in Moslem or Byzantine commercial regulations.

[42] W. Heyd, *Histoire du commerce du Levant* (Paris, 1885), II, 453.

SHIPS AND SHIPPING

10

The Merchant Marine of the
Venetian Republic*

THE theme of our colloquy is the study of documentary sources, which form a series and which permit a quantitative knowledge of the evolution of the merchant marine.

For Venice, the type of voyage for which we have the largest number of continuous documentary series is the voyage in convoy. Since the convoys were organized by the government, the registers of the senate and of the council inform us of the number of vessels entering into the composition of these annual convoys; in general, they indicate the tonnage, at least from about 1320.

Among the convoys, we need, nonetheless, to distinguish those which were formed by large round vessels navigated by sail, the cogs (*coche*). These cogs sailed in convoys only at a time of particular insecurity; but the merchant galleys almost always sailed in convoys, according to the orders of the senate, especially after 1380.

Since the senate organized yearly convoys of merchant galleys, their number and their tonnage can be tabulated each year according to their principal destinations. Such a table is much to be desired and I am happy to learn that one is in the course of preparation at the Centre des Recherches Historiques, Section VI of l'Ecole Pratique des Hautes

* Translation of "La Marine marchande et le trafic maritime de Venise à travers les siècles," in *Les Sources de l'histoire maritime en Europe du moyen âge au xviii siècle*, ed. by Michel Mollat (Actes du Quatrième Colloque International d'Histoire Maritime, Paris, May, 1959; Paris: S.E.V.P.E.N., 1962), pp. 7–32. (Translation by permission.)

Etudes, under the direction of Braudel, Tenenti, and Vivanti.[1] It is possible to present in a schematic form, as I have done in Table I, the number and tonnage of these galleys at representative dates about seventy-five years apart. The contrasts are striking, especially between 1490 and 1557.

TABLE I

MERCHANT GALLEY CONVOYS LEAVING VENICE
SELECTED YEARS, AT INTERVALS OF ABOUT SEVENTY-
FIVE YEARS

| Year | Number of vessels[a] | Tonnage[b] | |
		Average	Total
1335	26	150	3,900
1410	15	200	3,000
1490	19	250	4,750
1557	4	250	1,000

[a] These figures are not averages; they are those derived from the records for the years stated (A.S.V., Senato Misti, reg. 17, 48; Incanti galere, reg. 2). These years were selected as typical or representative in a special sense; namely, in these years the numbers designated were those normally considered desirable at that time. Over any ten-year period the number actually leaving per year on the average was considerably less. In the first and last of the ten-year periods, the average would probably be about one half of these figures.

[b] Tonnage means metric tons of commercial cargo carried. See my *Venetian Ships and Shipbuilders of the Renaissance* (Baltimore: The Johns Hopkins Press, 1934) pp. 15–16, 134, concerning the legal carrying capacity of merchant galleys. Because their legal capacity in *milliaria* seems to understate even the amount of merchandise actually carried, I have rounded off figures upward.

But the merchant galleys were only one special part of the Venetian merchant marine. Let us consider next the large round ships. In regard to these cogs, the record of convoys is, as far as I know, most extensive in the fifteenth century. It applies primarily to voyages to Syria and occasionally to voyages to the Black Sea and the English Channel. These convoys were composed entirely of vessels of 400 *botti* or more, many of them being for their day very big ships of 1,000 *botti* (600

[1] This table, covering the period 1332–1534, was subsequently published in *Annales (Economies, Sociétés, Civilisations)*, XVI (1961), 83–86.

tons). The administrative records, as well as other sources, make clear that sailing in convoy was the exception rather than the rule for these vessels, and the record of the size of the convoys is therefore useful chiefly in connection with other records to discover the number and size of the ships making comparable voyages in years when no convoys were organized.[2]

The planning of convoys created the best-preserved series of documents, but that series can be quite misleading unless ways are found to determine the relation between the amount and kind of traffic moving in convoys and the traffic carried by ships traveling out of convoy. The laws regulating navigation are a help in this connection, as are a few fragmentary statistical records. One of these fragments[3] is the oldest substantial compilation month by month and ship by ship that I have found, and it covers only those Venetian ships of 400 *botti* or more departing from Venice between October 19, 1557 and July 6, 1560. A comparison of these data from the mid-fifteenth and mid-sixteenth centuries should prevent the sixteenth-century decline of merchant galley convoys, shown in Table I, from creating a false impression. The decline did not apply to all types of shipping. The amount of traffic moving in the large round ships increased in the sixteenth century.

The shift from galley convoys to round ships, which seldom went in convoy, involved a change in Venetian navigation laws.[4] In the mid-sixteenth century round ships took over much of the traffic which had earlier been carried by merchant galleys. Behind the change in the laws lay changes in the flow of trade and also changes in shipbuilding, in the use of gunpowder, and in the political situation. The merchant galley was not in the sixteenth century as well adapted to political and naval conditions as it had been in the fifteenth century.

Because the planning of the voyages of merchant galleys was well recorded and the voyages of the cogs were less known, historians for some time misinterpreted the growth or decline in the size of the galley

[2] Estimates of this kind for routes in the middle of the fifteenth century appear in Table II, p. 24. This table permits comparison between the mid-fifteenth and mid-sixteenth centuries in regard to three important voyages: that to Syria and Cyprus, that to England, and that to Constantinople.

[3] The basis of Table I, p. 23. This table shows how these ships were employed in the middle of the sixteenth century.

[4] Before 1514 Venetians were not permitted to ship spices from the Levant to Venice except by convoys of galleys. From 1514–24, and again after 1534, the large caracks were allowed to bring spices from the Levant. A.S.V., Senato Mar, reg. 18, f. 29 (May 3, 1514); Arsenale, busta 8, ff. 2–3 (1524); Senato, Incanti Galere, reg. 2, f. 55 (Dec. 10, 1534); Arsenale, busta 9, f. 37 (Feb. 19, 1542–43).

convoys. They mistook it for an index of the growth or decline of the total movement of Venetian shipping or of the port of Venice. Now we know too much about these large round ships to continue in that error. As we learn more about the movements of these ships we recognize that the decline in the voyages of merchant galleys was out of all proportion to any decline of Venetian commerce in the first half of the sixteenth century. Conversely, the increase in the galley convoys during the fifteenth century is not necessarily in itself any indication of a general growth of trade.

Another danger now threatens, namely, that of overemphasizing large vessels, whether cogs or galleys, and ignoring the many smaller craft. Writing of the Mediterranean as a whole Professor Braudel has spoken of a triumph of small types over large at the end of the sixteenth century.[5] With regard especially to Venice and to vessels under 400 *botti* we should ask whether the smaller ships declined in number in precisely the decades when the number of large ships increased, namely, in the mid-fifteenth century and the mid-sixteenth century, and perhaps in other periods. Because there is more record of the large ships, we may be tempted to consider changes in the tonnage of such vessels as indicative of growth or decline in total traffic, mistaking a part for the whole because the part is better recorded, as was done in regard to merchant galleys.

It is with this problem of the relative importance of large and small vessels in mind that I turn to consider in general the sources which record, not voyages only planned, but voyages made. Five kinds must be mentioned:

1. Administrative records by port officials give the number and tonnages of all vessels entering and leaving, but no extensive series has been identified in the archives of the Republic. Many extracts and summaries can be found, as for the large ships of 1557 to 1560. But they vary in coverage and are of relatively late date.

The very inclusive figures for 1423 in the "political testament" of Doge Tommaso Mocenigo are isolated. For large ships of Venetian registry, which received state aid, the records of the Collegio and the Cinque Savii can probably supply the basis for quite an extensive series starting in the late sixteenth century, but for an earlier period or a wider coverage it is necessary to put together figures derived from a variety of administrative processes and from other sources.

---

[5] Fernand Braudel, *La Méditerranée et le monde méditerranéen au temps de Philippe II* (Paris, 1949), pp. 250–59.

2. Another obvious source for ship movements during earlier periods consists of the chronicles or diarists. The Venetian diarist Antonio Morosini gives an exceptional amount of information about shipping, which I have tabulated for 1404 to 1433 in Table II, using notes generously furnished me by Professor Gino Luzzatto. A similar tabulation of the shipping news in the diary of Marino Sanuto would contain much more, but it would still be subject to two important limitations that must be kept in mind in considering Table II. First, the figures he gives fall disproportionately to any drop in trade whenever the diarist's attention is distracted by personal preoccupations or events elsewhere; and, second, he is more interested in the spectacular than the ordinary and reports more about the large ships than about the smaller.

3. A third source, of course, is that of merchants' letters. If as extensive as the marvelous collection of Datini letters which Professor Melis is analyzing, they mention a larger proportion of the smaller craft than do any of the chronicles. But, as in the chronicles, the number mentioned from year to year may be determined by personal factors as much as by changes in the volume of shipping. How can we be sure that we have collected from them a list of all the vessels of any particular class of tonnage visiting a given port and especially of all the vessels of small tonnage? What minimum tonnage will be included in our figure?

4. That question of completeness has also bedeviled the use of a fourth and very valuable kind of material: notarial records. Eugene H. Byrne, who magnificently pioneered among Americans the study of Genoese notarial archives estimated the "total volume of Syrian trade" for some decades on the basis of surviving notarial records,[6] but more recent studies speak more cautiously of "indicazioni frammentarie e non di statistiche totali," to quote some words of Robert Lopez.[7] Concerning Venice, Alberto Tenenti and other specialists who know the Venetian notarial archives tell me that one can hope to find complete registers of notarial acts only for the period after 1560.[8]

---

[6] Eugene H. Byrne, "Genoese Trade with Syria in the Twelfth Century," *American Historical Review*, XXV (1920), 191–219. See Helmar C. Krueger, "Post-war Collapse and Rehabilitation in Genoa," in *Studi in onore di Gino Luzzatto* (Milan, 1950), I, 128, n. 1.

[7] Roberto Sabatino Lopez, "Settecento anni fà: Il ritorno all'oro nell'occidente duecentesco," *Quaderni della Rivista storica italiana*, no. 4 (Naples, 1955), 72.

[8] The wealth of these archives for the contracts of insurance appears in Alberto Tenenti's *Naufrages, corsaires et assurances maritimes à Venise d'après les notaires Catti et Spinelli (1592–1609)* (Paris, 1960).

TABLE II

SHIP DEPARTURES[a] FROM VENICE AS REPORTED BY ANTONIO MOROSINI.[b] (*1404–33*)

Year	Black Sea Galleys[d]	Black Sea Cogs	Syria and Cyprus[e] Galleys	Syria and Cyprus[e] Cogs	Egypt[e] Galleys	Egypt[e] Cogs	Western Mediterranean Galleys	Western Mediterranean Cogs	Atlantic Galleys	Atlantic Cogs	Others (not clearly stated) Galleys	Others (not clearly stated) Cogs	Total Galleys	Total Cogs	Both
1404	2		3		3[e]	1							8	1	9
1405[f]			3	6	3	1					2		8	7	15
1406	2	2	4	3	3				4				13	5	18
1407	3		4		3	1							10	1	11
1408	3	8	4	8	4	2			5			2	16	20	36
1409	3		3		3				5				14		14
1410	3		4		4				4	2			15	2	17
1411	3	2	4		4	1			4			2	15	5	20
1412	3		3		4		2	1	3	1			15	2	17
1413	2		4		3		1	1	4				14	1	15
1414	3		1	7	4	1	1	1	4	1			13	10	23
1415	3	4	4	18	4	2	1	1	4				16	25	41
1416	3	1	3	13	5	2	1	4	4	3		1	16	24	40
1417	2		4	10	5	3	1	1	4	1		3	16	18	34
1418	3		4	18	3	2	1		4				15	20	35
1419	2	3	4	15	3		1		4	1		6	14	25	39
1420[g]	3	1	4	15	4		1		4			2	16	18	34
1421	3		4	7	4	1	1		4	3	1	3	17	14	28
1422	3	3	6	4	3		1	5	4	1		1	17	14	31
1423	3	2	6	10	3		1	2	6[h]	3		2	19	19	38
1424	3	2	5	7	3		1		5				17	9	26
1425	3	2	4	8	5	2	2	1	5				19	13	32
1426	3		3	7	3	1	2		5	1		6	16	15	31
1427[f]	3			16	3			2	4	1	3	1	13	20	33
1428[f]	3		3	8	3	2			4				13	10	23
1429[f]	3			11	7	2			4		2		16	13	29
1430[f]	3		3	3	3	1	1		5		1		16	4	20
1431[f]	5		3	11	3								11	11	22
1432	4											6	4	6	10

TABLE II (*Continued*)

a Strictly speaking, the title should read "Departures planned," for I have counted all galleys put up for auction even when there is no further mention of them, but this distinction is not of much practical importance since the chronicle makes clear that most of the proposed voyages took place.

b A highly misleading feature of the table is the way the number of cogs (*navi or coche*) drops sharply in some years. This reflects Morosini's reporting, but it is no indication of the real number of clearances. For example, the drop from 20 in 1408 to 0 in 1409 does not mean that no cogs sailed from Venice in 1409. The departures of 1409 did not seem worth mentioning. Moreover, in a few cases, notably in 1404, the departures of cogs which Morosini mentions could not be included because he referred to them vaguely as "many," and, lacking any precise number, I entered no number on the table. On the other hand, the low figures for 1431–32 are significant, since those were years of war in which shipping was largely organized into convoys whose movements Morosini reported.

Before 1404 Morosini gives little maritime news. After 1404 he regularly reports on the state-owned galleys but mentions other vessels only occasionally until 1414. After 1414 he normally includes: (1) galley of Acqua Morte (Aigues-Mortes), (2) galleys of Flanders, (3) *navi or coche* of the Syrian spring *muda*, (4) galleys of Romania, (5) galleys of Beirut, (6) galleys of Alexandria, and (7) *navi or coche* of the Syrian fall *muda*. Other *navi or coche*, those leaving for Flanders, Tana, Valencia, notably, are not mentioned, even after 1414, unless their size, their richness, or some incident of the voyage was exceptional. Even less mention is made of voyages to Crete and Sicily.

When Morosini refers to a ship from Venice without indicating the date of its departure, I have counted it under whatever seems likely to have been the year of departure.

The table contains many arbitrary assignments of ships to one category or another. Apart from those explained in the numbered notes, the difficult classifications affected mainly voyages which Morosini mentions so rarely that such classifications have little significance.

In spite of all these weaknesses, the table gives a general impression which is probably correct. The figures are a more accurate indication of Morosini's interest in shipping than of the actual amount of shipping, but his interest was attracted by evidences of prosperity. His reports exaggerate the ups and downs but indicate correctly the good and bad years and the successively higher levels reached in the opening decades of the fifteenth century. A first peak was reached in 1408, a second in 1415, and a third perhaps in 1423, although there was no substantial drop before 1430, or 1432.

c In the few cases in which the convoy went to both Alexandria and Syria, it is counted under Egypt.

d *Bucentori* for Trebizond included.

e After 1415, Morosini sometimes mentions the galley carrying pilgrims to Palestine. When he does, it is included here because it frequently brought back some spices from Egypt.

f Classification of the galleys is difficult in these years: some went to both Beirut and Alexandria; some went to Crete to load spices that had been brought there from Egypt; some were primarily warships.

g Two months of this year are missing from the copy in the Marciana.

h Includes two sent to recover wares lost from previous fleet.

5. Fifth and finally, the reports of foreign envoys become extensive during the sixteenth century, and in the mass of the material from the seventeenth and eighteenth centuries there must be some nuggets of commercial statistics. The studies already published by Ruggiero Romano indicate these possibilities.[9]

The five kinds of sources I have just mentioned—Venetian administrative records, chronicles or diaries, the merchants' letters and account books, the notarial registers, and the reports of consuls or other foreign observers—all contain enough references to small vessels to persuade one of their importance, but I know of no series of any length stating the yearly total movement, including small vessels, until we come to the nineteenth-century administrative records. By the mid-eighteenth century, to be sure, we can find many extracts from the administrative records. Some samples are analyzed in Tables III and IV. They differ one from another in coverage. If we had the administrative records from which they are excerpts, we would be able to construct a group of series which in combination would reveal the changes in the total movement of the port, small vessels included. But we lack the series.

While we lack such records, it may be worth while to use some series of figures concerning the amount of taxes collected. These figures may give us an idea of the quantitative evolution of the trade, even if they do not furnish with precision the tonnage of the ships employed. Yearly receipts from the anchorage tax from 1529 to 1791 are presented in Table V.

The volume of shipping moving through the port was certainly one factor affecting the receipts from the anchorage tax, but unfortunately for our purposes it was not the only factor. Others were changes in (1) the tax rates, (2) the monetary unit, (3) the methods of collection, including the methods of judging tonnage, (4) the exemptions from and interpretations of the tax, and (5) the proportion paid by foreign compared to Venetian ships. Keeping all these factors in view as far as possible, as explained in the notes to Table VI, I will attempt to comment on some features of the series shown in Table V.

After some fluctuations, receipts rose to a maximum of 1,200 ducats in 1560. Although the rate of growth is slight for the period of thirty years as a whole (1529–60), it was 50 per cent during the twenty years from 1540 to 1560. Since the anchorage tax was collected on small ships as well as large, this increase in receipts shows that there was in that

---

[9] Ruggiero Romano, *Le commerce du royaume de Naples avec la France et les pays de l'Adriatique au XVIII*e *siècle* (Paris, 1951).

TABLE III

SHIPS PAYING ANCHORAGE TAX (1737–40).[a]

Type	Tax (ducats)	Number of Ships				Amount Paid (ducats)		
		1737–38	1738–39	1739–40	Average	1737–38	1738–39	1739–40
Venetian								
Ships and 4-masted vessels	8	33	26	41	33	264	208	328
Tartans and 3-masted ships	6	59	26	30	38	354	156	180
Tartans and 2-masted ships	4	27	29	25	27	108	116	100
Trabacolos	2	39	6	5	17	78	12	10
English								
Ships and 4-masted vessels	8	35	28	18	27	280	224	144
Ketches and 3-masted ships	6	11	11	5	9	66	66	30
Brigantines and 2-masted ships	4	3	11	4	6	12	44	16
Other (foreign)								
Ships and 4-masted vessels	12	6	6	13	8	72	72	156
Tartans and 3-masted ships	9	7	5	4	5	63	45	36
Tartans and 2-masted ships	6	15	17	9	14	90	102	45
Trabacolos	3	39	28	10	26	117	84	30
Total		274	193	164	210	1,504	1,129	1,075

[a] "Scosso fatto per conto del datio del ancoraggio da dì 11 Marzo 1737 sino dì 10 Marzo 1738" A.S.V., Cinque Savii alla Mercanzia, n.s., busta 3.

period growth not only in the trade with large ships but in the total movement of shipping.

A new schedule of anchorage taxes raised rates almost 50 per cent in 1581 and accounts for part but not all the rise between 1570 and 1587. The rise was resumed in the 1590's and reached its peak at 6,647 ducats in 1603. This well-attested figure is the high point in the series, and perhaps its most noteworthy feature. Receipts quadrupled from 1591 to 1603, although the only increase in rates in that period was one of 5 per cent across the board in 1595, and this was offset by measures taken in those years which reduced the rates applied to many foreign western ships.

Three influences probably worked together to effect the 300 per cent increase between 1595 and 1603.

TABLE IV

MOVEMENT AT THE PORT OF VENICE (1730–51)

Year	Anchorage Tax[a] (ducats of 124 soldi)	Anchorage Tax[b] (ducats)	Departures[c]	Arrivals[d]	Arrivals[e]					Ships Paying Anchorage Tax[g]				
					Ships[f]	Marci-lane[f]	Tartans[f]	Barche[f]	(Totals)	4-masted Ships[g]	3-masted Ships[g]	2-masted Ships[g]	Traba-colos[g]	(Totals)
1730	1,641													
1731	1,721													
1732					108	45	88	71	(312)					
1733					93	62	104	66	(325)					
1734					88	43	66	103	(300)					
1735					132	43	71	141	(387)					
1736	3,020				116	47	81	359	(603)					
1737		1,766	816 in 96 mo.	320	112	53	108	447	(720)	74	77	45	78	(274)
1738		1,185		315						60	42	57	34	(193)
1739		1,020		293						72	39	38	15	(164)
1740		1,305		243										
1741		751		284										
1742		987		281										
1743		945		217										
1744		1,026		199										
1745		878	808 in 85 mo.	183										
1746		679		198										
1747		877		246										
1748		786		230										
1749		1,302		270										
1750		810		260										
1751		950		222										

a See Table V.
b From the Dogana da Mar, Museo Civico Correr, Venice, Morosini Grimani, busta 496, f. 51.
c From the records of the Mag. dell'Armar (*ibid.*, ff. 175–76).
d From the records of the Mag. della Sanità (*ibid.*, f. 177).
e "Con mercanzie."   f *Ibid.*, f. 117.   g See Table III.

TABLE V

YEARLY RECEIPTS FROM ANCHORAGE TAX, 1529–1791

Years	Ducats of 124 soldi	Years	Ducats of 124 soldi
1529–31	750[a]	1607–9	5,210[ei]
1531–33	750[a]		
1533–35	950[a]	1618–20	1,701[ei]
1535–37	930[a]	1620–22	2,701[e]
1537–39	950[a]	1622	2,401[ej]
		1623	1,600[ejk]
1541–43	704[a]	1624–26	1,300[ej]
1543–45	895[a]	1626–28	750[e]
1545–47	896[a]	1628–30	1,000[e]
		1630–32	1,005[e]
1555	1,130[a]	1633	1,159[l]
ca. 1560	1,200[b]		
1569–70	1,039[c]	1637	1,160[l]
		1638	1,159[l]
1574	1,807[d]		
		1641	1,029[l]
1587–89	2,006[e]	ca. 1660	300[m]
1589–91	1,760[e]		
1591–93	1,500[e]	1670–80	430[n]
1593–95	1,850[e]	1680–85	425[en]
1595–97	2,014[e]	1685–90	685[en]
1597–99	2,513[e]	1690–91	600[en]
1599–1601	2,953[e]	1692–1702	850[en]
1601–3	3,930[efg]	1702–12	1,500[emp]
1603–5	6,647[efh]	1712	1,725[q]
1605–7	4,760[e]	1712–16	1,725 (2,291)[qr]
1720–22	1,700[t]	1762	917
		1763	913
1728	1,664[t]	1764	754
1729	1,613[t]	1765	837
1730	1,641[t]	1766	1,109
1731	1,721[t]	1767	784
		1768	1,037
1736	3,020[uv]	1769	964
1737	2,404 (1,040)[uvw]	1770	741
1738	1,256[uvw]	1771	494
1739	1,089[uvw]	1772	586
1740	1,212[uw]	1773	693
1741	944[uw]	1774	769
1742	862[uw]	1775	952
1743	1,003[w]	1776	593
1744	1,196[w]	1777	720
1745	1,064[w]	1778	556
1746	710[w]	1779	501
1747	775[w]	1780	500
1748	824[w]	1781	373
1749	1,127[w]	1782	474
1750	1,016[w]	1783	145
1751	988[w]	1784	180
1752	792[w]	1785	207

TABLE V (*Continued*)

YEARLY RECEIPTS FROM ANCHORAGE TAX, 1529–1791

Years	Ducats of 124 soldi	Years	Ducats of 124 soldi
1753	845[w]	1786	191
1754	702[w]	1787	298
1755	497[w]	1788	118
1756	196[w]	1789	574
1757	329[w]	1790	703
1758	584[w]	1791	280
1759	305		
1760	1,199		
1761	1,137		

[a] 1529–55, A.S.V., Arsenale, busta 133, ff. 105, 121–22, 140–41; busta 134, ff. 400–5; busta 135, ff. 12, 34–35, 50–51, 66, 78–79; busta 136, f. 1; these documents record the auctions by the Patroni e Provveditori all'Arsenale to the following *dazieri* or tax farmers: Vicenzo di Juane del Castello, 1529; Nicoleto Mustochin, 1531; Nicoleto Mustochin and Janeto di Vissa, 1533; Lunardo Sandeli de Michiel, 1535; Vizenao de Zane del Castello, 1537; Piero Polito, 1541; Polidoro Campana, 1544; Vettor Missocha, 1535.

[b] 1557, 1561, *Bilanci Generali*, vol. I, t. 1, p. 592.

[c] 1569–70, *Ibid.*, pp. 236–40, by the addition of several items.

[d] 1574, Museo Civico Correr, Archivio Donà della Rosa, busta 217, f. 262. The *aggiunte*, whose collection is included in this figure, but were not included in the earlier auctions, amounted by 1570 to 42.5 per cent. They were consolidated into the higher schedule of taxes issued in 1581. See n. a, Table VI.

[e] 1587–1702, A.S.V., Cinque Savii alla Mercanzia, n.s., busta 3; this document contains several copies of a compilation of the prices at which the anchorage tax had been farmed to the following *dazieri:* Giacomo Viviani, 1587; Battista Fede, 1589; Anzolo de Piero da Ven, 1591; Marcello Laguroni, 1593; Cesare Ferro and Anzolo Marioti, 1595; L. Battista Rospini, 1599 and 1601; Ludovico Bucali fo de Messer Emanuel, 1603; Francesco g. Battista dell'Angolo, 1605; Bostolo Cardinali, 1607. See also Arsenale, busta 137, f. 141. After 1607, the tax was not farmed but collected by the government directly (*per S*[a] *Sig*[a]) until: Zan Fisolo, 1618; Paolo Guaschi, 1620; Agostino Briosa, 1622; Eugenio Conduliner, 1623, who transferred it to Zuane Fondi; Francesco Fondi, 1624; Bostolo Guarinomi, 1626 and 1628; Domenigo Mazarol, 1630. Then for quite a long period it was not farmed, until the *inquisitori* all'Arsenal took it in hand and auctioned it to: Domenico Cimegatto, 1680; Nicolò Trevisan g. Simon, 1685; Domenico Cimegatto, in 1690, 1692, and 1702; Cimegatto seems to have had the farm of the tax for at least twenty years.

[f] 1601 and 1603. The precise figures given in the list in busta 3, above cited, are given also in a sheet in the Archivio Donà della Rosa, busta 217, f. 277.

[g] 1601. A lower figure, 2,454 ducats, is given in *Bilanci Generali*, vol. I, t. 1, p. 370, but presumably as an amount collected assigned to the Arsenal, not as the auction price.

[h] 1603. The peak figure for that year is both confirmed and shown to have been an overestimate by the *daziere* or tax farmer, presumably based on high collections in 1602 (Arsenale, busta 137, f. 92). The tax farmer having failed, in Oct. 16, 1606, the Patroni e Provveditori all'Arsenale called for payment by his guarantors, demanding from each his share, figures which multiply out to the same figure given in the list in busta 3, above cited, namely, 6,647 ducats.

Notes to Table V continued

ⁱ 1608. A higher figure, 5,513 ducats, is given in *Balanci Generali*, vol. I, t. 1, p. 421, as assigned to the Arsenal.

ʲ 1618–26. In a *riposte* to the senate, the Cinque Savii in 1626 (ser. 1, busta 147, ff. 41–42) gave the four figures for the four contracts since 1618 as follows: 1,700, 2,400, 1,700, and 1,500 ducats. On the lowering in 1607 and 1626 of the taxes on foreign ships, see n. a, Table VI.

ᵏ 1623, reauctioned at this lower figure, to the cost of Agostino Briosa, the *daziere* who had bid 2,401 ducats the year before.

ˡ 1633–41, *Bilanci Generali*, vol. I, t. 1, pp. 486, 503, 516, 562, amounts collected.

ᵐ 1640–70. The list in busta 3, cited n. e, says that until 1680 no one would bid for the tax and it was collected for the government without a tax farmer, yielding only 300 ducats a year. The figures for the 1630's from the *Bilanci Generali* indicate that such a low yield was not true of the whole period of collection on government account (*per Sᵃ Sigᵃ*) but it may have become true during the war for Crete. Lower taxes on foreign ships in 1607 and 1626 contributed to the drop from 6,647 ducats in 1603 to 750 ducats in 1626. A relaxation of enforcement after 1633 is suggested by the new regulations passed by the senate on May 13, 1633, after no one had bid on the tax, leaving it to ship captains to declare the size, on oath, of their ships (busta 3).

ⁿ 1670–1712. A.S.V., Cinque Savii, n.s., busta 3, includes another compilation for these later dates in which "V.C." (*valore currente*) is clearly indicated for all prices. The figure 425 for 1680 is specified to be *senza aggiunte*. The figures for 1702 and following include all *aggiunte*. I am not sure just when they were included, but the tax of 7 soldi per lira imposed since 1628 is specified in 1702, and the 3 soldi tax added in 1706 was included in 1712 and accounts exactly for the rise then from 1500 to 1725. (See busta 3, esp. Cimegatto's bid dated March 30, 1702, and actions dated May 19, 1712 and March 30, 1714; see also, A.S.V., Arsenale, busta 144, f. 31.) The 7 soldi per lira account for 35 per cent of the rise from 425 ducats in 1680 to 1,500 ducats in 1702. Some of the increase can be attributed to better enforcement, including a return to inspection to estimate ships by officials of the Arsenal. See busta 3 and Biblioteca Querini Stampalia MS. CLIV, Cod. 130, Cuore Veneto legale, sotto Ancorazo, ff. 59–60.

ᵖ 1709–10. That 1,500 ducats were the price in 1709 and 1710 is confirmed by A.S.V., Deputati ed Aggiunti alla provision del denaro, busta 392, numero interno 28, under expected collections by the Arsenal, Sept., 1709, and in busta 395, Bilancio, 1710.

 q 1712–14. Busta 3 contains many papers concerning the offer of a "Consorzio di Parcenevoli" to farm the tax, apparently to avoid annoyances that had developed while Cimegatto was *daziere*. The figure 1,725 ducats is their bid. Collections were by the Masser dell'Arsenal, at least until 1715.

ʳ 1712. The higher figure, 2,291 ducats, is calculated from a record of collections by harbors (Lido, Malamocco, etc.) in busta 3 and is a better indication of collections. Another sheet in busta 3 gives 2,217 ducats.

ᵗ 1720–31, from other loose sheets in busta 3; better figures for 1716 to 1736 are much to be desired.

ᵘ 1736–91, collections on government account (*per Sᵃ Sigᵃ*), compiled with the very generous and expert guidance of Dr. Ugo Tucci from the fifty-five volumes in the A.S.V. of Bilanci delle Rendite e Spese, Rendite dell Dominante. Those of 1736 and 1737 "all'Off. delle Cinque Savii," the rest "Del Nuovo Stallagio." The figures for 1740, 1745, 1750, and 1755 are published in *Bilanci Generali*, III, 10. All figures are for *ducati effectivi* and for the twelve months beginning March 1 of the year given. *Ibid.*, III, xxix–xl.

ᵛ 1736–39. Part of the explanation for double and conflicting figures for 1736–39 is given by a sheet in busta 3, which reads as follows:

Notes to Table V continued

Notes to Table V continued

"Scosso fatto per Conto del Dacio dell' Ancoraggio nelli anni"	Da primo Marzo sino tutto Febbraio [in ducati]			
	1736	1737	1738	1739
Nell'Officio Cinque Savii Mercanzia	3020:10	–	–	–
Nell'Officio Suddetto che fu esato in questa cosa sino al tempo della regolazione essendo doppo stata devoluta tal discossione all'Off. Novo Stallagio	–	1039:14	–	–
Nell'Officio Novo Stallagio come Sa	–	1364:14	1256	1089
	3020:10	2403:14	1256	1089
Soldo Passato all'Arsenal di ditta Raggione	2276:10	2011:17	1062:3	1027

Widely fluctuating figures in the decade 1730–40 are probably due to the change in rates and in administration in that period rather than to changes of comparable amplitude in the magnitude of traffic. See Tables III, IV, and VI.

ʷ 1737–58. Different figures for each of these years, but following roughly the same pattern of ups and downs, and of about the same magnitude, are given in a list certified by Ludovico Prandis, "Masser alla Dogana da Mar," in Museo Civico Correr, Arch. Morosini Grimani, busta 496, f. 50. Whether a different fiscal year accounts for the difference is doubtful, but that does seem a likely explanation of the difference between the figures given here and those given in Table III for 1737, 1738, and 1739. The figures in Table III, showing collections at the new rate, are closely comparable to those given above for collections for the three years at the Novo Stallagio.

A memorial (copy in busta 3) says that the new system of *alboraggio* was adopted by a *terminazione* of Feb. 22, 1736 (old style), because there was so much dispute over tonnage; that in the two years before the new regulation 3,561 ducats were collected; that in the two years after the new regulation 2,213 ducats were collected; and that the drop was due to small vessels that escaped the tax by removing their "bompresso che é l'alboro di prova."

New rules about measuring and estimating ships may have caused a rise in registered tonnage beyond any rise in real tonnage. The auction contract of 1555 said ships were to be estimated "di tutto il portar di basso" (i.e., according to the capacity of the hold) as provided by rules laid down in 1531. Regulations of the seventeenth century, in contrast, emphasized that upper decks and stern castles were to be included.[10] Although other factors that also account for the rise are better attested, the effect of stricter enforcement of the law is not to be excluded.

More surely important was the increase in the trade in this period. It is indicated independently by the receipts from the customs tax on

[10] A.S.V., Arsenale, busta 139, f. 1; Senato Mar (Aug. 28, 1601); and Cinque Savii alla Mercanzia, n.s., busta 3.

overseas trade called "the six per cent." That tax rose almost 100 per cent between 1584 and 1602 and declined after 1604.[11]

The combined evidence of the anchorage tax records and of "the six per cent" attests the extent of the revival of Venetian trade in the last decade of the sixteenth century. But the rise in receipts from the anchorage tax was sharper than the rise in trade. It was so because foreign shipping contributed an increasing proportion of the movement of the port. New rules were approved in 1601 for enforcement of the higher rates on foreign ships, particularly on Greek competitors in the Levantine trade[12] and on ships which claimed Venetian ownership but had not assumed all the obligations of Venetian registry. The ships of most western nations were encouraged to come from their home ports to Venice by being allowed to pay as if Venetian, but the English paid as "foreign" until 1607 because the English taxes on Venetians were felt to be discriminatory. After repeated petitions, the English were allowed to pay Venetian rates after October, 1607. By that time English shipping was so important at Venice that the tax farmer who had bid in the tax the month before was able to show that collections were 2,174 ducats, 19 grossi less than they would have been had not the rate for the English been changed. Even after that deduction the tax yielded 3,000 ducats, much less than the peak of over 6,647 ducats reached about 1603, but still twice the figure of 1591.[13]

Letting the English pay as Venetians may have made the farming of the tax unattractive to tax farmers, for after 1609 it was collected directly by the government for almost ten years, and when it was auctioned again in 1618 the price was down from 3,000 to 1,700 ducats. After a recovery about 1620, it fell and then reached a new low in 1626 when taxes on foreign ships were very much reduced. But the drop from over 6,000 ducats in 1603 to under 1,000 ducats in 1626 reflects not only lower rates for foreign ships but also fewer ships arriving; indeed the diversion of foreign ships to other ports was the reason given for lowering the taxes.

The gaps in the series in the mid-seventeenth century prevent it from showing any detail in regard to the decline during the war for Crete,

[11] From 65,000 ducats in 1584, these receipts exceeded 118,000 ducats in 1602. In 1616 they had returned to 64,000 ducats. A series from 1580 to 1618 is to be found in A.S.V., Cinque Savii, n.s., busta 98. The essential data are confirmed by the Notario di Collegio and by the documents in Bilanci Generali (*Documenti finanziarii della Repubblica di Venezia*, ser. II) , vol. I, t.l.

[12] Senato Mar (Aug. 28, 1601, and Sept. 7, 1629) .

[13] Arsenale, busta 137, f. 141 (Jan. 22, 1609–10) . See also notes to Tables V and VI for the dates in question.

but of the decline it leaves no doubt. The apparent revival, from about 400 ducats in 1670 to 1,500 ducats in 1702, is partly illusory, that is, partly the result of tax increases and monetary adjustments which made a Venetian ship of a given size pay twice as many silver ducats in 1712 as in 1620 or 1589 (when the yearly yield of the tax was about the same). But compared to the receipts at the end of the Cretan war, those of the last decade of the seventeenth century reflect some real recovery, for they show a rise of 100 per cent, of which only 35 per cent can be accounted for by higher taxes.

In the 1730's there is a break in the series, for a new tax schedule and a new system of administration were introduced in 1737. The rise to 3,000 ducats about 1736 and relapse thereafter are probably due to the changes in the extent to which small vessels were required to pay (see Table IV). When receipts had fallen back to 1,000 ducats, it was explained by saying that the new system of rating ships according to the number of masts made it easy for small ships to avoid the tax by taking down the *bompresso,* or forward mast.[14]

This episode illustrates the difficulties in using the total receipts from the anchorage tax as evidence of the total movement of the port, or of the movement of all ships above a specified size. The lower limit specified in the law had different meanings in practice at different times. Corrections for such variations could be made more satisfactorily if one had the series of records, which certainly existed at one time, classifying the various ships which paid anchorage. Data of this kind for a few years (1732–40) are shown in Tables III and IV. There are also some interesting data, difficult to interpret, available for the last year of the sixteenth century.[15] As more such fragments are found, the series showing receipts from the anchorage tax may be of help in linking them together. At least it may serve, as chronicles such as Morosini's do for earlier periods, to suggest the upward or downward movements over substantial periods and to indicate the turning points.

The problem of the small vessels remains to be solved. Records of convoys planned and reports of chronicles tell so little about them that their importance has to be estimated from other sources, of which tax records, such as those of anchorage taxes, are one kind among many. Together with business papers, notarial registers, consular reports, and other administrative records, the tax records may help us toward a better knowledge of the total volume of shipping.

---

[14] See notes to Tables V and VI. For the customs reform of this time, see D. Beltrami, "La crisi della marina mercantile veneziana e i provvedimenti del 1736 per fronteggiarla," *Rivista internazionale di scienze sociali,* L (1942), 304–18.

[15] Tenenti, *Naufrages,* app.

TABLE VI

Anchorage Tax Rates.[a]

	1529		1581	
	ducats		*ducats*	*grossi*
Venetian ships				
250 *stara* (25 *botti*) and under (once)		20 soldi		6
250–499 *stara*, per valuation (once) per 100 *stara*		10 soldi		10
per anchorage (each voyage)		20 soldi		6
500–699 *stara*, per valuation (once)	1	2 grossi	1	12
per anchorage (each voyage)	0.5		1	
per *i levanti* (each voyage)		14 soldi		–
700–999 *stara*, per valuation (once)	1	2 grossi	1	12
per anchorage (each voyage)	1		1	15
per *i levanti* (each voyage)		14 soldi		–
1,000 *stara* (100 *botti*) and over, per valuation (once)	1	2 grossi	1	12
per *il don.* (once) per 100 *botti*	1		1	10
per anchorage (each voyage) per 100 *botti*	1.5		2	4
per *i levanti*		14 soldi		–
Foreign ships				
250 *stara* (25 *botti*) and under (once)		20 soldi		6
250–499 *stara*, per valuation (once) per 100 *stara*		10 soldi		10
per anchorage (each voyage)		20 soldi		20
per *i levanti* per 100 *stara*		13 soldi		–
500–699 *stara*, per valuation (once)	1	2 grossi	1	12
per anchorage (each voyage)	0.5		1	16
per *i levanti* (each voyage) per 100 *stara*		13 soldi		–
per 100 ducats of freight, etc.	3		4	6
700–999 *stara*, per valuation (once)	1	2 grossi	1	12
per anchorage (each voyage)	1		2	16
per *i levanti* (each voyage) per 100 *stara*		13 soldi		–
per 100 ducats of freight, etc.	3		4	6
1,000 *stara* (100 *botti*) and over, per valuation (once)	1		1	12
per *il don.* per 100 *botti* (once)	1		1	10
per anchorage per 100 *botti* (each voyage)	1.5		3	–
per *i levanti* per 100 *stara* (each voyage)		13 soldi		–
per 100 ducats of freight, etc.	3		4	6

[a] *Anchorage taxes of 1529–81 and 1581–1737 compared.* The earliest formulation of an auction contract is that of 1529. It listed various taxes that had previously been decreed by the senate and in 1525/26 were ordered auctioned by the Arsenal for its benefit (Senato Mar, reg. 20, f. 190, Jan. 10, 1525/26). The arrangement of the items in 1529 is very different from that in 1581, since in 1529 the first taxes mentioned are those applying to both domestic and foreign ships, and these items have to be added to those mentioned later that are applicable only to Venetian or only to foreign ships. When

Notes to Table VI continued

these additions are made, the total taxes for 1529 are as indicated (A.S.V., Arsenale, busta 133, ff. 105, 121, 140; busta 135, f. 12, 34–35, 50–51, 66, 78). In 1555 the auction contract was drawn up in a new form, presenting the taxes in the same order used in 1581 (A.S.V., Arsenale, busta 136, f. 1; *Bilanci Generali*, vol. I, t. 1, p. 631, from Notatorio di Collegio, reg. 53, f. 34, May 10, 1581). But, the amount of tax is generally given in 1555 in lire and soldi di piccoli, counting 1 ducat equal to 6 lire, 4 soldi, i.e., about 5 soldi for 1 grosso. On this basis the amounts given in 1555 are the same as those of 1529 except that the small charges *per el boletin* are specified in the 1555 auction. This charge was the same for foreign and Venetian ships. The taxes *per i levanti* are more clearly labeled. They represent a tax previously collected by the *extraordinari e levanti*. See Senato Mar, reg. 18, f. 138, Nov. 6, 1516.

The rates for 1581 are taken from the Notatorio di Collegio, reg. 53, f. 34, May 10, 1581. The document is printed verbatim in *Bilanci Generali*, vol. I, t. 1, p. 631, except for a typographical error which makes the anchorage tax per voyage for Venetian ships read as 1 ducat, 6 grossi, whereas it should read 6 grossi.

While making relatively few changes in the basic rates of its indirect taxes, the Venetian Republic when in need of money ordered a percentage increase on all taxes, except specified exceptions. These *aggiunte* were appropriated to special purposes. Between 1493 and 1522 *aggiunte* of 3 grossi in the ducat (i.e., $\frac{3}{24}$) were levied, and between 1544 and 1560 *aggiunte* of 6 soldi in the lire ($\frac{6}{20}$), a total of 42.5 per cent (*Bilanci Generali*, vol. I, t. 1, pp. xlix, 580–83, 593–95, 632). But there is no mention of these *aggiunte* in the auction contracts of 1529–55, and there is no reason whatsoever to think they are included in the collections auctioned in 1529–55. In contrast, the figure for the anchorage tax in 1574 is said explicitly to include *aggiunte*. The general tax revision of 1578–81 abolished the *aggiunte* previously levied (except "il grosso per ducato del lazo delle monete") and raised rates to make up the difference. See *Bilanci Generali*, vol. I, t. 1, pp. xcviii, l, 621. The table shows that anchorage taxes were raised a little less than 50 per cent.

The most substantial discrimination in favor of Venetian as against foreign shipping was the tax per 100 ducats of freight, a tax not levied on Venetians, but amounting to 3 ducats per 100 ducats in 1529 and 4.25 ducats in 1581 for "foreign" ships, after a 10 per cent allowance. See the report of the Cinque Savii at the time of the removal of this tax (Cinque Savii, n.s., busta 3, Sept. 2, 1626; Senato Mar, filze, Sept. 9, 1626, with other papers).

The main purpose of this discriminatory tax was to prevent foreign vessels from taking the trade between Venice and the Levant from Venetian ships; that is clear from the report of the Cinque Savii, busta 137, ff. 42, 46, 152. Exemption from it, i.e., the right to pay the same anchorage taxes as the Venetians, was granted readily to most of the western nations. These exemptions and other changes in the application of the law are described below. (It should be noted that some changes in the rules were made in effect by the way the Patroni e Provveditori all'Arsenale, who were in charge of the collection of the anchorage tax, decided particular cases.)

Exemptions and changes in application. 1529–31. Exempt practically from the beginning by decision of the Patroni e Provveditori all'Arsenale were "tutti li burchi, feranti e barche che condurranne dentro di questa Città sali, legne da fuoco, scaglia per far Calzina, e robbe dell'Arsenale." Also exempt were those bringing government property in general, if not over 50 *botti*. The quotation is from the printed booklet of Sept., 1620, in Senato Mar, filze, Sept. 9, 1626. See also Cinque Savii, n.s., busta 3, and Cuore Veneto Legale, Biblioteca Querini Stampalia, MS. CLIV, cod. 130, f. 46, for the action by the Patroni e Provveditori all'Arsenale, Jan. 30, 1530/31.

Later papers in busta 3 of the Cinque Savii refer to all ships under 250 *stara* (i.e., 25 *botti*) as exempt. They were so by the law (see table) except for the fee for being so certified. Probably that was not enforced on all small craft. Note that 25 *botti* are almost exactly equivalent to 16 metric tons, and that *quadri* in 1817 distinguish between vessels over and under 16 tons.

Notes to Table VI continued

Another exemption referred to later but probably applied from the beginning is that of ships which brought no cargo. The possible importance of these exempt categories is suggested by figures of the number of ships entering and leaving about 300 or 350 years later, taken from Eugenio Baratto, "Le Vicende del Porto di Venezia dal 1797 al 1869" (unpublished dissertation, Istituto *Universitaria di Venezia*, 1928):

Arrivals	*1817*	*1850*
With fire wood	1,143	830
With salt	219	141
With stone	–	406
Empty	279	98
With merchandise	1,456	1,958
Total	3,097	3,433

Departures	*1817*	*1850*
Loaded	1,125	1,375
Empty	1,294	1,600
Total	2,419	2,975

1531. Venetian instead of foreign rates were granted to the ships of the kingdoms of Naples, Spain, and other dominions of Charles V, by senate action, Jan. 13, 1530/31. See Cinque Savii, busta 139, ff. 165–66.

1544–49. Venetian instead of foreign rates, or even less, were paid by Portuguese ships under old privileges that were reaffirmed in regard to particular cases in 1544 and 1549. Dates of actions are Feb. 15, 1543/44, Apr. 27 and May 7, 1549. Copies of the above actions are in Cinque Savii, n.s., busta 3, and their observance is confirmed by reports of the Cinque Savii, ser. 1, busta 137, ff. 42, 46; busta 139, f. 166.

1554. Venetian instead of foreign rates were granted to all ships that unloaded grain to the extent of half their cargo (Senato Mar, reg. 32, f. 170, Oct. 29, 1554).

1570. Special wartime exemptions permitted Venetians to load on foreign ships.

1574. Exemption from anchorage taxes was accorded to foreign ships that brought from Iviza and Trapani all their ballast in the form of salt, by action of the Council of Ten, Jan. 28, 1574/75. The language is ambiguous but seems to mean that these foreign ships did not have to pay even the anchorage taxes paid by Venetian ships.

1578. Payment of only half the foreign rates was granted to the ships of the Monastery and Island of St. John of Patmos.

1586. Venetian instead of foreign rates were granted to French ships by senate action, Jan. 23, 1585/86 or Aug. 6, 1586 (Cinque Savii, n.s., busta 3; confirmed by reports, ser. 1, busta 142, f. 26; earlier reports in busta 137, ff. 42, 46, 152, 177, dated 1581 and 1585). Although after this date the ships of France, Spain, etc., are sometimes referred to as exempt (busta 3, n.s., Cinque Savii alla Mercanzia), earlier reports of the Cinque Savii (ser. 1, busta 137, ff. 42, 46, 152) and the printed regulations in Senato Mar (filze, Sept. 9, 1626) make clear that the privilege which had been granted to Spanish, Portuguese, and French ships was that of paying the same rates as Venetian ships.

1595. Exemption from anchorage taxes was accorded to foreign ships bringing a full cargo of grain from beyond the Straits of Gibraltar, by action of the senate, Sept. 29, 1595. See Cinque Savii, ser. 1, busta 139, ff. 165–66.

1596. Venetian instead of foreign rates were granted to Dutch ships. This is my interpretation of the effect of interpretations made by the Patroni e Provveditori all'-Arsenale and the Collegio, May 17 and Aug. 27, 1596, and those in 1600–1 mentioned in Cuore Veneto Legale, ff. 46–48 and references to "olandese and fiamminghe" in later records of the Cinque Savii (i.e., ser. 1, busta 139, ff. 165–66).

Notes to Table VI continued

Notes to Table VI continued

1597. Venetian instead of foreign rates were granted Danzig vessels by senate action, Aug. 5 or 9, 1597, and this was later interpreted as applying to all "tedeschi." See Cinque Savii, ser. 1, busta 142, f. 26.

1601. Enforcement of foreign rates on Greek ships was strengthened, and exemption from anchorage taxes was extended to ships bringing their ballast as salt from any part of Sicily (Senato Mar, filze, Aug. 28, 1601). This was later interpreted to mean all ships bringing foreign salt (Cinque Savii, n.s., busta 3).

1607. Venetian instead of foreign rates were granted English ships by action of the senate, Oct. 19, 1607. Various reports on the problem are in Cinque Savii, ser. 1, busta 142, f. 26, Sept. 13, 1607; busta 139, ff. 165–66, Sept. 13, 1597; busta 147, ff. 41–42.

1626. Removal of the tax per 100 ducats of freight previously levied on foreign vessels and increase of the tax per 100 *botti* from 3 ducats to 3 ducats, 4 grossi, were decreed by senate action, Sept. 9, 1626 (Senato Mar, filze, Sept. 9, 1626). A summary of developments to Sept. 30, 1630 is the *Capitoli . . . stampati* of that date in Cinque Savii, n.s., busta 3.

1595–1706. The removal in 1626 of the tax on freight collected by foreign ships was the only substantial change in the rate structure between 1581 and 1737, but across-the-board increases were made as follows (and the 1 grosso per ducat ordered in 1572 continued): in 1595, 1 soldo per lira (i.e., 5 per cent); between 1619 and 1635 various provisions about the kind of coin that would be accepted culminated in 1635 with the requirement that 20 per cent be added to all payments made in *moneta corrente* or *valore corrente*, as were payments of anchorage taxes; there were also the following increases:

Jan., 1628/29	1 soldo per lira.
Nov., 1629	1 soldo per lira.
Aug., 1630	1 soldo per lira.
Aug., 1645	1 soldo per lira.
July, 1648	1 soldo per lira.
Aug., 1668	1 soldo per lira.
May, 1695	1 soldo per lira.
Apr., 1706	3 soldi per lira.

With these *aggiunte* and the 20 per cent for *moneta corrente*, the rates were just about doubled (*Bilanci Generali*, vol. I, t. 1, pp. li–lii. This is confirmed by a loose undated sheet in busta 3, in which someone figured that the anchorage tax for 400 *botti* would be 18 ducats, 11 grossi, instead of 8 ducats, 16 grossi.

1737. In 1737 an entirely new structure of rates combined with an entirely new way of estimating (i.e., rating) vessels was drawn up by the Deputazione al Commercio. The new rate structure, classifying ships mainly by the number of masts, is shown in Table III. A summary of the rates made in 1728 classified ships by size, as in 1581, but stated the rates in lire and soldi. (See Cinque Savii, n.s., busta 3.) In appearance, therefore, there was a sharp break in 1737, a shift from lire and *botti* to *ducati* and *alberi*, but I think it was more a change of form than of substance, for the figures in Table IV, while they show a drop both in tax receipts and in the volume after 1737, suggest that the relation between the size of tax receipts and the volume of movement was not greatly changed by the new tax structure of 1737. If we assume that the intent in 1737 was to preserve the rate of tax while changing the form, at least on Venetian ships, and that "aggiunte e lazo della moneta" have been absorbed, and, ignoring payments made only once, we calculate from those paid every voyage, we find the following approximate equivalents:

4-masted ships	= vessel of 185 *botti*.
3-masted ships	= vessel of 130 *botti*.
2-masted ships	= vessel of 80 *botti*.
1-masted ships	= vessel of 50 *botti* (i.e., 30 metric tons).

11

Naval Architecture,
about 1550*

THE way of life of the master craftsmen who shaped the ships of medieval or early modern times can generally be known only in the mass, their "mystery" but guessed at from its products. But some of the foremen ship carpenters of the Venetian Arsenal may be known individually, for the affairs of the ablest builders of war galleys became affairs of the state; and some slight records of them survive, while equally distinguished framers of stout merchantmen had no such connection through which unconsciously to record their rivalries and triumphs. Moreover, these galley builders of the Venetian Arsenal were the authors, or direct inspirers, of a group of treatises through which some secrets of their craft are revealed.

Such a foreman ship carpenter was Pre Theodoro de Nicolò. In 1544 the Council of Ten ordered that he be given one of the docks or sheds in the Arsenal in which to build such ships as the lords of the Arsenal might direct.[1] He thus became one of the dozen construction chiefs under whom the shipbuilding in the Arsenal was then organized, and would appear to have but little claim to more notice than his fellows of that rank were it not for a manuscript preserved at the Marciana entitled "Instructione sul modo di fabricare galere."[2] Its provenance is revealed by the reference (f. 33) to Francesco Bressan, foreman of the shipwrights' department (1540–70), and the whole secret of its author-

---

* From *The Mariner's Mirror*, XX (1934), 24–49. (By permission.)
[1] Archivio di Stato di Venezia, Arsenale, busta 9, f. 50.
[2] Biblioteca Nazionale, Venice, MS. Ital., Cl. IV, Cod. 26. This manuscript is occasionally cited in A. Jal, *Glossaire nautique* (Paris, 1848).

ship is revealed (f. 32) by the heading, "Galee che o facto sopra de me, Pre Todaro,"[3] that is, "Galleys that I, Pre Todaro, have made under contract."

Theodoro opened his notebook with the invocation, "In the name of God and of the glorious Virgin Mary I begin this book of measures of galleys both great and light, and of *fuste* and *bregantine* and *fregade,* and ships of every sort, and masts and spars and rigging and anchors." The treatise preserved nevertheless deals almost entirely with the shaping of the hulls of ships. Its chief contribution to our knowledge of sixteenth-century vessels is to be found in the attention given to other types besides the light galleys.

Theodoro's instructions are generally extremely cryptic and would be quite unintelligible except for the diagrams which accompany them, and for the explanations afforded by other Venetian treatises on shipbuilding. There are three other such treatises of prime importance dating from the fifteenth and sixteenth centuries—the *Fabrica di galere* of about 1410 partly published and translated by Jal,[4] the notes of Giorgio Timbotta of about 1445 published and translated by R. C. Anderson,[5] and the *Visione di Drachio* used by Contr'Ammiraglio L. Fincati.[6] I am deeply in debt to the students of these documents for the aid they furnish to an understanding of Theodoro's notes.

The Venetian state records not only identify the author of the *Instructione;* they also throw some light on two of the other three treatises. The earliest, the *Fabrica di galere,* refers in a section near the end, which Jal did not publish, to a galley of Theodoro Baxon, who may reasonably be identified with the Master Bassanius of Greek extraction who was esteemed the ablest galley builder in the Arsenal at the opening of the fifteenth century.[7] Apparently he died in 1407, for the senate then ordered eight of his galleys preserved for emergencies that they might meanwhile serve as models to other masters. Some of

[3] A.S.V., Arsenale, busta 135, ff. 141–42; his name is written "Pre Thodoro."

[4] Auguste Jal, *Archéologie navale,* 2 vols. (Paris, 1840). MS. in Bibl. Nazionale, Florence, Coll. Magliabecchiana, MS. Ital., Cl. XIX, Cod. 7.

[5] "Italian Naval Architecture about 1445," *The Mariner's Mirror,* XI, 135 ff.

[6] *Le Trireme* (2d ed.; Rome, 1881), reprint from *Rivista marittima.* Two documents of less value are in the Marciana: MS. Ital., Cl. IV, Cod. 5379, written by Piero di Versi about 1444 (Jal suggested that the part concerning sails was a copy from the *Fabrica,* but the two do not correspond), and MS. Ital., Cl. VII, Cod. 378, written in the sixteenth century by Alessandro Picheroni della Mirandola, mainly an explanation of a design for building galleys with two tiers of oars, one above the other.

[7] Similarly a later foreman's name is written Bressan, Brexan, and Brixiensis.

them remained in the Arsenal until 1431.[8] The *Fabrica di galere* may therefore be assigned with some assurance to the first thirty years of the fifteenth century. It describes exactly the types of vessels of whose construction in the Arsenal there is mention in the state records about 1410 and omits such types as the *galee bastarde* which were built there in the thirties. Since the author makes frequent reference to the cost of materials delivered at Venice, or specifically at the Arsenal, and devotes a large part of the whole manuscript to sail making and rigging, one is tempted to believe that he may have been the "admiral" of the Venetian Arsenal about 1410.

The latest of the four treatises, which is dated 1593, was believed by Fincati to be written under a pseudonym by a son or pupil of the famous foreman Francesco Bressan. This idea was suggested by the title, *Visione di Drachio,* and by the manner in which the treatise is written, the author pretending that the instructions were given him in a dream by Francesco Bressan. But Baldissera Drachio Quintio was a real person. In 1607 he was a member of a committee to select the best model of a galleon from among those presented by the masters of the Arsenal.[9] Three other compositions by him are preserved, *Recordi intorno la casa dell'arsenale,* full of suggestions for improving the organization of that shipyard,[10] *L'ammiraglio del mar,* explaining the duties of a Venetian "admiral" of a fleet, and *Ammiraglio de Baldissera Drachio Quintio,* describing the functions of the "admiral" of the Arsenal.[11]

Considered in connection with these other treatises on shipbuilding, Theodoro's *Instructione* possesses a double interest. He describes types of vessels which are not mentioned in the other treatises, and the terms of his directions contain suggestions concerning the technique employed by the Venetian craftsmen in the middle of the sixteenth century. Like the authors of the other documents, Theodoro gives instructions for building the standard light galley. He also gives some measures for the smaller-oared vessels used in patrols, and for the larger war galleys built for commanders. Specifications for early long ships are relatively numerous, while specifications for round ships of the fifteenth and sixteenth centuries are rarer and less complete. I have

---

[8] The careers of some of these shipwrights of the Arsenal are described in my *Venetian Ships and Shipbuilders of the Renaissance* (Baltimore: The Johns Hopkins Press, 1934).

[9] A.S.V., Arsenale, busta 137, f. 115.

[10] Arsenale, busta 533.

[11] Bibl. Nazionale, Venice, MS. Ital., Cl. IV, Cod. 177.

therefore chosen for publication, and for such translation as my capacity permits, the instructions for the round ships, *navi* and galleon, and for the intermediate types, the oared galleon and the great galley. To make comparison easy some of their measures have been tabulated below.

Type	*Length on deck stem to stern (ft.)*	*Beam (ft.)*	*Floor (ft.)*	*Depth (ft.)*
Fusta of Francesco Bressan	82	12	6½	4
Light galley	122	14½	–	5
Light galley	122	15	8	–
Galley for a general	138	16½	–	5½
Galley for a *Provveditore*	126	15½	–	5
Four-oared galley for a general	137	16¼	8	5⅛
Great galley	138	23	12	9
Rowed galleon, two men to an oar and two oars to a bench	145	27	9	9
Rowed galleon	90	18	–	6
Rowed galleon	100	21	7½	6½
Great galleon	135½	33	11	11
Merchantman	71½	20	7	6½

The rendering of many passages of the instructions is conditioned by one's conception of the methods employed by the shipwright in working out his design. Some discussion of pertinent parts of the craft of the shipwrights is therefore necessary to explain the translations.

The diagrams in Theodoro's notes show that the curve of the midship frame was determined by dividing the depth from the first deck into three equal parts. The four dividing lines were the beam, the *siepie,* the *trepie,* and the floor. The *siepie* and *trepie* were the widths at two thirds and one third of the depth above the keel, respectively. The measures of the four dividing lines determined the curve of the midship frame. If the proportions between them were once determined, these same proportions might be applied constantly even if the actual measures of the vessels varied slightly. Thus the shipwright arrived at a principle of design which, if once judged sound on the basis of experience, might be applied to all vessels of the same type. The finding of such principles of proportion would have been much more difficult if the curve had been determined, as it was in the fifteenth-century treatises, by giving "half-beams" at intervals of 1 ft. or ½ ft. along the depth.

Theodoro's drawings of stem and sternpost are not equally revealing for they leave some doubt concerning the method of finding the curve. The line connecting the scarf and the spot where the deck line cuts the stem or sternpost (Fig. 1) is reminiscent of the method employed in the earlier documents where the diagrams plainly indicated that the curves were drawn out by a series of offsets from the right triangle of which this line formed the hypotenuse. On the other hand, the indication of the *chalcagnol* and the drawing of the line dividing the right angle of the triangle—these two features are suggestive of the method described by Crescentio in 1602.[12] Here again the later of the two methods was a simplification of such a character that fewer measures were used to determine the curve. In consequence the later method made it easier to arrive at rough empirical rules concerning the mathematical proportions between these measures, rules applicable to ships of varied dimensions. While the exact method employed by Theodoro remains in doubt, his diagrams do indicate that he used fewer measures than the Venetian shipwrights had employed a century earlier.

This tendency toward a reduction in the number of measurements necessary to determine the lines of the ship is apparent in the instructions for narrowing or heightening the frames before and abaft of the midship frame. The earliest treatise, the *Fabrica di galere,* gives some measures of height and width for the "tail frames" and the frames 18 ft. before and abaft the midship frame. Complete specifications for the design of the individual frames, if given in these terms, would have involved an enormous number of measures, and it would have been very difficult to reduce their relations to simple rules of proportion applicable to ships of even slightly different sizes. But already in Timbotta's notes there is mention of a device which enabled the shipwright to derive from a few measures the design of nearly all the frames. The measures given by Theodoro imply the use of a similar geometric device.

Theodoro's method may be called that of the *partison.* The shipwright started with his design of the midship frame. That served as a basis from which to figure out the shape of the other frames, but he must modify his design in order to give such shapes to the other frames as would very gradually narrow and heighten the ends of the ship. The

[12] Bartolomeo Crescentio, *Nautica Mediterranea* (Rome, 1602) , p. 9; cf. Jal, *Glossaire nautique,* s.v. *sgaramento.*

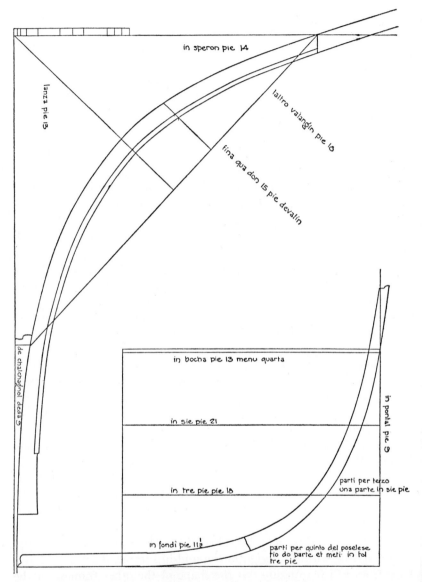

Fɪɢ. 1. Sketches from Theodoro's *Instructione*. Stem and midship frame of a great galley.

problem of narrowing will serve as example. He first determined the amount of narrowing to be made at the tail frame. The tail frame was probably the last frame forward or aft which formed a true floor timber. The frames before or abaft the tail frames were V- or Y-shaped.[13] But the essential was simply that it should be a frame near the end of the ship whose position on the keel was known.

After the location of the tail frame, the first measure to be determined was the extent to which the lower part of the tail frame should be narrower than the corresponding part of the midship frame. This measure might be fixed by tradition as a certain part of the floor or some other measure of the ship. The shipwright must then know how many frames there were to be fastened to the keel between the midship frame and the tail frame—say forty, as in the bow of Theodoro's great galley. He then faced the problem of making each of these successive forty frames slightly narrower than the preceding so as to effect at the tail frame the total amount of narrowing desired. Probably he worked out a separate design only for every fifth frame, so that he had a total of eight frames to be designed. To guide him in this operation he marked off on the base of the midship frame a line which was equal in its total length to the total amount of narrowing to be made at the tail frame, and which was divided into eight progressively smaller fractions. These divisions are roughly indicated in Figure 2.

He then made the first of his designed frames narrower than the midship frame by the amount of the smallest of the eight fractions, the second by the amount of the two smallest fractions, and so on to the tail frame. The division of the line of given length into a given number of progressively smaller fractions was made by a geometric device such as the *meza-luna* described by Crescentio and pictured in Timbotta's notes.[14]

The *Visione di Drachio* mentions four different ways in which the design of the frames fore and aft are to be made to vary progressively from the basic design, that of the midship frame, and he calls all four *partisoni*. The same four ways of varying the design of the frames are mentioned by Theodoro, although he, like Timbotta, calls only one of them *partison*, namely the narrowing. It is my conclusion that all four of these ways of modifying the shaping of the frames were worked out

[13] The amount of narrowing at the tail-frame—*partison*—is usually approximately a quarter of the floor. It was applied on each side of the keel. The diagrams show that the floor timbers amidships began to curve upwards about half-way between the keel and the point from which the floor measure was taken.

[14] Crescentio, pp. 14–18; Anderson, p. 154.

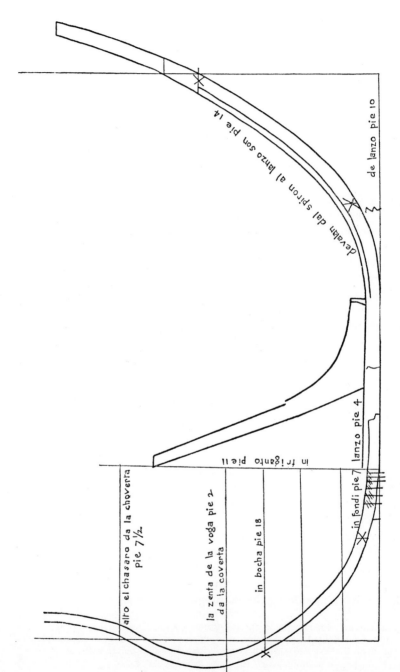

FIG. 2. Sketches from Theodoro's *Instructione*. Stem, sternpost, and midship frame of an oared galleon.

de lanzo pie 10

devalan dal spiron al lanzo son pie 14

in frigánto pie 11

lanzo pie 4

in fondi pie 7

in bocha pie 18

la zenta de la voga pie 2 da la coverta

alto el chasaro da la choverta pie 7½

by geometrical diagrams like the *meza-luna,* but that the first to be so worked out was that for narrowing the frames, the *partison del fondo,* and it is for that reason that it is referred to by Timbotta and Theodoro simply as *la partison.*[15]

The *stella* was a measure which governed the heightening of the frames fore and aft so as to lift both ends of the deck slightly above the center.

Of the *partisone del ramo* Drachio speaks as follows:

> Principiera nel capo di sesto da prova et terminera nelli forcami che sono appresso quelli della mezaria, et serve la dita solamente nelli forcami. Questo ramo e ragione che dilata et allarga la parte superiore della galea et gli da spalle overo quartiero nel petto di detta galea.

> [It] begins in the tail frame of the prow and terminates in the upper part of the frames which are near those of the center, and is used only in the upper part of the frames. This *ramo* is a measure which expands and widens the upper part of the galley, and gives it shoulder or space in the breast of the said galley.

Elsewhere Drachio says that the *ramo* enters into the design of the upper part of the frames at the mark for the top clamp. I take the sense to be that the *ramo* caused the top of the hull to narrow less rapidly than the floor.

The purpose or effect of the *schorer del sesto* or *schorer* I have been unable to determine. Drachio says that it was applied to the upper parts of the frames from the middle to the prow.

These four measures governing the variations of the design of the frames fore and aft from the midship frame would be derived by the shipwright one from another. For example, Drachio says of the *partisoni* to be applied to the poop of the light galley that the *partisone del fondo* would be one sixth of the beam, the *ramo* one fifth of the *partisone del fondo, il schorer* twice the *ramo,* and *la stella* one sixth of the *partisone del fondo.*

Crescentio writing in the Neapolitan tradition mentions only two of these four ways of varying the shapes of the frames, whereas Theodoro a half century earlier uses all four, and all except *il schorer* were mentioned an additional century earlier by Timbotta.[16] Apparently

---

[15] Crescentio, pp. 20–21, uses a similar association of terms. He calls the narrowing the *brusca* and the heightening the *brusca della stella.*

[16] Anderson, pp. 149, 150.

ramo and *schorer* were long known to the Venetian craftsmen and reduced by them to a mathematical basis, although not so used at Naples. Such slight refinements in design may have had much to do with the high reputation of the Venetian galley builders.

THE GREAT GALLEY

The use of the great galley was introduced at the end of the thirteenth century. The *Fabrica di galere* describes the two types sent on merchant voyages about 1410—those of the measures of Flanders and those of the slightly smaller measures of Romania. By 1480 the galleys of the smaller measures had gone out of use, and the size of the others had been increased so that they had a capacity of five or six hundred thousandweights. In 1481 the senate ordered the shipwrights not to make them with a capacity of more than 450 thousandweights, about 210 deadweight tons.[17] But since the shipwrights still showed an inclination to enlarge these ships to such an extent as to make it impossible for them to use their oars even in port, the senate again ordered a reduction of size in 1520 by limiting the length to 132½ ft.[18] The masters decreased the other measures accordingly, the beam by 1½ ft., the depth by ½ ft. But the artillery, the rigging, and the equipment carried on deck was kept as before so that the ships became less stable. For this reason the earlier measures were again authorized by law in 1549, namely, length 137½ ft., beam 23 ft., depth 9 ft.[19] These are almost exactly the measures of the two great galleys described in the following passages from Theodoro's instructions.[20] His specifications appear applicable, therefore, both to the great merchant galleys of 1500, the time when these ships were most famous, and to the great war *galeazze* which played so interesting a part in the battle of Lepanto.

> Commezeremo prima galie grosse. Da rioda a rioda son longa passa 27 e pie 3. Reaviso como galie grosse se parti per sesto dela bocha. Sie fia 23 sano farano passa 27 et pie 3, tanto vol eser la dita galia longa.
>
> In bocha vol esser pie 23, in fondi pie 12, in trepie pie 19, in siepie pie 22, in pontal pie 9.
>
> Ano de partison a pupa pie 3 quarta ½. Ano corbe n° 45 et a prova ano corbe n° 40 in partison. Son erto el sesto mezo pe.

[17] A.S.V., Senato Terra, reg. 8, f. 114.
[18] Senato Mar, reg. 19, f. 126.
[19] Senato Mar, reg. 30, f. 37, files, Feb. 17, 1548.
[20] Ff. 1, 36; superscript letters refer to Fig. 3; all punctuation has been added.

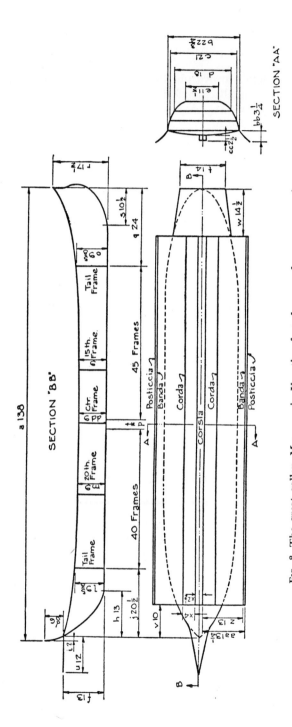

FIG. 3. The great galley. Measures in Venetian feet; letters refer to passages in text.

Ano de ferir a pupa pie 24 e do terzo. Ano de ferir a prova pie 12½.

De palmeta a prova pie 10ᵛ e de palmeta a pupa pie 14½.ʷ

In spiron son alto pie 13, aversi in palmeta a prova pie—. Erta in triganto pie 17½. Aversi in triganto pie 14.ᵗ La centa son basa a pupa pie 3.

La timonera son longa pie 5, son grossa 3 quarta de pe, son larga un pee 3 quarta.

Aversi la corsia a prova pie 2½.ˣ Da la corsia a la corda son pie 4,ʸ da la chorsia a la banda son pie 13,ᶻ e da la corsia a la postiza son pie 13 quarto.ᵃᵃ

Son alta la postiza a prova pie 3 e do adeda metando el morello sul chonudo [?] de la lata. Son alta al mezo pie 3 e quarta.ᵇᵇ Son alta a pupa pie 3 menu quarta.

Son erta la corsia al mezo pie 2½,ᶜᶜ a prova pie 2 e meza quarta.

La schaza vano a late 22. La porta de marangon vano a late—.

Son grasa la banda uni terzo pie. La chorsia son grossa mezo pie.

Questa e la rason de meter in voga. De la zovela da prova al primo scermo son pie 3½, e de la zovela da pupa al primo scermo son pie 3½, e de la postizo a l' altro son pie 3½.

Ano de stella mezo pe a prova, e a pupa mezo pe e do adeda. Dal 15 commenza la stela et legno in ramo, et chusi a prova. Ano de legno in ramo—.

A prova l' asta tute do son deda 14½ largi et grossi deda 10 e mezo.

The following is an attempt at an explanatory translation:

We will begin first [with] great galleys. From stem to sternpost [on deck] is 27 paces and 3 ft.[21] I remind you that great galleys are derived by design from the beam. Six times 23 they know will make 27 paces and 3 ft.; so much should be the length of the galley.

The beam should be 23 ft., the floor 12 ft., the *trepie* 19 ft., the *siepie* 22 ft. The depth is 9 ft.

The narrowing of the frames aft from mid-frame to "tail frame" is 3 ft. and half a quarter [foot]. There are 45 frames in which this narrowing is to be effected and forward 40 frames

[21] Venetian measures: 1 pace = 5 ft.; 1 foot = 16 in. (*deda*); 1 Venetian ft. = 1.1 English ft.

from mid-frame to tail frame. The [fore] tail frame is ½ ft. higher than the midship frame.[22]

The distance of the after tail frame from a perpendicular dropped from the sternpost at the deck level is 24 and ⅔ ft.[23]

The distance of the fore tail frame from a perpendicular dropped from the stem at the deck level is 12½ ft.[24]

The open deck forward is 10 ft. and the open deck aft is 14½ ft.

The height of the stem measured vertically is 13 ft. The width is [lit. "opens"] at the open deck forward—feet. The height of the sternpost measured vertically is 17½ ft. The width at the transom is 14 ft. The wale is low at the stern 3 ft.

The timber of the gallery overhanging the stern abaft the rudder is 5 ft. long, ¾ ft. thick, 1¾ ft. wide.

The width of the *corsia* forward is 2½ ft.[25] From the *corsia* to the *corda* is 4 ft. From the *corsia* to the *banda* is 13 ft., and from the *corsia* to the *apostis* [or outrigger frame] is 13¼ ft.

The *apostis* is 3 ft. and 2 in. high in the bow, putting the measuring rod on the *chonudo*[26] of the deck beam. It is 3¼ ft. high in the middle. It is 3 ft. minus ¼ high in the stern.

The *corsia* is 2½ ft. high amidships, at the bow 2⅛ ft.

The mast trough goes at beam 22. The carpenter's hatch goes at beam—.

The *banda* is ⅓ ft. thick. The [timbers of the] *corsia* are ½ ft. thick.

These are the measures for arranging the rowing. From the fore yoke[27] to the first tholepin is 3½ ft., and from the after yoke

---

[22] Literally, the design is ½ ft. high. I have given the above reading because the measure corresponds with that given later for the *stella*.

[23] This guess as to the interpretation of *ferir* is based on the following: In the Timbotta MS, *Mariner's Mirror*, XI, 139, is the expression, "E fiero con la qudiera chorba da pope lonzi dal pionbin pie 23 meno quarto." That appears in Anderson's translation the usual way of giving the distance of the tail frame from perpendiculars dropped from bow and stern. Another passage, *op. cit.*, p. 150, reads, "E de l' inferir la chorba dale onze quela da prova pie 4." In the *Fabrica di galere*, f. 77, one reads, "Fieri com la chodera chorbe de pope lonzi dal mezo passe 7 pede 1." On the basis of the similarity of "ferir" to the terms in the above passages, I have taken *ferir* to refer to the distance of the tail frames. The most likely results are obtained by considering that it refers to the distance from the perpendiculars dropped from stem and stern.

[24] The measure 20½ ft. given in the following selection seems more reasonable.

[25] The *corsia* was the gangway running fore and aft down the center of the ship. The *corda* and *banda* were apparently stringers let into the deck beams.

[26] Unidentified unless it stands for *cholo*, "end."

[27] The extra heavy deck beam at each end of the space occupied by the rowers.

to the first tholepin is 3½ ft., and from the central tholepin [of each group of three] to the next [central thole pin] is 3½ ft.

The heightening of the frames forward [between midship frame and tail frame] is [at the tail frame] ½ ft., and aft it is ½ ft. and 2 in. From the fifteenth [frame] begin the heightening of the frames and the widening at the tops of the frames and similarly in the bow. The widening of the upper part of the frame is—.

The timbers of the stem are both 14½ in. wide and 10½ in. thick.

The second description of a great galley which I have selected gives fewer measurements for the deck but more for the hull.

> Rason de galia grosa la qual fago adeso. Rason de galia grossa. Prima da rioda a rioda son passa 27 pie 3.[a] La rason son chavado per sesto dela bocha. In bocha pie 23 menu quarta,[b] in siepie pie 21,[c] in trepie 18.[d] In fondi pie 11½.[e] Meti te in scquaro, parti per quinto el fondi dal poselese et tio parte n° 2 et meti in trepie. Parti el trepie per terzo et meti una parte in siepie. In pontal pie n° 9.[dd]
>
> In speron pie 13.[f] Dal speron in su son pie 6.[g] Lanza la dita asta pie 13.[h] Ano de valangin pie 16 dal lanzo al speron et va fuora pie n° 2 in zema.[i]
>
> De ferir a prova pie 20½[j] tanto aversi el chavo de sesto. Ano de partison pie 2 et deda 10. Ano de schorer pie 1½ et legno in ramo pie 1 e deda 4. Ano de stella dede 10. Chomanza dal vinti a dar la stela et legno in ramo. Son chorbe in partison n° 40.
>
> Et a pupa ano de partison longa pie 3. Son chorbe in dita partison n° 45.[n] Ano de stela deda 10, ano de legno in ramo deda 8, schorer uni pe. Chomanza la stela et legno in ramo dal 15 et ano uno chorb in mezo.[p] Et de ferir a pupa pie 24.[q]
>
> Et el chanpo son deda 9 e qalche chosa piu.
>
> L' asta de pupa son alta pie 17½,[r] lanza 10½.[s] Aversi in triganto pie 14.[t] Longo el chastello pie—.
>
> Aversi in zovo a pupa pie 18 e deda 10. Aversi in zovo da prova pie 18.
>
> Ano de ziron pie 12.[u]
>
> Ano de chorsia in luze pie—. Erta la chorsia pie 2 e quare 3, grosse la chorsia deda 10.

Measures of the great galley I am making at present. Measures of a great galley. First, from stem to sternpost is 27 paces and 3 ft.[28] The measures are derived by design from the beam. Beam

---

[28] I am quite convinced by the analogous passage in the *Visione di Drachio* that this is the measure on deck. although there is a suggestion that *prima* might be

is 23 ft. minus ¼ [foot], beam two thirds of the depth above the keel is 21 ft., one third above the keel, 18 ft. Floor is 11½ ft. Draw it out in the square. Divide the base line by fifths from the mark and take two parts and put it in the *trepie*. Divide this *trepie* by thirds and put one part in the *siepie*.[29] Depth is 9 ft.

The height of the stem is 13 ft. The stem rises 6 ft. above the beak [and the deck line]. The stem rakes 13 ft. It is 16 ft. along the curve [?] from the [scarf] mark to the beak [or deck line] and goes outside 2 ft. at the top.[30]

The distance of the fore tail frame from the perpendicular is 20½ ft., as much as the width [of the tail frame]. The narrowing of the frames forward is 2 ft. 10 in. The *schorer* and the widening of the tops of the frames are 1½ ft. and 1 ft. 4 in. The heightening of the frames [forward] is 10 in. Begin at the twentieth [frame] to heighten [the frames] and widen the tops. There are 40 frames between the midship frame and [fore] tail frame.

The narrowing of the frames aft is 3 ft. There are 45 frames between the midship frame and the said tail frame. The heightening of the frames is 10 in., the widening at the top 8 in., *schorer* 1 ft. Begin the heightening and widening of the tops at the fifteenth (frame). There is one frame amidships. The distance of the after tail frame from the perpendicular is 24 ft.

And the space between the ribs is 9 in. and something more.[31]

The sternpost is 17½ ft. high, rakes 10½ ft. The width at the transom is 14 ft. The length of the sterncastle is—ft.

The width at the after yoke is 18 ft. 10 in. The width at the fore yoke is 18 ft.

The distance from the *corsia* to the *banda* is 12 ft.[32]

---

translated "keel" in Jal, *Glossaire nautique* (Paris, 1848), s.v. *primo*. But Jal cites only Neapolitan usage.

[29] The only way that I have thought of by which the derivation of the *siepie* from the *trepie* can be made to check is to assume that the shipwright drew out half a cross section, divided the *trepie* apparent on his diagram into thirds and added one of these thirds, i.e., 3 ft., to the whole *trepie* and thus obtained the measure for the whole *siepie*.

[30] Projects 2 ft. beyond the perpendicular drawn through the spot where the deck line cuts the stem.

[31] If there were 9 *deda* or 0.62 English ft. between the ribs, the ribs must have been about 0.56 English ft. wide, for with 87 ribs in 102.85 English ft. (93.5 Venetian ft.), the "space and room" would be 1.2 English ft.

[32] Equating *ziron* with the *giron* in Timbotta's notes. *Ziron* may refer to the length of oar inboard.

The width of the *corsia* outside [?] is—feet,[33] the height of the *corsia* is 2¾ ft., the thickness of the *corsia* [timbers] 10 in.

THE OARED GALLEON

Three different types of ships were called galleons, *galioni,* by the Venetians: the warships used on the rivers, the large round ships designed especially for military use, and a type of Cretan merchantman. The earliest of these mentioned are the galleons used on the rivers during the Italian wars of Venice in the first half of the fifteenth century. Flotillas of these ships were built at that time in the Venetian Arsenal, although there is relatively little record of their construction there a century later. These earlier ships were very likely essentially similar to the following galleon described on f. 21:

> Rason de un galion che voga a remi.
> Longo de timon a speron passa n° 20. In bocha pie 21. In siepie pie 18 e do terzi, in trepie pie 15 e ma[n]cho un terzo. In fondi pie 7 e quarta. In pontal pie 6½. La tolda son alta da la choverta pie 7½. Ano una zenta sora el magier de bocha de pie 2, et la va i bachalari siti.
> Vol saver el valangin va la scquara che son butado et la te mostra el tuto.
> De ferir a pupa pie 24. Ano de stella pie 2. Alta in triganto pie 11½. Lanza l' asta de pupa pie 7. Aversi in triganto pie 11 (?). Ano de charoso a pupa pie 6.
> Aversi la centa de la voga a pupa pie 9½. Aversi in centa del chasaro pie 8. Aversi de sopra pie 6.
> Aversi in chavo de sesto in magier de bocha pie 15. Aversi in la zenta de la voga a la dita chorba pie 16½, in la zenta de chasaro pie 13½.
> Ano de partison pie 2 et ano chorbe in dite partison n° 30 et chusi a prova chomo a pupa. A prova chomenza dal 5 a darge la stella et legno in ramo.
> Alto in spiron pie 9, lanza pie 10.
> De ferir a prova pie 19, et ano de stela a prova pie 1 a chavo de sesto. In paraschasola a prova pie 5. De palmeta a prova pie 17.
> De legno in ramo a la chorba de chavo de sesto do terzi de pe.

---

[33] One would expect here, on the basis of other instructions, a statement of the width of the *corsia*, but I cannot identify the expression *in luze* except to imagine that it serves to contrast the outside measure with that, given by Timbotta, taken inside between the two upright planks of the *corsia*.

Ano de partison a prova pie 2. Ano chorbe in partison n° 25 et resto in mezo da una chorba de le onze al altra son pie 4 et chascha in mezo 4 chorbe.

Measures of a galleon rowed by oars.

Length from rudder to beak 20 paces. Beam 21 ft. Width at two thirds of the depth above the keel 18⅔ ft., at one third above the keel 15 ft. minus ⅓. Floor 7¼ ft. Depth 6½ ft. The top deck is 7½ ft. above the [first] deck. There is a gunwale 2 ft. above the top clamp and there go the brackets [supports of the outrigger frame].

[If] you wish to know the curve [of the side] go to the square that is drawn [in the diagram] and it will show you all.

The distance of the after tail frame from the perpendicular is 24 ft. The heightening of the frames is 2 ft. The sternpost is 11 ft. high. The sternpost rakes 7 ft. The width at the transom is 11 ft. [Reading 11 or 19 doubtful.] The rising of the ship's floor at the poop is 6 ft.

The width at the gunwale of the rowers' deck at the poop is 9½ ft. The width at the strakes of the castle is 8 ft. The width at the top [of the bulwarks] is 6 ft.

The width at the tail frame at the top clamp is 15 ft. The width at the gunwales of the rowers' deck at the said frame is 16½ ft., at the strakes of the sterncastle 13½ ft.

The narrowing of the frames is 2 ft. and there are 30 frames in which the said narrowing is to be effected both in the bow and in the stern. At the bow commence with the fifth [frame] the heightening [of the frames] and the widening of the tops.

The stem is 9 ft. high, rakes 10 ft.

The distance of the fore tail frame from the perpendicular is 19 ft., and the heightening of the frames at the tail frame is 1 ft. The ceiling is 5 ft. [above the keel] in the bow. The open deck forward is 17 ft.

The widening of the tops [of the frames] is ⅔ ft. at the tail frame. The narrowing of the frames forward is 2 ft. There are 25 frames in which this narrowing is to be effected, and that leaves amidships, from one of the frames of which the design is drawn out to another, 4 ft., and there are amidships four frames [all of the same design, i.e., that of the midship frame].[34]

---

[34] Giuseppe Boerio, *Dizionario del dialetto veneziano* (Venice, 1867), s.v. *onza*. The design of every fifth frame was worked out geometrically. The earlier reference to thirty frames forward must be taken to mean thirty frames between midship frame and tail frame, while this passage shows that the narrowing was not begun until the fifth frame.

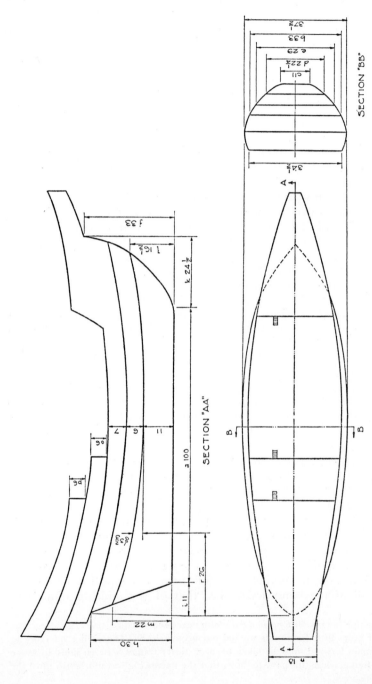

Fig. 4. The great galleon. Measures in Venetian feet; letters refer to passages in text. Other measures taken from Fig. 5.

THE GREAT GALLEON

The first great galleon built for the *signoria* of Venice was constructed between 1526 and 1530 by Matteo Bressan. It may have been a further development of the large round ships called *barze* which Leonardo Bressan, foreman of the shipwrights of the Arsenal, had been building for the previous thirty or forty years. Matteo's galleon was esteemed a highly satisfactory warship. When in 1547 it was finally declared unseaworthy and was broken up, the senate ordered the

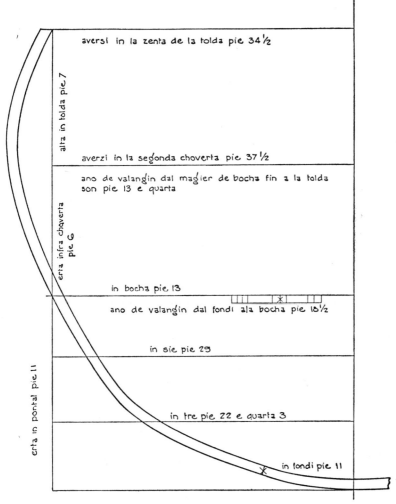

FIG. 5. Sketch from Theodoro's *Instructione*. Midship frame of a great galleon.

experts to record carefully its measurements, that its design might guide future makers of galleons. Two more ships of the same type were immediately ordered, but the order was not executed until 1554. Pre Theodoro's name is among the list of shipwrights considered when, at this latter date, a foreman was selected to take charge of building a galleon, but after Theodoro's name it is written that he was passed over because he was ill.[35] Giovanni Maria Spuazza was chosen. The galleon which he built capsized while issuing from the port of Malamocco on its maiden voyage in 1558.[36] Another galleon begun by the humanist Vettore Fausto about the middle of the century and not launched until 1570 was little used after its first voyage for fear it also would capsize. Apparently the effort to construct ships which would be fast under sail and would carry a heavy load of ordnance on the upper deck and castles led to the building of unstable vessels.

Theodoro gives these instructions[37] for a galleon at f. 26:

Questa son la rason de galion grande.

Longo in cholomba passa n° 20,[a] in bocha pie 33,[b] in trepie 22 e quarta,[d] in siepie pie 29.[e]

La partison de sesto a pupa: parti per quinto et buta via el piu che restaria parte do, tanta partison vol a pupa; a prova, parti per terzo et buta via el piu che seria una parte, tanta partison vol a prova.

La stela se dano a questo modo: parti el to fondi per terzo et tio una parte et dage tanta stela a chavo de sesto chusi a pupa chomo a prova. Mesura chon tuta la cholomba. Legno in ramo: a prova dege um pe de legno in ramo et a pupa mezo pe.

L' asta da pupa son alta pie 30,[h] lanza pie 11.[i] Ano de charoso la dita asta pie 12.

L' asta da prova son alta pie 33,[j] lanza pie 24 e ½.[k] Parti la to alteza per quarto et buta bia una parte che resta vi a pi 24½, et segna el to sallso [?] et fa el to valangin tanto quanto son la to asta alta, et accorda el lanzo con l' alteza tu fara belisimo.

Son alto el magier de bocha a prova pie 16½,[l] et son alto el magier de bocha a pupa pie 22.[m]

La paraschosola e alta a prova pie 9. Parti per quarto de quella da pupa. zoe del charozo, et buta via una parte restera parte n° 3, in tuto saria 9 pie alta la paracosola a prova.

[35] A.S.V., Arsenale, busta 135, ff. 141–42.

[36] A.S.V., Arsenale, busta 135, ff. 141–47; Pantero Pantera, *L'Armate navale* (Rome, 1614), pp. 41–43, says a sudden gust of wind sent all the artillery to one side. There were also complaints of overloading.

[37] Superscript letters refer to Fig. 4.

A darge l' ingornado a le chorbe, tio el to morello a la chorbe
de chavo de sesto da poselese a poselese a la chorbe de chavo de
sesto et fa el to valangin quanto e la to misura che ti a tolto. At
fa chusi a tute le to chorbe.

Fa ch' el to chavvo de sesto averza tanto quanto la nave e in
bocha al magier de bocha. Fa ch' el to balador sia longo quanto
aversi la nave in bocha, zoe in regia.

Fa la to sogia sia a scquara per in fin l' asta, de dagi de saido
[*or* caido?] pie 5. Da la sogia a la zenta son pie 2.

El stilo son longo pie 16. Ano el dito stilo pie 6.

Aversi in triganto pie 18.[n]

El magier de bocha son alta a prova pie 16½, el magier de
bocha son alto a pupa pie 22.

El primo chasaro e alto pie 6,[o] et chusi el segondo.[p]

Aversi la to galion a chavo del brando pie 34.

[The following is in different ink.] Ferir a pupa pie 26. Ferir
a proba pie 12 e quarta 3.

These are the measures of a great galleon.

Length in the keel 20 paces, beam amidships at the first deck
33 ft.,[38] *trepie* 22¼ ft., *siepie* 29 ft.

The narrowing-to applied in design aft: divide [the floor
measure] by fifths and throw away the most so that there will
remain two parts, so much narrowing ought to be made aft; for
the bow divide by thirds and throw away the most so that there
will be one part, so much narrowing ought to be in the bow.

The heightening of the frames is to be given in this fashion:
divide your floor by thirds and take one part and give so much
heightening to the tail frames both fore and aft. Measure with
all the keel. Widening of the tops of the frames: at the bow give
1 ft. of widening to the tops of the frames and in the poop ½ ft.

The sternpost is 30 ft. high, rakes 11 ft. The rising of the
ship's floor at the sternport is 12 ft.

The stem is 33 ft. high, rakes 24½ ft. Divide its height by
fourths and throw away one part so that it remains (that) there
are 24½ ft., and make your *sallso*,[39] and make your curve as far
as your stem is high and arrange the rake in accordance with
the height and you will do beautifully.

The top clamp is 16½ ft. high at the prow and the top clamp
is 22 ft. high at the stern.

---

[38] The diagrams show that this was not the maximum width; that was at the
second deck and was called the *regia*.

[39] Apparently some point marked on the right triangle in which the design of the
stem was drawn out.

The ceiling is 9 ft. high at the prow. Divide by fourths that of the stern, namely the rising of the floor at the sternpost, and throw away one part; there will remain three parts. In all the ceiling at the prow will be 9 ft. high.

To give tumble home[40] to the frames, take your measure at the tail frame from one guiding mark to the other guiding mark[41] on the tail frame and make your curve according to the measure you have taken. And do the same at all your frames.

Make the width of your tail frame [at its maximum width] as much as the ship's beam at the top clamp. Make your forecastle as long as the beam of the ship, that is, at its maximum width [at the second deck at the midship section].

Make your binding strake horizontal through into the [stern] post, and give it 5 ft. of sheer [in the bow]. From this strake to the wale is 2 ft.[42]

The projection of the forecastle is 16 ft. long. The said projection is 6 ft. [high *or* wide?].

The width at the transom is 18 ft.

The top clamp is 16½ ft. high at the prow, the top clamp is 22 ft. high at the stern.

The first sterncastle is 6 ft. high and so the second.

The width of your galleon at the top of the deadwork is 34 ft.

The distance of the after tail frame from the perpendicular is 26 ft. The distance of the fore tail frame from the perpendicular is 12¾ ft.[43]

A MERCHANTMAN

The large round ships used in commerce were commonly called *navi*. They were not built in the Arsenal but in the private shipyards of Venice. The manner in which Theodoro was assigned a shipyard in the

[40] Assuming that *ingornado* here corresponds to *ingahonada* in Timbotta; Anderson, p. 155. I take the sense of the following to be that the inboard curve of the tops of the frames was in some way determined by the curves of the lower parts of the frames.

[41] Both Jal, *Glossaire nautique*, s.v. *posselexe de la paraschuxula,* and Fincati, *Rivista marittima*, XIV, 350, give *posselese* as meaning simply any mark made on a timber to fix the point from which measures were taken. Similar points appear on Theodoro's sketches marked with an X.

[42] A risky rendering partly suggested by the corresponding part of the instructions for the *navi*. I am also indebted to R. C. Anderson for suggestions concerning the meaning of this paragraph, but it would be unfair to hold him in any way responsible for the above form of translation. To just what timber *sogia* refers is not clear to me.

[43] This figure does not make sense, being less than the stem rakes.

Arsenal—by special action of the Council of Ten instead of by the Arsenal officials—implies that he had not spent all his life in its service, but had been previously employed in private shipyards where it is to be expected he would have gained experience in the construction of merchantmen. On the other hand, the specifications for the merchantman, in f. 27, appear to contain fewer of those slight variations from simple rules which are to be found in the instructions for the galleys.[44]

> Rason de una nave de bocha pie 20.[a]
> Questa son la sua rason de una nave de passa 10 in cholomba.[b]
> In bocha pie 20, in trepie pie 13½,[c] in siepie 17½.[d] In fondi pie 7.[e]
> In pontal pie 6½.[f] Erta in la segondo choverta pie 5.[g] Erta in tolda pie 6.[h]
> Ano de partison pie 2 menu quarta. Ano chorbe in partison n° 25, et chusi a pupa.
> Ano de ferir a pupa pie 18 et chusi a prova,[j] che seria tanto le nave aversi in siepie.
> Averzi in regia pie 23.[k] Aversi de sora el morto pie 17.[l]
> Ano de stela a pupa pie 2 a chavo de sesto et chusi a prova.[m]
> A darge l' ingornado, va et tio a chavo de sesto da poselese a poselese, zoe el fondi, et poi fa um valangin. Questa son la sua rason.
> Et erta in chavo da pupa pie 18,[n] lanza pi 6½. Ano de charozo pie 6½.[o] Aversi in triganto pie 13.[t] Erto el magier de bocha a l' asta de pupa pie 13.[p]
> L' asta da prova son alto pie 20,[q] lanza pie 15.[r] Parti la tua alteza per quarto et poi buta via una parte che te rimaniera 15, et fa um valangin quanto son l' asta alta, et poi achorda dove son el lanzo et l' alteza ti fara um bel chavo.
> Son alta la paraschosola a prova pie 4½. Son alto el magier de bocha a prova mezo pe per passo de quel che son a pupa, che seria alto pie 11½.[s]
> Aversi a chavo del brando tanto quanto son la nave in bocha.
> La sogier del balador son longa tanto quanto la nave averzi in regia et ano de sentinado pie 3. Et butate a squara la sogia per in fina al chavo da pupa.
> Questa nave sera la merchandantia.
> S' ti vol saver butar el chostado, varda chomo son questo e poi ti fara anche ti.

These are the measures of a ship of 10 paces in the keel.
Beam 20 ft., width at one third of the depth above the keel 13½ ft., at two thirds above the keel 17½ ft. Floor is 7 ft.

---

[44] Superscript letters refer to Fig. 6.

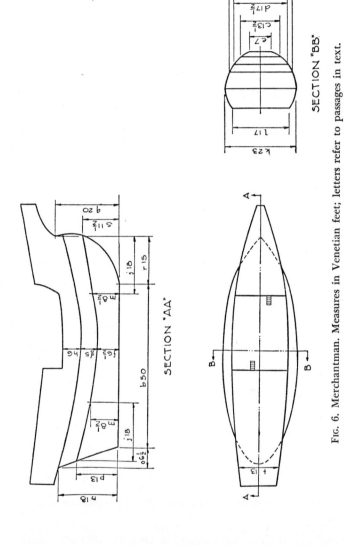

SECTION "AA"

SECTION "BB"

FIG. 6. Merchantman. Measures in Venetian feet; letters refer to passages in text.

Depth 6½ ft. Height of second deck 5 ft. Height of upper deck 6 ft.

The narrowing of the frames is 2 ft. minus ¼. There are 25 frames in which this narrowing is effected, and so aft.

The distance of the after tail frame from the perpendicular is 18 ft. and so in the bow, which will be as much as the half beam of the ship at two thirds of the depth above the keel.

The maximum width at the midship section is 23 ft. The width at the top of the deadwork is 17 ft.

The heightening of the frames aft is 2 ft. at the tail frame and so in the bow.

To give [the frames] tumble home, go and take [measure] at the tail frame from one marked point to the other marked point, namely, [of *or* at] the floor and then make a curve. These are your measures.

And the sternpost is 18 ft. high, rakes 6½ ft. The rising of the ship's floor aft is 6½ ft. The width at the transom is 13 ft. The height of the top clamp at the stern is 13 ft.

The stem is 20 ft. high, rakes 15 ft. Divide your height by fourths and then throw away one part so that you will have left 15, and make your curve according to the height of the stem and then arrange where are the rake and the height and you will make a fine stem.

The ceiling is 4½ ft. high at the prow. The top clamp is, at the prow, ½ ft. per pace of that which it is at the stern, which will be 11½ ft.[45]

The width at the top deck is as much as the beam of the ship [at the first deck].

The strakes of the forecastle are as long as the maximum width of the ship at the midship section. It has 3 ft. of sheer.[46] And you run the [binding] strakes horizontal through to the sternpost.

[45] Meaning ½ ft. per pace lower.

[46] This reading of *sentinado* is suggested by its use in the following very interesting passage in the *Visione di Drachio* concerning the construction of the *cantier*, i.e., the piles upon which the keel was laid. Fourteen such piles were driven, projecting 2 ft. above the ground. "Dapoi, torrano una staziola, overo maestra, che sii dritta, lungha, che arrivi almeno alli tre pali, et debanno principiar a prova a levellar in squara tutti li ditti pali insino all' ultimo palo a poppe segnando la detta livellatione. Fatto questo si alzerano sopra il livellado da prova deti n° otto et at pope deti n° dodeci, che sarano li ditte altezze fuori di squara, lasciando poi calar la trizuola nella mezaria; tenendo pero forti li capi della detta tezuola cosi a prova come a poppe sopra le segni fuori di squara, et lascierano calar la terzuola et in simil modo li darano il sentinato al cantier, segnando immediate per la via della trizuola nelli pali, et sara il detto sentinato deti n° dieci."

This ship will be a merchantman.

If you wish to know [how] to draw the [curve of the] side [or center frame] note how this is,[47] and then you will do so also yourself.

[47] A reference to the accompanying diagram (Fig. 7)?

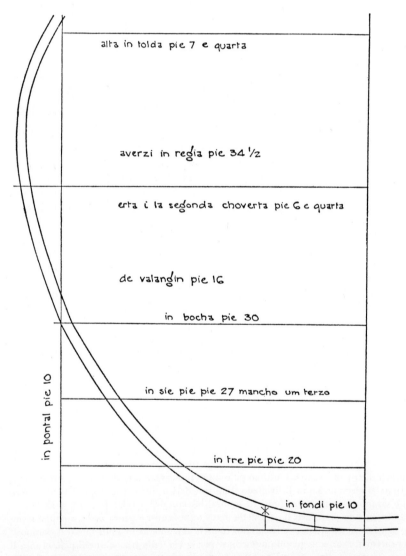

alta in tolda pie 7 e quarta

averzi in regia pie 34 ½

erta i la segonda choverta pie 6 e quarta

de valangin pie 16

in bocha pie 30

in pontal pie 10

in sie pie pie 27 mancho um terzo

in tre pie pie 20

in fondi pie 10

Fig. 7. Sketch from Theodoro's *Instructione*. Midship frame of a merchantman.

12

From Biremes to Triremes[*]

WHEN writing my *Venetian Ships* in 1933 I said that the Venetian galleys were triremes after 1290, following Sanuto the Elder, called Torsello.[1] R. C. Anderson has questioned the date,[2] and a study of the Venetian regulations of the early fourteenth century now leads me to the conclusion that this is too simple a way of describing a change that was in fact quite gradual. Indeed what Sanuto Torsello says in detail is that before 1290 the Venetian galleys were nearly all biremes; then some smart men discovered they could put three to a bench, and "at present," he said, writing sometime between 1306 and 1321, nearly all have three to a bench and some even four or five. He recommended four to a bench as a method that had been given considerable trial and which increased the speed, but obviously he doubted whether any governing council would accept such a proposal.[3]

Much light is thrown on the process of change from bireme to trireme by two provisions in the regulations made by the Venetian senate on January 18, 1303, regarding privately armed galleys leaving that year for the Levant. One passage reads: "The masters of the galleys must hire bowmen, [selected] according to the rules made by the Councils, 30 for each galley, and they must row the galleys *ad terzarolos*, so that, counting the third oars (*terzarolos*) and the other oars,

---

[*] From *The Mariner's Mirror*, XLIX (1963), 48–50. (By permission.)
[1] *Venetian Ships and Shipbuilders of the Renaissance* (Baltimore: The Johns Hopkins Press, 1934), p. 9.
[2] Note in *The Mariner's Mirror*, XXXVI (1950), 154.
[3] Marino Sanuto Torsello, *Liber Secretorum Fidelium Crucis super Terrae Sanctae recuperatione et conservatione* (*Gesta Dei per Francos*, Hanover, 1611), pp. 57, 65, 77. He uses not only the expression "ad terzarolos," but also, p. 65, "ad quartarolos" and "ad quintarolos."

each galley accordingly rows with 166 oars." And again later: "The masters of the galleys must have 180 men for each galley, among them 30 bowmen with their bows, who nevertheless shall be obliged to row. And each galley shall be rowed *ad terzarolos,* so that in consequence they row with 166 oars at least, as has been said."[4]

One hundred and sixty-six oars equally divided between the two sides of the galley gave eighty-three to a side. Since that figure is not divisible by three, we must suppose that some benches had only two oars although most benches had three. Probably there were on each side twenty-five benches manned by three men on each bench and four with only two men. That gives a total of twenty-nine benches to a side and of 166 oarsmen for both sides.

For the galleys going to the English Channel in 1327 the number was raised to 175 rowers out of a total crew of 200.[5] Since these galleys were no longer than those sent to the Levant in 1302,[6] it is reasonable to suppose that they too had twenty-nine benches on each side. In that case there were three men to a bench and one extra oarsman available as a substitute.

The form of these regulations clearly implies that the addition of a third man and a third oar to a bench was not at that time so usual that it could be assumed. It was something extra required by government regulation in order to give to these galleys the status of vessels especially well armed. The Genoese merchant galleys of the time, which were privately operated, had crews of about 150,[7] and some Venetian galleys were also privately operated with much smaller crews.[8] Probably they had only two oarmen to a bench, at least on most benches. Roberto Lopez says that the third man and third oar were added to give speed in battle and suggests that this was first done by Benedetto Zaccaria about 1300.[9]

---

[4] A.S.V., Senato Misti, reg. 1, ff. 186–87, now published in *Le Deliberazioni del Consiglio dei Rogati (Senato)*, *Serie Miztorum,* vol. I (Monumenti storici pubblicati dalla Deputazione di Storia Patria per le Venezie, n.s., vol. xv; Venice, 1960), pp. 89, 90.

[5] *Ibid.,* p. 327, no. 45.

[6] Lane, *Venetian Ships,* Table B.

[7] R. Doehaerd, *Les Relations Commerciales entre Gênes, la Belgique et l'Outre-ment* (Institut Historique Belge de Rome, *Etudes d'histoire économique et sociale,* vol. IV), III, 965; "Les Galères gênoises dans la Manche et la Mer du Nord," *Bulletin de l' Institut Belge de Rome,* vol. xIx, doc. XX.

[8] *Le Deliberazione,* pp. 129, 452.

[9] Roberto S. Lopez, *Storia della colonie genovesi nel Mediterraneo* (Bologna, 1938), pp. 54, 55.

A characteristic of the transition, as is evident from the passages quoted, is the use of the bowmen to pull on the third oars. There is an interesting comment on this practice by the Catalan admiral and soldier Muntaner who wrote a chronicle from 1325 to 1328. After describing a battle in 1285 in which bowmen played a vital part he added:

> And, assuredly, I wish you all to know (and he who tells you this has been in many battles) that on the enlisted cross-bow-men depends the issue of the battle after the galleys tie up the oars. . . . And whilst the galley-slaves [?] row, the cross-bow-men are occupied with their cross-bows, for all Catalan cross-bowmen are people who can renovate a cross-bow and everyone of them knows how to put it together, and how to make the light darts and bolts, and how to twist and tie the string, and he understands all that pertains to a cross-bow. . . . Therefore it is not necessary that the cross-bowmen row like tersols; or if they do, they lose their dexterity with the cross-bow. And, be-sides, the enlisted cross-bowmen do another useful thing; when they see that a sailor in the topmast or a man rowing on his bench is tired and wants to eat or drink, he will come forward and ply his oar for pleasure, until the other man had done what he wished and is refreshed. And thus all cross-bowmen go rested and fresh and make the crew keep fresh. I do not say that, in a fleet, there should not be ten galleys in a hundred with tersols, in order that these might overtake any galleys they come upon.[10]

Muntaner's comment implies that in the 1320's the usual practice was three oarmen to a bench, and he recommends it for the pursuit squadron, but in order to have more bowmen in the main battle he is quite ready to leave most of the galleys operating as biremes.

That bowmen on the Venetian galleys were ordinarily expected to row also is evident from a special provision for exempting from rowing any member of the Great Council who wished to go as bowman on a galley fleet leaving for Romania in the summer of 1301.[11] At the end of the century, in contrast, all the bowmen carried on the galleys were

---

[10] *The Chronicle of Muntaner*, trans. by Lady Goodenough, 2 vols. (Haklyut Society, ser. 2, vol. 47; London, 1920) , chr. 130, pp. 330, 331. The fact that Lady Good-enough translated as "galley slaves" (p. 346) in spite of references to paying the crews (p. 337) casts doubt on the accuracy of her terms, but the passage cited is substantially the same in the translation by J. A. Buchon in vols. 5 and 6 of *Collec-tion des Chroniques Nationales Françaises*.

[11] A.S.V., Maggior Consiglio, Deliberazione, Magnus et Capricornus, f. 17.

expressly forbidden to row or perform any other tasks not connected with bows.[12]

Although the change from two oarsmen to three oarsmen on each bench, like the sharp separation of bowmen from oarsmen, did not occur all in one year, it appears that all Venetian galleys were from the beginning of the fourteenth century so constructed that there was room for three men and three oars to each bench. The enlargement of hull and the adjustment of the outrigger to make this possible are probably the changes first made about 1290 which Marino Sanuto the Elder referred to as the change from bireme to trireme.

[12] *Ibid.,* Senato, Commissioni, reg. 4, formulari, f.51.

13

Merchant Galleys, 1300–34:
Private and Communal Operation*

DETAILED regulation of commerce and industry is more characteristic of the later Middle Ages than of the earlier medieval centuries. If we think of the whole Middle Ages as an epoch when such
regulation was prevalent, it is largely because more records for the later
Middle Ages are preserved. For the earlier centuries the records are less
complete but they suggest there was an earlier period of free enterprise
centering in the time of most rapid economic growth, the twelfth
century. This freedom was not due to any social theory favoring free
enterprise and probably not to deliberate intent of any kind. In large
part is was due to neglect—to the lack of administrative machinery
sufficient to enforce any regulation and to the inability of those
claiming authority to know what was going on in time to regulate it.
Because European economy was expanding rapidly attention was
focused on seizing some of the innumerable opportunities, rather than
on denying those opportunities to others or regulating the way they
were used. Freedom may have stimulated growth; certainly growth
created the opportunities which stimulated freedom.[1]

* From *Speculum*, XXXVIII (1963), 179–205. (By permission.)

For the opportunity to study in Venice in the spring of 1959 and 1961, I wish to
express my gratitude to the John Simon Guggenheim Foundation.

I wish to thank also the staff at the Archivio di Stato di Venezia, especially Dr.
Raimondo Morozzo della Rocca, Dr. Ugo Tucci, Dr. Luigi Lanfranchi, Dr. Maria
Francesca Tiepolo, Dr. Bianca Strina, and Dr. Giulia Mirabella for their gracious
and valuable assistance.

[1] A. B. Hibbert, in *The Cambridge Economic History of Europe* (Cambridge,
1963), III, 181 ff.

In Venice, however, private enterprise was mixed with a tradition of state supremacy, and a readiness to adopt communal management of any activity which those in power thought necessary and individual enterprise was not supplying satisfactorily. Government monopolies and direct government participation in trade were in the tradition inherited from Ptolemaic and Roman times and transmitted by Moslems and especially by the Byzantine empire. The merchants who ruled Venice were quite ready to adopt these methods through the government which they controlled. In time, direct government operation and free private enterprise became submerged by regulated private enterprise, but the development occurred only gradually.

Since maritime transport was basic to all Venice's other industries and to her power, it received constant attention from the governing councils of the commune. In the measures taken by these councils one finds a distinction between the galleys which were equipped with oars and the types of ships which depended entirely on sails. The galleys used in trade, *galee da mercato,* became after 1329 subject to a particular kind of close regulation formulated in the contracts through which galleys owned by the commune were chartered to private operators. Charter contracts of this kind proved so satisfactory that they were put up to auction nearly every year from 1329 to 1534. But before 1329, or perhaps 1325, there were no such auctions. At that time Venetian policy was fluctuating between two extremes; merchant galleys were either communally owned and operated, or privately owned and operated with relatively little supervision. The aim of this paper is to examine the nature of private operation and direct communal operation at the beginning of the century, and to show how they led to a sort of compromise, the annual auction for private operation of galleys built and owned by the commune.

I

Before considering the details of this problem, it is useful to place it in its setting by describing in general terms the five different ways in which the various branches of the shipping industry were organized at one time or another during the whole period 1300–1500, namely: (1) *free* voyages of ships privately owned and operated; (2) *regulated* voyages of ships privately owned and operated; (3) *licensed* voyages of ships privately owned and operated; (4) voyages of communally owned ships *auctioned* for private operation; (5) direct *communal* operation of communally owned vessels, which was more important than has generally been supposed.

The free voyaging—"navigazione libera," as Professor Luzzatto has called it—was not exempt from all regulation.[2] The general codes of maritime law, such as that promulgated by Doge Ranier Zeno in 1255, specified the number of crew required for ships of various sizes and a host of other details. Every year some voyages were forbidden or encouraged because of the political situation or the grain harvests. By "free voyaging" we mean those that were planned by private individuals subject to these rules but with the times of sailing, the routes, the freight rates, and the choice of vessel determined by private agreements.

Unless provision was made for one of the other ways of organizing shipping, we may assume that free voyaging was in effect. It applied in the western Mediterranean and to any voyages into the Atlantic made before the commune of Venice began in 1314 to subsidize and regulate galley voyages to the North Sea. During most years the shipping of the Adriatic was operated by such private initiative, subject to general regulations that protected Venice's lordship of the gulf. Much trade along the coasts or from island to island in the Ionian and Aegean Seas was also little guided by any governmental decisions.

While all that we would call tramp shipping was left to this free voyaging, ships serving the main lines to the Levant had less liberty. If they carried the more valuable kinds of cargo—cloth, cash, bullion, spices, and other "light wares"—they made "regulated" voyages. The times at which they might load in the Levant to come to Venice were specified by law even if the operation of the ships depended entirely on individual initiative. The loading periods and the fleets which loaded at these times were called *mudue* or *mude*. There were two *mude* a year, in spring and fall. Their dates varied from one region to another and according to the type of vessels loaded.[3] Because of the precious cargoes they carried, the government paid particular attention to protecting the galleys or round ships of the *mude*. Sometimes the government determined the freight rates and other economic conditions for these "regulated voyages."

When closer control seemed desirable all the vessels planning to go

---

[2] Gino Luzzatto, *Storia economica di Venezia dal XI al XVI secolo* (Venice: Centro Internazionale delle arti e del costume, 1961) , pp. 47–56; and "Navigazione di linea e navigazione libera nelle grandi città marinare del Medio Evo," in his *Studi di storia economica di Venezia* (Padua, 1954) , pp. 53–57.

[3] See Chap. 9, above.

for a particular *muda* were required to register in advance. Their owners had to post bond as assurance that they would actually sail. When the applicants were subject to approval by an appropriate governmental body they formed what I have called a "licensed voyage." Since this approval was more explicitly provided for in some cases than others, it is hard to draw the line precisely between the regulated voyages and licensed voyages.[4] Typically, the regulated voyages were open to all ships as long as they observed the rules of the *mude*. On licensed voyages the number of vessels was determined by the senate. Those approved were placed under an admiral, a *capitano,* appointed by the commune, who was instructed to lead the fleet on a specified itinerary and make sure that the ships were at all times adequately manned and armed.[5]

Whether the fleet navigated as a unit under a single command and whether it was under a unified economic management were connected but different questions. The former was a military or nautical problem; the latter a problem in business management. The records have

---

[4] As a matter of general principle it might be said that no vessel could leave Venice without the permission of the government and that all departures were registered in the sense that the law required inspection of crews and cargoes. See pp. 237–51. It was an ancient rule that the *Consoli dei Mercanti* could require ships which had begun to accept freight to give security to guarantee their fulfillment of their obligations. *Ibid.,* and A.S.V., Capitolare dei Consoli, cap. 38, 85. They required security of ten *solidi per milliarium,* according to the copy of Zeno's Code at the Library of Congress, Washington, D.C., Law Division, M.S. V46, a provision added to this early copy of the code and there numbered cap. clxxxvi. The same principle was extended to merchant galleys in 1303 when they were required to post security of 2000 *libre* at the ducal palace. This is my reading of A.S.V., Senato Misti, reg. 1, f. 186. I began this study before the publication of this surviving fragment of reg. 1 of Senato Misti and wish to acknowledge my indebtedness to Signora Mirabella of the Archivio di Venezia for her aid in reading this register and other documents. It has now been published in *Le Deliberazioni del Consiglio dei Rogati (Senato) serie Mixtorum,* i: Libri l–xiv, ed. by R. Cessi and P. Sambin, Monumenti Storici pubblicati dalla Deputazione di Storia Patria per le Venezie, n. s., XV (Venice, 1960). The transcript made for me by Signora Mirabella reads: "cuiuslibet galee antequam arment," which makes better sense in the context than "cuiuslibet galee comunis, quam arment," as one reads in *Deliberazioni,* I, 86, no. 309. (Where there is no conflict in readings I cite hereafter this edition by Cessi and Sambin, since it is most available.) Genoese galley masters were required to post a similar bond. See J. M. Pardessus, *Collection de lois maritimes antérieur au dix huitième siècle* (Paris, 1828–45), iv, 439. An example of enforcement of the Venetian requirement to post bond is in A.S.V., Grazie, reg. 1, no. 438.

[5] For a good example of a licensed fleet of cogs in 1405, see A.S.V., Senato Misti, reg. 47, f. 7; for a similar fleet of galleys in 1333, see Senato Misti, reg. 16, f. 3.

sometimes been misinterpreted because the two have not been distinguished. "Armentur per Comune" and "armentur per divisum" were
contrasting terms that meant literally "let there be armed by the
Commune" and "let there be armed separately."[6] "Armentur" meant to
man and equip—most specifically it meant to lay out the cash payments
of advance wages necessary to enlist a crew. "Armentur per Comune"
meant that the Arsenal would supply the ships, the state treasurers find
the coins for the payroll, and government officials enroll the crew.
Freights and expenses were then all for the account of the commune.
"Armentur per divisum" meant that a number of private individuals or
family partnerships acting through joint ventures would furnish the
vessels and enroll crews for the galleys, each of which would then be
operated for the profit or loss of the individual or partnership which
had "armed" it. When the ships were ready to sail, the senate could
decide to what extent they needed to keep together as one fleet.

If each galley master was planning separately how to keep down his
expenses and how to obtain a full cargo, there might be difficulties in
keeping the ships together as a single fleet. One way to meet these
difficulties was to pool freights and expenses. These pools were most
fully developed in the fourth way of organizing transportation enterprises, namely with ships communally owned but auctioned for private

[6] The contrast is particularly clear in the passages printed in *Deliberazioni*, I, 58–60
(June–July, 1302), which show the equivalence of "per divisum" and "cum galeis
singularum personarum," and pp. 84–85 (Dec.–Jan. 1302–3). *Per divisum* is also
used to mean individually "armed" in the regulations made to prevent *armatores*
from freighting wine beyond the legal limit as cargo under the pretense that it was
part of the supplies for the crew. *Ibid.*, I, 327, no. 44. Authorization to arm *per
comune* was generally accompanied by authorization to spend. Such provisions had
to be made months before the galleys sailed. Orders about convoys could in contrast
be issued at the last moment. *Ibid.*, I, 138, no. 127. Misinterpretation of some of the
resolutions I have just quoted, and of others, by applying *per divisum* to the navigation instead of to the business administration is found in Antonio Scialoja, "Un
precedente medioevale dei "Pools" marittimi," in *Studi in Memoria di Bernardino
Scorza* (Rome, 1940), p. 755, no. 6, reprinted also in Scialoja's *Saggi di storia del
diritto marittimo* (Rome, 1946); and in Roberto Cessi, "Le relazioni commerciali
tra Venezia et le Fiandre nel secolo XIV," in his *Politica ed economia di Venezia
nel Trecento* (Rome, 1952), reprinted from the *Archivio Veneto* (1914), pp. 92,
96, 100.

That *per divisum* meant private ownership and operation is evident also in the
return to private enterprise after 1309. The commune then sold its galleys for private
operation. The *rubrica* of the senate's decree reads: "Armentur per divisum et
dentur armare volentibus" (*Deliberazioni*, I, p. 134, no. 88). It was provided in 1312
"quod iste galee armate specialium personarum debeant ire, stare, et redire in con-
serva pro sua securitate" (A.S.V., Maggior Consiglio, Deliberazioni, Presbiter, f. 65 t.)

operation with special orders and privileges for the specific voyage for which they were chartered. They were governed by regulations much like those mentioned above for privately owned ships when they were licensed for specified *mude;* but there was more assurance that the regulations concerning the use of the vessel would be observed by the galley master, as it was not really his vessel. It was his only for the one voyage and under conditions specified in the auction contract concerning the cargo, the crew, the route, and loading, and the upkeep of the vessel. The admiral, the lords of the Arsenal, and other officials charged with enforcing these provisions were in the position of safeguarding the use of state property. The terms of the auction narrowly restricted the sphere of decision of the galley masters even as a group, and the pooling of freights limited more narrowly their range of activity as individual businessmen, but they were in posts of honor, which they had obtained by competitive bidding, and in which they were trying to make a profit for themselves and their partners.[7]

In the fifth form of organization, the galley master, *patronus,* was a salaried official chosen by the commune and sworn to operate the galley for the commune. He swore that he would be present whenever wares were loaded in order to record them, that he would search through the straw in the hold to make sure nothing was hidden, and would keep the hatches bolted down when he and the ship's clerk were not present. He reported on the commercial aspects of the voyage to the doge.[8] Under

---

[7] Scialoja, *Saggi;* my *Venetian Ships and Shipbuilders of the Renaissance* (Baltimore: The Johns Hopkins Press, 1934) , p. 14 n. 23; see also pp. 36–55 above; Jules Sottas, *Les messageries maritimes de Venise aux XIV et XV siècles* (Société d'éditions géographiques maritimes et coloniales; Paris, 1938) , pp. 120 ff.; Alberto Tenenti et Corrado Vivanti, "Le film d'un grand système de navigation: Les galères vénitiennes, XIV–XVI siècles," in *Annales: Économies-Sociétés-Civilisations,* xvi (1961) , 83–86, a geographical preview of an extended study of these auctions.

[8] The duties of a *patronus* of a communally operated galley are specified in detail in *Deliberazioni,* I, 63–65; A.S.V., Senato Misti, reg. 1, f. 163, Aug. 18, 1302; and in the oath of the *patronus* printed in Luigi Fincati, "Splendor e decadenza della marina mercantile di Venezia," *Rivista marittima* (1878) , pt. 2, pp. 165–71. Admiral Fincati says the document was communicated to him by B. Cecchetti, and was found in the Atti dei Proc. di San Marco, Amministrazione degli Instituti Pii Riuniti. Parchment copies of similar oaths for commanders of other types of vessels were generously called to my attention by the present director of the archive, Count Morozzo della Rocca, in Miscellanea Atti diplomatici e private, busta 7 and 9; but we could not find the original of that printed by Admiral Fincati. Its authenticity is to be inferred, however, from its similarity to these other oaths, and from the identity between many of its provisions and the clauses of the regulations of Aug. 18, 1302, in Senato Misti. In dating the oath, the year is omitted. We have only: Aug. 10,

this system of direct communal operation the crew was hired by the same officials who enrolled men for the war galleys and they received pay and rations from these armament officials or from the treasurers.[9] Hiring and disciplining at sea was done by the *capitano,* to whom the galley master reported.[10] Freights were collected at Venice by a special group of customs officials called the *extraordinarii.*[11] The *patronus* was thus an administrative officer reporting to other elements in the communal hierarchy. Unlike the *patronus* of a privately operated galley, he had not invested any of his money to man and outfit the galley; the capital necessary for that purpose had been provided from public funds.

These five methods of organizing maritime transportation were differently applied to different types of vessels. Free voyaging was the general rule for nearly all the smaller sailing ships, at least after the thirteenth century, and also for many of the larger round ships—the cogs and caracks of the fourteenth and fifteenth centuries.[12] But the cogs and caracks carrying cotton and other "light wares" in the eastern Mediterranean were operated either in "regulated" voyages or in more tightly organized "licensed" fleets. Such fleets of cogs were very frequent in the first part of the fifteenth century.[13] By that time the merchant galleys were almost all owned by the commune and chartered by annual auctions for private operation. In the early fourteenth century, in contrast, there were a large number of merchant galleys in private hands. A few of these galleys operated under free voyaging, generally manned by a crew that was small for a galley and using relatively few

---

thirteenth indiction. This thirteenth indiction came in 1300, 1315, and 1330. I believe the correct date is 1330, for the oath contains a clause, the reason for which will be discussed below, regarding the obligation of the *patronus* for wares damaged on board. This was enacted by the Maggior Consiglio, June 17, 1324 (M. C., Delibera-zioni del Maggior Consiglio, Fronesis, f. 135, old numbering). Direct communal operation of merchant galleys had practically ceased in 1330, but there had been occasion for drawing up the oath for the commander of such a vessel for the voyage to Romania regularly nearly each year for a decade before 1329, and in 1330, prob-ably in August, galleys at Ragusa were empowered to load freight to come to Venice (*Deliberazioni,* I, 425, no. 166).

[9] The oath above cited and that of the *ufficiali al armamento* in the Miscellanea atti above cited, busta 9, no. 327. See also M.C., Deliberazioni, Fronesis, f. 155.

[10] Senato Misti, reg. 1, f. 163. Initial enrollment was the responsibility of the *ufficiali al armamento.*

[11] M.C., Avogaria di Comune, Deliberazioni del Maggior Consiglio, Liber Magnus, f. 52 t; A.S.V., Miscellanea Codici, no. 131, 132.

[12] Luzzatto, *Studi,* pp. 56–57.

[13] The examples cited above in n. 5 and in my *Venetian Ships,* pp. 255–56.

200 *VENICE*

oars.[14] But most of the privately owned galleys were used for regulated or licensed voyages. These galley voyages of the early fourteenth century were organized much as were the regulated and licensed voyages of cogs a hundred years later. There were also in the early fourteenth century some voyages of communally owned galleys and they were operated directly by the commune.

Direct communal operation was not then anything new. It was the commune which had contracted in 1201 to furnish a huge fleet for the Fourth Crusade. In 1268 it offered to rent to Louis IX ships that it owned as well as some belonging to Venetian nobles.[15] In the thirteenth century, before the development of the type of ship which came to be known as the *galea da mercato,* the commune of Venice owned and operated some large round ships which carried wares for Venetian merchants.[16] Although the evidence concerning the thirteenth century deserves more study, the methods then used appear to have been at one extreme or the other: private operation of vessels privately owned or communal operation of vessels communally owned. At the opening of the fourteenth century Venetian policy was still wavering between these alternatives.

II

How to organize the galley voyages—whether by communal management or individual initiative, and under what basic rules—was very much an open question at the beginning of the fourteenth century. It came before Venice's governing councils nearly every year in relation to one or another of the areas in which Venetian shipping was active. From this point of view there were four such areas: (1) the Adriatic, (2) the Black Sea and what was then called Romania, approximately Constantinople and what we call Greece, (3) Egypt and *Oltremare,* and (4) the West. "Beyond the sea" (*Oltremare*) meant not only Palestine but all the lands which had once been conquered by the Crusaders. In practice it meant at this time Cyprus and Lajazzo, the port of the kingdom of Lesser Armenia which became of major

[14] Examples of references to such galleys, all in the 1320's, are Avogaria di Comune, Deliberazioni del Maggior Consiglio, Brutus, ff. 52 t, 86 t; Grazie, reg. 3, f. 10; R. Predelli, *I Libri commemoriali, Regesti* (in Monumenti storici publicati dalla R. Deputazione Veneta di Storia Patria, ser. 1, Documenti), I, 270, no. 457.

[15] A. Jal, *Archéologie navale* (Paris, 1840), mémoire 7.

[16] The oath of a salaried *patronus navis comunis* going on a voyage to Accon in 1282 has much detail concerning how he and his *socius* (a second *patronus,* I presume) should collect freights (Misc. Atti Diplomatici e privati, busta 7, pergamena no. 235).

commercial importance when the Christians lost their last port in Palestine by the Mameluke capture of Acre in 1291. There is justification for lumping under the heading "West" such diverse places as Tunis, Sicily, the Balearic Islands, and Atlantic ports, for in 1300 separate lines to these various areas had not been developed, although Venetian shipping was penetrating westward from the Ionian Sea.[17]

Immediately after the conclusion of the peace with Genoa in 1299 there was intense concern about the safety of the voyages to Apulia.[18] The carefully armed fleet sent in the fall of 1300 contained both "galee comunis" and "galee specialium personarum."[19] Within two years that voyage was turned over to private enterprise with plans for three convoys a year, each consisting of at least three galleys. Cash and some wares were to move only by galley.[20] But the plan did not work; private initiative failed to arm that many galleys. First two, then one galley was declared sufficient.[21] Soon the route was opened to unarmed ships, and since they were not limited to specified sailing seasons, in 1306 galleys also were permitted to sail whenever they wished.[22] The Adriatic was thus gradually turned over to free voyaging.

During the first decade of the fourteenth century voyages west were also left to private enterprise. The two other areas, Romania and *Oltremare,* were those in which various systems of organizing regulated convoys were tried out.

As long as Venice remained at war with the Byzantine empire, which had not been included in the peace made with Genoa in 1299, operation by the commune was preferred in that area. In 1301 Venice also had reason to fear the Sicilian fleets off Greece.[23] Early in that year, the senate decided that ten to twenty galleys, as many as could be made

[17] Regions beyond "capud de Porsano" (Capo Bruzzano in Calabria) were lumped together in a number of regulations concerning shipping (*Deliberazioni*, I, 95; p. 441, no. 4; A.S.V., Senato Misti, reg. 15, f. 100).

[18] *Deliberazioni*, I, 7–10.

[19] A.S.V., Maggior Consiglio, Deliberazioni, Magnus et Capricornus, f. 11, Oct. 15 and Nov. 23, 1300. Special provisions for the arming of galleys going to Apulia begin "Quod cercatores galearum Apuliae et specialium personarum pro utilitate Comunis et specialium personarum"—which implies that there were both kinds of galleys in the fleet.

[20] *Ibid.*, p. 61, no. 221, although p. 62, no. 222, might appear in conflict. In view of what follows it seems best to interpret it as a rejection of a proposal to reconsider.

[21] *Ibid.*, p. 74, no. 270; p. 82, no. 296.

[22] *Ibid.*, p. 80, no. 289; p. 111, no. 102; A.S.V., Avogaria di Comune, Deliberazioni del Maggior Consiglio, Magnus, f. 11.

[23] Paolo Sambin, "La politica mediterranea di Venezia alla fine della guerra del Vespro," *Atti del Reale Istituto Veneto di Scienze, Lettere ed Arti,* CIV (1944–45), p. 2, 972–93.

ready, should be armed to go to the Levant. Part were privately armed, part armed by the commune, but they were all under orders of the admirals appointed by the government.[24] Three galleys were to remain in the Adriatic, three to go to Crete, Cyprus, and Armenia for trade, and the rest were to turn northward in the Aegean to pillage the lands of the Byzantine emperor. When the fleet from Armenia was returning in May, the other squadrons were ordered to go into the Ionian Sea to protect it from possible attack by the Sicilians, and to provide additional transportation for wares which had accumulated at Crete and Modon for shipment to Venice.[25]

The spring fleet being safely back in the Adriatic, the senate debated for several days in July, 1301, how the fall voyage should be organized. Some senators favored finding five or six private galleys which would be operated by their merchant owners, but the final decision was that six be outfitted by the commune.[26] Before they left in October or November, a seventh was added to take care of the large amount of merchandise that had been presented for loading.[27] All went as far as Crete, whence three or four went on to Lajazzo. Although the possibility of diverting these galleys for a raid on Constantinople was considered, this was in effect a purely commercial voyage. All the galleys, except possibly one, were nevertheless operated directly by the commune.[28]

When the time came to prepare the spring and fall fleets of 1302, the senate again rejected proposals that galleys be armed "per speciales personas" or "per divisum" and voted instead for arming "per

[24] Both private and public galleys are referred to in a resolution which seems to apply to this fleet (A.S.V., Maggior Consiglio, Deliberazioni, Magnus et Capricornus, f. 13 t) . Private operators received loans from the Bailo of Negroponte. *Deliberazioni,* I, 10, no. 47. The commune pawned salt in order to have the cash for "arming" its galleys. *Ibid.,* p. 14, no. 57. "Galee nostri Comunis" are also mentioned, *ibid.,* p. 11, nos. 48, 49.

[25] *Ibid.,* p. 14, no. 56; pp. 17, 18, 21–25; p. 32, no. 113; p. 34, no. 117.

[26] *Deliberazioni,* I, 35–36; A.S.V., Senato Misti, reg. 1, f. 131 t; Scialoja, *Mem. Scorza,* pp. 755–56, interpreted this as an unsuccessful effort to find private operators who were ready to go.

[27] *Deliberazioni,* I, 43, no. 159.

[28] *Ibid.,* p. 40, no. 143, 148; A.S.V., Senato Misti, reg. 1, f. 140; Sambin, *op. cit.,* p. 983. The galley which Marino Morosini had recently built to replace one seized by Sicilians was proposed for the voyage, to sail in convoy but be privately operated. A proposal concerning how freights would be distributed in that case was defeated. *Deliberazioni,* p. 36, no. 128, *Regesti, Libri Commemoriali,* ed. Predelli, vol. I, lib. 1, nos. 44–46.

Comune."[29] The fleet of twelve galleys, leaving in April, 1302, had a combined military and commercial assignment. Four vessels were to be detached at Monemvasia to go to Cyprus and Armenia. The others were to wage war in the Aegean, but at least one of these was to load merchants and their wares from Greek ports on the return voyage.[30] In the fall of 1302 a new fleet was outfitted for trade to *Oltremare* and for this fleet the senate drew up detailed rules regarding the duties of a salaried galley master.[31] Meanwhile, the galleys making raids in the Aegean carried the war into the Dardenelles and were so successful that the Byzantine emperor sued for a truce.[32]

After peace was restored in 1303, communal operation was discontinued for a few years; but it was resumed in 1305 for the fleet going to Cyprus and Egypt.[33] Alexandria had been added to the termini of the eastern voyages after appeals to the pope for permission.[34] Then, after Venice in 1306 entered into a league with Charles of Valois for the restoration of the Latin empire, all galley voyages eastward became governmentally operated.[35] Again the movement of the galleys was guided by three objectives: to pass around Greece safely in spite of the threat of Sicilian fleets, to plunder profitably Byzantine territories in the Aegean, and to trade with Greece, Cyprus, Armenia, and Egypt.

The complication of achieving all these three objectives is presented especially clearly in 1308 because that is one of the few years for which we have the record of the letters sent by the doge and his council. These letters give a glimpse of many aspects of communal operation. There

[29] *Deliberazioni*, I, 48, nos. 172, 173; p. 59, nos. 211, 213.

[30] *Ibid.*, pp. 50–52, no. 183.

[31] *Ibid.*, p. 59, no. 213; pp. 63–65, nos. 226, 227; p. 70, no. 248; and see above, n. 8. As in 1301, merchants going to Negroponte were to be disembarked at Patras. Later there was debate whether a galley being sent in the fall to Constantinople to carry the ambassador to negotiate peace should be allowed to carry merchandise (*ibid.*, pp. 79–80).

[32] Cronica Justiniana (Bibl. Naz. Marciana, Venice, MS. Lat., Cl. X, cod. 237) f. 60 t; Sambin, *op. cit.*, p. 985.

[33] *Deliberazioni*, I, 112–14, nos. 119, 121, 123, 129, 131, 135; I, 117–20, nos. 177–80, 194–95, 197.

[34] Sambin, *op. cit.*, pp. 994–95; *Deliberazioni*, I, 104; and the text of one of these decrees preserved in the Capitolare Vicedominorum Ternarie (Bibl. Naz. Marciana, Venice, MS. Lat., Cl. V, cod. 6) f. 33 t.

[35] On the league, Camillo Manfroni, *Storia della marina italiana dal trattato di Ninfeo alla caduta de Constantinopoli*, pt. 1 (Leghorn, 1902), pp. 229–30. On private galleys going to the Black Sea in 1305 and 1306, see *Deliberazioni*, pp. 107–8, 115–16, and p. 118, nos. 180, 183, 185.

were as many as five admirals commanding various fleets, all of which had been armed directly by the commune, and the ducal council strove to keep all five informed and acting in concert. They were ordered to gather at Modon and decide whether the dangers were sufficient to justify restricting commercial operations by keeping the fleet together. It was assumed that almost certainly a fleet would be sent to *Oltremare* but it was not to visit any of the Syrian ports which were under the Mameluke sultan unless it numbered as many as seven vessels. If the galleys did separate and some went to Egypt, the *capitano generale* was to accompany them with three of his war galleys and was authorized to take men off other ships to be sure that his own were well armed. It was easier to make such a provision when all the crews were in the pay of the commune, whether on trading galleys or war galleys. These fleets were to be supplied with biscuits by the duke of Crete at such a price that there would be neither gain nor loss. How they were financed is indicated by the orders to the *capitani* going to Alexandria and Cyprus to pay out of the freights they would collect overseas 400 *bizanti* and 600 *sarazenati*, respectively, to specified merchants, evidently men from whom the commune had borrowed the money spent in Venice on outfitting and wages. The balance from collection of freights was to be invested in pepper for the return voyage. The *capitano* going to Alexandria was also instructed to buy various drugs desired by Gualtieri, a state-salaried physician. On their return these galleys were to load in Crete and southern Greece the wares ready there for shipment to Venice. This merchandise could also be loaded by some of the galleys which had been employed meanwhile in purely military operations in the Aegean and Ionian Seas.[36]

Military demands or threats produced a fair number of other instances of communal operation during the first two decades of the fourteenth century[37] but private operation became the general rule

---

[36] *Lettere di Collegio, 1308–1310,* ed. by G. Giomo (Miscellanea di Storia Veneta, ser. 3, t. i) , pp. 271–382, nos. 16, 35–55, 64. That the payments were for drafts which the council had sold in Venice to merchants willing to take payment overseas is suggested by the wording, "satisfacere creditoribus . . . et debent recipere suam solutionem dies xv postquam vos applicueritis in Cypro" (nos. 39, 40) .

[37] As explained in n. 50, there are difficulties in dating some of the references to fleets. Although the following references to communal operation (1308–18) may not, therefore, in all cases be assigned to the right years, they seem worth noting:

In 1311–13 to *Oltremare* and Egypt without detail as to years, see *Deliberazioni,* p. 135, nos. 96–97; p. 138, no. 127; and compare the edition of the *rubriche* by Giomo in *Archivio Veneto,* xvii (1879) , 260.

after 1302. Under the provisions made in 1303, privately owned galleys were operated in the Levant on "regulated" voyages.

The loading periods of the privately operated galleys, their *mude,* were regulated somewhat differently from those of the round ships which made similar voyages. In both spring and fall galleys were allowed to load at a later date than were round ships.[38] No unarmed galley could load just before or just after the fully armed galleys.[39] Coin and specified kinds of valuable merchandise, such as western cloth, could be carried only on the galleys, and if "light wares" of any kind were imported to Venice on round ships they were subject to a duty of 5 per cent which was not paid for wares imported on the galleys.[40]

The advantages given to operators of galleys were counterbalanced by many obligations, some in favor of the crews, but even more in favor of the shippers. The galley masters were forced to act as common carriers. They were required to load all merchandise presented as long as they had space; refusal to accept wares was subject to a fine of 5 *libre* per bale or 10 *libre* for each kantar refused. The galley masters could not charge freights higher than those which had been fixed for the communally operated galleys. They were supposed not to favor them-

---

In 1313 all galleys were taken over briefly by the commune. See A.S.V., Maggior Consiglio, Deliberazioni, Presbiter, f. 104.

In 1315 and 1316, voyage unspecified (*ibid.*, Clericus Civicus, f. 20; *Deliberazioni,* p. 162, no. 183; p. 164, no. 205).

In 1316 galleys which had been on patrol "ad custodiam nostrorum" were ordered on their return to load wares offered at Valona and ports along the way to Venice (A.S.V., Maggior Consiglio, Deliberazioni, Clericus Civicus, f. 36).

In 1318 galleys of the commune to Negroponte and Constantinople (*ibid.*, p. 185, nos. 95–96).

[38] The spring loading period in regions beyond Crete was, for example: for galleys, Apr. 1 to May 15; for *navi,* Mar. 15 to Apr. 15 (*Deliberazioni,* I, pp. 85–86, no. 308; p. 93, no. 318).

[39] *Ibid.*, p. 104, no. 11. The round ships are referred to as *disarmate* because they were without oars and with much smaller crews than the galleys. At the beginning of the fourteenth century some galleys were operated as "unarmed," but to do so they had to have special permission if they had crews of more than twenty-five. On the other hand, more than sixty men certainly were necessary to make a galley "armed," and the standard under Venetian law was 180 (*ibid.*, p. 129, no. 25; p. 138, no. 130; p. 362, no. 38; A.S.V., Grazie, reg. 3, f. 10; M.C., Deliberazioni, Clericus Civicus, f. 11 t). My references to galleys always mean armed galley unless otherwise specified.

[40] Avog. di Com., Delib. del M.C., Magnus, f. 8 t, 6, 39 t; M.C., Deliberazioni Magnus et Capricornus, f. 41; *Deliberazioni del Maggior Consiglio di Venezia,* ed. R. Cessi, in *Atti delle Assemblee Constituzionali Italiane,* II (R. Accademia dei Lincei; Bologna, 1931), 72; Senato Misti, reg. 15–16 copia, f. 97; *Deliberazioni,* pp. 85–86; p. 93, no. 318.

selves or their partners over other shippers in any way such as by allowing more weight of heavy freight with each bale of cloth. As had been the case when the galleys were operated by the commune, the galley master had to provide passage for each merchant who shipped as many as ten bales or paid as much as 20 *solidi grossorum* of freight, allowing him space 2 ft. in breadth and permitting him to bring on board without extra charge a quilt and mattress (not weighing more than 30 *libre* between them), a casket, a valise, and arms for himself and his servant.[41]

While these provisions remind us that many merchants still traveled with their wares, they may give an exaggerated impression of how much that was the case. Even if much trade was already organized by resident merchants who shipped wares to agents resident overseas, as seems likely, the galleys were still important as passenger ships. Many merchants moving their base from one city to another preferred galleys to round ships, not only because the galley voyage was safer but because it was more interesting. The galleys stopped at more trading centers along the way and so gave better opportunities to meet people and see the sights.

As a rule, round ships did not sail together in convoys, but galleys were under definite obligation to do so. They were ordered to keep together as far as Coron and to wait a day along the way for any of their number wishing to unload at Corfu or Chiarenza. After they passed around Morea and spread out to different ports, there were to be at least two convoying each other whenever that was possible. On their return they were expected to come together again at Coron or Modon into a single "caravan."[42]

A main burden of sailing in convoy was the obligation to wait for other ships, since each day of operation cost the operators heavily in pay and food for nearly 200 men, as well as uncalculable amounts in business lost. Thus in 1303 a partnership headed by Marco Barbo and Andrea da Mosto objected violently to having to await at Negroponte, which was as far as they intended to go, for the arrival of a galley operated by a partnership headed by Marco Contarini and Marco Morosini, which was going to Thessalonica. Special arbiters appointed by the doge settled the dispute by ordering the one galley to wait for the

[41] *Deliberazioni,* I, 87–91.

[42] *Ibid.,* p. 85, no. 307, for galleys to *Oltremare;* and Avog. Com., Delib. dei M.C., Magnus, f. 9 t, for extension of the rule to galleys going to Alexandria or the Byzantine empire.

other, but these judges recognized that the galley of Ca' Barbo might suffer heavy loss because the galley of Ca' Contarini delayed at Thessalonica, and therefore they required the latter to pay a sort of "demurrage fee," namely 25 *solidos grossorum* for each day that the Barbo galley had to wait after it was ready to sail. The *baiulo* and his council at Negroponte were to certify the day when the Barbo galley was really ready to sail and the day when the Contarini galley arrived.[43]

Whenever ships sailed in convoy they were under single command, that of a *capitano*. If no other provision was made, the galley masters took turns acting as *capitano*.[44] The primary functions of this official were nautical and military; he issued the orders to sail or anchor and to attack or avoid engagement if another fleet was encountered. He was also charged with enforcing the special rules made for the safety of the ships under his command,[45] but the duty of inspecting to see that the number of crew, their arms, their rations, the reserve of provisions, and the conditions of loading were according to the legal requirements fell mainly on various officials in Venice, on the rectors in Venetian colonies, and on some of the merchant passengers generally called the *navigatores*. For example, the regulations in 1303 provided that two merchants on each galley be chosen overseas by the rectors to check the ship's stores and the daily rations given the crew. They were to keep the crew at full strength by hiring additional seamen as needed. Even when a galley was sailing alone and there was no *capitano*, such *navigatores* were appointed by the merchants and the galley master.[46]

The authority of the *capitano* over the vessels thrown together in convoy on the regulated voyages may have been slight or sparingly exercised. Certainly there are more records about inspections by officials in Venice and about the committees of merchant passengers

---

[43] A.S.V., Libri Commemoriali, reg. 1, f. 37; summarized in Predelli's *Regesti*, vol. I, lib. 1, no. 128.

[44] In 1303 the senate voted that the doge and council should appoint a *capitano* of every galley (*Deliberazioni*, I, 85, no. 305). Since a galley commander was called *patronus* or *comitus*, I interpret this resolution as an affirmation of the principle that every armed galley should be under the jurisdiction of some government-appointed official, and the ducal council was responsible.

[45] In both Zeno's Code of 1255, cap. lxxiii, lxxv, lxxvi, and in the forms for the commissions given *capitani* by the doge, A.S.V., Senato, Commissioni, reg. 4, it is evident that the *capitano* was responsible above all for the safety of the galleys.

[46] *Deliberazioni*, I, 87–91; p. 115, no. 78; *Delib. del M.C.*, ed. Cessi, III, 153. On the inspecting officials at Venice, see pp. 246–51, below.

than about these admirals of the regulated fleets.[47] In 1319 we hear of a galley of Ca' Contarini at Corfu which was supposed to be part of a convoy commanded by Fantin Dandolo, an experienced admiral. Nevertheless the Contarini galley decided on its own to attack a Corfiote vessel. The parties damaged also ignored the admiral. They asked and obtained reparation from an agent of the Contarini partnership.[48]

In spite of the mass of legislation applying generally to "regulated voyages," each individual galley had considerable freedom in deciding questions connected with a specific voyage. The general rules having been laid down, the owners of a galley could decide for themselves without any further action by the senate whether they would send their vessel on a spring or fall voyage, or both. They could pick their ports of call and change their routes subject only to the contracts they had made with shippers. The obligation to go in convoy applied only in case there was another galley going to the same ports at the same season. Each galley was competing with others in trying to keep down expenses, obtain customers, and make a profit—in short each was a separate business venture.

On the licensed voyage there was more collective action. One way to overcome the difficulties of operating many galleys together as a single fleet was to pool all freights and expenses. Eventually such pooling was required by law for both licensed and auctioned fleets, but it probably began by private agreements, as was certainly the case in this same period among the Genoese, whose laws also required that galleys wait for each other so that two at least might sail in convoy.[49] Pooling freights was made easier when specified "licensed" vessels were given by the senate a monopoly for a season of a particular voyage.

The first examples of such licensed voyages appear to be those to

---

[47] On inspections of merchant galleys in Venice, see A.S.V., Maggior Consiglio, Deliberazioni, Magnus et Capricornus, f. 11, 13 t, 41; Clericus Civicus, f. 97, and on the rectors overseas, *ibid.*, f. 98. Also, *Grazie*, ɪ, nos. 55, 95, 185. In later *Grazie*, to be sure (A.S.V., reg. 3) there are condemnations of *patroni* made because of violations reported by the *capitani*, but these are in the 1330's, when even the galleys going to Armenia can be considered a licensed fleet, and after a new regulation made in 1329 tightened the *capitano's* control of the collection of freights by forbidding a *patronus* to load any wares without having a specific permit, a *boletta*, from the *capitano*.

[48] A.S.V., Libri Commemoriali, reg. 2, f. 93, summarized in Predelli's *Regesti*, vol. I, lib. 2, no. 171.

[49] Renée Doehaerd, "Les galères génoises dans la Manche et la mer du nord à la fin du XIII et au début du XIV siècle," *Bulletin de l'Institut Historique Belge de Rome*, xɪx (1938), doc. xx, xxɪɪɪ; Pardessus, *op. cit.*, ɪv, 496, 501; Scialoja, *Saggi*, pp. 255–56.

Flanders. Although the Venetians may have sent ships to the North Sea earlier, 1315 is the first date at which we can feel sure that Venetian galleys made the voyage as an organized fleet.[50] Because of difficulties with the routes through Lombardy and Germany, the commune was willing in 1314 to give much encouragement to entrepreneurs who would open an alternate route to western markets and "French" woolens.[51] Those who would register and post bond as assurance that they would actually make the voyage were offered in return an outright subsidy of 12 or 15 *libre grossorum* a month and were loaned 10,000 *libre* to help them meet the large advance wage payments necessary to recruit a crew. They had to load wares at freight rates fixed by the government. No minimum or maximum number of galleys going was fixed by the senate; probably it had reason to believe that two or three galleys would announce for the voyage.[52]

In 1317 and 1318 private operators of Flanders were given a new form of subsidy, the use of state-owned galleys, rent free. The leader of the Atlantic enterprise at this point seems to have been Dardi Bembo. A proposal that he and Michele Dolfin made in 1317 for operating the galleys was accepted. Their fleet was given the right to export Cretan wine as well as spices and silks, and to bring back French cloth, but it

[50] Roberto Cessi, "Le relazioni commerciali tra Venezia e le Fiandre nel secolo XIV (cited above in n. 6), p. 80, accepted 1313 as the date of the first senatorial enactment concerning a voyage to Flanders. This date, and 1314 for the actual voyage, was that decided on by A. Schaube, "Die Anfänge der venetianischen Galeerenfahrten nach Nordsee," *Historische Zeitschrift,* ser. 3, v (1908), 30. Schaube inferred dates from the paging of the rubrics as then published by Giomo, and to confirm these dates he used Giomo's "Regesto di alcune deliberazioni del Senato Misti," *Archivio Veneto,* XXIX (1885), 403 ff., and XXX (1886), 179 ff., in which he cited nos. 303 and 304 as evidence of dates in Misti, IV, but ignored nos. 305 and 306, which show that entries in that volume were not all in chronological order. Cessi also ignores this uncertainty in his recent edition of these rubrics but he now places the crucial rubric under the date November, 1314, *Deliberazioni,* I, 152, no. 72, and puts later references to the departure of these galleys under 1315. His new dating seems more consistent with such indications as I can find elsewhere, as in the Deliberazioni of the Maggior Consiglio, about later voyages. It leaves us no evidence for earlier years and none for 1316 except that there was a resolution throwing the voyage open to anyone who would post bond assuring that he would go through with it (*ibid.,* I, 164, no. 206). I know no evidence of whether any went, but the sea route received additional stimulus from the fact that the king of France banned Flemings from the fairs of Champagne in 1315. Doehaerd, *op. cit.* pp. 8–9. Also, famine in northwest Europe drew grain ships from the Mediterranean in 1316 (Schaube, "Die Anfänge," pp. 46–47).

[51] Cessi, pp. 78–79, and Schaube, p. 38.

[52] *Deliberazioni,* I, pp. 152–53, no. 73, 74, 79.

had no legal assurance of monopoly.[53] The command of the outbound fleet was entrusted by the senate to Gabriel Dandolo, who was going as ambassador to negotiate privileges at Bruges, but on the return voyage Dardi Bembo was in command, as we hear because of an episode at Majorca. On the outward voyage, the three galleys took with them three Greek slaves "liberated" from the Majorcans—stolen, so the latter claimed. When the galleys stopped at Majorca on the way back, Bembo refused to give up the three Greeks. Instead, so said the Majorcans, his galleys carried off five more.[54]

For 1318 new galleys were ordered. The government gave the contract for their construction to Dardi Bembo, Gabriel Dandolo, and Michele Dolfin, and then entrusted their operation to Dardi Bembo, Gabriel Dandolo, and Andriolo Baseio. The galleys were constructed larger than the measures stipulated, able to carry more cargo, but Bembo and his associates were voted a pardon for that offense by the Great Council.[55]

So successful was this venture that there seemed no need of subsidy to keep the voyage going in 1319, except that the commune paid high for

[53] *Ibid.*, I, p. 167, no. 250; p. 170, no. 283, 284; p. 172, no. 309; M. C., Deliberazioni, Clericus Civicus, f. 54.

[54] Predelli, *Libri Commemoriali, Regesti,* vol. I, lib. 2, no. 219, and in A.S.V., reg. 2, f. 86 t. Schaube, p. 50, places the incident at Majorca a year later.

[55] M.C., Deliberazioni, Clericus Civicus, f. 133 t (Jan. 14, 1317–18) for the government buying of the galleys; *ibid.,* f. 140 (Mar. 28, 1318) for the sale of that of Ca' Dolfin; *ibid.,* f. 144 t (Apr. 5, 1318) for the pardon. It refers to galleys "quas comune dedit eis pro viagio Flandriae quas fieri fecit ad mensuras galee Francisco Barbo." The three accused pleaded successfully that it was not possible to make two galleys alike in all their measures, which shows they were held responsible for the construction. Perhaps they had to pay rent of 10 *libre grossorum* a month, for a rubric which Cessi dates December, 1317, provides for accepting the offer of Marino Zeno and supplying him with a galley at that rent if he needs it (*Deliberazioni*, I, 185, no. 89). Cessi in "Le Relazioni commerciali," p. 87, following Schaube, pp. 49–50, interprets this as applying to the Flemish voyage. The word "Flanders" does not appear in the rubric itself, however; it was inserted by the editors because of the heading under which the rubric appears. But from that context it could equally well apply to a special galley going to Marseilles or Aigues-Mortes. See Giomo's edition in *Archivio Veneto,* xix, 93. Schaube also mistakenly applies to the Flemish galleys the decision to have the senate elect two *patroni* (see p. 51). They were I believe for the two "gallee comunis" going to Negroponte. See above n. 37. He believed there were two fleets in 1318, one of two galleys going to Bruges, the other of three galleys to Antwerp (*ibid.,* pp. 51–52). Because of the uncertainty over the dates of the items referred to in the rubrics, my account is guided as far as possible by the indications of the Deliberazioni del Maggior Consiglio. Flemish sources record the arrival in Antwerp in May, 1318; see Schaube, "Die Anfänge," p. 50.

the passage of a new ambassador to Flanders.[56] The commune having sold off in November, 1318, the galleys that had made the voyage that year, five new galleys, which went heavily armed, were provided by private operators who again included Bembo.[57] The fleet called at Southampton and there a fight developed between its crew and the townsmen which led to the interruption of all calls at English ports for the next five or six years.[58]

The voyage continued with Bruges or Antwerp as terminus. When the political situation made the selection of port difficult it was left to a council of the galley masters and the *capitano,* or to the merchants, galley masters, and *capitano,* sometimes represented by an elected group called the Council of Twelve. Inevitably the operators of this fleet had to be given more independent discretionary powers than were allotted to fleet commanders in the Levant, where there were many other Venetian officials nearby. The *capitano* of the Flemish fleet appears to have been rather an agent of the whole body of merchants and *armatores* than an agent of the senate.[59] He commanded a rather powerful force, for in fixing the size of the fleet in 1322 and 1327 the senate required that they be "at least six,"[60] carrying more than 1,200 armed men.

While the Flemish voyage was thus developing under private initiative and management, the Black Sea voyage was also expanded but under communal management. An important new eastern terminus for the voyage was obtained by a treaty with the emperor of Trebizond in 1319.[61] Although for several years previously fleets going to the Black

[56] *Deliberazioni,* I, 199, no. 265–66; p. 204, no. 317, 319, 320; p. 205, no. 324, 327, 331. A.S.V., Maggior Consiglio, Deliberazioni, Fronesis, f. 15 t.

[57] *Ibid.,* Fronesis, copia, f. 9 on the sale. There are two conflicting rubrics for the senate's action about these galleys, both referring to lib. V, f. 88 of the lost registers of the senate. See Giomo's edition in *Archivio Veneto,* xvii, 267, and xviii, 53. Only one of these two rubrics is printed in the *Deliberazioni,* I, 198. Bembo's interest appears from the provision that "illis di Ca Bembo et Tingo et sociis" be paid 10 *libre grossorum* out of the customs collected from the galleys. This was about two thirds of the passage money for the ambassador, assuming, as I do, that the latter had been expressed in *libre ad grossos* (*Deliberazioni,* p. 205, no. 324, 327; p. 211, no. 406).

[58] Schaube, "Die Anfänge," pp. 53–56; Alwyn A. Ruddock, *Italian Merchants and Shipping in Southampton* (Southampton Records Series; Oxford, 1951), pp. 25, 141–42.

[59] *Deliberazioni,* I, 232, no. 137, 140, 143; p. 334, no. 117; p. 366, no. 78.

[60] *Ibid.,* p. 240, no. 229; p. 327, no. 41.

[61] Wilhelm Heyd, *Histoire du commerce du levant au moyen âge* (2 vols., Paris, 1885), ii, 100–2.

Sea had been under private operation, the fleet sent out in the spring of 1320 to take advantage of the new treaty was operated by the commune.[62]

In the 1320's the galley voyages settled into a pattern which held with few changes for about a decade. A demand for such stabilization had been vigorously voiced in the preamble to a decree passed by the Great Council in March, 1321.

> Because of the continual changes and variations that are made in outfitting galleys, the merchants and men of Venice cannot tell with any assurance what to do, with one thing being ordered one day and changed the next, which results in much evil and danger to the land, and the men of Venice either do not dare make their investments (*facere facta sua*) or if they make them are much disappointed because of later changes, to their great damage and with grave danger to all those on voyage because the galleys do not return in due season to Venice but are navigating in Winter.

Accordingly, the Great Council ordered the senate to elect five *savii,* later called the *Savii ai Ordini,* whose duty it was by December 8 to draw up in writing the arrangements to be made for the following year in regard to arming galleys (*ordinum galearum armatarum*), and they and the ducal councilors, the doge, and the *capi* of the Quarantia were to make the necessary motions in the senate and vote on them before the end of December so that the merchants would know what they could count on.[63] Thus were the senate and its steering committees instructed to act as a planning body for the Venetian mercantile and shipping community.

The five *Savii ai Ordini* were told to plan concerning spring and fall *mude* to Romania and *Oltremare*. In 1321 and 1322 merchant galleys were sent for both *mude;* but after 1323 we hear of galleys only for the fall *muda*. The fall fleets included more than twice as many ships, however, as when two fleets a year were sent. In 1328, for example, ten went to the Black Sea and eight to *Oltremare*.[64]

---

[62] The senate proposed that the commune construct galleys and transfer them in some way not specified to private operators (M.C., Fronesis, ff. 26 t, 31; *Deliberazioni,* I, 213, no. 421. That plan must have fallen through since the senate later voted that the commune arm itself four galleys (*ibid.,* pp. 214–15, no. 437, 450, 451) .

[63] M.C., Fronesis, ff. 58 t–59.

[64] See notes to Table I.

TABLE I

MERCHANT GALLEY FLEETS, 1320–34.[a]

Year	Destination					
	Oltremare		Flanders		Romania and Black Sea	
	No.	Operation	No.	Operation	No.	Operation
1320	–	regulated	–	licensed	–	communal
1321	–	regulated	–	licensed	–	communal
1322	–	regulated	–	licensed	–	communal
1323	–	communal	–	licensed	–	communal
1324	–	regulated	–	licensed	–	communal
1325	–	regulated	–	licensed	–	auctioned
1326	–	regulated?	–	licensed	–	communal
1327	–	licensed	–	licensed	–	communal
1328	8	licensed	4	licensed	10	communal
1329	8	licensed?	8	licensed	–	auctioned
1330	7 or 8	licensed		none	8	auctioned
1331	8	auctioned	7	licensed but canceled	6	auctioned
1332	7–9	auctioned	9	licensed	8–10	auctioned
1333	6–7	licensed		none	10	auctioned
1334	8	auctioned	8	licensed	10	auctioned

[a] The series of surviving registers of the *Deliberazioni* of the senate begins in 1332. From that year on a complete tabulation of the galley voyages planned has been made by A. Tenenti and C. Vivanti, *op. cit.* (n. 7 above), in *Annales* (1961). In attempting to tabulate the earlier voyages some help is found in the *Deliberazioni del Maggior Consiglio*, but one must rely mainly on the *Rubriche* for the lost registers of the senatorial *Deliberazioni*. They are difficult to use for this purpose even in the new edition by R. Cessi and P. Sambin. The entries in this ancient index are only headings and sometimes give a misleading impression of the action taken. The entries can be dated only by inferences from the page references and there is no assurance that all items were in chronological order (see n. 50 above and my review in *Speculum*, XXXVIII (January, 1963). Some rubrics have several page references, some none. For these reasons a year-by-year tabulation before 1320 would be excessively full of gaps or guesses and even for later years some of the interpretations embodied in the table are doubtful.

1320. To Constantinople and Black Sea, communal. *Deliberazioni*, I, 214, no. 437; p. 225, no. 58; M.C., Deliberazioni, Fronesis, ff. 31, 34 t. To Flanders and probably to *Oltremare* (Cyprus and/or Armenia), private. *Deliberazioni*, I, 220, no. 3, 4.
1321. Black Sea voyages, communal, spring fleet. Fronesis f. 53 t°, 54 (in Nov., 1302); f. 56; *Deliberazioni*, I, 227, no. 74. Fall fleet, Fronesis, f. 62 t°, 73. To Flanders and *Oltremare*, private, *Deliberazioni*, I, 237, no. 191; pp. 228–29, no. 86–96.
1322. Black Sea communal spring fleet. Fronesis, f. 84; *Deliberazioni*, I, 242, no. 245, and 250–51, no. 37–39, 82, 65. Fall fleet planned but canceled, *Deliberazioni*, I, 252, no. 65, 74, 77, 79, 95. Flanders, private, *ibid.*, I, 240, no. 229. Lack of provision regarding *Oltremare* implies that galleys went there privately operated.
1323. One *muda*, communal to Romania and Cyprus leaving in May. *Deliberazioni*, I, 263, no. 210; pp. 270, 273, no. 295, 338. Private to Flanders, p. 267, no. 260.

Notes to Table I continued

1324. One *muda* only planned, *ibid.*, p. 277, no. 389. Communal to Trebizond, *ibid.*, p. 272, no. 327; p. 278, no. 403; p. 288, no. 62, 63. Private to Cyprus, *ibid.*, p. 289, no. 78; p. 293, no. 128. Private to Antwerp, *ibid.*, p. 276, no. 382; p. 283, no. 4. Avog. Com. Brutus f. 17.

1325. All privately operated. To Provence, *Deliberazioni*, I, 302–3, no. 40, 43, 46, 47; p. 307, no. 101. To Flanders, *ibid.*, p. 300, no. 11. To Cyprus, *ibid.*, p. 296, no. 165; p. 302, no. 44. To Trebizond, auctioned, *ibid.*, p. 300, no. 21; p. 304, no. 74, 76; M.C. Deliberazioni, Fronesis, f. 162.

1326. Return to communal operation to Trebizond. M.C. Spiritus. f. 2 t; *Deliberazioni*, I, 309, no. 130, 133; p. 313, no. 178. To Flanders, *ibid.*, p. 312, no. 164, 166; p. 315, no. 205; to Armenia, p. 313, no. 177.

1327. Private to Flanders, *Deliberazioni*, I, 327, no. 41, 43 with the formula "volentes armare . . . faciant se scribi," which clearly shows private ownership as well as operation, although Cessi in *Arch. Ven.* (1914), p. 38, speaks of an auction. Also, pp. 334–35, no. 117, 118, 121, 122, 130; p. 343 no. 207, Dardi Bembo, *capitano*, communal to Constantinople, *ibid.*, p. 332, no. 91; Avog. Com. Brutus, f. 59 t°; Armenia, "volentes armare faciant se scribi," *Deliberazioni*, I, 328, no. 53–55.

1328. Fall voyages: To Armenia, 8 galleys *per divisum*, *ibid.*, p. 361, no. 32. To Black Sea, 10 galleys *per comune, ibid.*, p. 361, no. 30; pp. 364–65, no. 57, 70. Private operation to Flanders was voted down first but later approved for 4 galleys. *ibid.*, pp. 360–61, no. 21, 33; p. 363, no. 39–40, 54; p. 365, no. 76. They were still out in the early months of 1329, *ibid.*, p. 374, no. 181–82.

1329. One communal galley taking merchandise to Crete, *ibid.*, pp. 375–81, nos. 196, 197, 201, 209, 251, 258. To Flanders, 8 galleys "compareant armare volentes," *ibid.*, pp. 374–76, no. 178, 179, 185–93. To Cyprus and Armenia, 8 galleys, "per speciales persones," *ibid.*, p. 383, no. 286; p. 388, no. 10; p. 396, no. 114. To Black Sea, communal galleys chartered for private operation, *ibid.*, p. 378, no. 228; p. 382, no. 266, 267; p. 394, no. 95; p. 397, no. 127. The patrolling fleet of Capitano Culfi was used to take to Sicily cash with which to buy wheat and was ordered when he returned to Venice to disarm to bring any merchandise left at Coron or ports between Coron and Venice for which no room had been found either in the galleys of Constantinople or those of Cyprus (*ibid.*, p. 382, no. 269, 272).

1330. To Cyprus and Armenia, 7 or 8 galleys "per armatores . . . probati," *ibid.*, pp. 404–5. To Trebizond, 8 galleys, "dentur per Comune ad naulum volentibus armare . . . per incantum," *ibid.*, p. 409, no. 283–84; pp. 423–24, none to Tana. Communal galleys from Ragusa, *ibid.*, p. 425, no. 166.

1331. To Cyprus and Armenia, 8 galleys or more, "armentur per speciales persones que galee accipiantur a Comuni," *ibid.*, p. 433, no. 251, 253; cf. p. 427, no. 186. To Black Sea, 6 galleys "que tollantur a Comuni," p. 433, no. 251, 252; p. 448, no. 88, of which two to Tana, p. 454, no. 162. On extra galleys as convoy and finding crews, *ibid.*, p. 446, no. 63; p. 448, no. 94; p. 449, no. 105; p. 456, no. 197; and Maggior Consiglio, Spiritus, f. 48. For the voyage to Flanders it was voted late in 1330 to send 7 galleys or more of the *armatores* registering, but early in 1331 they were ordered not to sail (*Deliberazioni*, I, 432, no. 240, 241; p. 435, no. 276; p. 442, no. 8).

1332. To Cyprus, 7 galleys auctioned, *ibid.*, p. 468, no. 340, 341; p. 469, no. 355; and A.S.V. Senato Misti, reg. 15, f. 3. To Constantinople, 8 galleys, *ibid.*, Misti, reg. 15, f. 3, and *Deliberazioni*, I, 467, no. 335; p. 469, no. 356. Permission to hire 1,000 of the crew in Dalmatia, M. C. Spiritus, f. 59 t°. To Flanders, 9 galleys or more, *Deliberazioni*, I, 461, nos. 255–56; Schaube, "Die Anfänge," pp. 71–73.

1333. A.S.V., Senato Misti, reg. 16, f. 3; Maggior Consiglio, Deliberazioni, Spiritus, f. 64.

1334. A.S.V., Senato Misti, reg. 16, copia, ff. 95, 97–98, 104, 105.

Broadly speaking, we can say that the three fleets of merchant galleys sent out every year during the 1320's operated each under a different system: the galleys to Cyprus and Armenia made "regulated" voyages; those to Flanders were licensed fleets, those to Romania and the Black Sea were operated directly by the commune (see Table I for detail). There was then a total of about twenty-five merchant galleys leaving on these three routes, while other galleys more or less armed and acting as cargo and passenger ships sailed around the Adriatic, to Tunis and other ports in Barbary, and to southern France. Being less regulated, these "free" voyages of galleys, like those of the many round ships of the time, are less well recorded.[65]

When the alternatives of communal or private operation were presented to the senate or were thrashed over by two or three councilors as they drafted a proposal, many appeals to general principles or particular interests must have been tossed back and forth. No chronicler or official record has left even a hint of the oratory. The medievalist may regret having no Hansard, but even if he had full records of debates he would discount them heavily, as does a modern student of the *Congressional Record,* and seek "real explanations" rather in the circumstances of the case.

Military demands or threats explain nearly all the instances of communal operation from 1305 to 1320. Indeed, the need for military action was so frequent and unpredictable that it alone might seem sufficient reason to make communal action the general rule. Direct governmental operation had other advantages also. These appear in the regulations concerning crews and cargo. Although there were such regulations for both communally and privately operated galleys, the latter are more detailed, revealing more fear of violations.[66] A galley

[65] A glimpse into the variety of shipping is provided by measures taken when alarming news was received in August, 1315. The Great Council ordered all unarmed ships leaving that fall to sail together in convoy with the galleys. But large ships were given permission to leave separately on the grounds that they could not very well travel in convoy with the small. Nine were named: a *cocha* going to Tunis, a *banzonus* waiting outside the port, a vessel going to the Marches for horses, an unarmed galley going to Ragusa with a cargo of wood, and the *naves magnas* of Ca' Pentolo, Ca' Pisani, Ca' Capello, Ca' Viadro, and of Ser Onustade Trevisano. The number of small ships left was still so large as to make such an unwieldy convoy that the admiral in charge, Fantin Dandolo, was given permission to split it up if he wished. A.S.V., Maggior Consiglio, Clericus Civicus, ff. 11 t, 12, 14 t.

[66] Compare the regulations for communally operated galleys cited above in n. 8, and those for privately operated galleys in *Deliberazioni,* I, 87–91, and also in the provisions made later for auctioning state-owned galleys for private operation, collected in Senato, Commissioni, reg. 4, formulari.

master named by owners might be tempted to hire at cut rates seamen who lacked some of the arms they were supposed to have. The salaried master, on the other hand, one elected and reporting to the doge and council, had every motive to wish his galley as proudly armed as possible. As an official of the state he could be forbidden to trade on his own account and would then have no wares of his own competing for space with the wares of other merchants. It was easier under communal operation to assure that the galleys treated all shippers alike and fulfilled their duties as common carriers.

If to all these considerations is added the general principle that governments do not readily give up functions they have taken over, it will seem surprising indeed that communal operation was ever abandoned. But there was in Venice no separation between a class of business executives and a class of government bureaucrats. The same individuals operated the fleets whether they did so separately ("per divisum") or by common action ("per comune"), on behalf of private partnerships or on behalf of the commune. Dardi Bembo, the leading entrepreneur of the galleys of Flanders just after 1315, was sent to France as ambassador in the 1320's to assure rights of trade and in 1327 was the admiral of the fleet going to Romania.[67] In 1333 a Marino Capello was the head of a private partnership which undertook to operate seven of the eight galleys sent to Flanders that year. Then he was named by the state the admiral of the fleet.[68] The profit of its merchants was professedly the aim of Venetian policy. In the early years of the century when the senate was debating whether galleys should be armed separately or communally, it enjoined an *ad hoc* planning committee to consider ways and means "quod nostri mercatores vadant ad lucrandum." On this principle they decided that year in favor of communal operation.[69] Later, communal operation was abandoned, partly in order to increase private profits and partly because of administrative difficulties which developed when the commune itself operated the ships.

A number of such difficulties appear in connection with the voyages to Constantinople in the 1320's. If the commune was the operator, it had to supply the working capital. The burdensome expenditure was not the cost of the galleys themselves but the cash outlay to enroll a

[67] *Deliberazioni*, I, 302, no. 42; p. 343, no. 207; A.S.V., Avog. di Comune, Delib. M.C., Brutus, f. 72 t; 81 and 81 t.

[68] Senato Misti, reg. 16, copia, ff. 90–91, 132.

[69] *Deliberazioni*, I, 35, no. 123, 125.

crew.[70] This enrollment was called *ponere bancum,* meaning literally to place a bench or table. In the Piazzetta, along the waterfront between the arcade of the ducal palace and the two columns, shipmasters were accustomed to set up tables with money on them and give out advance wage payments to seamen who signed on.[71] For the communal galleys it was the paymasters from the Ufficiali al Armamento or the Treasury who set up tables. When the commune was sending a fleet like those going to the Black Sea in the 1320's, they had to have money bags containing at least 100,000 of the large silver pennies called grossi. That would enable them to pay 1,000 men for fifty days at the rate of 2 grossi a day. Finding this amount of cash was not always easy. In 1308, as we have seen, the state had borrowed from private parties with promise of repayment at the eastern terminus.[72] One suspects that that could be a costly method. In 1320, funds not being found elsewhere to finance the spring voyage, the Great Council ordered that the necessary amount be taken from the wheat office, which at this time was acting as a kind of bank, receiving large deposits on which it paid interest at about 10 per cent, and using the funds not only to buy wheat but for other investments.[73] The loan from the wheat office was to be repaid from the freights collected by the galleys and if they did not suffice the commune assumed the obligation of making up the difference. The same method was authorized again for the fall voyages.[74]

A new source of financing was tried in 1323. It was a standing rule of Venetian public finance that all receipts above a certain sum should be deposited by the treasurers with the *procuratori* of San Marco, there to be kept for paying the interest on the public debt and retiring the debt. When more was accumulated there than was immediately needed to pay the interest, it might be borrowed. (Originally only the *officiales super auro* could borrow from the grossi thus deposited. They could use them to buy gold which, when coined, could be used to repay the

[70] Cf. the relative costs of galleys and operating expenses in claims. A.S.V., Libri Commemoriali, reg. 2, f. 154 (mentioned in Predelli's register, I, 263, no. 422).

[71] The scene is described in Nani's manuscript, Biblioteca Universitaria, Padua, M.S. 161, vol. I, f. 231. On rates of pay, see end of Chap. 16, below.

[72] See above, n. 36.

[73] On the wheat office, see Gino Luzzatto, *I prestiti della Repubblica di Venezia* (Accademia dei Lincei, Rome, *Documenti finanziari della Repubblica di Venezia,* editi dalla Commissione per gli Atti delle Assemblee Costituzional Italiane, ser. 3, vol. I, pt. 1, 1929), pp. lxxv–lxxviii nn.

[74] A.S.V., M.C., Deliberazioni, Fronesis, f. 30 t, f. 46.

procuratori.[75] But practically speaking the coin could be borrowed by anyone to whom the Great Council instructed the *officiales super auro* to lend it.) In June, 1323, a special commission of three nobles was appoined to get the galleys off and were empowered to borrow 10,000 *libre* from this source[76] (10,000 *libre ad grossos* is about 385 *libre grossorum*, which is a little less than 107,000 grossi). It was tapped again in 1324.[77] During the next couple of years there seems to have been no difficulty finding the funds, but in the spring of 1327 the Great Council authorized the borrowing of more than 16,000 *libre* from the *procuratori* or from the wheat office.[78] In addition to both these sources, borrowing of 5,000 *libre* from a fund for dredging and drainage was authorized in 1328.[79] Money was really hard to find that year. The wheat office did not have enough capital from private sources to fulfill its basic function of buying the grain needed to maintain a reserve. A forced loan was used to replenish its capital, and this operation was repeated in 1329.[80] But in that year the paymasters could use for war galleys all the funds they borrowed to recruit crews. By turning over to private individuals the operation of the galleys going to the Black Sea, the commune had turned over to them also the problem of finding the cash with which to enroll a crew.

No doubt the Venetian commune could have raised the capital to finance the voyages of the merchant galleys without placing any strain on its credit. It could have done so either by forced loans through long-term bonds or by more expensive short-term loans. But that would not have been in accord with the fiscal policy which the nobles ruling the commune were following in those years. Between 1313 and 1334 the funded public debt was reduced by something like one third or one half the large sum to which it had risen in 1313 because of the war of Ferrara. This reduction drove up the price of government bonds so high that they yielded their purchasers only 5.5 per cent in 1323 and again in 1333. By such bonds the government could probably have

[75] Luzzatto, *Prestiti*, Doc. 25; Roberto Cessi, *Problemi monetari veneziani*, in ser. 4 of the *Documenti finanziari* cited above, Doc. 44.

[76] *Ibid.*, Doc. 81; Fronesis, f. 110.

[77] *Ibid.*, f. 135 t.

[78] M.C., Deliberazioni, Spiritus, f. 14; Avog. di Com., Delib. del Maggior Consiglio, Brutus, f. 53 t, 66 t.

[79] Brutus, f. 82 t, 83 t, 84. Not all so borrowed was for merchant galleys: some was "pro ponendo banchum pro armatis maris," but the 5,000 *libre* from the "denari depositi paludum et ageris possint accipi mutuo pro armata Trapesonde."

[80] Brutus, ff. 87, 101–2, 97 t, 99, 106, 107.

raised capital more cheaply than could private operators. But to do so would have conflicted with the prevailing policy of reducing the financial burdens on the treasury, keeping high the price of government bonds, and leaving in the hands of private citizens a large amount of capital for their economic activities.[81]

Another kind of difficulty in communal operation arose in connection with the hiring and disciplining of the crews. They were hired by the naval paymasters, who were nobles serving in this office for a term of three or four years. They received little regular salary but were allowed to keep part of the penalties which they collected from enlisted crewmen who did not fulfill their obligation.[82] The "take" of the paymasters was raised from 6 pennies in the pound to 12 pennies in 1314, and by 1328 they had arranged, perhaps without explicit authorization, to take 27 pennies in the pound on fines, 16 pennies as fee from each man they enrolled, and 28 pennies out of the settlement of additional wages or loans to be repaid at the end of the voyage. Their salaries were raised and these fees cut in half, but in 1329 they were still making collections which the *advocatores communis* claimed were illegal and the paymasters insisted on trying to take, saying that they were customary.[83]

All the crew, even the oarsmen, were of course free men, not slaves, and the penalties for jumping ship had hitherto been pecuniary. Fines, however, no longer seemed sufficient in 1329 and judges were ordered to impose jail sentences.[84] Many seamen were imprisoned for debt, either because they accepted loans from ship captains beyond their capacity to repay, or because they failed to report at the times when their ships were due to sail, or for some other reason. But good seamen were relatively scarce in Venice in the 1320's. Since filling out the crews was difficult, men in prison were released in order that they might serve at

---

[81] Luzzatto, *I prestiti*, pp. lxxiii, cxxviii. From various data given by Luzzatto, I estimate that the debt was reduced from 2.8 million lire a grossi in 1313 to 1.8 million in 1334.

[82] A.S.V., Compilazione leggi, busta 24. A fourteenth-century copy of the oath demanded of these officials is in Misc. atti diplomatici e privati, busta 9, Pergmanea 327. Although Senato Misti, i, ff. 163–64 refers to the *Camerlenghi* as paying the crew, the *pagatores* are mentioned as performing this function for communal galleys in M.C., Deliberazioni, Fronesis, f. 155.

[83] M.C., Deliberazioni, Presbiter, copia, f. 292; Avog. Com., Deliberazioni del Maggior Consiglio, Brutus, f. 82; Compilazioni leggi, busta 24.

[84] M.C., Deliberazioni, Spiritus, f. 37, incorporated in the Venetian statutes, lib. VI, cap. 69.

the oar. There was thus a kind of debt slavery for many of the poorer members of the crew.[85]

The eagerness of the paymasters to collect their "cut" made them push claims against seamen even in cases where the Great Council was willing to grant pardon. For example, one sailor in service with the fleet on patrol contracted to go on the next voyage of merchant galleys to the Black Sea. When he failed to report it was because the vessel on which he was serving meanwhile had been taken by the Genoese.[86] Nevertheless the paymasters attempted to collect the fine to which he was liable.

A private shipmaster might have arranged a compromise in such a case, perhaps by agreeing with the seaman that what he had received as advance wages should be deducted from his pay on some later voyage under the same master. With seamen scarce but bound by debts, labor contracts could be most effectively concluded and enforced by ship captains who had future voyages in mind and could make workable compromises between present debts and future services. The paymasters were too tightly bound by regulations and by their personal interests in imposing and collecting penalties. Moreover, the paymasters did not sail with the galleys. Recruitment was probably easier for the private galley master who was himself going to command the vessel so that the crews knew under whom they would be serving.

In addition to financing the voyage and recruiting and disciplining the crew, the private operator relieved the government of many worries concerning the collection of freights. Under communal operation the individual galley master had no personal interest in how much was collected, although if he found wares smuggled aboard under the straw in the hold he received one quarter of their value as his reward.[87] His task of commanding the crew could be made easier by winking at their stowing something extra here and there, besides the chest or sack which each had a right to bring aboard. Just when communal operation was being abandoned there were complaints that the galleys from Romania and the Black Sea were carrying in this way much merchandise which paid no freight.[88]

---

[85] On the shortage, see the plea of the *patroni* in Grazie, reg. 3, f. 60, and the many permits to hire in Dalmatia, e.g., M.C., Spiritus, f. 48. On recruiting from the prisons, see *ibid.*, f. 45 t, and *Capitolare dei Signori di Notte*, ed. by F. Nani Mocenigo (Venice, 1877), no. 113, 243, 266.

[86] Avog. Com., Deliberazioni del Maggior Consiglio, Brutus, f. 67; Grazie, reg. 3, f. 23.

[87] The reward is not in the regulations of 1302 printed in *Deliberazioni*, I, 87–91, but in the oath printed by Fincati, cited above n. 8.

[88] Avog. Com., Deliberazioni del Maggior Consiglio, Brutus, f. 112 t.

The complaint came from the *extraordinarii,* officials created in 1302 expressly to collect the freights from the communally operated galleys.[89] When they had not much business of that kind, the *extraordinarii* busied themselves with such varied duties as the Feast of the Marys, the repair of the breakwater at the Lido, and the distribution of the reparations collected from the Byzantine emperor.[90] Their office gained more maritime importance (about 1320–21), however, when the commune undertook operation directly of the galleys of Romania.[91] They collected the freights paid in Venice and the *patroni* then had to load the wares for which they issued a receipt, a *bulleta.*[92] If freight was paid overseas, it was collected by the *capitano,* who issued the *bulleta* for the loading or unloading.[93] Although the *patroni* were strictly charged with keeping a record of all wares loaded, they were not personally concerned with collecting the freights, and being salaried officials they had no personal interest in seeing to it that all freights were paid.[94]

A crisis in freight collections occurred in 1321 as a result of measures taken to drive out of circulation underweight grossi. All government offices were ordered, in October, 1321, not to accept any payments except in full weight grossi. It then proved impossible to collect customs duties or the freights on the galleys of Romania. To keep goods moving and business going, the *extraordinarii* were instructed in November to make out bills to the merchants and release their wares to them on the receipt of good and sufficient security.[95] This gave legal status to a method which we find described later but which had probably begun between private operators and shippers earlier. Bankers pledged the necessary amounts so that shippers could receive their wares, sell them, and receive payments by transfers on the books of the bank.[96] But of course other kinds of security, gold coin, or other

[89] *Ibid.,* Magnus, f. 52 t.

[90] Fourteenth-century copies of their *capitolari* are in A.S.V., Misc. Codici, no. 131, 132.

[91] Cod. 131, cap. xxviii; Avog. Com., Deliberazioni del Maggior Consiglio, Neptunus, f. 167.

[92] M.C., Deliberazioni, Fronesis, f. 101 t; Spiritus, f. 14; Codici Brera, no. 132, f. 5 cap. 3 (1320).

[93] Although not stated explicitly in the regulations of 1302 or in the galley master's oath printed by Fincati (n. 8 above), it is spelled out in the captain's commissions at the end of the century, and is implied by the passages in the *Lettere di Collegio* cited above, n. 36.

[94] Fincati, *loc. cit.,* and Senato Misti, I, ff. 163–65.

[95] Misc. Codici, 131, cap. 27; M.C., Deliberazioni, Fronesis, f. 81 t, 82 t.

[96] Described in the senatorial decree of Nov. 3, 1342, printed in full in Scialoja, *op. cit.,* p. 758 n.

valuables could also be accepted by the tax-collecting and freight-collecting officials. In Venice's general practice of farming taxes, salaried officials computed the amount of the tax and received the security. The tax farmer's function was to pass on the adequacy of the security offered and arrange to collect on it if necessary. Without such a tax farmer the customs yielded less.[97] A private operator of a merchant galley could fulfill the same function even if the computation of the freight bill and the exaction of the security were the responsibility of the *extraordinarii*.

The allotment of damages because of goods lost or spoiled was closely connected with the collection of freights and was also handled through the *extraordinarii*. If the loss was the result of a storm, the shipper might claim recompense from the "general average" levied on other shippers. If the loss was due to proved negligence, compensation could be sought from the ship operator, in this case the commune. But who would be in court to represent the commune in such a suit or in case a claim was made on the ship in allotting the general average? In February, 1324, claims were being made against the commune because of damage to bales on one of the galleys of Trebizond, and the *extraordinarii* were told to represent the interest of the commune. But in June the *patroni* chosen to command the galleys going that year were required to respond in court for the commune, and to pay personally if any wares were lost or damaged because not loaded where they should have been. Only in case the *patronus* was blameless would the commune pay for the damaged wares.[98]

The financing, the recruitment of the crew, and the collection of the freights—all three created difficulties under communal operation. These difficulties were overcome when the galleys of Romania and the Black Sea were shifted in 1329 from communal to private operation under an arrangement which was subsequently applied in its basic features to all the merchant galleys. Communally owned galleys were

[97] *Bilanci Generali* (*Documenti finanziari della Repubblica di Venezia*, ser. 2, Commissione per la pubblicazione dei documenti finanziari della Repubblica di Venezia: Accademia dei Lincei, Rome), vol. I, pt. 1, p. xliii.

[98] M.C., Deliberazioni, Fronesis, ff. 127, 135 (old numbering) and the oath printed by Fincati, *op. cit.*, par. 14. In April, 1329, the Maggior Consiglio voted to pay 45 *libre grossorum* partly out of charity but also "pro omnibus que tangere possit comune" as a result of a whole galley having had to be ransomed from the Turks after it ran aground. Avog. Com., Deliberazioni del Maggior Consiglio, Brutus, f. 102. I presume the ransom was being collected from a general average levied on the whole fleet as is more clearly the case in a similar accident in 1325–26. M.C., Deliberazioni, Spiritus, ff. 1 t, 2.

chartered to those *armatores* who would bid highest for the right to arm and operate them for the year.

This auctioning of communal galleys for private operation secured some of the benefits of both systems previously in use. The private partnership which bid in the charter for the year undertook to find the big outlays of cash needed to man and outfit the galley, just as private operators were already doing for the voyages to Flanders and Armenia. In hiring crews the galley masters could be more flexible than the naval paymasters in making advances and loans, in exacting or waiving fines, or in doing whatever seemed practical to secure men. And since they were members and agents of profit-seeking partnerships, the galley masters had a strong personal interest in seeing that all the goods on board paid freight.

On the other hand, the recording of freights and the actual handling of payments was still in the hands of the *extraordinarii,* and this was probably an advantage. It gave assurance to shippers that the galley masters would not play favorites by collecting lower freights from some than from others. Certainly it put the government in a position to pay out of the freights collected according to the order of priority it might establish among the creditors of the galleys, and to distribute the balance among the members of the partnership operating the galleys. First priority was naturally given to the commune itself, which took whatever had been bid for the galley and a certain amount for wear and tear on rigging and fixings.[99]

Another advantage of the new system of auctioning galleys established in 1329 was that it avoided the frequent transfer of galleys from public to private hands and vice versa by sale. This overcame the discontent caused during the previous decades by the commune's buying and selling according to the evaluation put on the vessel by experts, presumably by the lords of the Arsenal.[100] In a few cases we have the full record of their estimate,[101] and there were many others of

[99] Misc. Cod., 131, cap. 37; the auctions recorded in Senato Misti, reg. 15 ff.; and *Deliberazioni,* I, 284, no. 16.

[100] *Deliberazioni,* I, 120, no. 211; p. 134, no. 88; p. 135, no. 93; A.S.V., M.C., Deliberazioni, Presbiter, f. 79 t, 110 t; Clericus Civicus, f. 133 t, 140; Avog. Com., Delib. del M.C., Magnus, f. 4.

[101] A.S.V., Libri Commemoriali, reg. 1, ff. 158, 162. The "corpo" and "coredi" were estimated separately. The galleys of Ca' Loredano here referred to were first bought by the commune (*Deliberazioni,* I, 135, no. 98) and then sold back to the original owners under the provision probably of 1312 (*ibid.,* p. 137, no. 115) so that the date Predelli guessed for the estimates (they are lib. 1, no. 464, in his *Regesti*) needs to be changed.

which we hear only indirectly. Sales were often made with more than a year in which to pay, and when payment proved difficult the debtor could be granted an extension as a special favor by vote of the Maggior Consiglio.[102] There must have been suspicion of abuses in the sales of new galleys, for the Maggior Consiglio complained of such sales a number of times and increased the safeguards. After 1323 any sale on term of a galley or of equipment was illegal unless the galley had already made five voyages, or the sale was voted by all six of the ducal Councilors and by three fourths of the Maggior Consiglio.[103]

There were no comparable restrictions on the acquisition of privately built galleys by the commune. Presumably it was done frequently when galleys were needed for the war fleets and we have seen that it was done in 1317 in order to charter the galleys on favorable terms for the voyage to Flanders.[104] The commune recognized an obligation to buy privately owned galleys in case it did not permit them to operate, for some assurance of this sort was needed if private building was to be encouraged.[105]

By 1330 the government was no longer interested in having galleys privately built. Since the end of the Second Genoese War the communal Arsenal had tripled its size by the addition of the Arsenale Nuovo. The commune was then equipped to maintain and outfit a large fleet of its own.[106]

Accordingly the auctioning of communal galleys for private operation was extended in 1331 and 1332 to the voyage to Cyprus and Armenia.[107] The state was then supplying about fifteen galleys each year for commercial voyages. For a while the government still showed consideration for the owners of private galleys. In 1333, when no galleys were licensed for Flanders, those that had made that western voyage the previous year were invited to register for a licensed voyage to Cyprus

---

[102] M.C., Deliberazioni, Presbiter, ff. 73, 79, 110; Clericus Civicus, f. 38; Avog. Com., Deliberazioni del M.C., Brutus, f. 46, 97 t; *Grazie*, ı, no. 435.

[103] Avog. Com., Deliberazioni del Maggior Consiglio, Magnus, f. 13; Maggior Consiglio, Deliberazioni, Fronesis, ff. 109, 134 t.

[104] M.C., Clericus Civicus, f. 133 t, 140; see above n. 55.

[105] *Deliberazioni*, I, 116, no. 159; p. 135, no. 93; p. 276, no. 381–83. In his "Relazioni commerciali," *Politica ed Economia*, p. 99, Cessi gives this rubric a different interpretation which seems to be based on reading "elevare" as if it were equivalent of "armare."

[106] Lane, *Venetian Ships*, pp. 130–31.

[107] *Deliberazioni*, I, 433, no. 251, 253; p. 448, no. 95, p. 427, no. 186; A.S.V., Senato Misti, reg. 15, ff. 3, 7, 13.

and Armenia.[108] The Flemish voyage itself was not transformed from a licensed private voyage into a privately operated fleet of communally owned galleys until more than a decade later.[109]

How and why state-owned galleys, privately operated, finally replaced all the privately owned licensed fleets is a story beyond the scope of this paper. By carrying the story to 1330 we have reached the point at which the Venetian aristocracy had devised to its satisfaction a means of dispensing with direct communal operation. The auctioning of merchant galleys enabled Venice to retain most of the benefits of private operation while concentrating the construction and possession of these vessels in the hands of the commune.

One may ask at this point why the Venetians did not adopt an obvious alternative way of dispensing with communal operation. Why did they not do as the Genoese did and turn over to private enterprise not only the operation of the galleys but also their construction and ownership? Of course the galleys which were used for long-distance trade were at this time also the foundation of the war fleet. Both Venice and Genoa restricted the size of the galleys in order that they should not be too large and unwieldy to serve as good warships.[110] Famous Genoese admirals and ship operators, such as Benedetto Zaccaria, armed their own galleys for the service of their commune in time of war or to serve foreign princes.[111]

---

[108] A.S.V., Senato Misti, reg. 16, f. 3.

[109] Scialoja, in *Memoria Scorza* cited above, p. 786.

[110] Hence the penalty from which Bembo received pardon, as noted above. Venetian limits: Avog. Com., Magnus, f. 7 t; *Regesti dei Libri Commemoriali*, ed. Predelli, vol. I, reg. 2, no. 135. Genoese limits, Pardessus, *op. cit.*, IV, 445, interpreted by Jal, *op. cit.*, I, 251–78. In the Venetian records there is no clear evidence before 1318 of a differentiation between galleys designed for trade and those designed for war or patrol. In the 1330's three types were distinguished: light galleys for patrolling the gulf, galleys of the measures of Flanders, and those of the measures of Romania, Trebizond, or Alexandria. Giomo, "Rubriche," *Archivio Veneto*, XVII, 259, 262; XIX, 100; *Deliberazioni*, I, 372, no. 162. Concerning the enlargement of galleys about 1290 permitting more cargo and three men to an oar, see pp. 189–92. I felt justified in using "Merchant Galleys" in the title of this paper because, even when considering those not distinguished in structure from war galleys, I have dealt with their use by merchants.

[111] Renée Doehaerd, *Les Rélations commerciales entre Gênes, la Belgique et l'Outremont d'après les archives notariales génoises aux XIII et XIV siècles* (Études d'Histoire économique et sociale, Institut Historique Belge de Rome, II; Brussels and Rome, 1941), I, 148, 224–26, 233; Roberto S. Lopez, *Storia delle colonie genovesi nel Mediterraneo* (Bologna, 1938), pp. 44, 49, 50, 52, 58, 62; and *Genova Marinara nel Ducento: Benedetto Zaccaria ammiraglio e mercante* (Messina, 1933), pp. 29–30.

Obviously galleys had both a military and a commercial value. It would be difficult to decide which was in that age preferable economically: for the galleys to be owned by the managers of their mercantile voyages and to be rented to the government when military needs were dominant, as at Genoa; or, as at Venice, for the galleys to be owned by the state which wanted them for military purposes and to be rented for mercantile uses when they were not needed for war. But there was a political as well as an economic aspect to these alternatives. Genoa provided an example of how private ownership and private management in the military establishment made it easier for factions to tear the state apart. The lesson may well have been evident to the Venetians at the time. The private fleets which the Zaccaria, Grimaldi, and Doria used for trade, war, piracy, and rebellion had no counterparts at Venice. In wartime the Venetian commune took ownership of the ships in its fleets, and it decided to become the owner in time of peace of the galleys used in trade—at first only in part but later more and more extensively until these vessels became a government monopoly. Communal ownership of galleys expressed the solidarity of the Venetian nobility and strengthened that solidarity. The system of annual auctions, combining advantages of private operation with communal control and ownership, was a vital element in giving to the Venetian government the efficiency and stability which distinguished it from so many other Italian city-states of the fourteenth century.

14

Maritime Law and Administration,
1250–1350*

I

"CON lo statuto del Doge Zeno la legislazione marittima di Venezia raggiunse il suo massimo splendore." With these words the modern Italian historian of medieval maritime law, Professor Riniero Zeno, paid tribute in 1946 to the revision of the Venetian maritime code made by Doge Rainier Zeno in 1255.[1] But the praise of Doge Zeno's Code should not be taken to mean that its provisions remained unaltered and were applied through the subsequent glorious centuries of Venetian maritime activity. On the contrary the regulation of Venetian shipping contained in the records of the Venetian senate, of which the continuous series begins in 1332, reveals a picture of the Venetian merchant marine and its practices which is substantially different from that derived from the Code of Doge Zeno. Professor Zeno recognizes that modifications were made in Zeno's Code. He says: "Altre aggiunte furono fatte nel 1302, 1328, 1343, e riunite dal Doge Andrea Dandolo nel libro VI," of the statutes of Venice.[2]

There were in fact many maritime statutes passed between 1255 and 1343 besides those of the years Professor Zeno mentions. To some extent they rendered the Code of Zeno obsolete and contributed to its gradual dropping out of use. In the eighteenth century, when a new

* From *Studi in onore di Amintore Fanfani*, 6 vols. (Milan: Dott. A Giuffrè, 1962), III, 21–50. (By permission.)

[1] Riniero Zeno, *Storia del diritto marittimo italiano nel Mediterraneo* (Pubblicazione della Fondazione Scialoia per gli studi giuridici, 3; Milan, 1946), p. 164.

[2] *Ibid.*

Venetian code, the "Codice per la Veneta Mercantile Marina," was compiled in 1786, the Consolato del Mare compiled in Catalonia in the late thirteenth century was better known to Venetians than was their own thirteenth-century code.[3] As Giuseppe Stefani, the historian of insurance at Venice, has recently written, "When and how ancient Venetian Maritime Statutes fell into desuetude is a historical problem so far unsolved."[4] Without attempting any complete solution of that problem, I hope to contribute to it by these comments concerning Venetian maritime laws and regulation between 1250 and 1350 and the branches of the government responsible for them. My main purpose is at the same time to lay some of the groundwork for understanding the revolutions which occurred during that period in the techniques of maritime transportation, the protection of convoys, and the status of sailors.

Let us consider first the surviving copies of Zeno's Code. Walter Ashburner, in arguing that the importance of the Rhodian Sea Law is indicated by the large number of manuscript copies, says that the maritime statutes of Zeno, in contrast, survive in only three manuscripts.[5] This is not exact, for even a quick search reveals others in Venice as well as one in Washington. True, there are three that are earlier and more complete than the others. In two fifteenth-century copies, obsolete statutes have been pruned away, as is explained by the following note at the end: "Item nota quod hec navium statuta sunt deflorata de multitudine statutorum navium, nam hec sola sunt oportuna et fece alii non utuntur."[6] The Code of Jacopo Tiepolo, only about twenty years earlier in date, was also considered useful. It

[3] *Ibid.*, p. 195; Vettor Sandi, *Principii di storia civile della Repubblica di Venezia* (Venice, 1755), pt. 1, II, 864; pt. 2, I, pp. 243–46; P. S. Leicht, "L'elaborazione del codice della veneta marina mercantile," in *Scritti vari di storia del diritto italiano* (Milan, 1948), II, t. I, 274–80.

[4] Giuseppe Stefani, *Insurance in Venice: From the Origins to the End of the Serenissima* (Assicurazione generale di Trieste e Venezia; Venice, 1956), I, 173.

[5] Walter Ashburner, *The Rhodian Sea-Law* (Oxford 1909), p. xlviii.

[6] The two copies to which this note is appended are: Archivio di Stato di Venezia (cited hereafter as A.S.V.), Capitolare della Corte dell'Esaminador (which was analyzed and partially printed by Predelli and Sacerdoti) and in the Biblioteca Marciana at Venice, MSS. Ital., classe II, cod. 50, dated about 1477. There are extensive extracts in a Venetian translation at the Marciana, MSS. Ital., classe II, cod. 93, and a sixteenth-century copy at the Museo Civico Correr, Archivio Gradenigo, busta 193. I am endebted to the Dottoressa Maria Francesca Tiepolo of the Archivio di Stato di Venezia for help in locating copies of the statutes and of various *capitolari* cited below. In addition to the four cited above, there are the three copies which Ashburner had in mind and which are discussed below, nn. 8–10.

survives in at least four copies, and Tiepolo's Code, not Zeno's, was incorporated into the first printed edition of Venetian statutes.[7] Tiepolo's Code was less elaborate and may for that reason have been preferred in the fifteenth century when changes in the techniques of rigging, loading, and warfare made both of these old codes obsolete in part.

Of the three oldest copies of Zeno's Code, two were used by Predelli and Sacerdoti in 1902 for their invaluable edition. At the time of their edition the third was in the Phillips Collection in England and they reported the information concerning it furnished them by its possessor.[8] It is now in the Library of Congress in Washington, D.C., available to all scholars.[9] It contains the *Statuta tarretarum* as well as the *Statuta navium*. The two statutes are numbered consecutively and have a total of 187 chapters. By some experts the manuscript has been assigned to the thirteenth century.[10] Its contents suggest that it was compiled about 1300. Whatever the date of the manuscript, it certainly was not the source of the two fourteenth-century manuscripts in Venice, one of

[7] The oldest copy of Tiepolo's Code is that in the Marciana, MSS. Lat., cl. V, cod. 130. Other copies at the Marciana are MSS. Ital., cl. II, cod. 41; and MSS. Ital., Z (Fondo antico Zanetti) 31. There are also an Italian translation at the A.S.V., Misc. Cod., no. 446 and a Latin version in the Museo Civico Correr, Arch. Morosini Grimani, no. 272.

The first printed edition of *Statuti Veneti,* containing a translation into Venetian of Tiepolo's statutes, was that of Filippo di Piero of 1477. There are copies in the Law Office, Library of Congress, Washington, D.C., and the Morgan Library, New York (called to my attention by Mrs. Louise Buenger Robberts) as well as those mentioned in A. Valsecchi, "Bibliografia analitica della legislazione della Repubblica di Venezia," *Archivio Veneto,* IV (1872), 259. In regard to copies in the Marciana, Valsecchi reports as one copy what are really two copies. One copy is the book which has the *segnatura* CIX 540221 and is without handwritten additions. Another copy forms part of MSS. Ital., cl. II, cod. 50, which contains many handwritten additions including the copy of Zeno's Code cited above in n. 6, beginning at f. cxvi, old numbering.

Later editions of the Venetian statutes omit all maritime statutes earlier than the corrections of Francesco Dandolo re-enacted by Andrea Dandolo. Valsecchi, p. 265. See *Archivio Veneto* III, 19 ff. on manuscript copies of Venetian statutes.

[8] *Gli Statuti Marittimi veneziani fino al 1255,* ed. by R. Predelli and A. Sacerdoti (Venice 1903), p. 13 n. Their edition also appeared in *Nuovo Archivio Veneto,* n.s., vols. IV–VI (1902–3). They printed as most authoritative the text in A.S.V., Misc. Cod. 527, but showed also the variants in the manuscript at the Biblioteca Querini Stampalia, Venice, cl. IV, cod. i.

[9] Law Office, MS. V 46.

[10] It is described with a photograph in the Library of Congress's *Quarterly Journal of Current Acquisitions,* VIII, 4 (August, 1951), 41.

which is tentatively dated 1323 by Sacerdoti, the other about 1350 or after, because the Library of Congress manuscript omits some important chapters found in the other copies. It omits the chapters numbered 20, 21, and 30 in the edition of Predelli and Sacerdoti of the *Statuta navium* and chapter 42 of the *Statuta tarretarum.* The only chapters in the Library of Congress copy which appear not to be in the other two fourteenth-century manuscripts are either (a) redundancies, e.g., chapter 9 in the numbering of the Library of Congress copy, (b) mistakes, chapters 118 (there are also many minor variations in spelling which are mostly mistakes, as "De coriis sciocis" instead of "De coriis siccis," for the equivalent of Sacerdoti's chapter 110), and (c) the final chapters.

Some significant new material is in the concluding chapters of the copy in Washington. They are there numbered 185, 186, and 187. The last of these is a copy of the law passed by the Maggior Consiglio, December 31, 1292, giving the *judices comunis* jurisdiction in disputes over freighting contracts even in cases in which the goods had never been loaded on board ship.[11] The inclusion of this law suggests that the compilation was made about 1292, and that the compiler intended to add pertinent laws passed since 1255 of which he had knowledge. It suggests also that the compilation was made for the *curia comunis,* or for some member thereof. An alternate possibility, however, is that it was made for the magistracy which lost the jurisdiction awarded to the *judices comunis,* namely the *consoli dei mercanti,* or if not for the magistracy itself, for an individual holding the office of consul.

This latter alternative is favored by the content of the other two additional chapters, numbers 185 and 186. Chapter 186 appears to be an elaboration of the power of the *consoli* to require of all vessels which had announced their voyages and begun to load that they give security which would be forfeit if they did not leave port and make sail as they ought.[12] Since it is a provision not previously published, as far as I know, I present the complete text:

> CLXXXVI. Hoc ordinamentum inventum fuit scriptum in quadam cedula. Ut non admieteretur fuit hic scriptum.
>
> Ordinamus quod omnes naves que exiverint extra culfum ex quo inceperint naulizari usque ad octo dies, patroni pignus x

---

[11] *Deliberazioni del Maggior Consiglio di Venezia,* ed. by Roberto Cessi (Accademia dei Lincei, Commissione per gli atti delle assemblee costituzionale italiane, Atti delle Assemblee Costituzionale Italiane dal Medio Evo al 1831, ser. 3, sect. 1; Bologna, 1950), III, 15.

[12] A.S.V., Capitolare, Consoli dei Mercanti, ch. 38, 85.

solidi pro unoquoque milliario dare et deliberare in manibus consulum teneantur in auro vel argento seu lapidibus preciosis sive seta vel opera sete, quod si extra portum naves non extraxerint et velum non fecerint et alia que facere tenentur in penam suprascriptam incurrant. Et si in manibus consulum dictum pignus non posuerint, infra dictum terminum octo dierum penam v sol. incurrant pro unoquoque milliario. Et nostri consules infra quattuor dies dictam penam v sol. accipere teneantur. Et si aliquis eorum rebellus fuerit ad dictam penam solvendam, Dominus Dux sacramento cum consilio suo teneantur, infra duos dies postquam eis nunptiatum fuit per consules eius accipere dictam penam sol. v pro quolibet milliario et in super pro pena liber xxv et pignus antedictum solidi x pro unoquoque miliario, ut superius dictum est et deliberare dictum pignus in manibus consulum mercatorum.

Chapter 185 of the Library of Congress manuscript also relates to the power of the *consoli,* at least in part. It begins with a sentence reserving to the doge and his councils, *minori et maiori,* authority to resolve or amend any obscurities in the law. This sentence appears in both the *Statuta navium* and the *Statuta tarretarum,* and is as published in the edition by Predelli and Sacerdoti on pp. 166–67. In the Library of Congress manuscript additional sentences follow of which the gist seems to be that the doge and his council have used their reserved authority to give to the *consoli* authority to exempt from the above statutes those small *tarrete* which could not operate if they had to observe the laws about loading and crew provided in the statutes. For small vessels a provision such as that requiring a crew of at least twenty-five for the smallest class of *tarete* (ch. 16 in the edition of Predelli and Sacerdoti) would have been unbearable. Hence the *consoli* were empowered to make other rules concerning the cargo and the crews of these small vessels. The text of chapter 185 reads:

> CLXXV. De potestate quam habet dominus dux et consilium minus et maius declarandi obscuritatem que esset in predictis statutis.

> Si autem in predictis statutis nostris aliqua obscuritas alicubi fuerit, potestatem habemus nos dux, cum nostro consilio minori et maiori, declarandi et reformandi ipsas obscuritates sicut bonum videbimus.
> Nota quad dictum statutum modo fuit spacificatum: Nos dux cum nostro consilio minori et maiori obscuritatem dicti statuti taliter declaramus. Nam volumus et ordinamus quod per consoles nostros possit et debeat dari ordo predictis tarritis parvis

que ordinem caricandi et marinariorum ferre non possunt. Caricandi et habere marinarios secundum quod pro ipsis consolibus vel maiori parte bene videbitur, et cum illo ordine a scribanis et patronis earum accipere sacramentum.

There is no date on this authorization to the consuls to modify the *Statuta tarretarum*. Indeed, the date of that code itself is doubtful. Professor Zeno questioned whether it was promulgated under Doge Zeno, remarking that the mere fact of finding it copied immediately after Zeno's *Statuta navium* in a manuscript at the Archivio di Stato did not prove that it was formulated at the same time.[13] Indeed, it was obviously composed somewhat later than the *Statuta navium* because it makes frequent reference thereto. Its contents shows that it was a simplification, suitable for the smaller, simpler vessels, and applying the same principles. But its substance at least was in force before the death of Doge Zeno in 1266, for a law passed in that year by the Maggior Consiglio referred to the requirement that *tarete* have 3 ft. of freeboard, a requirement found in the *Statuta tarretarum*. This requirement, like the demand for crews of twenty-five, was impractical for very small *tarete,* and it also was made subject to modification by the *consoli* so that they might make for these vessels the rules they thought best.[14]

II

Although it may seem like a diversion, it will be helpful at this point to give here some explanations concerning the types of vessels in use, for some regulations applied to one type, others to a different type. Zeno's *Statuta navium* applied only to what are commonly called round ships. It was not applicable to long ships such as galleys, in spite of the repetition in chapter after chapter of the assertion that it applied to all vessels *(ligna)* of 200 *milliaria* or more. Of course some chapters could be applied to both types and probably were, for example, chapter 37 (according to the numbering of Predelli and Sacerdoti) , requiring the master to take an oath that he will not sell any of the rigging. But clauses concerning what could be loaded between decks, such as chapters 47 and 48, conclude with the phrase: "Hoc intelligimus in

---

[13] Zeno, pp. 160–61.

[14] Delib. M.C., ed. Cessi, II, 254. This authorization to modify for the small *tarete* the rules about freeboard is contained also in the Capitolare dei Consoli dei Mercanti, cap. 59, although I have not found in that *capitolare* the authorization to them to modify for the small *tarete* the rules about crew and cargo, unless cap. 66 be considered an adaptation of such a law. Cf. in Delib. M.C., ed. Cessi, II, 256.

nave et banzono et buzonave vel alio ligno a ducentis milliariis et inde supra." Yet it obviously applies only to a ship with two decks, and could not apply to a galley. The phrases "alio ligno" or "quolibet ligno" are intended, as I see it, to prevent a shipmaster from avoiding obedience by pointing to some new feature of the ship's rigging and claiming that the ship was of a different type from those named. But the types for which it was intended were the two-decked, two-masted lateeners, such as that represented in a beautiful miniature on the copy of Zeno's Code at the Biblioteca Quirini Stampalia, vessels which the Code assumes will range from 200 to 1,000 *milliaria* in carrying capacity. In the mid-thirteenth century there were two or three ships at Venice which actually were of about 500 metric tons capacity (1,000 *milliaria*) and probably more than a dozen of about 200 tons.[15] I will here use the term *buzonavis* to cover all these two-decked, two-masted lateeners.

In the fourteenth century, the *buzonavis* was gradually replaced by a type called *cocha,* the cog. The new type had a mainmast with a large square sail. Probably many Mediterranean *coche* used lateen sails on a small mizzen mast, but this is doubtful, and the rig of the cog was certainly so completely different from that of the *buzonavis* that the rules in Zeno's Code about sails could not possibly be applied to the *coche.* The larger *coche* had two decks and high castles.[16] In function they were the successors of the *buzonavis* and in regard to armament and overloading they presented somewhat similar problems for government regulation. The transition from the one type to the other is obscured by the fact that both were commonly referred to as *naves* or *navi,* as were later types which combined square and lateen rig.

In contrast to the *buzonaves* and the *coche,* the *tarete* were vessels of only one deck.[17] Some of them were of more than 200 *milliaria* (the *Statuta tarretarum* provides for *tarete* as large as 400 *milliaria*) and

---

[15] See my *Venetian Ships,* pp. 35–40.

[16] *Ibid.,* pp. 37–38; R. Morton Nance, "The Ship of the Renaissance," *The Mariner's Mirror,* XLI (1955), 180–93; Guilleux la Roerie, "Introduction à une histoire du navire," *Annales: économies, sociétés, civilizations* (Jan.–Feb., 1963), p. 150. The earliest reference to a *cocha* or *chocha* that I have seen in Venetian records is in 1315. A.S.V., M.C., Deliberazioni, Clericus Civicus, originale f. 59, new paging.

[17] In the edition of Predelli and Sacerdoti chapters numbered (1–12) tell much of the size and rig. They indicate a ship of one deck, as does the chapter (31) on loading. Chapter 40 of the Capitolare dei Consoli dei Mercanti mentions maximum measures about as follows: beam, 18–20 ft.; depth, up to 10 ft.; partial deck or shelter deck above, 4 ft. Note that no length is given. The measures stated are apparently an attempt to prevent building as *tarete* ships so high and wide that they should have been *buzonaves* with two decks. Such building would have evaded regulations intended for larger ships but not applicable to *tarete.*

those of 200 *milliaria* and over would have been obligated to obey many of the complications of Zeno's Code if the simpler *Statuta tarretarum* had not been composed for them. The *tarete* also had two masts, and several different kinds of sails were used interchangeably on each mast, as on the masts of the *buzonaves*. Aside from their having only one deck, what distinguished the *tarrete* structurally from the *buzonaves* was their straighter lines, and in many cases their greater length in proportion to their breadth.[18]

Buzonaves, coche, and *tarete* were all what we call round ships. They were equipped with sails, not oars, although the use of sweeps might occasionally be important in maneuvering the smaller vessels. Moreover, *buzonaves, coche,* and *tarete* were what the Venetians called unarmed ships. Obviously the expression "unarmed" is not to be taken literally but relatively. A section of maritime regulations entitled "Rules for Unarmed Ships" is full of specifications concerning the number of lances, cuirasses, helmets, shields, and various kinds of engines of war that had to be carried by these unarmed ships.[19]

When the Venetian regulations call a ship unarmed they mean that it had neither the crew nor the equipment of a galley. Generally speaking, armed ships mean galleys. The essential in arming them was putting on board a large crew, 150 to 250 men, who then provided both fighting power and rowing power.[20] The proper outriggers and deck furnishings were essential in order to use the large crew effectively in

---

[18] Albertis calls the *tareta* a cross between the galley and a small round ship such as the *tartane* of later date. The measures he gives indicate that some at least are very long compared to their width. Enrico Alberto d'Albertis, *Le costruzioni navali e l'arte della navigazione al tempo di Cristoforo Colombo* (Raccolta di doc. e studi pub. della R. Com. Colombiana, pt. IV, vol. I; Rome, 1893), pp. 16–18, 213. See also August Jal, *Archéologie navale* (Paris, 1840), II, 221–23. Jal distinguishes between *nefs-tarides* and *galée-taride.* About 1320 we have the following description which may apply only to a special class of *tarete:* "Moreover there is a ship good for carrying the aforesaid provision and wood, the taretes, which are used at the present time by the Genoese at Pera, both because they carry much and because they can be manned easily by a few sailors, and also because, when the sails are spread, they sail quickly across the sea: this is because having long hulls they go better close hauled, and they gain with the wind against them better than other, shorter ships."
Marino Sanuto (the Elder), called Torsello, *Liber Secretorum Fidelium Crucis super Terrae Sanctae recuperatione et conservatione,* in *Gesta Dei per Francos* (Hanover, 1611), p. 58.

[19] In the Capitolare of the Officiales de Levante, described below, A.S.V., Codici Brera 263, f. 35.

[20] A law of 1290 (*Delib. M.C.,* ed. Cessi, III, 262) distinguishes between "navis, tarita, et banzonus incaibatus" on the one hand and "quodlibet lignum armatum a viginti remis et inde supra" on the other.

rowing and fighting. This equipment and crew were the essential of arming a vessel. A long low vessel with one deck might be either a galley or a *tareta;* even if a galley, it was not armed unless it was manned and equipped for battle.[21]

All armed vessels were under different or additional regulations just because they were armed. Sometimes the Venetians armed their galleys by communal action; sometimes galleys were armed by individual action. In the former case the galley masters were chosen by the governing councils; in the latter case the galley masters were chosen by the owners and outfitters of the galleys.[22] In either case, armed galleys were nearly always operated in convoys under admirals chosen by the commune and according to military or commercial plans formulated by its governing councils.

In short, from the point of view of maritime laws and regulations there were two main categories in the merchant marine—those armed galleys which carried merchants and their wares, and the unarmed ships. Among the latter were the *buzonaves,* the *tarete,* and also any galleys operating unarmed, that is with small crews.

III

Zeno's statutes were designed for the types of unarmed ships in use in the mid-thirteenth century and not for the galleys then used. His codes began immediately to be modified by new legislation regarding *buzon-aves* and *tarete* and before long it was supplemented by an extensive system of regulation of voyages by merchant galleys.

Several organs of government took a hand in modifying the maritime

[21] "The prohibition of constructing *galeam vel tarretam de bandis vel lignum currens*" (in *Delib. M.C.,* ed. Cessi, II, 74 in 1282) shows that a *tareta* could be turned into something like a galley by the addition of an outrigger. On *banda,* see p. 173. But a galley might be considered an unarmed ship if it lacked sufficient crew. With provisions concerning "navigia disarmata" in 1315 which permitted the larger vessels to leave outside of convoy, clearance was also given to "Galea Ser Marco Mauroceno que vadit Ragusium cum lignamine, quia similiter est magna" (A.S.V., Maggior Consiglio, Deliberazioni, Clericus Civicus, copia, f. 22) . More definite references to unarmed galleys are in G. Giomo, "Le rubriche dei Libri Misti del Senato perduto," *Archivio Veneto,* XIX, 104, a permit to galleys to leave with unarmed ships if they carry no more than twenty-five men in the crew, and, *ibid.,* p. 109, a permit to Marcus Soranzo "super suo galea disarmata possit portare homines L, Giov. Michiel LX."

[22] Many cases of "armentur per comune" and "armentur per divisum" or "volentes mittere . . . faciant se scribi" are mentioned in the *rubrica* of Senato Misti published by Giomo, e.g., *Archivio Veneto,* XVIII, 316, 320. The surviving fragment of reg. 1 of Senato Misti (A.S.V.) gives a regulation for each system, ff. 163-65, 186-87.

laws. Most important at first was the Maggior Consiglio. The records of its *deliberazioni* have survived for the period subsequent to 1282 and those prior to 1300 have been published by Professor Roberto Cessi, but the lack of indices and of adequate rubrics for most years after 1282 makes it difficult to find all the maritime legislation they contain.[23] The Maggior Consiglio not only approved the alterations in the basic law, such as the *aggiunte* approved under Doges Francesco Dandolo in 1328 and Andrea Dandolo in 1343; it made many new regulations of maritime police and during the first decades of the fourteenth century sometimes made the kind of decisions organizing convoys which later in the century were regularly made by the senate.[24]

The senate made detailed regulations for particular fleets in its earliest register, but only a part of that register has survived and the next thirteen are missing, so that this rich treasury of information on maritime affairs is not available as a continuous series until 1332.[25]

The administration of the merchant marine received considerable attention directly from the doge and his ducal council.[26] It was also part

[23] Roberto Cessi has described the earliest records in the introductions to his edition, which is cited in n. 11 above (cited thereafter as *Delib. M.C.*). Subsequent to 1282, four series at the A.S.V. record the decisions of the Maggior Consiglio: (1) In the archive of the Maggior Consiglio the original registers are difficult to use because (i) although entries are roughly in chronological order, many items are out of order, (ii) there are some lacunae, (iii) dates are given in a way that does not make them easy to find, (iv) difficulties with the handwriting are increased by discoloration and by the crossings out of laws officially canceled. (2) In the same archive are clear copies made in the sixteenth and seventeenth centuries in which the chronology is easy to follow, canceled items are included, and the pagination of the original is given. They are generally accurate, although I found some slips, e.g., "naulo" for "navilio" in the law of February 8, 1303, new style. There is an index which is useful but not exhaustive. (3) The archive of the Avogaria di Commun, Maggior Consiglio, Deliberazioni, contains a series of registers of which the earliest was compiled about 1309. From that date they are approximately contemporary copies from the M.C. originals, but omit the laws already canceled. In some registers the arrangement is chronological, in some topical.

The originals in the records of the Maggior Consiglio are of course the best source for its actions. In regard to the form in which laws were in some measure obeyed for some time, the series of *deliberazioni* in the Avogaria is as good a source.

[24] A.S.V., M.C., Deliberazioni, Magnus copia, f. 361 (March 5, 1308); Presbiter, copia, f. 167 (March 31, 1312); ff. 240–41 (Sept. 8, 1313).

[25] Senato Misti, reg. I, ff. 163–65, 186–87.

[26] M. Roberti, *Magistrature giudiziarie veneziane e i loro capitolari fino al 1300* (Monumenti storici pubblicati per la R. Deputazione Veneta di Storia Patria, XVII, ser. 2, Statuti, II; Venice, 1909), II, 27, 48; *Delib. M.C.*, ed. Cessi, II, 26–27, 31, 43; III, 332; A.S.V., Maggior Consiglio, Delib., Magnus, copia, f. 29; Spiritus, copia, ff. 240–41, and Senato Misti, reg. 1, ff. 163–65 where the ducal council is charged with hearing the report of income and expenses of the galleys operated *per comune*.

of their duties to enforce the decisions and collection of fines for various subordinate administrative boards.

Of these subordinate magistrates the most intimately associated with merchant shipping in the thirteenth century were the *consoli dei mercanti*. Their importance is evident throughout Zeno's statutes,[27] is emphasized by the provisions added to the copy of these statutes in the Library of Congress, and is reflected in the early chapters of the *capitolare* of the *consoli*.[28] During the six centuries of their existence the activities of these *consoli* varied considerably. One basic function was their jurisdiction over contracts in restraint of trade. They were responsible as judges for levying criminal penalties on those making illegal contracts, that is, monopolistic combines among foreigners or between foreigners and some Venetians harmful to other Venetians. To this basic original function was added many special duties from time to time: supervision of the woolen and silk industries, of banking, insurance, and exchange. They were called on for advisory opinions on commercial policy, often jointly with the *provveditori di comun*.[29] But in the third quarter of the thirteenth century the main concern of the *consoli* was with the Venetian merchant marine.

One responsibility of the consuls was to estimate and record the carrying capacity of each vessel. The rating thus given it determined the amount of crew and equipment the ship was required to carry. This duty was prescribed in the oldest *capitolare* of the *consoli,* possibly compiled before 1240,[30] and remained with the consuls until it was shared with the Arsenal in the sixteenth century.[31] A rule for measuring in specified ways to determine the dimensions of the ship and

[27] The consuls are mentioned in ch. 32–36, 40, 41, 44, 52–53, 73, 83, and 98 of the edition by Predelli and Sacerdoti. One suspects that the consuls acted in some instances in which the doge and his council are the authority referred to, for example, in naming a fifth member to the committee in charge of ballasting the ship in case the required four members could not agree (Ch. 3).

[28] The copies of the *capitolare dei consoli dei mercanti* are relatively late in date. That in A.S.V. is a compilation finished in 1506. In the Museo Civico Correr is an exact copy thereof, with additional laws down to 1590. The chapter numbering is the same in both copies. Regulation of ships, especially their registry, bulks large in the section on the consuls in the "Liber Comunis," *Delib. M.C.*, ed., Cessi, II, 252–57.

[29] Sandi, *Principii di Storia Civile*, II, 787–90.

[30] Capitolare, Consoli dei Mercanti, ch. 35, where it is specified that provisions are being copied from the "capitulari antiquissimi." This chapter comes before the earliest of the dated chapters, which is dated 1240.

[31] See Lane, *Venetian Ships*, pp. 247–49; Senato Mar, reg. 1, f. 86; reg. 18, f. 138. Sandi, *Principii di Storia Civile*, II, 793, mentions the *savii sopra li conti* among the seventeenth-century magistracies competing with the *consoli dei mercanti* "per estimar li navigli."

calculating the rating of capacity by a formal mathematical rule was in use in the fifteenth century, but originally the *consoli* depended on their individual judgments of how deeply the vessel could safely be submerged and on the records of the shipmasters and the *scribani* concerning how much cargo had been put aboard when the vessel was down to its load line. A decision was reached by vote of the majority, each individual *console* using his own judgment, according to the oath prescribed in their *capitolare:* "Omnes naves, et ligna, quas extimabo, bona fide extimabo, de quot milliariis esse videbitur mihi."[32] If a Venetian built a ship in one of the Venetian possessions overseas, a similar rating of the vessel was made by the nearest Venetian rector.[33]

The amount of cargo the ship could properly carry having been determined by the *consoli,* a load line was marked on the side of the vessel. Two ways of indicating how deeply the ship could safely be submerged were used, one for galleys and *tarete,* the other for vessels of more than one deck. On the former there were iron rods or some other form of marker extending downward from the lowest point of the deck or gunwale. Laws prescribed the amount of freeboard, that is, how many feet and inches of this marker must be visible above the water.[34] On ships of more than one deck, the line was determined by placing a cross on the outside at the level of the first deck.[35] The laws then stipulated for various kinds of ships and voyages how far below the surface of the water the cross might be submerged.[36]

Much inspection was required to prevent vessels from taking on too much weight and submerging the markers to an illegal extent. The *consoli* were instructed to go themselves to the waterfront or to send someone to see that the round ships leaving in important convoys were

---

[32] In the *Statuta navium* of Zeno there is no detail about the procedure in estimating and rating each vessel of 200 *milliaria* and over. More detail and the quotation are found in the Capitolare, Consoli dei Mercanti, ch. 35. In the *Statuta tarretarum,* the first chapter provides that all *tarete* be rated, those already built and those to be built, even those under 2,000 *milliaria,* and that record be made of the number of *milliaria* they could carry, accepting the sworn statements of the *scribani* as to how much was loaded when the vessel was down to its load line, namely 3 ft. of freeboard.

[33] Code of Zeno, ed. by Predelli and Sacerdoti, ch. 101.

[34] A.S.V., Senato Misti, reg. 1, ff. 163–65, 186–87; Codice Brera 263, f. 56, regarding galleys. On *tarete,* their *statuta,* Predelli and Sacerdoti, ch. 1, and A.S.V., Capitolare, Consoli dei Mercanti, ch. 40, 59; *Delib. M.C.,* ed. Cessi, II, 254, 256.

[35] That the place of the cross was determined by the level of the first deck is to be inferred from Zeno's statutes, ch. 93, ed. by Predelli and Sacerdoti, which provided a heavy fine for raising the lower deck after the completion of the ship.

[36] *Ibid.,* ch. 61–66. Also in Ziani's law on loading, ed. by Predelli and Sacerdoti, p. 48.

not loaded excessively.[37] Many other officials besides the *consoli* were ordered to check on the load lines. The *statuta* of Doge Zeno gave the *scribanus* and the merchant passengers authority to enforce the regulations. For each vessel loading overseas, a ballasting committee consisting of the shipmaster, the mate, and two merchants—with a third merchant added in case the four could not agree—was in charge of ballasting the vessel. The scribe and the merchants on this committee were charged individually with measuring the degree of submersion of the cross, and if it was excessively submerged with estimating the amount of excessive cargo. The shipmaster was then liable to a fine of twice the freight on that amount of cargo. The fine was calculated by using the highest rate of freight paid by any cargo.[38] Shippers who were also passengers had double reason to try to enforce the law: overloading placed their lives as well as their goods in danger, since it was frequently a cause of shipwreck.

At the beginning of the fourteenth century the markers showing how deeply a galley was loaded were closely watched to prevent overloading. How closely is suggested by a provision in a law of 1300 increasing the obligation of the galley masters to carry arms for their vessel. As compensation they were permitted to load the galley one inch deeper in the water.[39] Enforcing the loading laws on galley masters was not the concern of the *consoli dei mercanti,* however; it was the obligation of other officials who appear to have had at first the simple title of *cercatores galearum.*[40]

[37] A.S.V., Capitolare, Consoli dei Mercanti, ch. 36.

[38] Doge Zeno's *Statuta navium* (ed. by Predelli and Sacerdoti) , ch. 4, 42. Although the statute says "mensurabunt vel extimabunt," it is evident that they are not estimating the capacity of the ship by taking its basic measures, for the same words are used in clauses instructing the *consoli* and others to measure vessels after they are loaded, and after their rating has been determined (*ibid.,* ch. 42, 44–47) . Consequently the measuring referred to was the measuring of the degree of submersion of the cross. This is confirmed by provisions for what to do if waves prevent measuring (ch. 46) and prohibition on the masters to place anything above the cross so as to interfere with the measuring (ch. 38) . The estimating referred to may mean the estimate of excess cargo which determined the amount of the fine.

[39] A.S.V., Maggior Consiglio, Deliberazioni, Liber Magnus et Capricornus, originale, f. 11, Oct. 15, 1300. The general rule seems to have required 2 ft. of freeboard for the communally armed galleys, and 2½ ft. for those privately armed and operated. Senato Misti, reg. 1, ff. 163–65, 186–87; Codici Brera, 263, f. 56.

[40] They had their own *capitolare,* which forbade them to conduct inspections except when acting in pairs. For a special emergency the doge and council were authorized to appoint assistants with whom they could act. A.S.V., Maggior Consiglio, Deliberazioni, Liber Magnus et Capricornus, f. 10, originale (Sept. 3, 1300) . They are also mentioned as inspectors in *ibid.,* f. 11, 11 t.

While the load lines of the galleys were closely watched, those of the round ships apparently received little attention at the beginning of the fourteenth century and by 1375 the vessels were no longer even marked with the cross so often referred to in the thirteenth-century codes. Much which those codes prescribed in regard to rig and structure had become obsolete because the *buzonavis* had been replaced by the cog. The thirteenth-century rules about sails were no longer enforced and the *consoli* also failed to apply to the cogs the rules requiring that they be marked with a cross to show their proper loads. The *consoli* continued to give each vessel a rating which determined its complement of crew, arms, etc., but this was done by taking the ship's measures and calculating its size by a mathematical formula. When in 1375 it was ordered anew that the round ships also be marked so that their proper load line could be quickly determined, the enforcement was given not to the *consoli* but to a different agency, the *officiales Levantis,* of whom we will have much to say shortly.[41]

Closely connected with the inspection of loading on round ships, which was part of their responsibilities in the thirteenth century, was the authority of the *consoli* over the *scribani*. These scribes or clerks were the officials on each ship who kept the record of the ship's crew and cargo. All of them had to be examined and approved by the *consoli,* before whom they took the oaths of office specified in Zeno's statutes.[42] In the thirteenth century the ship's scribe was assigned to it by the *consoli* instead of being selected by the shipmaster or ship-owners.[43]

The authority of the *consoli* extended to many other matters. When the governing councils of Venice had declared the seas open, it was the duty of the *consoli* to see that ships got off within the specified sailing season and to prevent them from leaving at forbidden times. They

[41] Senato Misti, reg. 34, f. 165 (Feb. 27, 1374/75) , and on the rating of ships by the consuls, Capitolare, Consoli dei Mercanti, ch. 200, 247.

[42] Zeno's Code (ed. by Predelli and Sacerdoti) , ch. 41, 42, 35.

[43] Capitolare, Consoli dei Mercanti, ch. 37, reads: "Debeo cum sociis meis elligere et dare scribanos omnibus navibus que debentur habere scribanos secundum statum et concedere eis certam mercedem pro suo labore." Later the *scribanus* appears to have been chosen by the *patronus,* as was the general custom; see Zeno, pp. 266–70. That the change was taking place at Venice in the fourteenth century is indicated by a provision in 1315, although in regard to galleys, that if the *patronus* is not satisfied with the *scribanus* the *patronus* can choose another and the rejected is to have another post on the galleys. A.S.V., Maggior Consiglio, Deliberazioni, Clericus Civicus, copia, f. 120, June 17, 1315.

could levy fines to enforce orders concerning the times of sailing.[44] It was also their responsibility to fine shipmasters who loaded excessively, or in forbidden places, who did not stay with their ship, or who fired one crew member and hired another without the permission of the majority of the merchants on board, or appointed a ship's scribe contrary to the rules.[45] They were responsible also for fining any merchant-passenger who refused to serve when elected to the committee of five prescribed by Venetian laws to decide doubtful questions during the voyage.[46] While the *consoli* gave the sentences imposing the fines, the obligation to enforce their collection fell on the doge and was executed by his *gastaldi,* or in some cases by the *signori di notte.*[47] Condemnations for violations of the maritime laws could also be made by the *advocatores comunis,* and of course by the ducal council itself.[48]

Originally the *consoli* had had not only administrative oversight of the merchant marine but also general judicial authority in disputes between merchants on land or sea.[49] The Venetians did not clearly separate administration from such judicial functions, as, for example, the settlement of a dispute between a shipmaster and a shipper or a member of the crew; but, in general, disputes among the parties to a voyage were judged either by arbiters agreed to by the parties to the dispute or by one of the *uffizi di palazzo,* which had developed out of the doge's court.[50] This ducal court was divided at the time of Sebastian

---

[44] A.S.V., Capitolare, Consoli dei Mercanti, ch. 85 (1287) ; Avvogaria di Comun, Deliberazioni del Maggior Consiglio, Cerberus, f. 63 (1288 and 1298) .

[45] Zeno's *Statuta navium* (ed. by Predelli and Sacerdoti) , chs. 32–33, 35, 41, and Capitolare, Consoli dei Mercanti, ch. 43.

[46] *Ibid.,* ch. 73.

[47] Roberti, *Magistrature giud.* (Padua, 1906) , pp. 78–80; Sandi, *Principii di Storia Civile,* II, pp. 808–10; and innumerable chapters of Zeno's *Statuta navium;* e.g., ch. 73 contains the clause, "et si eam auferre non poterunt [i.e., the *consoli*] nos cum nostro concilio, infra quindecim dies postquam in noticia fierit nobis datum, ipsam penam auferre vel auferri facere teneamur." See also ch. 116.

[48] The *advocatores comunis* are charged with the execution of penalties in the laws under Doge Ziani in 1227 (Predelli and Sacerdoti, p. 48) and are given general powers to proceed against violations in Zeno's *statuta,* ch. 98, 118, and powers with reference specifically to sailors in ch. 90 and 112. They were the highest ranking officials charged with law enforcement under the doge; the functions of the *consoli* were much more specialized. Roberti, *Magistrature giudiziarii,* I, 179–81.

[49] Sandi, *Principii di Storia Civile,* II, 787; *Delib. M.C.,* ed. Cessi, II, 252.

[50] Roberti argued that before 1255 disputes were always settled by an arbiter chosen by the parties to the dispute. He so interprets the reference to *iudices* in

Ziani into two *curie,* that *del proprio* and that *dei giudici del comune,* later called *giudici del forestier.* In the second half of the thirteenth century, most cases involving maritime law were assigned to the *giudici del forestier.*[51] In July, 1255, they were given authority to impose penalties on shipmasters to force delivery of wares to merchants. In 1264 they were given obligatory jurisdiction over all cases about ships (*ad rationem navium*) involving judgments of less than 10 lire and optional jurisdiction when the sum was larger. In 1273 they were given exclusive jurisdiction over both foreigners and Venetians in disputes with shipmasters about freights, the equipment of ships, routes, and similar matters.[52] In 1292 they were given jurisdiction over freight contracts even when the wares were not actually loaded on shipboard.[53] They were made responsible for determining penalties against either shipmaster or crew for violations of wage contracts and for requiring the execution of the penalties by the *signori di notte* (*domini de nocte*).[54] A later draft of their *capitolare* summarized by saying that they judged suits "ad rationem navium."[55]

One of the general statutes of the *giudici del forestier* provided that in judging suits involving foreigners, they decide according to what was provided by treaties; if there was no treaty, then according to the statutes; if there were no applicable statutes, then according to custom; and if there was no established custom, then according to their conscience. The same order of authority was also applied explicitly to cases of maritime law, except that when no foreigners were involved no treaty need be considered.[56]

Tiepolo's Code of 1229, ch. 43–45. See Roberti, *Magistrature giud.,* I, 191 n. He believed that other references to *iudices* should be interpreted as references to these arbiters. But ch. 45 in Tiepolo's statute does not say how the judges are chosen, and in regard to disputes to be settled overseas it explicitly gives jurisdiction to "duca, potestas vel bailus per nos" or whomever they designate, in any place where there are such offices. This implies that a similar authority was held by the ducal court in Venice. In Zeno's statutes, ch. 83–86 admit of the same interpretation. Roberti found no specific reference to the *giudici del comune* or *del forestier* prior to July 20, 1255, less than a month before the promulgation of Zeno's Code in August of that year. Therefore the law of that July may have been the first which gave the *giudici del forestier* jurisdiction in cases involving maritime law.

[51] Roberti, *Magistrature giud.,* I, 182, 189–92; II, 105–17.

[52] *Delib. M.C.,* ed. Cessi, II, 205; Roberti, *Magistrature giud.,* II, 105, 112–14.

[53] Roberti, *Magistrature giud.,* II, 117, and here above, sect. I, n. 11.

[54] *Ibid.,* I, 192; II, 114; and see A.S.V., Archivio del Forestier, Perg. B. I.

[55] Roberti, I, 189–92; II, 105.

[56] *Ibid.,* II, 105, ch. 4, 5; Zeno's *Statuta,* ch. 97.

In spite of the large jurisdiction in maritime law acquired by the *giudici del forestier,* the *consoli* retained authority over many disputes. In Zeno's Code, where the authority of the *giudici* was affirmed, it was made subject to the powers given the *consoli.*[57] They were the authorities in cases where a shipper claimed his wares had been damaged by water,[58] and in cases of salvage.[59] Their general jurisdiction over exchange transactions of all kinds probably extended to loans on bottomry made by a master offering his ship as security. A glimpse into the relations between the jurisdiction of the *consoli dei mercanti* and that of the *giudici del forestier* is provided by a case brought to the Maggior Consiglio in 1358 by Doge Giovanni Dolfin. A ship whose master had died at Constantinople had been brought back to Venice by its crew, who had then sued the ship for their wages. The *giudici del forestier* had given judgment favorable to the seamen, but the ship was in the hands of the *consoli dei mercanti.* The *consoli* said that all the value of the ship was needed to pay exchanges that the shipmaster had drawn in Constantinople. The doge protested that no one could have a better claim against a ship than the seamen who had had possession of it and had brought it home by their own labors. The Maggior Consiglio backed up the doge, although only by a vote of 310 to 81, 101 abstaining. Thus was established the principle, entered in the *capitolare:* "Quod creditores virtute mercedis aliis creditoribus preferantur."[60]

IV

The time and attention that the *consoli* gave to shipping must have been very considerable in the mid-thirteenth century, but many of the duties which took them from the Rialto to the waterfront—that is, to the anchorage in front of the ducal palace—were transferred later in the century to other magistracies.

In 1279 the inspection of unarmed ships to see that they carried the required arms was transferred to the *domini super mercationibus Levantis.*[61] These officials were sometimes referred to simply as the

---

[57] Ch. 86, 98 (Predelli and Sacerdoti).

[58] *Ibid.,* ch. 52–53; and Capitolare, Consoli dei Mercanti, ch. 46.

[59] Capitolare, Consoli dei Mercanti, ch. 46, 105.

[60] *Ibid.,* ch. 191, and M.C. Novella, originale, f. 57, Feb. 18, 1357/58.

[61] *Delib. M.C.,* ed. Cessi, II, 218; A.S.V., Cod. Brera, 263, f. 35–36. On this *capitolare,* see below n. 84.

Levanti.[62] They had been created to supervise trade in Levantine wares[63] and continued to enforce rules about who could take part in the Levant trade at the same time that they inspected the armament of merchantmen.[64] They were so much concerned with contraband that their office was in 1285 combined with that of the *domini de contrabannis,* although immediately separated again.[65] In 1288 the *Levanti* were ignored in a new regulation concerning the kind or number of bows to be included in the armament of the ships; the enforcement was assigned to another administrative board concerned with trade, the *cattaveri,*[66] but in 1291 when the head armor required for sailors was changed from hoods to hats, the *Levanti* were cited as the authorities on armor.[67] Although the enforcing authority of *consoli, contrabanni, capitanei postarum, cattaveri,* and *Levanti* overlapped, the *Levanti* were those directly responsible for inspecting large round ships on the eve of their departure. Their authority was not limited to vessels going to Syria and for cotton; it extended to all Venetian unarmed ships, and in 1339 the *Levanti* were given authority to inspect also the ships of cities subject to Venice, presumably Dalmatian and Greek cities, whose ships were said to be operating without proper arms;[68] but the armament that most concerned these officials was that of the big ships that went out to the Levant to bring back cotton.

Whenever one of these ships was about to sail, a member of the *Levanti* accompanied by his clerk and two pages went aboard and ordered all the crew mustered for his inspection.[69] If there were not as many men as there should have been for the size of the ship, according to its official rating which the *Levanti* received from the *consoli,* or if the crew did not include a proper number of bowmen, or included too many boys, or did not have all the arms prescribed, the inspecting

[62] In the reorganization in 1516 of the estimating and rating of ships and the anchorage tax. A.S.V., Senato Mar, reg. 18, f. 138; see Chap. 10, Table VI.

[63] Roberto Cessi and Annibale Alberti, *Rialto: l'isola, il porto, il mercato,* p. 234; *Delib. M.C.,* ed. Cessi, II, 289–91. Their number was reduced from three to two in 1280. *Ibid.,* p. 291.

[64] A.S.V., M.C., Magnus, copia, f. 115, 118. Biblioteca Marciana, MS Lat., cl. 5, cod. 6, Capitolare della Ternaria, f. 34.

[65] *Delib. M.C.,* ed. Cessi, III, 125. On the creation of the Three against Contraband, see *ibid.,* II, 220.

[66] *Ibid.,* III, 210.

[67] *Ibid.,* III, 301.

[68] A.S.V., Codici Brera, 263, f. 41.

[69] *Delib. M.C.,* ed. Cessi, III, 333; A.S.V., M.C., Deliberazioni, Spiritus, originale, ff. 44–45 (Feb. 3, 1330/31). To ships going within the Adriatic they could send a clerk and a page to inspect. Codici Brera 263, f. 41, Aug. 28, 1339.

magistrate would report to his colleagues and the *Levanti* could then levy a fine up to 50 lire. They would receive a quarter of the fine.[70] Collecting it was up to the *signori di notte,* who received another quarter.[71] If the *ufficiale di Levante* found all the men prescribed by law, each with the arms appropriate to his rank, and the additional arms which the shipmaster had to provide, all there in the arms room, still he was ordered to take precautions. He was to lock and seal the arms room and give the key to the shipmaster with order not to open the door until the ship was at sea and to make anyone who took arms out put them back. A representative of the merchant shippers, called the navigator, was to inspect the room after the ship had been three days at sea.[72] Such elaborate provisions for enforcement in 1309 clearly imply that violations occurred.

The regulations which the *Levanti* were charged with enforcing reflected the changes in weapons and armor in the late thirteenth and early fourteenth centuries. Their *capitolare* included chapters concerning armament from Zeno's Code,[73] but also later provisions requiring more crossbows and more body armor, at least on the higher-paid members of the crew.[74] As crossbowmen became specialized out from the other seamen, it was required after 1331 that two out of ten of the crew, at least, be bowmen.[75] And the responsibility for providing arms and armor was gradually shifted from the individual seaman to the shipmaster.[76]

[70] That the *Levanti* should keep a record of the estimates of size made by the *consoli* appears from M.C., Deliberazioni, Fronesis, originale, f. 140, Sept. 24, 1324.

[71] *Delib. M.C.,* ed. Cessi, II, 218. There are references to their inspections and to condemnations for having insufficient crew in *Grazie* (ed. Favaro), reg. 1. no. 95, and A.S.V., Grazie, reg. 3, f. 15; reg. 5, ff. 14, 16, 20, 44, 62.

[72] A.S.V., Cod. Brera 263, ff. 40–41. In 1280 passenger shippers were ordered to inspect the books of the *scribanus,* who was to keep a record of all arms. Violations were to be reported to the rectors; there was no mention of the *Levanti.* But already in 1293 the *Levanti* were ordered to put in their *capitolare* their duty to inspect and give an inventory to the committee of three merchants, the *nauclerus,* and the *scribanus.* These five were all put on oath to inspect within five days of going to sea in order to be sure that the arms were where they belonged. Delib. M.C., III, 333, Feb. 26, 1292/93.

[73] A.S.V., Cod. Brera, 263, ff. 36–37, contains copies of ch. 27, 29, and 30 of Zeno's Code.

[74] Cod. Brera, 263, ff. 34–35.

[75] *Ibid.,* f. 35; M.C., Spiritus, originale, ff. 44–45. Earlier laws of 1280, 1288, and 1290, requiring more arms for high-paid seamen but not requiring bowmen as a separate category are not included in the surviving copy of their *capitolare* (Cod. Brera, 263), but see *Delib. M.C.,* ed. Cessi, II, 70; III, 210, 262.

[76] *Delib. M.C.,* ed. Cessi, III, 333; A.S.V., M.C., Deliberazioni, Magnus copia, f. 32; Spiritus copia, f. 97.

Since the *Levanti* had to inspect ships to see that they were properly armed, it was natural to entrust them also with inspection to prevent overloading, and to prevent stowage in forbidden places or by forbidden methods. This duty was one which the *Levanti* shared with the *cattaveri*. The chief new law that they were called on to enforce in the early fourteenth century concerned specifically the loading of cotton. Emphasis on cotton suggests an explanation for the neglect in regard to round ships of the load line required in Zeno's Code. If large round ships were being built mainly to carry cargoes of cotton, there was little danger that they would be sunk too low in the water by such a light cargo. Instead the dangers were that they would load between decks and above decks in forbidden places and that they would employ mechanical methods to compress the cotton excessively in stowing it below decks. Using screws to compress a row of bales so as to squeeze in more bales could damage the cotton and could even be carried to the point of springing the ship's planking and causing leaks.[77] The thirteenth-century codes contain some reference to mechanical methods of loading and unloading cotton.[78] Fourteenth-century laws applying to both galleys and round ships distinguished between loading by hand and by lever or screw (*ad brachia, ad cuneum*) and limited the amount of loading by screw according to the age of the ship.[79]

In so far as these laws and others about loading applied to galleys, their enforcement did not fall within the jurisdiction of the *Levanti*

[77] The screwing of cotton in a modern cargo vessel is described in Thomas Rothwell Taylor, *Stowage of Ship Cargoes* (U.S. Bureau of Foreign and Domestic Commerce, Department of Commerce Miscellaneous Series, 92; Washington, 1920). A Venetian regulation of 1302 was headed: "Non possit ponere in galeis plus ad cuneos quam ad brachia taliter quod non infrangant aliquam catenam nec levare copertam." A.S.V., Cod. Brera, 263, f. 56.

[78] In the regulation of loading under Pietro Ziani in 1227 (*Gli Statuti marittimi*, ed. by Predelli and Sacerdoti, p. 47) stowing *ad trabem* (with levers) is subject to approval of local officials. See also *ibid.*, Statuto di Tiepolo, par. 18.

[79] The distinctions between sacks of cotton loaded by screw (*ad cuneos*) and by hand (*ad brachia*) is made in 1300 in regard to the loading of galleys (Senato Misti, reg. 1, ff. 163–65) and very elaborately for round ships, according to the age of the vessel, in July 28, 1332. See Senato Misti, reg. 15, f. 27. This law is in the *capitolare* of the *Levanti*, A.S.V., Codici Brera, 263, ff. 37–38 misdated July 18, 1322, and in the *capitolare* of the *cattaveri*, where it is dated correctly.

There are two very similar copies of a *capitolare officialium cattaveris* compiled and written in the fourteenth century; one in the Archivio di Stato di Venezia, Ufficiali al Cattaver, busta 1; the other in the Library of Congress, Washington, D.C., Law Office, MSS. V42. In the manuscript at the Library of Congress the regulations about the stowage of cotton are on ff. 119, 122.

until their office was consolidated about 1330 with the *officiales de super denariis de Rascia.*[80] Strange as it may seem in view of their title, these officials, originally instituted to prevent the coins of the Balkan despot of Rascia from being accepted as the equivalent of the Venetian grossi,[81] were in 1304 charged with inspecting privately armed galleys.[82] The need for such inspection was increasing. In the first decades of the fourteenth century, galleys with crews of 150 to 200 each were organized into convoys for many voyages. They were all commanded by admirals appointed by the commune and followed routes and procedures specified in detail by the Maggior Consiglio or the *quarantia* and senate. Sometimes the individual galleys were operated communally, sometimes under private management for private profit.[83] In the former case, their inspection was primarily the responsibility of the galley master appointed by the *armatores,* by private parties who were seeking a profit on the voyage. Strict inspection by government officials was needed to make sure that they did not overload, that they carried all the arms they were supposed to, paid the crew fully at official rates, etc.[84] In 1300 the officials called *cercatores galearum* inspected both communal and private galleys,[85] but from 1304 to about 1330 inspection of pri-

---

[80] The first mention I have yet found of the consolidation is in A.S.V., M.C., Deliberazioni, Spiritus, copia, f. 156, March 3, 1334.

[81] Roberto Cessi, *Problemi monetari veneziani* (R. Accademia dei Lincei, Documenti finan. della Rep. di Venezia editi dalla Com. per gli Atti delle Assemblee Cost. Ital., ser. 4, vol. I; Padua 1937) , doc. 57, 60, 68.

[82] A.S.V., Avogaria di Comun, Deliberazioni del M.C., Magnus, f. 41.

[83] Innumerable references to the two systems appear in "Le Rubriche dei Libri Misti del Senato perduto," ed. by G. Giomo, *Archivio Veneto,* vols. 17–27.

[84] Compare the provision for the privately operated galleys and communally operated galleys in Senato Misti, reg. 1, ff. 163–65 and 186–87.

[85] A.S.V., M.C., Deliberazioni, Magnus et Capricornus, f. 10, 11, 11 tᵛ. These *cercatores* probably formed part of "illi de super armamento" referred to in *Delib. M.C.,* ed. Cessi, II, 228–29, 332, and in A.S.V., Avogaria di Comun, Deliberazioni del Maggior Consiglio, Magnus, rubriche. In 1302 there is a reference to an inspection by the *pagatores,* who were perhaps the same officials; *Grazie,* reg. I (used in proof through the courtesy of Dr. Luigi Lanfranchi) , no. 336. These *pagatores* were certainly part of the *officium de super armamento;* the first paragraphs of the lost first volume of the *capitolare* of the *provveditori all'armar* were largely devoted to these officials. See A.S.V., Prov. all'Armar, reg. 10, rubriche, s.v. Pagadori. See also Compilazione leggi, busta 24. Since they paid the crews on communal galleys, they also levied fines on seamen who failed to serve after receiving pay. A.S.V., *Grazie,* reg. 3, ff. 23, 24, 41 *et passim.* Their disciplinary authority was sometimes extended from state galleys to private galleys. *Delib. M.C.,* ed. Cessi, III, 332. Probably they inspected communal galleys and did so not only to see that all the crew paid were aboard but also to see that the vessels were properly armed and loaded. Before 1304 they may

vate galleys was assigned to the *officiales grossorum de Raxia.*[86]
Many of the rules enforced by the *officiales grossorum Raxie* were
derived from the decrees passed by the senate each year concerning the
convoys for the year. In these decrees many clauses were repeated with

---

have inspected also such private galleys as there were. The *cercatores* referred to in
1300–1 are probably the same officials who are also called *pagatores.*

This interpretation is supported by the oath sworn to by the *ufficiali al armamento;* see the thirteenth-century parchment in A.S.V., Miscellanea atti diplomatici
e privati, busta 9, no. 327, kindly called to my attention by Dr. Raimondo Morozzo
della Rocca, director of the Venetian archive.

[86] I know of no surviving records of the *officium grossorum de Raxia* except those
incorporated in Brera 263. If there are any others they might, surprisingly enough,
be valuable not for monetary history but for maritime history.

The regulations to be enforced by the *Levanti* were collected in a *capitolare* about
1375 and the contents of this document, Cod. Brera, 263, is one indication of the
functions of the *Levanti.* To be sure this surviving copy of their *capitolare* is full of
mistakes in the dating of laws. It is on paper in a cursive hand without embellish-
ments. Presumably there was a more handsome parchment copy of the *capitolare*
of the *Levanti* comparable to the *capitolare* of about the same date of the *cattaveri*
(see above, n. 77). It is to be hoped that the parchment copy was more accurate,
but it probably contained very similar material.

The *capitalare* of the *Levanti* was divided into six *libri.* The first two *libri* contain
regulations concerning contraband and the kind of voyages permitted to the Levant,
i.e., the functions of the *Levanti* before 1279 (see above n. 63).

Book III contains the regulations concerning the arms and crew required on
unarmed ships. One of the first chapters, III, ff. 35 t–36, is largely a word-for-word
copy of chapter 27 from Zeno's Code. This is another bit of evidence that Zeno's
Code was accepted as the basic law and was considered as still in force in the second
half of the fourteenth century unless it had meanwhile been modified. The standards of Zeno's regulations appear in many other chapters, for example, one of f. 35,
dated 1311, stating that any vessel *(lignum)* big enough to be rated by the consuls
must have a crew of at least twenty-five. The figure is that given in Zeno's statute for
the *tarete* (see above), ch. 16; and it is significant that the *Levanti* applied it, not to
navi, but to unarmed galleys or any other *lignum,* which means, in my view, any
vessels that were like galleys in being relatively long and low, and having only one
deck, as were the *tarete,* but were considered unarmed because they carried less
crew and arms than if they had been fully equipped and manned for the use of
oars. But most of the regulations in Book III are modifications of Zeno's Code made
desirable by changes in the techniques of warfare and ship construction.

Book IV concerns mainly the internal management of their office but includes
some regulations concerning moneys.

Book V contains regulations for arming and loading merchant galleys. It was copied, presumably, from the *capitolare* of the *officiales denariorum Rascie.*

Book VI appears a miscellany.

little change from year to year.[87] For the galleys leaving in 1317, the Maggior Consiglio itself made very detailed provision for inspection by the *officium super grossis Raxie*. The *armatores* were to have their galleys "in Canali a trageto Sancti Gregorii usque ad Sanctum Nicolaum de Littore" with all arms, men, and stores aboard. They were to be inspected only between sunrise and sunset. If they lacked their complement of men and arms or did not measure the proper amount of freeboard, the galleys' *armatores* were to be fined and extra cargo removed. On return voyages they were required to bring certificates from Venetian officials overseas showing that they had been inspected there before departure. If they lacked these licenses, the galley masters were to be fined and in all these fines the *officiales de super grossis Raxie* would have a share.[88]

Their consolidation with the *Levanti* was itself a sign that their duties had become less heavy about 1330. Shortly thereafter the combined agency was doing so much less business than formerly that in 1334 it was instructed to meet only in the mornings, instead of both mornings and afternoon.[89] In fact a new system of operating convoys of galleys had been worked out. We find it in effect for the Levantine voyages in the 1330's, for the Flemish voyage in the 1340's. The galleys and the material equipment for their armament were supplied by the communal Arsenal and the operation was entrusted to whatever individuals bid highest for the right to receive the freights and pay the expenses of crew and supplies for the voyage indicated.[90]

Under the system of leasing state-owned galleys for specified voyages, inspection of their armament was left to the *capitano* chosen for the fleet and to the Arsenal. The inspection of their cargo was entrusted to the *domini extraordinariorum*. This magistracy had been created in 1302 in order to inspect and collect freights, not from private galleys, but from galleys operated by the commune. The resolution of the

---

[87] This was true of the resolutions for auctioning galleys contained in the surviving registers of Senato Misti, 1332 ff. I believe that the same was true earlier. The surviving fragment of reg. 1, ff. 185–86, contains a resolution of Jan. 17, 1303, providing for a convoy of privately operated galleys. The provisions it contains concerning how much each merchant-passenger might take with him is identical in substance to that in the *capitolare* of the *Levanti* dated June, 1302.

[88] M.C., Deliberazioni, Clericus Civicus, copia, 177–79.

[89] *Ibid.*, Spiritus, copia, f. 156, March 3, 1334.

[90] Some legal aspects of the system are described by Antonio Scialoja, "Un precedente medioevale di 'Pools' marittimi," in *Studi in memoria di Barnardino Scorza* (Rome, 1940) .

Maggior Consiglio that created the agency said merely, "quod eligantur tres super racionibus extraordinariis et super cercandis galeis."[91] They soon acquired the entirely unrelated function of supervising the important Venetian festival called the feast of the Marys, but they expanded their collection of galley freights so as to collect for the galleys leased by the state.[92] Since these freights included in effect the customs duties, the *extraordinarii* became in the course of time customs collectors.[93] To follow that evolution would take us too far afield.

By the middle of the fourteenth century only the principles applied in Zeno's Code to assure safety at sea were valid; its detailed provisions were obsolete. Ships were still required to carry crew and arms according to their size, but the rules about the number of men and the kind of armor and weapons gradually changed. In the regulations against overloading the load line was no longer of primary importance for the large round ships; new rules about where cotton could be placed and how much mechanical compression could be used in loading it were more important. Submersion of the load line was a problem only for the merchant galleys. For both round ships and galleys, technical improvements in shipbuilding and in warfare gave occasion for much new legislation and for new administrative boards concerned with maritime affairs: the *officiales de Levante,* the *officiales denariorum Rascie,* the *Extraordinarii,* and the *cattaveri.*

The complex pattern made by these magistracies in the first three decades of the fourteenth century is evident in the outline opposite. This outline by no means includes all the officials concerned with Venetian shipping in the fourteenth century. It omits customs officials such as the *vicedomini maris* and the *vicedomini ternarie.* It omits also the *provveditori di comun* who were given a general mandate to enforce maritime regulations early in the fourteenth century[94] and for

---

[91] A.S.V., Avogaria di Comun, Deliberazioni del M.C., Liber Magnus, f. 52 t. Their earliest *capitolare,* A.S.V., Misc. Cod., 131 gives the title *domini extraordinariorum.*

[92] The two earliest *capitolari,* Misc. Cod., 131 and 132, are especially important for their record of the freight rates established. But ch. 3 in Misc. Cod. 132, f. 5, shows how collecting freights led them into enforcement of maritime regulations generally. Before giving a merchant a receipt they were to require of him an oath that he had no merchandise brought illegally. Ch. 14 of Cod. 132, f. 7, orders them to collect double freight on any wares in forbidden places or not entered on the ship's manifest. Ch. 22 and 23 show that they administered the levying of some expenses on the general average *(per varream).* In 1357 they were ordered to collect freights from the Flemish galleys. *Ibid.,* ch. 28, f. 10.

[93] Sandi, *Principii di Storia Civile,* II, 771–72.

Organization of Venetian Shipping about 1304–30.
Armed galleys, including merchant galleys:
Private
  Patroni pay crews and collect freights.
  Officiales denariorum Rascie inspect crews, arms, and loading.
Communal
  Officiales super armamento (*pagatores*) pay and inspect crews.
  Extraordinarii inspect cargoes and collect customs and freight.
Both
  Capitani of galley fleets and *cattaveri* enforce regulations concerning loading.
Unarmed ships, private:
  Consoli estimate size, give rating, enroll *scribani.*
  Patroni pay crews and collect freights.
  Levanti inspect crews, arms, and loading of cargoes.
  Cattaveri and others also enforce regulations concerning cargoes.

some years received the pledges required of private galleys before their departure.[95] And there were other officials in other parts of the Venetian lagoons. In fourteenth-century Chioggia an official called the *scabellus* recorded not only sales of salt and leases of real estate but also all shipping contracts.[96] I know of no provision at Venice for such a complete record of ship charters or freighting contracts in spite of the large number of boards then active in supervising the merchant marine.

The officials most prominent earlier, the *consoli dei mercanti* mentioned in Zeno's Code, had become relatively inactive in maritime affairs in the fourteenth century but they had by no means lost all their importance. They continued until the sixteenth century to be responsible for giving each ship an official rating according to its size. And although the *giudici del comune* or *del forestier* formed the court responsible for applying maritime law to disputes between a shipmaster and his crew or his shippers, the *consoli* retained important areas of jurisdiction, for example, over salvage and insurance. Zeno's Code was so detailed that one can hardly say that the amount of regulation had

---

[94] M.C., Delib., Magnus et Capricornus, copia, f. 111.

[95] Giomo, "Regesto di alcune deliberazioni del Senato Misti," *Archivio Veneto,* XXXI (1886), 187, no. 252; Grazie, I, no. 438.

[96] Archivio antico di Chioggia, busta 25, f. 133. For knowledge of this official and of the archivio antico di Chioggia, I am endebted to the generous helpfulness of Dr. Ugo Tucci.

increased between 1255 and 1350, but it had been "modernized." The agencies administering the regulations had multiplied, and the modifications needed because of new techniques in rigging, loading, and armament had been made partly by new regulations and partly by custom without explicit legislation.

15

Cotton Cargoes and Regulations against Overloading[*]

REGULATIONS to prevent the overloading of merchantmen are of interest in giving some indication of the importance of various kinds of cargo as well as in expressing the degree of sophistication and the nature of the concerns of the regulatory authority.

The Venetian maritime laws of the thirteenth and fourteenth centuries show the particular importance then being assumed by an exceptionally light bulky commodity, cotton.

The earliest surviving Venetian statutes made provision against a vessel carrying too heavy a cargo. Laws required that each vessel be marked with a load line and stipulated the degree of immersion.[1] During the thirteenth century rules were developed for indicating this load line in one way on river barges, in another on the galleys and *tarete*, and in a third way on vessels of more than one deck. Vessels plying the rivers were marked with a nail by agents of the *consoli dei mercanti* to show how deeply they could legally be submerged.[2] On the

---

[*] A translation of "Cargaisons de coton et réglementations médiévales contre la surcharge des navires—Venise," *Revue d'histoire économique et sociale*, XL (1962), 21–31. (Translation by permission.)

[1] *Gli Statuti marittimi veneziani fino al 1255*, ed. by R. Predelli and Adolfo Sacerdoti (Venice, 1903), p. 48, in the statutes of Pietro Ziani. This edition of the statutes appeared first in the *Archivio Veneto*, n.s., IV–V (1902–3).

[2] *Deliberazioni del Maggior Consiglio di Venezia*, ed. by Roberto Cessi (Accademia dei Lincei, Commissione per gli atti delle assemblee costituzionali italiane, Atti delle Assemblee Costituzionali Italiane dal Medio Evo al 1831, ser. 3, sect. 1, Bologna, 1950), III, 15.

253

seagoing vessels having only one deck, namely the galleys and *tarete*, there were iron rods or some other form of marker extending downward along one of the sides. In general, *tarete* were required to have 3 ft. of freeboard; but since that was too much to require for the smaller *tarete*, the consuls were empowered to modify this rule.[3]

Galleys were naturally more closely regulated since they were low vessels and were used for the most precious cargoes. They were required to have three iron rods on each side, marked with a scale in inches, Venetian inches, sixteen to the Venetian foot, and having the seal of San Marco at the ends to prove their authenticity. These rods were fastened against the outside of the hull, perhaps partly hidden by the supports of the outrigger but sufficiently visible for inspection.[4] The amount of freeboard, measured from the *catena* was varied somewhat by special provisions for special circumstances, but in general at the beginning of the fourteenth century it was $2\frac{1}{2}$ ft. for privately operated galleys and 2 ft. for the galleys operated directly by the state. The difference indicates that on privately operated galleys the profit motive created more danger of overloading.[5] Penalties were graded at so much for the first inch and twice as much for each subsequent inch. The measuring of the submersion in inches was taken quite seriously; special permission to load heavily enough to submerge an extra inch was granted as compensation for having to carry extra arms.[6] When it was proposed to modify the rules as a favor to the pope and the king of Naples, it required action by the Maggior Consiglio.[7]

On the high round ships of more than one deck the load line was

[3] Archivio di Stato di Venezia, Capitolare dei Consoli dei Mercanti, ch. 59; Compilazione leggi, busta 150; *Delib. M.C.*, ed. Cessi, II, 254. Another way of stating the submersion was 1 ft. from the top of the *catena;* Capitolare dei Consoli dei Mercanti, ch. 40; and on the meaning of *catena,* see below nn. 5, 14.

[4] A.S.V., Senato Misti, reg. 1, f. 186: "Et debent dicte verete [sic, vergette] figi in costate de extra in loco ubi erit galea magis bassa."

[5] *Ibid.* reg. 1, ff. 163–65, 186–87: "Et quaelibet galea debeat habere de vivo a catena que est magis bassa ab oro de supradicte catene usque ad aquam pedes ducs e dimidio." In this context *catena* seems to mean a clamp or timber tying together the tops of the frames. There is support for this reading in the *capitolare* of the *ufficiali di Levante,* A.S.V., Cod. Brera, 263, f. 56, where similar regulations about freeboard read: "quelibet galea habere debeat de vivo a catena sive lata." This regulation provides penalties of 100 *libre* for the first inch and 200 *libre* for each additional inch illegally submerged.

[6] A.S.V., Avogaria di Comun, Deliberazioni del Maggior Consiglio, Magnus, f. 1 (Dec. 18, 1300).

[7] A.S.V., Maggior Consiglio, Deliberazioni, Presbiter, copia, f. 246 (Oct. 6, 1313).

shown by putting a cross on the outside at the level of the first deck.[8]
Whether the position of the cross was determined entirely by the
construction of the frame of the vessel, so that the load line was in effect
fixed by the shipwright, or whether the *consoli dei mercati* adjusted
the position of the cross when they estimated the carrying capacity of
the ship is open to some doubt, but I believe that structure determined
its position. The upward reaching arm of the cross must have been
marked to show a scale of feet, so that the cross may have been merely
the lowest of a series of crosses.[9] How deeply this cross, or lowest cross,
might be submerged varied with the age of the ship, its cargo, and its
destination. For ships within the Adriatic loaded with foodstuffs or salt,
there was no restriction provided the shippers were satisfied.[10] Ships
loading foodstuffs within the gulf, but planning to go outside the
gulf, or those loading *valonia* for tanning and carrying no merchants
could submerge the cross 2½ ft. and no more.[11] The other ships, those
that carried merchants and went on distant voyages, could submerge
the cross only 2 ft. according to the statutes of Tiepolo of 1229.[12] Ranier
Zeno elaborated that rule to allow for differences in the age of ships:
for the first five years they could submerge the cross 2½ ft., from five to
seven years, 2 ft., after seven years only 1½ ft. For any cargo loaded
beyond these limits the shipowners were liable to a fine of double and
freight of the wares illegally loaded.[13]

Although these regulations were a major concern in the thirteenth
century, this enforcement ceased altogether during the first part of the
fourteenth century except in regard to galleys. By 1375 round ships
were no longer even marked with the cross, and new rules were necessary to re-establish the practice.[14]

Load lines were of little importance when the main wares being

---

[8] This location of the cross seems to me a necessary inference from ch. 93 of Zeno's
statutes (*Gli Statuti,* Predelli and Sacerdoti, as cited).

[9] *Ibid.,* p. 48.

[10] *Ibid.,* statuta de Tiepolo, ch. 22; statuta de Zeno, ch. 63.

[11] *Ibid.,* Tiepolo, ch. 23, 24; Zeno, ch. 65, 66.

[12] *Ibid.,* Tiepolo, ch. 20.

[13] *Ibid.,* Zeno, ch. 61.

[14] A.S.V., Senato Misti, reg. 34, f. 165, Feb. 27, 1375. In this law the location of the
load line was specified as follows: "Omnibus navigiis unius coperte ponatur unum
signum, quod sit inferius catenis ubi sunt inferiores uno digito per traversum.
Navigiis vero de duabus copertis a vii^e butis infra ponatur unum signum inferius
catenis una quarta pedis. Navigiis autem a vii^e butis supra ponatur unum signum
inferius catenis medio pede."

loaded were of light weight and large bulk, as was cotton. Already in the thirteenth century bulky cargoes had become of such importance that the early codes contain restrictions not only on the weight to be loaded but also on the space, and these restrictions had been particularly strict for vessels coming from the chief cotton-producing areas.

The main purpose of these restrictions was to prevent merchandise from being loaded on the top deck where it would interfere with the handling and defense of the ship and to restrict the loading between decks so that there would be plenty of room for adequate quarters and food for the crew and a place where arms could be placed conveniently and be available. The space set aside for carrying food and drink was called the *glavam* in the thirteenth century, although in later centuries *glavam* or *giava* or *iava* applied to any compartment in the hold, so that one spoke of the *iava del maragon,* the ship carpenter's hold; and when used without specification in description of the great merchant galleys, *glavae* meant the largest divisions of the hold, those used for merchandise.[15] In contrast the thirteenth-century codes impose penalties if the *glavam* is encumbered by merchandise, and then specify for various loading zones how much of the area between decks must be set aside as *glavam,* that is storeroom. Ships whose cargo was food, namely, wheat, wine, oil, meat, or cheese, could load the whole area between decks; they had no need of a separate room for stores, and it seems likely that because of this rule ships trading only within the gulf escaped, as a practical matter, this restriction on where they loaded.[16] There is no clause specifying the size of their *glavam.* In general, the longer the voyage, the larger the storeroom. According to the code promulgated under Ranier Zeno in 1255 ships going to the area east of a line drawn from Alexandria in Egypt to Adalia in Anatolia had to leave the whole space between decks for stores and passengers.[17] This was the voyage on which the space between decks was most needed for crew and passengers, for food and drink, and for arms and for organizing defense. But this was also the area in which very light cargo, especially cotton, needed space.

Eighty years later the cotton had won. New regulations in 1332 increased penalties for loading on the top deck and imposed new restrictions on the ways of loading, but explicitly provided for filling

---

[15] A.S.V., Arsenale, busta 1, sheet entitled "l'Ordine che se osserva a far le seraglie all' dett galie grosse"; A.S.V., Cattaveri, busta 2, ch. 4, f. 11 in 1360; Senato Misti, reg. 50, f. 120 (1414).

[16] *Gli statuti*, Zeno, ch. 47–48, 68–70, 88.

[17] *Ibid.,* ch. 70.

with cotton most, at least, of the space between the first and second decks.[18] To some extent changes in arms and in rigging and a subsequent reduction in the size of crews may have been responsible, but the change may have been due simply to the persistent interest of shipowners in carrying larger cargoes.

The desire of the shipowners (about 1330–50) to load as much cotton as possible is evident in the steps taken at that time to limit the use of mechanical pressure to pack bales in tighter. The attention given the problem shows that in the voyage *ultra mare,* that is, to Cyprus, Lesser Armenia, Syria, and Palestine, there was not enough heavy cargo offered by shippers to balance the offerings of light cargo, namely, cotton. The shipmaster had to carry ballast, but in addition he could pack in all the cotton bales the vessel could possibly carry without any danger of submerging the ship too deeply.

The resulting problem is that which in modern treatises on stowage is called "screwing" cotton.

> This is simply a method of compressing the cotton by the use of jack screws so that it will occupy less space. It was formerly used not only on cotton cargoes but on many other cargoes of light-measurement freight, but has been largely abolished because the additional pressure caused strain in the vessels, and more particularly because it consumed time and money.[19]

> Formerly it was not uncommon for the master of the sailing vessel to spend several extra days in loading in order that he could squeeze in the largest possible amount. He would use screws on hemp, wool, cotton, and similar commodities, and it became a matter of pride to set more bales by screwing than a rival master could.[20]

In the following description the process seems one which might have been used in much the same way six centuries ago:

> In flooring off the hold of a ship, a few bales are placed on edge between stanchions. A long post is placed in an upright position in the wing of the ship, and a screw is inserted between the post and a board placed against the cotton. The screw is turned by hand until it is completely out, and the cotton is then "tommed off" with a screw and post at one side and a "dolly" at

[18] Senato Misti, reg. 15, f. 27.

[19] Thomas Rothwell Taylor, *Stowage of Ship Cargoes* (Bureau of Foreign and Domestic Commerce, Miscellaneous Series, no. 92; Washington, D.C., 1920), pp. 40–41.

[20] *Ibid.,* p. 51.

the other in order to hold the space gained while the screw is taken out. After the removal of this screw, there are tommed in as many bales as the space will contain.[21]

Too much screwing damaged both cargo and ship. Merchants contended that bales of wool should not be pressed in any other direction than that in which the wool was packed into them[22] and that cotton also might be damaged by compression.[23] Both cotton and wool would thus require extra labor for shaking them out before they could be washed and spun. In extreme cases there was danger to the ship. In the mid-nineteenth century, Stevens' standard treatise on stowage cautioned: "Great attention is required to see that as much as possible is put in the hold; but occasionally time is lost in screwing hard to gain a little space; it frequently results in breaking posts and starting beams or stanchions, and it has been known to rend a ship at sea."[24]

To avoid these dangers, the Venetian statute of July 28, 1332 specified what proportion of bales might be loaded by hand and by screw—literally, by arm and by wedge, *ad brachia et ad cuneum*.[25] Since we cannot be sure whether jack screws or some other apparatus was used, I will translate *ad cuneum* hereafter as "by press." Venetian rules varied according to the age and dimensions of the vessel. Those over twelve years old could load only by hand, not by press. Any other ships could load at least as much by press as by hand. Except in the tiers next to the walls,[26] they could load one or two more sacks by press according to their age and the depth of the hold, but two extra sacks (per tier) were permitted only if the hold was 9 ft. deep and the ship less than eight years old. Between decks these ships could load only one extra sack by press.

If the method of screwing the sacks was roughly similar to that pictured above, one way of evading the intent of the law would have been to put very large bales in first, screw them as tight as possible, and then by hand place in between them an equal number of very small

[21] *Ibid.*, p. 41, where there is a description also of screwing wool.

[22] R. W. Stevens quoted, *ibid.*, p. 42.

[23] *Ibid.*, p. 53.

[24] Robert White Stevens, *On the Stowage of Ships and Their Cargoes* (London, 1873), pp. 142–43.

[25] Capitolare dei Cattaveri, ch. 148. I have used both the copy in A.S.V. and that in the Library of Congress, Law Division, and have checked the text with that in Senato Misti, reg. 15, f. 27. The copy in the Capitolare dei Levanti (A.S.V., Codice Brera, 263) contains many serious mistakes.

[26] "Pillis que fient ad muratas" is the phrase I have translated as "tiers next to the walls." Whether *muratas* means the outside walls or partitions of the ship could be questioned, but I presume it means the former.

bales. That trick and other methods of making the compressed bales excessively large and the hand-packed bales excessively small were forbidden by specifying that those loaded by hand must weigh at least 550 lb. Venetian (330 lb. English), and those loaded by press might not weigh more than 700 lb. Venetian (462 lb. English). Although I have referred to bales, because it is the familiar term, it would be more accurate to speak of sacks. Venetian ships going to Palestine, Syria, and Cyprus for cotton customarily took with them canvas sacks in which to load the cotton. How much the cotton was repacked on board the ship is questionable. Merchants were ordered to present their cotton in sacks weighing between 500 and 700 lb. Venetian, but the law contains one passage which seems a reference to some kind of a baling machine or more probably simply a frame or harness used in packing the sacks, and each ship was required to have one. The law of 1332 required it to be 5½ ft. long and 3¾ ft. in diameter. An amendment in 1333 raised the length to 6 ft.[27] Such a frame or harness could hold a sack containing 32 cu. ft. to 38 cu. ft. of cotton, and that volume of cotton, even if very lightly packed, would weigh the minimum required, 500 Venetian lb. (330 English lb.).[28] Any use of weights or levers in the hand-loaded sacks was strictly forbidden.[29]

Use of levers, screws, windlasses, tackle, or other mechanical means of

[27] Senato Misti, reg. 16, copia, f. 95 (Dec. 14, 1333).

[28] Stevens, pp. 29–30, says that cotton from Alexandria when not compressed weighed 5 tons per 850 cu. ft. If we assume that the cotton the Venetians loaded by hand had the same density, then 330 lb. English would fill only 25 cu. ft. In contrast, bales of 700 lb. Venetian (462 lb. English), would have filled 36 cu. ft. when hand packed before compression. When compressed into 32 cu. ft., 462 lb. had a density equivalent to 155 cu. ft. per ton, or 5.5 tons per 850 cu. ft., somewhat more than a standard American bale. More than a century later, sacks imported by Nicolò Barbarigo averaged almost exactly 500 lb. Venetian. His account books are described in my *Andrea Barbarigo, Merchant of Venice* (Baltimore: The Johns Hopkins Press, 1944).

[29] I give here my translation of a passage from the law of July 28, 1332; Senato Misti, reg. 15, f. 27: "In each of said ships of whatever age and condition, sacks loaded by hand must weigh at least 500 lb., and those loaded by press cannot weigh more than 700 lb. And in each ship there must be rigged up a harness at least 5½ ft. long and at least 4 minus ¼ ft. wide at the mouth; and the sacks loaded by hand are not to be compressed in any way or manner with weights or squeezed or loaded with a windlass but ought to be loaded only by men's arms." The Latin is "Intelligendo quod in qualibet dictarum navium cuiuscumque temporis et conditionis fuerint sachi qui ponentur ad brachia sint librarum 500 vel inde supra et sachi qui ponentur ad cunium non possent esse ponderis ultra librarum 700 et debeat in qualibet navi ordiri pectorale de pedibus quinque cum dimidio per longitudinem ad minus et bucam fieri de pedibus quatuor minus quarto per latitudinem ad minus, nec possint sachi ponendi ad brachia ullo modo vel ingenio suppressari cum calcis vel stringi seu poni cum argano sed solum poni debeant ad brachia hominum."

some kind in loading was certainly no novelty in 1332. In its regulations for the merchant galley voyages in 1302 to 1303 the senate had
ordered that no more be loaded by press than by hand.[30] The earlier
codes do not mention the press or screw (*cuneus*), but as early as 1227
the use by the shipmaster of beams (*trabes*) in loading was made
subject to oversight by the local Venetian governor.[31] In Tiepolo's code
there is a more definite statement of how beams and windlasses are to
be used.[32] There is nothing comparable in Zeno's code, curiously
enough, unless we interpret as a penalty for excessive compression the
payments which the shipmaster is there ordered to make to the shippers
in case he unloads cotton and wool *per pilum*.[33] Although *pilum* here
probably means a pole used as a lever, possibly it means a hook of some
kind. Or perhaps the use of a boom as a kind of crane to drag bales up
over the side and across the deck to the hatch was considered damaging.
Lack of comparable provisions in later laws suggests that the prohibitions on these various uses of booms, capstans, or windlasses in loading
soon lapsed.

The law of 1332 against the excessive pressing in of cotton bales was
taken seriously for some decades, at least if we may judge from its
presence in the statute books of the enforcing officials and from mention of it in later legislation.

The officials for the Levant trade imposed fines on merchants whose
bales were below the minimum, and objected when the offending
merchants applied to high councils for pardon. The officials protested
that whenever they found sacks underweight the merchants said it was
because they had been cleaned, and that when sacks were found over-
weight the merchants said it was because the sacks were wet. But two
merchants were pardoned in 1334.[34] In 1340 an effort was made to
improve enforcement. Ship captains had discerned a loophole. They
went ashore leaving a mate in charge and encouraging him to accept
bales and stow them in disorderly fashion. When they themselves came
aboard they ordered the cotton all moved around and stowed away
properly—and in the process squeezed the bales some more. To stop

[30] Senato Misti, reg. 1, ff. 163–65, 186–87.

[31] *Gli Statuti*, p. 47, in the regulations on loading issued under Doge Pietro Ziani.

[32] *Ibid.*, p. 58, Statuta de Tiepolo, par. 18. I would translate the passage, which is
difficult to interpret, as follows: "We order that every ship should be so loaded that
each boom (*trabem*) is worked by one capstan (*rustica*) and all the rope which is
worked by that capstan is to be worked in four turns (*in quarta*) with two levers
(*stangis*) each of which is 11 ft. and not more."

[33] *Ibid.*, Statuta navium of Zeno, ch. 54.

[34] A.S.V., Grazie, reg. 5, f. 48, June 5, 1334.

this practice fines were levied on the master of any ship on which the bales had been moved after the first stowage: a fine of 1,000 lire for vessels carrying up to 800 sacks and 2,000 lire for vessels carrying more than 800 sacks (equivalent to about 560 metric tons).[35]

By 1412 the concern with excessive screwing seems to have abated. Then a new complaint was made of violation of the law of 1332. *Patroni* profited from their violations by conniving with their accusers to receive back half the fine and to collect on additional freight for the illegally loaded bales more than they were fined. But the new and stiffer penalties applied only to placing wares on deck.[36]

The decline of interest in stowage under pressure coincides in time approximately with the revival in 1375 of the regulations about the load lines of round ships. The conjunction suggests that the Venetian shipmasters had found some heavy freight with which to balance their load on the voyage back from Syria. Certainly they had been for some time under economic pressure to do so. For ships going out from Venice, the movement east of metals and timber as well of such light cargo as bales of cloth presented a possibility of a balanced cargo.

On the galleys, each merchant who shipped eight bales of cloth had a right to ship one *milliarium* of heavy goods.[37] For the return voyage from *ultra mare* to Venice, shipowners had reason to offer low freights to heavy cargoes which would take the place of the sand or rock that otherwise would have to be put in as ballast. Perhaps at one time or another alum from Egypt or salt from Cyprus supplied the heavy cargo needed. One wonders what was the nature of the "ashes" (*cenere*) which are mentioned in the fifteenth century as a prominent part of the cargo on the ships from Syria. Outside of their use in glass works these "ashes" were probably a basic product for developing the soap industry of Venice. By the fourteenth century the Venetians already considered soap as an industry which helped the development of the merchant marine.[38] It is also true that the merchant marine helped the development of the soap industry.

The need of the ship operators to balance their cargo has frequently been the stimulant to new forms of interregional exchange. With cotton demanding so much space on the ships returning from *ultra mare* in the fourteenth century, the Venetians had reason to search the

---

[35] Senato Misti, reg. 19, f. 26. Also in the Capitolare dei Cattaveri.

[36] Senato Misti, reg. 47, f. 98.

[37] Senato Misti, reg. 1, f. 186–87.

[38] *Capitolare Vicedominorum Ternarie* (Bibl. Naz. Marciana, Venice, cl. V, cod. 6, coll. 2380), f. 50, t. 9.

Levant for some heavier kind of freight. How they solved their problem is one question among many which have been raised but not resolved by this examination of the Venetian medieval regulations.

In spite of the unresolved questions, the general nature of the government's intervention is clear. Enactments were mainly in the interests of shippers and went into considerable technical detail, but, in the course of time, enforcement of this or that part of the legislation lapsed either when it seemed unnecessary or when it was persistently opposed by the shipowners. Safety at sea was a general interest, but the shipowners and their representatives, the shipmasters, were less devoted to it than the government.

16

Diet and Wages of Seamen in the Early Fourteenth Century*

THE diet and the wages of seamen are useful historical bench marks in the history of welfare economics.[1] They are among the few standards which are stated numerically in the sources concerning the wageworkers. They provide a relatively international standard, and one which perhaps will prove, on inquiry, to have been relatively stable.

The earliest figures I know concerning the rations of seamen are those recorded by the elder Marino Sanuto, called Torsello. About 1320 he wrote an extensive plan for a crusade against Egypt and as part of his extraordinarily complete logistic planning, he computed the provisions needed for the fleet. These, as Sanuto himself tells us, have been calculated according to the rations distributed on the Venetian galleys at the time.[2] Table I shows the rations per day and their nutritional value.

* A translation of "Salaires et régime alimentaire des marins au début du XIV° siècle: Vie matérielle et comportements biologiques," *Annales: économies, sociétés, civilisations* (Jan.–Feb., 1963), pp. 133–38. (Translation by permission.)

[1] In his article, "L'alimentazione degli equipaggi nelle antiche marine italiane," *Rivista marittima*, LXIV (July, August, 1931), R. Alberini treated the same problem with different coefficients of conversion. His conclusions are essentially identical: the food on board was amply sufficient.

[2] Marino Sanuto, called Torsello, *Liber Secretorum Fidelium Crucis Terrae Sanctae recuperatione et conservatione (Gesta Dei per Francos,* Hanover, 1611), pp. 60–64. On this Sanuto, see P. Molmenti, *La Storia di Venezia nella vita privata* (Bergamo, 1927), I, 240.

TABLE I

DAILY RATIONS ON VENETIAN GALLEYS, ABOUT 1310.[a]

Ration	Cost	Venetian Measure	Total (incl. water, etc.)	Protein	Fats	Carbohydrates	Calories	Cost	Weight	Calories
			Quantity						Percentage	
	piccoli		*gr.*	*gr.*	*gr.*	*gr.*	*cal.*	*%*	*%*	*%*
Ship biscuit (*Panis biscocti*)	6.5	1½ *libre*	715	76.7	2.1	591.3	2,674	50.8	49.7	68.4
Wine (*vini*)	3.4	¼ *libra*	536	–	–	2.7	375	26.5	37.2	9.6
Cheese (*casei*)	1.0	1 *oncia*	40	10.0	12.0	0.7	159	7.8	2.8	4.0
Salt pork (*de porcinis carnibus salitis*)	1.3	$\frac{33}{80}$ *oncie*	52	3.2	39.6	0.0	367	10.2	3.6	9.4
Beans (*fabae*)	0.6	$\frac{1}{40}$ *quartarolae*	98	24.5	1.8	56.5	340	4.7	6.7	8.6
Total	12.8		1,441	114.4	55.5	651.2	3,915			

[a] Conversion from Venetian measures into grams: Comparison of Sanuto Torsello's discussion of the measures for *biscoti* with that in Bartholomeo de Paxi, *Tariffa de pexi e mesure* (Venice, 1503) leaves no doubt that Sanuto's "libre panis biscoctis" are the Venetian *libre grosse* which equaled 477 gr. See Angelo Martini, *Manuale di Metrologia* (Turin, 1883). On the other hand, the *libra vini* was $\frac{1}{40}$ *bigoncia* according to the multiplications which Sanuto makes to arrive at figures of yearly consumption. It must therefore have been a wine measure distinct from the *libra grossa*. Angelo and de Paxi refer to such a *libra* as the smallest wine measure, although they do not give it as $\frac{1}{40}$ *bigoncia*. I have calculated the *libra vini* as $\frac{1}{280}$ of an *anfora* of 600 liters so that the ration of ¼ *libra* was a little more than half a liter. Paxi says also that cheese and meat were measured by the *lire grosse* and that the *quartarola* of beans was $\frac{1}{16}$ of a *ster*. Since a *ster* of wheat weighed 132 *libre*, and since wheat and beans are of about the same density (having similar stowage factors of about 50), I have considered a *ster* of beans to have weighed 132 *libre* also, and the *quartarola*, 8¼ *libre*.

Content in calories and in protein, fats, and carbohydrates is computed from Charlotte Chatfield, *Proximate Composition of American Food Materials* (U.S. Dept. of Agriculture, Circular, no. 549, Washington, D.C., 1940), with the following equivalents: for *panis biscocti*, water crackers, unshortened; for *de porcinis carnibus salitis*, salt pork, medium; for *caseis*, a rough average of Cheddar and Parmesan cheese; and for *fabae* beans, dry seeds, broadbeans. Wine is computed as 70 cal. per 100 gr., according to Michel Cépède and Maurice Lengellè, *Economie Alimentaire du Globe* (Paris, 1953), p. 624. In computing the percentage of calories from each nutritive element, I used the table given by Cépède and Lengellè, p. 126.

The total cost per day, as well as the cost per item, is given by Sanuto.

If they really received 114.4 gr. of protein and a total of 3,915 calories a day, the Venetian crews of the Middle Ages were reasonably well fed. The calories in the food (excluding wine) came 71.3 per cent from carbohydrates, 14.3 per cent from fat, and 14.4 per cent from protein.

A kind of pork and bean soup helped to make it a balanced ration. Sanuto Torsello gives some details on its distribution. For each man of the galley company the *scribanus* furnished the cook with 3 ounces of meat each Sunday, and half this amount on each of the first four days of the week, Friday and Saturday being fast days. With this salt pork the cook made a vegetable stew—usually beans, I suppose, for when he gives the details of the rations, Sanuto says: "fabae vel alicuius alterius leguminis" ("Beans or some other vegetables"). But with the exception of Sunday, the day of general distributions, the pieces of meat in the stew or in the bean soup were distributed on one day to half the crew and on the following day to the other half. "Thus," continues Sanuto, "they will each have [solid] meat three days a week and share in the broth of the meat on five days. The other days, Friday and Saturday, vegetables will be cooked and the soup distributed." If a fast day fell on the first of the week, the distribution of meat for that day would be postponed until the next feast day.[3]

The distribution of meat and cheese to the galley crew is confirmed by other sources from the early fourteenth century. It is specified by Venetian laws of 1302–3 which are to be regarded as typical. On privately operated galleys two of the merchants were appointed and charged under oath to make sure that the men received the due amount of meat,[4] and on communally operated galleys the *capitano* was responsible for seeing that each galley master fed his crew as specified by law, as is evident from one instance in which a galley master was condemned for twice failing to give out cheese as required.[5] The legal code widely used in the western Mediterranean, the "Consolato del Mar," required that the crews be fed meat on Sundays, Tuesdays, and Thursdays, and *minestra* on other days.[6]

Handing out the soup and meat to the men on the benches of a galley must have given many occasions for favoritism and for brawling. The

---

[3] *Ibid.*, p. 63.

[4] *Le Deliberazioni del Consiglio dei Rogati (Senato), Serie "Mixtorum."* vol. I, edited by R. Cessi and P. Sambin (Monumenti Storici pubblicati della Deputazione di Storia Patria per le Venezie; Venice, 1960), pp. 64, 90.

[5] Archivio di Stato di Venezia, Grazie, reg. 5, f. 18.

[6] R. Zeno, *Storia del diritto marittimo nel Mediterraneo* (Fondazione V. Scialoia per gli studi giuridici, no. 3; Milan, 1946), pp. 279–80.

Elder Sanuto advised that, under the direction of the mate, three crewmen be appointed to do it, one stationed in the poop, one amidships, and one forward. He thought it wise to rotate these jobs. Distributing the bread and cheese was simpler, since supplies for several days could be given out at one time.

How far the rations that Sanuto reports as regulation were in fact usually supplied is of course another question. He admits that the men could operate with less, on a bread ration of 15 or 12 ounces a day. "Indeed," he says, "I was in a fleet in which only 9 ounces were given to each man; but that is the extreme limit; and when such a severe emergency at a particular time and place had passed, it was made up to the men of the ship's company by the government either in money or in other things. And the men buy out of their own money from time to time wine and food as they wish when they are in a place where they can get them."[7]

After estimating the amount of food needed per day per man, and totaling up the amount for a year and for an *armata* of 1,000, 10,000, and 100,000 men, Sanuto works out the costs, and he admits that his figures are approximate. After arriving at the figure of 12$\frac{4}{5}$ piccoli (*denari parvi*) per man per day, he multiplied by 360 to arrive at the round figure of 12 soldi di grossi for the year, saying that he was not going to add anything for the other 5$\frac{1}{4}$ days of the year, since many small matters had also not been considered and since supplies would, God willing, be plentiful overseas.[8] His estimate of the cost seems low if we consider that the amount which a galley master might charge a passenger for board was set at 64 piccoli for a merchant and 32 for his servant (about 1317).[9]

---

[7] *Liber Secretorum,* p. 63.

[8] *Ibid.,* p. 64. During the period in which Torsello wrote (1306–21), Venetian coins and moneys of account had a stable relation to one another: 1 ducat = 24 grossi; 1 grosso = 32 piccoli. In the period 1330–50 the old grossi were disappearing from use but the grosso continued as a money of account equal to $\frac{1}{24}$ ducat or to 32 piccoli. The number of piccoli to a ducat fluctuated between 768 and 840 but did not rise above the latter figure until after 1360. Consequently the piccoli (*denari parvi*) which I have used as a common denominator to facilitate comparisons can be considered about $\frac{1}{24}$ of the grosso of 2.1 gr. of fine silver or $\frac{1}{768}$ of a gold ducat of 3.5 gr. of fine gold. See Frederic C. Lane, "Le Vecchie monete di conto veneziane ed il ritorno all'oro," *Atti dell'Istituto Veneto di Scienze, Lettere ed Arti* (Scienze morali e lettere), CXVII (1958–59), 72–76; Gino Luzzatto, *Studi di storia economica veneziana* (Padua, 1954), pp. 268–69; G. A. Zanetti, *Nuova raccolta delle monete e zecche d'Italia* (Bologna, 1775), IV, 169–76.

[9] *Deliberazioni,* cited above, I, 170, no. 282–83. The maximum permissible charge for a merchant was raised in 1330 to 3 grossi, but that for a servant was kept at 1 grosso (*ibid.,* I, 407, no. 253).

A suspicion that Sanuto Torsello was underestimating costs arises also from the nature of his writing. Since he was trying to stir the pope and others to undertake an expedition against Egypt, he had an interest in not overstating the costs. The difference between 32 and 12$\frac{4}{5}$ piccoli is undoubtedly considerable. Is it more than the difference today between what a transatlantic line has to spend on the food eaten by a member of its crew and what it charges its lowest-class passengers for food? A shipping expert might be able to supply an answer.

The wage rates Sanuto Torsello gives seem relatively low:[10]

	grossi / month =	*piccoli / day*
Lowest-paid oarsmen	48	51–52
Bowmen and trumpeters	60	64
Highest-paid oarsmen (aft, setting stroke)	72	83
Mates (*nauclerii*)	90	96
Galley master	180	192

Other sources indicate that the standard pay generally for bowmen and crewmen about 1300 to 1330 was 80 to 96 piccoli (2$\frac{1}{2}$ to 3 grossi) a day,[11] and a galley master's salary was fixed in 1302 at 240 grossi a month, considerably above Torsello's figures.[12] But other indications concerning a minimal living standard at the time are not out of line with Torsello's figures. A usual living allowance for widows was 20 ducats a year, the equivalent of about 42 piccoli a day,[13] and unskilled hewers of stone were paid about 48 to 60 piccoli.[14]

If Sanuto Torsello is low in his estimates of both wages and the cost of living, his errors balance each other from one point of view. If the lowest-paid oarsman received 51 piccoli a day and his keep on the galley, which cost 12$\frac{4}{5}$ piccoli, we may say that he received a total of 63$\frac{4}{5}$ piccoli (not counting his claim to booty from battle or to freighting space on a merchant galley). If his family at home spent on food somewhat more but not twice as much, say 20 piccoli a day, then a total of 32$\frac{4}{5}$ piccoli, more than half of what he received went for food. This makes no allowance either for unemployment part of the year or for earnings by other members of his family or for what he might gain by

---

[10] *Liber Secretorum*, p. 75.

[11] A.S.V., Maggior Consiglio, Deliberazioni, Magnus et Capricornus, f. 17; *Deliberazioni*, I, 469, no. 337, 338, 344.

[12] A.S.V., Senato Misti, reg. 1, f. 163; *Deliberazioni*, I, 63.

[13] Luzzatto, *Studi*, pp. 285–97, esp. p. 297.

[14] Rudolf Gallo, "Contributi alla storia della scultura veneziana," *Archivio Veneto*, ser. 5, XLV (1949), 19. A highly paid artist received 504 piccoli a day, the ordinary skilled stone worker an average of 120 piccoli a day.

trading with wares carried in his share of shipping space or from booty. If a diet as good as that specified by Sanuto—bread, wine, cheese, meat, and vegetables, yielding 3,920 calories a day—could indeed be purchased for 12⅘ piccoli, then the 51 piccoli plus food received by even the lowest-paid seaman could not be called starvation wages, and the seaman who received 96 piccoli a day plus his keep was relatively well off.

These are highly tentative estimates. I hope that they can be corrected and rendered more meaningful by confrontation with similar comparisons.

INDUSTRY AND GOVERNMENT

17

The Rope Factory and Hemp Trade in the Fifteenth and Sixteenth Centuries*

FROM the early fourteenth to the late eighteenth century a rope factory was operated by the Venetian Republic. This factory was called the Tana, because located in the building known by that name, a long narrow structure which formed the southeast side of the Arsenal. The Tana received for sortage and taxation all the hemp or cordage brought to Venice.[1]

The institution of a manufactory in the Tana was a consequence of the care with which the *signoria* watched over the maritime life of its people. The safety of the cargoes of wealth, for which the Venetian merchants "held the gorgeous East in fee," might in some storm depend on the strength of a single anchor line, and the last hope of the proudest merchantman might be based on the honest workmanship of some distant craftsman. The state had not faith enough in human nature to let this rope maker go unwatched. For the sake of supervising

---

* From *Journal of Economic and Business History,* IV (1932), 830–47. (By permission.)

[1] For general descriptions of this warehouse-factory see Giovanni Casoni, "Forze militari," in *Venezia e le sue lagune* (Venice, 1847), I, 153, and Mario Nani Mocenigo, *L'Arsenale di Venezia* (Rome, 1927), pp. 20, 27, also published in *Rivista Marittima* (April, 1927). For its use as a customhouse, see also Biblioteca Querini-Stampalia, Venice, Mss. Ital., cl. iv, cod. 150, ff. 106–107, 124, 379. This manuscript is entitled "Il cuore Veneto legale" and is so cited below. It is a topically arranged compilation of the regulations of the Arsenal made by Bernardo Lodoli in execution of a decree of the senate of October 11, 1641, and approved by a decree of the senate of August 23, 1703. See also Archivio di Stato di Venezia (cited hereafter as A. S. V.), Senato Mar, reg. 22, ff. 33–34, reg. 27, ff. 1–2; Arsenale, file 9, f. 38.

him, it became involved in a manufacturing venture which might otherwise have been left to private enterprise.

The equipment of the Tana as a manufactory of cordage was simple. It may be called a factory, nevertheless, inasmuch as many laborers worked together there in co-operation under centralized direction and an imposed discipline. Such machineless factories attract interest because of the extent to which they reveal the existence of industrial problems commonly considered to have been the result of the introduction of machinery. The grouping of many workers within one structure, where they become factory hands performing tasks set by the minds of others, became a prominent feature of economic life only after industrial technique came to be dominated by power machinery, but many of the difficulties resulting from the herding together of workers appear in advance of the advent of power-driven machinery. The machineless factories established in France in the seventeenth and eighteenth centuries are well known.[2] There is an apparent difference between the object of the Tana and that of the French examples. In the latter the factory form of organization was adopted to insure, by collective training and supervision, a finer quality of output in the production of luxuries than could be obtained if the artisans were scattered about in their homes. Ropes were no luxury in Venice, yet it was the same need of the best workmanship which caused their manufacture to be organized in factory form. "The manufacture of cordage in our house of the Tana . . ." declared the Venetian senate, "is the security of our galleys and ships and similarly of our sailors and capital."[3]

Moreover, the Tana affords a much earlier example of factory organization than the French concerns, for it was established in 1303,[4] and the basic regulations for supervising the spinning date from 1332–38.[5] During its exceptionally long life—nearly five centuries—its organization was continually elaborated through the formulation of an ever increasing amount of explicit regulation. Initially the Tana was placed under the charge of two *uffiziali al canevo* who were to oversee personally and directly the vital aspects of its activity,[6] but so simple a system would be expected to become impractical in a large plant.

[2] Germain Martin, *La grande industrie sous le règne de Louis* xiv (Paris, 1898), and *La grande industrie en France sous le règne de Louis* xv (Paris, 1900).

[3] "Cuore Veneto legale," f. 532. See also A. S. V., Senato Mar, reg. 26, ff. 58–59.

[4] Casoni, *op. cit.*, vol. I, pp. 153, 104–5.

[5] "Cuore Veneto legale," ff. 254, 445.

[6] *Ibid.*, f. 379. The number of *uffiziali* was soon increased to three.

Accordingly, the restriction of these head officials to office duties and the creation of a number of minor officials—developments completed during the sixteenth century—may be taken as an indication of increased production at the Tana. In 1558 the titles of the head officials were changed to Visdomini alla Tana and their pay quadrupled,[7] changes which may be taken as signs of the more elevated status deserved by the heads of the enlarged enterprise. The construction between 1579 and 1583 of an imposing new building more commodious than the old is another suggestiõn of expansion.[8] Thereafter neither the size nor organization of the factory changed greatly. In the late eighteenth century the number of supervisory officials was the same as in the sixteenth. The practice of laying down written rules to govern the processes of production was considerably extended, covering then for the first time the laying of the ropes; but in many departments the elaboration of written rules reached the point where it lacked economic significance and represented only the growing addiction of all branches of Venetian administration to that bureaucratic habit.[9] For the Tana, while in many respects typical of the machineless factories, presented also peculiarities of a governmental industrial enterprise.

It is difficult to draw a distinct line between the field of activity of this state factory and that of private enterprise. Since the state was engaged in the cordage business for the purpose of securing high quality, the Tana was primarily engaged in the manufacture of high grade hemp.[10] It was expected that practically all cordage made for the

---

[7] Casoni, *loc. cit.*

[8] *Ibid.*, pp. 110–11. This new Tana was in the form of one huge hall 316 meters in length, 20 meters in width, divided into 3 aisles by 84 great columns, and overhung by galleries. The architect was Antonio da Ponte, designer of the famous Ponte di Rialto. The prints reproduced by Nani Mocenigo, *op. cit.*, show it located on the site of the old Tana which in the print of Jacopo de Barbari of 1500 appears to have been almost as large as the new structure.

[9] See the printed regulation in the unnumbered files of the *inquisitori al Arsenale*, A.S.V., dated 1774 and 1784. The same supervisory officials are mentioned in the regulations of 1774, p. 11, as those described below. The master hemp dressers had been divided into two groups: *spatolatori*, beaters, and *pettinatori*, combers. A separate establishment, the Tanetta, had been created for using the lowest grades of hemp.

[10] It is necessary to refer in general terms to high and low grade hemp because the names of grades underwent change of meaning. In the fourteenth century the three grades mentioned were "bon," "refudio," and "stoppa longa" ("Cuore Veneto legale," f. 195). In the sixteenth century the grades prepared for the Arsenal were "refudio," the highest, "mocado" and "sorte," "sotto-sorte," and "coperte" (A. S. V., Arsenale,

larger ships would be made there, for such ropes could be made only out of high grade hemp.[11] For a long time, however, the Tana did not have a monopoly of that field of activity, and, on the other hand, while the manufacture of lower grades of hemp into smaller ropes was generally left to private enterprise, the Tana repeatedly engaged therein likewise, in order to satisfy the demands of the state arsenal.[12] The Tana was given a monopoly of the manufacture of bowstrings[13]—another application of the principle that the requisite of excellence in the product occasions close supervision of the laborer. While there was a tendency for the state to extend its activity and compete more and more with private enterprise, there were frequent reactions against the policy of letting the Tana use low grade hemp. All distinction between the fields of private enterprise and state activity was removed for a time, however, when an oppressive private monopoly appeared in the industry.

The exorbitant prices asked by private monopolists were a source of difficulty throughout the first part of the fifteenth century. At that time practically all the hemp used at Venice came from Bologna, and from this regional monopoly of the supply followed a monopoly of the trade

---

file 2; Senato Terra, reg. 3, ff. 77, 136; Senato Mar, reg. 5, f. 170). In the eighteenth century regulations the following three grades are mentioned, "mocado," "prima sorte," "seconda sorte." See printed regulations in A. S. V., Inquisitori al Arsenale, unnumbered files. I take it that the change of the names of the grades does not mean, as might appear, a progressive deterioration of the hemp, but instead a migration of names by elevation of standard.

[11] On the expectation that all high grade hemp would be manufactured in the Tana see "Cuore Veneto legale," ff. 106–8. A rule, made in the fourteenth century and frequently re-enacted with added penalties, required that all ropes weighing 50 Venetian lbs. or more be made of the best hemp ("Cuore Veneto legale," ff. 195–197). Itemized lists of the ropes needed on galleys and round ships in a fifteenth century treatise (Biblioteca Nationale, Florence, Coll. Magliabecchiana, Mss. Ital., cl. xix., cod. 7, ff. 10, 31, 39, 50–51, 90) show that even the biggest ships carried but a few weighing as much as 10 lbs. per pace (of five Venetian feet) while almost all of the cordage ranged from 2 to 6 lbs. per pace. Therefore I take the 50 lbs. to refer to the total weight of the rope, and the restriction to mean that practically all the cordage for ships had to be made of this high grade hemp, and consequently was expected to be made in the Tana. One Venetian foot equals 1.1 English ft.; 1 Venetian lb. (heavy) equals 1.05 English lb. (Angelo Martini, *Manuale di Metrologia*, Turin, 1883).

[12] A. S. V., Arsenale, file 5, first series of chapters, chapter 54, and A. S. V., Senato Terra, reg. 3, f. 16. Contrast the prohibitions in "Cuore Veneto legale," ff. 106–8.

[13] A. S. V., Arsenale, file 5, first series of chapters, chap. 87.

by a few importing merchants.[14] In 1422 the senate complained that the whole trade was in the hands of one Florentine who held the Venetians at his mercy.[15] At other times the trade was controlled by combinations of Venetian merchants. This control of the hemp supply reacted on the organization of the cordage industry so as to bring the craftsmen into dependence on the merchants. The latter controlled all branches of the trade from the purchase of the raw material to the sale of the finished product.[16] They raised the price and threw a burden on Venetian shipowners and the Arsenal, which aroused the government, particularly as the profits of such overcharging frequently went to foreigners.

To break this monopoly the Tana as early as 1407 was ordered to manufacture all grades of hemp for any shipowner. But the order could only be effective in case a way was found by which the Tana might obtain an adequate supply of raw material. A measure was authorized which aimed to accomplish this and by drastic means, namely, by allowing the officials of the Tana to supply any spinner who lacked material by taking hemp from those who had it stored in the Tana and paying the price for which hemp had last been sold in Venice.[17]

Although this measure was repealed within the year of its enactment,[18] during the fifteenth century the hemp monopoly was broken. In part this was accomplished by laws directly forbidding combinations to trade in hemp and forbidding the purchase of more than 100 thousand-weights by any one man during one year.[19] Moreover, the development of the hemp production of Montagnana, an episode of economic statecraft described below, struck at the root of the difficulty. By 1503 the hemp of Montagnana competed sufficiently with that of Bologna to drive down the price of the latter from 28 to 20 ducats per thousand-weight.[20] Bologna hemp remained the best and was indispensable for

---

[14] A. S. V., Senato Misti, reg. 47, ff. 109, 145; reg. 54, ff. 79, 149; reg. 55, f. 6; reg. 58, f. 182; Senato Terra, reg. 1, ff. 119, 163.

[15] Senato Misti, reg. 54, f. 79.

[16] *Ibid.*, reg. 47, f. 109; Senato Mar, reg. 1, f. 218.

[17] Senato Misti, reg. 47, f. 109.

[18] *Ibid.*, f. 145. The repeal was urged under the subterfuge that the law had demanded sale at the same price for which the hemp had been bought in Bologna, although it contained no such stipulation. Under this pretence liberty was granted to those bringing hemp to Venice to have it manufactured by whomever they wished and to sell as they pleased.

[19] Senato Terra, reg. 1, f. 120, reg. 3, f. 73; Senato Misti, reg. 47, f. 109; Senato Mar, reg. 20, f. 170.

[20] A. S. V., Arsenale, file 2, batch of loose papers on hemp.

the finer mooring cables, but the hemp of Montagnana could be substituted for it in a sufficient number of uses to take the edge off the demand for the Bologna product and keep down its price.[21] No complaints of "monopolists" were made during the sixteenth century.

Meanwhile the state had become thoroughly in favor of extending the activities of the Tana, either with the aim of improving the quality of the cordage in use—the professed purpose—or because of fiscal interests. In 1515 the Tana was given a monopoly of the manufacture of all sizeable ropes.[22] In 1525 an effort was made to attract as much business as possible, not only from Venetians but also from foreigners, by cutting the charges for manufacture and improving the accounting.[23] In 1580 the monopoly of the Tana was extended to cover all but the very lowest grades of hemp.[24]

Even when the Tana did not work up into ropes all the hemp deposited there it at least performed one essential function, that of sorting and grading the hemp. Sorting may be considered the first stage of manufacture since it was closely associated with the heckling or hackling process by which the longer finer fibres were separated out. Grading was of the utmost importance. Unless it was carefully done the rules concerning the grade of hemp to be used in different types of rope would have been valueless.[25]

The various grades were kept separate throughout the ensuing process of manufacture. This presented a special problem in the handling of materials. A further complication in the recording and arrangement of materials was involved by the presence in the same building of the property of the state and that of numerous private parties. Indeed, in the sixteenth century, the care in the arrangement and recording of the grade, ownership, and amount of the materials received, manufactured, and distributed was a major problem in the management of the Tana. An explanation of the measures taken to meet this problem leads,

---

[21] *Ibid.*, and Marino Sanuto, *I Diarii* (Venice, 1879–1903) , vol. iv, col. 631.

[22] "Cuore Veneto legale," f. 110, specifically all weighing 50 lbs. or more. See n. 11.

[23] Senato Mar, reg. 20, f. 170.

[24] A. S. V., Arsenale, file 2. This law of 1580 provided that all "refudio" and "mocado" were to be manufactured in the Tana. Earlier, in 1542 (Senato Terra, reg. 3, f. 16) and in 1555 (Arsenale, file 2) , it had been ordered that the lowest grade of hemp be removed as soon as it had been sorted out.

In addition to its domestic monopoly the Tana enjoyed protection from the competition of foreign states (Senato Mar, reg. 23, f. 109) .

[25] "Cuore Veneto legale," ff. 106–7, 195.

therefore, to a description of the internal organization of the factory at that time.[26]

All bales received at the Tana were to be opened and sorted within two days after their receipt. An official known as the weigher recorded the amount in duplicate or triplicate, giving copies to the authorities and the owner. The amount, quality, and ownership of the hemp received was recorded by one of the hemp officials, the highest officials of the Tana, and similarly by one of the bookkeepers. These entries, and all subsequently necessary, were recorded first in the journal or day book and then in the appropriate account in the ledger.[27] The hemp was carried to the storeroom assigned to its grade. If more hackling and dressing were necessary, it was given to the masters of the craft to be prepared for the spinners.[28] At this and every ensuing stage of manufacture the material so given out to the craftsmen was weighed by the official weigher, and the appropriate entry was made in the journal and ledger at the main office, and in his own book by the craftsman concerned.[29] The work of the master hemp dressers was inspected and graded by four inspectors. If unsatisfactory work was found, the craftsman responsible might be fined or required to do it over at his own expense. Above the four inspectors were the foreman and subforeman of the Tana, also responsible for seeing that the hemp fibers ready for the spinners had been properly graded.[30]

The hemp thus graded and stored in the Tana might be sold by one merchant to another—this being duly recorded on the books of the main office—and, if the material was not of that grade of which the Tana had a monopoly and if all taxes and payments for labor had been made, it might be taken out by the merchant to be manufactured by the craftsmen who worked outside the Tana. If the owner decided to have it manufactured in the Tana his next step was to pay in advance

[26] There is danger in the assumption that improvements in organization were first introduced at the time at which they are mentioned or formulated by official decrees. For that reason there has been little attempt in the description below to trace chronologically the progress in industrial management in the Tana. Instead the aim is to show what problems of industrial management were encountered and met before the seventeenth century.

[27] Senato Mar, reg. 20, f. 170 (dated 1525). A regulation dated 1332 required the bookkeeper to do the weighing ("Cuore Veneto legale," f. 550).

[28] Senato Mar, *loc. cit.*; and similar regulations dating from the early fourteenth century in "Cuore Veneto legale," ff. 106–7.

[29] Senato Mar, *loc. cit.*

[30] "Cuore Veneto legale," ff. 109, 595. Regulations dated 1419, 1449, and 1488.

the cost of the labor and have it sent to the spinners.[31] The spinners worked in two separate rooms. One of these rooms was reserved for first grade hemp, the other for second grade; and if Bologna hemp was being spun in one of the rooms that of Montagnana might not be spun there at the same time.[32] Markers on the spindles showed what kind of hemp had been used thereon.[33] Thus the different grades of hemp were segregated throughout the process.

Because of this segregation it was possible to mark the ropes according to the grade of hemp used in their manufacture which left no doubt that they were what they pretended to be. Cables for mooring or other uses in which they might be under water were made only of the best Bolognese hemp and bore a white wool label. Ropes of second grade Bolognese hemp had a black label, first grade not Bolognese a green, second grade not Bolognese a yellow. Thus was the ultimate purchaser and user protected from fraud in what might be for him a matter of life or death.[34]

The regulations for the spinning of the yarns afford the clearest illustration of the industrial problems of this pre-machine factory. Although the laying of the ropes is mechanically the most interesting part of the process of manufacture, it was before 1525 so directly under the supervision of the foreman and subforeman as not to be the subject of formal regulation.[35] With the expansion of the Tana in 1525 this part of the work was turned over to private enterprise. Thereafter a well-to-do craftsman bid in at open auction both the collection of the customs duties on rope and hemp and the direction of rope-laying with all the associated dues and expenses.[36] But the work was still carried on in the Tana subject to the supervision of the foreman, and the unskilled laborers employed were not engaged and discharged at the will

---

[31] Senato Mar, *loc. cit.*, regulation dated 1525. Cf. regulation of 1365, "Cuore Veneto legale," ff. 106–107.

[32] A. S. V., Arsenale, file 136, ff. 3–5; "Cuore Veneto legale," ff. 126–127, regulation of 1555. The principle of separation of grades during manufacture is also manifest in a regulation of 1365 (*ibid.*, ff. 107–8).

[33] These markers are mentioned in a decree of 1572 threatening one year in irons at the oar of a galley to whoever removed them (Museo Civico Correr, Venice, Mss. iii, cod. 330, Capitolare dei Visdomini della Tana, f. 8).

[34] "Cuore Veneto legale," f. 123, regulation of 1531.

[35] "Cuore Veneto legale," ff. 335–36, 445. A *masser* and a *capo de manuali* are mentioned in 1502 and 1504 as assisting in supervising this work (A. S. V., Arsenale, file 133, ff. 32, 11; reg. 136, f. 16).

[36] Senato Mar, reg. 20, ff. 170–71; A. S. V., Arsenale, file 133, ff. 80–81, 143; file 135, f. 16.

of the contractor but taken by lot from a list made up by the heads of the Arsenal and the Tana. Their choice was determined more by principles of charity or patronage than by the fitness of the workman for the job.[37] The effort of the state officials to insure the efficiency of the laborers was, therefore, directed mainly towards the hemp spinners, and it is in connection with their work that the supervision of the craftsman in the factory was carried to greatest detail.

The hemp spinners of Venice were all members in their craft guild whether they worked in shops of their own or in the Tana,[38] but in neither case were the masters economically independent, for the "monopolistic" control of the hemp supply was accompanied by the domestic form of industry, or putting-out system, the draftsmen being dependent on merchants who bought hemp and sold rope.[39] Therefore, craftsmen who worked outside were in much the same situation as the masters working in the Tana, in that they also did not own the material on which they worked and were paid by the piece.[40] The difference in conditions lay in the manner in which their work was regulated and supervised. In his own shop or home the only checks upon the care of the workman were the need of satisfying the merchant to whom the yarn or rope was delivered and the monthly visits of the Gastaldo of the gild.[41] The supervision in the Tana was far more strict.

There the bobbins were marked so that the work of each spinner might be readily identified.[42] Removing these marks or using a spindle which bore the sign of someone else were cardinal offenses punishable by whipping and banishment from the craft for ten years.[43] The fineness of the threads was stipulated for each grade of hemp in terms of the

---

[37] Senato Mar, reg. 23, f. 111. At least until 1535. Thereafter the contractors, although they still took workers by turn from a list, themselves chose the men to be added to the list whenever one inscribed thereon died. But a new proposal made about 1570 still refers to the workers as "vecchi ballotai" (A. S. V., Arsenale, file 136, ff. 91–92).

[38] "Cuore Veneto legale," f. 329, regulation of 1334.

[39] Senato Misti, reg. 47, f. 109. Clearly stated in law of 1407.

[40] Piece rates in the Tana were adjusted in 1525 as follows (Senato Mar, reg. 20, f. 171):

Dressers were paid 12 l.; will be paid 10 l. per thousandweight

Spinners were paid 17 l.; will be paid 15 l. per thousandweight for 1st grade hemp

Spinners were paid 20 l.; will be paid 17 l. per thousandweight for 2nd grade hemp

[41] A. S. V., Giusticia Vecchia, file 87, Registers of Suits, reg. 102, f. 104 (1528).

[42] "Cuore Veneto legale," f. 254. This basic rule dates from 1338.

[43] Museo Civico Correr, Mss. iii, cod. 330. Capitolare dei Visdomini della Tana, on title page, "Capitolar Restaurato sotto le qui sottoscriti Giudici al Mag.to Ecc.mo della Tana," f. 1 (1559).

number of threads which could be included in a rope of which one pace would weigh one pound, and the workers were required to come up to that standard.[44] No bobbin was to weigh more than 150 pounds.[45] The marked spindles permitted the foreman and subforeman to inspect the work, discover the inefficient workman, and punish him by a fine.[46] But that alone was not enough, for the spinners might, and sometimes did, spin the first threads on the spindle too coarse and cover the outside only with good yarns. This was prevented both by having the foremen watch the yarns as the bobbins were unwound to make the strands and by requiring the four inspectors to make at least two complete tours of inspection each day.[47]

Since all these craftsmen were paid by the piece there was no need of any supervision to punish idleness. On the contrary, complaint was made that some spinners, in their eagerness for gain, worked so fast that they wasted materials and did inferior work. In consequence an approximately equal division of materials to all the workers was ordered. This arrangement, however, not only slowed down the fast workers but put pressure on the laggards to speed up, so that despite the piece-work system of payment there was a tendency to require all to work at a uniform speed.[48]

Thus the craftsman transferred to the factory was subject to much

[44] The treatise in the Biblioteca Nationale, Florence, Coll. Magliabecchiana, Mss. Ital., cl. xix, cod. 7, f. 48, describes the ropes made in the Tana as follows: "All the cordage which is made at Venice at the Tana [which is] of three strands is of 12 threads to weigh one pound to the pace, and if it be of four strands is of 9 threads weighing one pound to the pace. Highest grade hemp [*el fior de chanevo*], if it is sixteen threads and three strands, one pace will weigh one pound and if of four strands and 12 threads will weigh one pound. An anchor weighing one thousand pounds needs a cable of 80 paces and to have 120 threads per strand and to weigh 10 pounds per pace if of second grade hemp, and if of highest grade hemp it will have 160 threads and will weigh 10 pounds per pace." This treatise apparently dates from the early fifteenth century. Regulation of 1488 requires the thread to be spun thinner, the best hemp so that 18 threads can go into one strand, the second best hemp so that 15 threads can go into one strand of the standard pound-pace of rope ("Cuore Veneto legale," ff. 109, 254). Assuming a three strand rope is understood, this means 54 threads in the standard pace-pound rope of best hemp, 45 threads in the similar standard rope of second best, while the passage quoted at length above implies 48 and 36 threads respectively. The regulation of 1488 was still the standard in 1570 (Museo Civico Correr, Mss. iii, cod. 330, f. 8).

[45] "Cuore Veneto legale," f. 254, regulation of 1332.

[46] *Ibid.*, f. 445, regulation of 1488.

[47] *Loc. cit.*, and Senato Mar, reg. 26, ff. 38–39 (1541).

[48] Museo Civico Correr, Mss. iii, cod. 330, Capitolare dei Visdomini della Tana, f. 3 (1560).

closer supervision and was forced to adjust his speed to that of the group. Moreover, here, as in the adjoining Arsenal, the congregation of so many workers in one place created a special police problem where economic rancor might be added to the normal incentives to stealing, quarreling, and willful destruction. Such offenses occasioned special punishments, and to prevent them the workers were forbidden to leave their appointed places except at specified times.[49]

Moreover, the removal of the craftsman from his home shop prevented him from using fully the assistance of his family, and altered the nature of the apprentice system. For a time the government aspired to have no apprentices at all in the Tana, only masters. All the work would then be that of trained masters, not that of members of their family passed off as their own. Apparently it was hoped that masters working outside the Tana would rear a sufficient supply of new masters.[50] When that was found not to be the case, workers in the Tana were permitted to take apprentices,[51] but the acceptance of apprentices and the regulation of their training period ceased then to be merely an affair between the master and his guild. Instead the conditions of apprenticeship were dictated by the authorities of the Tana.[52]

To such an extent was the master craftsman subordinated to the managerial personnel. Was the management equal to its responsibility? Since the highest officials of the Tana, the *uffiziali al canevo,* or the *visdomini alla Tana,* were in the sixteenth century kept busy with bookkeeping and management of the cash,[53] direct supervision of the workers was the business of a foreman, a subforeman, four inspectors, and some chiefs of spinners.[54] The duties of the last-named consisted in giving out the hemp and receiving and weighing the bobbins of yarn.[55] The inspectors were chosen two from the hemp dressers and two from the spinners. At first they had been the graders of the hemp received, but after 1488 four other craftsmen were designated as sorters, and the

[49] *Ibid.,* ff. 1–2, 8 (1559).

[50] A. S. V., Senato Mar, reg. 20, f. 172. This is the policy implied by regulations of 1525.

[51] *Ibid.,* reg. 21, f. 27; "Cuore Veneto legale," ff. 320–321 (1531).

[52] *Ibid.,* f. 131 (1558).

[53] A. S. V., Senato Mar, reg. 20, ff. 170–171, "Cuore Veneto legale," ff. 170, 379. These officials were subordinated to the lords of the Arsenal (Senato Terra, reg. 6, f. 11; "Cuore Veneto legale," f. 611; A. S. V., Arsenale, file 136, ff. 3–5).

[54] Other specialized employees of the Tana in 1555 were the bookkeepers, the office-boys, a *masser* or shipper, the doorkeepers, and a custodian in charge of the store-rooms (A. S. V., Arsenale, file 136, f. 15; "Cuore Veneto legale," ff. 435, 612).

[55] Museo Civico Correr, Mss. iii, cod. 330, ff. 1, 3, 7 (1559).

inspectors could devote themselves to the oversight of the workers.[56] The foreman and subforeman were mainly concerned in the laying of ropes but were also responsible for all departments.[57]

In this state factory there was no employer whose own eagerness for profit spurred him on to detect any lack of honesty or zeal among these supervisory officials. Probably the worst that could happen, the cause of most inefficiency, would be to have such offices sold to men satisfied to live on the fees assigned them. Yet in 1510 the Council of Ten ordered the office of inspector sold. At that time the very life of the state was threatened by the League of Cambrai so that it was natural for the state to seek money from every possible source. When in 1544 the office was again to be filled by the election of the ablest applicant, it was stipulated that the new inspector pay 20 ducats for two years to the person who had bought the office more than thirty years before.[58] But generally, all the technical supervisors in the Tana were elected from the ablest craftsmen by the hemp officials and the lords of the Arsenal.[59] But the evil state into which the Tana might fall through the improper selection of foremen was apparent in 1541, when it was discovered that not only the four inspectors but also the foreman were neglecting their duties to work on their own account as spinners. What was worse, they were taking fees from the other workers in return for their complaisance in neglecting all inspection.[60]

But such abuses can not be considered typical. Serious and continuous deficiency in the products of the Tana would certainly have reached the ears of the *signoria* since the Arsenal and the state merchant galleys were among the largest users of its products. In view of the difficulties involved in such an industrial establishment and of the likelihood of protest from the admiral of the Arsenal[61] or from the captains of the galley fleets in case poor cordage was produced, there does not appear to have been an undue amount of complaint, nor is there much evidence of what would, in that time, be regarded as serious inefficiency.

In the Tana thus organized is to be seen a hybrid form of industrial

---

[56] "Cuore Veneto legale," ff. 109, 595.

[57] *Ibid.*, f. 445; A. S. V., Arsenale, file 133, f. 11.

[58] A. S. V., Arsenale, file 135, f. 72.

[59] *Ibid.*, file 6, f. 96 (1476), file 135, f. 10 (1535); Museo Civico Correr, Mss. iii, cod. 330, ff. 7, 11 (1567–76).

[60] Senato Mar, reg. 26, ff. 38–39.

[61] This official was both the technical head of the Arsenal and the official especially in charge of rigging.

organization, a mixture of craft tradition and state supervision. The economies made possible by linking together under one control the successive steps in the manufacturing process were not entirely different in kind from those effected by the "vertical trust" of modern times, namely the elimination of rehandling and reselling. These the putting-out system might effect. But such savings must have been comparatively infinitesimal. A far more important advantage of this miniature vertical combination was the possibility of controlling continually through all the work the grade of the materials employed.

There was manifest in the Tana but little of the spirit of speed and efficiency associated with the modern factory. Had the state management tried to introduce such a spirit it might have come in conflict with the guild spirit. But the main purpose of the Tana was high quality— careful grading of the material, honest workmanship, and a standardized and reliable product. On that ground the purposes of the guild and the state were in agreement.

In connection with the Venetian cordage trade another illustration of the working of state interference in business is afforded by the Montagnanese hemp industry, the enterprise by which the government loosened the yoke of the Bolognese monopoly.[62] Although various attempts had been made during the first part of the fifteenth century to revive the growing of hemp in this region between Padua and Mantua,[63] it was only after 1455, when envoys from Montagnana solicited aid in the co-operation of the *signoria,* that extensive provision was made for introducing the new crop.[64] The most detailed and probably the most important part of these provisions concerned the drainage of a marsh belonging to the commune and the maintenance of the ponds

---

[62] Montagnana was not the only place where the Signoria tried to raise up a competitor with Bologna. The planting of hemp near Treviso was carefully fostered for a time but never produced more than 50 thousandweights (Senato Terra, reg. 5, ff. 109, 135, reg. 6, ff. 13, 85; A. S. V., Arsenale, file 6, ff. 2, 24, 35–36, 60, 76–77; file 7, ff. 43–44) , and was abandoned in 1554 on the ground that it was not of the desired quality (A. S. V., Arsenale, file 10, ff. 24–25) .

During the brief period when Ravenna was under Venetian dominion an attempt was made there similar to that at Montagnana (A. S. V., Arsenale, file 6, f. 37; Senato Terra, reg. 8, f. 34) . An attempt was even made to develop the possibilities of Cyprus (Senato Mar, reg. 11, f. 36) .

[63] A. S. V., Senato Mar, reg. 47, f. 112; reg. 54, ff. 79, 149; reg. 59, f. 14.

[64] Senato Terra, reg. 3, ff. 177, 181.

The regulations for the Montagnanese industry by two authorized nobles are in a batch of papers concerning hemp in A. S. V., Arsenale, file 2. For later provisions see *ibid.,* file 6, f. 11.

for soaking the hemp to separate the fibers and so prepare them for market. Aside from the proper management of the streams, it was in the technical education of the farmers that the state was most useful. The peasants of the district were obliged to sow part of their fields to hemp and in return were offered a bounty for all hemp delivered at the Tana. The time and manner in which the land was to be cultivated, the seed sown, and the crop harvested and prepared, were all specifically regulated. These may be viewed not as burdensome restrictions but as measures for the education of farmers unaccustomed to the new crop and ignorant of the proper system of cultivation. Once the farmer had been educated these technical stipulations were repealed.

The turning point in the venture came when about 1476 the services of a Bolognese were secured to teach the Montagnanese the methods of growing and harvesting the hemp in use in his native district. The luring of experts from foreign states was a common phase of the mercantilism of the times and it was essentially by this method that Venice broke the monopoly of Bologna. The expert in question, Michele di Budrio, was punished for his migration by perpetual banishment from the Papal States and confiscation of his property there, but he was richly rewarded by the *signoria*. At least four generations of his descendants served as salaried supervisors of the hemp industry of Montagnana and Cologna. They brought seed from Bologna and taught the subjects of Venice how to dress the hemp after the Bolognese fashion so that eventually the usual additional dressing given at the Tana was omitted.[65]

A further aid given by the state to the new industry was the creation of an annual hemp market at Montagnana. All the fifteenth-century regulations implied that the hemp should be brought to the Venetian Tana for sale,[66] but a law of 1476 contained the germ of a local market, in that it ordered one of the lords of the Arsenal to visit Montagnana every September to see that the regulations were enforced.[67] That visit became the occasion of the purchase of the hemp needed by the Arsenal and so grew into an annual market.[68] In 1503 the supervisor at Montagnana was required to maintain a warehouse in which the hemp for sale at the time of the annual visit could be deposited.[69] That standard-

---

[65] *Ibid.*, file 2, file 6, f. 53, and file 7, f. 10; Senato Mar, reg. 35, f. 70, and files, March 31, 1561; Senato Terra, reg. 36, f. 96; Sanuto, *op. cit.*, vol. iv, cols. 1, 631.

[66] A. S. V., Arsenale, file 2; Senato Terra, reg. 5, f. 60, reg. 7, f. 87, reg. 12, f. 110.

[67] A. S. V., Arsenale, file 6, f. 11.

[68] Senato Terra, reg. 27, f. 43.

[69] A. S. V., Arsenale, file 6, f. 53.

izing of the wares which was essential for the market appears in the provision for two weighers and two sorters, one of each brought from the Tana by the visiting lord of the Arsenal and the others chosen by the Council of Montagnana. In the market thus created, the Arsenal naturally occupied a privileged position, for no one else was allowed to buy or load the hemp of Montagnana until the lord of the Arsenal had finished his purchases.[70] But in a good year the crop might be twice as large as the needs of the Arsenal, so that there was plenty of room for the activity of private merchants after the Arsenal had been supplied.[71]

The importance to Venice of the proper functioning of the local producers' market thus created was clearly revealed in 1531. The senate did not appreciate the value of the marketing mechanism which it had unconsciously set up until in that year they tried to avoid the expense of sending a lord of the Arsenal to Montagnana and simply proclaimed that all hemp must come to the Tana or be confiscated. The result was disastrous. Although some 600 to 700 thousandweights of hemp were prepared at Montagnana, only 227 thousandweights reached the Tana, and the Arsenal had to pay 22 to 25 ducats where before it had paid 14 to 16 ducats per thousandweight. Naturally in 1532 a lord of the Arsenal was again sent to Montagnana.[72]

Once again the marketing machinery was upset by the government towards the close of the sixteenth century during the general rise of prices. When the lord of the Arsenal was sent to Montagnana in 1533 the price at which he was to buy hemp was fixed by law at what was professed to be a fair average of what had been paid.[73] The fixing by law of the price at which the state would buy does not seem to have done any harm to the industry before 1565.[74] The price so determined might not represent the relation of immediate supply and demand as closely as would a free market price, but the legal price was varied so as to encourage or discourage production in accordance with expected future demand. During the middle of the century the price ranged

[70] Senato Terra, reg. 27, f. 43.

[71] *Ibid.*, f. 150. In 1533 the Arsenal was to buy 300 out of 600 thousandweights. The merchants who bought after the Arsenal had filled its needs were required to bring the hemp to the Tana, but there may be some doubt whether they did so, since in 1557 a large appropriation for the purchase of hemp by a lord of the Arsenal was urged on the ground that it would prevent the hemp going to other countries (Senato Mar, reg. 33, f. 160).

[72] Senato Terra, reg. 27, f. 43.

[73] *Ibid.*, f. 150.

[74] See mention of good supply prepared in Senato Mar, reg. 28, f. 116; reg. 32, f. 106; reg. 33, ff. 48, 96, 160; reg. 37, f. 71.

from 13 to 16 lire the hundredweight, and from 700 to 800 thousand-weights were produced each year.[75] But when all prices began to mount rapidly at the end of the sixteenth century with the increase in the amount of precious metal in Europe, then the legally fixed price disrupted the market. Every increase meant an addition to the cost of the Arsenal, so that the *signoria* was slow to make the sizeable increases which the occasion demanded and the prices fixed by law did not rise naturally in conformity with other prices, but only belatedly after repeated petitions from the growers.

The effects of this unsound policy were keenly analyzed by Bertini Contarini, the lord of the Arsenal sent out in 1591.[76] Government price fixing on a fiscal instead of an economic basis had resulted in the Arsenal receiving only 200 thousandweights. Since the government price was artificially low, much of the hemp which was grown was not brought to the local "Tana" or official warehouse but disappeared from the public market through contraband selling. Since it was more profitable to raise wheat than to raise hemp for the government's price, no fields not obligated to hemp were sown therewith, as many had been previously. Even the renters of the marsh land which had been irrigated by the state especially for the purpose of raising hemp found it so much more profitable to grow wheat than hemp that they bought licenses to do so.

Thus state interference appears to have been beneficent in reviving the industry, but when corrupted by the fiscal exigencies of the government such interference became a nuisance and an oppression. The constructive work of educating the farmers proved more lasting, however, than the disruption resulting from the abuse of the marketing machinery. In the eighteenth century the hemp production of the region had more than regained its former capacity.[77]

[75] *Loc. cit.*, A. S. V., Arsenale, file 2.

[76] In A. S. V., Arsenale, file 2. There also is a note on the amount of hemp obtained 1590–93. The average for a year is about 180 thousandweights. In 1588 the legal price was 18 l. 6s.; by 1594 it was 24 l.

[77] Papers in A. S. V., Arsenale, files 536 and 537, show that the price paid by the state rose to 30 l. in 1638 and fell to 25 l. in 1670 and that the average yearly production 1791–94 was about 1,000 thousandweights.

18

Medieval Political Ideas and the
Venetian Constitution*

THE constitution of the Venetian Republic can be considered emi-
nently successful, for it endured 500 years, whereas the much-
admired constitution of the United States has not yet lasted 200. The
ideals and theories behind the American constitution, the arguments of
such founding fathers as Madison and Adams, are extensively recorded.
In contrast, the men who shaped the Venetian constitution have left no
direct statement of their political ideas.

After the governmental structures of Venice had proved their staying
power, there was no lack of theorizing about them. Not surprisingly,
Florentines, rather than Venetians, took the lead. Francesco Guicciardini and Donato Giannotti idealized the Venetian constitution, contrasting it with the unstable institutions of Florence under which they
suffered. In reaction to their observations and to the less complimen-
tary comments of Machiavelli, Venetians such as Gasparo Contarini
and Paolo Paruta elaborated what may be called the classical theory of
the Venetian constitution. Subsequently it was idealized by republicans
in seventeenth-century England and damned by republicans and Bona-
partists in eighteenth-century France. The fullness and eloquence of
these later commentators interfere with describing the Venetian constitution in the terms in which it probably appeared to the Venetians
while the basic institutions were taking shape in the twelfth, thirteenth, or early fourteenth century. Lacking any reasoned expression of

* In a shortened form this paper was read before the History of Ideas Club at The
Johns Hopkins University, February 12, 1965.

the thoughts of the Venetian founding fathers, we are tempted to attribute to them the conceptions developed later by men who either contemplated their handiwork admiringly and praised it as a balance between monarchy, aristocracy, and democracy, or else condemned it as the gradual usurpation of power by a class-conscious oligarchy.

The alternative I will attempt here is to examine political thought that was contemporary with the formation and crystallization of the basic features of the Venetian constitution.

I

For this purpose it is pertinent to signalize two periods in its development: one about 1200, the other about 1300. The earlier of the two periods was initiated by the assassination of Doge Vitale Michele II in 1172. That was the last violent revolution to occur in Venice. Venetian chroniclers of a generation or two later were already so ashamed of it that they tried to gloss it over as the act of a madman, although it followed a riotous popular assembly during which a doge, just after his return from a disastrous naval expedition in the Aegean, failed notably to receive support from the principal men of the community. After 1172 the government of Venice was conducted by the co-operation of twenty to forty men, persons outstanding because of their wealth and political or naval experience, drawn from about as many families. In form Venice continued to be a monarchy ruled by an elected doge and a popular assembly, but the doge did not try to act contrary to the advice of the leading men, and they controlled the assembly. While the doge was the most powerful of the leaders, he could not override the others. The limitations on him were formally strengthened by the revision of his coronation oath in 1229. Other constitutional mechanisms through which this result was obtained were a series of councils of which the smallest and most influential was the Ducal Council of six members, and the largest, sometimes with 400 to 500 members, was called the Great Council.

In the second period, between 1297 and 1323, the limits on the doge's power were more precisely defined, the structure of councils was given the form that remained unchanged for about 500 years, and the assembly of the people became a mere formality. Participation in law-making and in elections was restricted to that fraction of the population who were members of the Great Council, which now became a body of 1,000 to 2,000 with a membership that in 1323 was declared fully hereditary. After that date, any effort to change this basic constitutional structure was liable to be punished by the powers of the Coun-

/

cil of Ten. After the changes about 1200 the Venetian constitution had retained monarchic and popular elements. The changes about 1300 accentuated the aristocratic element and did so in a way which reduced to a minimum the factional strife that weakened most of the Italian republics.[1]

Lacking Venetian political theorists of early date, we can follow a method Nicolai Rubinstein applied to Florence and seek political ideas in the city's chroniclers.[2] Venetian traditions even earlier than 1200 are strongly republican—I might almost say democratic. They began their history with legends of San Marco and early patriarchs, expressing the feeling that their origins as a group lay in the Christian communities of the Roman Empire. They applied what Walter Ullmann calls the ascending theory of government even to their ecclesiastical organization, referring frequently to their patriarch, that of Grado, as being chosen by *clero et populo*. It was their means of asserting their ecclesiastical independence of the rival patriarch of Aquileia.[3] For the creation of an independent political unity a crucial step was the election of the first doge. The earliest chroniclers, even John the Deacon who wrote about A.D. 1000, described this as the decision of all the Venetians. He assigned to the people also the choice of doge and the decision to establish the capital at Rialto.[4] Later chroniclers are quite specific that it was the people of Venice who made and unmade doges and approved constitutional changes, at least until 1268.[5]

By "the people" they obviously did not mean the lower classes in distinction from an upper class; they meant the whole of the laity at least and most frequently the whole community acting as a whole. A conception of "the people" as the source of political authority was part

[1] Heinrich Kretschmayr, *Geschichte von Venedig,* vol. I (Gotha, 1905), ch. 9; vol. II (Gotha, 1920), ch. 11; Giuseppe Maranini, *La constituzione di Venezia* (2 vols., Rome, 1932); Roberto Cessi, *Storia di Venezia: II, Dalle origini del Ducato alla quarta crociata* (Venice: Centro Internationale delle Arti e del Costume, 1958), pp. 408–17, 442–47.

[2] Nicolai Rubinstein, "The Beginning of Political Thought in Florence, a Study in Medieval Historiography," *Journal of the Warburg and Courtauld Institute,* V (1942), 198.

[3] *Croniche veneziane antichissime,* ed. by G. Monticolo (Fonti per la Storia d'Italia; Rome, 1890), pp. 39–40, 76 n.; Andrea Dandolo, *Chronica per extensum descripta,* ed. by Ester Pastorello (Rerum Italicarum Scriptores, t. XII, pt. 1, 2d ed.; Bologna [1940]), pp. 9, 10, 51, 55, 76, 79, 90–91, 100.

[4] *Croniche ven. antichissime,* pp. 91, 98–99, 105, 106, 129, 148.

[5] *Historia ducum Veneticorum,* ed. by Simonsfeld (Monumenta Germaniae Historiae, SS, XIV), pp. 80, 89, 94; Martino da Canale, *La cronique des Veniciens,* in *Archivio Storico Italiano,* ser. 1, VIII (1845), 317, 345, 363, 691; Dandolo, *Cronica,* pp. 105–6, 118, 207–8, 252, 259, 302–3, 317.

of the tradition inherited from Roman law historians and was given
new expression in the revival of Roman law that began at Bologna in
the eleventh century. Although the general recognition by these civil-
ians that "the people are the only ultimate source of political authority
and of law" was counterbalanced by their teaching that the Roman
people had by the *lex regia* transferred this power to the emperor, some
of the *glossatori* maintained that the people retained the power to create custom which had the force of law.[6] The Venetians felt that they as
a community had done that legitimately for themselves.

While these lawyers are the most likely source of any general theories
in the minds of the Venetians who from 1172 to 1226 established in
Venice what was in effect an aristocracy, one cannot exclude the possibility that some Venetians may also have known Aristotle's *Politics.*
Although it was not yet directly influencing Latin schoolmen, it was
known and discussed in the Byzantine Empire throughout the Middle
Ages, and since many Venetians had a knowledge of Greek sufficient for
purposes of business and diplomacy, leading Venetians may well have
been familiar even in the twelfth century with Aristotle's very suggestive compendium of Greek political ideas and experience.[7] In that case
the Venetians could have drawn inspiration from Aristotle in balancing as they did about 1200 the three elements of monarchy, aristocracy,
and democracy. More likely, in case Aristotelian doctrines influenced
the Venetians at all in their constitution making, their influence was
felt only after Aristotle's *Politics* was translated into Latin by William
of Moerbeke and extensively expounded by Western schoolmen in the
second half of the thirteenth century, most notably by Thomas
Aquinas. They could not then have helped to shape the reforms made
about 1200. The balanced constitution enjoyed by thirteenth-century
Venice was probably created without the aid of Aristotelian theories.

II

The political thought of Thomas Aquinas was like that of Aristotle
not only because it was in part derived from Aristotle but also because

---

[6] R. W. and A. J. Carlyle, *A History of Medieval Political Theory in the West*
(Edinburgh, 1909) , II, 57–59, 63–66; Walter Ullmann, *Principles of Government and
Politics in the Middle Ages* (London, 1961) , p. 281; Werner Goez, *Translatio Imperii*
(Tubingen, 1958) , pp. 386–89; Francesco Colasso, *Medio evo del diritto,* I (Milan,
1954) , pp. 182–83, 198, 209.

[7] Ernest Barker, *Social and Political Thought in Byzantium* (Oxford, 1957) , pp.
136–39, on Michael of Ephesus, *ca.* 1070–80.

Thomas was for his own part interested in many of the same problems. Thomas did not discuss problems of universal empire or feudalism. He discussed those of various political communities—cities, provinces, kingdoms—within a universal church.[8] Like the ancient Greeks, Thomas extolled civic life as natural and good, enabling men better to develop in their relations one with another their many excellent natural qualities. As a Christian, Thomas Aquinas of course did not stop there. The purpose of organized society was not merely a virtuous life on earth; it was also preparation for the life to come and the enjoyment of God. For this purpose political organization was supplementary to ecclesiastical organization, and natural law was but one part of divine law; yet within this basic framework derived from his Christian faith, Thomas in discussing problems of government appealed as Aristotle had to reason and experience.

Did Aquinas's political conclusions provide support for the kind of constitution which the Venetians had already created? Were the changes which the Venetians made about 1300 in accord with, or in defiance of, Thomas's judgments?

The six forms of government distinguished by Aristotle are frequently referred to by Aquinas: namely, three forms of unjust government, tyranny, oligarchy, and democracy, and in contrast three forms of just government, kingship, aristocracy, and polity. In Question 105 of the *Summa Theologica*, Aquinas presents as the best type of government a mixture of the three just forms, arguing that such a mixture preserves the best features of each form: monarchy supplying unity, aristocracy rewarding merit, and popular participation ensuring peace by making all men set value on the state and by making them more ready to defend it. "This," he says, "is the best form of constitution (*politia*), which results from a judicious admixture of kingship (*regno*) in that one person is the head of it; of aristocracy (*aristocratia*) in that many participate in the government according to their virtue or capacity; and of democracy or popular rule (*democratia, id est, potestate populi*) in that rulers may be elected from the people and the whole population has the right of electing its rulers. Such was the form of government which was established by divine law."[9]

In using these words Aquinas was referring to the government which

[8] Thomas Aquinas, *Select Political Writings*, ed. by A. P. d'Entrèves, trans. by J. G. Dawson (Oxford, 1948) (cited hereafter as d'Entrèves), p. xxv, where d'Entrèves says: "There is no open mention, in the whole of St. Thomas's work, of the idea of a universal empire."

[9] *Ibid.*, p. 149.

God established among the Hebrews, but it would seem that they are at least equally descriptive of the Venetian government after the reforms of about 1200. Venice was then in form an elective monarchy with all the people joining in the election of the doge and in approving the laws, while at the same time outstanding men were given extra power through the councils which advised the doge, and the doge himself had power enough to give unity to the administration. At least Venice seems nearer to the ideal mixture pictured by Aquinas than any other Italian city of the time.

But Venice had already gone further in limiting the power of its monarch, the doge, than Thomas Aquinas would have judged wise. Checks and balances are not a feature of Aquinas's ideal mixed forms. He says nothing about the aristocratic element limiting the power of the monarch, or of the people restraining the aristocrats. In the *Summa* Aquinas speaks only of blending the good qualities of each, not of checking their evil tendencies by skillful mixture. We must turn to his other writings to seek his attitude toward such a limiting of the monarch.

In the treatise of kingship which he began about 1260 for the king of Cyprus, Aquinas reviews the six forms of government, and declares flatly that kingship is the best.[10] This is sometimes regarded as in conflict with the passage I have quoted from the *Summa,* but the conflict disappears when we realize that the mixture recommended in the *Summa* is not a mixture designed to limit the power of the monarch. Kingship is the best, declares Aquinas, both in principle and in practice. In principle, it resembles God's government of the universe; it

[10] Thomas Aquinas, *On Kingship, to the King of Cyprus,* trans. by Gerald B. Phelan, revised with an introduction by I. Th. Eschmann (The Pontifical Institute of Medieval Studies; Toronto, 1949), I, 1; II, 3, 4 (II, 14, 15) (cited hereafter as *On Kingship*). Eschmann in his introduction maintains that *De Regno* is the correct form for the treatise which Thomas wrote. It is usually called *De Regimine Principum,* but that title should apply, Eschmann argues, only to the composite in which the fragment written by Thomas and the later treatise generally assigned to Tolomeo of Lucca were put together. *De Regno* is certainly the more convenient form of reference and since I have quoted some of Phelan's translations I have adopted this usage and cite the chapters giving first Eschmann's numbering and then in parentheses the numbering in the Parma edition when it is different: Thomas Aquinas, *Opera Omnia secundum impressionem Petri Fiaccadori Parmae, 1852–1873* (New York, 1950). On the dating of Aquinas's works and William of Moerbeke's translation see *On Kingship,* pp. xxix–xxx; Thomas Gilby, *Principality and Polity: Aquinas and the Rise of State Theory in the West* (Chicago, 1958), pp. 82, 95, 267; and esp. M. Grabmann, *Die Werke des Hl. Thomas von Aquin* (3 ed.; Munster, 1949), p. 333, who dates the *De Regno* in 1265–66.

is as natural as the rule of the human body by one head, and as the V of flying geese. In practical terms he argued that it was the form most likely to produce peace, justice, and the general welfare.[11]

In all the discussions of government by Thomas and his followers the form of government—whether it should be by the One, the Few, or the Many—was treated as distinctly secondary. The important question was whether it was a just government. The justice of the government was determined by whether it served the general welfare or sought only the welfare of the ruler, be that one man, or a few who use power to enrich themselves, or the many plebeians who oppress the rich. In serving the general welfare the just government will of course observe the natural and divine law.[12]

His practical argument in favor of monarchy is that it is more likely to promote the welfare of the whole through unity and peace. Aquinas recognized that history as he knew it, and examples in his own time, proved that kingship was very likely to turn into tyranny, and he declared tyranny the very worst form of government, saying that the concentration of power in a single person which was so mighty a force for unity and justice in a kingship became in a tyranny a mighty force of oppression and injustice. The main practical problem of government was how to secure the advantages of a uniting monarchy while avoiding a tyranny. As he put it, "Danger thus lurks on either side. Either men are held by the fear of a tyrant and they miss the opportunity of having that very best form of government which is kingship; or they want a king [try for the ideal] and the kingly power turns into tyrannical wickedness."[13]

But if experience shows the dangers of monarchy, it also shows that any other form of government is even more likely to turn into a tyranny. Where several men share the power, as in a aristocracy, one of them is likely to seek his own welfare, disregarding that of the state as a whole. The ambitious perverter of the regime seeks power for himself, the aristocracy becomes divided; the dissension among the leaders is followed by the multitude until a tyrant emerges. So it happened in ancient Rome and often also in his own time. He concludes: "In general, if one carefully considers what has happened in the past and what is happening in the present he will find that more men have held tyrannical sway in lands previously governed by many rulers than in

---

[11] *On Kingship,* I, 1, 2, and II, 2 (I, 13).

[12] Gilby, *Principality,* p. 294–310.

[13] *On Kingship,* I, 2–4, esp. p. 21.

those governed by one." In short, tyrannies have arisen more in republics than in monarchies.[14]

This thought may have served to confirm the Venetians in keeping their monarchic form of government. Its relevance to Venice is not lessened by the fact that the Venetian doge was elected, for Aquinas never speaks of kingship as hereditary. He speaks always of the king's being chosen either by the people, that is, the community, or by some superior, and he stressed the importance of choosing the right kind of man.[15]

In the treatise on kingship which he left unfinished, Aquinas promised to explain how the government should be arranged and the king's power limited so that he would not turn into a tyrant.[16] In fact he never wrote such a section, but the ideas he expressed elsewhere imply disapproval of the amount of limitation which the Venetians had already by 1229 imposed on their prince.

What he would have written had he finished the treatise on kingship would have reflected his belief regarding the relation of the king to the law. When he discusses the nature of law in the *Summa Theologica,* Thomas distinguishes divine and natural law from man-made law. Natural law is embedded in the nature of things and can be known by man through reason. Positive or man-made law is not true law at all if contrary to natural law, but man-made laws are necessary to provide for particular cases, that is, for adaptation to circumstances of the principles which constitute natural law. Since the purpose of man-made law is to provide for the general welfare, a monarch who does not govern according to positive laws in harmony with natural law is not a king but a tyrant.[17]

But in what sense can a king, a true king, be called subject to the law? To answer that question, Aquinas distinguished between the directive power of law and its coercive power. The ruler is subject to the directive power of natural law through his reason and conscience. In the judgment of God he will be held responsible for breaking the law. But the ruler is not subject to the coercive power of man-made law: "A ruler is said to be above the law with respect to its constraining force:

---

[14] *Ibid.,* I, 5 and 6, esp. p. 23.

[15] *Ibid.,* I, 6, p. 27, and more specifically in the *Summa Theologica,* I, II, 105, 1.

[16] *On Kingship,* I, 6. Eschmann (p. xviii) argues persuasively that Aquinas intended to insert the treatment of how to moderate or limit the king's power at that point in chapter 6 before the discussion of how to get rid of a tyrant. That he postponed writing it may indicate, it seems to me, that he was indeed uncertain how to limit the king without also hobbling the king's power to assure peace and unity.

[17] *Summa Theologica,* I, II, 91.

for nobody can be constrained by himself; and law derives its power of constraint from the power of the ruler. So it is said that the prince is above the law, because if he should act against the law nobody can bring a condemnatory judgment against him."[18] To test the meaning of this argument, the Carlyles and Gilby envisage English institutions and say that it means no more than Bracton's dictum that no writ can run against the king.[19] It is at least equally pertinent to test its meaning by envisaging how it applies to the institutions of the Italian city-states and specifically Venice. In Venice a condemnatory judgment could indeed be made against their prince, the doge, just as in many Italian communes a penalty could be inflicted on a *podestà*. The doge of Venice was liable to be fined by the state attorney and his councilors.[20] But in that case, a Thomist might contend, the doge was not really the ruler; the real ruler was that body able to inflict the penalty, in this case the Ducal Council, or to speak in Aristotelian terms, the aristocracy. A king subject to the coercive power of the law was no true king, he was a mere magistrate.[21]

This comparison of Thomas Aquinas's ideas with those implicit in the Venetian constitution shows both similarities and differences. In form Venice was an elective monarchy with all the people joining in the making of the laws and in the election of the doge, who gave unity

[18] *Ibid.,* I, II, 96, 5. The quotation is from Dawson's translation—d'Entrèves, p. 139.

[19] Carlyles, V, 475–76; Gilby, p. 289. Eschmann argues (pp. xxx–xxxi, xxxvii) that Aquinas was writing with conditions on Cyprus particularly in mind and that Book I, ch. 6, "urges the principles of limited monarchy" as laid down in the Assizes of Jerusalem which were applied in the Cour des Liges of the Kingdom of Cyprus. But he offers no evidence to support such an assumption. It seems to me more reasonable to argue that the conditions of disunity and dissension in the crusading kingdoms were among those experiences with aristocracy that Thomas cited in ch. 5 in arguing that monarchy was superior to aristocracy, and that his statement in the *Summa* that the king was above the coercive power of the law excludes his acceptance of such limitations, of which La Monte wrote: "While in the West the kings listened to their councils, in the East they were bound by their decisions." John L. La Monte, *Feudal Monarchy in the Latin Kingdom of Jerusalem, 1100 to 1291* (Cambridge, Mass., 1932), p. 95. On the alleged conflict between Thomas's monarchic theories and Quest. 105, see also Charles Howard McIlwain, *The Growth of Political Thought in the West from the Greeks to the End of the Middle Ages* (New York, 1932), pp. 330–31 and n. E. Gilson, *Le Thomisme* (5 ed., Paris, 1948), p. 456, concludes that he believed the best form "la monarchie, pourvu qu'elle soit completée par ce qu'ont de bon les autres règimes." (Note that he says *completée,* not *freinée.*)

[20] Kretschmayr, *Geschichte,* II, 89; Maranini, I, 199–200; Vettor Sandi, *Principii di storia civili della repubblica di Venezia* (10 vols., Venice, 1758–72), pt. I, vol. II, p. 712.

[21] Accordingly, Egidio Colonna, *De Regimine Principum* (Augsburg, 1473), Lib. III, pt. 2, ch. 2, says that the real rulers of the Italian cities are the people who elect and punish the *signori* and *podestà* who appear to rule.

to the administration, while at the same time the outstanding men were given extra power through the doge's council and the Great Council. Looking at these aspects, Thomas might have considered it an ideal constitution. But in fact the Venetians had limited the power of the doge far more than the reasoning of Aquinas approved, and in the two generations after his death the Venetians, disregarding that reasoning, stiffened the aristocratic character of their government.

On the other hand, the general tenor of thought of those generations could have found support in Aquinas's basic attitude toward rational constitution making. It is noteworthy that he discussed government as if it could be man-made, that is, a work of art, to use Burckhardt's famous but misleading expression. Certainly Aquinas sometimes referred to governments as situations given men by God, nature, or custom, but he also spoke of men making decisions about what form of government they would have. To be sure, he envisaged only three alternatives: (1) rule by a just king, (2) rule by a tyrant, and (3) a government which was not monarchical and would therefore succumb quickly to dissension and become a tyranny. He failed to recognize that the Venetians were in the process of proving that there were other possibilities, or that the third alternative was not as bad as he thought. Because he defined kingship in such a way as to exclude the existence of constitutional bodies which could compel a king to obey the law, Aquinas left only a few possibilities open, but he did present them as alternatives among which men could choose and should choose on the basis of reason and experience.

III

During the two generations after Thomas's death, these alternatives were discussed by several writers influenced by him and directly by Aristotle also in some cases. Six need to be mentioned here. The three most relevant to the Venetian constitution are Tolomeo of Lucca (1303), Paolino of Venice (1314), and Marsiglio of Padua (1324). One, Egidio Colonna (Giles of Rome), wrote with France primarily in mind: but we will find him relevant as background, for his influential *De Regimine Principum* was written as early as 1285.[22] The remaining two were the Florentines, Remigio dei Girolami and Dante Alighieri.[23]

---

[22] Carlyle, V, 74–75.

[23] Charles T. Davis, "An Early Florentine Political Theorist: Fra Remigio de'Girolami," *Proceedings of the American Philosophical Society*, CIV, no. 6 (1940), 662–76.

Although concerned with the problems of universal empire, they expressed the intense civic spirit of Florence. Their eloquence and despair over the factionalism of their city might well have persuaded any Venetians who read them that Florence was worth considering as an example of the evils to be avoided.

More relevant to Venetian institutions were the arguments of another Tuscan, Tolomeo of Lucca (Bartolommeo Fiadoni), an apologist for popular governments of the Florentine type. Tolomeo was a disciple and companion of Thomas Aquinas near the end of the latter's life and completed in 1303 the tract *De Regimine Principum,* incorporating into its first books Thomas's treatise *On Kingship.*[24] Here Tolomeo took as his starting point for a defense of popular government the distinction which Thomas had made between the directive and the coercive power of the law. He combined it with a parallel distinction between what I will call regal government and constitutional government, *regimen regale* and *regimen politicum.* In a regal government the king carries the laws in his breast; he is bound by what Thomas called the directive power of the natural law but it is the king who decides what natural law requires and formulates its application in positive law. In constitutional government on the other hand the prince rules according to the laws established by the people, by the community.[25] Neither Thomas nor Tolomeo equated regal government with tyranny. A king, even an absolute monarch, was unlike a tyrant because the king ruled in the interest of the whole and according to the law, but under a regal government the positive laws the king enforced were those he made and could change.[26]

Tolomeo sharpened the contrast between regal and constitutional

[24] *Enciclopedia italiana,* s.v. Bartolomeo Fiadoni; M. Grabmann, "La scuola tomistica italiana nel xiii e principio del xiv secolo," *Rivista di filosofia neo-scolastica,* XV (1923), fas. 22–23, pp. 120–27; *Die Annalen des Tholomeus von Lucca,* ed. by B. Schmeidler (Monumenta Germaniae Historicae, SS, n.s., VIII; Berlin, 1930), pp. xxxi–xxxii. Schmeidler says Tolomeo wrote his part of *De Regimine Principum* between May, 1302 and September, 1303, but uses some of the very words he used in his "Determinatio compendiosa de iurisdictione imperii," composed in 1281.

[25] Thomas Aquinas, *Opera Omnia,* XXI, 367; I. *Pol.,* Lect 1 and 10. Gilby, 197–98, treats Thomas's conception of *principatus politicus* as the equivalent of Tolomeo's. Walter Ullmann, *Principles of Government and Politics in the Middle Ages* (New York, 1961), p. 254, says cautiously that Thomas "coined the new term *regimen politicum.*" It is difficult to decide how far the exposition of Aristotle's ideas in Thomas's lectures are to be considered expression of Thomas's own conclusions.

[26] Egidio Colonna, *De Regimine Principum* (Augsburg, 1473), Lib. III, pt. 2, esp. ch. 29, also denounces tyranny as so defined but favors a king who is only under the natural law, not subject to positive law.

government by emphasizing that in a constitutional government the ruler could be coerced into obeying the laws established by the community.[27] His analysis of constitutional government is like that Sismondi presented in his *Histoire des républiques italiennes du moyen âge* as the theory of political liberty.[28] All power is derived from the people, rulers are strictly accountable to the people, and honors are distributed to each citizen in turn according to merit.[29] Office holders are bound by oaths and penalized for violating them. They serve for only short terms to insure rotation. In saying that regal governments give fiefs whereas constitutional governments pays salaries, Tolomeo was deliberately contrasting the Italian cities, where even the *podestà* was on a salary, as was the doge of Venice, with such kingdoms as France and Naples.[30]

As to which was better, regal or constitutional government, Tolomeo's position is ambivalent. Constitutional government is milder, its officials less able to restrain the lawless, and for that reason regal government is better for many countries. Indeed, Tolomeo goes so far in one passage as to say, as Aquinas had, that in the actual generally corrupt conditions of the world regal government usually works better. But his heart lies on the other side. Under wise and virtuous men like the ancient Romans, the government was constitutional. When men were in a state of innocence, before the Fall, the government was constitutional.[31] In Italy, constitutional government was the only alternative to tyranny. "Men of strong spirit and bold hearts," he wrote in this connection, "with confidence in their own intelligence cannot be ruled except by a constitutional government, including therein what is commonly called an aristocracy." They will not willingly submit to one-man rule, when it occurs it has to be imposed as tyranny, which, he admitted, had always been the case in Sicily, Sardinia, and Corsica, and was occurring also in Lombardy. In this connection occurs one of the few specific references I have seen in treatises on government of that time to the Venetian constitution.

[27] Tolomeo, *De Regimine Principum* published in Thomas Aquinas, *Opera Omnia*, XVI, Lib. II, ch. 8 and 9; III, 20; IV, 1. Thomas Aquinas had clearly implied that the *regimen politicum* was not a monarchy in our sense for he said it was a government in which men took turns being first rulers and then subjects. I *Pol.* 10.

[28] J. C. L. Sismonde de Sismondi, *Histoire des républiques italiennes au moyen âge* (Paris, 1840) , X, ch. 8.

[29] *De Regimine,* IV, 7: "Laudabilis igitur politia est in qua secundum merita unicuique civi vicissim distribuntur honoras."

[30] *De Regimine,* II, 10; IV, 1, 7, 8.

[31] *De Regimine,* II, 9; cf. Gilby, *Principality,* pp. 287–91.

Tolomeo wrote: "In the regions . . . which are today called Lombardy no one has been able to hold office for life other than by tyranny, except the Doge of Venice, who however has a limited power *(temperatum regimen)*. Hence rulers with limited terms receive more support in those regions."[32] Obviously he is forced to treat Venice as an exception. He does not wish to classify it as a regal government, since the power of the doge was so limited by councils, and therefore he must recognize it as an exception to his general rule that there must be rotation in high office in constitutional governments.

The life tenure of the doge was the only exception at Venice to Tolomeo's principle that rotation in office was characteristic of constitutional government. The twenty or thirty other men who really governed Venice held their high offices, such as that of ducal Councilor, for only six months or a year and were debarred from being re-elected to the same post. The Venetian system of drawing lots to form nominating committees was designed to prevent factions from controlling these nominations and thus to assure nominations that agreed with the principle laid down by Tolomeo that offices be distributed to citizens according to their merits. All those elected were bound by oaths, as Tolomeo recommended, and subject to penalties if they violated the regulations they had sworn to abide by. Even the doge was bound by oath, indeed his oath, the *promissione,* was the keystone of the constitution. The subjection of all to the law, even the mightiest, was reinforced in Venice shortly after Tolomeo wrote by the creation in 1310 of the Council of Ten.[33] The extreme example of calling a ruler to account was given in the mid-fourteenth century when the Council of Ten condemned Doge Marino Falier to be beheaded. In all these respects, Venice's institutions were the kind that Tolomeo declared appropriate to a constitutional regime.

In concluding his final book, Tolomeo admitted constitutional government might be corrupted, but defended it by saying that it was good as long as the right kind of men were chosen for office. What were the right kind? Those from the middle class, said Tolomeo. He wrote, "The proper men, as Aristotle explained in his *Politics,* are the mid-

[32] *De Regimine,* IV, 8. Tolomeo's statement recalls that of Aristotle, that the barbarians endured despotic rule because they were more servile in nature than the Greeks (*Politics,* III, ix, 3). Cf. R. Koebner, "Despot and Despotism: Vicissitudes of a Political Term," *Journal of the Warburg and Courtauld Institutes,* XIV (1951), 277–79.

[33] Kretschmayr, *Geschichte,* II, 76–90; Sandi, *Principi,* pt. I, vol. II, pp. 721, 898; pt. II, vol. I, pp. 31–35.

dling men (*mediocres*) of the city, that is, not the most powerful for they are likely to become tyrants, and not those of the lowest conditions, because they at once turn it into a democracy. For when they think themselves on top, forgetful and ignorant of government, they are swept under by the false leadership of low scoundrels who do not provide for their subjects and who are presumptuous and bold in oppressing others, so that constitutional government is corrupted and disrupted."[34] Although recalling Aristotle, Tolomeo's words applied to contemporary Italian cities in which the self-styled *popolo,* having seized power, was concerned with defining membership in their own ranks. Most cities had begun to exclude the formerly "most powerful," as Tolomeo now advised. Venice was distinctive in neither barring great families from office nor sending into exile any substantial faction. It did act in accord with Tolomeo's views, however, when it excluded the lower classes from political activity by gradually suppressing during the fourteenth century the popular assembly, the *concio.*

When Tolomeo speaks of government by "the people" it is clear that he does not count everyone as part of "the people." The most striking illustration of this is his reference to Egypt as a place where the people elect their ruler. By "the people" he clearly means the Mameluke soldiery, who in fact did the electing, and he shows his familiarity with the way this soldiery recruited new members, namely by buying likely young men on the slave market. In discussing Egyptian government he never seems to have thought of including the mass of the Egyptians among "the people."[35] He probably thought of them as slaves, as far from citizenship as the domestic slaves then common in Italy, or the tenants in its countryside, or the Greek serfs on Cyprus or Crete. There was never any question in the minds of any of the men I am discussing of equal political rights for all men. There is no reason to think such an idea ever contributed to political issues in Venice, but Tolomeo's praise of the middle class shows that by 1303, when he was writing, the question of where to draw a line so as to exclude from citizenship those below was recognized as a problem by some political thinkers.[36]

[34] *De Regimine,* IV, 8. Aristotle gives (IV, ix) a much longer encomium of middle-class government.

[35] *De Regimine,* IV, i.

[36] There is no indication in Thomas Aquinas's discussion that he thought that political activity of the lower classes presented any problem. Probably it did not in his day when merchants and shipowners were happy to have craftsmen and seamen shouting support for them in the piazza. But Aquinas expounded without demur what Aristotle said about the exclusion of laborers and artisans from citizenship (*Opera Omnia,* vol. XXI; III *Pol.* Lect. iii) .

IV

Among the six political writers already mentioned, all more or less contemporaries of Tolomeo, only one was a Venetian, Fra Paolino. To be sure Tolomeo himself had ended his life as bishop of Torcello, the former commercial center in the Venetian lagoons, but he was then at least a septuagenarian. Paolino, in contrast, knew Venice like a native, was a member of Venice's Franciscan friary, served as its ambassador to Naples, wrote a chronicle very important for Venetian history, and dedicated his treatise of government to a Venetian noble, Marino Badoer, duke of Crete, 1313 to 1315.[37] His Venetian patriotism shows in one passage which appears in all the copies of his chronicle: "The people of Italy cannot and should not live in subjection because liberty has its seat in Italy. But in the most admirably perfect state of Venice (*regnum Venecie*) which is foremost among the most important parts of Italy, Italian liberty is preserved in superior degree."[38]

Paolino's treatise on government followed the basic plan and many of the lines of thought of Egidio Colonna's *De Regimine Principum* but Paolino abbreviated Egidio's longwinded treatise into a brief tract that might conceivably be read by a young man of action about to take a responsible position. It is written in the Venetian dialect and divided into short chapters each containing a few injunctions baldly stated and often illustrated with a memorable incident. Apart from the dialect, its most Venetian characteristic, perhaps, is its practicality. Paolino emphasizes the importance of finances and of the food supply. Among his maxims are: Take pains to do no great injury to anyone, nor yet many small injuries, for many small injuries count as a grave wrong, just as many small expenses add up to a large expenditure. Keep calling attention to the dangers that confront the city, whether from enemy attack, from possible loss of merchandise and profits, or from shortage of food. Point them out not because you are afraid of them, but so that the citizens, fearing the dangers, will not be seditious (ch. 71). He concludes: Be loved by your subjects.

Paolino simplified the Aristotelian description of the six forms of

[37] *Enciclopedia italiana*, s.v. Bartolomeo Fiadoni; Tolomeo da Lucca, *Annales seu gesta Tuscorum*, ed. by B. Schmeidler (Monumenta Germanicae Historiae, SS. n.s., VIII; Berlin, 1930), p. xx; Fra Paolino Minorita, *Trattato de Regimine Rectoris*, ed. by Adolfo Mussafia (Vienna and Florence, 1868), intro.

[38] Ester Pastorello in her edition of Andrea Dandolo, *Chronicon per extensum descripta* (Rerum Italicarum Scriptores, 2d ed., XII, pt. 1; Bologna, 1940), p. xxxv-vi.

government by saying that the three perverted forms were government by a tyrant, by the rich, and by the poor; the three good forms were rule by one man alone, by a few men of virtue, and by the many who were rich (ch. 67). That might be called an optimistic view, worthy of a prosperous city like Venice. Venetian also, one is tempted to say, is his view of how men came together to form a city. The first city, he opined, was built by Cain because he and his sons having turned robbers needed a strong place in which to protect their booty from those they had despoiled (ch. 65).

A few of the chapters in which Paolino departs from Egidio's pattern of argument can be taken seriously as showing differences in their political views. Most notable is their different treatment of the relation of the ruler to the laws. Egidio had argued that the "laws were in the breast of the king," and in this connection he had elaborated Thomas Aquinas's distinction between regal and constitutional government before it had been taken up by Tolomeo of Lucca. Egidio did not believe a king could change natural or divine law, nor violate them without becoming a tyrant, but he did maintain that one of the functions of the just ruler was to interpret natural law and apply it to the situation in his kingdom. He went on to declare that it was better to be ruled by a good king than by good laws because a good king would follow the just laws anyhow and would in addition moderate and supplement the laws wisely in applying them to particular cases.[39] The conclusion follows logically enough and is not so contrary to Aquinas's position as the Carlyles represent.[40] But Paolino of Venice showed no interest in such logical games. He ignored that part of Egidio's tract, and put in its place some arguments for the practical value of written laws. They are the means of preserving the counsel of wise men and of having their wisdom readily at hand even after they have passed on. Justice depends on the availability of such wisdom. Laws are more certain and less affected by the loves and hates of individual judges. Moreover, when a written law is followed, the judgment arouses less hostility against the ruler since the condemnation is not his work but that of the law.[41] Although some of these arguments are suggested by Aristotle, Paolino's emphases suggest the relatively impersonal style of government developing at Venice and a readiness to make the ruler subject to the law, as Tolomeo had done.

[39] Egido Colonna, *De Regimine Principum* (Augsburg, 1473), III, pt. 2, ch. 29.
[40] Carlyle, V, 75–76.
[41] Contrast the emphasis in Paolino, *Trattato*, ch. 75–80 with that in Egidio, *De Regimine*, III, pt. 2, ch. 24–29. Cf. Aristotle, *Politics*, III, ch. 6, 9, 11, 12.

In discussing monarchy Paolino omits Egidio's argument for hereditary monarchy, saying nothing about how the monarch should be chosen (ch. 68). He devotes many chapters to the roles of councilors who can, he says, give to a monarchy all the advantages of an aristocracy, preventing the ruler from being deceived or ignorant (ch. 69–70). Since Venice was still a monarchy in form, Paolino's arguments in favor of one-man rule were not of a kind to be offensive to his compatriots. Yet Paolino's terse little treatise is not a defense of the Venetian political system, in which the councilors were elected, controlled the prince, and turned what was formally a monarchy into an aristocracy. Paolino assumes that the councilors of whom he speaks will be chosen by the prince and he advises him regarding what kind to appoint: able men, friendly to him, but willing to tell him the truth. There is no discussion of representation or of rotation in office. And the people are to obey the ruler as the body obeys the head (ch. 83).

V

In Venice's closest neighbor, contemporary with Paolino, lived the ablest political thinker of that generation, Marsiglio of Padua, whose thought reflected the speculative power generated in Paris, the democratic institutions of his native Padua, and the example of integrated government presented by Venice.[42]

Marsiglio's thinking started from the Aristotelian conception of the state as the natural outgrowth of man's needs. For his development man formed various social orders. Marsiglio distinguished six such fields of organization within a community: the agricultural, the indus-

---

[42] Marsilius of Padua, *Defensor Pacis,* ed. by C. W. Previté-Orton (Cambridge, 1928); Marsilius of Padua, *Defensor Pacis,* trans. with intro. by A. Gewirth (2 vols., Records of Civilization; New York, 1956). Quotations in Latin are from Previté-Orton's edition, in English from Gewirth's translation. McIlwain, *Political Thought,* pp. 297–99, minimizes the role of Marsiglio in writing the *Defensor Pacis* and the relevance of that work to Italian conditions. Something must be allowed to McIlwain's contention (pp. 304–5 and n.) that departures from Aristotle reflect Roman practices and could have been derived from Roman law or Cicero. But I find convincing Previté-Orton's interpretation as expressed in the *English Historical Review,* XXXVIII (1923), p. 16, where he says Marsiglio was "so much more an understanding disciple of Aristotle than were his forerunners" because of "his upbringing at this critical time among these communes, . . . His lawgiver is merely the *arengo* or *parlamento* of an Italian city." A clear example of his favoring current Italian practice over that approved by Aristotle is in his treatment of artisans as citizens. See below, n. 45.

trial (*artisanal, artificium*), the military, the financial, the ecclesiastical, and the political (*iudicialis seu consiliativa*) (I, v, 1). In Aristotle
(*Politics*, VII, vii), these same six appear, but are hardly more than
occupations. In Marsiglio they are based on occupational differences
but amount to more than that because they are called *officia* or
ordines.[43]

Human welfare required that the relations between these six orders
or subsystems be such as to assure peace (I, ii and xix). That would be
secured only if the political order was supreme and controlled all the
others (I, xv, esp. 8 and 14). Marsiglio was as concerned with the
dangers of dissension and strife, as insistent on peace, as either Thomas
Aquinas or Dante Alighieri, as his title shows, but Marsiglio thought
the key to peace was not a universal pope or emperor but the sovereignty within each community of its political organization, the *pars
principans*, over all competing organizations. He returned to that
theme in the ringing appeal with which he ended *The Defender of the
Peace*. He was of course preoccupied with ecclesiastical claims to power,
with the efforts of churchmen to determine for themselves their relations to the rest of society instead of letting these be determined by the
government. But in the history of the Italian communes there were
many other struggles which Marsiglio may have had in mind, although
he does not specifically refer to them, namely, the contests of the Italian
communal governments with the seignioral controls over agriculture,
with military entrepreneurs, and with artisan guild organizations
within their walls. While these had disrupted the peace in Padua and
many other Italian communes, Venice had been able to avoid any
armed conflicts of that sort, partly because of its peculiar maritime
structure and economy, partly because its Byzantine tradition and the
continuity of its political life had made its political organization
stronger than any groupings of artisans or of landlords and tenants.
The guilds permitted at Venice were definitely subject to the doge and
his councils. In accordance with its Byzantine traditions, the Venetian
government exercised much control over its churchmen, more than in
most western states, even if not as much as Marsiglio advocated. In

---

[43] In his edition of the *Defensor Pacis*, p. xv, Previté-Orton calls them "orders." To
Marsiglio, the varied capacities and occupations of men were only the material
cause of these orders; their formal and efficient causes involved human legislation
(I, vii, 2). The governing part or order should be the most highly organized; it
should have a unity which in any of the other parts would be harmful (I, xvii, 2),
but some measure of organization in the other parts or orders is implied by even
comparing them in this way with the ruling part (*pars principans*).

these regards and in its deep respect for written laws, Venice may well have appeared to Marsiglio as a model.

When he considers how the government should be organized (i.e., how the political part of society should be structured) Marsiglio discussed the six forms mentioned by Aristotle in a way that shows explicitly his admiration for the Venetian constitution. In an early draft he cited Venice as an example of some of the benefits of elective monarchy. Popular election, he said, gave more assurance that the office would go to a man of the necessary virtues. Moreover uncertainty over his successor would give him an additional incentive to act for the public welfare since he would wish to make a record that would help his children to succeed him. Marsiglio continues (I, xvi, 13) : "Hence too he will take greater care that they [his children] be virtuous and well educated; and the children considering this fact, will aim with greater effort at the virtues and the performance of their duties. Hence it is very likely that a son brought up to be similar to his father in virtue will be named to the rulership because of his merit and the obedience customarily given to him, so long as the son has such a character, as fully appears in the Dukes of Venice." When he wrote the last phrase, he may have had in mind Doge Pietro, the son of Doge Sebastian Ziani, and Doge Lorenzo, the son of Doge Jacopo Tiepolo. Later he crossed it out, perhaps regretting such praise of Venice.[44]

Marsiglio's elected monarch was to be definitely subject to advisers and to the law, as was the doge of Venice. Marsiglio repeats with approval Aristotle's story of the Spartan king Theopompus who replied to his wife's reproaches that he was leaving their children a smaller rule than he had received, because of the creation of the ephors, by saying, "Not at all, for the power I give to them will be more lasting" (I, xi, 8; cf. Aristotle, *Pol.*, V, xi). Marsiglio clearly went further than Thomas Aquinas in making the king subject to the law, declaring the king should be subject to penalties decreed and executed by the sovereign people (the legislator) or a person or persons appointed by the people for that purpose (I, xviii, 3).

While finding much admirable in the thirteenth-century constitution of Venice—its subordination of other social organizations to the government, its election of the doge, and its holding of him strictly to account—Marsiglio's thought offered no support for the kind of changes the Venetians were making during his lifetime, for Marsiglio emphasized the will of the people. He distinguished the three healthy

[44] *Defensor Pacis,* ed. by Previté-Orton, p. 80 n.

from the three diseased forms of government not only by the fact that the healthy forms were for the benefit of the whole people but also by their being in accordance with the popular will (I, 8). There has been much debate over what Marsiglio meant by "the people," which he frequently calls "the whole citizen body or its weightier part (*universitaten civium aut valentiorem partem*)." In one passage he specified: "By the weightier part I mean to take into consideration the quantity and quality of the persons in that community over which the law is made" (I, xii, 3; Gewirth, I, 182–89). He did not believe in one man, one vote; he did not mean by *valentiorem partem* merely a numerical majority. Nor did he include all inhabitants in the citizen body; like Aristotle he excluded slaves, immigrants, along with women and children. But in the light of contemporary practices and the changes going on in Venice and Padua his doctrines imply opposition to the aristocratic trends. While he too used *populum* to mean the whole community, Marsiglio stressed including the whole, and not restricting the number who could participate in the sovereign power of lawmaking and electing the ruler (I, xii, 5–7; I, xv, 2). Those who did not participate were in the position of slaves, he said, subject to the will of others, and one of his few references to manual workers shows that he does not favor treating them as the equivalent of slaves.[45] They should participate in the lawmaking. Marsiglio stated the arguments commonly used in favor of aristocracy and against democracy, namely that most men are stupid, many of them vicious, and that it is easier to secure agreement among a few than among many. But he gives these arguments only to refute them.[46] A contemporary Venetian could hardly have interpreted his theories otherwise than as hostile to changes made about 1300 and favorable to the old Venetian constitution, that established a hundred years earlier, when the people, assembled in Saint Mark's and shouting their sentiments, seemed of real importance in determining the choice of doge and when important

---

[45] In I, xii, 2, while discussing whether the making of laws should be in the hands of men learned in the law or of the general body of citizens he refers to manual workers who must devote all their efforts to acquiring the necessities of life ("Mechanicorum . . . qui ad acquirenda vite necessaria suis operibus habent intendere"). He concludes, in I, xiii, that a few elected wise and learned men should propose and draw up the laws, but that the laws should be subject to approval by the whole body of citizens, for the multitude, he argues, can pass sound judgment on what they are to use, just as ships and houses can be judged by men who use them but are incapable of building them. In this connection Gewirth points out, "His main arguments are directed against those who would deprive the *vulgus* of power." Gewirth, pp. 181–82, 192–93. Contrast Aristotle, *Pol.*, III, 5.

[46] Gewirth, I, 199–203.

laws were submitted not merely to the Great Council but to the popular assembly.

VI

For an argument in favor explicitly of the aristocratic character of the Venetian constitution, we must turn from the schoolmen to a Roman lawyer, Bartolus. Writing about 1350 he declared that the best form of government depended on the size of the city-state.[47] For a small city such as the Perugia in which he lived and even for Siena and Pisa, he thought a popular government best.[48] For a very large city ruling a great empire, such as imperial Rome, monarchy was preferable; and for cities "of the second rank" as he called them, such as Venice, an aristocracy was best. Of such a city, he argued, "to be ruled by a king is not appropriate and to have such a large multitude in an assembly is dangerous so that it is wise that they be ruled by a few, that is, by the rich and good men of the city." He cited the senate of early Rome as well as the governments of Venice and Florence as examples, and then came to the pith of his argument, "For although they are said to be ruled by the few, I say that they are few compared to the whole population of the city, but they are many compared to [those ruling] in other cities and because they are many the people are not resentful of being governed by them. Also because they are many they are not easily divided against themselves; moreover many of them are men of moderate wealth who are always a stabilizing force in a city. So this kind of government of the few is better when the city has grown to the second degree of size.[49] Bartolus's description of the good form of government by the few is curiously reminiscent of the Venetian friar Paolino's description of the good form of government by the many, "namely, the many who are rich."

The Venetian aristocracy became in the course of time strictly hereditary. The arguments that might have been used to support the inheritance of political rights by a few are given by Egidio and Marsiglio in discussing whether kingship should be hereditary, namely, that when political rights are hereditary the rulers are more devoted to the state because they know their sons will inherit control of it, that the sons are brought up to assume responsibility, and that the people are more obedient because ruled by men belonging to famous families.

[47] C. N. S. Woolf, *Bartolus of Sassoferrato* (Cambridge, 1913), pp. 174–81.

[48] Bartolus, *Tractatus de Regimine Civitatis*, in *Consilia, Questiones et Tractatus,* which is vol. X of *Opera* (Basel, 1588), par. 15–19, 22.

[49] *Ibid.*, par. 20.

Egidio Colonna had used these arguments to defend the French hereditary monarchy,[50] but Marsiglio gives them only to refute them.[51] Paolino, the Venetian popularizer of Egidio, made no mention of them in
any connection, and I find no evidence that anyone, even Bartolo,
applied them to Venice during the fourteenth century, although they
do appear in the sixteenth-century encomiums.

VII

The conclusions from this examination of the political thinkers most
likely to have had influence in Venice during the formation of its
constitution, or to have reflected ideas then current, must be largely but
not altogether negative. It shows no theoretical discussion preceding
and justifying the constitutional arrangements distinctive of Venice,
although there was considerable *ex post facto* praise of the sort of
balanced constitution which the Venetians had created about 1200 and
this suggests that the success of Venice under that constitution may
have had some influence on such thinkers as Thomas Aquinas and
Marsiglio of Padua. It shows almost no support for the aristocratic
reforms of about 1300, not even after the event: Tolomeo's praise of the
middle class was directed against both those above and those below;
and Marsiglio favored participation by even the "mechanics" in the
approval of laws; only Bartolo, belatedly, praised Venice for being
aristocratic.

Yet this examination of political writers suggests one conclusion of
importance for the interpretation of Venetian constitutional history.
In the changes made about 1300 under Doge Pietro Gradenigo, the
crucial provision proved to be the reform of the Great Council in 1297,
which was later called the "closing," the *serrata*. It gave more weight to
heredity than had been done previously in determining the membership of that council and at the same time enlarged it greatly. During
the next generation or two, the enlarged Great Council replaced the
general assembly, the *concio*, as the sovereign representative of the
Venetian people. Was the reform of 1297 a move by an aristocratic
party deliberately designed to exclude lower classes from any share in
the government?[52] Or was it an adjustment in the governmental machinery which made no change and intended no change in the location

---

[50] *De Regimine Principum*, III, ch. 5.

[51] *Defensor Pacis*, I, xvi.

[52] The view of William Roscoe Thayer, *A Short History of Venice* (Boston and
New York, 1908), ch. V; see also Götz Freiherr von Pölnitz, *Venedig* (Munich, 1951),
ch. 7, 8.

of effective political power?[53] That is a crucial issue in Venetian constitutional history. Our survey supports the second rather than the first interpretation.

The main concern of the political thinkers was not whether government should be by the One, the Few, or the Many. Even those who declared themselves clearly in favor of a monarch as did Aquinas or in favor of subordinating the monarch to the people, as did Marsiglio, treated the *form* of government as a secondary matter. The only really Venetian writer, Paolino, saw no conflict between praising Venice and praising monarchy. What really mattered to all the writers mentioned was that some means be found to avoid the evils of dissension and tyranny. If these writings indicate at all the general ideas that were in the minds of Piero Gradenigo and the men who reformed the Venetian constitution about 1300, they indicate that these men were worried about dissensions that would lead to the tyranny of a faction first and then of a *signore*. The Gradenigo and the other leading families had been occupying all the high offices for centuries and no doubt expected to continue to occupy them. They had been securing the ratification of their elections and of the laws they proposed by the general assembly of the people gathered in San Marco or its piazza. This kind of popular assembly, although clearly favored by Tolomeo and Marsiglio, was proving itself vulnerable to manipulations and intimidations which opened the way in other cities to tyranny. In Venice the development of the Great Council prevented such manipulation. Very possibly its enlargement by the recognition of hereditary rights of membership, while not at first excluding the admission of new men, and its subsequent displacement of the popular assembly as the sovereign authority were thought of as simply a better way of organizing popular participation in the government while lessening the dangers of factionalism. Then, during the fourteenth century there was a gradual growth of conscious conflict over participation by the lower classes and acceptance of new men into the ruling class. But factional fights within the ruling class were at the beginning of the century both the main danger in fact and also the main concern of those reshaping the constitution. They were not yet worried that the theme of popular sovereignty would interfere with their power and felt no need for an aristocratic theme of government.

This view of the political atmosphere of Venice finds some confirmation in the chronicle of Andrea Dandolo, doge of Venice, 1343 to 1354.

[53] F. C. Hodgson, *Venice in the Thirteenth and Fourteenth Centuries* (London, 1910), ch. 9; Roberto Cessi, *Origini del ducato veneziano* (Naples, 1951), ch. 11.

This Dandolo, the friend of Petrarch and a learned lawyer, was one of the twenty to forty men who took turns in the highest offices and managed the Venetian state during the very period when the popular assembly was being suppressed. The Dandolos are commonly reputed to have been leaders in that movement. The chronicle which Andrea Dandolo composed at the end of his life became the basis for all the subsequent Venetian histories.[54] Yet this chronicle emphasizes popular sovereignty and the role of the people, people as well as nobles, in creating the Venetian constitution. For example, in telling of the election of the first doge, which the apparent source, Giovanni the Deacon, said was the action of all the Venetians, Andrea specifies that the common people (*plebeii*) as well as the leading citizens (*proceres*) took part.[55] The decision to move the capital to Rialto was made "by the common decisions of the Venetians (*Venetici communi decreto*)," said Giovanni, whereas Andrea Dandolo specifies that it was made by the popular assembly (*in concione publica*), by the very popular assembly that in Andrea Dandolo's own day was being shoved aside.[56] And Andrea is also more explicit than his sources in ascribing to this popular assembly a vital role in the election of Sebastian Ziani in 1172.[57] If he exaggerated the role of the people in events of his time, one might discount it, arguing that he was party to a conspiracy to make them unaware of how completely real power had passed into the hands of a hereditary aristocracy. But he had no such motive for emphasizing the role of the common people or of the popular assembly in the traditional turning points of Venetian history centuries earlier. He writes as if unaware of any ideological conflict between partisans of aristocracy and partisans of more popular government. Indeed no Venetian chronicle gives any evidence of any such conflict until later in the century.

Analysis of Venetian chronicles and Venetian official records must serve as the main basis for understanding Venetian political life; contemporary political theorists can serve only a supplementary function. In that role these theorists indicate little concern with rule by one class over another and much concern with preserving peace by controlling factions.

[54] Dandolo, *Cronica*, ed. by Pastorello, cited above; F. Thiriet, "Les chroniques vénitiennes de la Marcienne et leur importance pour l'histoire de la Romanie greco-vénitienne," *Mélanges d'Archéologie et d'histoire publiée par l'École Française de Rome* (Paris, 1954), 241–92.

[55] *Cronache veneziane*, cited in n. 3 above, p. 91; Dandolo, pp. 105–6.

[56] *Cronache veneziane*, p. 106; Dandolo, p. 139.

[57] Dandolo, p. 259; cf. Monumenta Germanicae Historiae, Scriptores, XIV, 80.

Part Two

EUROPEAN COMMERCE

19

Colbert and the Commerce of Bordeaux*

WHEN France emerged from the domestic conflicts and the wars against the Habsburgs which had absorbed her energy for a century, Holland and England had seized the economic opportunities offered by the newly discovered lands. Moreover, they profited more than any other country from the development of industry made possible by the expansion of markets. From a France hindered until then from taking its share in the new economic life, Colbert wished to create the most powerful state in the world. To this end it was necessary to endow it with colonies, to extend its trade, and to create industry on a large scale. Likewise he attempted to attract money into the kingdom—this *pecunia nervus belli*—and he hoped thus to give to the young king an economic might sufficient for supporting his politics of magnificence. What part in this grandiose dream could be played by the bourgeois of Bordeaux, who did little else than to sell their wines and liqueurs to the English and Dutch who came to buy them? In the seventeenth century as in the Middle Ages and even more than today the wealth of the Bordelais came from the sale of wine.

Colbert thoroughly recognized the importance of this commerce. He requested his agents, both those who were at Bordeaux and those who passed through, to inform him carefully of the quantity of wine exported. He demanded that one of them send him a report each fortnight.[1] The question interested him not only from the commercial but especially from the financial point of view. His economic theory, the mercantilist doctrine, appeared clearly in the following passage:

* "Colbert et le commerce de Bordeaux," *Revue historique de Bordeaux,* XVII (1924), 169–90. (Translation by permission.)

[1] G.-B. Depping, *Correspondance administrative sous le règne de Louis XIV* (Paris, 1850), III, 528–58.

To judge well whether the province has been generally over-
burdened, it is necessary that you pay close attention to the
wine and goods which will be exported during this winter. In as
much as money comes abundantly into the kingdom by that
path, it is certain that if the same quantity is exported as last
year, the province will not be in a bad way.[2]

Just as the pharaoh of Egypt fixed his taxes according to the crest of the
Nile, Colbert would have liked to estimate his own according to the
value of Bordeaux's wine exports.

Colbert's administration did a great deal to facilitate the internal
commerce on which the rise of external commerce partly depended.
Opening the navigation of the Dronne, the Lot, and the Garonne,
abolishing tolls, helping the commerce of the Dordogne, especially at
Bergerac, discovering copper and iron mines, completing the canal of
Deux-Mers, all these attempted projects would have been profitable to
Bordeaux.[3] More important was the establishment of tar manufacture
in Landes. The enterprise was directed by the Sieur Lombard who was
one of Colbert's most capable collaborators at Bordeaux and whom the
Marquis de Seignelay called "extremely intelligent and effective."[4]
With the help of three Swedes whom Colbert had brought in for this
purpose, he instructed the inhabitants of Landes in the manufacture of
tar and other resinous products. This work of Colbert had immediate
and durable results because it survived the disastrous wars at the end of
the century.[5] The tar and pitch industry was regulated by statutes
according to the principles of Colbertism, particularly in 1672 by an
ordinance of the Intendant d'Aguesseau.[6] One part of the product was
sent directly to Rochefort for the navy and another was exported
through Arcachon and Bayonne, but Colbert wished that as much of
the tar as possible be sent to Bordeaux where he was able to find a
common and easy market.[7] Thus he was able to develop goods of
exportation which drew money into the kingdom and to facilitate the
growth of the maritime industry.

Far from being satisfied that Bordeaux was only a center for exports,

---

[2] *Ibid.*, III, 201.

[3] The correspondence on these subjects is found in P. Clément, *Lettres, instructions et mémoires de Colbert* (Paris, 1861 *et seq.*) , II, Part 2, 548; and Depping, III,
201, and IV, 4 ff. and 31–33. See also F.-M.-J.-F. O'Reilly, *Memoires sur la vie publi-
que et privée de Claude Pellot* (Paris and Rouen, 1881) .

[4] Clément, II, Part 2, 24.

[5] Bazin de Bezons, *Mémoire concernant la généralité de Bordeaux,* p. 154.

[6] Arch. départ de la Gironde, C. 3., 671, where one finds a list of manufacturers of
pitch drawn up by Lombard.

[7] Depping, III, 72, 694, 859, 861; Clément, III, Part 1, 406.

Colbert desired to see it play a role in his grandiose dream of maritime expansion. Persistently he wrote to the intendants of the necessity to encourage the Bordelais to construct ships, or even to buy them if necessary, and to conduct large-scale commerce and distant voyages in competition with the Dutch and the English. He was well aware that he could not attain his goal immediately, and wrote to d'Aguesseau that if he succeeded in increasing the number of ships of the Bordelais by two, three, or four each year, that would represent "considerable progress."[8] Monsieur de Pontac, the First President of Parlement, who was wealthy and "greatly endeared to the service of the king," helped him, but the task was difficult.[9] The Marquis de Seignelay, who was at Bordeaux at the time of the fair in 1670, although expressing admiration for the seven or eight hundred vessels at anchor in the harbor, wrote to his father: "There are not three Bourgeois of Bordeaux who have their own ships."[10]

In effect Colbert collided with the commercial habits of the Bordelais. The Intendant, Bazin de Bezons, describing how they conducted their commerce in 1697, indicated that it was exactly the same in 1660. He distinguished three classes of merchants: the first composed of French and not numerous, the second and largest composed of naturalized foreigners who enjoyed bourgeois privileges before the uprising of 1675, and the third consisting of foreigners who returned enriched to their own lands. What was most significant was that the majority of Bordelais acted as agents for the foreign merchants and did little on their own account.[11] A dispute which arose in 1665 during the war between Holland and England gives us a glimpse of the organization of this commerce. The English took several Dutch ships which were transporting wine belonging to merchants of Bordeaux. When the latter asked for reparations, Colbert wrote to de Pontac that he suspected that the Bordelais had lent their names to the Dutch who were the true owners of the wine. Indignantly the bourgeois replied that the wine was truly theirs and added somewhat naïvely: "The trade of the Dutch in this province has not been large in comparison with that of the Bourgeois."[12]

---

[8] Clément, II, Part 2, 548.

[9] Depping, III, 364. On the subject of M. de Pontac, see Depping, II, 126.

[10] Clement, III, Part 2, 24.

[11] Bazin de Bezons, pp. 102–3. See Alfred Leroux, *La colonie germanique de Bordeaux* (Bordeaux, 1918), pp. 23 and 24, on the subject of the Dutch, and T. Malvezin, *Histoire du commerce de Bordeaux* (Bordeaux, 1892), II, 305, for a list of merchants.

[12] Arch. munic. registre de la Jurade, BB, 1665, January 26 and 27.

Moreover, the bourgeois were especially concerned over their customs privileges. An act of Colbert suggesting restriction of these rights was immediately the occasion of a delegation to Paris in protest.[13] When as a part of his design to bring order into the finances Colbert wished to verify the right to that status of all claiming to be bourgeois, the Intendant wrote him that it would be of no use since all trade would be in the hands of those who made good these claims.[14]

All of these indications lead us to the same conclusion: the bourgeois attended to the purchase and sale of wine, and benefiting from the advantages which their privileges provided, they made such good profits that they had no reason for becoming involved in distant affairs. A letter in 1664 from the magistrates of Bordeaux to Colbert demonstrates that the bourgeois were more interested in maintaining their privileges than in undertaking new enterprises. In the beginning they lavished gratitude for the interest which the king bore towards commerce. But all of a sudden, their tone changed, and they observed that after they had paid so many taxes, they were not left with enough wealth with which to conduct trade. Finally they protested against the tax on tobacco, liqueurs, etc., with a sincerity beyond all doubt.[15]

At first Colbert enacted some general regulations for pressuring the merchants into large-scale trade. On September 10, 1664, the magistrates received a royal letter, which they were required to publish at the meeting of the Cent-Trente, announcing the creation of the Council of Commerce. It emphasized the great facility which the king wished the merchants to have in presenting to him their views on the subject of commercial development; it designated Colbert to attend to these matters; and it mentioned the orders which the king had given to the tribunals and ambassadors for assuring prompt justice to the merchants. Finally it informed of his intention of giving subsidies to merchants who acquired ships for trade. On March 1, 1665, the magistrates transcribed on their register the decree of the Council of Commerce of December 5, 1664, which provided the details of those promises. The decree gave subsidies to those who ordered ships to be built, who bought them abroad, who made voyages in the Baltic to Norway or to Russia, and who transported settlers to the New World. A commissioner was to be named at Bordeaux for distributing these rewards. To organize the representation of merchants before the king, Bordeaux

---

13 *Inventaire sommaire des registres de la Jurade,* II, 485 ff.
14 Depping, I, 691.
15 Depping, III, 11.

was joined with La Rochelle and Bayonne, thus forming one of three sections each of which would have a permanent deputy at the court. The bourgeois should assemble at the end of January and elect a regional chamber from which the king would choose its representative at Paris.[16] The register of the magistrature for January and February, 1666–1667, however, contained no mention of the elections that it should have conducted according to the decree. Although Colbert had indicated the way, Bordeaux was to await until the following century before receiving a Chamber of Commerce.

Colbert did not limit his efforts to this general ordinance, however. The tradition established by Richelieu and the example of the rich Dutch republic induced him to choose the method of large privileged companies for extending trade and developing colonies.

Although without great importance for the future of Bordeaux, the formation of the East India Company was the source of some activity. Its establishment was due neither to the necessity of producing a direct trade with lands where French products could find outlets as was the case of the Compagnie du Nord, nor to the fact that France already possessed productive colonies overseas; rather it was motivated simply by the jealousy which the prosperity of the Low Countries engendered in Colbert. And Colbert did not ask Bordeaux for managers and shipowners to take active part in the company, but only for capital. This is why membership in the company was not limited to the bourgeoisie but was opened also to the clergy, nobility, lawyers, and judges. Churchmen and nobles had been for a long time the possessors of numerous and fertile lands, and riches were also to be found in the hands of royal office-holders, since for centuries the wealthiest bourgeois had aimed at little else than to purchase a position in Parlement or in one of the financial courts. The merchants themselves could easily subscribe because the wholesale purchase and resale of wine required and produced fluid capital. Their fortunes were not tied up in ships, as were, for example, those of the merchants of Saint-Jean-de Luz.[17]

If the Bordelais possessed the money, that did not mean that it was easy to obtain it from them. On June 25, 1664, the magistrates received a letter from the king and the directors of the company which explained the utility and advantage of the company for all those who wished to enter and ordered that the letter be read to a general meeting. The magistrature complied and on the morrow the great bell

---

[16] Arch. munic. registre de la Jurade, for the dates mentioned.
[17] See their response to Colbert, in Depping, III, 354.

summoned the council of the Cent-Trente. After the public reading, the assembly asked for copies of the letter and time to consider, but nothing more was done before autumn.[18] At this point the Intendant, Claude Pellot, intervened, making known to the magistrates the displeasure of the king and letting it be understood that their privileges would be placed in question.[19] Colbert wrote that if they did not enroll "the king will examine the privileges of the Bourgeois with such severity that without doubt they will be deprived of most of them."[20] Monsieur de Pontac pressed the magistrates and the judge of the Exchange and on November 10 he on his part wrote that the king would examine their privileges.[21] On November 13 the magristrates reconvened the Cent-Trente and urged them to subscribe to the company which the king had established "for the glory and advantage of religion and state." We should notice that they attempted to arouse patriotism and not commercial ambition. It was finally decided to return the matter to the various municipal bodies so that each could seek subscribers from among its members.[22] Monsieur de Pontac wrote that the meeting had demonstrated great enthusiasm.

Some difficulties soon appeared. Monsieur de La Chèze, Receiver General, did not wish to contribute because he had already subscribed to the West India Company. Perhaps influenced by jealousy which the lawyers held against the officers of finance, Pontac exaggerated the bad effect of such an example. He was equally shocked that the members of the Cour des Aides wished to enroll together under the name of their procurator general and thus to evade the payment of 1,000 livres each. At Parlement, however, the presidents subscribed: de Pontac for 6,000 livres, Montesquieu Grimaud and Salomon for 3,000 each. "It seems to me that the gentlemen of our group are greatly disposed to obey the commands of His Majesty," wrote de Pontac, but after having received all the subscriptions, he thought it necessary to offer an excuse for not obtaining more. He suggested to the members of the Chambre de l'Edit to subscribe before they had to be "prompted" by the orders of the king, and the Protestant counselors took his advice. The Lieutenant-General, Monsieur de Saint-Luc, emphasized the poverty of the provincial nobility, but considered it inexcusable that the Cour des Aides had contributed only 21,000 livres. Moreover. he sug-

[18] Arch. munic. registre de la Jurade, BB 164.
[19] Depping, III, 72.
[20] Lavisse, *Histoire de France*, VII, Part 2, 240.
[21] Depping, III, 358–60.
[22] Arch. munic. registre de la Jurade.

gested mass assessments in the small towns. The members of the clergy wished to be excused on the pretext that it was in conflict with their profession.[23]

As to the merchants, the judge and consuls of the Exchange persuaded them to join in. On January 10, 1665, Larcebaut, the First Consul, presented to the magistrates two documents signed by the bourgeois in which they subscribed a total of 108,400 livres.[24] Since these lists no longer exist at the Municipal Archives, it cannot be determined who were the largest subscribers. Later at the time of the elections the names of 111 subscribers were mentioned, but not all contributed 1,000 livres each, if the following remark of Monsieur de Pontac can be trusted: "Some individuals among the Bourgeois who did not possess enough to offer the entire sum of 1,000 livres could join together to place the total under the name of a single individual."[25]

The threats and exhortations had not been without result. The subscriptions of all the Bordelais attained 400,000 livres,[26] and Colbert informed the Magistrature that His Majesty was "indeed satisfied."[27]

Next it was necessary to elect a local treasurer to receive the payments. The Sieur de Jean, having been authorized by the Parisian directors of the company, requested confirmation by the magistrates, who convoked a meeting of those concerned. Although de Jean had been approved by the Parlement, the Cour des Aides and the Trésoriers de France, and although Colbert had written in his behalf, he was not chosen by the bourgeois. It was contrary to the statutes of the company that the local treasurer be named by the Parisian directors, and perhaps the bourgeois were discontented with this interference in their affairs. Paul Lestrilles was chosen as treasurer and confirmed by the Parlement.[28] Then those concerned turned their attention to the election of the directors, of whom five were to be chosen by the merchants and one by the members of Parlement. The merchants first selected Saint-Luc because "it was necessary to strengthen [the company] with the counsel, credit and authority of persons of quality and predisposed to maintaining a project so useful to the public good." Davançons was chosen

---

[23] Depping, III, 360–63.

[24] Arch. munic. registre de la Jurade.

[25] Depping, III, 361.

[26] H. Weber, *La compagnie française des Indes* (Paris, 1904), p. 131, n. 3, according to the report of Charpentier, but this figure seems to me to be a little high and Charpentier was advertising for the company.

[27] Arch. munic. registre de la Jurade, January 27, 1665.

[28] Arch. munic. registre de la Jurade, January 13 and February 4, 16, and 18, 1665.

to assist Saint-Luc, and Duribaut, Judge of the Exchange, Lafon, Lavard and de Jean for the four other posts.[29]

In June, 1666, more than a year after the call for subscriptions, the majority of them were not yet paid. The directors in Paris wrote to de Jean, who in turn persuaded the magistrates to assemble the bourgeois to make them comply. The register of the magistrature contains no report of the meeting. Again, in February, 1667, Colbert ordered the Directors Lafon and de Jean to enforce the payment of the first third. Lafon and de Jean consulted with the First President, the Lieutenant-General, and the Intendant, who believed that the magistrature was charged with the authority to enforce collection. Finally in March the magistrates commanded the Commissioner of Police to visit the houses of the bourgeois concerned to collect the payments.[30] Two years later, in April, 1669, de Pontac, who had been so enthusiastic in the beginning, protested that it was not just to require the members of Parlement to pay the second third because in this case they would be treated worse than those who had subscribed nothing.[31]

As for the activities of the company, they do not concern us because Bordeaux took no part in them. Bordeaux only furnished it with capital, and did so not as a fruitful commercial enterprise but as a public duty and one imposed.

The creation of the West India Company coincided with that of the East India Company, but its organization prompted no commercial drive at Bordeaux, and it appears that the merchants of Bordeaux had no part in the subscription. Although only the Cour des Aides and the Receiver-General contributed[32] and des Forges, a Farmer-General,[33] entered it for 8,000 livres,[34] Bordeaux was more important for the activities of that company than for those of the East India Company. The company sent a ship from Bordeaux to the American islands in 1665.[35] The fact that the departmental archives of the Gironde contain an announcement which declared the departure from La Rochelle of three vessels and which specified the conditions applicable to those who

[29] Arch. munic. registre de la Jurade, April 27, 1665.
[30] Arch. munic. registre de la Jurade, June 26, 1666, February 26, and May 21, 1667.
[31] Depping, III, 415.
[32] Depping, III, 362, n. 8.
[33] S. des Forges, formerly of the Reformed Church of Bordeaux, is mentioned in the fifth book of the Consistory of the Reformed Church of Bordeaux, fol. 176.
[34] Stewart L. Mims, *Colbert's West India Policy* (New Haven, 1912), p. 81. Professor Mims shows that very few of the subscribers came from merchants.
[35] Mims, p. 95.

wished to establish themselves in the territory of the company, indicates an attempt to recruit settlers from the Gironde.[36] I have transcribed it in part because it conveys a clear idea of the conditions offered the Bordelais who emigrated to America in the seventeenth century. After the opening portion of the document which is half destroyed and which has reference to Cayenne, one reads:

> Those who wish to go to Martinique, Guadeloupe and to the other islands of America either for settlement or for working at their trade will be transported and fed on the aforesaid ships according to the customary manner for the sum of fifty livres each, one half to be paid immediately and the other six months after their arrival at the above mentioned islands.
>
> Those who wish to establish dwellings on the above mentioned islands will also be provided with as much land as they can cultivate and have cultivated. Moreover, these lands will be granted without any payments and with exemptions from all obligations for three years. The Company will likewise furnish and advance wood, materials, negroes and beasts.
>
> For those who prefer to go to the aforementioned island of Cayenne than to Martinique, Guadeloupe, and the other islands and will engage themselves in the service of the Company for three years, they will be transported and fed for the above length of time. They will have the customary wages, and if they desire to reside there at the end of the above three years, they will be given as much lands in ownership as they are able to cultivate.
>
> The artisans and craftsmen who voyage to Cayenne or the other islands of America will be considered as masters in such towns of France where they wish to live after they have practiced their arts and crafts in America during the time set down by the grant and verified by the Parlement. Tools will be supplied to those who do not have them.
>
> The inhabitants of the above mentioned islands and the main-land of America for their advantage will be able to export to France all the goods which they extract from the exploitation of their lands and to import from France foodstuffs, goods and merchandise which they need for the maintenance of their families and residences on the vessels of the Company. To facilitate the sending and receiving of such goods and merchandise the Company will acquit them of all import and export tolls for the payment of a reasonable sum which would cover

[36] Arch. départ., C 3784.

both the freight of the merchandise and the demands of the tolls.

All artisans, craftsmen, or manual laborers who wish to be engaged in the service of the Company in the aforementioned lands and those who wish to travel in the aforementioned ships to establish residence there should present themselves to the office of the General Directors situated at Paris or in the seaports to the directors and commissioners for the Company, who have sufficient authority to agree with applicants over the above conditions which will be punctually executed.

Done at the office of the General Directors of the West India Company in Paris, the eighth day of August 1664.

In 1671 Brunet, one of the directors of the company and a collaborator of Colbert, passed through Bordeaux to organize a branch of the company there and to order the purchase of beef in the Haute-Guienne.[37] The company had a warehouse at Bordeaux of which Lombard was the representative. In September and November, 1671, he loaded two ships of the company, one the "Afriquaine" of 200 tons, the other the "Marianne" which was built in Holland and whose tonnage, to judge from its cargo, was about the same. Each ship was armed with a half-dozen cannons, a dozen muskets, pikes, and the like. This was truly a Bordeaux enterprise because a good part of the crew came from the region. Moreover, four employees of the Company and seven passengers embarked on the "Marianne." Among the latter was Monsieur Puilauzy who afterwards conducted considerable trade on his own account. The instructions of Brunet lead us to believe that the main cargo consisted of lard and beef to which were added some merchandise belonging to the bourgeois.[38] Moreover, Brunet encouraged merchants outside the company to send ships to the islands, and in 1671 some eleven ships were dispatched. The activity of these independent merchants was significant. When in 1669 Colbert took charge of granting passports, the private ship operators began to replace the company.[39]

In addition Brunet helped the Bordeaux refineries to improve their operations. At that time there were three refineries in the city: one established in 1663 by Daniel d'Hierguens, another in 1645 by Jean Vermeron,[40] and a third recently begun by Huguelas and Dobreil. To protect them Colbert decided that the sugar of Nantes should pay the

---

[37] Depping, III, 528.
[38] Arch. départ, fonds de l'Amirauté de Guienne, 6 B 64.
[39] Mims, pp. 176, 225.
[40] Arch. munic., II, carton 26, titre *Raffineries*.

same import dues as those of Holland. It was his wish that each province refine its own sugar.[41]

Three vessels of the company, eleven ships sent by the independent merchants in 1671, fifteen in 1672,[42] a new refinery—all these together constituted only a rather modest beginning, but it was the beginning of a commerce which acquired great importance in the following century. The details which we have mentioned above demonstrate that the company worked together with the merchants at the start and fully justify the judgment of Professor Mims: "Thus the West India Company was the means of transition from the period of Dutch commercial supremacy to that of the growth and development of French commerce."[43]

A third organization, the Compagnie du Nord, completed the system planned by Colbert for extending trade. Already French products found outlets in the Baltic countries, but it was the Dutch intermediaries who realized the profit. Colbert wanted this trade to be conducted by the French and their vessels, and since the wine of Bordeaux was the most important of French goods consumed by the northern lands, it would seem that the project should have stimulated the commercial interests of the Bordeaux merchants.[44] But as we have seen they were busy with the sale and consignment of wine but not with its transport.[45] The prosperity of their business depended entirely on the opportunities to sell wine at a good price. This price was only high when the demand was great and that depended in turn on the Dutch and English through whom the wine was exported. Any decrease in the number of ships which reached Bordeaux or any tariff on wine levied in reprisal by the English or Dutch would have struck the wealth of Bordeaux at its root.

Colbert never desired to decrease this trade, but he thought it would be better for the Bordelais to transport their wine themselves and on their own ships to the northern consumers. To their former profits they would thus add those which they derived from maritime commerce. But the system of Colbert raised one difficulty: because of the fertility

---

[41] Depping, III, 200, 859.

[42] Arch. départ., fonds de l'Amirauté, 6 B 64 and 6 B 65.

[43] Mims, p. 181.

[44] A correspondent of Colbert wrote him that the office of the company should be at Bordeaux or La Rochelle because it could transport wine or salt. P. Boissonnade, *Histoire des premiers essais de relations économiques directes entre la France et l'État prussien pendant le règne de Louis XVI,* p. 170.

[45] See Malvezin and Bazin de Bezons, *passim.*

of the lands in the Bordelais, the chances for profit of a shipowner were not as favorable as for a merchant. Undoubtedly some of the merchants were obliged to become shipowners and to make ocean voyages, but the richest merchants who owed all their fortune to the sale of wine did not wish to commit themselves to hazardous enterprises which would have jeopardized their business. To compete with the Dutch went not only against their habits, but against their interests. That is why we shall discover later that Colbert collided precisely with those who possessed the capital of which he had most need for the success of his plans.

The Compagnie du Nord was established in 1669 with the co-operation of several merchants from La Rochelle. Colbert said that he would have assigned the directorship to the merchants of Bordeaux if the men of La Rochelle would not accept his conditions,[46] but in fact the Rochelais directed the company and only established a branch office at Bordeaux in 1671.[47] The energetic Intendant Claude Pellot set to work vigorously. He sought subscriptions not only at Bordeaux but also at Bayonne, Saint Jean-de-Luz, Ciboure, Bergerac, and Montauban. Without doubt his account to Colbert was partial, but he shows us the divisions among the bourgeois and their jealousy towards La Rochelle. The richest bourgeois and in particular de Jean and Duribaut were opposed to the formation of the company, maintaining that the Dutch would take revenge by placing a tax on wine and that all the embarkings and loadings would be performed at La Rochelle. Pellot suggested various means for making them subscribe: for example, by deposing de Jean, who was Director of the East India Company, or by threatening Chanevas, Postal Director, who was worth 400,000 to 500,000 livres, with loss of his position; or finally to oblige all those who wished to retain their bourgeois privileges to join the company at the rate of 1,000 livres. Two or three Portuguese Jews were disposed to accept, and their community subscribed 10,000 livres. Not entirely satisfied, Pellot wrote that he had tried personally to make persons enter. He attempted to exact subscriptions from the villages exempt from the taille, apparently not distinguishing very clearly between such subscriptions and taxes. Colbert approved of the idea of forcing the bourgeois to subscribe at 1,000 livres. There was a wave of discontent, but Pellot was of the opinion that the protests were not justified. He scolded the bourgeois for unwisely spending 40,000 to 50,000 livres to send a delegation to the king.[48] That reveals the problem: the bourgeois were ready to

[46] Clément, II, 466.
[47] Boissonnade, p. 77.
[48] Depping, III, 412–18.

spend money for maintaining the privileges from which they drew their fortunes in their habitual commerce, but they did not wish to lend their money in support of the new trade which Colbert wished to develop.

Not all of the bourgeois, however, opposed this distant commerce. Taking advantage of the decree of December, 1664, certain merchants sent ships to the northern lands. In a ceremonious assembly at the City Hall on November 27, 1670, Lombard read the names of those who should receive rewards for having sent several vessels. The register does not furnish the names of those receiving premiums but it indicates several of those present at the meeting: Rosse, Judge of the Exchange; the Consul Saige; Lestrilles; Cornut; d'Arbis; Denisart, and Lamarque.[49] A letter of Colbert further informs us that Lombard and Noguez also constructed ships.[50] It was the beginning of a new kind of activity.

Thus it appears that Colbert's first efforts to create a trade between Bordeaux and the northern lands were seconded by some of the Bordelais but were opposed by the great majority. We will find this true also in the history of the Privileged Company of Bordeaux,[51] which was organized in 1671 at the request of certain townsmen. Who were these Bordelais who were the initiators? The minutes of the magistrature furnishes an incomplete list of the signers of the articles of the Company: Lobard, Merier, Loustau, Coudert, Cornut, Reveu de Reveu, Paraberc, Laléonnarde, François Saige, and Navarre. We know that Lombard, Cornut, and Saige were among those who had attended the distribution of subsidies to those who had made a northern voyage, and they also traded with the American islands. Mercier had been recommended by Pellot at the time of the subscriptions for the Northern Company. None of this is precise because the loss of Colbert's correspondence preparatory to the formation of the company does not permit the naming of the founders with any certitude.

The purpose envisaged for the company was specified in its articles: "A Company of commerce and for the manufacture and construction of several ships able to provide for the trade of this Company as well as that of all the other merchants and shippers who wish to load them for the transport of the goods of the province." As to the regions where it

---

[49] Arch. munic. registre de la Jurade. It indicates that a list of payments was to be found in the possession of Brisson, the royal notary. His name does not appear in the numerical repertory of notarial minutes court rolls.

[50] Depping, III, 201.

[51] Arch. munic. registre de la Jurade for August 27, 1671, furnishes the articles of the company.

should direct its activities, the islands of America, New France, and the northern lands were named in particular. In part the company was formed to satisfy the complaints of the Bordelais who said that the Compagnie du Nord would conduct all its business at La Rochelle. In effect the Rochelais had completely taken over the direction of that company, and since Bordeaux was equally important in the plan which Colbert had designed for trade with the north, it seemed wholly natural that he had wished to establish an individual company there. The article which follows shows to what extent the privileged company of Bordeaux was the heir of the Northern Company:

> Those who have signed up to invest in the Compagnie du Nord will be absolved of the payments they promised by placing in the aforesaid Company [of Bordeaux] a third of the sum previously pledged provided that the third is not less than a thousand livres, and with the condition that the subscription to the said Compagnie du Nord will become of no effect and value and will be restored to them by those who hold it and who thereby will be completely and validly discharged.

Other articles were designed to assure capital: it was necessary to subscribe 2,000 livres to be elected a magistrate or a judge of the exchange and 1,000 livres to be elected a consul or to receive bourgeois status (an alternative was to invest that amount in a ship or the Compagnie du Nord). Foreigners born outside of the kingdom could not receive bourgeois status "except by placing 2,000 livres in the aforesaid company." Anyone of whatever nationality or condition could invest as much money as he wished provided that the total was not less than 500 livres. A reserve fund was to be constituted from the revenues of the exchange's communal building. Each year for ten years 3,000 livres should be paid in to this reserve by the receiver, or tax farmer.

The company was to have a board of directors with an office at the exchange consisting of the judge, consuls, and six investors, with a treasurer, a bookkeeper, a keeper of the warehouse and four inspectors of accounts. All the investors should assemble once each year to replace one-half of the directors by a plurality of votes. If any vessel was lost, the cost was to be borne by all the company. The first division of profits would take place after three years. At that time the profits of the first year would be distributed, and a similar settlement would be made at the end of each year thereafter, always leaving the profits of the two last years to serve as a reserve fund for the company. The payments would be made with the use of drafts drawn by the directors on the treasurer, who would authenticate them so that they could be negotiated as were bills of exchange. The text contained still more details on the qualities and functions of the directors and on the distribution of profits, but the page is half destroyed. Finally the articles offered detailed rules for deciding disputes between members and for judging frauds.

In addition to the funds which were to be built up from the revenues of the exchange, other financial advantages were accorded to the company: reduction in a number of taxes, the promise to pay the subsidies mentioned by the decree of 1664, permission to cut in the forests, paying a reasonable price, trees selected as suitable to the construction of ships. Other privileges were designed to appeal to Bordelais sentiment: for example, the right to call itself "The Privileged Company of Bordeaux" and the right to fix on its vessels and flags the blazon of the city. In January, 1672, Colbert accorded other advantages which had been suggested by the Intendant d'Aguesseau. All those who subscribed 4,000 livres would be granted bourgeois status and enjoy this privilege for their merchandise. Creditors of the city who invested their credits in the company would be paid first.[52]

The first ship of the company was finished in March, 1672, and was built by François Saige, whose yard was at the end of the Chartrons. The launching of the vessel was the occasion of a solemn celebration. Hugla, Judge of the Exchange, Comte, the First Consul, and Maillos, Secretary of the Company asked the magistrates to choose its name. The two magistrates delegated for the ceremony, Loustau and Sabatier, christened it "La ville de Bordeaux," and the ship bore the arms of the city carved on her stern and embroidered on her standard.[53] Colbert took great interest in the affair, writing to de Sève, the new Intendant: "I have seen that the founding of a yard for the construction of ships begun by the Sieur de Sage [sic] has succeeded very well. Concerning this I tell you that there is nothing so important for the good of commerce as to give support to this establishment. Moreover, you should give it particular attention by urging strongly those who are interested to devote themselves to it in order that the project for which they formed their company be completely executed." In the rest of the letter he concerned himself with a question of detail, what salary the master carpenter should receive.[54]

[52] Clément, II, 642.
[53] J. de Tillet, *Chroniques historiques et politiques de la ville et cité de Bordeaux* (Bordeaux, 1718), and Arch. munic. registre de la Jurade. March 5.
[54] Clément, II, Part 2, 661; Depping, III, 862.

Thus when the war with Holland began in 1672 Colbert had realized a portion of his program, that belonging to what might be called the period of the companies. The East India Company had solicited part of its capital at Bordeaux; the West India Company had contributed to the beginnings of trade with the islands; the Compagnie du Nord had made way for the Privileged Company of Bordeaux through which certain of the bourgeois attempted to fulfill the ambitions of Colbert.

The war dealt a serious blow to the commerce of Bordeaux, whose prosperity depended in great measure on foreign markets. Early in February Colbert instructed the Intendant to confer with the principal bourgeois on the best means for protecting their trade. They advised continuing it with naval escorts for which Colbert promised to issue the necessary orders. Actually, however, the port was sometimes open and sometimes closed. The difficulty arose from the bourgeois' unwillingness to pay the cost of the escorts. As a consequence the majority of the departing ships were taken by the Dutch.[55] The news of bankruptcies increased, but Colbert advised the Intendant not to take such rumors too seriously.[56] The newly established insurance company (Chambre d'Assurance) collapsed, but Colbert judged that this failure had the same causes as that of the Chambre of Paris. Having become too eager because of their first profits, the merchants had overextended their insurance. Colbert advised the Intendant to work slowly towards its rehabilitation. It appears that in spite of several mentions of revived businesses[57] the war produced a serious crisis for the commerce of Bordeaux.

The privileged company of Bordeaux received a mortal blow by losing its four ships, but the war was not the only cause of its failure. Quarrels had quickly risen among the investors. Colbert wrote in October, 1673: "I learn, however, from the letters written to me from this city that the Judge and Consuls who are naturally the directors of the privileged Company, rather than laboring hard for its establishment, offer a bad example to the other habitants by refusing to pay the sums set down by the rules made for the foundation of the Company."[58] In effect the regulations which made subscriptions to the company necessary in order to be elected a magistrate, judge of the exchange, or consul had introduced into it bourgeois who had no enthusiasm or

---

[55] Clément, II Part 2, 661; Depping, III, 862.
[56] Clément, II, Part 2, 662; Malvezin, II, 369.
[57] Clément, II, Part 2, 675.
[58] Clément, II, Part 2, 681.

were even hostile to it. We can doubt whether their capital did more good for the company than their dissensions brought it harm, but Colbert commanded the Intendant to enforce the rules and to prevent anyone who had not subscribed from becoming a magistrate.

The opposition of the bourgeois expressed itself in a meeting convoked by the magistrates on 17 March 1674.[59] Colbert had written that the king would entertain arguments in favor of abolishing the company if they were presented to him by the magistrates and the most notable merchants. The city clerk referred to the members of the meeting as "very intelligent and the most part investors in this company."[60] They decided "with a common voice" to request the king to abolish the company and to re-establish the rights of the bourgeoisie as they existed in 1664. At the end of the minutes of the proceedings of the meeting is found a list of reasons for which the abolition of the company had been requested. There is no indication that these reasons were drawn up by the assembly and the bitterness of their tone argues against it. Probably they were written by Duboscq, who had been the city clerk since 1654, and express the point of view of the rich bourgeois belonging to the old families hostile to Colbert's whole program. Although these arguments are partial, they furnish us with important evidence concerning the failure of the company.

> The first is that since this company has been solely the work and creation of the ambition of certain Bourgeois, only envy and division among the investors has resulted. . . .
>
> The second reason is that the majority of the investors were drawn from the less eminent and substantial of the city, while the chief merchants withdrew from that society in order to have no part in its disorders. . . . and that if some of the more important Bourgeois did participate, it was only out of compliance with the will of the King, not to say constraint, which is absolutely opposed to commerce which ought always to be free.
>
> The third reason is that the great losses suffered by this Company demonstrate its slight usefulness to the province. Three of its four vessels were lost and the fourth has been ransomed from the enemy. . . .

[59] Arch. munic. registre de la Jurade.

[60] He gives the following names: Borie, Barbot, and Comet, lawyers; Paul Lestrilles, de Jehan, Philip Minvielle, Hugla, Nouguès, Sabatier, Vallous, judge of the Bourse; Partarrieu and Darbis, consuls; Pontois, Lafourière, Decoud, Villate the elder, Poncet, Saige, François Saige, Guiteronde, Minvielle, Pudifer, Cogol, Ripote, Larchebaut, Lafosse, Mantalaut, Delas, Garegues, Bonneau, and Taussin.

And if, notwithstanding these losses, it has survived to the present, it is due to the adroitness of the officers who find profits for themselves in the salaries they receive or by the jobs which they give to their followers and by the management of the treasury which they use to ease their own personal difficulties.

The fourth reason mentioned is the restriction of the number of persons who could hold public office in the city, because the rule which rendered subscription to the company obligatory resulted in a decrease of the number of the bourgeois.

Finally, the self-interested conduct and the lack of loyalty which have appeared in the conduct of those who composed this Company has shown clearly that their actions are far from the original motives professed at its establishment. This situation has entirely repelled the best merchants, who ordinarily do not enter any trade except with complete freedom and with some confidence in the persons with whom they are engaged.

Do we have here the reasons submitted to Colbert? In any event he did not allow himself to be convinced easily. In a letter of October, 1674, he endeavored to show the new Intendant de Sève, who was unfavorable to the company, that it might lead to some important advantages, and he added: "It will be difficult to persuade me of the contrary unless you have stronger and more convincing reasons than all those of which I am aware." But his letter of November 23, 1674, was a little less intractable. "In an affair of this sort," he wrote, "it is necessary to make a decision quickly for it can produce in the course of time inestimable benefits to the state if supported as it ought to be, and it can also perish through failure to settle the disputes which have begun over this Company." He ordered de Sève to investigate the reasons of both parties and give his opinion.[61] In the end the magistrates won out and the company disappeared, a victim of the war and the hostility of the bourgeois.

After the war, trade revived, especially that of the American islands, which expanded considerably. Although it could not be compared in tonnage with the exportation of wine, it was later destined to become more important, and it accustomed the Bordelais to making long ocean voyages. Since a passport was necessary for participation in this trade, registrations exist in the collections of the Admiralty of Guienne and permit us to draw up the following table:[62]

[61] Clément, II, Part 2, 687.
[62] Arch. départ. fonds de l'Amirauté, 6 B 64 and ff.

Year	Number of Vessels	Tonnage
1671	13	1,320
1672	15	1,255
1675	7	505
1676	17	1,760
1677	22	2,475
1678	18	1,836
1679	22	2,020
1680	15 (incomplete)	1,240
1681	20 (incomplete)	1,465
1682	32	2,655
1683	30	2,355
1684	39	3,470
1685	49	4,069
1686	28	2,435
1687	33	3,080

Notable is the steady rise from the end of the Dutch war until the year following the revocation of the Edict of Nantes, when trade declined 43 per cent. A comparison between the names of shippers and those which are found on the register of the consistory of the Reformed Church of Bordeaux from 1669 to 1670 leads me to the conclusion that half of this commerce was in the hands of Protestants.

Those figures provided by the passports are somewhat higher than those obtained from the register of departures. Keeping this fact in mind we can make several comparisons with the trade that other French merchants conducted with the islands. In 1672 fifteen passports were registered at Bordeaux as against eighty-nine for all of France. In 1683, when thirty were issued at Bordeaux, there were 205 French vessels trading with the islands. From August, 1685, to August, 1686, fifty-eight ships left Nantes, while forty passports were issued at Bordeaux.[63]

The increase of trade was accompanied by prosperity for the sugar refineries. Here is a comparison of the consumption of raw sugar at Bordeaux with that of other French cities:[64]

	livres
All of France	17,700,000
Rouen, eight refineries	4,500,000
La Rochelle, four refineries	2,400,000
Nantes, three refineries	2,000,000
Bordeaux, three refineries	2,000,000

[63] Mims, pp. 241, 248.
[64] Mims, p. 263.

As to trade with the north, the register of departures does not furnish, in my opinion, reliable information on the part played by the shipowners of Bordeaux.[65] Therefore we cannot confidently affirm that any important trade resulted in Bordeaux from the grandiose ambitions of Colbert, except the beginning of commerce with the American islands. It is doubtful that even this survived the War of the League of Augsburg. The memoir drawn up by Bazin de Bezons in 1697 makes no reference to it. He says: "There are no French vessels which carry the goods of this province to foreign lands."[66] This statement provides brutal testimony of the fact that the wars had destroyed what little of truly French trade Colbert had, despite the ill will of most of the bourgeois, succeeded in developing.

[65] If one reads in the register "La Marie-Anne de Bordeaux," does that prove that the owner was of Bordeaux? In several cases no name of a city is indicated with that of the ship, but such instances are rare. See Arch. départ., 6 B 288 and ff.

[66] Bazin de Bezons, p. 106.

20

The Economic Meaning of the
Invention of the Compass*

THE discovery of America by Europeans appears most obviously the outstanding result of the development of the mariner's compass, and Samuel Eliot Morison's biography of Columbus has emphasized anew Columbus' dependence on the compass. Although Columbus made a pretense of understanding how to determine his position from the sun and stars, he had not in fact mastered the methods of astronomical navigation that the Portuguese were in the process of working out. He relied entirely on dead reckoning. His ability to describe accurately where he had been and to find the same island again on a new crossing of thousands of miles of ocean depended on the accuracy of his estimates of speed and on the correctness of his record of courses plotted by the compass. To be sure, mere dead reckoning on voyages of such length, subject to the pull of ocean currents and complicated by changes in the magnetic variation, was almost sure to lead to grave errors unless the navigator had a personal uncanny "feel" for the signs of the sea, as did Columbus. The more scientific methods being developed by the Portuguese were no doubt necessary for a regular flow of ordinary voyages. Quadrant or quarterstaff as well as compass and chart were necessary for the settlement and exploitation of the American continent. Yet the discovery itself is tightly linked to the use of the compass.[1]

* American Historical Review, LXVIII (1963), 605–17. (By permission.) The author presented this paper in an earlier form to the session at Venice, September, 1962, of the Sixth International Conference on Maritime History.
[1] E. G. R. Taylor, The Haven-Finding Art: A History of Navigation from Odysseus to Captain Cook (London, 1956), Chap. vii; Samuel Eliot Morison, Admiral of the

My concern here is not with transoceanic voyages, however; it is with the more immediate effects of the invention of the mariner's compass, and especially with the century between 1250 and 1350.

The immediate effects were most important in the Mediterranean. There the use of the compass went hand in hand with the creation of nautical charts of unprecedented accuracy and the compilation of the navigating tables called *tavole di marteloio*. The charts are commonly called portolanos although that name more properly belongs to the written sailing directions that were compiled for the Mediterranean as a whole in the middle of the thirteenth century, at about the same time that the first portolan charts were composed. In the early fourteenth century these charts had reached a high standard of accuracy for all the Mediterranean. They depicted the Atlantic less accurately and either omitted or misrepresented the shores of the North Sea and the Baltic. The navigating tables, for use in reducing a zigzag of tacks to a single compass bearing, were already referred to by Raymond Lull about 1290, although the earliest known examples are in Venetian manuscripts of the fifteenth century.[2] Charts, tables, and compass used together reduced the errors of sailing by dead reckoning. They formed a new technique of navigation which was characteristic for the Mediterranean and was so well fitted for that sea that even in the mid-sixteenth century the compass was the only instrument there considered necessary.[3]

The immediate practical consequence in the Mediterranean of the invention of the compass was more navigation during winter months. In summer, Mediterranean sailors were able to plot their courses fairly

---

Ocean Sea: A Life of Christopher Columbus (2 vols.; Boston, 1942) ; and on the inadequacies of dead reckoning, C. V. Sölver and G. J. Marcus, "Dead Reckoning and the Ocean Voyages of the Past," *Mariner's Mirror*, XLIV, No. 1 (1958) , 18–34.

[2] Taylor, *Haven-Finding*, Chap. v; *Il Compasso da Navigare*, ed. Bacchisio R. Motzo, Facoltà di Lettere e Filosofia della Università di Cagliari, VIII (1947) , introd.; Konrad Kretschmer, *Die italienischen Portolane des Mittelalters* (Berlin, 1909) , pp. 50–80.

[3] Ugo Tucci, "Sur la pratique vénitienne de la navigation au xvie siècle," *Annales: Économies, sociétés, civilisations*, XIII (Jan.–Mar. 1958) , 72–74; Commandant Avelino Teixeira da Mota, "L'Art de naviguer en Méditerranée du xiiie au xviie siècle et la création de la navigation astronomique dans les océans," in *Le Navire et l'économie maritime du moyen âge au xviiie siècle principalement en Méditerranée*, ed. Michel Mollat (Paris, 1958) , pp. 129–38; see also Alberto Tenenti, *Cristoforo da Canal: La Marine vénitienne avant Lépante* (Paris, 1962) , p. 42.

accurately using the sun by day and the stars in the clear Mediterranean nights. There is no reason to think that they had ever been afraid to put out beyond the sight of land in the summer. During fair weather they could lay their courses by the stars.[4] That early sailors "hugged" the shore is a landsman's idea, as Professor Eva Taylor and Admiral Morison agree; a sailor's fear of rocks and reefs near the coast made him prefer to stand well out to sea.[5] The trade to Crete and Cyprus from Egypt and Phoenicia at the dawn of history shows at how early a date Mediterranean sailors were prepared to go out of sight of land. In the twelfth century, voyages were made from Marseilles to Alexandria circling west and south of Sicily but avoiding at the same time the hostile African shore.[6] So long as the nights were clear these seamen were not afraid of losing their way even on a long voyage.

The compass was initially a means of countering overcast. "The mariners guide themselves in obscure nights by the needle," says a typical thirteenth-century text, "which is the means . . . to show them how to go in bad weather as in good."[7] In the Mediterranean the "bad weather" comes between October and April. Modern hydrographic office reports show that the Mediterranean skies are on the average about one-half covered in those months and seldom overcast in summer.[8] If the climate has changed appreciably during the last two thousand years, as some experts say and others deny, the storm track of the Northern Hemisphere sometimes swung further south than at present. Such a swing, bringing more variable winds and more cloudiness in the Mediterranean, may have occurred about 1300 A.D., but that is uncertain.[9] In part of antiquity, winds and weather may have been

[4] Léon Denoix, "Les Problèmes de navigation au début des grandes découvertes," in *Le Navire et l'économie maritime du Nord de l'Europe du Moyen-Âge au* xviiie *siècle,* ed. Michel Mollat (Paris, 1960) , p. 132.

[5] Taylor, *Haven-Finding,* 4; Morison's review of Miss Taylor's book in *Isis,* XLIV, Part 3 (1958) , 352–53; also G. J. Marcus, "The Mariner's Compass: Its Influence upon Navigation in the Later Middle Ages," *History,* XLI, No. 1 (1956) , 16–17.

[6] Adolf Schaube, *Handelsgeschichte der romanischen Völker des Mittelmeersgebiets bis zum Ende der Kreuzzüge* (Munich and Berlin, 1906) , p. 153.

[7] Quoted in John Forsyth Meigs, *The Story of the Seamen* (2 vols.; Philadelphia and London, 1924) , I, 268; cf. Taylor, *Haven-Finding,* p. 94.

[8] U.S. Hydrographic Office, *Sailing Directions for the Mediterranean* (2d ed., 5 vols.; Washington, D.C., 1952) , V, 13, on the Aegean; see the tables in other volumes for various ports elsewhere, e.g., IV, 242–45.

[9] Arguments for the change are presented by Ellsworth Huntington, for example, in his *Civilization and Climate* (New Haven, Conn., 1924) , pp. 327, 358, 401; and by Gustaf Utterström, "Climatic Fluctuations and Population Problems in Early Mod-

worse than they are now. The Greeks and Romans pulled their long ships ashore between October and April and tied up their heavy merchantmen.[10] It was not only storm they feared; it was also rain, clouds, and fog.

In the twelfth century and at the beginning of the thirteenth the seas were still closed in winter. A desire not to have vessels at sea between October and March is evident in the early records of the Italian cities. Venetian convoys sent to the Levant were so timed as to avoid the winter months. One fleet left about Easter and returned in September. A second fleet, called the fall or winter *muda,* left in August, wintered overseas, and returned the following spring, often reaching Venice in May. The early statutes of Pisa contained the rule that if a ship made harbor on or after the first of November the ship captain could not put to sea again prior to March 1 without the consent of the merchants on board.[11] From Genoa there was an annual caravan to Syria and Egypt leaving in September, reaching Egypt in October, wintering there, and returning late in the spring. It was expected at Genoa by St. John's Day, June 24.[12]

In the fourteenth century we find a different rhythm of voyages. Venetian fleets were making two round trips a year. The fleet left in February and returned in May, normally; the second convoy left about August 1 and was due back before Christmas.[13] Thus there was no need for either fleet to winter overseas. The Genoese ordered their galleys, at least, to make two voyages a year also, if going to Cyprus or the Aegean,

---

ern History," *Scandinavian Economic History Review,* III, No. 1 (1955), 19–21; see also C. E. P. Brooks, *Climate through the Ages* (New York, 1949), p. 301; H. C. Willett, "Long Period Fluctuations in General Circulation of the Atmosphere," *Journal of Meteorology,* VI, No. 1 (1949), 35, 49–50; and Karl W. Butzer, "Climatic Change in Arid Regions since the Pliocene," in *History of Land Use in Arid Lands,* ed. L. D. Stamp (Paris, 1960), pp. 43–47.

[10] Lionel Casson, *The Ancient Mariners: Seafarers and Sea Fighters of the Mediterranean in Ancient Times* (New York, 1959), pp. 39, 234.

[11] Walter Ashburner, *The Rhodian Sea-Law* (Oxford, 1909), pp. cxliii, cxlviii; *Fonti per la Storia di Venezia,* sez. IV, *Archivi Privati, Famiglia Zusto,* ed. Luigi Lanfranchi (Venice, 1955), p. 26.

[12] Schaube, *Handelsgeschichte,* pp. 153–54.

[13] *Le Deliberazioni del Consiglio dei Rogati (Senato),* Serie "Mixtorum," I, ed. Roberto Cessi and Paolo Sambin, Monumenti Storici pubblicati dalla Deputazione di Storia Patria per le Venezie, n.s., XV (Venice, 1960) [hereafter cited as *Delib. dei Rogati*], 60, No. 219; 85–86, No. 308; 93, No. 318; 169, No. 275; see also nn. 41–44, below.

one leaving in February, the other between mid-August and mid-September.[14] At Pisa the notarial records begin already in the 1280's to show ships leaving at all times of year, even in the dead of winter.[15] Thus the traditional "closing of the sea in winter," which had persisted in the Mediterranean during several thousand years, was shattered by the compass.

Of course one should not exaggerate the abruptness of the change. Some voyages had been made in winter in earlier centuries,[16] and winter navigation continued to be less pleasant and less safe in general than summer sailing. When *savii ai ordeni* were established at Venice in 1321 to make specific provision year by year for the voyages of the merchant galleys, one of the objectives specified in the law defining their duties was that the galleys should return in due season and not navigate in winter.[17] As late as 1569 wrecks were blamed on navigation in the dead of winter ("su'l cuor dell' invernata"), and a law was passed forbidding Venetian ships to leave Venice or any port in the Levant between November 15 and January 20.[18] This law was then an anachronism,[19] but let us note that it did not interfere with the schedule for two round trips a year established about 1300. Under that schedule also departures between November 15 and January 20 were avoided. The spring fleet was not to leave Venice until the very end of January, and the fall fleets were scheduled to depart from their Levantine ports by the middle of November. But all through December ships would be coming home through the Ionian and Adriatic Seas. Al-

[14] *Monumenta Historiae Patriae, Leges Municipales* (2 vols.; Turin, 1838–76), Institucio Offici Gazarie, II, 340–41.

[15] David Herlihy, *Pisa in the Early Renaissance: A Study in Urban Growth* (New Haven, Conn., 1958), pp. 107–108. Dr. Sobhi Y. Labib informed me that Arab sources show the closing of the sea in winter to have been observed at Alexandria also until the thirteenth century but not thereafter. See his forthcoming "Handelsgeschichte Ägyptens im Spätmittelalter."

[16] R. H. Dolley, "Meteorology in the Byzantine Navy," *Mariner's Mirror*, XXXVII, No. 1 (1951), 10–13, gives weather reports about 900 A.D. from the Gulf of Iskanderun indicating local voyages there in the dead of winter.

[17] MS, Archivio di Stato di Venezia, Maggior Consiglio, Deliberazioni, Fronesis, pp. 58–59.

[18] Law of June 8, 1569, in *Parte prese nell'Eccelentissimo Conseglio di Pregadi con diverse leggi cavate dal Statuto in materia de navi e sua navigatione* (Venice [1644]), pp. 17–18.

[19] As is noted by Tucci, "Navigation au XVIᵉ siècle," p. 77. The prohibition was repeated in 1598, but repealed in 1600. See Alberto Tenenti, *Venezia e i corsari, 1580–1615* (Bari, 1961), pp. 136–37.

though ideally all ships would be in home port during January, in fact, according to various chroniclers and according to Jacques Heers's compilation of material from the Datini archive for 1383–1403, the arrival at Venice of galleys from Alexandria was spread between November 11 and January 24.[20]

Even if the sea still remained closed for a brief period, which varied somewhat from place to place, the gain of a few months for navigation could be of considerable importance. Because of the nature of the prevailing winds in the eastern Mediterranean there was much advantage in being able to sail during some of the more cloudy months. Returning from Egypt, for example, vessels leaving between May and October faced almost steadily northerly and northwesterly winds. To reach Italian ports they had to take a roundabout route going first to Cyprus or at best to Rhodes, and then working west. This was the route taken in antiquity by the Roman grain ship *Isis* described by Lucian.[21] In the fifteenth century Florentine merchant galleys also went by way of Rhodes.[22] Only late in the fall, in October and November, are easterly winds to be expected off Alexandria.[23] The schedules set for the Venetian galleys in the fourteenth and fifteenth centuries enabled them to take advantage of these winds. A sixteenth-century Venetian round ship, of which we have the log, returned from Alexandria by the direct route south and west of Crete, leaving October 21 and reaching Corfu November 7, 1561.[24] The Venetian galleys frequently left later, as we have seen, and did not reach Venice until mid-winter. On the other

---

[20] Jacques Heers, "Il commercio nel Mediterraneo alla fine del sec. XIV e nei primi anni del XV," *Archivio storico italiano*, CXIII, No. 2 (1955), 166. The very spotty record of arrivals, 1404–1423, in the chronicle of Antonio Morosini shows arrivals at the end of November or in December. (Gino Luzzatto, "Vi furono fiere a Venezia?" in *Studi di storia economica veneziana* [Padua, 1954], 206.) On the usual rhythm of Venetian voyages, see also Frederic C. Lane, "Ritmo e rapidità di giro d'affari nel commercio veneziano del Quattrocento," in *Studi in onore di Gino Luzzatto* (4 vols.; Milan, 1949, I, 254–58.

[21] Lionel Casson, "The *Isis* and Her Voyage," *Transactions of the American Philological Association*, LXXXI (1950), 43–48.

[22] Wilhelm Heyd, *Histoire du commerce du levant au moyen âge* (2 vols.; Leipzig, 1886), II, 487; Armando Sapori, "I Primi viaggi di levante e di ponente delle galere fiorentini," *Archivio storico italiano*, CXIV (1956), 90.

[23] U.S. Hydrographic Office, *Sailing Directions* (2d ed.; Washington, D.C., 1951), IV, 241; U.S. Hydrographic Office, Henry H. Gorringe, *Coasts and Islands of the Mediterranean Sea* (3 vols.; Washington, D.C., 1879), III, 284.

[24] Relazione di un patrizio veneto [Alessandro Magno] del viaggio di Cipro, di quell'isola, et di altri viaggi, MS. 1371.1 (V.a.259), in the Folger Shakespeare Library, Washington, D.C.

hand the Genoese using round ships about 1400 usually left Egypt in February or early March, taking advantage of southerly winds that blow in those months.[25] Both Venetians and Genoese avoided the northwest winds of the summer months. For the sake of favorable winds they took the risks of being at sea in cloudy weather.

Probably the chief economic importance of the compass in the Mediterranean was that it led to more voyages per year. In transportation between Venice and the Levant, being at sea in winter months made all the difference between two voyages a year instead of one. It enabled ships to transport twice as much each year and keep crews more continually employed. In regard to the Levantine voyages in general, it may be said that starting the spring voyages before winter was over and letting the fall voyages run into December gave sailors more favorable winds. That same schedule was selected again when convoys were established late in the seventeenth century.[26]

The winds and clouds of the Mediterranean made the compass important in that sea especially in connection with winter navigation. Weather conditions were different in the Indian Ocean and in the waters lying to the west and north. The development of the compass did not have the same impact in those seas that it had in the Mediterranean.

In the Indian Ocean the regularity of the monsoon winds was such that they alone sufficed to give the sailor his sense of direction.[27] The navigators who crossed the open sea between India and Arabia had no need of a compass in order to steer their course. They were favored by constant winds and by clear skies at least during the season of favorable winds. For voyages ranging north and south from Persia to Zanzibar, the Arabs learned how to find their latitude from the stars. When Marco Polo, Fra Mauro, and Niccolò de Conti report that the navigators of the Indian Ocean did not use the magnetic compass, even in the fifteenth century, but depended on the polar star, we can take that as evidence, not that the Arabs had never heard of the mariner's compass, but that the compass was not of practical importance in the Indian Ocean. It was not much needed to find direction, and position was determined less by dead reckoning with compass and chart than by

[25] See Heers, "Commercio nel Mediterraneo," 170. In his *Gênes au xvᵉ siècle* (Paris, 1961), p. 300, he speaks of a "ralentissement hivernal," but says of it, "ce sont les marchands qui l'imposent aux marins, non les éléments."

[26] Ugo Tucci, "La Marina mercantile veneziana nel Settecento," *Bollettino dell'Istituto di Storia della Società e dello Stato, Fondazione Giorgio Cini,* II (1960), 5.

[27] Denoix, "Problèmes de navigation," p. 132.

stellar observation.[28] "Under clear tropical skies . . . the celestial
bodies nearly always give sufficient guidance."[29]

If cloud, fog, and rain were what made the compass important, its
use might be expected to revolutionize the methods of navigation in
the often overcast seas of Northern Europe. But the North Sea and the
Baltic are both shallow, and in those waters seamen found their way by
knowledge of the sea's floor. A lead covered with tallow was lowered to
bring up a sample of sand or mud as well as to learn the depth. The
experienced ship captain could find his way by lead and line. The same
method had long been used in the Mediterranean where possible.
Herodotus mentions its use by ships approaching the Nile Delta, and
the medieval portolan books describe its use in the upper Adriatic. But
off the coast of Syria or of Liguria a ship would very quickly be out of
soundings; most of the Mediterranean is too deep to be navigated by
lead and line. The contrast between the Mediterranean and the Baltic
in this respect is obvious on any modern map which shows the one-
hundred-fathom line. Its significance for the navigator is spelled out on
the fifteenth-century map of Fra Mauro where a legend north of Germany reads: "In this sea they do not navigate by compass and chart but
by soundings."[30]

As in his reference to the navigation of the Indian Ocean, Fra Mauro
may be understood to mean, not that the compass was unknown in the
Baltic, but that it was not in common use there. Whether the Vikings
used a magnetized needle to find north is a matter of dispute. Leo
Bagrow, founding editor of the cartographic journal *Imago Mundi*,
believed that they did;[31] G. J. Marcus firmly asserts that they did not,
that the long voyages of the Irish and Norse in the North Atlantic are
evidence of the relative unimportance of the compass, proof that no
compass was needed to embolden seamen to sail out of sight of land.

[28] Taylor, *Haven-Finding*, pp. 123–28.
[29] George Fadlo Hourani, *Arab Seafaring in the Indian Ocean in Ancient and Early
Medieval Times* (Princeton, N.J., 1951), p. 109; cf. Alan John Villiers, *Monsoon
Seas* (New York, 1952), p. 56. A similar conclusion regarding medieval methods of
navigation in the Indian Ocean was presented to the session of the Sixth International Conference on Maritime History, Venice, September 1962, by Michel Mollat
in reporting on the session of the Sixth International Conference on Maritime History that had met in July 1962 at Lourenço Marquès. In the session at Lourenço
Marquès the Commandant Teixeira da Mota presented a thoroughgoing study of
navigation in the Indian Ocean. The proceedings of the session at Lourenço Marquès will be published at Lisbon; those of the session at Venice will be published
by the Fondazione Giorgio Cini in Venice.
[30] Taylor, *Haven-Finding*, pp. 21–29, 35, 107, 131.
[31] Leo Bagrow, *Die Geschichte der Kartographie* (Berlin, 1951), p. 48.

His evidence regarding the Norse voyages seems conclusive. Indeed, the opinion that the Norse used a compass seems to lean too heavily on the mere assumption that they could not have made such long voyages without it and the fact that loadstones were exported from Scandinavia.[32] But although the Norse voyages to America were made by taking directions from the skies, compasses became known in the north in the thirteenth century, and after 1300 contemporary chronicles no longer contain references to ships that had completely lost their bearings, as was common in the earlier sagas.[33] The compass became a useful auxiliary to soundings, while the latter remained the chief reliance of the navigator in the north. The supreme importance of the sounding line as late as 1449 is illustrated by the case of a Danzig ship bound for Lisbon that was placed under arrest in Plymouth, England. To prevent it from trying to leave, it was deemed sufficient to take away the ship's lead and line.[34]

The addition of a compass to the equipment of the vessels sailing the waters west and north of Europe made less difference, therefore, than has commonly been supposed. But some of the sailing routes passed off the continental shelf and were out of soundings. The most important commercially was the crossing from Cape Finisterre, Spain, to England or the Channel. How an accurate compass bearing for this voyage was to be combined with soundings is set forth in the oldest English book of sailing directions, compiled in the mid-fifteenth century on the basis of earlier materials. Somewhat condensed and modernized in language it reads as follows: "When you come out of Spain, and when you are at Cape Finisterre set your course north northeast. When you reckon you are two thirds of the way across [to England] if you are bound for the Severn you should go north by east until you come into soundings. If you then find 100 fathoms deep or 90, then go north until you sound again [and find] at 72 fathoms fair gray sand. And that is the ridge that lieth between Cape Clear [Ireland] and [the] Scilly [Islands]. Then go north until you come into soundings of ooze, and then set your course East North East or else East and by North. . . ." These directions for

---

[32] This seems to me the gist of the arguments reported by Edmund O. von Lippman, *Geschichte der Magnetnadel bis zur Erfindung des Kompasses gegen 1300* (Berlin, 1932), pp. 39–42. Cf. *Isis*, XIX, Part 3 (1933), 441; see also Heinrich Winter, "Who Invented the Compass?" *Mariner's Mirror*, XXIII, No. 1 (1937), 95–102.

[33] Marcus, "Mariner's Compass," pp. 17–20. "The Early Norse Traffic to Iceland," *Mariner's Mirror*, XLVI, No. 3 (1960), 179 n., and "Hafvilla, A Note on Norse Navigation," *Speculum*, XXX, No. 4 (1955), 601–605; see also Taylor, *Haven-Finding*, pp. 65–85, and Denoix, "Problèmes de navigation," pp. 131–32.

[34] Marcus, "Mariner's Compass," p. 24.

combining a look at the sea's floor with compass bearings suggest how helpful the compass could be, especially in an overcast, when crossing outside the feared rocks of Brittany on the way from Spain and the Mediterranean to England and the Netherlands.[35]

A trade route of less commercial importance which also went out of soundings and in whose development the compass was "a prime factor" was that from England to Iceland. There is explicit mention of "needle and stone" on the ships making this voyage from Bristol. Compasses were also used on fishing vessels operating far out in the Atlantic.[36]

Navigation throughout the winter in the Mediterranean and safer voyages from the Mediterranean around Spain to England and the Netherlands appear to have been the main immediate advantages from the development of the compass. It is significant that the evidence for both of these advances comes in the closing decades of the thirteenth century. The first evidence of commercial voyages directly from the Mediterranean into the English Channel are the contracts made by Genoese galley masters in 1277 and 1278.[37] No doubt Basque, Galician, and Portuguese sailors were familiar earlier with the Bay of Biscay, but it seems significant that a large expansion of the Portuguese trade with the north falls under King Dinis who reigned from 1279 to 1325.[38] When the Venetian Senate in 1314 offered a subsidy to Venetian galleys that would make the voyage to Flanders, it was a sort of testimonial to the relative security of the route.[39]

After a survey of the notarial cartularies of Pisa, David Herlihy concludes that the opening of the seas in winter began in the Mediterranean just about 1280. Even as late as 1272–1274 he found trade following "heavily," as he put it, "the rhythm of the seasons," whereas already in the years before 1284 this rhythm ceased to be clearly reflected in the cartularies. Ships left all year around.[40]

---

[35] Taylor, *Haven-Finding*, p. 135; Marcus, "Mariner's Compass," pp. 23–24.

[36] Marcus, "Mariner's Compass," pp. 23–24.

[37] Renée Doehaerd, "Les Galères gênoises dans la Manche et la Mer du Nord à la fin du xiii° et au début du xiv° siècles," *Bulletin de l'Institut Historique Belge de Rome,* XIX (1938), 10; Alwyn A. Ruddock, *Italian Merchants and Shipping in Southampton, 1270–1600* (Oxford, Eng., 1951), pp. 19–21. For the commercial reasons why these voyages began at this time, see Robert S. Lopez, "Majorcans and Genoese on the North Sea Route in the Thirteenth Century," *Revue belge le philologie et d'histoire,* XXIX, No. 4 (1951), 1163–79.

[38] Bailey W. Diffie, *Prelude to Empire: Portugal Overseas before Henry the Navigator* (Lincoln, Neb., 1960), pp. 33–48.

[39] See Chapter 13.

[40] Herlihy, *Pisa*, pp. 107–108.

Neither at Venice nor at Genoa have the notarial registers for the period been analyzed from this viewpoint, but at Venice the regulations for convoys show the change beginning in the 1290's and completed when a new set of regulations was issued in 1302–1303 after the conclusion of the Second Genoese War. In 1283–1288 the dates for the opening of the port were set between March 9 and April 15.[41] In 1290 and 1291 it was fixed at February 18;[42] in 1292 the port was declared open on January 12. A change decreed in 1292 in the laws governing commercial investments in *colleganze* was desirable, so said the preamble, because two voyages a year were being made instead of one. The use of a new type of vessel for commercial voyages, a larger type of galley, was the reason given for ability to make two voyages a year instead of one.[43] No doubt the new schedule of voyages required faster ships, or ships less entirely dependent on the winds. Necessary also was a commercial organization permitting a quick turn-around. Even so, ships had to leave for the first voyage before the winter was finished and returned from the second after winter had set in again.[44]

In short, those changes in European shipping services that can most reasonably be associated with the invention of the compass fall in the period 1270–1300. Significantly, this is also the period in which we find the first clear reference to the use of nautical charts and navigational tables, and the period to which is assigned the oldest of these charts, the *carta Pisana*. It is just a few decades after the date to which Bacchisio Motzo in his fundamental study, *Il Compasso da Navigare,* assigned the composition of the master portolan, the unification of the port book for the whole Mediterranean, and the drawing of the first nautical chart of the whole sea from Gibraltar to Constantinople and Damietta.[45]

I have hitherto been purposefully vague about just what I was referring to as the "invention of the compass." There were several steps in its development. As Abbott Payson Usher has shown with many

[41] *Deliberazioni del Maggior Consiglio di Venezia,* ed. Roberto Cessi, in *Atti delle Assemblee Constituzionali Italiane,* Academia dei Lincei (Bologna, 1934), III, 25, 62, 103, 169, 198.

[42] *Ibid.,* pp. 257, 290–91, 311.

[43] *Ibid.,* pp. 357–58.

[44] See notes 13, 20, and 39 above. Although galleys were not sent for the spring *muda,* at least not usually after 1322, round ships made spring voyages in the 1320's, leaving sometimes in January or even possibly December, as is shown by the laws forbidding these "unarmed vessels" to load in the spring any wares reserved for the galleys. (See *Delib. dei Rogati,* ed. Cessi and Sambin, I, 242, No. 249; 264, No. 228; 469, No. 347.)

[45] *Compasso,* ed. Motzo, cited in n. 2 above, pp. xxvi–xlix.

examples in his *History of Mechanical Inventions,* it is useful to distinguish four stages in invention: the posing of the problem; the assemblage of the elements of a solution; the union of these elements in a new way by an act of insight which constitutes the essential "breakthrough"; and the critical revision and perfection of the solution. A "compass" which was no more than a magnetized needle attached to a chip floating in a bowl of water was in use in both China and Europe in the twelfth century. But this may be said to represent only the first stage, the posing of the problem, just as the "water commanding" engine of the Marquis of Worcester or the jet fountain of Solomon des Caus is said by Usher to represent the first stage toward the invention of the steam engine. They were unsatisfactory patterns, setting minds to work to find better.[46] Other elements had to be assembled to "set the stage": the division of the horizon into thirty-two or more points and various ways of mounting the needle so that it could swing freely and yet come to rest, even on the deck of a ship at sea.

Some of the elements that went into the invention of the mariner's compass may have come from China to the West. A needle magnetized to point north and south is mentioned earlier in China than anywhere else. Already in the thirteenth century a compass of some kind with twenty-four points was important in voyages across the South China Sea.[47] But the various elements used in the compass—the magnetized needle, wind roses, and so on—probably developed independently in

[46] Abbott Payson Usher, *A History of Mechanical Inventions* (rev. ed.; Cambridge, Mass., 1954), pp. 63–72.

[47] The magnetized needle is mentioned in China earlier than in Europe, but "As to the common story that it (the compass) had been brought from China by Arab sailors, there is no evidence whatever to support it." (Taylor, *Haven-Finding,* p. 96.) Most Westerners agree with her, but the "story" is declared "probable" by Hourani, *Arab Seafaring,* p. 109, and reaffirmed in the article based on Chinese sources by Li Shi-hua, "Origine de la Boussole," *Isis,* XLV, Part 2 (1954), 187–96. On the other hand, Gaston Wiet *et al.,* "L'évolution des techniques dans le monde musulman au moyen âge," *Journal of World History,* VI, Part 1 (1960), 31, make no such definite claim, saying only "nous savons que la boussole était utilisée dès le XIII° siècle par les marins musulmans." Gabriel Ferrand, in his *Instructions nautiques et routiers arabes et Portuguais* (3 vols.; Paris, 1921–28), III, 124, concluded from the contributions to this volume, which he edited, that he could claim the wind rose for the Arabs if not the compass, but Taylor, *Haven-Finding,* pp. 15, 53–56, 98, traces the origins of the wind rose back to the Greeks. On the Norse, see notes 31–33 above. For the theory that knowledge of the magnetic needle came to Western Europe from China across Asia, see Lynn White, Jr., *Medieval Technology and Social Change* (Oxford, Eng., 1962), p. 132.

several regions, and there is no evidence that the Arabs put the elements together into a new and more useful combination.[48] The problems of navigating being what they were in the Indian Ocean, there was no pressing need to do so.

In the Mediterranean there was need. There we find in the treatise on the magnet written by Peter Peregrinus in 1269 descriptions of several ways of putting together magnetized needles, pivots, and arrangements to relate the needle to the points of the horizon and even the path of a ship. Peter does not, however, describe a compass in which the wind rose or compass card is attached to a magnetized needle in such a manner that when placed on a pivot in a box fastened in line with the keel of the ship the card would turn as the ship changed direction, indicating always what course the ship was on.[49] Consequently there is an inclination to honor tradition and assign to a later date, about 1300, and to Amalfi the attachment of the needle to the compass card.[50] Perhaps this was part of the "critical revision" made after the essentials of the solution had been found. The evidence leaves room for doubt concerning the form taken by that "act of insight" which first related in a practical way the direction of a free-swung needle, the wind rose with thirty-two or sixty-four points, and the course of the ship.

The opening of the seas in winter about 1280 or 1290 and the safer crossing of the Bay of Biscay clearly point to the most important part of the invention having been made shortly before those dates. Indeed, it must have been made about the time when Peter Peregrinus was writing. Whether this break-through consisted indeed of the attachment of the compass rose to the needle, which may have already been in practice at sea, but was not known or not clearly understood by Peter, who was no sailor, or whether it was indeed added about 1300, seems to

[48] According to Li, "Origine de la Boussole," p. 195, the first Arab reference to a compass is by Bailak al-Qabajaqī, who wrote about 1282 and referred to having seen it used in the Mediterranean in 1242. What Bailak describes is a floating cross of wood attached to a temporarily magnetized needle. Bailak says that in the Indian Ocean a floating fish was used. The fish suggests the Chinese floating compass, but that is no new combination. Li (p. 194) says the "dry compass" had been invented in China, but was reintroduced from Japan as a novelty in the seventeenth century.

[49] Motzo, *Compasso,* pp. cix–cxiii.

[50] Denoix, "Problèmes de navigation," p. 135. An elaborate wholehearted defense of the Amalfitan tradition, considering the addition of the compass card the essential, is presented by A. d'Arrigo, "La Bussola amalfitana," in *Annali dell'Istituto Universitario Navale, Napoli,* XXVI, No. 4 (1957), 247–72.

me problematical.[51] I am inclined to follow such authorities as Konrad Kretschmer and Commandant Denoix and assign to 1300 or thereabouts the attachment of the compass card to the needle, considering it part of the revision and elaboration of the invention after the crucial break-through had occurred.[52] There was considerable improvement in the mapping of the Mediterranean between the time of the *carta Pisana,* presumably 1270, and that of the maps which Petrus Vesconti of Genoa made about 1320 for the Venetian publicist Marino Sanuto Torsellinus. A parallel perfection of the compass seems probable.[53]

The essential in the process of invention must have occurred earlier, however, whether at Amalfi or elsewhere, and its practical consequences were already evident in European waters. Apart from any effects it may have had on navigation in the China seas, the use of the compass had by 1300 aided the quickening of transportation in two important respects: more and safer voyages from the Mediterranean to the English Channel and more movement of shipping in the Mediterranean during the winter months.

[51] In his introduction to *Compasso* (pp. cxiii–cxiv), Motzo argues that the union of needle and compass card was already made before 1269, even by 1250, since the sixty-four points of the compass used in the sailing directions would not be practical otherwise. But Motzo also gives (lxxvii) a description of a technique of combining compass and map, which he seems to think may have been used earlier, and then says it was in use when the first nautical charts were created. Recognizing the strength of the Amalfitan tradition, Motzo credits Amalfi with importance in the twelfth century in spreading the use of the magnetized needle (pp. cxv–cxvii). Taylor, *Haven-Finding,* p. 92, follows Motzo in putting Amalfi's importance early, in what I have called the posing of the problem.

[52] Kretschmer (*Italienische Portolane,* pp. 73–81) places this improvement at Amalfi, but after reviewing the controversy about the inventor, considers it unlikely that he was named Flavio Gioia.

[53] Youssouf Kamal, *Monumenta cartographica Africae et Aegypti* (16 vols.; Cairo, 1926–51), IV. See Kamal, *Hallucinations scientifiques (les portolans)* (Leiden, 1937), p. 15, for his judgment that the compass was not a prerequisite or even the inspiration for the construction of the charts, but merely made their use in navigation more practical.

21

Tonnages, Medieval and Modern[*]

I

TONNAGES are of prime importance in economic history not only in estimating changes in the shipping industry's own employment of men and resources but also in estimating the relative importance of various trade routes and the relative prosperity of various periods. To evaluate the figures used in such comparisons it is essential to know what is meant by a "ton." Too often historical studies refer to "tonnage" without making clear what is meant, although the word has meanings so different one from another that a ship's tonnage measured in a ton of one kind is often two or three times its tonnage measured in a different kind of ton.

The ordinary man in the street thinks first of a weight. Perhaps in America he thinks first of the short ton of 2,000 lbs., but let us hope he thinks of what is called in Britain and America the long ton of 2,240 lbs., for long tons are the measure of weight used with reference to ships. The metric ton of 1,000 kg. is practically the same as the long ton (1 m.t. = 2,240.6 lbs. avoirdupois and 1 long ton = 1.016 m.t.). The best way to compare medieval and early modern statistics of shipping, it will here be argued, is to convert them as far as possible into estimates of carrying capacity measured in metric tons, or into deadweight tonnage.

Since conversion is often difficult, historians are justified in repeating what they find in their sources even if they are unable to say what kind of a "ton" is meant, so long as they make clear what they are doing. Whenever the same unit is used for all the figures in a set, comparison may be valuable within the set. Wider comparisons, however, require

* *Economic History Review*, Second Series, XVII (1964), 213–33. (By permission.)

identification of the units used and conversion to a common denominator.[1] Unfortunately different kinds of modern tons have been employed in such comparisons, and "ton" is sometimes used without sufficient identification. It would be a great help if students of maritime history could establish a common usage with clear equivalents in many languages. In the hope of moving towards such an agreement I present this explanation of various kinds of tons, giving some equivalents in French and Italian.

It is necessary to distinguish six kinds of tonnage.

(1) The measure most used in modern statistics of shipping is gross registered tonnage (*tonneaux de jauge brute, tonnellata lorda di stazza*). This is a statement of the amount of enclosed space on a ship. It was introduced by the British Merchant Marine Act of 1854 (effective 1855) embodying the ideas of the engineer G. Moorsom. Elaborate measurement and calculations were used to determine the total cubic feet of closed-in space, and each 100 cu. ft. (2.83 cu. m.) was counted as one ton.[2]

Moorsom's conception was clear cut, and mathematical skill by that time was sufficient to determine adequately the total enclosed space, but previous practices had created some attitudes that were difficult to overcome in practice. The purposes of estimating registered tonnage were fiscal and commercial. In these connections, tradition related tonnage to the carrying capacity of the ship. Carrying capacity and closed-in space are two distinct concepts, for there is on any ship some enclosed space which cannot be used. Moorsom estimated that in every 100 cu. ft. of enclosed space only 75 cu. ft. were available for cargo, the other 25 per cent being occupied by either beams, knees, and other

---

[1] Jacques Heers, in his *Gênes au XV siècle* (École Pratique des Hautes Études, VI section, Centre de Recherches Historiques: Affaires et Gens d'affairs, XXIV [Paris, S.E.V.P.E.N., 1961]), 453–54, gives a useful comparison of Venetian-Syrian trade about 1460 with the total maritime trade between the Mediterranean and the English Channel at that date, and Spanish American trade about 1560, using deadweight tons (*tonnes metriques de port*). Ruggiero Romano, "Per una valutazione della flotta mercantile europea alla fine de secolo XVIII," *Studi in onore di Amintore Fanfani* (6 vols.; Milan, Giuffré, 1962), V, 575–91, published a valuable survey made in the *tonneaux de mer* described below, and compares those figures with others in *nostra tonnellata, tonnelate di stazza bruta*, and *t. di portata effetiva* but without making clear the differences.

[2] Walther Vogel, *Die Grundlagen der Schiffahrtsstatistik* in *Veröffentlichungen des Instituts für Meereskunde* (Berlin, 1911), Heft 16, pp. 1–9; G. Moorsom, "On the new Tonnage Law, as established in the Merchant Shipping Act of 1854," in *Transactions of the Institution of Naval Architects*, I (London, 1860), 128–40.

timbers, or ship's stores and the like. Over the years law-makers have compromised so that some space is not counted even in estimating gross registered tonnage. Nearly all space is counted in gross tonnage, however; the chief result of the traditional desire to relate registered tonnage to income-yielding cargo capacity was the development of a second kind of registered tonnage, the net registered tonnage.[3]

(2) Net registered tonnage (*jauge nette, stazza netta*) is an estimate derived from gross registered tonnage by deducting from the total enclosed space a portion devoted to engines, crew's quarters, etc. The difference between gross registered tonnage and net registered tonnage is of course much greater in steamships than in sailing vessels and it has varied with the many modifications in ship propulsion machinery and rules of registry. For a sailing vessel about 1870 it was only 4–5 per cent.[4]

During the second half of the nineteenth century the British method of estimating gross and net registered tonnage in terms of units of 100 cu. ft. was imitated around the world, although there were slight variations from one jurisdiction to another in the spaces excluded from measurement. Where the metric system is used, the registered ton of 100 cu. ft. is reckoned as 2.83 cu. m.

(3) Entirely different is the concept embodied in displacement tonnage. This is the weight of the sea water displaced by the vessel (figuring that 35 cu. ft. of sea water weighs 2,240 lbs.). There are two kinds of displacement tonnage. Light displacement tonnage (*déplacement lège, dislocamento leggiero*) is the weight of water displaced by the vessel when entirely unloaded. It is the equivalent of the weight of the ship itself. Displacement tonnage loaded (*déplacement en charge,*

---

[3] Moorsom, pp. 134–35. J. Bes, *Chartering and Shipping Terms* (5th ed.; Amsterdam, 1951), pp. 168–70, makes a distinction between "gross tonnage" which includes all enclosed space, and "gross registered tonnage" which allows deduction for staircases, waterclosets, etc.; but most references to gross tonnage are to gross registered tonnage measured according to the rules of some registering authority, e.g., U.S. Bureau of the Census, *Historical Statistics of the United States* (2nd ed.; Washington, 1960), p. 439.

[4] George C. V. Holmes, *Ancient and Modern Ships* (rev. ed., 2 vols.; London, 1906), II, 208; Bes, pp. 202–3; William H. White, *A Manual of Naval Architecture* (2nd ed.; London, 1882), p. 49. A deduction from the gross tonnage of sailing vessels for the space occupied by crew's quarters was first authorized in 1867. The remarks of Moorsom and of the chairman of the meeting of the Institution of Naval Architects make clear that they thought sufficient allowance for existing crew's quarters was made in setting the divisor as high as 100 cu. ft. But the law of 1867 was intended to encourage better quarters.

dislocamento a pieno carico) is the weight displaced when the vessel is loaded to its designed draught. Displacement tonnage is used mainly for battleships and in estimating the amount of construction (labor and materials) involved in building various vessels. I doubt whether it was used in merchant shipping statistics before the nineteenth century.[5]

(4) The difference between light displacement and displacement loaded is called deadweight tonnage. It may be defined as the weight of the additional water displaced because of loading cargo. It is of course the same as the weight of the cargo.[6] For ordinary wooden sailing vessels the deadweight tonnage was about half the displacement loaded, that is, the weight of the cargo and the weight of the ship itself were about equal.[7]

Before displacement was used in determining the weight of either the ship or the cargo, the weight of the cargo was determined by weighing and counting the units loaded. This method of calculation also yielded a valid estimate of deadweight capacity, as it is called, or deadweight tonnage (*port en lourd, portata lorda*).[8]

[5] Paul Gille, "Jauge et tonnage des navires," in *Le Navire et l'économie maritime du XV au XVIII siècles,* Travaux du Colloque d'Histoire Maritime, 1956, ed. Michel Mollat (Paris, S.E.V.P.E.N., 1957), p. 85. In contrast, Walter Ashburner, *The Rhodian Sea Law* (Oxford, 1909), pp. cliii–v, treated the estimates of Venetian ships in *milliaria* as estimates of displacement and even considered it debatable whether the ratings of ancient ships in *modii* referred to the weight of the cargo or the displacement loaded. But I agree with the naval architect, Paul Gille, that neither the Ancients nor the Venetians could have determined the displacement of their vessels. Ashburner used displacement tonnage as an explanation of Venetian statutes of 1252 prescribing how many *kantars* could be carried by ships of various ratings in *milliaria,* but the passage is better explained by considering the *kantar* a kind of freight ton, and the *milliaria* as indicative of deadweight tonnage.

[6] F. G. Fassett, Jr. (ed.), *The Shipbuilding Industry in the United States* (2 vols.; New York, The Society of Naval Architects and Marine Engineers, 1948), I, 64; Harold F. Norton, "Freeboard, Tonnage, and Capacity," in *Principles of Naval Architecture,* eds. Henry E. Russell and Lawrence B. Chapman (2 vols.; New York, The Society of Naval Architects and Marine Engineers, 1942), I, 13, distinguishes gross deadweight which includes the weight of the crew and some fuel, and the cargo or net deadweight which, not including these, gives the weight of commercial cargo.

[7] Gille, p. 96.

[8] Fassett (ed.), p. 64; Moorsom, p. 133, used the expression "deadweight cargo," but any such expression as "deadweight cargo tons" seems to me ambiguous, for statistics of cargoes transported are frequently given in short tons, as in *Historical Statistics of the United States,* 2nd ed., series Q, pp. 210–37, where only those for the Panama Canal are in long tons. On the other hand, when "deadweight tonnage" is given for ships, long tons of 2,240 lbs. are always meant.

(5) Measuring the maximum cargo not by weight but by volume gives the measurement freight tonnage (*tonneau d'affrêtement, tonnellata di nolo*). In modern usage the comparable measure is often called bale capacity, cubic capacity, or measurement capacity and is stated in cu. ft. In ancient and medieval times the capacity of a ship was commonly stated in the units actually loaded. Wine was so important a cargo that the large wine cask called in England the tun or ton and weighing about 2,240 lbs. was the most commonly used unit. A 100-ton ship meant a vessel that could load 100 of these casks. Since the cask measured about 40 cu. ft. (1.13 cu. m.), freight rates on light bulky commodities were set in England in this unit, called a "freight ton." Cargo that pays according to its volume is called measurement cargo. For some kinds of measurement cargo, 42 cu. ft. are considered one ton in freight rates; but the "freight tonnage" of a ship is what Moorsom called the amount of "measurement cargo at 40 feet to a ton which a ship can carry."[9] This English freight ton, which to remove all ambiguity I will call a measurement freight ton, equals in the metric system 1.13 cu. m. or 1,132 liters.

(6) Although officials and shipowners understood by tonnage the amount of cargo that could be loaded, they did not always rate a ship by observing what was put aboard. They took measurements of the ship's keel, beam, etc., to estimate its size. For a time these methods of estimating were regarded as subject to correction in case actual loading proved they were incorrect. But even the counting of cargo actually loaded was not necessarily a firm basis for a ship's rating. The number of deadweight cargo tons it would carry depended on how deeply it could safely be submerged. This might vary with the voyage, the age of the ship, and the judgments of shipwrights, masters, and officials. How many measurement freight tons a ship could carry depended on how much space was used for commercial cargo and how much for ship's stores, crew's quarters, arms, and propulsion. These varied with the length and circumstances of each voyage and with the design of the ship. Thus there was plenty of room for arguments and accommodations between shipowners, charterers, and taxing authorities. Gradually official estimates came to be determined largely by taking specified measures and calculating according to fixed rules. These rules might give fairly accurate estimates for a ship of one design but not for a ship of a different design. The rules varied from country to country and

---

[9] Moorsom, p. 133; Holmes, II, 205. "Freight ton" is the expression used by White, p. 67, and Robert Riegel, *Merchant Vessels* (New York, 1921), p. 138.

even within the same country for various purposes. Those ratings which were determined by official rules of measurement I will here call "old registered tonnage." There were of course many different kinds of old registered tonnage. Since they were based on measuring, English writers sometimes call them "measured" tons, and in French and Italian they are a kind of ton *de jauge* or *di stazza,* just as are modern registered tons.[10]

In view of their different meanings we have thus distinguished six kinds of tonnage:

(1) Gross registered tonnage (modern, for total enclosed space).
(2) Net registered tonnage (modern, for income-yielding enclosed space).
(3) Displacement tonnage light (modern, for weight of the ship itself).
(4) Deadweight tonnage (for weight of maximum cargo).
(5) Measurement freight tonnage (for cubic volume of maximum cargo).
(6) Old registered tonnage (old, official, for size of ship).

The different results obtainable are illustrated by the standard Liberty ship, the "workhorse of the fleet" in World War II. It had the following tonnages:[11]

Gross registered tonnage	7,185
Net registered tonnage	4,380
Displacement tonnage, light	3,600
Deadweight tonnage	10,500
Freight tonnage (bale capacity of 468,000 cu. ft. divided by 40)	11,700

Such an example underlines the fact that a ship's net registered tonnage and its freight tonnage are very different. Although both are statements of the volume of freight the ship is judged able to carry, the modern registered ton, gross or net, is 100 cu. ft. whereas the freight ton is 40 cu. ft.

[10] Ralph Davis, *The Rise of the English Shipping Industry in the Seventeenth and Eighteenth Centuries* (London, 1962) , pp. 395–96; Gille, pp. 92–98.

[11] René de Kerchove, *International Maritime Dictionary* (2nd ed.; Princeton, N.J., 1961) , *s.v.* Liberty ship; Gerald J. Fischer, *A Statistical Summary of Shipbuilding under the U.S. Maritime Commission during World War II,* Historical Reports of War Administration, United States Maritime Commission, No. 2, issued by the Commission in 1949, Table A–1. Because it was designed for quick construction and large carrying capacity in an emergency, the Liberty ship had a very large deadweight tonnage compared to its displacement light.

G. Moorsom and other authorities, 1860–70, estimated that the relation between the various tonnages then in use was such that a typical merchant sailing vessel of one or two decks would have tonnages in the following proportions:[12]

Gross registered tonnage	100
Net registered tonnage	96
Displacement, light	150
Deadweight tonnage	150
Freight tonnage	187½
Old registered tonnage	90–120

With this range of difference in tons it is desirable to make clear which is meant when referring to a modern "ton" and to try to find out which conception is expressed in estimates from former times.

II

In medieval and early modern sources it is often difficult to know whether the figures given refer to deadweight carrying capacity, to capacity in freight tons, or to some old conventional registered tonnage. The three were not always clearly distinguished. A survey of some important early ship measures will include examples of how two or three of these conceptions were combined.

Such a survey needs to distinguish two types of vessels: the rowed ships called galleys and the "round ships" dependent entirely on sail. The different armament and equipment of the galleys created special

---

[12] Moorsom, pp. 133–35, quotes an official government paper giving the conversion formulae:

1 gross reg. ton under the tonnage deck = 1⅞ freight tons

1 gross reg. ton under the tonnage deck = 1½ deadweight tons.

The tonnage deck is the upper deck in all vessels which have fewer than three complete decks and is the second deck from below in other vessels. Bes, *op. cit.*, p. 202. Moorsom explains that the conversion factor of 1⅞ is obtained by estimating that out of every 100 cu. ft. of enclosed space only 75 cu. ft. is available for cargo and 75/40 = 1⅞. The conversion factor of 1½ for deadweight he derived from the empirical rule that on an average 67 cu. ft. below tonnage deck is needed for every ton of deadweight cargo safely carried. Then: gross reg. ton times 100 divided by 67 (= × 1½) = deadweight tonnage. On the old registered ton see below, n. 56.

For steamships, Isserlis says, "A rough and ready rule in common use for many years was 100 net tons = 160 gross tons = 240 deadweight tons." He gives a table of the variations of relations by types, 1914–1936. L. Isserlis, "Tramp Shipping Cargoes and Freights," *Journal of the Royal Statistical Society*, n.s., CI (1938), 62–63. For this reference I am indebted to Douglass C. North.

problems in rating them and they were important cargo carriers for only a relatively short time. I will consider them after examining the measures used in stating the size of round ships.

Since the earliest ratings of merchant ships were descriptive of their cargoes and wine was already in ancient times one of the more important cargoes, the size of ships was then described in terms of the containers in which wine was carried, namely the earthen jars, amphore. Just as we speak of a 2,000-ton ship, Cicero referred to a 2,000-jar ship; as we say a ten-thousand tonner, they said a myriamphore. Marine archaeology has shown that the jars in a cargo of wine were of a few standardized sizes—some of 19–20 liters, others of 26 liters (.92 cu. ft.). L'Ingenieur Paul Gille has figured that the latter, holding wine weighing 26 kg. (57 lbs. Eng.), themselves weighed 17 to 18 kg. (37–40 lbs. Eng.), increasing the weight to be transported by 65 per cent.

When wooden casks were substituted for jars there was a significant saving of weight, for a wine barrel weighed only about 8 per cent as much as its content.[13] The use of wooden casks established new average relations between weight and space in transportation. Those developed in the Anglo-French wine trade provide a basic frame of reference. The wine cask which the English called a tun and the French a *tonneau* contained about 240 to 252 gallons of wine (810–957 liters, 28.6–33.8 cu. ft.). Since wine has about the same specific gravity as water, the contents weighed about 2,000 lbs. (about 900 kg.). Allowing for the cask, the standard for the total weight of the tun became fixed in England at 2,240 lbs. (1,016 kg.), in France at 2,000 livres (979 kg.), an addition of about 8–10 per cent for the weight of the cask.[14]

A similar relationship seems to have been established in the Mediterranean in the thirteenth century or before. There the wine cask used in estimating the size of ships was called the *botta* or *botte* in Venice and Naples, and *boute* in Marseilles. As the generic English equivalent I use the word "butt." The butt of Naples contained about 470 liters,[15]

[13] Gille, p. 87.

[14] Dorothy Burwash, *English Merchant Shipping, 1460–1540* (University of Toronto Press, 1947), pp. 92, 95; Jacques Savary, *Dictionnaire universel de commerce,* Tome II (Paris, 1723), cols. 387–88. The specific gravity of wine is given as .993 in R. W. Stevens, *On the Stowage of Ships* (London, 1893), p. 114.

[15] Francesco Balducci Pegolotti, *La Pratica della Mercatura,* ed. Allan Evans, Medieval Academy of American Publications, No. 24 (Cambridge, Mass., 1936), p. 189, equates it with 64 *sestieri* of Paris. Yves Renouard, "Recherches Complémentaires sur la capacité bordelais au moyen âge," *Annales du Midi,* LXVIII (1956), pp. 220–24, gives the *sestier* of Paris as 7.45 liters. Since that is an eighteenth-century figure, the validity of the conversion depends on the Parisian *sestier* remaining unchanged since the fourteenth century.

that of Marseilles 480 liters,[16] and that of Crete used by the Venetians was in the thirteenth century of about 450 liters (15.9 cu. ft.) .[17] Genoa used the *baril,* 10 of which held 476 liters (16.9 cu. ft.) .[18] The corresponding units of weight were at Genoa 10 *cantars* equivalent to 476 kg. (1,048 lbs.) and at Venice the *milliarium,* equal to 477 kg. (1,050 lbs.) .[19] The *milliarium* of Venice and the *botte* of Crete seem to have been equated around 1300 by adding to the weight of the wine about 6 per cent to allow for the weight of the cask.[20]

The relation of the content of the cask to the total weight of the full cask was only one part, however, and the simpler part, of the problem in relations of weight and space created by the invention of the wooden cask. The other part of the problem is the relation between the cask of a given weight and the space that the cask occupied. Because of the shape of the cask and the shape and structure of the ship's hull there were empty spaces between casks and about timbers. Counting these spaces it is estimated that a cask weighing 2,240 lbs. (1,016 kg.) "occupies" 57–67 cu. ft. (1.6–1.9 cu. m.) .[21]

Estimates vary because "occupies" can be variously interpreted. The content of such a cask was only about 34 cu. ft. (.95 cu. m.). The cylinder occupied by the cask, allowing for the size of the cask itself and its bulging shape, was estimated as 40 cu. ft. (1.13 cu. m.) . But when all empty spaces around timbers and between casks are considered, the 2,240-lb. cask was said to "occupy" about 60 cu. ft. (1.7 cu. m.) .

The problem of equating a weight with a space occupied arose first

[16] E. Baratier et I. Reynaud, *Histoire du commerce de Marseilles,* II (Paris, 1951), pp. 742–43 n.

[17] The earliest indication I have found concerning the size of the Cretan *botte* is a resolution of the Venetian Senate of 1385 which equates the *botte* to 3 Venetian *bigoncia* (450 liters). See Archivio di Stato di Venezia, Senato Misti, reg. 38, fol. 26; Angelo Martini, *Manuale di Metrologia* (Turin, 1883) , pp. 817–22.

[18] Pietro Rocca, *Pesi e Mesure antichi di Genova e del Genovesato* (Genoa, 1871), p. 108. An excellent work based in part on a study of the measuring instruments that have been preserved. At Barcelona ships were rated in a *bota* of 10 *quintas.* The equivalent of the modern Catalan *quinta* is 40 kg. but that of the medieval *quinta* is unknown according to C. Carrère, "Le droit d'ancrage et le mouvement du port de Barcelona au milieu du XV siècle," in *Estudios de Historia Moderna,* III (1953) , 91.

[19] Rocca, p. 110; Martini, pp. 224, 817–22.

[20] This is to be inferred from the application to vessels over 200 *botti* of rules made for vessels over 200 *milliaria.* See nn. 24 and 30 below and Chapter 14 for discussion.

[21] Moorsom as cited in n. 12 above, gives 67; Norton, *op. cit.,* I, 72, gives 57; Gille, *op. cit.,* p. 59, gives 56; experts of the Royal Navy in 1626 estimated 60 cu. ft. (Michael Oppenheim, *History of the Administration of the Royal Navy* [London, 1896], p. 268) .

in connection with setting freight rates. If the cargo was as heavy as wine or heavier than wine, it paid so much per ton by weight, but the shipowner would not accept at that rate a lighter cargo such as cotton, for he then would collect little even from a full ship. To persuade the ship to take a cargo lighter than wine, a shipper had to pay approximately as much for the space his cargo occupied as did the shipper of wine casks. In England the space obtained by paying for a ton of freight became standardized fairly early at 40 cu. ft. This was the freight ton. But 40 cu. ft. was only about two-thirds or at most four-fifths of the space which the 2,240-lb. cask really "occupied" or used up. The low figure may have been due partly to a different conception of "occupied space," and partly to the ability of the shipmasters to collect relatively high freights from the shippers of light goods.[22] It probably reflected also the nature of English shipping in medieval times.

The relation between a ship's capacity in deadweight tons and its capacity in measurement cargo tons depends on the design of the particular vessel, the size of its timbers, the kind of cargo loaded, the nature of the voyage, and other factors that vary from ship to ship and voyage to voyage. Most of the traffic of northern Europe and much of that of the Mediterranean was in small single-decked vessels which made short voyages and allowed little or no space below deck for stores, arms, or quarters for the crew or passengers. If such a ship was loaded to its deadweight capacity with 100 casks each weighing a ton, it probably had no usable space left below deck. The master was not willing to replace wine with a lighter cargo unless he was sure of being paid at least as much by the shipper of lighter cargo.

Larger ships with two or three decks were in use in the thirteenth century, however, at least in the Mediterranean. They carried much light cargo and reserved much space for arms, supplies, and quarters for crew and passengers. These two-deckers or three-deckers had deeper draft, of course, than the one-deckers and could carry more deadweight, but the upper decks increased their cubic capacity more than it did their weight-carrying capacity. They had more space to sell and could profitably set a different relation of weight to space. Certainly the English equivalence of 1 ton of weight to 40 cu. ft. was quite unrealistic in stating the amount of space they provided. Somewhat more useful in indicating the relative size of such vessels was the equivalence adopted

---

[22] Burwash, *English Merchant Shipping, 1460–1540,* pp. 88–94. She calls it the "cargo ton," and gives evidence of its development as a unit of general meaning in freight contracts, but she has no real explanation p. 95, of why 40 cu. ft. was used instead of 60 cu. ft.

later in France where the *tonneau de mer* (979 kg. or 2,158 lbs. Eng.) used as a freight ton was considered 42 *pieds cubes français* (1.44 cu. m. or 51 cu. ft. Eng.), although this *tonneau* contained not quite 28 *pieds cubes*.[23]

The variability of the factors which determined for a particular ship on a particular voyage how much of heavy cargo or of light cargo it might load is clear already in the thirteenth-century Venetian maritime statutes. They provided against two different kinds of overloading. (1) A ship carrying a heavy cargo such as salt might be submerged too deeply even if much of the space below deck was empty. This danger was met by regulations concerning submersion of the load lines which were marked on all ships. The minimum freeboard differed according to the age, cargo, and destination of the vessel, and so accordingly did the deadweight that could legally be carried. (2) In the fourteenth century light cargoes, mainly cotton, became so important for many Venetian large ships that there was no temptation to submerge them too deeply. Regulations about loadlines were almost forgotten, many ships were not even marked with the cross which served as Plimsoll line. On the other hand, stricter regulations were enacted concerning the places where merchandise might and might not be loaded. The purpose was to reserve adequate space for arms, stores, and crew's quarters. The rules varied with the voyage, and the Mediterranean was divided into four loading zones. The zone involving the longest voyages and subject to the most hazards of war and piracy was that east of an imaginary line drawn from Alexandria to Adalia in Anatolia. Ships loading in that zone were forbidden to place any cargo above the lowest deck; all space between decks was to be left free for supplies, arms, passengers, and crew. Ships not going so far east, but yet going outside the Adriatic, were permitted to load certain kinds of light wares between decks, provided specified spaces were left unencumbered by merchandise. The reserved space was defined one way for ships going west of the toe of Italy and another way for voyages east in the Ionian and Aegean Seas. Within the Adriatic rules were relaxed; it was traditional that two-deckers carrying wine, oil, meat, cheese, or grain within the gulf could load them between decks.[24] A ship's carrying capacity in

---

[23] Gille, pp. 99–100, and Gille, "La Jauge au XVIII siècle," in *Les Sources de l'histoire maritime en Europe*, Actes du Quatrième Colloque International d'Histoire Maritime, Paris, 1959, ed. M. Mollat (Paris, 1962), p. 466.

[24] See Chapters 14 and 15 for discussion; also *Gli Statuti marittimi veneziani fino al 1255*, eds. R. Predelli et Adolfo Sacerdoti (Venice, 1903), and in *Archivio veneto*, 1902–3, Statuto of Pietro Ziani, and Statuti of Jacopo Tiepolo, caps. 48, 49, 71, 72.

freight tons thus varied, legally, according to the loading zone, just as the deadweight capacity of many vessels varied, legally, according to their age.

Practical calculations by ship captains of what their vessels could actually safely carry, as well as laws, caused the deadweight and measurement cargo capacity to differ not only from ship to ship but on different voyages of the same ship. Consequently, the tendency to use for convenience a measuring unit that combined two conceptions of carrying capacity, such as the English-Biscayan ton or the early Mediterranean butt, was paralleled by an opposing tendency to use for accuracy either an unmistakable unit of weight or a clearly distinct volumetric measure.

Where heavy cargo was the most important, ships were rated according to their deadweight capacity. This was true at Genoa where the *cantar* equal to 47.6 kg. (105 lbs.) was used. A heavy cargo, alum, provided cargo for some very large round ships, as Jacques Heers has shown. The Genoese had a dozen or more vessels of 1,000 deadweight tons (1,000 *tonnes metriques de port*) in the mid-fifteenth century. They were used mainly on the voyage from Chios to the Channel.[25] Since alum (specific gravity 1.7) was the principal cargo they were loaded down to their maximum draft long before all their space below decks was filled, leaving plenty of room for cotton or silks or crew's quarters.[26] Since they hardly ever used their full cubic capacity, they were rated according to their deadweight capacity, that is, the amount of weight they could carry.

During the fourteenth, fifteenth, and sixteenth centuries wine casks and units of liquid measure in the Mediterranean underwent considerable change. The Genoese *baril* increased so that it held about 55 liters in 1455 and 59 liters in 1523,[27] but ship measures at Genoa were stable because they were based on the *cantar*. When the butt was used, it was regularly equated to 10 *cantars*.[28] As late as the sixteenth century a French observer speaking of all the Mediterranean but familiar chiefly

[25] Jacques Heers, *Gênes au XV siècle*, pp. 268–69; Heers, "Types de navires et spécialisation des trafics en Méditerranée à la fin du Moyen Âge," in *Le Navire et l'économie maritime du Moyen-Âge au XVIII siècle principalement en Méditerranée*, Travaux du Colloque International d'Histoire Maritime, 1957, ed. Michel Mollat (Paris, S.E.V.P.E.N., 1958), pp. 107–17.

[26] Stevens, *Stowage*, p. 114.

[27] Rocca, pp. 110 and 67–72, where he gives a detailed account of how the wiles of tax-dodging tavern-keepers and other factors kept enlarging the size of the wine measure.

[28] Heers, *Gênes*, p. 269.

with Marseilles and Genoa said that whereas Atlantic seamen reckoned in tons, in the Mediterranean they reckoned in butts, each of 950 *livres* Fr. (465 kg.).[29]

At Venice there was a more complicated development. Since light cargo became more important than heavy during the fourteenth century, the unit of volume, the *botte,* became for a time more important than the unit of weight, the *milliarium.* Before the end of the century, the rules concerning manning, arming, taxing, or hiring, which had been stated in terms of *milliaria* in the thirteenth-century codes, were stated in *botti.*[30] The Republic of Venice continued thereafter to use this butt as its ship measure and in doing so tried to combine a unit of volume and of weight.

The butt which the Venetians used in this way was no longer, however, based on the old Cretan *botte* of about 450 liters (15.9 cu. ft.). The size of the cask used in Crete varied, but early in the fifteenth century it contained about 159 gallons (600 liters or 21.2 cu. ft.) and at that size became the basis of the standardized ship measure.[31] Adding about 8 per cent for the weight of the cask, I estimate the Venetian *botte* weighed 640 kg. (1,411 lbs. or .63 long ton). For comparison with

---

[29] Auguste Jal (ed.), *Documents inédits sur l'histoire de la marine à XVI siècle* (Paris, 1842, extrait des *Annales maritimes et coloniales,* July, 1842), pp. 39–40.

[30] A.S.V. Capitolare dei Consoli dei Mercanti, cap. 1, 164, 200, 247. Rules formerly applying to vessels over 200 *millarii* were after 1362 applied to all vessels over 200 *botti.* This suggests that when the wine casks of Crete called *botti* grew larger, the ship measure which had earlier been equated with both *milliarium* and *botte* stuck to the *botte* and grew larger with it.

[31] The wine casks used in Crete varied considerably in size. The largest, of 55 *mistati,* were considered standard in 1432 (A.S.V. Senato Misti, reg. 58, fol. 125), whereas *botte* of about 45 *mistati* were common earlier, in the fourteenth century, and later, about 1480. (Senato Misti, reg. 38, fol. 26; Senato Mar, reg. 9, fol. 162.) The Cretan *mistate* equalled .015 *anfore* of Venice (= 9 liters according to Bartholomeo de Paxi, *Tariffa de pexi e mesure* (Venice, 1503), no paging, but a manuscript "Tarifs" of 1454 shown to me at the Archivio di Stato, Venezia, by Dr Ugo Tucci, for whose help I am very grateful, gives equivalents that make 1 *mistate* equal to 10.7 liters. This *tariffa* then resolves the discrepancy by saying that 100 *mistati* Candioti repoured make of clear wine, if old, 1¾ *anfore* (1,050 liters); if new 1½ *anfore* (900 liters). The older wine yielded more clear wine because the dregs, being more thoroughly settled filled less space. Allowing for the space filled by both clear wine and dregs, I estimate the *mistate* of Candia as 11 liters. A *botte* of 55 *mistati* was then 605 liters. That the Cretan *botte* at its largest, not in its smaller versions, was that used in rating ships is shown by the relation of the *botte* to the grain measures, explained below, and by the figures used in the rules to determine ratings from the ship's measure. See Frederic C. Lane, *Venetian Ships and Shipbuilders of the Renaissance* (Baltimore, 1934), Appendix I.

the English freight ton, we may add 20 per cent, as did the English, which gives 720 liters (.72 cu. m. or 25.4 cu. ft.) . This is a little less than the estimates of Corazzini[32] and Gino Luzzatto.[33] But for comparison with the French *tonneau de mer,* it would be reasonable to add 50 per cent, and say that the Venetian *botte* "occupied" or "used up" about 900 liters (.9 cu. m. or 31.8 cu. ft.) .[34]

A confirmation of this interpretation of the *botte* is found in the examination of grain measures and their use in indicating the size of ships. Cargoes of grain had been important for centuries at Venice and become more so in the sixteenth century when we find the Venetian bushel, the *ster* (or *staio,* plural *stera* or *staia*), frequently used in rating ships. The capacity of the *ster* was about two and a third Imperial bushels (83.3 liters) and the Venetians considered a *ster* of wheat equal to 132 *lire* (138.6 lbs. Eng. or 62.9 kg.) .[35] This gives a specific gravity for wheat of .74, which is reasonable.[36] When used in rating ships, the *ster* was regularly considered one-tenth of a *botte,*[37] which implies that 10 *stera* either weighed the same as one *botte* or that they occupied the same space, or both. According to the estimates given above based on the wine measures, 10 *stera* were indeed almost exactly one *botte* by weight and occupied within 10 per cent of the same amount of space.

In Europe as a whole grain measures were almost as much used as wine measures to indicate a ship's capacity and they expressed a similar relationship between weight and space occupied. Grain could be poured into the hold leaving no empty spaces such as those around the wine casks, but the specific gravity of wheat was about .75 while that of wine was about .99. Other grains had a specific gravity less than that of

---

[32] Francesco Corazzini, *Vocabolario nautico italiano* (Turin, 1900–1907) , I, 335, gives: 1 *botte* = 28 cu. ft.

[33] Gino Luzzatto, *Studi di storia economica veneziana* (Padua, 1954) , pp. 42–43 n., gives 1 *botte* = .7 to .75 *tonnellata.*

[34] A similar conclusion is to be drawn from a passage generously called to my attention by Dr. D. Sella found in A.S.V. Cinque Savii alla Mercanzia, n.s., busta 836*b,* a deposition of two merchants in 1584. They equate two *botti* of wine with one English ton and since they also distinguish the freight paid on wine in these terms from the freight on raisins, which was in tons of 2,240 lbs., I interpret the passage to mean, as Dr. Sella suggested to me, that two *botti* of wine occupied as much space as one English ton. The space "occupied" by the English ton was estimated at 56–67 cu. ft. (see n. 21 above) so this indicates that the *botte* "occupied" 28–33 cu. ft.

[35] Lane, *Venetian Ships,* pp. 245–46.

[36] *Enciclopedia italiana,* XVII, 731, says a hectolitre of ordinary wheat weighs 73–75 kg.

[37] Lane, *Venetian Ships,* p. 246.

wheat; Walther Vogel calculated that it was .765 for wheat and .73 for rye.[38] Where contemporaries give the number of pounds in a bushel, that evidence is to be respected, but in general it seems reasonable for convenience in rough calculations to convert dry measures for grain into measures of weight assuming a specific gravity of .75 and rounding off on the lower side. If a ship was loaded to its maximum draught with grain but left some space for crew's quarters or stores, its specific gravity as a whole must have been somewhat less, perhaps about 6.8–6.9, as is implied by the French equating of the *tonneau* weighing 979 kg. (2,159 lbs.) with 1.44 cu. m. (50.8 cu. ft.).

One of the regions where grain-carrying capacity was the most-used way of stating a ship's size was Sicily, a major exporter of wheat. Ships were rated in *salma*, but unfortunately more than one *salma* was in use in Sicily and it is often difficult to know which was meant.[39] For the exports from the kingdom of Naples, particularly Apulia, grain was measured in *carri*, each of about 2,000 liters (70.6 cu. ft.) equivalent to 1,500 kg. (3,307 lbs.) of grain.[40] The *carro* was used for estimating ship size also at Ragusa, whose merchant marine became very important in the sixteenth century. Converting to deadweight tonnage measures we may call the *carro* equal roughly to 1½ tons.[41]

The size of the Hanseatic and Dutch ships which plied the Baltic was also for a long time expressed by estimates of how much grain they could carry. The Hanseatic grain measure, the *last*, was a volumetric unit which had an equivalent in pounds, like the early English ton. *Last* meant at first the load of a four-wheeled wagon. When it was somewhat more precisely defined, the standards set varied from port to

[38] Walther Vogel, *Geschichte der deutschen Seeschiffahrt*. Bd. I, Von der Urzeit bis zum Ende des XV. Jahrhundert (Berlin, 1915), p. 557. Stevens, *On the Stowage of Ships* (London, 1858), pp. 16–17, gives the stowage factor of wheat as 21, about the same as that for wine, 20, thus allowing for broken space in loading wine casks.

[39] Heers, *Gênes*, pp. 274 and 334–5, and Heers, *Le Livre de comptes de Giovanni Piccamiglio, homme d'affaires génois* (1456–1459) (Paris, 1959), p. 21, refers to a *salma* which he equates with 200 kg. but Paxi, *Tariffa*, ed. of 1557, pp. 26–27, describes a *salma pizola o generale di Sicilia* equal to 3¼ *stera* of Venice (270.7 liters or 139 kg.) and a *salma grossa di Sicilia* equal to 4 *stera* of Venice (333.2 liters or 233 kg.).

[40] De Paxi ed. of 1557, p. 23, and in the unpaged edition of 1503, gives the *carro* as equal to 22⅔ *stera* of Venice. Marino Sanuto, *I Diarii* (Venice, 1879–1903), III, 1455, gives it as 22 *stera*, which is 1,833 liters.

[41] Jorjo Tadic, "Le port de Raguse et sa flotte au XVI siècle," in *Le Navire et l'économie maritime du moyen âge au XVIII siècle principalement en Méditerranée*, Travaux du Deuxième Colloque International d'Histoire Maritime, 1957, ed. M. Mollat (Paris, S.E.V.P.E.N., 1958), pp. 14–15, 26.

port and within the same port for different commodities. In Danzig, for example, 3 *lasts* of herring equalled 4 *lasts* of rye, and the *last* of rye, equal to 3.105 cu. m. or 2,257 kg. (4,975 lbs.), was used to rate ships. At Hamburg in the seventeenth century the grain *last* was 3.159 cu. m. (111.5 cu. ft.), but for rating ships there was a special *Schiffslast* equal to 2,000 Hamburg pounds (1,935 kg. = 4,266.9 lbs. Eng.). At Amsterdam, grain was measured using the *Kornlast* of Danzig of 3.105 cu. m. or 109.6 cu. ft. but ships were rated according to the weight they could carry in *Schiffslasten* of 2,000 Amsterdam pounds (1,976 kg. or 4,356.3 lbs.). This situation seems to be the result of a shift away from an ambivalent measure, which expressed a rough equivalence of volume with weight, towards two distinct measures: the *Kornlast* which measured volume and the *Schiffslast* which told how much a vessel could carry without submerging its loadline excessively.[42] There is some evidence that the ships were of such a design that the deadweight capacity could not be accurately determined when the cargo was grain, for the vessel would be full before it was submerged to its loadline, and could then load some lumber on deck. But when a heavy cargo was loaded, such as the salt which formed the main return freight from the Bay of Biscay, then the deadweight tonnage could be definitely determined. This is suggested by the records of a ship constructed in Koenigsberg in 1559 which left on its first voyage after paying only part of the taxes due on it but with the proviso that it would pay more on its return if the rating then given it proved it owed more. It returned with 166 *lasts* of salt and accordingly paid on a rating of 160 *lasts*.[43]

Generalizing roughly, we can say that the Hanseatic and Dutch *Schiffslast* equalled about 4,480 lbs. (2,032 kg.) and that the *Kornlast* became by the seventeenth century a measure of volume equal to about 112 cu. ft. (3.2 cu. m.).[44] A ship's capacity in the two *lasts* was the same when the specific gravity of the cargo was roughly .63.

This was about the same as the relation between weight and space occupied which developed at Bordeaux. About 1300 a very large cask was in use, the *tonneau*, holding about 800 liters to 900 liters (28 cu. ft. to 32 cu. ft.), as well as smaller casks called *pipes* and *barriques*. Later the very large casks went out of use but, as Yves Renouard has shown,

---

[42] Walther Vogel, *Geschichte der deutschen Seeschiffahrt*, Bd. I, pp. 554–58.

[43] Pierre Jeannin, "Le tonnage des navires utilisés dans le Baltique de 1550 à 1640 d'après les sources prussiennes," *Le Navire et l'économie maritime du Nord de l'Europe du moyen âge au XVII siècle*, Travaux du Troisième Colloque d'Histoire Maritime, 1958, ed. M. Mollat (Paris, S.E.V.P.E.N., 1960), p. 50; Aksel E. Christensen, *Dutch Trade to the Baltic about 1600* (Copenhagen and The Hague, 1941), p. 343.

[44] Vogel, *Deutsche Seeschiffahrt*, Bd. I, pp. 558–59.

the *tonneau* was still used as a unit of reckoning according to the formula: 1 *tonneau* = 2 *pipes* = 4 *barriques*. The content of the *barrique* was so maintained that the amount of wine in a *tonneau* became about 960 liters (33.9 cu. ft.) weighing 960 kg. (2,116 lbs.).[45] We would expect 5 to 10 per cent to be added to allow for the weight of the cask. A sixteenth-century French author in generalizing about ship measures said that the *tonneau* weighed 19 to 20 *quintals*, that is 1,900 to 2,000 *livres Fr.*[46] When the rules for measuring and rating ships were standardized for all France under Colbert, the *tonneau* of 2,000 livres (979 kg. or 2,158 lbs. Eng.) was considered standard. For some time the amount of space effectively occupied, taking into account the shape of the casks and the broken space around the beams in the ship's hull, may have been differently estimated from port to port, but the ordinance of 1681 fixed 42 *pieds cubes Fr.* (1.44 cu. m. or 50.8 cu. ft.) as the size of the *tonneau de mer*.[47] Accordingly, this French *tonneau* was approximately one-half of a *last* by volume as well as by weight and was so considered by contemporaries (more precisely it was .495 of an Amsterdam *Schiffslast* and .477 of the Danzig *Kornlast*).

Such commercially used measures of carrying capacity were for centuries used in assigning to vessels official ratings which in a sense might be called registered tonnage, but a separate and distinct "registered ton," recognized as of different size, appears relatively late. When such a ton does appear, it is based on taking specified dimensions and applying an arithmetic formula. Rough rules of that kind had been in use among shipwrights long before they acquired any official status. A fifteenth-century Venetian shipwright's notes contain the formula $(K \times B \times D)/6$, where the keel was measured in Venetian paces, the beam and depth in Venetian feet and the result is the capacity in *botti*. In England there was an old ship's carpenter's formula: $(K \times B \times D)/100$ = tonnage. Such rules were useful to a ship's carpenter in planning the construction of a vessel of a given size, although it is difficult for us to use them in determining the size of the butt or ton, unless we are informed as to the places in the ship's structure from which the meas-

[45] Yves Renouard, "La capacité du tonneau bordelais au moyen âge," *Annales du Midi,* LXV (1953), 395–400; Renouard, "Recherches complémentaires sur la capacité bordelaise au moyen âge," *Annales du Midi,* LXVIII (1956), 195–205. Equivalents in *sestier* of Paris, *barils* of Genoa, etc., work out to values ranging from 755 liters to 885 liters. A value of 960 liters is derived from the Bordeaux system of counting 1 *tonneau* equal to 4 *barriques,* each of 240 liters.

[46] Jal, *Documents inédits,* as above cited, pp. 39–40.

[47] Jacques Savary, *Dictionnaire universel de commerce,* Tome II (Paris, 1723), cols. 387–88. *Encyclopédie méthodique: Marine* (3 vols.; Paris, 1783–87), II, 553–54, presents the standardization of this conventional figure as favourable to the *armateurs*.

ures were taken. A more complicated Venetian rule used the hoops of the butt as well as a measuring rod. Although this latter rule had official status, Venice does not seem to have developed official ratings in registered tons different from the generally recognized carrying capacities, at least not before the late sixteenth century.[48]

A precisely defined method of measuring and a conventional mathematical formula had some advantages over empirical estimates of carrying capacity. An official rule gave a constant, whereas the actual cargo capacity varied, as has been explained, with the kind of voyage, the age of the ship, how deeply it should be submerged, how much space was needed for arms, stores, and crew's quarters, and on other factors which also depended on somebody's judgment. To avoid high port dues and expensive obligations in regard to crew and armament, shipowners wanted as low a rating as possible; but when they were renting their ships to the government they wanted a higher rating. Without precise official rules there was too much room for controversy or collusion between ship-masters and officials.

A clear-cut early example of a registered ton distinct from the commercial measures in use was the *tonelada* introduced in Spain during the sixteenth century. At the beginning of the century *toneladas* of about the same size as the French *tonneaux* were in use in Spain. That of Seville was 1.4 cu. m. (49.4 cu. ft.) and another of the Biscayan ports was of about 1.7 cu. m. (60 cu. ft.). When the oceanic voyages were organized by the Spanish, the tonnages of ships were recorded, Chaunu implies, according to how they had been rated in various ports in the local measures; but there was a tendency to use the larger units which gave a ship a lower tonnage. The lower rating was reported by the ship's captain because it made the ship's obligations less. The ton in use about 1550 was that from the Biscayan ports, about 1.7 cu. m. This was an estimate of cargo-carrying capacity, a measurement freight tonnage. It was derived from counting the number and size of the casks or chests put on board. Perhaps it was still determined in that manner in the mid-sixteenth century. But there was another way of determining the ship's size, namely by taking measure of its keel, beam, etc. This gave what I would call an old Spanish registered tonnage. Chaunu concludes that the figures so obtained, although expressed in *toneladas,* were not a statement of how many *toneladas* the vessel could carry but a statement of the total enclosed capacity, including the upper decks but not the sterncastle and forecastle. He therefore likens it to modern gross

---

[48] Lane, *Venetian Ships,* pp. 247–49; and on the old English rule, John Lyman, "Register Tonnage and its Measurement," *American Neptune,* V (1945), 224.

registered tonnage. The Spanish old registered tonnage was set by law as a specified number of cubic feet or cubits. Its size changed when the length of the cubit changed. Such a change in measures was made in 1590 and the Spanish old registered ton was thereafter 2.6 cu. m. (91.8 cu. ft.). Believing that the change from a ton of 1.4 cu. m. or even 1.7 cu. m. to 2.61 cu. m. is too great to have occurred overnight by royal decree, Chaunu argues that a sort of registered ton based on the ship's measures had been gradually replacing the measure of cargo capacity in *toneladas* for about forty years, and he provides a table of conversion factors ranging from .7 to 1.2 to show the gradual change. His table, he says, permits conversion from a measure of carrying capacity to a measure of total enclosed space and it includes also allowances for other variations due to imperfections in the sources.[49]

Chaunu's *taux de ponderation* are useful in reducing all his figures to a common base so as to make the comparison between them more meaningful, and that is his main purpose.[50] He has introduced a complication which I find confusing, however, in taking as that common base the modern gross registered ton of 2.8 cu. m. (100 cu. ft.). This seems to me unfortunate for two reasons: (1) I doubt whether the Spanish old registered ton of 2.6 cu. m. (91.8 cu. ft.) used after 1570 was really a measure of all the enclosed space in the vessel in the same sense as is the gross registered ton introduced by Moorsom. To determine the extent of similarity it would be necessary to examine the Spanish rules of measurement. I cannot find anywhere in Chaunu's monumental work an analysis of these rules in relation to the structure of the ship.[51] (2) Chaunu's figures invite comparison with other figures concerning shipping movements of the fifteenth to eighteenth centuries. For such comparisons, conversion into modern gross registered tonnage leads to a round-about method introducing new chances of error. More practical would seem to be a conversion into the French

---

[49] Pierre Chaunu, "La tonelada espagnola au XVI et XVII siècles," in *Le Navire et l'économie maritime du XV au XVIII siècles,* Travaux du Colloque d'Histoire Maritime, 1956 (Paris, 1957), pp. 75–80; Huguette and Pierre Chaunu, *Seville et l'Atlantique, 1504 à 1650,* 8 vols.; École des Hautes Études, VIe Section, Centre de Recherches Historiques: Ports–Routes–Trafics, No. VI, I (Paris, 1955), 132–46; VI (Paris, 1956), 29–30. Michael Oppenheim, *History of the Administration of the Royal Navy,* gives from Admiral Duro the ton of Seville as 53.44 cu. ft. (1.513 cu. m.) and the Biscayan ton as equal to 1.2 tons of Seville.

[50] Chaunu, *Seville et l'Atlantique,* in Vol. VI, in addition to that given in Table 129 and explained in Vol. I, pp. 132–46, he uses a different "taux de conversion," having approximately the same range, in Table 13 to show the average size of ships.

[51] He mentions them, *Seville et l'Atlantique,* I, 140, 145, as does Oppenheim, pp. 132–33.

tonneau de mer of 1681. Since this was about the same as the Spanish *tonelada* at the beginning of the century it should be possible to use for the seventeenth century his *taux de ponderation* in reverse.

If the Spanish figures were first converted into *tonneaux de mer,* they would then become roughly comparable to those in English dead-weight tons, for contemporaries equated the *tonneau de mer* with the weight of 2,000 *livres Fr.* (979 kg. or 2,158.3 lbs.) as well as with 42 *pieds cubes Fr.* (1.44 cu. m. or 50.8 cu. ft.).

Any comparison with English shipping statistics involves a wide margin of error. The English figures are in "tons burden," which Davis considers a synonym of "deadweight tonnage." That the two terms were always synonymous is doubted.[52] Probably what was called "tons burden" in common usage was a rough statement of what the vessel could carry in either units of weight or of cubic capacity. The rough equivalence must have been made on the assumption that 2,240 lbs. = 56–60 cu. ft. (not 40 cu. ft.). Comparison between English statistics and those of other countries cannot usefully be made by employing the English freight tons of 40 cu. ft. (1.13 cu. m.), for that was not even roughly equivalent to the space "occupied" by 2,240 lbs. of cargo.

English ratings of vessels in cubic capacity are made more confusing by the development of the old English registered tonnage. The English rules for calculating registered tonnage developed from those used by the Royal Navy in hiring private vessels. The tonnages attributed to vessels in commercial usage, based on capacity in deadweight tons, were obviously understatements of the cubic capacity of these ships in freight tons. When a ship was hired by the Navy, one-third was added to what was called its "tonnage." The larger figure was called its "ton and tonnage." The use of "ton and tonnage" seems to have been an effort to show how many more "tons" (i.e., units of 40 cu. ft.) the ship could carry if loading a close-fitting cargo such as coal than if loading casks of wine. Although it was sometimes called, in flat contradiction to modern usage, "deadweight," instead of "ton and tonnage," it seems to have been an estimate allowing for the vessel's greater capacity in freight tons.[53]

---

[52] Ralph Davis, "Merchant Shipping in the Economy of the Late Seventeenth Century," *Economic History Review,* 2nd ser., IX, No. 1 (1956), 61; Davis, *The Rise of the English Shipping Industry in the Seventeenth and Eighteenth Centuries,* pp. 7 n., 49, 74, 395–96. The doubt is expressed by W. Salisbury in his review in *The Mariner's Mirror,* XLIX, No. 3 (August, 1963), 236.

[53] Oppenheim, pp. 30, 132–33, 268. Suppose a ship had a capacity below deck of 20,000 cu. ft. and was so shaped that cargo weighing 333 long tons would submerge

In determining the rating of the vessels it hired, the Royal Navy adopted the old carpenter's rule $(K \times B \times D)/100$, but there was much discussion regarding where precisely the dimensions should be measured, whether inside or outside the planking, for example. Customs officials did not object in theory to the rules used by the Navy but found it hard in practice to take the specified measures on a loaded vessel, especially the depth and the length of the keel. They were satisfied to measure the length on deck and the beam. Then they considered the depth half the beam and used a simple formula, adopted also by the Navy in 1677:

$$\text{Registered tonnage} = \frac{\text{Length on deck} - \frac{3}{5} \text{ beam} \times B \times \frac{1}{2} B}{94}.$$

Substantially this formula was applied to all merchant shipping by the tonnage law of 1773 and thereafter British shipping statistics came to be in registered tons thus determined.[54] Although it had disadvantages it was re-enacted with relatively slight changes in 1786, 1819, and 1833, and adversely affected the design of ships. To avoid the higher ratings that would come from increasing the beam, shipowners had vessels built excessively long, deep, and narrow, "all more or less crank."[55] The registered tonnage, called Builder's Old Measurement (B.O.M.), diverged considerably from the real carrying capacity expressed in either deadweight or freight tons.[56]

The inadequacy of the rules governing old British registered tonnage makes analysis of shipping statistics from 1773 to 1855 an especially difficult problem and it is rendered more complicated by the introduc-

it to its designed draft. If it loaded that weight in wine casks, each cask would occupy about 60 cu. ft., allowing for broken space, etc., as explained above, n. 21. Since $60 \times 333 = 20,000$, the vessel could in that sense be called of 333 tons burden in either deadweight or measurement cargo capacity. But if its capacity were calculated in measurement freight tons of 40 cu. ft. it would be rated 500 tons. Adding one-third to the 333 tons burden would give 444 as "ton and tonnage."

[54] Oppenheim, pp. 30, 132–33, 266–68; Lyman, p. 225.

[55] C. N. Parkinson, ed., *The Trade Winds, a Study of British Overseas Trade during the French Wars, 1743–1815* (London, 1948), pp. 33, 94, 145; Lyman, pp. 224–25, 230.

[56] Moorsom, p. 130, said that the total existing registered tonnage in 1854 (based on Builder's Old Measurement) was about the same as the registered tonnage would be under his new rules, but for "individual ships evasion of tonnage to the amount of 10 or 15 per cent was easily effected under the old rules." Conversion factors of 1.11 to 1.38 are used to convert from registered tonnage to deadweight tonnage by Abbott Payson Usher, "The Growth of English Shipping, 1572–1922," *Quarterly Journal of Economics*, XLII (May, 1928), p. 467.

tion of steam. But before 1773 British tonnages are commonly given in deadweight tons or in "tons burden" that were roughly equivalent, and comparisons with other fleets are possible. For the whole medieval and early modern periods such comparisons can best be made, on the whole, by using carrying capacity in metric tons as common denominator. The following equivalences are approximate, but more decimal places would misrepresent the accuracy of the figures with which one has to work:

1 metric ton burden = 1 deadweight ton,
= 1 *tonneau de mer*,
= ½ *last*,
= 1 *tonelada* of Seville of 1520,
= .6 Spanish registered *tonelada* of 1620,
= ⅔ *carro* of Ragusa and the Kingdom of Naples,
= 1.6 *botti* of Venice,
= 2 *milliaria* of Venice,
= 20 *cantars* of Genoa.

III

Determining the tonnage of galleys in order to compare their commercial activity with that of other types of vessels is difficult because of their heavier construction and the importance on the galley of space not enclosed. Having no second deck, the galley had to make its one deck serve for crew's quarters, for the transport of their possessions, including some large chests of merchandise, and above all for armament, in which might be counted the power of propulsion from working the oars. Before special mercantile types of galleys were developed, the galleys built primarily for war were sometimes used for transport. In that case they carried less than 50 metric tons of cargo.[57] To call them 50-ton ships would be to misrepresent their size, however, just as reporting the deadweight tonnage of a particular Navy transport as 2,000 tons would misrepresent its size in an instance in which it had nearly the same dimensions of keel and beam as a Liberty ship of 10,000

---

[57] The larger galleys that came into use early in the fourteenth century carried about 50 metric tons of cargo in the hold. Renée Doehaerd, "Les Galères génoises dans la Manche et la Mer du Nord à la fin du XIII et au début du XIV siècle," in *Bulletin de l'Institut Historique Belge de Rome*, XIX (1938), Doc. XIX, XXV, XXI, and below, n. 61.

deadweight tons, but had only 2,000 deadweight cargo capacity because of armour and powerful engines.[58]

When engaged in purely peaceful commercial operations, the galley had advantages from its oars comparable to those which an auxiliary motor later gave a sailing vessel. The heavier types of merchant galleys depended on their sails most of the time and generally waited in harbour for fair winds like any other sailing vessel; but when working their way out of a harbour, when caught by a calm, or when in danger off a lee shore they could assert some independence of the wind. They could therefore operate more nearly on schedule than other vessels of the Middle Ages. It would be desirable to insert a conversion factor allowing for their greater efficiency, but I know no way of setting a figure for it. In any case, we would need statements of their carrying capacity as basic data to which to apply such a conversion factor. Whenever their carrying capacity is given, it is in units of weight.

Larger types of galleys fully able to carry 50 metric tons or more developed at the end of the thirteenth century when the bireme was gradually replaced by the trireme.[59] Some of those being built for commercial voyages were too large from the point of view of the Venetian and Genoese governments. Although these galleys could carry more, they were too slow for the battle fleet and too clumsy to be as safe as they might have been for trading voyages. In their attempts to limit size, the Genoese and Venetian governments specified desired dimensions.[60] The Venetians also stipulated the maximum cargo. About 1305, when the merchant galley was not yet differentiated from a large war galley, maximum cargo in the hold was set at the equivalent of 50 metric tons;[61] in 1320 for the voyage to Flanders at about 110 metric tons;[62] in 1356 at about 140.[63]

At Venice all merchant galleys came to be called great galleys (*galee grosse*) while the standard war galleys were called light galleys (*galee sottile*), but at Genoa a distinction between great and light galleys was applied within the merchant galleys, at least during the first half of the

[58] Fischer, *Statistical Summary*, U.S. Maritime Commission, cited above, n. 11.

[59] See pp. 189–92 for discussion.

[60] Lane, *Venetian Ships*, p. 236, and pp. 225–26, above, for discussion.

[61] *Le Deliberazioni del Consiglio dei Rogati (Senato)*, Serie Mixtorum, Vol. I, eds. R. Cessi and P. Sambin, Monumenti storici pubblicati dalla Deputazione di Storia Patria per le Venezie, n.s., XV, No. 158 (Venice, 1960), 131, 115.

[62] *Delib. dei Rogati*, I, 228, 242.

[63] Archivio di Stato di Venezia, Senato Misti, reg. 27, fol. 105. The Arsenal was ordered to build galleys of 300 *milliaria grossorum*, not 400 as wrongly stated in my *Venetian Ships*, p. 16, when I depended on the work of Cessi there cited.

fourteenth century. In order to rank as a "light galley" a vessel must not exceed specified measures. Certain voyages were reserved for these light galleys. As their dimensions show, many of the Genoese light galleys were not much smaller than some of the merchant galleys used by the Venetians and called "great galleys."[64] What the Genoese called *galee grosse* probably operated as did those the Venetians referred to as *galee disarmate:* they did not rank as fully armed galleys because they lacked sufficient crew and for that reason, as well as their dimensions, lacked the defensibility and manoeuvrability of the state-approved vessels.[65]

During the next century the Genoese abandoned the use of merchant galleys while the Venetians sent out more and more fleets and increased the size of the individual galley. About the middle of the fifteenth century there were also Florentine, Catalan, and even Burgundian galleys operating. Their carrying capacities have to be inferred in many cases from their dimensions.[66] In making such inferences it is useful to work backwards from the sixteenth century when both the basic dimensions and the carrying capacity of the Venetian galleys are known. The latter was then about 280 metric tons, almost twice that of the approved fourteenth-century galley.[67]

If one asks when the substantial increase in size above 170 tons took place, the answers depend on whether certain crucial Venetian regulations refer to the heavy pound or the light pound. The heavy pound (equal to 477 grams) was used for salt, metals, etc.; the light pound (equal to 301 grams) was used for spices, cotton, and such relatively

---

[64] M. Pardessus, *Collection de droit maritime* (6 vols.; Paris, 1828–45), IV, 445–47, 450, 456–57, 512–13.

[65] On Genoese crews, *ibid.*, pp. 439–40; on Venetian unarmed galleys, see p. 235, n. 21, above. A Genoese "galea grossa de Fiandra" is referred to in 1329 in Renée Doehaerd, *Les Rélations commerciales entre Gênes, la Belgique et l'Outremont d'après les archives notariales génoises,* Vol. III of *Études d'histoire économique et sociale,* IV Institut Historique Belge de Rome, Brussels and Rome, pp. 1, 162.

[66] Heers, *Gênes,* p. 270.

[67] Marino Sanuto calls 400 to 440 *colli* the cargo of a galley and reports that the galleys of Alexandria in 1501 brought an average of 428 *colli* per galley; in 1502, 410 *colli*. Sanuto, *I diarii,* IV, 49, 260, 281; V, 78. Merchant records show that the *collo* equalled about 1,090 lbs. Eng. (495 kg.) so that the spice cargoes were 450,000 to 470,000 lbs., roughly 230 metric tons, and we must allow for some other cargo. This accords with the indications of A.S.V. Senato Terra, reg. 8, fol. 114, cited in n. 74 below. In 1520 the size was limited by reducing the length to 132½ feet, Ven. (Senato Mar, reg. 19, fol. 126) but it was increased again in 1549, as were other measures correspondingly. Senato Mar, reg. 30, fol. 37 and files under 17 Feb. 1548/9. These

TABLE I. SIZE OF MERCHANT GALLEYS

Date	Type	Length	Breadth	Depth	Index ($L \times B \times D$)	Legally below deck	Cargo in metric tons Total commercial cargo (estimated)
1318	Venetian, for voyage to Cyprus	40.4	5.3	2.4	513.9	—	110
1320	Venetian, for voyage to Flanders	40.4	5.7	2.4	552.7	90	115
1333	Genoese light merchant galley	40.5	4.75	2.1	404.0	—	90
1356	Venetian, for Flanders	—	—	—	—	140	170
c. 1420	Venetian, for Flanders	41.2	6	2.7	667.4	140	170
1422	Florentine large merchant galley	42.2	7.9	2.8	933.5	200	240
1454	Genoese *galee bastarde*	41.25	5	2	412.5	—	100
1481	Venetian merchant galley					220	260
c. 1500–20	Venetian merchant galley	47.8	8	3.1	1,185.4	240	280
1520–49	Venetian merchant galley	46.1	7.5	3	1,037.2	—	260
1549–59	Venetian merchant galley	47.8	8	3.1	1,185.4	—	280

For sources see nn. 57–76.

bulky goods.[68] In the fourteenth century the laws limiting the cargoes of galleys explicitly declare whether they are expressed in the heavy pound or the light pound. Sometimes one is used, sometime the other.[69] In regulations of the fifteenth and sixteenth centuries the kind of pound is not specified. One might assume that the heavy pound is meant because that assumption accords with other facts when applied to the many references to *milliaria* in the thirteenth-century Venetian maritime statutes. But there are two kinds of evidence indicating that the light pound is referred to in a law of 1440 which complains that the galleys exceed 500 *milliaria* and requires that they be reduced.[70] (1) The dimensions of Venetian galleys in the opening decades of the fifteenth century were not very much larger than they had been in 1320.[71] It is clear then that they doubled in size, approximately, some

larger measures are almost the same as those given with detail about their application in a shipbuilder's notes of mid-century. See pp. 163–70 for discussion.

[68] De Paxi, ed. of 1557, p. 23; Lane, *Venetian Ships*, p. 245.

[69] See nn. 61 and 62 above.

[70] The law (Senato Misti, reg. 60, fol. 249) set future limits between 400 and 440 for the largest type of galley. A smaller type sent to the Tana and Trebizond carried 300 to 320 *milliaria* at that time. Senato Mar, reg. 1, fol. 13. A contemporary chronicler, Antonio Morosini, gives the same *portada* for the galleys but also does not specify whether they are *miera* of the light or heavy pound.

[71] The dimensions attributed to the early fifteenth century are from the Fabrica di Galere which it is difficult to date precisely, but which refers to galleys built by Baxon, who was active in the Arsenal in the first years of the century. See pp. 164–65.

time during the fifteenth century. See table on p. 369. (2) A law about freight rates in 1453 is accompanied by a notation calculating how much freight would be collected on 430 *milliaria*.[72] Since freights were set in thousandweights of the light pound,[73] this indicates that as late as 1453 the legal load of the holds of these galleys was only about 150 metric tons. Of course the galleys were not perfectly standardized in size, the laws not perfectly obeyed, and the change gradual, but the evidence above cited indicates that the increase in size occurred mainly shortly before 1480 when the merchant galleys reached the dimension that became standard in the sixteenth century.[74]

The "tonnage" of great galleys should be thought of as more than twice the commercial cargo indicated on the table if "tonnage" is considered a measure of the size and total capacity of the ship, since one should consider for that purpose not only the commercial cargo in the holds but also the armament, equipment, crew, and passengers. There were relatively large compartments below deck reserved for food and for arms, as well as cabins for the officers and their friends. On deck were the crews of 180 (in 1307) to 210 (after 1412) and their personal possessions, including some large chests. Contemporaries who took these things into account considered the galley of about 1500, for which the table gives 260 or 280 metric tons, as the equivalent of a round ship of about 1000 *botti,* namely about 600 metric tons burden.[75] In the same way a fourteenth-century galley with 150 metric tons of cargo in the hold was considered the equal of a round ship of 500 *botti,* about 300 metric tons burden.[76]

---

[72] A.S.V. Senato Terra, reg. 3, fol. 75.

[73] *Delib. dei Rogati* (ed. Cessi) , I, p. 152, No. 74; Pegolotti (ed. Evans) , p. 144.

[74] In 1481 on complaint that the galleys were of 500 to 600 *milliaria* and too big to be manageable, the maximum was set at 450 *milliaria.* A.S.V. Senato Terra, reg. 8, fol. 114. Whatever its intent, this law must have been interpreted as meaning 450 *milliaria grossorum* in view of the sizes indicated about 1500. See n. 67 above.

[75] *Relatione del S. Pietro Martire, Milanese, recate nella italiana di Carlo Passi* (Venice, 1564) , p. 8.

[76] A.S.V. Senato Misti, reg. 58, fol. 27 (May 18, 1383) . The galleys built by the Florentines in 1422 were said by the contemporary chronicler, the same who gives their dimensions, to be "di portata di 400 botti." Sapori interprets this for reasons he does not make clear to mean that they were of 400–450 *tonnellate.* Armando Sapori, "I Primi viaggi di Levante et di Ponente delle galere Fiorentine," *Archivio storico italiano,* CXIV (1956) , 77.

Part Three

THE COST OF PROTECTION

22

National Wealth and Protection Costs*

S POKESMEN for modern imperialism repeat the faith of the mercantilists that war is an instrument which can and should be
used to increase national prosperity. In that tradition, arms are also
viewed as a means to the high end, power, but wealth is said to depend
on power just as power depends on wealth. Accordingly, one school of
writers regards the defeat of the Spanish Armada as a fact of major
importance for the increase of the wealth of Britain. Another school,
more devoutly attached to the faith of Adam Smith, minimizes the
economic consequences of military successes.[1] A reconciliation of the
conflicting traditions is hardly to be expected, but perhaps more could
be done than has been done to apply the economists' traditional style of
thought to some aspects of non-peaceful behavior. Before attempting to
describe in these terms specific historical situations, it is necessary to
clarify the starting points of the analysis.

* This paper was read at the meeting of the American Historical Association in
December, 1940, and published with other papers presented at that meeting in Jesse
Clarkson and Thomas C. Cochran (eds.), *War as a Social Institution: The Historian's Perspective* (New York, 1941), pp. 32–43. Before he was aware of this plan
of publication, the author had submitted a longer version to the *Journal of Social
Philosophy and Jurisprudence* (see below, Chapter 23), but he eliminated from that
more theoretical version the details included in this paper concerning the price of
spices before and after the Portugese discoveries. Both these articles are included
here because of differences of content and phraseology. (This paper is reprinted by
permission.)

[1] The efficacy of the use of force is not, of course, the only point at issue between
the two traditions. The general conflict and its implications in historical writing
were stated particularly clearly and thoughtfully by George Unwin. See, for example,
his remarks on the assumptions of Professor W. E. Lingelbach and the assertions of
B. Hagedorn. *Studies in Economic History: The Collected Papers of George Unwin*
(London, 1927), pp. 134–35, 168, 215–16. Unwin even denied that force was a decisive factor in the expansion of Britain. *Ibid.*, pp. 341–43, and cf. pp. 23–28, 224–25.

An essential charge on any economic enterprise is the cost of its protection, its protection from disruption by violence. Different enterprises competing in the same market often pay different costs of protection, perhaps as tariffs, or bribes, perhaps in some other form. The difference between the protection costs forms one element in the income of the enterprise enjoying the lower protection cost. This element in income I will call protection rent. Just as differences in the fertility of land produce rents for the owners of the more productive fields, so differences in the difficulties of protection produce rents for the enterprises which are more easily or efficiently protected. To the categories traditional with the economists, that is, wages, interest, and land rent, can be added for present purposes the category protection rent.[2]

How a change in protection costs could shift a carrying trade from one nation to another is illustrated by the trade of the West Indies at the time of Colbert. At the beginning of his ministry the trade of those islands was conducted almost entirely by Dutch enterprise, and there is every indication that under free competition without the interference of armed force the Dutch would have continued to underbid competitors. At Colbert's direction not only was the Dutch trade declared illegal, but a fleet of three naval vessels was sent to seize the Dutch ships visiting French islands. This use of armed force caused the Dutch some loss, threatened them with more losses, and increased the cost of "protection" for those Dutch who continued to trade as smugglers. At the time of Colbert's death some 200 French ships were receiving passports each year for voyages to the French West Indies. By raising the protection costs of the Dutch, Colbert had given the French the advantage of a protection rent and so made the West Indies trade profitable for French enterprises.

But profits for French enterprises trading to the French West Indies did not necessarily mean a profit for France as a whole—did not necessarily mean any increase in the total national income of France. The protection costs compared so far were those of private French trading enterprises and those of private Dutch trading enterprises. In order to discuss French national income, a way must be found of balancing against the profits made by French traders to the West Indies such items as the cost to France of maintaining naval squadrons there. In short we must consider protection costs from the point of view of the nation.

---

[2] The way protection is usually dismissed by economists is illustrated by L. M. Fraser, *Economic Thought and Language* (London, 1937) , p. 210 and n.

As soon as we adopt this point of view, it is necessary to stretch the meaning of the word protection. Under national protection costs are to be included not only what is spent by a nation for the defense of the economic enterprises of its own members, but also what the nation spends in raising the protection costs of competing enterprises of other nations. Besides protection costs which are obviously defensive—such as the cost of convoys for defense against pirates—there are others which may be called offensive protection costs. Perhaps to include these the term "political costs" would be preferable, but the word "political" is too vague. The phrase "national protection costs," whatever the verbal contradiction in applying it to aggressive actions, at least preserves the suggestion of the use of armed force. I shall use it to cover all the expenditures by which a nation seeks to create protection rents in favor of its own enterprises. In modern times many such expenditures, for example the expense of maintaining a permanent navy, may be regarded as overhead costs. Allotting the cost of a navy to various branches of trade would be as difficult to a cost accountant as the problem of allotting the cost of a dam between its various uses for power production, irrigation, and flood control, but perhaps no more puzzling. This difficulty is less in the study of medieval and early times because force was then more commonly exerted in direct connection with particular commercial activities and there is more basis for estimating how much a particular branch of trade added to national protection costs.

To discover the effect on national income, involves considering also the national opportunity cost of the new enterprises, that is, the cost of violating the law of comparative advantage. As Adam Smith argued so convincingly in similar cases, goods could have been more cheaply obtained in the West Indies, and West Indian wares could have been more cheaply obtained in France, if the transport had been left to the Dutch, and that French capital and labor which was in fact diverted to the West Indies trade had been allowed to find employment according to "the system of natural liberty." The profits of the new French enterprises were being paid for not only in royal outlay on the naval squadron, but also in the higher freights on shipments between France and the West Indies.

Only by dealing with all these factors can one estimate, even roughly, the effects of Colbert's West Indian policy on French wealth. Against the addition to the national income embodied in the profits of the French West Indian traders and shippers must be balanced a formidable array of losses. First, obviously, there is the big deficit of the

French West India Company, which pioneered the voyage; then the cost of employing a French naval squadron. Since the exclusion of the Dutch from the West Indies was one of the reasons for the outbreak of the war between France and Holland in 1672, some part of the expense of that war would have to be considered also. To allow for the national opportunity costs, the price of sugar to French consumers would have to be investigated, and if the islanders are counted part of the French nation, we must add the loss they suffered in paying prices for supplies two or three times as high as those previously charged by the Dutch. Even in authors sympathetic to Colbert the evidence presented fails, when all these factors are considered, to indicate that any gain in national income resulted during Colbert's lifetime from the capture of the trade.[3]

A more complicated case of seeking to increase national wealth by the use of military power is the temporary capture of the spice trade by the Portuguese. Protection costs were always especially prominent in determining who should handle the spices which moved from the Indian Ocean to Europe. In the second half of the fifteenth century most of them were carried by Arab merchants from India to Jeddah in the Red Sea. There they came under the protection of the Soldan of Egypt and passed through his lands, paying dearly on the way for his protection, until at Alexandria they were sold to the Venetians and other Europeans. When the Portuguese reached India by circumnavigating Africa, it was feared that they would ruin the Venetians by selling for less than the prices the Venetians were accustomed to charge. The often-quoted Venetian merchant banker, Gerolamo Priuli, prophesied in his diary that the Portuguese would be able to undersell the Venetians because the spices brought around Africa would not have to pay the high taxes levied on the spices which passed through Egypt.[4] Priuli expected the Cape route to prove cheaper because of lower protection costs.

This is *not* what happened. The Portuguese did *not* set their prices below those common at Venice in the fifteenth century. True, the Portuguese did, for a short time, capture most of the spice trade, but by methods which raised prices rather than lowered them. The Portuguese king attempted to prevent by armed force the passage of any spices

---

[3] Stewart L. Mims, *Colbert's West India Policy* (New Haven, 1912) ; and Charles Wolsey Cole, *Colbert and a Century of French Mercantilism* (New York, 1939).

[4] Girolamo Priuli, *I diarii* (Vol. I, Città di Castello, 1911; Vol. II, Bologna, 1933), in *Rerum Italicarum scriptores,* 2d ed.; II, Tome XXIV, Part III, 156.

from India to the Red Sea or Persian Gulf. He staked his hopes of profit on securing a monopoly. Although his success was not complete, Portuguese seizure of sources of supply, the destruction of Arab ships, and the risk of capture for others was sufficient for some decades to raise greatly the protection costs of the Red Sea route. Consequently, the Portuguese king was able to sell for prices higher than those the Venetians had received in the fifteenth century before Vasco da Gama rounded the Cape.

Since Priuli's prophecy has often been mistaken for a true statement of what happened, it may be worth while to give a few details on the price of pepper, that "king of the spices" which the Portuguese king tried hardest and most successfully to monopolize. Prior to the war between Turkey and Venice in 1499, pepper was selling at Venice for 42 to 57 ducats a *cargo*. War and speculation then drove the price up momentarily to 131, but that was a most exceptional figure.[5] For more than a half century before the interference of the Portuguese, the typical Venetian wholesale price had been about 50 ducats.[6]

When news reached Venice in November 1501 that the Portuguese had sunk Arab spice ships, pepper again rose at Venice and for a few years remained between 80 and 100. From this high level the price fell, first at Lisbon and then at Venice after the return of Vasco da Gama's second fleet. The king of Portugal fixed his price in 1506 at the equivalent of 52 ducats a *cargo,* and in 1509 Venetian prices were only slightly above that figure.[7] In short, the first shock of Portuguese interference raised prices at Venice. As soon as the Portuguese voyages were in full operation prices dipped to, but not below, the fifteenth-century level. This conclusion is based primarily on quotations of the Venetian

[5] Priuli, *Diarii,* I, 16, 48, 65, 75, 143, 159, 238; II, 74, 111; Marino Sanuto, *I diarii,* eds. Rinaldo Fulin and others under the auspices of the R. Dep. Veneta di Storia Patria (Venice, 1879–1903), III, col. 1445.

[6] This conclusion is based not only on the quotations for the few years given by Priuli but also on quotations for more than a dozen scattered years earlier in the fifteenth century, quotations found mainly in merchants' letters and account books in the Archivio di Stato at Venice. I am indebted to the Social Science Research Council for a grant-in-aid which made it possible to use material in Venice.

[7] Priuli, *Diarii,* II, 335, 431; Rinaldo Fulin, *Diarii e diaristi veneziani* (Venice, 1881), pp. 165–68, 174, 178, 188, 191–92, 203, 206, 208, 211; Sanuto, *Diarii,* V, cols. 133–34, 319, VI, col. 384, XI, col. 672; Eugenio Alberi, *Le relazioni degli ambasciatori veneti al senato* (Florence, 1863), XV or Appendix, 13, in the report of Vincenzo Quirini; J. Lucio de Azevedo, *Epocas de Portugal Economico* (Lisbon, 1929), pp. 94–95, 110, 127.

wholesale market but agrees with what little evidence is available concerning the prices paid by English and German consumers.[8]

During the twenty years after 1506 the general trend of pepper prices was upward, more steeply upward than can be explained by the influx of precious metals from America to Europe. The prices charged at Antwerp by the Portuguese rose about 66 per cent between 1509 and 1527.[9] At Venice the pepper received from Egypt was selling as high as 110 ducats a *cargo* in 1520 and, in hopes of buying more cheaply at Lisbon, Venetian galleys were ordered to call there. But when the galleys reached Lisbon in January 1522, one of the merchants wrote home that Lisbon prices were so high no one would think of buying for cash although there might be some barter. Pepper was selling at Lisbon at the equivalent of 83 ducats a *cargo*,[10] well above the fifteenth-century Venetian price of 50 ducats. These prices show that the tight grip which the Portuguese had on the pepper trade in the fifteen twenties did not depend on their selling more cheaply than the Venetians had sold in the fifteenth century. The Portuguese had seized the pepper trade by increasing the protection costs of their Arab and Venetian competitors.

But at the same time the Portuguese king had created for his own spice-trading enterprise some high protection costs also, the costs of overawing Indian princes, seizing trading posts, and maintaining naval control of the Indian Ocean. These were the king's means of raising the protection costs of his competitors and were therefore what I have called an offensive protection cost comparable to the cost of the fleets which Colbert sent to patrol the West Indies. But whereas in Colbert's France the profits of the private French traders to the West Indies and the cost of the naval squadron fell on enterprises entirely separate in their direction and their accounting, in Portugal the bulk of the profits from the sale of spices came into the hands of the same entrepreneur who paid the offensive protection cost, namely, the king. This cost appeared in the deficits of the *Estado da India* and in the expenses for sending out from Portugal soldiers and warships for operations in

---

[8] In the recently published studies of the price revolution, the only series of pepper prices I have found sufficiently complete in these years are those for Klosterneuburg. A. F. Pribram, *Materialien zur Geschichte der Preise und Löhne in Osterreich* (Vienna, 1938), I, 615. Pepper prices for Cambridge are given in J. E. Thorold Rogers, *A History of Agriculture and Prices in England* (Oxford, 1882), III, 521.

[9] Braamcamp Freire, *Maria Brandão, a do Crisfal: Vol. II, A Feitoria de Flandres* ("Archivo Historico Portuguez"), VI, 414; VIII, 24.

[10] Sanuto, *Diarii,* XXXIII, 177–79.

India. Hence, historians have some basis for estimating the financial results of this royal enterprise which combined spice trading with military action. Charles de Lannoy figured that by 1580 the king obtained at the most 250,000 ducats a year net from the spice fleets, a figure which allowed for wrecks but did not allow sufficiently for the many cases of spending one to three hundred thousand ducats in reinforcing the Indian army and navy.[11] Lucio de Azevedo, taking into account all the military expenses, asserts, "The truth is that only in the period of conquest did India pay its cost . . ." and then, as he says, only by booty, tribute, prizes and the ransom of Moors.[12] Historians of the Portuguese empire seem generally agreed that the riches prophesied by Albuquerque proved a mirage. Long before the Spanish conquest of Portugal the inefficiency of the Portuguese system of government and trade was such that the costs of the Indian empire, added to the then considerable loss of ships, threatened to consume all the spice profits of the king. The offensive protection costs of the royal Portuguese enterprise were proving excessive.

Meanwhile the progressive inefficiency or corruption of the Portuguese government in India and the efforts of the Ottoman Turks lowered somewhat the protection costs of the Red Sea route. At times the protection costs of the Portuguese king may have been the higher, a possibility which helps explain the revival of spice exports from Alexandria to Europe in the second half of the sixteenth century.

About 1560 Venice and other Mediterranean ports regained a substantial part of the spice trade.[13] Why, one might ask, did not the king of Portugal lower spice prices as soon as the Venetians or French threatened to take his business? Was not the all-water route around the Cape cheaper from a purely economic point of view, so that he could undersell the Venetians even if he did fail to keep the protection costs of the Red Sea route as high as in 1520? The greater economy of the Cape route, apart from protection costs, is difficult to demonstrate. Contradictory assertions on the subject are easy to find,[14] but any calculation which ignored protection costs would be irrelevant to the

---

[11] *Histoire de l'expansion des peuples européens* (Brussels, 1907), I, 191–202.

[12] *Epocas de Portugal economico,* p. 155; cf. also pp. 118–31. Francisco Antonio Correa, *Historia economica de Portugal* (Lisbon, 1929), I, 194–95.

[13] See Chapter 2 above for discussion.

[14] A. H. Lybyer, "The Ottoman Turks and the Routes of Oriental Trade," *English Historical Review,* XXX (1915), 587; François Charles-Roux, *Autour d'une route: l'Angleterre l'isthme de Suez e l'Égypte au xviii siècle* (Paris, 1922), pp. 14–15; Halford Lancaster Hoskins, *British Routes to India* (Philadelphia, 1928), pp. 9, 43.

present problem. In trying to cut off the Red Sea route the Portuguese king had assumed high protection costs for his own enterprise. He could not later lower spice prices substantially and still cover his own costs—not, at least, while his Eastern empire was so thoroughly permeated with inefficiency and corruption. That much at least is clearly implied by the statements of Azevedo and others concerning Portuguese finances.

Turning now from the Portuguese capture of the spice trade and the nature of that "capture" to its effects on the prosperity of Portugal, we enter the field of conjecture, one in which profits from the spice trade and from pure plundering can hardly be distinguished. When Lucio de Azevedo says that the cost of the Indian empire exceeded the receipts, he seems to include under the costs the salaries and pensions with which the Portuguese king rewarded the nobles who conquered and governed the empire. In so far as these rewards came directly or indirectly from the empire, they made the income of the nobles greater than it would otherwise have been and accordingly they represent an addition to the national income. Royal officials in India also increased their revenue illegally from booty, bribes, and private trade. The revival of the Red Sea route did not interfere with these illegal forms of revenue, since Portuguese officials could grow rich on the bribes paid them for their "protection" of Arab traders. There seems no doubt that Portuguese national income increased for a time. Even the Portuguese kings, whatever the condition of their treasury, so enhanced their credit through the possession of spices that they were able to borrow extensively from international bankers and suspend payments in the grand manner, like their fellow sovereigns, in the third quarter of the sixteenth century.

Before deciding whether the Portuguese military action in India was profitable to the nation, one must consider in this case, as in connection with Colbert's activities, the opportunity cost. Could Portuguese capital and labor, assuming the same geographic discoveries and the same skill in navigation, have been used more profitably in some other way than that to which it was directed by military action in the Indian Ocean? Admittedly it is difficult for even a lively historical imagination to conceive how Portugal could have followed in this case "nature's simple plan," but the question must be faced if the Smithian point of view is to be dealt with at all. And some contemporaries did in fact conceive policies requiring far less military action. Gerolamo Priuli was not the only Venetian observer who considered whether the Portuguese might not operate advantageously, without enforcing a monopoly, simply because their new route would enable them to avoid the high taxes formerly paid in Egypt.[15] But the Portuguese soon showed that they intended to depend on force, and by basing their hopes of profit on raising the protection costs of their rivals, the kings of Portugal diverted Portuguese labor and capital from the commercial development of the voyage and focused the energies of their people on war, plunder, and the taking of bribes.

In the long run of fifty or a hundred years, a more peaceful policy, fostering a greater development of the Eastern trade, might have made the nation richer. Although the conquest of India increased Portuguese national income for a time, it was followed by a decrease later in the productivity of the nation's labor. It does not therefore supply a clear case of success in using armed force to increase the nation's prosperity.

But can we not find an opposite case, an example of a use of armed force which, although decreasing the national income temporarily, may have increased its productive capacity in the long run? The previous discussion of Colbert's West India policy considered its effects on French national income in the short run only. Looking at the policy from the long run historical point of view, Professor Mims concluded: "In reality their development [that of the West India colonies] proved to be the most valuable colonial asset which France possessed and contributed more to her commercial prosperity than any other single branch of trade."[16] By stimulating the French West Indian commerce Colbert fostered the development in France of a certain type of labor and capital which proved in the long run of a hundred years exceptionally productive.

By various measures, many of which depended on armed force, the mercantilists strove to increase the proportions of their nations' capital and labor devoted to oceanic commerce and to manufacturing for export. Thereby they diverted capital and labor from employments in which, according to nature's simple plan, they would have produced *at the time* more national income.[17] But oceanic commerce and manufacturing were to prove, in the long run of a couple of centuries, those

[15] Alberi, *Le relazioni,* XV or Appendix, 15–19; Leonardo de Ca' Masser, *Relazione sopra il commercio dei Portoghesi nell'India, 1497–1506* ("Archivio storico italiano"), Appendix, II, 34 (1845).

[16] *Colbert's West India Policy* (New Haven, 1912), p. 339. On the East India Company, cf. C. W. Cole, *Colbert and a Century of French Mercantilism* (New York, 1939), I, 523.

[17] The conflict between Colbert and conservative merchants, at Bordeaux at least, seems to me to have been such a conflict between the concern of the merchants with present profits and the ambitions of Colbert for the future. See Chap. 19, above.

branches of economic activity capable of the greatest expansion. The distinguished continuator of the Smithian tradition, Alfred Marshall, admits that the national income of England depended much in the eighteenth century, and even more in the nineteenth, on "the action of the law of increasing return with regard to her exports."[18] Colbert did not, to be sure, think in terms of "a law of increasing return" and he was more interested in power than in plenty. But in so far as Colbert diverted capital and labor from conspicuous consumption or from agricultural investments which were subject to the law of decreasing return, and directed them into commercial and industrial activities which in the future were to yield increasing return, his activity as a statesman did contribute to the future wealth of France.

Of course, armed force was not the only form of state activity used by mercantilists to canalize economic activities, and in many cases it is practically impossible to distinguish the particular effects which should be attributed to the use of force. All attempts at explaining secular trends in national wealth must be tentative because of the number of factors involved. Explanations in terms of a single factor are properly suspect, and economists may well condemn those which are simply references to military victories. But such victories do, in some cases, change the protection costs borne by a nation's enterprises and so affect both the distribution of income within the nation and the growth or decline of the whole national income.

[18] Alfred Marshall, *Principles of Economics* (8th ed.; London, 1936) , p. 672.

23

The Economic Meaning
of War and Protection*

B ECAUSE wars reduce national wealth in many ways it is often
said that even for the victors wars never pay and never
have paid except under quite primitive conditions. On the other hand,
one of the ways in which an individual may gain his livelihood is by
specializing in the use of force, and history records many groups of men
famous mainly for their efficiency in war who gained relatively great
wealth. Of course they had to live in a society with others engaged in
occupations more commonly called productive. Cannot a nation,
living in a relation of give and take with other nations, similarly add to
its income by showing superiority over others in its ability to use force?
Some of its capital and labor will have to be diverted from other
employments, but it may be argued that under some circumstances war
is the employment which will be most productive of national income.
Although economists have done little to define the conditions under
which the use of force may be the most advantageous of occupations,
their usual method of theoretical analysis seems applicable to this
problem so long as it is admitted that the use of force may be productive of a utility. That utility is protection.

Every economic enterprise needs and pays for protection, protection
against the destruction or armed seizure of its capital and the forceful
disruption of its labor. In highly organized societies the production of

*Journal of Social Philosophy and Jurisprudence, VII (1942), 254–70. (By per-
mission.) See the prefatory footnote to Chapter 22, above.

this utility, protection, is one of the functions of a special association or enterprise called government. Indeed, one of the most distinctive characteristics of governments is their attempt to create law and order by using force themselves and by controlling through various means the use of force by others. The more successful a government is in monopolizing all use of force between men within a particular area, the more efficient is its maintenance of law and order. Accordingly, the production of protection is a natural monopoly. The territorial extent of this monopoly is prescribed more or less loosely by military geography and historical circumstances. Breaks in the monopoly occur, as when there is an insurrection or a boom in the rackets of gangsters, but such rival enterprises in the use of force substitute monopolies of their own if successful. These illegal monopolies may be quite transitory and highly localized, perhaps as fleeting as that of the stick-up man who finishes his robbery before the policeman comes around the corner. When, as in that exteme example, no protection is given against immediate additional seizure by the same bandit or some other user of violence, it is a clear case of plunder. Both the history of nations and the stories of gangsters contain plenty of borderline cases, but clearly force is not only used in plundering but also in preventing plundering, and a government which maintains law and order is rendering a service in return for the payment it collects.

The cost of producing this service varies greatly and affects the size of the real national income since the amount of goods and services other than protection which can be distributed to the nation is reduced when more capital and labor is employed in the production of protection.[1] Sometimes, as in the recent Spanish civil war, internal conflicts prevent any single enterprise from securing general recognition as the only legitimate monopolist of force and so reducing its costs. Sometimes fear of powerful neighbors causes more to be spent on arms. In the United States the amount of our nation's capital and labor now being employed for the production of protection is strikingly larger than the amount so employed a few years ago. Some nations have lower protection costs than others because of their cultural heritage or geographic position. A nation with easily defended frontiers, for example, may have a lower protection cost due to this gift of nature. The United States still devotes to the production of other goods a larger proportion of its productive capacity than does Great Britain, and our geographic

---

[1] Assuming no change in the extent to which the nation's capital and labor is employed in some form of production.

position has, so far, enabled us to enjoy more protection while paying less for it.[2]

Thus broadly stated from a national point of view, the importance of protection as a factor in production is easily recognized. But from the point of view of private economic enterprises the relation is frequently obscured. The ordinary economic enterprise operating within the territory of a government which has a monopoly of the use of force pays for protection in the process of paying taxes. Of many an individual entrepreneur it can be said that he does not normally "vary the *amount* of 'law and order,' or security, by variations in the taxes he pays." To him, ". . . law and order is in general a free good, in the sense that any payment which must be made for it will presumably come out of general taxation and will not be counted as specific expense of production at all."[3] In this way economists generally dismiss protection from their calculations. But even for individual economic enterprises, protection costs are variable and to a significant extent affect the earnings of such enterprises. What they pay in taxes can in some cases be reduced by paying for protection in some other form—by lobbying, by bribes, or even by revolution.[4] To be sure, changes in protection cost are not often effected by an individual entrepreneur acting by and for himself alone. They are generally effected by group decision and group action. The decisions are made by governments in consultation with and for the benefit of a group of enterprises. They involve action in the forum and perhaps on the battlefield as well as in the market place or factory, but in so far as they are attempts to gain a utility at minimum cost they are subject to economic analysis. When an associate of Cecil Rhodes estimated that "good government" in the Boer states would bring a saving of six shillings per ton on gold ore production costs and an increase in consequence of $12,000,000 a year in dividends, we may say that protection was being included by an entrepreneur among the factors of production and the principle of substitution was about to be applied.[5]

For individual enterprises engaged in international trade protection hardly ever appears a free good. Costs of protection are vital factors in production since their variations frequently determine profits. Competing enterprises are subject to different governments, and pay in taxes

[2] This article was written and submitted before December 7, 1941. [Editor of the *Journal*]

[3] L. M. Fraser, *Economic Thought and Language* (London, 1937) , p. 210 and note.

[4] *Ibid.*, note.

[5] Parker Thomas Moon, *Imperialism and World Politics* (New York, 1926) , p. 174.

and tariffs different costs of protection. Usually they pay at least two governments for protection and not infrequently they hope that the action of one government, which they call their own, will effect a reduction in what they pay to another government. For that purpose they can afford to increase their payments to their own government if their total protection costs, the sum of their payments to both governments, will be reduced.

To isolate the element in business profits which results from minimized protection costs, imagine a case of various enterprises competing in the same market and having the same costs except that they pay different costs of protection. The sale price of their product will be high enough to cover the highest protection cost, namely that of the marginal producer whose offering is needed to satisfy the demand. The profits of the enterprises enjoying lower protection costs will include the difference between their protection costs and that of the marginal competitor. This difference I will call protection rent. Just as differences in the fertility of land result in rents to owners of more fertile fields, so differences in the ease of securing protection result in returns to enterprises which enjoy cheaper protection, returns for which the best name seems to be protection rent.[6]

The simplest illustration of such a protection rent is provided by enterprises competing under a tariff differential. For example, Hawaiian sugar was admitted to the United States free of duty from 1876 to 1890 while to meet the American demand much sugar was being imported from Cuba or Java. These full duty imports were the marginal supply and fixed the price. The Hawaiian producers received a

[6] The term protection rent seems preferable to the term protection profit because this element in income arises so largely from conditions which are beyond the control of the individual entrepreneur and are unaffected by his ability as a business manager. Admittedly the analogy to land rent is imperfect. Land rent normally refers to what an entrepreneur pays for the use of land, whereas protection rent does not refer to what an entrepreneur pays for protection, for that payment is here called protection cost. In the case outlined in the text, the protection rent is paid by the consumer; it is what he pays to secure the offering of the producer whose offering is marginal by reason of high protection costs.

If we look at protection rent from the point of view of the nation, instead of looking at it as in the text above from the point of view of individual enterprises, we may say that protection rent for a nation arises from the geographical or cultural conditions which make the production of protection easier for one nation than for another. These conditions may be called gifts of nature or gifts of history. Whether the protection rent will be collected by the government or will be passed on to private enterprises depends, as is indicated below in note 10, on the form of government.

protection rent of two cents a pound.[7] Other examples abound in the history of the wealth of nations and the analysis of a few instances in which protection rents determined major changes in international trade will assist an analysis of the possibilities of increasing national income by the use of force.

The Venetians obtained in 1082 a charter exempting them from all tariffs in the Byzantine Empire and thus secured a differential in their favor even against the Greeks. These privileges were secured by placing the Venetian navy at the service of the Byzantine emperor in his war against the Norman king of Sicily. For more than a hundred years they were renewed or elaborated by continued use of Venetian arms, sometimes against the enemies of Byzantium, sometimes against the Byzantine emperor himself to compel renewal of the charter. The privileges were used in trade between different parts of the Byzantine Empire and between that empire and other markets of the Levant as well as in trade between East and West. The Venetians alone did not satisfy all demands for commercial interchange within so large a field. Although their earlier chief rivals, the Amalfitans, were soon reduced to insignificance, the Venetians continued to have competitors, not only the Greek and Jewish subjects of the Byzantine emperor, but also new groups, the Pisans who paid a tariff of 4 per cent and the Genoese who paid the usual 10 per cent until 1155 and then 4 per cent.[8] Since such merchants found the trade worthwhile they too must have been necessary to meet the demand. Among them were the "marginal producers." The Venetians were able to sell wares at prices which must often have been higher by reason of the higher protection costs of less privileged traders. Consequently the profits of the Venetian merchants in that area were swelled by fat protection rents procured for them by their government's use of its naval power.

At a much later date, the trade of the French West Indies at the time of Colbert illustrates how a government could, by changing protection

---

[7] Frank William Taussig, *Some Aspects of the Tariff Question* (Cambridge, Mass., 1915), Chaps. iv and v. The protection rent was, to a certain extent, a result of the strategic geographical position of the islands.

[8] H. Kretschmayr, *Geschichte von Venedig* (Gotha, 1905), I, 361–64; Adolf Schaube, *Handelsgeschichte der romanischen Völker des Mittelmeergebiets bit zum Ende der Kreuzzüge* (Munich and Berlin, 1906), pp. 226, 229. For the full story of Venetian-Byzantine relations see Kretschmayr, I, Chaps. vii and viii; Schaube, pp. 19–25, 223–47; Wilhelm von Heyd, *Histoire du commerce du levant au moyen âge* (Leipzig, 1886), I, 116–20, and Richard Heynen, *Zur Entstehung des Kapitalismus in Venedig* (Stuttgart and Berlin, 1905), Chaps. iii–v.

costs, shift a carrying trade from one nation to another. The trade of the French islands was almost entirely in the hands of Dutch enterprises when Colbert became minister, and there is every indication that the Dutch would have had no difficulty holding their own against possible French competitors if there had been no appeal to force. Under Colbert's direction the Dutch trade was declared illegal and a fleet of three naval vessels was sent to seize any Dutch ships visiting the French islands. This caused the Dutch some loss, threatened them with more, and increased the cost of protection of those who continued to trade as smugglers. When Colbert died, some two hundred French ships were receiving passports each year for voyages to the French West Indies. The rise in the protection costs of the Dutch had made the trade profitable for French enterprises by giving them protection rents.[9]

But profits for French enterprises trading to the West Indies, or for Venetian enterprises trading in the Byzantine Empire, did not necessarily mean a profit for France or Venice as a whole—did not necessarily mean any increase in the totals of their national incomes. To consider the effects of these uses of force on national income, a way must be found to balance against the protection rents of the Venetian traders in the Byzantine Empire the cost of the naval action which secured their privileges, to balance against the profits made by French traders to the West Indies such expenses as that of maintaining naval squadrons there. In short we must investigate the *national* protection costs in these cases. And we must first inquire further into what is to be included in these costs and what additions to national income besides protection rents they may produce.

When we adopt this point of view we can hardly avoid stretching the meaning of the word protection to include aggressive action. The cost of using armed force at sea and in lowering foreign tariffs must be counted, although protection on the high seas is not a natural monopoly and international trade, by definition, extends beyond the territory of any single government monopoly. In this connection there are some protection costs which are obviously defensive—such as the cost of convoys to ward off pirates; others—such as the cost of capturing ships of other nations engaged in competing enterprises—might be called offensive protection costs. But it would be useless to try to classify the suppression of smuggling as offensive or defensive action. Whatever the verbal contradiction involved in applying it to aggressive actions, one term is needed to cover both what a government spends to prevent

[9] Stewart L. Mims, *Colbert's West India Policy* (New Haven, 1912).

the plundering of its own enterprises and also what it spends in plundering enterprises of other nations; in attempting to create protection rents for its own enterprises, or in extending its monopoly of force so as to levy tribute.

By tribute it means payments received for protection, but payments in excess of the cost of producing the protection. The possibility of tribute arises from the fact that a government, like many another monopoly, does not need to sell its product at the cost of production. Most governments have been so constituted that ruling classes have been able to exploit these monopolies and raise the price of protection for other classes so as to increase their own incomes.[10] The tribute collected by one class from another need not in itself change the total of national income. It may merely move money from one pocket to another within the nation.[11] But tribute may be collected from outside the nation, and the income of a nation is increased by any sums which its ruling class is able to collect as tribute from members of some other nation. The Venetian penetration of the Byzantine Empire, for example, came to a dramatic climax in 1204. Finding a large supply of armed force, the knights of the Fourth Crusade, available for its purposes at bargain prices, Venice employed them to overthrow the Byzantine Empire and seize a portion of it. By that conquest the Venetians not only arranged to collect their protection rents for many more years but

[10] The possibilities are clarified by considering the two "ideal types" of states contrasted by A. De Viti de Marco, *Principii de economia finanziaria* (Turin, 1934), pp. 12–19. In the "ideal" popular state, in which all groups freely compete to arrive at power so that all equally shape the financial decisions of the government in their interests, the costs of protection for private enterprises would be equal to the cost to the government of producing their protection. In the "ideal" absolute state, or monopolistic state as De Viti there calls it, in which one man or one ruling class determines the financial decisions of the state entirely in their own interest, the government's monopoly of protection would be fully exploited. In the latter case the amount collected is not limited by the shape of the demand curve, since protection is a necessity, but it may be restrained by the danger that too high a tribute will stimulate attempts to break the monopoly, i.e., will attract invaders, stimulate smuggling, or provoke insurrection.

[11] If a ruling class collects more tribute and, while thus making its position more enviable, spends its added income on luxuries, it is more likely to be overthrown by invasion or insurrection. It has, in this sense, good reason to spend its increased income on armies or police forces. If it does so, the cost of production of protection in that society is thereby increased. Accordingly, the higher the tribute paid to a ruling class, especially a ruling class of military traditions, the higher is likely to be the cost of producing protection. Escapes from this vicious circle have come through the fact that most states have not been ruled simply by one all-powerful ruling class.

they also secured a sensational amount of booty and were enabled to levy tribute in the portion of the empire which passed under Venetian dominion. This tribute was paid by Greek subjects in taxes or in servile services and was received by Venetian nobles as manorial revenues or as salaries of government offices. Since it is readily admitted that plunder and tribute added to national wealth in earlier times, this conquest has been much emphasized. But the tariff privileges of the Venetians had gained them much wealth from the Byzantine Empire before they became strong enough to overthrow it; the growth of wealth in Venice during that period as a whole came less from booty and tribute than from protection rents.

The variety of uses to which may be put the force organized by governments makes the national cost of protection an overhead cost and creates the practical difficulties involved in allotting such costs. When the Venetians were fighting the Norman king of Sicily in 1081–84, they were acting not only to secure privileges in the Byzantine Empire but also to prevent the king from extending his rival monopoly of force over both sides of the Adriatic and Ionian Seas. Had he succeeded he would have been able to take plunder and tribute from the Venetians. The problem of allotting the cost of an army or navy is as difficult a problem in cost accounting as allotting the cost of a dam among its various uses for power production, irrigation, and flood control, but perhaps no more difficult. Defense of the home territory against the devastation of invasion may be compared to the prevention of floods in a populous country. At least such defense may be accepted as a starting point. Additions to national protection costs beyond that point may be judged profitable or unprofitable according to the amount they add to national income in the form of booty, tribute for the ruling class, or protection rents for privileged private enterprises. Colbert created a navy larger than was needed to prevent the plundering of France; its cost was predicated on the desirability of extending France's commercial and colonial empire. The cost of the portion of the navy used in the West Indies may fairly be alloted to whatever France gained by that commerce.

In estimating the cost to the nation of any acquisitions of booty, tribute, or protection rent, it is particularly important, and difficult, to reckon the opportunity costs. Allowance must be made for any violation of the law of comparative advantage involved either in the military effort or in the new enterprises created by the stimulus of the protection rents. For it is evident that all tariffs and forceful restraints involve less income immediately for someone than would have been gained if everyone concerned had acted freely, peacefully, without restraining or being restrained by force, and with a perfect eighteenth century reasonableness. As Adam Smith argued so convincingly in regard to similar cases, West Indian wares could have been sold more cheaply in France, and European wares would have been cheaper in the West Indies, if that trade had been left to the Dutch and if the French capital and labor, which was in fact diverted to the West Indies trade, had been allowed to find employment according to "the system of natural liberty." The protection rents of the new French enterprises were being paid for not only in royal expenditure on the naval squadron but also in higher prices paid by consumers both in France and in the French West Indies. On the other hand, the protection rents of Venetian traders in the Byzantine Empire, although dependent on the higher prices produced by the duties levied on their competitors, were not paid for in the main by Venetian consumers since relatively little of the merchandise found its ultimate market in Venice. The cost of the violation of the law of comparative advantage was borne by foreign consumers and was therefore no deduction from Venetian national income.

The only substantial opportunity cost to the Venetians was the opportunity cost of the war fleets by which their privileges were won. If the capital and labor employed in those war fleets had been secured by bidding for them in an open market against competing demands for their use in other activities—such as continuance of the trade without special privilege—then there would be no opportunity cost requiring special investigation. But most war fleets are not secured simply by competitive bidding in a free market and their costs are not therefore fully expressed by figures in a government budget. Although Colbert's navy was partly paid for at market prices and the squadron sent to the West Indies was too small to make the difference of great weight, the Venetian fleets which fought for and against the Byzantine Empire were major mobilizations of the maritime force of the nation. The government decided whether in a given year ships should be allowed to sail as usual or whether certain trades should be suspended and a fleet prepared for war. Roughly put, the choice before the Venetians was whether to withdraw their ships and crews from trade for certain years and use the same capital and labor during those years in fighting. The opportunity cost of a year's war was primarily the loss of the returns on a year's trade. War also risked damage to the ships and the loss of productive labor through casualties, but when successful, the Venetians may have made up for these losses by plundering the enemy.[12] Assuming they were going to have a successful campaign, the Venetian leaders might sometimes have calculated in the following terms: With our privileges, the employ of our merchants and seamen in the Byzantine Empire in trade yields each year 20 per cent more than it would if we had no privileges.[13] Employing those merchants and seamen as fighters for a year will mean a 100 per cent loss of return from them for this year but it will be worthwhile if it secures us our privileges for five years or more. Of course the Venetians did not work out the problem precisely this way and the sources do not permit us to calculate it in exact accord with attested facts. But it illustrates how it was possible for the Venetian use of force in securing tariff differentials to be productive of increase in Venetian national income. During the century after 1082 Venetian national income did increase very substantially. Other developments of that century helped, especially the rise of Western markets for Eastern products. That aided all the seaboard cities of the Mediterranean which were intermediaries in the trade, but Venetian commercial enterprise was then focused particularly on the Byzantine Empire and was very largely devoted to exchange within that empire and to the commerce between it and other markets of the Levant. To be sure, the Venetians acted partly for their own security, as has been explained, and our picture of how Venice grew rich in this general period is complicated by the events of the Fourth Crusade. Yet, everything considered, Venetian policy from 1082 to 1204 appears an unusually successful use of force to increase national income.

Colbert's capture of trade with the West Indies seems, by contrast, to

---

[12] This does not allow adequately, I confess, either for the directly received pains of fear, anxiety, or wounds, nor for the directly received pleasures of those who found satisfactions in killing and glory. Except when soldiers are hired for war in a free labor market, how do these satisfactions or dissatisfactions manifest themselves in action in such a way as to be measurable in prices or wages? Perhaps, even if they were reflected in the price of mercenaries, the pleasure one man may take in killing should not be counted part of the total satisfactions which form national income, but the pain caused by wounds should be counted as diminution of the total satisfactions? The question emphasizes the inability of economic analysis to deal with the relative worth of various satisfactions except in money terms and the resulting limitations of the meaning of national income as commonly used and as used here. Cf. Alfred Marshall, *Principles of Economics* (8th ed.; London, 1936), pp. 14–25, 57–60, 76.

[13] Although the tariff differentials were 4 per cent or 10 per cent, many more than one tariff were added to the price of wares sold during a year's trading.

have failed to produce any immediate gain in French national income. When we count all aspects of the national protection cost and the opportunity cost of the new enterprises, a formidable list of losses must be subtracted from the addition to national income embodied in the profits of traders to the West Indies. Besides the big deficit of the French West India Company which pioneered the voyage, there was the direct cost of employing a French naval squadron, and, since the exclusion of the Dutch from the West Indies was one reason for the outbreak of war between France and Holland in 1672, some part of the expense of that war would have to be included. To allow for national opportunity costs, the price of sugar to French consumers would have to be investigated, and if the islanders be considered part of the French nation, their losses in paying for supplies prices two or three times as high as those previously charged by the Dutch must be added. Even in authors highly favorable to Colbert the evidence presented indicates that a loss rather than a gain in national income resulted during Colbert's life-time from the capture of the trade.[14]

A case of attempting to increase national wealth by military power which presents enlightening similarities and contrasts with those just discussed was the temporary capture of the spice trade by the Portuguese. In the second half of the fifteenth century nearly all the spices reaching Europe from the Indian Ocean passed through the Red Sea and the lands of the Soldan of Egypt, paying him well for his protection on the way, before they reached the Venetians and other Europeans. After the Portuguese found the way to India around Africa, the Portuguese king decided to assume a royal monopoly of the most valuable spices. At the same time he attempted by armed force to bar the passage of all spices into the Red Sea. His success was not complete, but the destruction of some ships of Arab traders and the risk of capture for others was sufficient for some decades to raise greatly the protection costs of the Red Sea route. While he kept these costs up, the Portuguese king sold spices in the West at prices above those which the Venetians had charged in the later fifteenth century. So long as he raised the protection cost of the Red Sea route sufficiently, the king, as monopolist of the Cape route, could fix his price so as to secure the protection rent arising from the higher protection costs of his rivals.[15]

[14] Stewart L. Mims, *Colbert's West India Policy*; Charles Wolsey Cole, *Colbert and a Century of French Mercantilism* (New York, 1939).
[15] The Portuguese policy and particularly its effect on pepper prices is presented more fully in Chap. 22, above.

But in attempting to extend his government's monopoly of force over the Indian Ocean the Portuguese king assumed a heavy burden of expenditure which can properly be charged as protection cost to his own spice trading enterprise. The overawing of Indian princes, the seizing of trading posts, and the assertion of naval supremacy in the Indian Ocean were the king's means of raising the protection costs of his competitors, and such was the inefficiency of Portuguese methods of trade and government that these offensive protection costs soon proved excessive. The Ottoman Turks lowered tariffs in Egypt after they conquered it, and they challenged the Portuguese control of the Indian Ocean.[16] About 1560 a substantial part of Europe's spice imports again came through the Red Sea,[17] a sign that the protection costs of the Portuguese king were at times higher than those of his rivals on the competing route. Reviewing the economic history of the Portuguese in India and taking into account the military expenses, J. Lucio de Azevedo asserts: "The truth is that only in the period of conquest did India pay its cost . . . " and, then as he says, only by "booty, tribute, prizes, and the ransom of Moors."[18]

Tribute was an extremely important factor in this case and especially so if we shift our point of view to consider not simply the royal enterprise of governing and spice trading but the changes in Portuguese national income as a whole. When Lucio de Azevedo says that the cost of the Indian empire exceeded the receipts, he seems to include under the costs the salaries and pensions with which the Portuguese king rewarded the nobles who conquered and governed the empire. Whatever increase in the income of this ruling class came from charges levied on non-Portuguese subjects constituted an addition to national income. Royal officials in India did increase their revenue illegally also by booty, bribes, and private trade. This sort of corruption was probably the chief factor in undermining the profitableness of the royal monopoly, but it was a positive factor in national income. Although in political or legal theory they were part of the royal enterprise, the corrupt officials were from an economic point of view acting as entrepreneurs on their own. Each sold for his own profit the protection of the force at his disposal. The revival of the Red Sea route was not an interference with their income but a sign that they preferred selling their protection for bribes to Arab traders instead of extending it to the

[16] A. H. Lybyer, "The Ottoman Turks and the Routes of Oriental Trade," *English Historical Review*, XXX (1915), 586.

[17] See Chapter 2, above.

[18] *Epocas de Portugal economico* (Lisbon, 1929), p. 155; also, pp. 118–31.

king's monopoly as they were supposed to do. If we count all the increased income of the ruling class, legitimate and illegitimate, booty and tribute as well as protection rent, there seems no doubt that Portuguese national income did increase for a time.

The opportunity cost remains to be considered. With the same geographical discoveries and the same skill in navigation, could Portuguese capital and labor have been used more profitably in another way than that to which it was directed by military action in the Indian Ocean? Although it is hard to see how the Portuguese could have followed "nature's simple plan" in this case, any more easily than the Venetians could have adopted such a plan in dealing with the Byzantine Empire, some contemporaries did conceive policies requiring less military action. Observers at Venice—ironically enough now that Venice, three hundred years after the conquest of Constantinople, was no longer making wars pay—pointed out that the Portuguese might operate advantageously without attempting a monopoly of force, simply because the Cape route would enable the Portuguese to avoid the high customs levied in Egypt.[19] Instead, the Portuguese decided to seek their protection rents by raising the protection costs of possible rivals rather than by trying themselves to operate with protection costs below the existing level.[20] The consequent increase in the prices to Portuguese consumers of Indian products was of trifling importance since the bulk of these products was sold abroad. But less military action against Arab traders and the employ of more capital and labor in commercial activity might have increased the volume and the value of the Eastern wares which the Portuguese could offer for sale in Europe. Would the returns of such an expanded commerce have increased Portuguese national income more than it was increased by plunder, tribute, and the small trade actually developed?

To frame the question in this way suffices to suggest that a full estimate of opportunity cost involves two considerations which were passed over lightly in the cases discussed earlier. The first concerns the kind of capital and labor there was in Portugal, in other words nothing less than the character of Portuguese society in 1500. The activity in which the Portuguese then displayed superiority over other nations was

---

[19] Girolamo Priuli, *I diarii* (Vol. II; Bologna, 1933), in *Rerum Italicarum scriptores*, 2d ed.; II, Tome XXIV, Part III, 156.

[20] The motive of the Portuguese king may have been to add a new title to his name as João de Barros implies, *Da Asia* (Lisbon, 1727), Decada I, Part II, Libro VI, Cap. I, pp. 8–9; but this discussion is concerned with results of historic actions not with the motives.

not shrewd trading but bold adventuring both in navigation and in war. Because of the military and religious traditions of the Portuguese and their class structure, the crusading policy pursued in India may well have stimulated energies which obtained more wealth than the Portuguese could have gained by less bellicose means. A Venetian of 1500 was likely to believe that the Portuguese could gain more by a more peaceful policy because such might have been the case had the Portuguese ruling class been similar in character to the Venetian in 1500. At that date many Venetian nobles had become wedded to peaceful trade or to the management of country estates. They were no longer, as they had been three or four hundred years earlier when bullying Byzantium, equally efficient either as merchants or as sea raiders.

The second consideration is that two different answers are possible— one for the short run and one for the long run. The policy which the Portuguese adopted in India yielded so much tribute and plunder that a greater immediate increase in national income under a more peaceful policy seems improbable. But the king's attempt to conquer an Indian empire, and the closely connected decision to make the chief items in the trade a royal monopoly, diverted Portuguese capital and labor from the commercial development of the voyage and focused the energies of his people on war, plunder, and the taking of bribes and tribute. The large immediate rewards attracted the youth of the nation to these warlike activities which soon yielded diminishing returns. A royal policy which relied less on force and opened more opportunities for those with trading skill would have favored the development of mercantile capacities among the Portuguese. In the long run of a hundred or two hundred years these capacities might well have made Portugal richer. The possibility raises very complex questions since a change in the type of capacity possessed by a nation's labor, both managerial and manual, involves a basic change in social structure, in this case a decline of the military and a rise of the commercial and industrial classes. Because the ensuing centuries were to bring greater wealth to commercial and industrial nations, it is generally held that the conquest of India, although it increased Portuguese national income for a time, caused a decrease later by undermining the productivity of the nation's labor.

On the other hand, Colbert's West Indian policy, although in the short run it decreased French national income, is generally judged successful in the long run. Within a century after his death, the West Indies "proved the most valuable colonial asset which France possessed and contributed more to her commercial prosperity than any other single branch of trade."[21] The particular type of labor and capital which Colbert fostered by providing protection rents for West Indian traders became in the long run of a hundred years exceptionally productive. The same can be said of many of his efforts. After describing Colbert's East India Company, Professor Cole concludes: "The value of navigators who knew the routes to the East, of merchants who could carry on the Indies trade, of agents who had learned oriental ways, were all assets which did not appear on the balance sheet, but which formed a significant contribution from the Company of Colbert to its successors."[22] By a variety of measures many of which depended on force of arms, Colbert increased the proportion of his nation's capital and labor devoted to oceanic commerce and to manufacturing. He often diverted capital and labor from employments in which they would have produced more national income at the time. But manufacturing and oceanic commerce were to become more and more profitable as they attracted more and more labor and capital. In so far as Colbert drew resources away from conspicuous consumption or from agricultural investments which were subject to the law of diminishing returns and directed them into commercial and industrial activities which were in the future to yield increasing return, his activity as a statesman did contribute to the future wealth of his nation.

This contrast between short-run loss and long-run gain is present in many cases of mercantilism. Against England's immediate losses from enforcing the Navigation Acts, losses from higher freight rates and from naval action, may be put some of the advantage which the size of the British merchant marine later gave many British enterprises. Against the immediate cost to the British of winning and holding colonial outposts may be balanced not only any immediate return in protection rents, but also some of the benefits of the internal economies made possible to British industries in following centuries by the size of Britain's overseas market. The recent continuator of the Smithian tradition, Alfred Marshall, admits that the national income of England in the eighteenth century, and even more in the nineteenth century depended much on "the action of the law of increasing return with regard to her exports."[23]

During a long earlier period of history the chief hope of making war

---

[21] Mims, *Colbert's West India Policy*, p. 339.
[22] *Colbert and a Century of French Mercantilism*, I, 523.
[23] *Principles of Economics*, p. 672.

pay was tribute. In the Age of Mercantilism the wealth which govern-ing classes took directly for themselves from other nations became relatively small. As economic life became less largely agricultural and more intricately organized through differentiated enterprises, the profits secured by favored economic enterprises came to form a larger part of national income. Tribute became less important than protec-tion rents. The change made immediate success in increasing national income by military action less frequent, for protection rents were secured by violations of the law of comparative advantage which were usually to the detriment of all nations concerned. Yet in the long run military victories added more to national income when used to gain protection rent than when used to gain tribute. Tribute-paying em-pires yielded diminishing returns as they drew more manpower into the maintenance and extension of such conquests. The protection rents stimulated oceanic commerce and industries which found new markets from wider trade. In another epoch the premiums given commerce and industry might have been thrown away. In that particular period of social and technological change, the period of the expansion of Europe, those fields of enterprise yielded increasing return.

In more recent times the forms in which national income may be increased by military pressure on other nations have been enormously complicated and especially recently by exchange controls and market-ing quotas. At the same time the armed forces used by governments have been consolidated into enduring military and naval establish-ments so that national protection costs are even more largely overhead costs. A part of these costs may be allotted to security against invasion, but another part arises from desire for "a place in the sun" or for escape from "economic strangulation." Even if it were clearly demonstrated that military pressure never gained immediate additions to national income sufficient to justify the added cost, historical perspective emphasizes the extreme difficulty of guessing the results in the long run. The long-run success of present military efforts to increase national income depends on whether these efforts direct the labor of a victorious nation into those types of activities which will prove to be most produc-tive of increasing return during the technological and social revolu-tions of the future.

24

Force and Enterprise in the Creation of Oceanic Commerce*

Among the other excellent and extraordinary gifts that God has given to human kind is the knowledge of the motion of the spheres, the course of the planets and stars, and of the climatic zones under which is placed this marvelous world machine. With this knowledge we furrow that very great element, the water, and betake ourselves into almost any part of the world that we wish, with the same facility as if there were in the wide ocean a fixed road showing signs of its use, and a through highway.[1]

I

THESE opening words of a Venetian treatise on navigation written about 1560 summarize the impressive technological achievement that made possible oceanic commerce. In considering what was the role of government and what the role of business enterprise in making highways across the oceans for man's use, one is tempted to give the easy answer that governments played the major role. The activities of Prince Henry and King John II of Portugal,[2] the voyages of Colum-

---

* "Oceanic Expansion: Force and Enterprise in the Creation of Oceanic Commerce," in *The Tasks of Economic History*, Suppl. to the *Journal of Economic History*, X (1950), 19–31. (By permission.)

[1] Agostino Cesareo, "L'Arte della Navigatione con il regimento della tramontana, e del sole; e la regola del flusso, e reflusso del le Acque," MS in my possession. Another copy, dated 1570, is referred to in E. G. R. Taylor's edition of Roger Barlow, *A Brief Summe of Geographie* (London: The Hakluyt Society, 1932), Ser. 2, No. LXIX, p. 184 n.

[2] Edgar Prestage, *The Portuguese Pioneers* (London: A. & A. Black, 1933), chap. xiv.

bus, the development in the Spanish Casa de la Contratación of what C. H. Haring calls "a hydrographic Bureau and School of Navigation, the earliest and most important in the history of modern Europe"—all these and more could be cited as evidence of the role of government in the creation of oceanic commerce.[3]

Looking more closely at the great voyages of discovery raises doubts, however, about classifying these activities as either governmental or business enterprise. The doubts increase as one turns from the discoveries to examine the exploitation of their commercial possibilities. Whereas many historical papers relate to the last hundred and fifty years, the conquest of the oceans occurred some centuries earlier, at a time when neither governments nor business enterprises had assumed the forms now most familiar to us. In present thought there is an inclination to assume that government and business have existed as separate organizations. We identify as governments those organizations that are guided by considerations of power and general welfare, that use war and police as essential activities—while basing their authority also on appeals to moral sentiments—and that bring into existence systems of law and allegiance. We recognize as business enterprises those organizations that are guided by considerations of profit and loss to the enterprise, that use as their customary activities buying and selling and the organization of labor and techniques in the production of goods, and that bring into existence new uses of the means of production and new distributions of goods and services. Thus we are inclined to assume that all three criteria may be used to distinguish between the two types of organization. In terms of motives, the antithesis is between the profit-oriented activities of business and the power-oriented activity of government, or its provision for someone's conception of the general welfare. In terms of the methods employed, the contrast is between the buying, selling, and calculation of engineering costs in a business enterprise and the military action, the policing, and the judicial procedures employed by government. In terms of social consequences, the contrast is between the new goods and services created by business enterprise and the emergence of new laws and empires through the actions of governments. In examining the organizations actually existing in the western world about 1900 it is not too difficult to classify them according to all three criteria either as governments or as business enterprises. But in examining the oceanic expansion of the fifteenth

---

[3] Clarence Henry Haring, *Trade and Navigation between Spain and the Indies in the Time of the Hapsburgs* ("Harvard Economic Studies," Vol. XIX; Cambridge, Mass.: Harvard University Press, 1918), p. 35. Cf. also pp. 3–4, 298–314.

and sixteenth centuries, we cannot classify in this way the organizations initially involved.

This is especially true of the key innovating enterprises. Whether we consider their motives, their methods, or their consequences, we find that these enterprises usually combined characteristics of government with characteristics of business. The Portuguese pepper trade with India was, at least in the long period of the royal pepper monopoly, part and parcel of the same enterprise that waged war to build an empire. The Portuguese colonization of the islands off Africa and of Brazil was largely through grants to proprietors who were charged not only with organizing production on the lands granted them but also with police and protection. The conquest of Mexico and the conquest of Peru were initiated as profit-making enterprises financed by contracts stipulating how the profits were to be shared. These enterprises resembled government in some respects, business in others.

Of course, distinctions can be made, and it would be both possible and profitable to make them in legal terms. Using that approach, one might seek for the distinctions made by legal thinkers between activities of the state and activities that were based on rights of private property. Perhaps historians of public and private law can find recognized distinctions in those centuries between the usual sphere and attributes of governmental activity, on the one hand, and the usual sphere and activity of private enterprise, on the other; and perhaps exceptions could be taken care of by saying that for various purposes peculiar to the problems of oceanic expansion governments occasionally assumed certain activities and attributes of private enterprise, and, on the other hand, private enterprise took on some of the activities and attributes of government. Certainly it would be possible and profitable to follow through legal sources the development of these conceptions —to study the distinctions in constitutional law between the public property of the Crown and the more personal property of the prince, the change from feudal to more modern forms of land tenure, and the development of distinctions concerning public and private corporations. But the legal formulation of the distinction between government and private enterprise was far from being clear-cut at the time when oceanic expansion began. In its legal systems Europe was still close to feudalism. As Joseph Schumpeter has said, our words "state" and "private" enterprise can hardly be applied to the institutions of feudalism without creating a distorted view of those institutions.[4] Under

---

[4] Joseph A. Schumpeter, *Capitalism, Socialism, and Democracy* (2d ed.; New York: Harper & Brothers, 1947) , pp. 169, 201.

feudalism a state was in a certain sense the private property of a prince in the same way that the fief was the private property of a vassal. The feudal vassal was expected to collect from the lands and rights he held in fief more goods and services than he had to pay his suzerain, and to gain thereby a profit as his reward for defending the fief and rendering the service provided in the feudal contract. Princes and their vassals extended the jurisdictions of their courts, the cultivation of their fields, and the conquests of their arms as profit-seeking ventures. Later, much of the spirit and legal forms of feudalism were applied in oceanic expansion.

II

But I am less interested in legal formulas and theories than in a different aspect of the question. The problem that has most aroused my curiosity in this connection is the effect of the use of armed force on economic development. When and how did force-using enterprises become separate from the profit-seeking enterprises we call business? And in those numerous cases in which they were not separated, what were the effects on economic development of various uses of armed force?

The way in which force was applied to secure gain determined the economic success or failure of many of the innovating enterprises that created oceanic commerce. As an example, consider first the Portuguese circumnavigation of Africa. It presented an opportunity to organize the shipment of spices by that route in such a fashion that the cost of bringing the spices around Africa to Europe would be less than the cost of bringing them to European markets through the Red Sea and the Mediterranean. Since the taxes levied by the Soldan of Egypt were a large factor in the cost of the Red Sea route, the Portuguese king could collect an equivalent amount and still undersell the Venetians, provided transportation cost by the oceanic route was less than by the Red Sea route. Whether transportation by the oceanic route was or could have been made cheaper seems to me doubtful. It was never put to a test. The Portuguese crown did not try to resolve the problem in those terms. The Portuguese decided to apply military and naval power, with the twin objectives of gaining the glory of having an empire of India and gaining wealth. The king undertook to prevent forcibly any shipment of spices to the Red Sea, to secure a complete monopoly for himself, and to sell the spices in Lisbon at prices as high as or higher than those prevailing before the discovery of the new route. Accordingly, the profitableness of the oceanic route to India depended on whether the returns from the sale of the spices would yield sufficient revenue to support fleets and armies large enough to blockade the Red Sea route. It was not a question of size only, but of whether the armies and fleets would be used well in order to make the monopoly effective. In fact they were either not large enough or not sufficiently well organized. By the 1560's the royal Portuguese Indian enterprise was not proving profitable. Spices were again moving through the Red Sea in as large a volume as ever—an aspect of that continued commercial predominance of the Mediterranean in sixteenth-century Europe which has been brilliantly pictured in Fernand Braudel's volume.[5] Except in the opening decades, when enriched by the plunder of conquest, the Portuguese kings failed to gain the expected riches from the discovery of the oceanic route to India.[6] They had misjudged and badly organized their use of force in Indian waters. Although this very abbreviated account of Portuguese enterprise in India leaves out much, even a more extended analysis would, I believe, lead to the conclusion that the gain or loss of the Portuguese depended, not on technically determined costs of competing routes of transportation, but on the way in which force was applied to control the use of the competing routes.

From the point of view of the long run, Portuguese enterprises in South America were more profitable. In Brazil there was less occasion for investing so heavily in military and naval forces, but even in Brazil the way in which arms were used decided the fate of colonial enterprises. After a preliminary period in which the only Portuguese in Brazil were the cutters of brazilwood, the Portuguese crown divided the region among twelve colonial proprietors called the *donatários*. These proprietors were expected to fulfill the political function of keeping out the French. They had civil and criminal jurisdiction within their captaincies, the right to levy taxes, and the right to collect tithes from land granted to settlers. At the same time they engaged in what might be called the business enterprise of establishing sugar plantations. Their success in creating new supplies of sugar for the European market makes some of these *donatários* deserving of attention as innovating entrepreneurs. Within a century imitative entrepreneurs had extended the sugar plantations of Brazil so that they were Europe's chief source of supply. The first successful sugar plantations of Brazil were developed by those proprietors who were able to solve at the same

[5] Fernand Braudel, *La Méditerranée et le monde méditerranéen à l'époque de Philippe II* (Paris: Armand Colin, 1949).

[6] See Chapters 2 and 22 for discussion.

time the political and economic problems of bringing land, labor, and capital together in a profitable way.

One example of a successful proprietor was Martim Affonso da Sousa. Martim Affonso started his colony of São Vicente in the present state of São Paulo, in 1532, before he received his proprietary grant, at a time when he commanded a fleet sent by the Portuguese king to patrol Brazilian waters against the French. Tradition has it that he introduced in the next year the first sugar cane grown in Brazil, bringing sugarcane growers from Madeira, and that shortly thereafter, when he had received São Vicente as his *donatária,* he imported Negro slaves to work on the sugar plantations. But there is no direct evidence of the use of Negro slaves in Brazil that early. The main solution of the labor problem in the colony of São Vicente was the use of Indian slave labor. Martim Affonso allied with friendly Indians to wage war and secure slaves from other tribes, and hired enough soldiers to keep the upper hand.[7]

Another conspicuously successful proprietor was Duarte Coelho whose grant was at Pernambuco. A Brazilian writer about a generation later says that he expended on his colony thousands of *cruzados,* gained in India, which were well spent because his son received tens of thousands in revenue as a result.[8] A letter written by Duarte Coelho himself in 1550, sixteen years after he had received his grant, said that he had five sugar mills in operation and implied he was just beginning to make a profit.[9] How much of his investment during the previous sixteen years went into bringing settlers and supplies to his colony and how much was spent building mills and laying out cane fields is uncertain, but the evidence makes clear that a part was spent in hiring soldiers. Coelho had secured some labor for a time from the Indians by barter, giving them such items as cloth and iron tools in exchange for their labor. But in addition to these peaceful relations at certain periods with some of the Indians, his colony lived through periods of Indian attacks followed by the enslavement of Indians. Whether the Indian attacks were the result of efforts to enslave or whether Indians were reduced to slavery only after they turned hostile is left by the sources to our

[7] Alexander Marchant, *From Barter to Slavery: The Economic Relations of Portuguese and Indians in the Settlement of Brazil, 1500–1580* (The Johns Hopkins University Studies in Historical and Political Science, Series LX, No. 1; Baltimore: The Johns Hopkins Press, 1942), pp. 48–52, 77–78, 94.

[8] Gabriel Soares de Sousa, quoted in Marchant, p. 55.

[9] Duarte Coelho to John III, November 24, 1550, in *Historia da colonizacão portuguesa do Brasil,* ed. Carlos Malheiro Dias (3 vols.; Porto, 1924–26), III, 321.

imagination. This much is clear, however, not only in regard to the colony of Duarte Coelho at Pernambuco but in regard to the colonies of many other *donatários:* it was essential to be able to resist Indian attacks. Those enterprises that could not failed. Those proprietors who prospered were able both to resist the attacks and to acquire Indian slaves to labor on their sugar plantations. Among all the items of expenditure that had to be made by a proprietor in order to bring into existence profitable sugar plantations in Brazil, the hiring of soldiers was one of vital importance to the success of the enterprise.

These Portuguese enterprises in Asia and America have been presented as examples of force-using, profit-seeking enterprises. Many other examples in the transoceanic expansion of the Spanish, French, Dutch, and English invite analysis. When English and Dutch enterprises first penetrated the Caribbean, they came equipped to use force against the Spaniards. Armament was necessary to secure trade just as arms were necessary to secure labor, and in the first establishment of trade or of plantations in new areas, military and business activities were conducted by the same enterprise.

Very soon, however, at least in the Americas, the initial colonial enterprise began to subdivide into a number of more specialized enterprises, some of which were primarily concerned with war, police, and protection, while others specialized in trading, mining, or in agricultural production. In Brazil, for example, after about fifteen years in which efforts by the *donatários* had achieved a few successes and many failures in occupying the land, a governor-general was created. Although he did not take over all force-using (political) activities from the *donatários,* the organization headed by the governor-general was of a more specialized character than that of the *donatários* had been. He was concerned with war and police, not directly with the organization of sugar production. At the same time the grants of lands by the proprietors created enterprises in Brazil that were concerned with sugar production and that depended for protection, not on their own efforts, but on the *donatário* or the captain general.[10] Instead of all the problems of colonization being handled as by one enterprise, various aspects of colonizing activity were undertaken by more specialized agencies.

This development occurred much earlier in Spanish America. Columbus' first two expeditions were empowered to perform all the functions of colonization—discovery, government, conversion of the

[10] Marchant, Chap. iv.

Indians, mining, and the conduct of trade. The royal enterprise of which Columbus was the head contemplated activity in all these fields.[11] Again, when Ovanda was placed in charge in Hispaniola, his responsibility as royal governor included for a few years the direction of trade and mining as well as conquests and police.[12] The situation was very different twenty years later, after colonizing activity had grown larger. We can then see many more specialized enterprises operating in the colonial field. I will mention but a few: (1) royal governors collecting taxes and commanding troops in established colonies; (2) the Casa de la Contratación providing ships and arms to protect vessels going to the New World; (3) shipowners asking high freight from the Casa and from various shippers; (4) traders who bought wares in Seville, contracted for their shipment to America, and entered into *commenda* contracts with agents who went overseas with the wares to sell them in the colonies; and (5) conquistadors such as Pizarro operating on the geographical frontier of the Spanish empire and adding to the area of colonial enterprise.[13]

III

This development of differentiated enterprises within a colonial area seems to me comparable in many ways to the emergence within a single industry, such as the automobile industry, of many types of firms each specializing in furnishing parts or service in demand by other firms within the industry. In colonial activity in a transoceanic area, an activity which may be considered for the purposes of the comparison as one industry, government was one of the most important services

[11] Haring, pp. 3–4; Samuel Eliot Morison, *Admiral of the Ocean Sea: A Life of Christopher Columbus* (Boston: Little, Brown & Co., 1944), pp. 104–5, 355–56, 390–92, 430–44.

[12] Leslie Byrd Simpson, *The Encomienda in New Spain* ("University of California Publications in History," Vol. XIX; Berkeley: University of California Press, 1929), pp. 25–33.

[13] Haring, pp. 32, 49, 51, 201–6, 283; Roger B. Merriman, *Rise of the Spanish Empire in the Old World and the New* (4 vols.; New York: The Macmillan Co., 1918–34), III, 576–667; André-E. Sayous, "Partnerships in the Trade between Spain and America and also in the Spanish Colonies in the Sixteenth Century," *Journal of Economic and Business History*, I (February, 1929), 282–92; Sayous, "Les débuts du commerce de l'Espagne avec l'Amérique (1503–1518)," *Revue Historique*, CLXXIV (1934), 191–92, 195–97, 200–2. On mining enterprises and bullion merchants, see Earl J. Hamilton, *American Treasure and the Price Revolution in Spain*, 1501–1650 ("Harvard Economic Studies," Vol. XLIII; Cambridge: Harvard University Press, 1934), pp. 15–16, 26–28.

needed by the industry. The industry needed government in the crude sense of a use of force to provide protection from assaults and to impose forced trade or forced labor. Once colonies were well enough established, governmental organization to furnish these services became an enterprise separate from the other enterprises in the industry. On the other side, managing a plantation or farm also became a specialized enterprise. Shipping services likewise finally became distinct, although for a time they were performed either by the same enterprises that furnished protection or by the trading enterprises that marketed in Europe the products of the farms, plantations, and mines of America.

The analogy between the differentiation of enterprises in growing industries and in oceanic colonization suggests a formula by which to explain in economic terms why there was no such differentiation in precisely those colonial enterprises which were the trail blazers, those which were the clearest cases of dynamic innovation. Industrial firms cannot specialize until the industry has grown large enough to supply a market for a specialized product—whether that product be a form of a service or a component used in manufacture. Similarly, colonial enterprises did not specialize until there was, in the transoceanic area in question, a market for such specialized services as transportation, or trading, or the use of force.

To call the use of force an economic service raises some important problems that I have hitherto touched on only indirectly. Did the use of force only transfer wealth from one group to another and usually decrease in the process the combined total wealth of the two groups? Or did war and other forms of organized physical violence in some cases create wealth?

Two ways in which the use of force may affect the income of the persons or enterprises involved may be distinguished. First, application of force may result in a simple transfer of wealth from one person or enterprise to another. For example, when a gunman steals a watch or a treasure ship is taken by pirates, it is a clear case of plunder. Second, force may be used to create protection. Some colonial governments took plunder, but generally they assured to those in the colonies from whom they collected payments some protection against plunderers and against other governments. Giving this protection involved creating some kind of a rule of law. In creating a system of law and order the government performed an economic service; it created the utility that I have called protection.[14]

---

[14] See Chapter 23.

I think it may be accepted as a general proposition that every economic enterprise needs protection against the destruction or seizure of its capital and the disruption of its labor force. In creating protection under a system of law, governments imposed practices concerning the appropriation of land, labor, and other goods. Establishing these practices was part of the process of organizing production. If production, such as the growing of sugar cane or the mining of silver, was done by organizations separate from government, then the situation could be described by saying that the government created conditions favorable to the development of business enterprise. But when all activity in a colonial area was under one enterprise, labor and land were appropriated as part of the process of organizing production. An organization using force and producing goods for sale was making its own rules. Later, general rules about the appropriation of land and labor came to be used by other enterprises, which had to depend on the government in the cases when arms were necessary to enforce the appropriation.

Rules concerning the appropriation of land, water, patentable ideas, or labor can be called part of the law of property. When the practices enforced by property law include forced labor, the question arises whether these practices are not like plunder in merely transferring wealth from one person to another, but the same question might also be raised regarding application of force to appropriate land for private use. The whole problem is so large that I can only skirt the edge of it.

Plunder and forced labor were of such importance in early colonial activity that there is much truth in the assertion that Europeans gained wealth by taking it from colonial peoples. But that assertion does not explain why some uses of force contributed to economic development whereas other uses of force contributed little or nothing. The question on which I wish to focus attention is this: How distinguish those uses of force that contributed to economic development and those that did not? I cannot hope to give any full answer to that question, but I wish to direct attention to its importance and to suggest some concepts that might be useful in seeking an answer.

Can we not use in this connection the familiar concepts of increasing and decreasing returns? I venture to propose as a hypothesis that the enterprises which used force to plunder and to prevent the trade of rivals were in general subject to diminishing returns, but that many enterprises using force to create protection, including many that imposed forced labor, enjoyed the advantages of increasing returns.

The Portuguese activities previously mentioned can be described in these terms. Their enterprise of India seems to have encountered diminishing returns, for, under the policy the Portuguese adopted, efforts to increase their trade in pepper depended on tightening their blockade of the Red Sea. Outfitting fleets for that purpose was a use of funds that yielded decreasing returns. In Brazil, in contrast, a use of force created protection and a rule of law of such a character that, as the colony grew and produced more sugar, the proportion of the expenses of the whole colonial enterprise that was spent on protection became less. As the number of those receiving protection increased, its cost per unit in the colony declined, and government—the protection-producing enterprise—was operating under conditions of increasing returns.

That favorable condition did not last forever. A highly prosperous colony was an enticing prospect for plunder or conquest in the eyes of other European nations. When the Dutch invaded Brazil, protection costs in that area took on a new aspect. But that was eighty years after the arrival of the *donatários*. The colonial rivalries of the European powers are an important complication to consider in analyzing later economic development.

In very general terms, however, the principle of development can, I suggest, be stated as follows: The cost of producing protection, like the cost of producing other utilities, was affected by the size of the demand for it. Effective demand, able to pay the price, was very small in the area of a new colony when the enterprise started. So long as there was no demand except that of the first colonizers themselves, there was no economic basis for a specialized organization of government. Government and various kinds of business were all conducted by the same enterprise. When a colony was successfully established and began to grow, the market for protection increased. This expansion of the market led to increased division of labor that took the form of specialized enterprises. The force-using enterprise—government—then became one among many enterprises operating in that transoceanic colonial area. While it satisfied the demands of other enterprises for the service of protection, they satisfied its demands for the kinds of goods and services we usually associate with business enterprise. Production of both protection and other goods at lower unit prices gave opportunities for external economies to all the enterprises in the colonial area.

I have in mind in this connection the article entitled "Increasing Returns and Economic Progress," in which Allyn A. Young elaborated the theme that the main explanation of all economic progress in modern times lies in the increasing returns that result from the extension of the market, and that these increasing returns arise less through the internal economies of firms that expand as their industry expands than through the external economies created for each firm by the development of specialized firms producing at lower costs the components and services used in the industry.[15] This applies in a special way to early colonial enterprise. In initiating these ventures, a variety of activities—trading, transport, government, and farming or mining—had to be combined under one management. There was a notable lack of division of labor, especially in the field of managerial labor. Specializing by entrepreneurs or managers was not even sufficient to place the military man, the planter, and the merchant at the heads of different enterprises. But the kinds of ability and knowledge needed in a force-using enterprise were different from those needed in a peaceful business enterprise. Consequently when differentiation occurred and government separated from business, it was an important step in the increase of wealth through the division of labor.

On the other hand, combining the two types of managerial or entrepreneurial activity in the same enterprise was also highly productive in its own time. It was the method by which transoceanic colonization was initiated. Government and business entrepreneurship were combined in the innovating enterprises that created new spheres of economic activity. Those initial undifferentiated enterprises created the conditions of demand and supply that enabled more specialized and more efficient enterprises to appear. In addition to creating a supply of the service I have called protection, they created also a supply of seamen experienced in oceanic voyages and created the beginning of a supply of overseas products such as sugar and silver. Each element of supply was also an element of demand. The expansion of colonial markets should be understood to mean not only the overseas market for European manufactured goods but also the market for services to be performed in the colonies or on the oceans.

IV

In this paper I have touched on many broad issues in a partial, onesided way in order to deal with some aspects that have seemed to me important in understanding Europe's oceanic expansion. Part of the role of government in that expansion consisted in organizing the use of force, employing it sometimes in ways favorable to economic development, sometimes in ways less favorable. Only after the use of force was

---

[15] *Economic Journal,* XXXVIII (December, 1928) , 527–40.

applied in a colonial area in a way favorable to economic development was business organized into enterprises distinct from the organization of government.

In this discussion I may have given the impression that I overestimate in general the role of force in producing protection. Actually, it is of limited importance. In the long run, enterprises that produce protection depend less on brute force than on tradition, propaganda, and moral sentiments. Low protection costs generally depend on a government's skill in using ideas more than on its skill in using force. The role of naked force is not as important in most societies as it was in early colonial areas.

Also, I would not like to leave the impression that I underestimate all aspects of government other than protection. I have emphasized the combination in early colonial enterprise of only one characteristic of government, supplying protection, with various characteristics of business enterprise, including profit-seeking. Important also was the combination of the two kinds of motives, the profit-seeking associated with business enterprise and the larger objectives of national power or general welfare associated with government. In many cases it was only after enterprises based on both kinds of motives had started a colony that purely profit-seeking enterprises could be formed or prosper in the colonial area. Force and protection constitute only one aspect of government. It is an aspect important to economic development in any society, but an analysis focusing on that aspect alone cannot pretend to tell the whole story.

25

*Economic Consequences of Organized Violence**

IN the writing of economic history at present there is a tendency to focus attention on the quantity of material goods and of people. This is not because economists seriously maintain that the chief end of man is to produce a maximum population, each member of which has at his disposal a maximum amount of material things. I do not think many economists or economic historians hold such a materialistic belief—why then would they choose to be professors? We merely write as if we did, or at least we too often write so that we can be thus misinterpreted; and we are the more likely to be thus misinterpreted because the great political powers of the present, the United States and the Soviet Union, using different ideologies, each extols, paradoxically, its material productivity as proof of the force and validity of its ideals.

In the past a major concern in economic history—from Adam Smith and Karl Marx to Gustav Schmoller and Richard Tawney—has been dissecting the forms of justice and injustice in economic life. Many of its most enthusiastic students were attracted to economic history by this concern, sometimes passionately avowed, sometimes calmly assumed. They expressed it through indignation and satire, for as historians they wrote mainly about injustice, searching for more perfect justice by elimination, by examining alternatives. I hope we continue the search.

I have placed this profession of faith at the beginning because the way in which I will approach my main theme lays me open to the

* *Journal of Economic History,* XVIII (1958) , 401–17. (By permission.)

common misinterpretation. I wish to explore the possibilities of discussing governments as one among the many organizations producing goods and services, and specifically as the producer of a service I will call protection. I will leave aside initially any consideration of justice, will center attention on material wealth, and may even seem to speak cold-bloodedly of brute force.

I

Economic theory has dealt at length with some of the functions performed by the state, for example, with monetary policy, but has had relatively little to say about the military and judicial activity which may be regarded as the essence of government and which bulks largest in history. Economic theorists have generally traditionally defined their subject so as to exclude analysis of the use of violence. One of the tasks of economic history is to overcome that exclusion. Looking back over the centuries, or even if looking only at the present, we can clearly observe that many men have made their living, often a very good living, from their special skill in applying weapons of violence, and that their activities have had a very large part in determining what uses were made of scarce resources.

Men specializing in warfare appear very early in the history of the division of labor and were at an early date organized into large enterprises. In the use of violence there were obviously great advantages of scale when competing with rival violence-using enterprises or establishing a territorial monopoly. This fact is basic for the economic analysis of one aspect of government: the violence-using, violence-controlling industry was a natural monopoly, at least on land. Within territorial limits the service it rendered could be produced much more cheaply by a monopoly. To be sure, there have been times when violence-using enterprises competed in demanding payments for protection in almost the same territory, for example, during the Thirty Years' War in Germany. But such a situation was even more uneconomic than would be competition in the same territories between rival telephone systems. Competing police forces were even more inefficient than competing fire companies. A monopoly of the use of force within a contiguous territory enabled a protection-producing enterprise to improve its product and reduce its costs.

The use of violence, I am maintaining, is to be considered a productive activity, at least in some cases, and governments would have to be considered producers of a part of a total economic output even if they had no other function than the use and control of violence.[1] To be sure, an armed robber renders no service by his robbery; but the police that protect us from robbers, and the courts that protect the rights of the citizen even against the police, do, it is commonly agreed, render a service. Difficulties begin when we consider the racketeer who collects payments for "protection" against a violence that he himself threatens, and who actually supplies a sort of "black-market" protection in return, suppressing rival gangsters. Such borderline cases may not be important in analyzing the economic life of modern America, but they are far from negligible when we consider the violence-using and violence-controlling enterprises of Europe during the millennium between A.D. 700 and 1700. Which princes were rendering the service of police? Which were racketeers or even plunderers? A plunderer could become in effect the chief of police as soon as he regularized his "take," adapted it to the capacity to pay, defended his preserve against other plunderers, and maintained his territorial monopoly long enough for custom to make it legitimate.

Whether a government was engaged in pure policing and defensive war, or was in contrast a kind of "racket," imposing payments by its use of violence against those who refused to pay, is important from several points of view, some of which I will consider later.[2] Most actual govern-

---

[1] Strictly speaking, the production of protection depends on the control of violence; the use of violence is only one among a number of possible means to that end. Theoretically one might say that violence is productive when it is used to control violence and is not productive when it is used to transfer wealth from one person to another. In regard to advertising and salesmanship in general, a comparable distinction would declare them productive when they increase a consumer's knowledge of products available and of his own needs, but unproductive when they cause the consumer to misjudge the products available and to be confused about his own wants. It would be difficult to apply such a distinction in analyzing advertising budgets, and it would be similarly difficult to apply the first distinction in analyzing governmental budgets, for courts and police are used to collect taxes as well as to control robbers, and in the collection of taxes the control of violence is used to transfer wealth from the taxpayer to someone else. The question is: What does the taxpayer receive in return?

[2] If a government rendered no service except "protection," the taxes it collected might theoretically be divided into two categories: a part that were payments for the service rendered and another part that one is tempted to call plunder. How distinguish between them, even in theory?

(a) One might consider as payment for service only what had to be paid in order to be protected from third parties and call plunder all that was exacted under threat of violent seizure by the government itself. But this distinction would be of very limited usefulness. Only in some aspects of the feudal system and of early maritime trade did violence-controlling enterprises punish refusals to pay their

ments were probably a mixture. But in any case the payments that these governments collected were, from the point of view of the enterprises that made payments to them, the prices that they had to pay to avoid more severe losses. On the frontiers and on the high seas, where no one had an enduring monopoly in the use of violence, merchants avoided payment of exactions which were so high that protection could be obtained more cheaply by other means. On land or sea, the protection received was far from perfect; we might say that the service being rendered by the protection-producing enterprises was of poor quality and outrageously overpriced, but poor as it was, it was still for most enterprises most of the time a service for which they had to pay. Without it they could not operate. Although wasteful by ideal standards, the payments for protection were one of various kinds of waste built into the social organization.[3]

Some useful distinctions between payments proportionate to the service rendered and payments not proportionate to any service will appear from examining how the costs and income of the violence-controlling enterprise were affected by its monopolistic character. Once it had eliminated from the territory of its monopoly all competing specialists in the use of violence, it could reduce the costs of policing that territory and of exacting payments from its farmers, craftsmen, and local traders.[4] It could reduce the costs it incurred in producing

---

price, not by themselves using violence against refusers, but merely by leaving them exposed to the violence of third parties. Even governments that rendered good service *required* payments for it (but see n. 5 below on forced sales).

(b) One might consider as payment for service the amount the government collected to cover its necessary costs, all else as plunder. I attempt below some analysis along this line but do not in this connection use the word plunder. I would prefer to reserve it for the extreme case, namely:

(c) Plunder I would define as the exaction by a violence using enterprise of such large payments from another enterprise that the other enterprise is unable to keep up such payments and also maintain its production. I am inclined to stretch the phrase "payments for protection" to cover all exactions below this limit, even if they are in excess of real or necessary costs and are imposed by the violence of the collecting enterprise itself.

[3] Compare the discussion of military expenditure as part of national income, and the comparison with deceptive advertising, in Simon Kuznets, *National Product in Wartime* (New York: National Bureau of Economic Research, 1943), pp. 4–7.

[4] Crudely, this means only that military expenditures were higher in times of civil war, which is obvious enough. A more careful historical analysis would have to consider how changes in the art of war, in transportation, etc., have changed the advantages and disadvantages of scale for violence-using enterprises and thus have changed the amount of territory embraced by a "natural monopoly." In much of medieval Europe, governing more territory than one province brought disadvantages

and selling protection, unless there was a dangerous threat from out-side. Costs could be further reduced if the government acquired legiti-macy, either through mere time and custom, or through ceremonial and religious acts, or through any forms of appeal to opinion that established legitimacy and were less costly ways of controlling violence than expenditure on the police force.

Reduction in the costs of a protection-producing enterprise did not necessarily lead to any reduction in its exactions. Being a monopoly, it could keep up its "sales price" or even raise the price up to the point at which it encountered a kind of sales resistance, namely, difficulty in collecting taxes, or at which it invited the entrance of a competitor into the territory monopolized.[5] Lowering costs, while establishing the high-est prices the traffic would bear, gave the protection-controlling enter-

---

of scale. In contrast, by the seventeenth century it had become almost impossible for a government to maintain against outsiders its monopoly of even a single prov-ince unless its military establishment was strong enough to conquer a national kingdom. The size of the natural monopolies has changed, and there have been periods of competition and higher costs of protection while new natural monopolies in accord with new techniques were being established. In our age of atomic weapons there is perhaps no natural monopoly smaller than the whole world.

[5] To the objection that a "forced sale" is really no "sale" at all, and that con-cepts applicable to exchange do not apply, it may be answered:

(a) "Forced" is a matter of degree. At one extreme the "buyer" may have the alternative of payment or death, or taking extreme chances of dying. This choice faces not only those who pay for "protection" but also those who depend for water on a supplier who has a monopoly of the supply. During a desperate famine many buyers of food have only this choice. In some cases of illness patients are in this sense practically forced to agree to the fee asked. Such extreme cases may arise more often in the purchase of protection than in the purchase of water, food, or medical care, but the purchaser of protection has very often had other, less extreme, alter-natives.

(b) Admittedly, protection is not as easily divisible as is water, and the amounts paid to a monopoly for protection cannot so easily be varied in accordance with the amount received as is done when water is purchased from a monopoly. But many other goods and services are also of very limited divisibility. Again, the fees of a hospital which is the only one within reach come to mind. And there have been many historical situations in which the amount of protection may be said to have depended on the amount and form of the payment made. The amount of protection may be measured in time, in space, in the degree of risk, and in the range of the activities that are protected.

(c) Calling the taxpayer a purchaser of protection is no more inadmissible than saying that the servile laborers of an eastern German landlord were "selling" their labor services to their landlord, yet an economist describes that situation by saying: "The Lord of the manor was a monopsonist with a closed demand" (Walter Eucken, *The Foundations of Economics* [London: Hodge, 1950], p. 155). When laborers had

prise an excess of income over costs. This was a special kind of monopoly profit (or producer's surplus) which it seems appropriate to call, for convenience, by the name of tribute.

Of course if the violence-controlling enterprise behaved as a government should according to our democratic ideal, it would take no tribute. It would lower the prices charged for protection as fast as it was able to lower the cost. A government can be expected to behave that way if it is in fact controlled by its customers, as it is supposed to be in the theory of representative government. But during most of history govenments have not been democratic; the protection-producing enterprises were not controlled by the totality of other producers and consumers. They have been in the hands of a separate group or class pursuing distinct purposes of their own. In so far as they rationalized the economics of the violence-controlling enterprise, they pursued aims diverse from that of serving customers by maximizing the quality of their service and minimizing the price charged for it. Two other goals were in fact probably more frequently sought.

A great many protection-producing enterprises were controlled by the upper ranks of the army and police, in short, by their top management. In such cases we might say that their primary objective was preserving the life of the firm, and that maximizing size was more important than maximizing profits. Sometimes the rank and file of the army and other employees controlled or at least limited the policies followed, although their methods were different than those of modern labor unions. When employees as a whole controlled, they had little interest in minimizing the amounts exacted for protection and none in minimizing that large part of costs represented by labor costs, by their own salaries. Maximizing size was more to their taste also.

A different principle prevailed in those governments controlled by a prince or emperor so absolute that he could be considered the owner of the protection-producing enterprise. An interest in maximizing profits would lead him, while maintaining prices, to try to reduce his costs. He

---

to work for the landlord at the wage he offered or else have no means of livelihood, there was a "forced sale" with the "force" in the hands of the buyer.

(d) "Sales resistance" by taxpayers might take the form of flights into the "desert," as in Ptolemaic or Roman Egypt, or of serfs running away from their seignioral lords to towns where they could hide for a year and a day. It might take the form of local riots against tax collectors, or pot shots by moonshiners at revenuers. In border regions it could take the form of smuggling, so that a salt tax, for example, could be higher in the center of a kingdom than on the frontiers. These examples suggest that many taxpayers could find alternatives to the more excessive of the payments demanded.

would, like Henry VII of England or Louis XI of France, use inexpensive wiles, at least as inexpensive devices as possible, to affirm his legitimacy, to maintain domestic order, and to distract neighboring princes so that his own military expenses could be low. From lowered costs, or from the increased exactions made possible by the firmness of his monopoly, or from the combination, he accumulated a surplus, the kind of monopolistic profit which I am calling tribute.

Modern discussions of fiscal policies are full of references to their effect on full employment and the redress of social inequalities. In a modern context it may be shocking to consider government a profit-seeking enterprise. But in the feudal system a fief holder was expected to manage his fief with an eye to profit. The successful baron might disdain bourgeois haggling over merchandise, but he was an expert in using military and governmental means of making money. This mixed conception of private and public enterprise carried over from feudalism into the building of the absolute states at the end of the Middle Ages.[6] Moreover, in that period governments were so insecure and the limits of their territorial monopolies so uncertain that the princes at the head of protection-producing enterprises faced necessities that approximated those of competition. They often had to act on the principle of maximizing profits if their competitors were not to bid away from them their resources and their customers. Of course, while their situation was really that difficult, they enjoyed no monopoly and made no monopoly profit; but having surmounted it, as Louis IX did, the princes continued their pursuit of profit and organized a bureaucracy devoted to that aim. Between governmental enterprise and other kinds, the difference in regard to the degree and the principles of rationalization is considerable, but it is becoming less as more other enterprises become monopolistic and affected with a public interest. It was less, for converse reasons, during the period when European governments were more or less feudal, kings considered their realms personal possessions, and kings and chartered companies mixed trade and violence in their competition for colonial empires.

When a protection-producing enterprise operated at a profit, the profit or tribute generally went not to one person only, the prince, but to a group of which he was the focus, dispensing gifts, pensions, sinecures, and important offices. If a king had to spend all his income on army and police, then he had no profit, no tribute to keep or give

---

[6] Some aspects of the mixture of governmental and business enterprise and their gradual differentiation are considered in Chapter 24, above.

away—all his income was consumed in the costs of the governing enterprise. In fact, large profits were made in early modern times by the suppliers from whom princes bought military services, by the military entrepreneurs who undertook to recruit, organize, finance, and perhaps command bodies of soldiers.[7] Judicial and fiscal services as well as military forces were obtained from suppliers who used governmental powers for their personal profit.[8] Lacking effective bureaucracies, princely enterprises contracted out so much of their violence-using activities that subcontractors made large profits and the subcontractors should perhaps be considered the chief recipients of the tribute collected by maintaining at high level the exactions of government. And in addition the court of a Renaissance prince contained many favored courtiers who received in gifts and pensions much more than was necessary to enable or induce them to perform any service connected with protection.

What difference did it make to the rest of society, one may ask, so long as the exactions of the government were at the same level, whether it was or was not reducing its expenditure on violence? A large difference. Reduction in the costs of producing protection freed resources for other uses, whether or not the price was reduced. If there was a reduction in the cost of production and no reduction in price, the resulting profit or tribute could be spent in new kinds of consumption, or be hoarded or invested. This is what distinguishes tribute from the labor costs incurred in hiring generals, soldiers, police, tax collectors, and legal officers. As a practical matter the distinction would be difficult to apply, I suppose, in any statistical analysis of royal expenditure, but there was enough conspicuous consumption at Renaissance courts to indicate that a part of the revenue collected and dispensed in the king's name was not consumed on necessities, not even military necessi-

---

[7] Military entrepreneurs are being fruitfully studied by Fritz Redlich, who has nearing completion a two-volume work to be published by the Harvard University Press. By-products that have already appeared are "Der Marketender," *Vierteljahrschrift für Sozial- und Wirtschaftsgeschichte*, XLI (1954), 227–52; *De Praeda Militari: Looting and Booty, 1500–1815* (Beihefte 39 of the *Vierteljahrschrift für Sozial- und Wirtschaftsgeschichte*, Wiesbaden, 1956); and "Military Entrepreneurship and the Credit System in the 16th and 17th Centuries," *Kyklos*, X (1957), 186–93.

[8] Tax farmers are one example. The officeholder who uses his office as an enterprise of which he seeks to maximize the income is discussed in a different context but in terms significant in relation to my theme by Jacob von Klaveren, "Die historische Erscheinung der Korruption," *Vierteljahrschrift für Sozial- und Wirtschaftsgeschichte*, XLI (Dec., 1957), 291 ff.

ties. The expenditure of tribute for luxuries or wants previously unsatisfied stimulated new forms of production. If it was not spent on this kind of consumption, the tribute was available for investment, for a courtier's improvements of his landed estates, for example. High costs of producing protection were a drain on resources, high prices for protection merely diverted wealth from one group to another.

II

In addition to governments, other economic enterprises—those mainly concerned with producing goods and services other than protection—found opportunities for profits arising out of the way violence was used. These opportunities were created by the governments, primarily—by the fact that the prices charged by the violence-controlling enterprises were different for different classes of customers, there being some degree of customer control, or, to put it in more usual language, by the fact that the exactions levied by the government were different for different enterprises. One very important aspect of this is the fact that in the later Middle Ages land rents gradually become so distinct from the protection payments embodied in seignioral dues and taxes as to be susceptible to Ricardian analysis. I have no time for that subject, for I wish to explore another important aspect, the nature and source of the profits made in international trade.

The profits of a merchant engaged in trade over long distances were limited by the real or potential competition of other merchants. If one merchant or one group was as good as another in gathering information and guessing about supply and demand, the one able to operate with lower costs would gain larger profits. A very substantial part of costs was what had to be paid for protection and for insurance against losses that might be inflicted by violence-using enterprises if their exactions were not paid. Some trading enterprises secured more protection than others, or equally good protection at less cost, and this difference in their costs enabled them to make extra profits which I call protection rents.[9]

A simple example in a modern context will clarify what I have in mind. If two producers of copper sell at prices set by the London market and have the same costs of extracting, refining, and transporting ore, but pay different tariffs on the way to market, the one that pays lower tariffs receives protection rent.

[9] See pp. 383–87.

I would have no excuse for giving a special name to profits resulting from favorable tariffs if that were all I had in mind. But the situations in which I am interested were not that simple. All kinds of navigation laws were involved. The enterprises engaged in international trade or colonization during the later Middle Ages and during the first centuries of Europe's oceanic expansion had to make many kinds of payments to secure protection. I propose "protection rent" in order to have a term to apply to profits arising from differences in the whole range of costs incurred in using or controlling violence. These included convoy fees, tribute to the Barbary pirates, or higher insurance for voyages into pirate-infested waters, bribes or gifts to customs officials or higher authorities, and other kinds of smuggling costs. It included some expenditures by trading or colonizing enterprises to organize their own armed forces—from placing extra guns and soldiers on an individual ship to dispatching an army for the defense or even the conquest of a colony.

The diversity of ways in which enterprises could obtain protection enabled them to choose among alternatives, pay different amounts according to the choice made, and receive different kinds or degrees of protection in return. They could freight wares on heavily armed ships and pay low insurance, or freight on less defensible ships and pay high insurance. They could use ports where established treaties required them to pay high duties but in return gave reasonable assurance against seizure, or they could go to ports where no treaties applied and trust to their own guns, diplomacy, and well-placed bribes.

Operating with lower payments for protection was often the decisive factor in the competition between merchants of different cities or kingdoms and was achieved by complicated mixtures of public and private enterprise. The fleets of merchant galleys for which Venice is famous were successful partly because their sailing qualities were adapted to the seas in which they operated and partly because they were for a time the best solution to the problem of protection—not only safety from pirates, but a flexible marshaling of the flow of trade so as to secure favorable treaties and take quick advantage of them. Any effort to explain why Venice was more prosperous than its rivals, or more prosperous at some times than at others, must consider how far the Venetians were more secure, at less cost, from disruption by violence in their purchases of wares in one place, their shipments, and their sales in good markets.

During the Middle Ages and early modern times protection rents were a major source of the fortunes made in trade. They were a more important source of profits, I believe, than superiority in industrial techniques or industrial organization. The wealth gained in mercantile and colonial enterprise from protection rents gradually increased to the point where it began to rival that which governmental enterprises obtained from tribute.[10] Like the landlords, whom I have not time to discuss, merchants became recipients of a surplus which they could consume in luxuries or could invest. The amount merchants invested was relatively high. Their habits, abilities and involvements as traders made them on the whole the class most inclined to save and invest their part of the surplus product of the economy.

By surplus I mean that part of the total production which did not have to be consumed in order to maintain the existing level of production. The following three conclusions regarding surplus result from the foregoing analysis of the use of violence:

First, the higher the costs of production in the protection-producing enterprise, the less the surplus.[11] When violence-producing enterprises were controlled by employees, they made little or no effort to minimize costs, and as a result a large part of total production was consumed in militarism.

Second when the protection-producing enterprise was controlled by an absolute monarch, he had an interest in reducing costs. If he was able to do so, the surplus was increased, and much of it went to the monarch's court where it was available for conspicuous consumption or investment.

Third, in international trade and colonization competing mercantile enterprises paid highly variable amounts for protection, and those paying less received protection rents, a kind of profit which placed in their hands a part of the surplus production.

Since this third effect occurred later than the others, it suggests a stage theory of economic development, which I offer as a kind of prologue to the Schumpeterian sequence of capitalism, democracy, and socialism.

---

[10] Of course there was no sharp line between those who made fortunes by subcontracting governmental activities and those who traded with political privileges that yielded protection rents.

[11] *Ceteris paribus.* As I was reminded by H. J. Habakkuk, in a society where there is chronic underemployment of resources, increased military expenditure has often stimulated more production of other kinds so that the amount of surplus rose in time of war. But can it not be said that over the long run, other things being equal, a society that is able to attain a high level of employment of resources only by high military expenditure produces less surplus than if it were able to attain that same level of employment of resources with less military expenditure?

In my first stage anarchy and plunder dominate. Viking raids and feudal warfare reduce western Frankland almost to this kind of "primitive anarchy" about A.D. 900. The use of violence is highly competitive, even on land. The second stage begins when small regional or provincial monopolies are established. Agricultural production then rises, and most of the surplus is collected by the recently established monopolists of violence. When, as in twelfth-century feudalism, the monopolists formed loosely organized cartels constantly bickering over the production and market quota of each, the surplus is kept relatively small by the high military costs, and what there is of it is widely distributed among a tribute-taking class.

During a later phase of the second stage many tribute takers attract customers by special offers to agricultural and commercial enterprise. They offer protection at low prices for those who will bring new lands into cultivation, and special policing services to encourage trade such as that organized by the counts of Champagne for merchants coming to their fairs. When profit-seeking princes are able to consolidate larger, tighter monopolies, they reduce costs of production and increase the amount of tribute. Somehow in the process land rent becomes more clearly differentiated from taxes and seignioral dues. Production increases. A larger surplus, although mostly tribute, makes consumption more varied and stimulates interregional trade. Differences in what competing traders have to expend for protection gives rise to protection rents.

A third stage is reached when the merchants who collect protection rents and the landowners who collect land rents are getting more of the economy's surplus than are fief holders and monarchs. In this third stage the enterprises specializing in the use of violence receive less of the surplus than do enterprises that buy protection from the governments. Protection rent and land rent replace tribute as the chief sources of large incomes. Since successful merchants devote much of their income to capital accumulation, a higher proportion of the surplus is invested in expanding commercial enterprises, in agricultural improvements, and in new industries.

The passage from the third stage to a fourth occurs when technological improvements—industrial innovations—become more important than protection rent as a source of business profits. Violence-using and violence-producing enterprises come increasingly under the control of their customers as a whole; governments become more democratic. Credit formation—the creation of deposits, the floatation of bonds, and the whole mechanism of a capital market—having been created largely to serve protection-producing enterprises, now responds to the needs of the industrial innovator. We have reached capitalism of the Schumpeterian model, my prologue is finished, the curtain rises on the main show.

I confess that my capsuling of a thousand years of history into four paragraphs contains some grains of satire. No sequence of stages can enable us to predict the future or to explain particular past events. The stages are abstract models. A stage theory is only a device for emphasizing or overemphasizing some factors among many.

But I hope that my capsules contain some grains of truth. The four stages are distinguished by the changing relation of violence-using enterprises to the amount and distribution of surplus. They focus attention on the way the surplus was distributed among different kinds of producers, including the "producers," as I call them, of protection. The distribution of the surplus affected the way it was used—whether in new forms of consumption, in attempts at hoarding, or in agricultural, commercial, and industrial improvements.

These alternative uses of surplus, and its total amount, were important for economic growth. There has been so much fruitful study recently of the economic growth accompanied by industrialization which has occurred during the last two centuries that many modern preoccupations have been carried back into the study of ancient and medieval times with stimulating results. But with the longer perspective in mind, I would like to suggest that the most weighty single factor in most periods of growth, if any one factor has been most important, has been a reduction in the proportion of resources devoted to war and police. Those princes or statesmen who organized government in such a way as to reduce the costs of protection contributed to economic growth just as did the industrial or agricultural innovators who reduced the costs of other products. Entrepreneurial princes were all the more important because they were reducing not the cost of some luxury that was a small item in total consumption but the cost of a widely consumed necessity. In many centuries the main way in which governments influenced growth was through decisions that determined how much should be expended on the use and control of violence.

Debatable, however, is the effect on economic growth of the monarchs who maintained or raised their exactions while reducing their costs, and who thus collected as tribute a large part of the surplus available for capital accumulation. If all the tribute was used for conspicuous consumption, a term which seems particularly appropriate for the court of a prince of the *ancien régime,* growth was slowed by lack of investment. Merchants who gained protection rents from international trade and colonization, although not entirely inconspicuous in their consumption, probably had a lower propensity to consume. If so, lower profits for governments and higher profits for trading enterprises meant more capital accumulation and more growth.

I have used the device of a stage theory to emphasize the relation of violence-using enterprises to the distribution of surplus. Their relation to monopoly in economic life, basic in this connection, has other aspects deserving of even more emphasis.

In my fourth stage, which roughly corresponds to a commonly accepted model of industrial capitalism, monopoly appears in temporary forms as a result of technological and commercial innovation and attains relative permanence in those industries in which technology has so developed as to give monopoly decisive advantages. In earlier stages very few industries had undergone such technical development as to become natural monopolies, but government had already attained that status. I am tempted to call government the earliest natural monopoly. Priestly activities, another basic service industry, were widely organized on a comparable scale at as early a date, and irrigation was an even more compelling natural monopoly in some regions. But apart from special regional conditions concerning the use of natural resources, monopoly-inducing advantages of size were most effective on the two closely connected service-rendering organizations—priesthood and government.

Monopoly in one field can be used in seeking a monopoly in others; control of a basic ingredient can lead to control over finished products. Since protection is in a sense a basic ingredient in nearly every other product, a government could use its monopoly in its own field to establish monopolies in others. When irrigation as well as government and religion were combined into one huge, centrally directed enterprise, it reached out and became the monopolist of many other products, from salt to papyrus. Where there was no irrigation and where warriors and priests were separately organized, extension of monopoly into other fields was in part checked by disadvantages of scale, in part directed, as well as checked, by the influence of various consumer groups on the control of the protection-producing monopoly.

One aspect of the extension of monopoly is the effort of businessmen to become less "entrepreneurial" and more "bureaucratic," their desire for what have been called "security zones of investment, protective shells built with the use of political influence."[12] Another aspect is the

[12] W. T. Easterbrook, "Long-Period Comparative Study: Some Historical Cases," The *Journal of Economic History*, XVII (Dec., 1957), 574–75.

pressure from within the governmental enterprise itself to expand into fields which, although not directly involving violence, are closely connected with military power. Today atomic physics has become a sensitive field in which some scientific and engineering services are being monopolized by governments on the ground that national security requires it. In the nineteenth century railroad building had overriding military importance in many countries. In the later Middle Ages and early modern times the pressures for and against monopoly collided in maritime transportation, an industry then occupying a strategic position in both commercial and political rivalries. Efforts to protect shipping led to situations in which cargo space was under monopolistic control, and this control could be used to obtain a monopoly over the wares bought or sold at the ports of destination.

The links from monopoly of protection to monopoly of transport to monopoly of the products transported are all the more clearly revealed in the regulation of shipping by the commune of Venice because Venice broke the chain. Its government was firmly controlled by one group, mostly wholesale merchants, and they opposed monopolistic sales on the Venetian market. Transportation of wares from a Levantine port to Venice was not, as transportation, a natural monopoly. Purely from a navigational point of view it was more advantageous for ships to sail at various times on various routes and offer competing services. But because there were advantages of scale when organizing protection, ships were directed to sail in convoys in periods of danger and Venetian merchants were then required, if they wished to ship at all, to freight specified wares on these convoys only. When defense was thus monopolistically organized, only a limited number of ships could offer cargo space to shippers. Selected operators had to be given a monopoly. Since the ship operators were also merchants, they tried to use their control of cargo space to secure monopolistic advantages in buying or selling the wares shipped—at Cyprus or at Venice, for example. The Venetian government resisted such monopolies of merchandising by regulating the convoys as public carriers, and it had many difficulties indeed making the regulations effective.[13] In contrast, the enterprises of the Portuguese kings, the Dutch East India Company, and many others during the first two centuries of oceanic commerce

---

[13] Some aspects of the problem are discussed in Gino Luzzatto, "Sindicati e cartelli nel commercio veneziano dei sec. xiii e xiv," *Rivista di storia economica*, 1936, and in his *Studi di storia economica veneziana* (Padua: Cedam, 1954), pp. 195–200; in my *Andrea Barbarigo, Merchant of Venice* (Baltimore: The Johns Hopkins Press, 1944), pp. 45–52, 77–84; and in Chapter 3 above.

combined monopolies of protection, of transportation, and of products transported.

Since monopoly is more efficient in some fields, competition in others, their distribution in the economy affected the total output of wealth. But that is not their chief interest. The running battles between monopolistic and competitive tendencies in Venetian shipping, or in British colonial trade, to name but two examples, cannot be fully evaluated in terms of the effect on the output of goods and services. Monopoly affected not only efficiency. It brought with it more or less freedom and equality, more or less security and stability; and these qualities, quite as much as efficiency, determined the outcome of the conflicts between monopolistic and competitive forces. We cannot understand how the participants in the battle behaved without inquiring what they, in their time and their society, meant by freedom or security, and how they related it to happiness, virtue, and justice, which, with all their changing meanings, are the ultimates that men have striven for. And we in turn also evalute monopoly not only in terms of efficiency but also in terms of justice.

"Without justice, what is government but a great robbery?" declared Augustine. From his point of view he might have said the same of all kinds of economic organization, and in effect did: Without justice what is any business but thievery? Not government alone but many other organizations through which men receive the necessities of life are judged by standards of justice and liberty. Governmental monopoly of violence, even when in itself good, has led to the formation of other monopolies that were not good, either because they were not efficient, being in fields in which a monopolistic scale of operations had no advantages or because gains in efficiency, even if they occurred, were overbalanced by losses in liberty and justice.

In short, the function of government that I have been analyzing has at least two aspects. As producer of a necessary service, protection, the violence-using, violence-controlling enterprises affected the amount and distribution of material wealth through the costs incurred and the prices exacted. At the same time, being natural monopolies, they affected the extent to which monopoly prevailed in other fields of production, and in this way affected human relations throughout the whole economic organization.

This second aspect seems to me the more important because I regard knowledge of the social situations created by men's efforts to gain a livelihood and accumulate wealth as the bedrock of economic history. We want to know what men were like in the ordinary business of life, in their daily occupations—the kind of problems they faced and what they did about them. Connections between their daily lives and what they produced were very close indeed, so that part of our answer is found in statistics on the number of calories consumed, on the variety of their diet, and in their other material satisfactions. Explanations of craft routines, of the emergence of new techniques and of commerical practices also form part of the answer. But how men have dealt with each other in the process of production is more important than how they dealt with soil, plants, or tools. "Knowing what men were like" means, above all, knowing how they behaved toward other men.

How much they produced was one factor in determining how they behaved, but only one. The economic interpretation of history is a mistake, I think, because it declares that economics is the all-important cause. Concentration on economic growth would be a mistake if it were to imply that the quantity of material goods is the all-important result. Knowledge of changes in output and in techniques is vital, absolutely vital, but not so much for its own sake as because it is necessary in order to understand the social structure of production. In ultimate interest, the way men have dealt with each other in producing material goods is more important than the goods themselves.

Many of us, without believing in the economic interpretation of history, yet share the feeling that economic history is in some sense the most important part of history. We believe that knowing the economic life of any society is fundamental to understanding that society, not because the process of production has a unique causal importance shaping all other aspects of culture and being itself reshaped only by changes generated within itself, but, quite simply, because the qualities expressed in economic activities constitute the largest part of what life has been. Most men most of the time have been occupied in making a living. The values that existed for them, not merely as aspiration or as ideas to be talked about, but in action and as qualities of personal character, were those embodied in the daily activities by which they made their living. If bullying and fawning, arrogant command and servile obedience were the rule in economic life, that is the way men were—that is what society was like. Other themes—religious aspiration, artistic feeling, and creative intellectual vigor—reward endless historical investigation for their own sake, even when they have no discernible connection with social organization, but historians interested in justice, freedom, or any other qualities of social life have reason to give primary attention to the human relations entered into during the processes of production and distribution.

Part Four

HISTORY

26

Why Begin at the Beginning?*

FIRE ENGINES screeching down the street, windows flying up, small boys running and grownups pretending not to run. As a crowd gathers about the blazing building the question most heard from the lips of later arrivals is an historical question, "How did it start?"

Queries about the past arise spontaneously. Every effort at personal recollection may be considered an historical question and without the answers furnished by memory our lives would lack purpose and meaning. Quite rightly has history been described as an extension of memory. Though the memories of which history consists have become impersonal, or as we may say second hand, they can be just as important in influencing how we act as first hand memories. Our personal recollections determine innumerable day-by-day decisions; recent historical events sway our political judgments; remote historical memories affect our attitudes on the most basic questions. Our conceptions of where we are going and where we should go are entangled with our notions of where we came from.

So insatiable is man's interest in his distant past that imagination assists the weaknesses of memory. The Romans elaborated the legends of Romulus, Numa, and other early kings to explain the origins of familiar Roman customs. Where memory fails completely, imagination is given free rein. Among primitive peoples myth-makers tell their stories of the origin of the world, of man, and of the social customs of the tribe. What though the maker of myths knows nothing about it! Men demand a story nevertheless and if one soothsayer refused to invent, the people would find another less cautious, for they will not

* *Proceedings of the Middle States Association of History and Social Science Teachers,* An Address to the Middle Atlantic Association of History and Social Science Teachers at Philadelphia, May 7, 1937, XXV (1937), 73–77. (By permission.)

be satisfied without some kind of an answer to their questions about the past.

The position of a history teacher, whether in a college or in a high school, is not entirely different from that of the myth-makers of primitive peoples. We are bound to give the best answers we can to questions about the past. What started it? How did society become divided into the rich and the poor? How did civilization begin?

Perhaps my remarks are conjuring up for some of you a picture, which you find fantastic, of a teacher beset by interested young students who deluge him with questions so persistently that, turn and dodge as he may, he is unable to escape their inquisitiveness. All too rarely, whether in high school or college, does the teacher taste the joys and embarrassments of such overwhelming attention. Experience may have imprinted in our minds quite a different image, a classroom where the teacher is urging his own interest upon the students, with greater or less success, and where the questions asked seem concerned only with the understanding of a textbook and the passing of tests. Even if this be the picture etched by experience, it is really quite superficial. The very students who are most passive in the classroom may turn up later in life battling vigorously for some version of history, whether it be the first chapters of Genesis, or Weem's *Life of Washington,* or some version of why the Constitutional Convention created the Supreme Court. Historical questions are answered in many places besides the classroom. What we teach is only a foundation, more or less shaky and more or less complete. Throughout their lives our students will build on that foundation, adding a wall here or a turret there, according to the questions which arise during the varied experiences through which they pass.

From this point of view, the survey courses given in American colleges and universities have much the same function as the historical curricula offered by high schools. In neither case are we, the teachers, chiefly concerned with preparing pupils for advanced studies in history. Our main concern is to furnish the best possible second-hand memories on those historical subjects about which they are likely sooner or later to ask questions.

For the last seven years I have been in charge of the historical survey course required of all students in the College of Arts and Sciences of The Johns Hopkins University. In most American colleges a one-year survey course in history is demanded and the history department is therefore under an almost irresistible temptation to restrict the course to the period after 1648 or 1450, or at least not to go further back than the proverbial fall of Rome. The Johns Hopkins faculty decided to have a two-year survey, and unlike some two-year introductory courses, ours does not include elementary economics or American government. Fortunate in being allowed two years for a purely historical course, I resolved to start with the first appearance of man, and have given about a quarter of the course to what is commonly called ancient history. Seven years of trial, with some shuffling back and forth, have confirmed my belief in the advantages of beginning at the beginning. No doubt courses should be different at various colleges; high school curricula present detailed problems on which I am no expert; and the planning of a particular course is in general best left to those who are to teach it; but I do wish to urge here three reasons why youths who are not going to specialize in history should, somewhere in their studies, begin history at the beginning.

First, the more remote past often presents in simpler form the problems of the present. Take, for example, the most elemental of human problems, that of obtaining food. In modern life personal experience permits most of us to know directly only a fragment of the process by which we are fed. To my small boys it is simply a matter of coming to dinner when called; to my wife it is a problem of shopping and cooking. If we attempt to grasp the whole social process as it is now carried on, we find ourselves face to face with the AAA, scientific agriculture, co-operatives, foreign markets, and tariffs. How much easier it is when introducing the problem to turn away from these mysteries, and go back to begin at the beginning. Look at food supply from the point of view of the reindeer-hunters or of the first farmers in the Stone Age, examine a medieval manor or even the marketing system of a medieval town, and it is possible to present an elementary idea of the problem as a whole. Because the processes by which early societies gained their food were relatively simple, their study makes the elements of our modern problem easier to grasp.

Democracy and other types of government can similarly be introduced in simple but concrete form in connection with the history of ancient Athens or Rome. I would like to linger on this point but lack of time compels me to pass on to what is to me an even more important reason for urging that we begin at the beginning, a reason at which I have already hinted.

Sooner or later our students will make up a beginning anyhow, and that beginning will to a great extent determine for them the meaning of history. In any narration the opening episode is likely to stick in the mind and to color the whole story. The question "How did it start?"

was answered for millions of men through many centuries by the scenes in the Garden of Eden. The adventures of Adam and Eve fixed a certain interpretation of the whole of human experience. When the rationalists of the eighteenth century rejected the theological view of human destiny, Voltaire provided a different story of how it started, and Rousseau offered yet another. In our age of uncertain purposes and a great deal of historical evidence, professionals may not be ready to supply an answer as simple as those of Bossuet, Voltaire, and Rousseau. Non-professionals more certain of their aims and less bothered by evidence are not lacking to fill the gap.

There is now a disposition to restrict survey courses in colleges, and also, I believe, the high school teaching of history, to the period since the emergence of nations in the fifteenth and sixteenth centuries. Nationalism is thereby mistaken as the beginning and persists in dominating the story. Of course it is possible, while teaching only modern history, to take a different starting point and make some other theme, like class war, dominate the narrative, but nationalism is now of such interest that it is common to begin with the origins of modern nations, especially of our own. Since history inevitably takes the form of a narrative and the plot makes more impression on our students than do the generalized disavowals which the cautious textbook writer will place in his introductory chapter, the student may well be left with the feeling that all history is a history of nations. As teachers of history we lay ourselves open to the criticism that historians connive with history to place the nation between man and humanity.

Presumably these fragmentary courses, amputated to fit the exigencies of curricula and examinations, are not intended to answer certain ultimate historical questions, yet these questions should be directly faced somewhere in the educational system. Otherwise the fragment will be mistaken for the whole. Is history a record of progress? And if so what is the character of that progress? To what do we owe our civilization? Some sort of answer is demanded. If we, the professional dealers in second-hand memories, do not respond, the answers of such soothsayers as the politicians, the novelists, and the Sunday supplements will be accepted. Under the direction of their dictator, Turkish children are told that they are the descendants of the Hittites who were the source of civilization; Germans are nourished on the Nordic myth; and in America we have such books as Madison Grant's *The Passing of the Great Race*. Most popular misrepresentations of ancient history have a racial or nationalistic thesis which agrees very well with the preoccupations inculcated by limiting historical schooling to modern times.

No doubt classroom instruction will not root out the historical interpretations which are inspired simply by the wishes of the moment, but we can avoid encouraging them. It is our task to outline the whole story in accordance with the best evidence available. We are falling down on our jobs if we give only a fragment which encourages misrepresentation of the whole.

The mention of evidence brings up my third reason for urging that we begin at the beginning. It is in teaching the early history of man that we have the best chances to keep the student conscious of the sources. The pyramids, the palace at Cnossus, and the successive layers of the mound of Troy appear both as the vital facts in the case and as the star witnesses. To continually pop the question "How do we know?" in the midst of a discussion of the French Revolution is hardly practical anywhere except in a graduate seminar, but even the most elementary discussion about the men of the Stone Age can easily turn on questions of evidence. The methods by which archeologists have discovered the everyday customs of the Egyptians and the Sumerians constitute the main attraction of those studies for beginners. The findings of the excavators are material things, varied and interesting in themselves, and many of the important inferences from artifacts are relatively simple. To be sure, these inferences from archeological evidence are sometimes as ingenious as they are simple—for example, the inference that a people were immigrants from the north because the hearth was the central feature of their houses. But it is just this kind of statement which most strikingly suggests to the students that history is based on evidence, and that there is a distinction to be made between the evidence and the inferences drawn from it. All historians do some guessing. Because the guesses of the archeologist are so obvious and above-board they are most provocative of the pertinent question "How do we know?"

That question is quite as vital to the profession as the query "How did it start?" Though we are in some ways like the myth-maker we are also in this respect different. We do not ask that our stories be accepted on faith nor do we feel justified in relying entirely upon any artistic charm which we may give them to insure acceptance. Our craft is to make the facts speak for themselves, or at least to show that there is evidence supporting the facts through which we speak. It is our business as historians to be always ready to face the challenge "How do you know?" and as teachers it is our business to encourage, nay even to drill our pupils to hound us with that interrogation.

Unlike the question "How did it start?" the query "How do we know?" is not one that bursts forth spontaneously on all occasions. Readiness to ask it is one of the best tests for distinguishing the intelligent from the guillible. In the crowd attracted around the burning building by the rush of fire engines all sorts of reports about the source of the blaze will circulate unchecked by skeptical queries as to the basis of the rumors. The very success of the myth makers suggests that most people find it easier to believe than to question. Undoubtedly we should try in all social studies to stimulate the questioning attitude, and should encourage our students to receive skeptically what they are told about quite recent events; but, I believe, history teachers will find it easiest to arouse the critical habit when they are dealing with ancient history. It is by beginning at the beginning that we can most effectively drum into the students the pertinence of that basic question "How do we know?"

27

The Social Sciences and the Humanities*

THE vastness of the subject assigned me is so redoubtable that I must begin the discussion within what I feel to be relatively familiar territory, within my own field, history. If there is any frontier line between the social sciences and the humanities, then history lies across the frontier as a sort of buffer state, and some of the intellectual experiences of the historical profession may therefore be of interest. Facing an audience with members knowing more than I do about nearly every corner of this broad topic, I hope only to point out some similarities and contrasts in the methods by which human affairs are studied.

Briefly put, my theme is that the movement to ape the natural sciences which began about a hundred or seventy-five years ago has caused much misunderstanding and sneering or coldness along the frontier between the social sciences and the humanities, partly because too much emphasis has been placed on organizing knowledge in propositions of correlation or into propositions which in a sweeping way state the whole sequence of historical development. Recently, since the First World War particularly, that ideal of being scientific—which involved I believe inadequate understanding of what was basic in the natural sciences—has been on the decline, at least in historical study. There is some danger that this shift in the climate of opinion will lead to the building of a higher barrier between humanities and social sciences. Accepting with enthusiasm the slur that history is only literature, some historians are turning their backs on social science. But there is also hope that the present questioning of the "scientific" ideal will break

* Paper Read February 6, 1948 in the Symposium on Research Frontiers in Human Relations, Proceedings of the American Philosophical Society, XCII (1948), 356–62. (By permission.)

down the barrier and create understanding co-operation. The breaking of the barrier seems to me to depend on reaching a common understanding concerning the necessity of describing human relations in terms of motives and concerning the way to frame and test such propositions about motives. When we study past human action as a guide to future action, the most fruitful way to organize our knowledge into a general system is not through coefficients of correlation nor yet through sweeping developmental theories, but through what I will call structural propositions—models or types—which are constructed with close attention to their relation to historical realities. This method requires the resources of both the social sciences and the humanities.

Being a historian, I will use a historical approach to my theme, and take as my starting point the attitude towards science expressed by the presidential address delivered at the American Historical Association almost exactly forty years ago by George Burton Adams. The distinguished medievalist noted the rising clamor that history must be a science, or as he summarized it, the assertion that history is "the orderly progression of mankind to a definite end, and that we may know and state the laws which control the actions of men in organized society."[1] Regarding such a science Professor Adams was skeptical, but he made without reservations the following declaration of faith: "All science which is true science must rest upon the proved and correlated fact." Facts are the foundations, and he exhorted his hearers to collect them and pass them on to later builders, saying "the man who devotes himself to such labors, who is content with the preliminary work, will make a more useful and more permanent contribution to the final science and philosophy of history than will he who yields to the allurement of speculation and endeavors to discover in the present stage of our knowledge the forces that control society, or to formulate the laws of their actions." [2]

For about a generation historians were comforted by this faith that facts were the foundation and that if enough were collected someone someday might be able to build with them a science of history. Then arose haunting echoes of Emerson's dictum: "Time dissipates to shining ether the solid angularity of facts. No anchor, no cable, no fences avail to keep a fact a fact."[3] In language more precise, modern, and

[1] George Burton Adams, "History and the Philosophy of History," *American Historical Review,* XIV (1909) , 229–30.

[2] *Ibid.*, 235–36.

[3] Ralph Waldo Emerson, *Essays* (Boston: Houghton Mifflin, 1903) , p. 9 [Vol. II of the Centenary Edition of the *Complete Works*].

epistemological, the historian was told that not only his selection of what to study or narrate, but even his establishment of the fact itself depended on his preconceptions. The presidential address of Carl Becker in 1931, "Everyman his own Historian" breathed an atmosphere utterly different from that expressed by G. B. Adams in 1908. In the new climate of opinion, "the proved and correlated fact" was discovered to have been a theory in disguise all the time, or at least a compound partly of evidence and partly of the historian's emotions and preconceived ideas.[4] Consequently in our day historians are showing an interest in theories of history which even Arnold Toynbee has failed to satiate. The report of the Social Science Research Council's Committee on the theory and practice of historical study has also proved a best seller. It gives a broader view of developments which I am looking at only from a special angle.[5] As long as a historian could feel respectably although humbly scientific in his untheoretical collecting of facts, he was fortified to resist temptations to be literary, or philosophical, or scientific in ways requiring abstract thinking. Now that he has discovered that he is a theorist in spite of himself, he is more inclined to inspect what those who are theorists by deliberation have to offer.

To be sure, there were always some historians who deliberately theorized about history. They were seeking mainly laws of development. Although there are aspects of human affairs that seem recurrent—as was emphasized this morning by Dr. Marquis—the aspect of change which is the historian's main problem constitutes a development through successive stages or states each of which was made possible by that preceding and was prerequisite to that which followed. Accordingly, the expression "historical law" most frequently means a proposition which characterizes the direction and sequence of development. The nebular hypothesis is a historical law in this sense. Edward P. Cheyney used it thus when in his presidential address to the American Historical Association in 1923 he proposed six laws in history. His fourth law was a law of democracy, a tendency for all government to come under the control of all the people. His sixth was a law of moral progress.[6] A developmental proposition more complicated than any of Cheyney's, and one much more influential, was Karl Marx's sequence

---

[4] *American Historical Review*, XXXVII (1932) , 221–36.

[5] *Theory and Practice in Historical Study: A Report of the Committee on Historiography*, Social Science Research Council, Bulletin 54, 1946.

[6] Edward P. Cheyney, "Law in History," *American Historical Review*, XXIX (1924) , 231–48.

of class struggles. These broad theories describe change which is all in one direction. There is no assumption that we will go back from solid planet to gaseous nebula, from man to ape, from democracy to absolute monarchy, or from one form of class struggle to an earlier form, and start over. These historical laws or developmental propositions are not descriptive of sequences which are expected to repeat themselves.

Although the men who framed the best known developmental propositions, notably Karl Marx, claimed to be making history scientific, their "laws" were really too sweeping and did not in fact serve that end. If we inquire what is the purpose of making these developmental propositions, we find that some modest developmental theories are useful to be sure in making predictions, as is illustrated by the studies of population, but that the broader they are, the less is their predictive value. Even if the general direction of development in the past is well established empirically, there is little basis for telling what will occur in the immediate future. Economic history can say that the general trend has been towards more and more efficient production, but there have also been ups and downs. Knowledge of the general trend is not an adequate basis for short-range predictions. On the other hand, if we seek to use developmental propositions to predict far ahead, we are on weak ground logically. How sound is a long extrapolation forward of a curve of development when the curve is merely a chart of observed occurrences in the past and we do not know the factors which determined the occurrences? In the long run an entirely new factor may set matters going in an entirely new direction.

If developmental propositions based on the very slight knowledge which has as yet been gained of human affairs are of such little use in making practical prediction, why have they been formulated with so much pains? Examination of the propositions themselves indicates the answer. The main value of organizing on a large scale what was known about the direction and sequence of development was, and is, to formulate a conception of where we should go, and why. Every important general theory of historical development has been shot through with assertions as to what is worth while in the world, and it has also contained statements, capable of being proved empirically true or false, concerning the conditions under which good and evil have existed in the past and could or will exist in the future. That of Arnold Toynbee, which is most popular at present, illustrates the ethical and in a measure empirical character of these broad theories of development. I do not mean to disparage them on that account, for we need systematic thinking which harmonizes and strengthens our ethical beliefs. But that is not science, or at least not what was admired as science by social scientists who were following in the trail of the natural scientists and thereby becoming less and less concerned with ethics and more and more concerned with correlations which could be used to make hypothetical predictions. Social scientists were not attracted by "laws of history" which proved to be at best ethical systems and at worst mere wishful thinking.

Meanwhile some of the young historians who in 1908 dreamed of building a science of history were treading paths more nearly parallel to those of natural scientists. They turned away from developmental propositions, focused on recurrent aspects of historical events, and sought to find in these recurrences the basis for another kind of historical law more modestly called correlations. In the very next volume after that printing G. B. Adams' presidential address, the *American Historical Review* carried an article by Frederick J. Teggart. In this article of 1910, Teggart outlined an hypothesis for explaining historical changes in ways "verifiable by the processes of science."[7] In 1939 Professor Teggart published the results of his thirty years of effort to apply strictly "the methods of science to the facts of history," in a book entitled *Rome and China*. It bore the subtitle, *A Study in Correlation in Historical Events*.[8]

By 1939 much progress had indeed been made in finding and using correlations in historical research very much as they were found and used in natural science—observing variable phenomena and noting correspondences between a change in one factor and a change in other factors. To a limited extent the humanistic historical disciplines use correlations to make predictions much as they are used in experimental science. Archeologists note the correlations of certain types of pottery with the sequence of strata in buried cities and associate particular types of potsherds with the first use of metals, other types of pottery with the various evidences of trade, and so on. With the observed correlations as his basis, the archeologist will predict what types of potsherds will be found in later excavations and in association with what other artifacts. By digging he can subject his predictions to verifications.[9] Of course predictions made by these methods are not correct 100 per cent of the time, and actually the archeologist, like any scientist, will work out predictions concerning various sites and select

[7] Frederick J. Teggart, "The Circumstance or the Substance of History," *American Historical Review*, XV (1910), 715.

[8] (Berkeley: University of California Press, 1939.)

[9] Consequently, archeology might be called an experimental science. Cf. William Foxwell Albright, *From the Stone Age to Christianity*, (Baltimore, The Johns Hopkins Press, 1940), p. 24.

for excavation a mound concerning which he is in doubt, in order by his excavation to resolve the doubt.

The archeologist's use of this kind of historical prediction is more easily dubbed scientific because he deals with material remains, but the same methods are used by those whose sources are in written words. The historian who has studied guild statutes can make some pretty good predictions about what will be found in other guild statutes. Moreover, both a student of guild statutes and a student of Greek statues are in effect making statements, not about material things only, but about the people to whom their evidence is relevant. They are making predictive statements about human affairs in the past, and on the basis of a few cases forecasting what will be found in other cases. Perhaps we should call this special kind of prediction "historical prediction."

Frederick Teggart himself pushed far afield in using correlations as the basis for constructing a science of history. He was interested in the Roman Empire and the barbarian tribes on its borders. Since he wished to show that history could be organized as a science, as well as narrated as a branch of literature, he summed up his study not in a narrative but in a proposition of correlation, and marshalled his evidence with as little narrative as possible. He stated the correlation thus: "Within these decades [58 B.C. to A.D. 107] every barbarian uprising in Europe followed the outbreak of war either on the eastern frontiers of the Roman empire or in the 'Western regions' of the Chinese."[10] The significance of Professor Teggart's effort for our evaluation of method is in his way of explaining this correlation. He maintained that the wars in the East disrupted trade and so led to the barbarian uprisings in Europe. True to the "scientific" scheme of thought which he was trying to imitate, he looked for general laws about wars, trade, and the effects of the severance of trade. He wished there were such laws, confirmed empirically by other historical correlations in addition to his, for then his explanation could be comparable to the kind of explanation given by a physicist who explains Kepler's laws of planetary motion by referring to Newton's more generalized laws. But in fact Professor Teggart knew no such general laws about trade and war.[11]

[10] *Rome and China*, p. vii. Practically speaking, a fatal defect in Teggart's demonstration is his inability to establish that the events correlated—"uprisings" or "wars" —are similar one to another in the respects pertinent to the inquiry. See my review in *American Journal of Philosophy*, LXIII (1942), 356–57.

[11] His searchings for them are reported especially in his *The Processes of History* (New Haven: Yale University Press, 1918), and in parts of his *Theory of History* (New Haven: Yale University Press, 1925).

Instead he has to leave his explanation of the uprisings at the point where he has given us to understand that interruption of trade created barbarian discontent. Thus his need for explanation drove him to make some inferences about the state of mind of the people being studied.[12]

As soon as he began describing action in terms of the aims of the actors and their pattern of behavior as social types, he was no longer dealing simply in propositions of correlation; he was using structural propositions. Under structural propositions I include those of the sort that economists often call models and that Max Weber called ideal types. These models or types are analyses of action which use the concept of an actor with defined aims and methods so that his reaction to various conditions will form a consistent pattern and may be predicted. The actor referred to by the structural type of model may be either an individual or a social group. Professor Teggart's explanation implies a type of tribal society which profits from trade passing through its territory and reacts to the interruption of that trade by attacking neighbors.

I have taken up Professor Teggart's use of structural propositions precisely because of the remoteness of his theme. He did not have a position in the historical profession comparable to G. B. Adams, E. P. Cheyney, or Carl Becker and could not embalm his philosophy in a presidential address before the American Historical Association. From many points of view it seems strange, even bizarre, to test the possibility of making history a science by a theme requiring assertions concerning the behavior of ancient tribes in inner Eurasia of which almost nothing is known directly. But for that very reason Professor Teggart's intellectual adventure demonstrates incisively how the historian needs and creates types or models intelligible in terms of motives, even if there is no direct evidence that their counterparts existed in reality. If Frederick Teggart had chosen to correlate the making and breaking of alliances in modern times with the volume of trade between the countries involved, he would have found his sources full of evidence concerning the motives and social structures connecting alliances and trade. This evidence would have created other complicated problems of methodology. But in the sources for his *Rome and China* he found almost no evidence concerning the process by which interruption in trade led to war. His correlation was empirical, as nearly as he could make it; that

[12] The state of mind is not usually explicitly referred to, to be sure, but at least once he slips and refers to "suspicion" as the inspiration for an attack (*Rome and China,* pp. 240–41).

is, it was based on the evidence concerning what actually happened on the Roman and Chinese frontiers; but the structural proposition by which he explained the correlation was purely hypothetical. Professor Teggart devoted a lifetime to an experiment in method. The outcome seems to me to show the limitation of trying to explain history by correlations. It illustrates the inevitability of structural propositions in organizing historical knowledge.

A complete contrast to Professor Teggart's work in most every respect is that of the International Committee for Price History, yet the outcome of their investigations seems to me to confirm also the importance of structural propositions compared to mere correlations. These students of price history did not of course start out to collect data purely empirically and see what correlations would emerge, although that has been done to an imposing extent in the study of business cycles. Research in price history was guided very largely by the quantity theory of money. In a recent statement on the uses of price history, Earl J. Hamilton said, "Monetary theories that meet the test of logic and internal consistency are usually verified both by their authors and critics through an appeal to experience, and no phenomena are more illuminating than the behavior of prices over long periods of time."[13] He then analyzes a number of examples, to which might be added his own study of Spanish prices. But, as Professor Hamilton pointed out, these studies of correlations between prices and the quantity of money have not all substantiated the same theory. Consequently more and more emphasis is being placed on the mechanisms by which increases in gold, silver, or some other form of money, acted on the price systems.[14] This emphasis on "mechanism" has meaning both to the theoretical economist and to the historian. To the theoretical economist it means more attention to analytical models of aggregates by which to study prices. To the historian, it means more attention to the culture and the institutions of the various countries which received the gold and silver of the New World.

I have drawn one example from the field of history and another from the border at least of economics. Sociology will supply a third. Talcott Parsons in his *Structure of Social Action* analyzed the work of four scholars, partly sociologists partly economists, and concluded that al-

[13] Earl J. Hamilton, "Use and Misuse of Price History," in *The Tasks of Economic History,* Suppl. to the *Journal of Economic History,* IV (December, 1944), 52.

[14] E.g., Joseph A. Schumpeter, "Theoretical Problems of Economic Growth," in *The Tasks of Economic History,* Suppl. to the *Journal of Economic History,* VII (December, 1947), 5–6.

though they started from diverse intellectual backgrounds, the nature of the problems they were trying to solve drove all of them into using basically the same conceptual scheme, the scheme which I am calling structural propositions. Professor Parsons analyzes elaborately what is involved in this approach. Just as there are some concepts suitable in the study of matter—mass, motion, location, and so on—there are other concepts suitable to the study of human relations. The essential in the analysis of action are an actor, his aims or purposes, the conditions he faces, the means he uses, and the normative standard by which he relates the means to the end he has in view. The "actor" may be a person or a society.[15]

This conception can be expressed in various ways. It is in Robert M. MacIver's description of "dynamic assessment."[16] It was implicit in that part of Marx's system which was concerned with the *process* of change. It is dramatized in Arnold Toynbee's formula of challenge and response.[17] They are all examples of what I am now calling structural propositions. They explain the process of change by stating the relations between the different attributes or elements in various types of action.

Having illustrated my theme by pointing to some trends in history, economics, and sociology, I shall not venture further afield. From the conversation of friends who are students of literature and language, I have discovered that they have arguments about positivism which seem to resemble the arguments over the scientific nature of history. But if the large topic assigned me is to be covered, I must appeal to your competent imaginations to apply my suggestion to other areas of the humanities and the social sciences.

But, it may be objected, the test of any system of knowledge is its ability to make predictions. The study of correlations has enabled natural science to predict, and, as I pointed out with reference particularly to archeology, correlations are also the basis for much historical prediction about human relations. Will knowledge organized in structural propositions do as much?

In answer it is to be noted first of all that the kind and amount of actual, accurate prediction about human relations which can be based

---

[15] Talcott Parsons, *The Structure of Social Action: A Study in Social Theory with Special Reference to a Group of Recent European Writers* (New York: McGraw-Hill, Inc., 1937), pp. 731–36 and *passim*.

[16] Robert MacIver, *Social Causation* (New York: Ginn, 1942), Chap. xi.

[17] Arnold J. Toynbee, *A Study of History* (Oxford: Oxford University Press, 1935), I, 271–99, and, less mythologically, 299–301.

on correlations alone is extremely limited. For this purpose a distinction must be made between correlative propositions which are empirical, because they sum up our observation of past recurrences, and those that are hypothetical. They become hypothetical as soon as they include the phrase "other things being equal." In that form they cannot be applied directly to the world of human reality, either historical or contemporary, in which "other things" are never unchanged. Empirically observed correlations on the other hand, such as those to which I referred concerning types of pottery, have a relatively very narrow range; or else it becomes very hard to give any operational definition to the elements being correlated so that they can be identified in examining an additional historical event in which their presence is in question.

Structural propositions also are hypothetical or empirical. Those most familiar to the economist, which he calls analytical models, are hypothetical and often highly abstract. An example is the statement that the entrepreneur combines the factors of production so that the last dollar spent on each factor yields approximately the same return. An example more familiar to historians but of essentially the same analytical sort is Machiavelli's characterization of the power-seeking prince. At the other extreme there are structural propositions which are purely empirical, but in that case they are quite specific and refer to particular acts of individuals or social groups. Examples are Machiavelli's statements describing the deeds of Caesar Borgia in language which characterizes these acts as having the same attributes, related in the same pattern, as the acts of an ideal power-seeking prince. The theorist is more interested in the analytical model itself; the historian or any practitioner is more interested in the extent to which particular people or societies can be fully described in terms of one or another group of models. But theorist and historian have some common ground because they are both using the same kind of propositions, and in that sense "talk the same language."

The advantage of the structural propositions in regard to prediction is the way they allow for the uncertainties. The proposition which says: "In so far as the behavior being observed is that of such and such a type—a power-seeking prince or a profit-seeking entrepreneur—his actions will be such and such" invites considering what other models may apply to other aspects of the situation.

At least that is an aspect that appeals to the historian. I am not sure whether it appeals equally to the economist. A historian of the reign of Louis XI of France, for example, would investigate how far the people of that time acted like the princely type, how far like the feudal type, how far like "economic man," how far like craftsmen, how far like obedient Christians, and so on. I can put the same thing differently by saying that he is seeking to describe all sides of the life of the time. To do that at all well he must in any case use imagination and intelligence. The weakness of the historian usually is that he does not have clearly enough in mind the types, especially the social models, which have been developed by the social sciences through analysis and study of the present. Therefore he misses many clues. Especially the historian who insists that history is primarily literature is likely to be mentally equipped only with models that are old-fashioned and mainly political.[18] But the "new history" has done much to remedy that, and the historian recognizes that it is his function to seek to describe all the factors in the situation, and not to apply to the community as a whole conclusions drawn from one element only of the complex of forces shaping it. He is not exclusively concerned with any one model.

The historian's interest in applying several different models to the analysis of each situation he studies is part and parcel of his interest in the kind of proposition first mentioned, as the historian's main concern, the developmental. Although the sweeping developmental laws of history, both those of Edward Cheyney and those of Karl Marx, are on the whole in disrepute, no historian doubts the truth of what Cheyney called his second law, the law of mutability, of the impermanence of nations. This impermanence applies to the varieties of human behavior—feudalism, nationalism, democracy, and so on—which we try to understand by use of structural propositions. For one time one type, such as the feudal noble, for another time another type, such as Machiavelli's prince, is the more pertinent frame of reference for the historian of Italy. As time passes actual behavior becomes more and more like one type and less and less like another type, which finally ceases altogether to be relevant and disappears, as the feudal noble has disappeared. Analysis in terms of only one model would not be history, for it would not permit analysis of developmental change.

---

[18] In his presidential address to the American Historical Association, at the one hundred and fiftieth anniversary of the Constitution of the United States, Guy Stanton Ford said, "Awareness of what is being done in the other social sciences is a special obligation of him who would write the history of American democracy under a constitution conceived and adopted by an essentially aggressive pioneering people on the eve of an age of science and technology which has carried us farther from them than they were from the Greeks and Romans." For some suggestions to American historians, see *American Historical Review,* XLIII (1938), 268.

Social scientists studying the present have occasion also to use several models at once and to analyze development. Is it not necessary that they should do so in order to make the best use of correlations? The predictions which are soundest and most restrained are based not simply on the brute facts of correlation, as for example between changes in prices and in quantity of money, but also on knowledge of the process which created a relation between them; for study of the process gives some understanding of the purposes and forms of action without which the correlation would be very unlikely to occur. In other words, a correlation holds true only within a certain institutional framework. Study of the structure of action discovers what institutions are so essential that their absence would make recurrence of the correlation unlikely. Then it becomes pertinent to study the contemporary transition from one institution to another. Since the forms of social behavior are impermanent, the social scientist who has completed a voluminous record of correlations and is ready to hazard a prediction may find, when his statistics are all correlated, that his prediction has become historical, comparable in that respect to Frederick Teggart's correlation between wars in Asia and uprisings on the European frontier of the Roman Empire.

The purpose of my discussion has been to show the interlacing of the methods of various disciplines, and I have therefore been unable to restrict myself to a well-ordered vocabulary drawn from one discipline alone. Perforce I have had to yank words around and set them in strange company without taking the time which would be required for formal introductions and explanations. What I have tried to say would have been said by another student in different language in accordance with whatever was his training and background. The three kinds of propositions which I have called correlative, developmental, and structural are all useful parts of our knowledge of human relations. I have tried to suggest something about their relations to each other, and about the way the social sciences and the humanities meet in studying social types developmentally.

28

*Theoretical and Historical Interests**

AMONG the themes presented in the foregoing selections, the one that seems most worth commenting on in this conclusion is the contrast between a theoretical interest and a historical interest. Like most of the other issues concerning method in economic history, this contrast affects all knowledge about human action, but it is particularly important in our discipline because economic history depends, as its very name suggests, on the interaction of the two interests. Moreover, I believe it is a practical help to anyone undertaking a study in economic history to recognize that the theoretical interest and the historical interest, although often combined in the same individual, produce different results.

In his discussion of the comparative method it is apparent that Marc Bloch is interested in the particular instances examined, not merely as examples, but as interesting and worthy of study in themselves. Therein he reveals himself as basically a historian. A most eloquent formulation of this interest can be found in Clapham's inaugural lecture: "If the economic historian has his modesties in presence of the pure economist he also has his pride. He is proud because, by definition as a historian, he is one to whom the tangled variety of human life is attractive in itself; one who will study alterations in the tangle for the love of it, even when his information is such that he can never hope to pick out with assurance the forces at work, or measure exactly the changes brought about by the aggregate of them between dates x and y."[1] The selections from Arthur Spiethoff serve equally to make evident

* Concluding chapter, *Enterprise and Secular Change: Readings in Economic History,* Frederic C Lane and Jelle C. Riemersma (eds.) (Homewood, Ill., (1953), pp. 522–34. (By permission.)
[1] John H. Clapham, *The Study of Economic History* (Cambridge, 1929), p. 34.

that from the historical point of view a knowledge of particulars, or some segments of the past, is worth while in itself. On the other hand, what I here call the "theoretical interest" aims at finding generalizations and leads to the feeling that intellectual progress consists in perfecting generalizations, that every body of knowledge advances by being formulated more and more in general terms.

Few people will deny that generalizations are to some extent desirable. The wish to know some particulars about the past is quite as strong, however, as the desire to generalize. I think it should be granted that a knowledge of particulars is justified as an end in itself. Certainly our wish to know about the American Revolution is not based merely on a desire to generalize about revolutions, nor do we wish to know about campaigns of the Civil War merely in order to be able to formulate general rules of strategy and tactics. Both interests—the historical interest in particulars and the theoretical interest in reaching generalizations—are to be accepted as each being independently worth while.

Since I will be referring so often to the "particular" and the "general," I offer an illustration to make clearer what I have in mind. Consider the following series of statements, the accuracy of which is at the moment irrelevant. Assuming that they were all equally accurate, which would be of most interest? Which would be the most important contribution to knowledge?

> *Example A*
> 1. In 1300 Carrefour had a population of 1,000, its manufactures were sold to the immediate neighborhood only, and it contained 20 distinct crafts. In 1800 its population was 500,000, its manufactures were sold to distant markets, and it contained 2,000 distinct crafts.
> 2. An increase in specialization among industrial workers occurred in Europe between 1300 and 1800 as a result of the increase in the size of cities and the extension of their market areas.
> 3. The extent of division of labor depends on the extent of the market.

Obviously, the last statement is the one of most importance to anyone with theoretical interests. On the other hand, a person dominated by a historical interest will find the first or second statements the more interesting and consider them, if true, additions to the body of knowledge, which is his primary concern. As the contrast between the first and second sentences makes clear, the amount of generalization is a matter of degree, and there are many intermediate degrees of generalization, just as there are many shades of grey between black and white. Theoretical thought seeks truth with the maximum possible generality. Historical thought seeks truths that are of limited generality; it is, comparatively speaking, interested in particulars for their own sake. This difference in objective is no reason to call either type of thought inferior to the other. They spring from different interests, from different aspects of the desire to know.

Each type of thought makes use of the other. The theoretical draws on the knowledge of particular cases in order to discover general principles; the historical draws on theory in order to understand particular cases. But when they are thus helping each other, the contrast in their basic goals persists. To the theorist, particular historical cases are merely means to his end and have no real interest except in so far as they help him improve his generalizations. To the historian, the generalizations of the theorists are a means which interest him because they help him find out what he wants to know about particular past events.

In studying occurrences in the physical universe, theoretical interests generally dominate. For example: At 11:00 P.M. on January 16, 1943, the newly built steel tanker "Schenectady," while at its outfitting dock at Portland, Oregon, split across the deck and down both sides. The cracking of the steel was, like an eruption of a volcano, an individual historical event, a particular incident in time and place. A committee of engineering experts immediately conducted an investigation of the accident, and their report was an example of historical inquiry concerned with explaining, not human action, but a purely physical occurrence. They recorded the temperature and the change in temperature which occurred immediately before the cracking, the quality of the steel, the point at which the fracture began and the direction in which it proceeded, and the relation of the position of the fracture to the structure of the ship. All these particulars were noted in an effort to determine the causes of the fracture, the causes of this particular historical event. The search for causes was guided by some general theories about the nature of steel and the effects of welding on steel. The engineering experts, in their professional capacity, were interested in the particular historical event, the cracking of the "Schenectady," only in so far as its history would enable them to add to their general knowledge of the behavior of steel in ships. When on March 29, 1943, another tanker, the "Esso Manhattan," built in a quite different shipyard, split entirely in two on a calm day at the entrance to New York harbor, they were presented with another case study for the testing of their theories. All such cases, because entirely unplanned, I will call in a special sense "accidents." While studying the accidents, the experts planned to attach gauges to certain ships to measure stresses under various conditions; well-planned case studies of this kind are called "experiments." Statistics were compiled concerning the time, place, and characteristics of all fractures, even quite minor ones, in any of the thousands of welded ships in operation. As a result, then, of various kinds of historical study—general statistical surveys and closer examination of a few particular cases, some unplanned "accidents" and others planned "experiments"—new generalizations applicable to the problem were developed and in later years were applied to ship design and the setting of specifications for steel plate. From the point of view of engineering science or applied physics, the cracking of the "Schenectady" became merely one of many cases to be studied comparatively. Scientists were interested in the general conclusions concerning the effects of heat and cold on the crystalline structure of steel; the naval architects were interested in conclusions that would affect the design of ships and the writing of steel specifications. These conclusions were revised again and again in the light of new experience, while the particular event that had occurred at Portland, Oregon, on January 16, 1943, passed into "history."

When a science is based on experiments, that is, on the study of events which the scientists planned and can cause to happen again, the setting of a particular case in time and place becomes so unimportant that it is easy to forget entirely that historical records of particular events, namely, of the experiments, lie at the foundations of these sciences. In the natural sciences with a more descriptive character, such as geology, the description of past occurrences as such, of the unplanned events which I have called "accidents," is of more evident importance.

Whether the cases studied be human actions or physical events, the methods used in studying them are subject to the same logical requirements if the theoretical interest is to be served. To a large extent the methods used in compiling and analyzing the laboratory notebooks that are the historical records of the natural scientist can and do serve as models for those students of human behavior whose method is determined by their theoretical interest. Simiand's method is an example.

To be sure, even those students of human affairs whose interests are theoretical differ from students of the physical universe in one important respect: they tend to formulate generalizations in terms of human motives, interests, and attitudes. The theoretical interest does not necessarily exclude an interest in human motives, attitudes, and institutional patterns. On the contrary, even Simiand, in making generalizations about "social facts," included attitudes as an essential ingredient of these "social facts."

What are the consequences of this difference between natural scientists and students of human affairs? In answering that question, it is desirable to distinguish between verification and discovery. (1) Are generalizations about human conduct subject to different criteria of truth, to different logical standards in verification, from those applied in the study of the physical universe? My answer is "No." We may know by inner experience something about the human nature which is the subject of our generalizations, but this does not make it less necessary to apply the rigorous standards of verification developed by natural scientists. It makes it more necessary; for individuals differ as to their internal experience and accordingly are biased in one way or another. (2) When generalizations are first conceived, they are unproved hypotheses that come to the mind as flashes of insight. Some are sound, most of them are erroneous. Natural scientists recognize the importance of these "flashes of insight" quite as much as do the students of human affairs. We know little of this mental process, but it seems to me that the kinds of generalizations we make about human affairs are necessarily influenced by what we know of human nature from inner experience. Probably the influence is beneficial, and to that extent the student of man has an advantage over the student of physical things. But, for those with theoretical interests, this disadvantage is more than counterbalanced by the disadvantage already mentioned, namely, that our inner knowledge of human nature makes it very much more difficult to be entirely logical and accurate in testing and discarding the enormous output of "insights" which will not stand the test of verification.

In placing so much stress on verification, I may seem to deny the value of the sort of generalizations which cannot be verified. Unverifiable generalizations are exactly the kind which many readers of economic journals may, with some justification, associate with theoretical interests. There is, of course, a large output of economic theory which makes no claim that it can be verified by case studies, statistics, experiments, or any other empirical procedure. Indeed, some theorists claim that logical consistency is the one and only test of all generalization. Their activity seems to me comparable in many respects to that of mathematicians; they are concerned with ways of finding the logical consequences of certain assumptions, whether or not the conditions described in the assumptions exist, have existed, are likely to exist, or are utterly unlikely ever to exist. Economic theorists have approached most closely to the mathematicians in their methods, but such social theory as that produced by Max Weber in certain parts of *Wirtschaft und Gesellschaft* is similarly an elaboration of logical possibilities. As Spiethoff says, it is also pure theory. The usefulness of pure theory in building a body of knowledge about human affairs seems to me as undeniable as the usefulness of mathematics in our knowledge of the physical universe. But, to avoid misunderstanding, I must repeat that I have been using the expression "theoretical interest" to designate, not pure theory only, but all effort aimed at a maximum amount of generalization. I have had in mind particularly the effort to combine as much generalization as possible with conformity to fact. Scientists who make this effort and those in whom the historical interest dominates have a common interest in historical case studies.

What, then, is the method appropriate to a study of historical events under the guidance of a theoretical interest? In spite of the fact that it is dealing with human nature, the study is comparable in most respects to a scientific or engineering study of an "accident." In describing the events, the investigator selects aspects which seem likely to make it fit into some general category (for example, the category of prices or price levels) ; he seeks other concurrent events which there is some reason to think may occur in some general relation to the kind of event being described (for example, depreciation of the currency or population growth) and examines the relations of the various events to see whether an available generalization, such as the quantity theory of money, is confirmed or whether it needs modification in view of the new fact, and, if so, how. A theoretical interest in economic history calls for a selection of "test cases" by standards as near as possible to those used in experimental sciences. It calls for a continual use of the comparative method both in selecting new cases for study and in interpreting the results of each new case examined.

Are different methods appropriate for the investigator dominated by historical interests? He starts with a particular event (such as the American Revolution) in the center of his attention, but he, too, has some ideas about general causal relations. He, too, selects for description aspects of the event which classify it under known general categories, and he describes attendant circumstances which seem causally relevant. His selection of characteristics and circumstances depends on what general theories he has explicitly or implicitly in mind concerning events of that type. As an example, reconsider Collingwood's reference to the killing of Julius Caesar. The historian who describes it by using such words as "dictator," "Senate," "assassination," "republicanism," is thereby stating aspects of the event that place it in certain general categories. In so far as relevant generalizations about human behavior available in the general body of knowledge of his time are known to him, the historian uses such generalizations as aids in framing his description.

But, in regard to the choice of topics and the range of the investigation, there is a contrast between the procedures dictated by historical and theoretical interests. If the dominant interest is theoretical, then the investigator, in asking himself what he should investigate, starts thinking about some general relation, such as that between a rise in prices and an increase in the quantity of money; asks himself whether there are any cases to the contrary or whether the relation is the same in all cases; hits on a case in which it seems superficially that the relation is unusual, for example, a country in which there occurred during some period a large importation of precious metals without a comparable rise in prices; and inquires into the special circumstances of that case. Perhaps he finds evidence of increases in population and in the velocity of the circulation of money. His findings may suggest a slightly more sophisticated form of the quantity theory of money. Following up his theoretical interest, he would turn next to other cases of increase in population, cases which occurred with or without increasing velocity of circulation. He would compare the many cases, seeking to find what general statement could be made that would be true of all of them. His standard in selecting new cases to study would be their value in enabling him to frame a statement with a maximum possible amount of generality.

When the dominant interest is historical, however, the investigator starts with a question which is, to some extent at least, tied to a particular time and place, such a question as: How did London become the financial center of the world? He is interested in the historical question for itself, not because answering it will make possible a generalization applicable to other cases. He begins looking for attendant circumstances that seem causally pertinent to his problem—for example, the pattern of trade or the financing of wars or the location of gold production. His selection of these circumstances as pertinent to his problem implies, at least, some general theories about the relations between financial settlements, on the one hand, and trade balances, government finance, and flow of precious metals, on the other. To evaluate the circumstances and give a causal explanation of the rise of London as a financial center, a historian needs to know what the best generalizations are which the theorists have attained. But, since one man cannot do everything, a historian is less concerned with changing these generalizations than he is with applying them for the solution of his problem. If his theme is the London money market, he will not desert it for the sake of making case studies of other money markets, not unless his historical interest weakens and a theoretical interest takes the upper hand.

Historical interest is thus a consumer, rather than a producer, of broad generalizations. Only by giving second place to his historical interest can an investigator let his research be directed into the paths necessary to test a generalization, modify it according to new findings, test its new form, and present as the fruit of his labors a new or improved generalization, more universally applicable. Consequently, the historian does not basically bear the responsibility for the quality of the generalizations which form our knowledge about human action in general. He does not bear the producer's responsibility for the quality of the generalizations in use. But he does have a consumer's responsibility for the quality of the particular products he uses. He deserves to be reproached, if he treats, as sound, generalizations which have proved unsound. He needs to know the best of the theoretical thought of his time, and the investigator dominated by historical interest in economic events needs to know especially what his contemporaries with theoretical interests are thinking about economic behavior.

What most historians actually do most of the time is to use the generalizations which they find more or less explicit in the sources from which they construct the record. Perhaps there is less of that in the study of events that are so recent that we do not ordinarily think of them as historical, as was the cracking of the "Schenectady" for the investigating committee, but which are historical in the sense that they occurred once and for all in a definable time and place. Since our contemporaries are the sources of information on such events, however, we are quite likely to be affected by their general ideas, their theories. In examining the more distant past, a historian spends so much time working with the sources closest to the event that he can hardly fail to have in mind the general ideas there expressed—expressed even in the terms in which events are described—and to have no other generalizations to guide him unless he makes a deliberate effort to discover what generalizations about human behavior have been produced by the most recent thinkers on the subject.

Is it sound practice to introduce into the examination of past epochs general theories based on modern studies of society? Many of my historical colleagues seem to deny it; many passages in Collingwood's attack on the positivist methods in history seem to deny it. A history which consists essentially of reliving the past has no place for such theories, it is said. But Collingwood himself, when at work as a historian of Roman Britain, uses generalizations concerning the relation between methods of cultivation and the shape of the fields; and I doubt whether he would maintain that those generalizations were part of the thoughts of the Britons of Roman times. I see no reason why the study of money and prices in the sixteenth century A.D.—or in the sixth century B.C., for that matter—should be limited to aspects of events which were recognized by the people of the time. A good causal analysis of a past event should consider not only what the contemporaries thought was causally relevant but also causes which contemporaries knew nothing of but which are suggested by the modern body of knowledge about human affairs.

Nevertheless, historical interest leads to a living with the sources, and the investigator, trying as best he can to penetrate beneath deceptive rationalization, enters as far as possible into the attitudes and thoughts of those about whom he writes. Consequently, when faced with the problem of deciding which facts to present, of deciding, that is, what events are causally relevant to one another, he proceeds mainly by setting forth what was thought relevant by the people about whom he is writing. It would be a mistake to leave that out. The main interest now attached to the cracking of the tanker "Schenectady" is the human side of the event, the alarm it caused at the moment and the accusations exchanged by shipbuilders and steel manufacturers.

Generalizations in history and social science are, as we have seen, generalizations about human conduct. In framing them, we use our ability to participate in thoughts and feelings common to men generally. The use of what Germans have called *Verstehen* is indispensable, unavoidable, I think, in any striving toward general knowledge of human action. (And the process of striving to relive the past has other values; it can be justified on grounds that would be irrelevant here.) But a result of thus approaching events "from the inside" is to suggest to anyone of lively imagination a large number of conflicting generalizations. Distinguishing between the true and the false raises many difficulties, some of them basic problems of methodology which are still in dispute.

It must be admitted, therefore, that most causal explanations given by historians, even those given by as intelligent, widely informed, and careful a historian as Marc Bloch, have a very weak foundation in general theory. This is particularly true in regard to what Marc Bloch has called "particular causes," that is, the causes of differences in development when the two cases being compared are cases within the same general culture. An example is his description of the different combination of circumstances in England and France about the year A.D. 1100 and his explanation of the differences in social structure that appeared later when hereditary classes became more firmly established. Because the civilizations of France and England were of common origin, the differing circumstances in the two countries were relatively few. Yet they were enormous compared to the differences which an experimental scientist has to take into account when he analyzes and seeks a "particular cause." A chemist who put different combinations of substances into two test tubes and wrote in his laboratory notebook a comparative history of what happened when the test tubes were heated would be seeking a particular cause, namely, the cause of the difference in events in the two cases. In setting up his experiment, the chemist can create a degree of similarity between the cases which makes analyzing the cause of the difference relatively easy. The historian cannot thus simplify the difference between the cases being compared, and therefore descriptions of these differences occupy a prominent place in the historian's search for particular causes.

Moreover, the historian's interest compels him to seek particular causes even if he knows no general principles which can be applied to the case in question. According to the general logical theory of causality, a causal explanation is not well-founded unless the particular event or circumstance which is treated as the cause can be identified as a member of a general class of events or circumstances about which we have some general knowledge from other cases. The chemist's causal explanation of the different reactions in his two test tubes will be framed in terms of general categories, namely, chemical elements. The validity of the chemist's explanation depends on its being in accord with other cases and with the established knowledge concerning the properties of the chemical elements involved. The historian does not usually have a similarly well-developed system of classification to apply or knowledge of the pertinent general relationships. Although the economic historian is probably better off in this respect than the social historian, both are working in relative darkness. Nevertheless, it is part of the historian's function to explain as best he can, in the light of the inadequate general knowledge available to him, particular differences in historical development.

In the foregoing pages I have been concerned with analyzing the divergence of the historical and theoretical interest. For an economic historian to understand what he is doing, it is important that he recognize this divergence in lines of interest and recognize that both lines are worth-while ways of extending human knowledge. Many investigators start off on one line and then switch over to the other without fully realizing that they have changed their objective. They may start to test the truth of the hypothesis suggested by Max Weber's work, namely, that religious attitudes determine economic organization, or Marx's that economic organization determines religious attitudes; pick a particular case to work on, such as religion and business in the Netherlands in the sixteenth century; and end up more interested in the particular case than in the generalization with which they began. They may start out seeking a general proposition concerning factors producing change from one form of industrial organization, such as the putting-out system, to some other form, such as the factory system; pick a particular case to work on, such as the French cotton textile industry in the nineteenth century; and end up by writing a history of that industry, bringing in and explaining, as far as possible, a variety of the characteristics which that industry developed during the century—all of which is as it should be in a work dominated by historical interest in that particular historical "individual," the French textile industry of the nineteenth century, but which distracts the investigator from choosing and analyzing cases comparatively, as he should do if his dominant purpose is to discover valid generalizations. His final product should not be condemned, then, on the ground that it fails to arrive at any clear-cut theoretical result, unless, of course, he fails to realize how his aim has changed and presents his work as if it were a theoretical study. Similarly, the investigator whose examination of historical particulars is limited to those which for him have theoretical significance should not be reproached for having failed to include "all sides of the story," provided that he has included those pertinent to his theoretical inquiry, and provided, of course, that he does not claim that he has presented the whole history of an event when in fact he has studied only the side pertinent to the generalizations in which he is interested.

Although I wish to insist, above all, on the consequences of the difference between the desire to generalize and the desire to know about historical events, I must turn now to consider some consequences of the fact that the difference is a matter of degree. As illustrated by the series of sentences offered as examples at the beginning of this discussion, economic history as presented in the basic manuals on the subject emphasizes mainly statements of an intermediate degree of generality, such as the statement that the variety of specialized occupations multiplied in the growing cities of Europe in the nineteenth century because of the extension of their markets. These are historical statements because they apply to a particular time and place. They are also general

statements that summarize certain observed uniformities in the ocur-
rences within that time and place. Because of their degree of generality,
it is conceivable that they should be called "theories." They form a part
of what Spiethoff would call *anschauliche Theorie,* although to satisfy
his conception they have to be part of a general pattern or *Gestalt*
embracing the essential causal relationships. How to determine what is
"essential" seems to me the difficult point in his methodology, but I
cannot probe that point here. The question that interests me is this:
Are these "historical generalizations," as I will call those of this intermediate degree of generality, worth while because they are stepping-
stones to broader generalizations? Or are they worth while in themselves, that is, because they satisfy the historical interest? I believe the
latter.

How far is the historical interest to be satisfied by historical generalizations and how far is it to be satisfied only by relatively very specific
statements? To weigh the question in more specific terms, consider
another series of statements of varying degree of generality somewhat
more elaborate than that introduced at the beginning of this discussion.

Example B
  1. In March 1440 the Senate of the Venetian Republic voted
     to charter four great galleys to carry specified cargoes to
     London and Bruges.
  2. Nearly every year in the fifteenth century the Venetian
     government sent three to five galleys for the transport of
     high-priced cargoes on voyages to the English Channel.
  3. In the later Middle Ages the Venetian government sent
     merchant galleys to all the main seaboard trade centers of
     the Mediterranean and western Europe to assure the safety
     of precious cargoes.
  4. Medieval city-states made most elaborate provision for
     those branches of trade affecting most the income of the
     government, the supply of precious metals, and the food
     supply.
  5. Governmental action in regard to commerce is always most
     intense on those exchanges which are believed to affect the
     income of the government, and the suppy of food and of
     military stores, and the conditions of the currency.

Here, as in the earlier example, the last statement is in such general
terms that a person dominated by historical interest will consider it,
even if true, a less valuable contribution to knowledge than one of the

preceding statements. But which preceding statement? If the value of statements 1–4 does not lie in their enabling us to arrive at the final most general statement, or some better generalization on the same theme, how decide which of the preceding statements is of most importance? Having rejected the proposition that, of two statements of equal validity, the more general is always the more important, are we without any criterion of relative importance? Is there no way in which to draw the line, then, between history and antiquarianism?

Logically, I do not think there is any general universally valid answer. Because of the nature of our culture, certain historical generalizations are esteemed of interest in themselves. Any general statement about why industrialism increased in the early nineteenth century and how it affected the family or social structure is, if true, worth while, whether or not it is a steppingstone to some statement about the nature of industrialism which is of so sweeping a character that it will apply also to the twentieth century. The worker in economic history, whether graduate student or director of a research institute, takes his interests from daily converse with other participants in our culture. The striving to attain a maximum of generalization is one characteristic of that culture; the effort to know about man's past is another prominent feature. He therefore encounters certain historical generalizations as well as universal generalizations; and, according to his bent, he can consider either one the means, the other the end.

Perhaps some readers will deny that either is justified in its own right and will argue that a third interest, the desire to predict, is and should be stronger in our culture than either the effort to generalize or to wish to know particulars about the past. Many people believe that prediction is the essence of science, that attempts at prediction should dominate all study of human affairs, and that the rules for acquiring and organizing knowledge should be shaped accordingly. How far knowledge can be so organized is too large a question to be examined here, but it is my impression that efforts by social scientists to predict what will really happen next in the continuing stream of history have not been notably successful. The will to construct a systematic body of knowledge enabling us to predict social developments is based on faith, therefore, not on the amount of success already attained in making such predictions. Concern over ability to predict has been increasing in economic history, but it still shares the field with the two rival interests we have examined, the theoretical and the historical.

29

Some Heirs of Gustav von Schmoller*

THE value of Gustav von Schmoller's thought and its influence on economics and economic history have been the subject of many contrasting judgments. Joseph Schumpeter's writing in 1926 in the periodical known as *Schmollers Jahrbuch* compared favorably Schmoller's *Grundriss* (Basic Outline of General Economics) with the *Principles of Economics* by Alfred Marshall. "The *Principles* like the *Grundriss* contain in seminal form 90 per cent of that which can be accomplished now and in the immediate future and of what has thus far been accomplished, although not all this accomplishment has been directly linked to these works either through criticism or acceptance of them. They still remain inexhaustible mines of social insights. . . ."[1]

In the beginning of that same article, Schumpeter cited the Presidential Address of Wesley C. Mitchell before the American Economic Association in December, 1924, as evidence of the "living force" of Schmoller's ideas.[2] It is true that the American school of "Institutionalists" received encouragement during the first decades of this century from knowing that many of its sentiments were shared by scholars occupying the dominant chairs of economics in Germany. And Edwin F. Gay, who worked with Wesley Mitchell in establishing the National Bureau of Economic Research, had found in Schmoller's seminar the "intellectual home" that he had sought in Europe as a student.[3] On

* *Architects and Craftsmen in History, Festschrift für Abbott Payson Usher* (Tübingen: J. C. Mohr, 1956) , pp. 9–39. (By permission.)

[1] Joseph Schumpeter, "Gustav v. Schmoller und die Probleme von heute," *Schmollers Jahrbuch für Gesetzgebung, Verwaltung und Volkswirtschaft im Deutschen Reiche*, L (1926) , 388.

[2] *Ibid.*, pp. 337–38.

[3] Herbert Heaton, *A Scholar in Action: Edwin F. Gay* (Cambridge: Harvard University Press, 1952) , p. 39. Cf. pp. 61–62.

his return to the United States, Gay at Harvard, like Schmoller at Berlin, became, through his force of character and the pupils brought him by his position, the honored teacher of many of the leading economic historians of the next generation, and thus gave economic history in the United States a link with the head of the German historical school of economics. But both the Institutionalist School in economics and economic history in the United States had other roots as well. The specific influence here of the German historical school would be difficult to disentangle, and within that school the theories of Karl Bücher, being more sharply defined than those of Schmoller, seem to have had more influence, or at least to have stirred up more discussion. By the time that Edwin F. Gay as first president of the Economic History Association delivered his presidential address to fellow economic historians, he treated Schmoller's position as justified in its time but no longer valid in view of the progress recently made in economics.[4]

The high praise that Schumpeter bestowed on Schmoller in 1926 was primarily a tribute to the position which Schmoller, nine years after his death, then occupied within Germany. For almost two academic generations, during practically the whole life of the Hohenzollern Reich, Gustav von Schmoller had been the most influential German professor teaching economics. He had proclaimed himself the head of a school, the younger historical school. Moreover, as one of his students wrote on the hundredth anniversary of Schmoller's birthday, "Gustav von Schmoller was in a double sense a creator of a school. . . . Out of the academic recruits who pressed around his Chair, he trained up to the career of teachers a magnificent number of those gifted for economic science and, thanks to his authority and the influence of his friend Althoff in the Prussian Ministry of Education (Kultusministerium) they occupied before the war (World War I) the majority of the professorships of economics in Germany. Schmoller formed a school also in a wider sense and of even greater numbers, in that thousands on thousands of students from all faculties, especially students of law, public administration, and history listened to him and took away from his lecture room into their future professional activity enduring convictions concerning economic policy and social ethics."[5]

As head of a school, Schmoller became the target of a number of

---

[4] Edwin F. Gay, "The Tasks of Economic History," in *The Tasks of Economic History*, Suppl. to the *Journal of Economic History*, I (1941) , 13–14.

[5] Waldemar Zimmermann, "Gustav von Schmoller und der nationalökonomische Nachwuchs," *Schmollers Jahrbuch*, LXII (1938) , 733. On this article see also below, n. 62.

attacks, or was himself the initiator of controversies with prominent contemporaries. These attacks and counter-attacks made him the symbol of a program. He "triumphed" over his critics by consistently acting and speaking as if his side had been proved right. The controversy best remembered by economists was that with Carl Menger, leader of the Austrian school. In this *Methodenstreit,* Schmoller appeared as the arch-enemy of economic theory.[6] Antagonisms and personal loyalties then aroused were kept alive for years in methodological discussions. In the 1920's and 1930's German scholars frequently felt it necessary to define their position towards the historical school and its master, so that serious consideration—and reconsideration—of what Schmoller stood for is to be found primarily in German authors.

The accurate definition of Schmoller's ideas and the distinguishing of his ideas from those of his predecessors and contemporaries is in this connection neither easy nor necessary. Schmoller did not define his own positions in a thorough and logical fashion. For example, after reading his celebrated controversy with Menger over the place of theory in economics, one can still be in doubt as to what Schmoller meant by theory. The conceptions which Schmoller used to group the materials he presented in his final major work, the *Grundriss,* are drawn from many sources without being synthesized into a coherent system. I agree with Georg von Below's characterization of him as an eclectic.[7] Below considered eclecticism to be bad; Schmoller considered premature system-making to be worse. The great popularity which he enjoyed in his own time seems to have been due in no small measure— and with due allowance for his qualities of personality—to his acceptance of so much of the contemporary climate of opinion.

In considering Schmoller's influence, our main interest therefore is not his personal contribution to historical knowledge nor ideas which he originated, but his attitudes as head of an influential school. In broad terms I will attempt to summarize these attitudes in four sentences:

1. He disparaged theory and extolled historical research.

Although he did not in practice nor in words entirely condemn all kinds of theory, he dogmatically decried the body of economic theory of his time, and attacked especially the idea that the same body of theory

---

[6] *Enterprise and Secular Change: Readings in Economic History,* eds. Frederic C. Lane and Jelle C. Riemersma (Homewood, Ill.: Richard D. Irwin, 1953) , pp. 433–36, and references there cited and on pp. 543–44.

[7] Georg von Below, "Zur Würdigung der historischen Schule der Nationalökonomie," *Zeitschrift für Sozialwissenschaft* (1904) , pp. 155–56. Cf. pp. 802–3.

was valid for all times and places. At its best, the historical school spurred economists to give more attention to the empirical content of their schemata. At its worst, the historical school encouraged economists to turn to empirical study without any theoretical clarification of the concepts and questions that entered into their description and selection of facts.

A word of explanation is necessary concerning the adjective "historical." As used by the writers we will be considering, "history" refers to the present as well as the past. "Historical" research, as the term will be used here, means the study of events and conditions—past, present, or future—when they are viewed as part of the unique irreversible sequence of what actually has and will occur. Using "history" in this sense, we may say that for some Christians the Last Judgment in 4004 A.D. was part of history just as much as the Creation in 4004 B.C., and for Karl Marx socialism was an historical event just as much as feudalism.[8] Schumpeter was using "historical" thus to embrace the present when he said that the only tool of analysis developed by Schmoller's school was the "historical monograph."[9] The "historical" research advocated by Schmoller included descriptive studies of present condition, although he and his followers spent much time on research into the past.

2. He believed that economists should seek to understand the general causes of development from one type of social organization to another.

Although commonly called "economists," Schmoller, his predecessors and his followers, were so placed in the academic world that they were under constant pressure to embrace the whole field of social science. The "Historical economists" were generally members of faculties of law and the only members not teaching law. Their chairs often bore the name inherited from the Cameralist tradition, *Staatswissenschaft.* They had no colleagues in sociology or political science in the American sense. Their academic functions therefore led them into very general discussions of social evolution. In fact Schmoller's *Grundriss* sketches the development, not of economic institutions only, but of all social institutions.

In spite of the obvious futility of objecting to names well established by tradition, it should be noted that confusion has arisen from putting

---

[8] On the historical and spatialized concepts of time, see Abbott Payson Usher, *A History of Mechanical Inventions* (Rev. ed.; Cambridge, Mass.: Harvard University Press, 1954), pp. 46–47.

[9] Joseph Schumpeter, *History of Economic Analysis,* ed. from manuscript by Elizabeth Boody Schumpeter (New York: Oxford University Press, 1954), pp. 807–10.

the same label, such as "economics," on bodies of knowledge having varying content according to the national cultural background in which they developed.

3. He emphasized the *Geist*—the cultural, moral, or spiritual factors—as the essential in historical development.

This expressed itself in two ways: in causal explanation and in designating higher and lower forms of social life. Schmoller did not hesitate to pass moral judgments; he believed ethics an integral part of economics. The name that he preferred for his school was ethical historical,[10] and in the triumphant address he delivered when inaugurated Rector of the University of Berlin in 1897 he boasted that economics had again become a great moral political science.[11]

4. He was inclined to regard the state, especially the modern national state, as an expression of "moral" development, and as beneficient.

Schmoller's political and social program was expressed in the Verein für Sozialpolitik, the organization of German economists of which Schmoller was a founder, and which sought to guide the activity of the state in ameliorating the condition of the industrial working classes and integrating them into the rest of the nation.

None of these four attitudes was new in Schmoller's time nor peculiar to him and his school alone. The first two created some bonds of intellectual sympathy between the historical school and the Marxians, for although of course the Marxians were definitely in favor of theory, of their own kind, they attacked the same body of theory that Schmoller was attacking, and they too sought to explain social development in general terms. On the other hand, the last two attitudes itemized distinguished Schmoller sharply from the Marxians. Between him and the general body of economists of his time, especially the Austrian school, the chief cause of antagonism was the first and last mentioned of these four attitudes, most of all his disparagement of theory.

Now, two generations later, "the historical school has almost died out." Such is the opinion of a particularly well informed and sympathetic historian of economic thought, Edgar Salin.[12] But the ideas for

[10] *Ibid.*, p. 812. Compare Gustav Schmoller, *Grundriss der Allgemeinen Volkswirtschaftslehre*, I (Leipzig: Duncker & Humblot, 1908) , 123–24.

[11] "Wechselnde Theorien und feststehende Wahrheiten im Gebiete der Staatsund Sozialwissenschaften und die heutige deutsche Volkswirtschaftslehre," in *Schmollers Jahrbuch*, XXI (1897) , 1387–1408.

[12] In his "Nachwort" to Walter Eucken's *Grundsätze der Wirtschaftspolitik* (Bern and Tübingen: Francke/Mohr, 1952) , p. 381.

which the school stood have not died without issue. They have entwined with the ideas of other schools. I will examine how this has occurred in the work of four economists who wrote in the shadow of the Schmollerian tradition: Werner Sombart, Arthur Spiethoff, Joseph A. Schumpeter, and Walter Eucken.[13] No full analysis of the thought of any of these men is possible here. My theme is the relation of these men to the school that honored Schmoller as its founder and, more specifically, their positions in regard to the four Schmollerian attitudes enumerated above.

For a historian, one of the significant lessons that may be learned, it seems to me, from the controversies over the historical school is a clarification of the difference between two kinds of history: (1) a restricted economic history which examines how historical circumstances have affected economic life but renounces any attempt to explain the changes in historical conditions, and (2) a broader treatment which does seek to explain why historical conditions changed and thereby cuts loose from any moorings available in economics. Many of the confusions in the Historical School resulted from the attempt to apply to both the same concepts and methods.

I. WERNER SOMBART

The climate of opinion that Schmoller reflected was the robust self-assurance of the late nineteenth century, believing that evolution meant progress. Before 1917 when Schmoller died, even before 1914, the climate had begun to change. The new drift in sentiments and beliefs was expressed most brilliantly by Werner Sombart. As long as he was overshadowed by Schmoller's living presence, Sombart was considered a young radical, the "red professor" of Wilhelmenian Germany. Later Sombart voiced the varying but generally pessimistic moods of the Weimar Republic.

Sombart disdained any claim to succeed Schmoller as head of "the school." In the introduction to the first edition of *Der moderne Kapitalismus* in 1902, Sombart avowed that his honored teacher, Schmoller, would throw him out of the temple if he claimed to be using "historical method," for Sombart gloried in the fact that he was more theoretical

---

[13] There are others whom it would be interesting to discuss if time permitted, especially Georg Weippert, Alexander Rüstow, and Hans Ritschl and of course, in the older group, Max Weber, mentioned briefly below. Many are mentioned in Edgar Salin's *Geschichte der Volkswirtschaftslehre* (4th ed.; Bern, Tübingen: Francke/Mohr, 1951), pp. 143–70.

than Schmoller and thereby attained a superior synthesis.[14] Sombart declared strongly his debt to Karl Marx and reiterated it in his *Hochkapitalismus*.[15] He was, he stated in 1902, attempting to unite the methods of Schmoller and Marx. But Schmoller reviewed Sombart's first edition with the mixture of condescension, criticism, and pride appropriate to the work of a wayward but gifted pupil,[16] and in his *Grundriss* Schmoller referred depreciatingly to Sombart's many new analytical categories in order to conclude that Sombart's work was largely in line with his own.[17] Although Sombart insisted on his own originality and independence, the historical school followed Schmoller's lead in accepting Sombart as one of their leading lights. In fact we can almost say that they treated him as their star performer. *Schmollers Jahrbuch* issued a special number in Sombart's honor in 1932, and when that review devoted an issue to honoring Schmoller in 1938, on the one hundredth anniversary of his birth, Sombart's tribute to Schmoller was given the place of honor.[18]

Thus, although Sombart presented his *Kapitalismus* as a continuation and bringing to completion of the work of Karl Marx,[19] it was hailed rather as a continuation and fulfillment of the program of Gustav von Schmoller. Sombart, like Schmoller, criticized the economic theorists and believed history the proper subject of economic studies. He too saw in history the development of various forms of economic life for each of which a separate theory was necessary. Methods applied by Schmoller to separate aspects of economic and social history were applied by Sombart to the economy as a whole. Schmoller had laid down stages of development for many aspects: developmental sequences of industrial organization, of forms of property, of monetary

[14] Werner Sombart, *Der moderne Kapitalismus* (Leipzig: Duncker & Humblot, 1902), I, xxix.

[15] *Ibid.*, and III: *Das Wirtschaftsleben im Zeitalter des Hochkapitalismus* (Munich and Leipzig: Duncker & Humblot, 1927), xviii–xxii. Cited hereafter as *Hochkapitalismus*.

[16] *Schmollers Jahrbuch*, XXVII (1903), 291–300.

[17] Gustav Schmoller, *Grundriss der Allgemeinen Volkswirtschaftslehre*, II (1904), 669.

[18] What Sombart chose at that date to praise in Schmoller was the following: "die Überzeugug dass ein Wissen, . . . das nicht ein Grundsätzliches ist, das nicht seine Wurzel in den Mutterboden der Philosophie und der Geschichte treibt, ein Zweckwissen, ein Fachwissen, eine Technologie bleibt, aber nicht auf den Ehrennamen einer Wissenschaft Anspruch zu erheben das Recht hat" (*Schmollers Jahrbuch*, LXII [1938], 386).

[19] In Introduction to *Hochkapitalismus*, above cited, p. xix.

organization, and so on. They were only very loosely tied together in the main sequence of stages: village or tribunal economy, town economy, territorial economy, and national economy. Schmoller cut what may be called longitudinal sections through history. Sombart presented cross-sections which he called economic systems, each of which contained a particular pattern of organization, industrial, political, monetary, and so on. For Schmoller the contemporary stage of development was national economy or the economy of world empires;[20] for Sombart it was high capitalism or the beginnings of socialism.[21]

Although considered within the Schmollerian tradition, Sombart departed from Schmoller's position in many respects and he did so in two ways that widened the gap between the historical school and the main body of economists, at least, economists in other Western nations. On the one hand he paid homage to Karl Marx and accepted many specifically Marxian interpretations. On the other, when he departed from Marx, as he did in rejecting the materialistic economic interpretation of history, he did so on grounds not likely to be understood or appreciated outside of Germany. In practice Sombart, like Schmoller, emphasized the importance of what may be called psychological, motivational or spiritual causes; he treated capitalism as a creation of the capitalistic spirit *(Geist)*.[22] But Sombart considered Schmoller too much of a positivist, one who conceived the methods and goals of social

[20] *Grundriss*, II (1904), 668–69.

[21] *Hochkapitalismus*, pp. 1012–17. See Arthur Spiethoff's comparison of Schmoller and Sombart in "Die Allgemeine Volkswirtschaftslehre als Geschichtliche Theorie. Die Wirtschaftsstile," *Schmollers Jahrbuch*, LVI, Part 2 (1932), 905–24. Appropriately enough it is in this article within the *Festschrift* for Sombart that Spiethoff says, on p. 924, speaking of Sombart, "Er stellt eine eigenwillige Erfüllung kühnster Träume der Geschichtlichen Schule dar." Schumpeter said of Sombart's work, "Der ganze Wurf liegt in der Richtung des Schmollerprogramms und gab ihm einen neuen Impuls nach einer Richtung, die in ihm lag" (Joseph Schumpeter, "Sombarts Dritter Band," *Schmollers Jahrbuch*, LI [1927] 352).

[22] True, Sombart's first edition, with its emphasis on surplus value and ground rent as the sources of capitalism, is closer to Marx than is his second edition, in which not economic conditions but the capitalistic spirit is continually presented as the driving force creating capitalism; Schmoller, in his review already cited, criticized the first edition for retaining too much of the materialistic interpretation. But even in the Preface to that edition Sombart declared motivation to be the best explanatory principle. See Vol. I, pp. xvii–xxii. Cf. *Hochkapitalismus*, pp. xii, 7–9. See also *The Quintessence of Capitalism* (London: Unwin, 1915), pp. 42–53. In his review article on the second edition, A. P. Usher wrote, "Schmoller had always been an important factor in Sombart's thought, but in this work Schmoller becomes the dominant influence" ("The Genesis of Modern Capitalism," *Quarterly Journal of Economics*, XXXVI [1921–22], 526).

science to be the same as the methods and goals of the natural sciences. In regard to the controversy between Menger and Schmoller, Sombart declared that Menger had won the victory in logical argument, although Schmoller was correct in rejecting Menger's position. Schmoller was on the right side but did not understand the cause for which he was fighting.[23] Economics should follow the special methods and aims appropriate to the *Geisteswissenschaften,* the science of man as a maker of culture. Sombart's interpretation of *Geisteswissenschaft* led him towards methods which many economists condemned as reliance on intuition and art.

I will return to the methodological issue later. Here it suffices to note that Sombart's conception of the scholar's task was, like his temperament, very different from Schmoller's. Sombart felt himself to be an artist; he maintained that every important achievement in the science of man must be a work of art.[24]

II. ARTHUR SPIETHOFF

While Sombart was the most brilliant writer in the historical school, its titular head after Schmoller's death was Arthur Spiethoff, who had been Schmoller's assistant and succeeded him as editor of the Jahrbuch that was the mouthpiece of the school. Far more than either Schmoller or Sombart, Spiethoff, a specialist on modern business cycles, was at home in modern economic theory. He laid down a program of studies for the historical school, and restated the attitude of the historical school towards economic theory.

In doing so, Spiethoff was influenced by Sombart's position, by the recent achievements of the theorists (especially Schumpeter) and by the methodological writings of Max Weber. Although Max Weber's contributions are too complicated to be given more than a passing reference here, he certainly was one of the thinkers through whom Schmoller's work was transmuted into the forms in which it still has influence. Much of the significance of Max Weber lies in the fact that he began his scholarly life with studies in legal and economic history

[23] Sombart stated his methodological position first in the Prefaces in *Der Moderne Kapitalismus* and then at length in *Die Drei Nationalökonomien* (Munich and Leipzig: Duncker & Humblot, 1930). He commented on Menger's and Schmoller's *Methodenstreit* in the latter work, pp. 153–54. *Schmollers Jahrbuch* then devoted a complete issue, LIV (1930), 193 ff., to appraisal and criticism of Sombart's *Drei Nationalökonomien.*

[24] *Die Drei Nationalökonomien,* p. 339. " . . . alle geistwissenschaftliche Forschung ihrem innersten Wesen nach auf die künstlerische Gestaltung hindrängt."

and at its end was writing a general treatise on sociology. Finding that a formulation of the methods best in economic history required discovering those best for all history and all social science, he engaged in a long methodological investigation out of which he formulated through his "ideal types" the methods which he found to be giving the best results. "Economic man" can be considered as an example of an ideal type. Max Weber did not agree with Schmoller's disparagement of economic theory, except—an important exception—that in Weber's system of thought economic theory is only valid for a special ideal type and is applicable to show how realities approximate or differ from that ideal type.[25]

Spiethoff accepted the usefulness of Weber's ideal types for certain purposes. He considered the study of ideal types one form of pure economic theory and emphasized the importance and value of pure theory as it had been developed by theoretical economists. This was an important step towards the reconciliation of the successors of Schmoller with the successors of Menger.

Spiethoff clung to Schmoller's position, however, in insisting that pure theory alone was of too limited usefulness, that something more was needed. This something more Spiethoff also called *Theorie,* although our use of the word "theory" makes it difficult for us to recognize it as such. Indeed there are extreme difficulties in conveying Spiethoff's point of view through direct translation of his slogans. In stating a program for the historical school, he urged the replacement of pure theory by realistic theory or *anschauliche Theorie,* that is, the creation or discovery of "real types" instead of "ideal types."[26]

---

[25] Together with Sombart and Spiethoff, Weber is considered in "The Youngest Historical School," in Schumpeter's *History of Economic Analysis,* pp. 815–19. On his "ideal types" and their relation to Spiethoff's thought see the *Readings* edited by Lane and Riemersma, pp. 436–43, and works there cited.

[26] Arthur Spiethoff, "Die Allgemeine Volkswirtschaftslehre als geschichtliche Theorie. Die Wirtschaftsstile," in *Schmollers Jahrbuch,* LVI (1932), 891–924; Spiethoff, "The Historical Character of Economic Theories," *Journal of Economic History,* XII (1952), 131–39; Spiethoff, "Pure Theory and Economic Gestalt Theory; Ideal Types and Real Types," in *Enterprise and Secular Change: Readings in Economic History* (Irwin, 1953), pp. 445–63; and Spiethoff, "Anschauliche und reine volkswirtschaftliche Theorie und ihr Verhältnis zueinander," in *Synopsis, Festgabe für Alfred Weber,* ed. Edgar Salin (Heidelberg, 1948), pp. 560–664; and Spiethoff, "Gustav von Schmoller und die anschauliche Theorie der Volkswirtschaft," *Schmollers Jahrbuch,* LXII (1938), 400–19. In this last article, Spiethoff shows how Schmoller's work, particularly his treatment of business cycles, gave an "image of reality" in the sense of *anschauliche Theorie.* On p. 412 Spiethoff characterizes the goal of the historical school as "die idealtypische Theorie durch eine realistische zu ersetzen."

Edgar Salin, who coined the term *anschauliche Theorie,* suggested "essential (-intrinsic) theory" as an English translation.[27] Fritz Redlich has suggested and Spiethoff has approved the phrase "theory of economic Gestalt."[28] I believe that the thought they are trying to express will be better understood by English readers if they forego any use of the word "theory" in a translation. Common usage does not hold theory in such high esteem that they need feel they are losing caste by abandoning it. Hereafter, when I use the word "theory" without qualification I will mean pure theory. But pure theory is not the only kind of generalization that is used in, and shaped by, analysis of economic life. The problems that Spiethoff had in mind arise, it seems to me, when one starts to analyze a historical situation, past or present, and asks: What theories are applicable here? It arises also if one starts with a theory in mind and asks what situations have existed which can be explained by applying it. Even extreme champions of theory do not maintain that all their theories are applicable to all situations. They may claim that their theories are all universally valid, however, if they follow logically from the premises set forth. Spiethoff acknowledged that theory is universally true in this sense, truth being then, as in geometry, a question of logic. That leaves two questions. (1) Should a theory be called "valid," should it be called a "law," regardless of the extent that situations to which it is applicable exist or have existed? This being merely an argument over words, it deserves few.[29] (2) The second question has significance and seems to me to be the real point at issue, namely: What kind of general statements can be made about the real existence of conditions which in pure theory are considered as hypothetical? Or, to put it differently, what kind of general statements, if any, can be made about history, past or present, to show which portions of pure theory are relevant to which portions of history?

For example, some theories are relevant to one form of market relationships, such as bi-lateral monopoly, and not to another form, such as pure competition. Some are associated with particular institu-

---

[27] His *Geschichte der Volkswirtschaftslehre* (1951 ed.), p. 191. H. W. Singer proposes "all-round sociological theory." (*Ibid.,* p. 191 n.) T. W. Hutchison translated it by " 'intuitive' or descriptive theory," in Walter Eucken, *The Foundations of Economics* (Chicago: University of Chicago Press, 1951), p. 67.

[28] *Enterprise and Secular Change: Readings in Economic History,* p. 442 n.

[29] See the very useful comment of Fritz Redlich on Spiethoff's use of the word *Geltung,* and its translation, in the *Journal of Economic History,* XII (1952), 131. On the importance of *Relevanz* in *anschauliche Theorie,* see Salin, *Gesch. der Volkswirtschaftslehre,* p. 196.

tions, such as a central banking system. Some assume one kind of "needs" or motivation, others another kind. An investigation of historical reality will apply those theories which are relevant to explaining the kind of events being studied. The result may be said to consist of, on the one hand, statements that certain events occurred, and, on the other, statements of causal connections between them. These causal connections are not hypothetical (in the form: if A occurs then B will occur), but categorical or historical (in the form: because A occurred, therefore B occurred). The statements of causal connection are, in effect, statements that a particular theory has been found applicable. If the historical situation studied covers a large period, or if several historical situations are studied comparatively, and the same theory found to be relevant again and again, the statement of causal connection will still be in the historical form (repeatedly, because A occurred, therefore B occurred) but will be made in general terms.

Generalizations of this kind are well on the way towards what Spiethoff calls the creation of a "real type." And generalizations of this kind have in effect much the same meaning as saying that certain parts of pure theory are applicable to certain groups of real, historical situations. Whether such generalizations are called theory or taxonomy or historical analysis seems unimportant, they are useful.

Put it another way. Economics has been called a "box of tools." No workman is able to repair a machine, an electric circuit, or even a piece of furniture merely because he has a box of tools. In order to use his tools effectively, he has to know how the machine or circuit operates, or what kind of a piece of furniture he is working on.

Let us abandon the "box of tools" for another analogy. The principles of mechanics and electricity are the same for all machines and all electric circuits. But knowledge of the principles alone will not make a good repair man. Before he goes to work he must know the structure of the type of machine or circuit he is asked to repair.

These metaphors are not Spiethoff's way of presenting the matter. Again and again he asserted that a real type is an image of reality (*Abbild der Wirklichkeit*). For the purpose of forming an image of reality, pure theory is only a means to the end. If, on the other hand, the end sought is an abstract scheme of functional relations, then an undersanding of actual historical situations, even of recurrent situations, is only a means. The danger in pure theory, said Spiethoff, is that it is mistakenly believed to be an image of reality.

If the creation or discovery of real types proceeded only by the application of economic theory, then the difference between the historical school and the theoretical economists might quickly have become a harmonious division of labor. But there are two aspects which arouse real difficulties.

One is the intrusion of sociology, broadly interpreted. General statements about the applicability of theories to real situations become important in the formulation of social policy and in explaining past events. In both cases it is necessary to consider not only the economic interrelations, with which economic theory is concerned, but also the social and cultural aspects of the situation. Therefore *anschauliche Theorie* includes much generalization about the cultural and social situation as a whole, or, to put it differently, many generalizations stating which cultural and social theories are applicable to the particular historical situation being analyzed. It merges economics with sociology in the latter's broadest sense, even as Schmoller had done in his outline of general economics.

The second difficulty, closely connected with the first, arises in the search for some way of grasping the situation as a whole. This is essential in *anschauliche Theorie*. Translating the term as "theory of economic *Gestalt*" emphasizes the concern with the whole pattern.

The way in which an analyst obtains a view of the whole pattern in the situation being analyzed is variously expressed. One method may perhaps be best introduced by returning to the metaphor suggested by calling economic theory a box of tools. For the understanding of an apparatus on which tools are to be used, it is obvious to inquire as to the purpose of the apparatus. Of course, the metaphor is only a metaphor; society is not a machine. But there are many social institutions that are best understood in terms of their purposes—clubs, armies, and churches as well as business firms. Historians describe movements such as the Reformation or the American Revolution by analyzing the purposes and attitudes of the participants. An extension of this method leads to analysis of all history through an understanding of the dominant purpose or spirit manifest in action. Many German writers including Max Weber have analyzed the importance in some form or other of this kind of understanding, which they call *Verstehen*.

"Understanding" of the dominating spirit of an economic system was the key used by Sombart to determine the essentials of economic history. He did not accept the designation *anschauliche Theorie*, suggested by Edgar Salin, as a good term for characterizing his way of thinking;[30] Sombart preferred to speak of *verstehende Theorie* and

<hr>

[30] *Die Drei Nationalökonomien,* p. 202.

referred to his *Kapitalismus* as an "ideal type" in Max Weber's sense. But his way of describing capitalism was certainly an approach to what Spiethoff called a "real type." It was claimed as such by Spiethoff, who emphasized that Sombart analyzed reality whereas Weber's ideal types were, according to Weber's own formulation, a departure from reality, accentuating some features and not others in order to obtain a picture possessing inner consistence or coherence, and therefore fully accessible to the understanding (*Verstehen*) .[31]

The distinction between real type and ideal type is indeed likely to be blurred in any extensive historical analysis. As formally defined by Spiethoff, a real type is a general statement of what phenomena really occurred regularly together with a causal connection between them. The phenomena related to each other in the real type may be mere material circumstances, such as the volume of iron production and the number of bank notes in circulation, which are open to objective observation by methods comparable to those of natural science. But they may also be mental or moral attitudes or purposes. Spiethoff stressed the former, Sombart the latter.[32] There is a tendency, as I see it, to convert a real type into an ideal type whenever the picture of motivation, the pattern of aims and attitudes, is emphasized and is elaborated into a meaningful whole, disregarding incongruous and inconsistent elements that were (or are) present in the historical reality.

Spiethoff's own formulation of the task of *anschauliche Theorie,* his program for the historical school, was in some ways relatively modest. He did not, like Sombart, embrace all social theory under the name economics (*Nationalökonomie*) . He did not stress the explanation of historical evolution nor call for the further elaboration of developmental sequences. He proposed that attention be centered, not on stages as in Schmoller's time, but on what he called "economic styles." For example, he referred to "the economic style of town economy," "the economic style of free, capitalistic market economy," and so on.[33] A "style" was a highly generalized example of a real type. Although inclined to equate styles and periods, Spiethoff did not envisage a

[31] *Ibid., passim;* Spiethoff, in *Schmollers Jahrbuch,* LVI (1932) , 897–900, 911 ff.; and in *Synopsis,* p. 577; Lane and Riemersma in *Enterprise and Secular Change: Readings,* p. 441 n.

[32] *Synopsis,* p. 611.

[33] Arthur Spiethoff, *Boden und Wohnung in der Marktwirtschaft, insbesondere im Rheinland* (Jena: Fischer, 1934) (Vol. 20 in *Bonner Staatswissenschaftliche Untersuchungen*) , pp. 5–10.

developmental sequence of styles. But each economic style should be explained by the *anschauliche Theorie* appropriate to it; there should in this sense be separate theories for each style. These theories would state the essential causal connections characteristic of each style. Spiethoff did not define fully how the essentials of a style were to be distinguished from the non-essentials.[34] He stated clearly and emphatically the usefulness of pure theory and left room also for other methods, either the "understanding" to which Sombart had appealed or some form of that quality which Schumpeter called "vision."

III. Joseph A. Schumpeter

Schumpeter considered himself a "champion of theory."[35] A pupil of the Austrian school but also the author of important historical sociological studies before he left Austria, he was resuming in Germany has professorial career when in 1926 he wrote the article already cited on "Gustav von Schmoller and Today's Problems." He was then professor of public finance at Bonn where the chair of economic theory was held by Spiethoff. But Schumpeter also conducted a seminar on theory and was attempting in the shadow of the Schmollerian tradition to increase the interest of the Germans in theory, even the kind developed by the Austrians.[36] In accord with his purpose of reconciling the historical school to economic theory, Schumpeter in his 1926 article spoke as favorably as he possibly could of Schmoller and of Schmoller's program, explicitly revising some judgments he had expressed in 1914 in his *Dogmen- und Methodengeschichte*.[37] At Harvard in 1943 Schumpeter was under no such pressure to phrase his thought in a way

[34] In *Schmollers Jahrbuch*, LVI (1932), 896–97, he wrote: "Wollen sie doch arteigene Wirtschaftsgestaltung der Wirklichkeit zur Anschauung bringen. Was sie als arteigen angeben, muss wirklich für den einzufangenden Teilzustand wesenseigentümlich gewesen sein. Will man den Stil der mittelalterlichen Wirtschaft bestimmen, so muss man z. B. wissen, von welchen Antrieben zum wirtschaftlichen Handeln der Wirt geleitet worden ist. . . . Was "wichtig" und "wesentlich" war, wird sich nie zwingend erweisen lassen, die Zahl der notwendigen Stile und die Bestimmung jedes einzelnen wird immer weitgehend *vom Urteil des Forschers abhängen* . . ." (italics mine). Cf. *Synopsis*, pp. 639–40.

[35] Schumpeter, *History of Economic Analysis,* p. 819n.

[36] G. Haberler, "Joseph Alois Schumpeter, 1883–1950," in Seymour E. Harris, (ed.), *Schumpeter, Social Scientist* (Cambridge, Mass.: Harvard University Press, 1951), pp. 36–37. Schumpeter's early historical studies have been translated in *Imperalism and Social Classes* (New York: Kelley, 1951). On their composition, see *ibid.*, pp. ix–xi.

[37] *Schmollers Jahrbuch*, L (1926), 355n.; J. Schumpeter, *Dogmen- und Methodengeschichte* (in *Grundriss der Sozialökonomik*) (Tübingen: Mohr. 1914), pp. 108–9.

acceptable to the Schmollerians when he wrote the incomplete drafts and notes which after his death were skillfully put together to form his *History of Economic Analysis*.[38] But Schumpeter's doctrine regarding methodology seems to me basically consistent throughout his thirty years of writing on the history of economic thought, in spite of the shifts in emphasis.[39] He was strongly sympathetic with the methods of the theorists and with the aims and interests of the historical school. He was most interested in history,[40] and his *Business Cycles,* and *Capitalism, Socialism and Democracy* are notable for their combination of history and theory.[41] His earlier *Theory of Economic Development* built on pure theory, and in the Preface to the second German edition Schumpeter protested that it had no more to do with economic history than had all other economic theory,[42] but his protest was a sign of how much it had aroused the interest of economic historians, as it still does. Although Schumpeter's versatile individuality defies classification within a school, there is no space here for a balanced picture of his contribution to economics and I hope I may be pardoned if I here view him one-sidedly as a part of what he called "the youngest historical school." He was the most persuasive exponent of many of its basic conceptions.

He emphasized effectively the points on which the historical school

[38] *History of Economic Analysis,* editor's introduction, esp. p. vi.

[39] In his first work aimed specifically at a German public, in 1908, he said that both parties to the *Methodenstreit* had been right in their main contentions, but they had been talking about different problems. *Das Wesen und der Hauptinhalt der theoretischen Nationalökonomie* (Leipzig: Duncker & Humblot, 1908), pp. 6–7. See also pp. vii, xxi, 18, 32. Schumpeter's "methodological tolerance" is well set forth in Fritz Machlup, "Schumpeter's Economic Methodology," in Harris (ed.), *Schumpeter, Social Scientist,* pp. 95–101.

[40] In his notes for the *History of Economic Analysis,* p. 12, he wrote, "Of these fundamental fields, economic history—which issues into and includes present day facts—is by far the most important. I wish to state right now that if, starting my work in economics afresh, I were told that I could study only one of the three but could have my choice, it would be economic history that I would choose."

[41] *Business Cycles: A Theoretical, Historical, and Statistical Analysis of the Capitalist Process* (2 vols.; New York: McGraw-Hill, 1939); *Capitalism, Socialism, and Democracy* (2d ed.; New York: Harpers, 1947). On their composition, see *History of Economic Analysis,* p. v.

[42] Joseph Schumpeter, *Theorie der wirtschaftlichen Entwicklung; Eine Untersuchung über Unternehmergewinn, Kapital, Kredit, Zins und den Konjunkturzyklus* (Munich and Leipzig: Duncker & Humblot, 1926) pp. xiii–xiv. The subtitle was added to the second edition to make this point. On his distinction between history and theory, see in the English translation (1934), pp. 58–62, and most clearly in the first German edition (Leipzig: Duncker & Humblot, 1912), pp. 466–67, in the chapter which was omitted from the second edition.

and the theorists generally were drawing closer together. All could agree that the writers of historical monographs needed an understanding of the relevant theory; Schumpeter praised Spiethoff unreservedly for his competence in this respect and spoke warmly of the value of the total addition to historical knowledge to which the historical school had contributed.[43] There was general agreement also that not all theory was always relevant. Schumpeter wrote, "the historical or 'evolutionary' nature of the economic process unquestionably limits the scope of general concepts and of general relations between them (economic laws) that economists may be able to formulate."[44] And, since changes in social institutions had to be taken into account by economists, there was room for specialists on institutional developments. Schumpeter recognized this by adding what he called economic sociology among the fields fundamental for "economic analysis." He listed four: economic history, statistics, economic theory, and economic sociology.[45] He considered Schmoller, Weber, and Sombart economic sociologists,[46] but in so labeling them he was not excluding them from the temple of economics; he did not consider economic theory the whole of economic analysis.

Most economists would probably accompany Schumpeter thus far along the road of reconciliation between the historical and theoretical schools, making reservations only concerning terminology. More serious difficulties, only partly terminological, arise from the way in which he blurred the distinction between ideal types and real types. We may be grateful that he avoided the use of these ugly phrases, and yet doubt the usefulness of stretching the word "model," as he did, to cover both. In his Presidential Address before the American Economic Association in 1948, he said,

> The work (of model building) consists in picking out certain facts rather than others, in pinning them down by labeling them, in accumulating further facts in order not only to supplement

---

[43] *Schmollers Jahrbuch,* L (1926), 376–77; *History of Economic Analysis,* p. 810 ("Much of this work was no doubt rather pedestrian. But the sum total of it meant a tremendous advance in accuracy of knowledge about the social process"), and p. 813 (comparison with a physician's clinical experience), and on Spiethoff, pp. 804, 816, and 1126–27.

[44] *History of Economic Analysis,* p. 34.

[45] *Ibid.,* pp. 12–21.

[46] *Ibid.,* p. 812: "the Schmollerian economist was in fact a historically minded sociologist in the latter term's widest meaning." See also *Schmollers Jahrbuch,* L (1926), 369–71.

but in part also to replace those originally fastened upon, in formulating and improving the relations perceived – briefly, in 'factual' and 'theoretical' research that go on in endless chain of give and take, the facts suggesting new analytic instruments (theories) and these in turn carrying us towards the recognition of new facts. This is as true when the object of our interest is an historical report as it is when the object of our interest is to 'rationalize' the SCHRÖDINGER equation though in any particular instance the task of fact finding or the task of analyzing may so dominate the other as to almost remove it from sight.[47]

This description of economic analysis or model building is very similar to the analysis of Spiethoff's method which Schumpeter wrote in 1926 and which Spiethoff hailed as a description of *anschauliche Theorie*.[48] But Schumpeter did not distinguish two different kinds of theory, as Spiethoff had. Although Schumpeter recognized a distinction in regard to the "object of interest," which may be "a historical report," or "to 'rationalize' " an equation, he did not allot to each interest a separate method and he shows no favoritism as between history and equations.

If Schumpeter's models are to serve the same functions as those that Spiethoff claimed for real types, they must distinguish the essential in real historical situations, past or present. How is that done? Without attempting a full answer, Schumpeter approached the problem in his discussion of "vision." Before any form of model-building (before any kind of economic analysis) there must be perception of a set of related phenomena which we wish to analyze. "This mixture of perceptions and prescientific analysis we shall," he wrote, "call the research worker's Vision or Intuition."[49] It follows that real types depend on "vision" initially in selecting certain relations as more essential than others. But ideal types depend on vision also. The "vision" determines which general relationships are worth thinking about. Schumpeter insisted that vision necessarily precedes any study in pure theory as well as any analysis of a historical situation.

Vision comes to us mixed with value judgments in a compound that Schumpeter called ideology. Ideologies are socially conditioned; if

---

[47] "Science and Ideology," *American Economic Review*, XXXIX (1949), 350–51.

[48] *Schmollers Jahrbuch*, L (1926), 372–77 and especially 377n. Compare the description in the *History of Economic Analysis*, pp. 816–17, where he concluded that Spiethoff "actually developed 'realistic theories' of a certain type." Cf. *Business Cycles*, I, 6, 30–33.

[49] *American Economic Review*, XXXIX (1949), 350.

valid at all they are valid only for a particular historical situation. The
results of analysis, the facts and theoretical techniques developed in
working over the material proffered by the vision, are what constitute
the cumulative science having universal validity. Gradually, specific
ideological elements are eliminated since "fact finding and analysis . . . tend to destroy whatever will not stand their tests,"[50] but the
influence of ideology "shows nowhere more strongly than in economic
history which displays the traces of ideological premises so clearly,
precisely because they are rarely formulated in so many words and
hence rarely challenged. . . ."[51]

The concepts which Schumpeter uses in his own historical works are
very similar to what Spiethoff called real types. In defining capitalism
Schumpeter is asserting, as he explicitly recognized, that a number of
specified conditions have in fact (i.e., in history) occurred together—
for example, credit creation and innovations by means of borrowed
money. His definition implies "a statement of fact, namely, that the
defining characteristic gives the essence of a definite historical phenomenon."[52] The "capitalist process," which he depicted most broadly
in *Capitalism, Socialism, and Democracy,* is basically a pattern of causal
relations between a number of historical events or conditions: commercial society with credit formation, rational science, invention and innovation; private property; entrepreneurial profits; the bourgeois class,
family, and spirit; the structure of the late feudal state and the modern
national state, and so on. In analyzing the causal relations, the tools of
economic theory are used but they alone do not suffice. Much sociological theory is embodied in the description. And the main lines are
laid down by the acceptance as correct of a certain "vision," a vision
developed from that of Karl Marx, namely that "capitalistic evolution
will destroy the foundations of capitalistic society."[53] It is the vision

---

[50] *Ibid.,* p. 359.

[51] *Ibid.,* p. 358. On vision see also his *History of Economic Analysis,* pp. 41–42.

[52] *Business Cycles,* I, 223. Cf. *Imperialism and Social Classes,* p. 137 and n. Although Spiethoff's section of the youngest German historical school made much
of the contrast between "real types" and "ideal types," all branches of the German historical school were so much influenced by German idealistic philosophy,
that from an empiricist point of view they were all idealistic. Accordingly, Abbott
Payson Usher commented that in "Schumpeter's treatment of capitalism . . . the
primary features of the concept as an ideal culture type remains. It can be shown
that the retention of these features of the idealistic philosophy makes the tasks of
historical analysis more difficult" ("Historical Implications of the Theory of Economic Development," in Harris (ed.), *Schumpeter, Social Scientist,* p. 129).

[53] *Capitalism, Socialism, and Democracy,* p. 42.

which focuses attention, gives a view of the process as a whole and thereby supplies the principle of relevance that permits distinguishing the essential.

Schumpeter's *Capitalism, Socialism and Democracy* is a mixture of many currents. The similarity of his synthesis to that of Sombart is obvious but there are also sharp contrasts. I mention only two. (1) Schumpeter unreservedly accepted and applied the tools of economic theory which Sombart treated with scorn.[54] (2) Schumpeter rejected Sombart's emphasis on the capitalistic spirit and presented man's economic activities as the prime mover of the whole historical process.[55] It follows that "rising capitalism produced . . . the mental attitude of modern science . . . ,"[56] and "all the features and achievements of modern civilization are, directly or indirectly, the products of the capitalistic process."[57] In these two respects, Schumpeter departed further than did Sombart from the Schmollerian tradition, but there is much in Schumpeter's view that recalls Schmoller's attitude and makes it fitting that Schumpeter should praise Schmoller as often as he did.[58] Both Schumpeter and Schmoller admired capitalistic enterprise and entrepreneurs, both disliked the kind of socialism that Marx had predicted, and both sought an explanation of the passage from one social organization to another through an interplay of causes such as the form of the state, of the family, of property, and of ideas, as well as of the class structure. In Schumpeter's analysis all these strands are

[54] Although Schumpeter criticized Sombart's attitude towards theory he also praised Sombart's achievement (Joseph Schumpeter, "Sombarts Dritter Band," *Schmollers Jahrbuch,* LI [1927], 349–69). *Cf. Das Wesen und der Hauptinhalt der theoretischen Nationalökonomie,* p. 18; *Theory of Economic Development* (Cambridge, Mass.: Harvard University Press, 1934), p. 59; *History of Economic Analysis,* p. 818. Sombart returned the compliment in replying to the criticism in *Die drei Nationalökonomien,* pp. 303–4.

[55] *Capitalism, Socialism, and Democracy* (2nd ed.; New York: Harpers, 1947), pp. 121–23. *Cf. Imperialism and Social Classes,* p. 145. In *Business Cycles,* I, 228, Schumpeter criticized the "unrealistic" views of Sombart and Max Weber.

[56] *Capitalism, Socialism, and Democracy,* p. 124.

[57] *Ibid.,* p. 125.

[58] Schumpeter praised Schmoller's *Grundriss* not only in 1926 but in 1943, writing, "Into a framework that did not depart fundamentally from oldest tradition, he fitted the rich materials of social history, giving for every type or institution a sketch (in some cases, a masterly sketch) of its historical evolution on the lines of his personal theory of it . . ." (*History of Economic Analysis,* p. 813). And in *Business Cycles,* I, 229, after again criticizing M. Weber and W. Sombart, Schumpeter praises Schmoller, "whose sober realism prevented him from kicking up the dust of spurious problems."

intertwined; in Schmoller's *Grundriss,* which instead of focusing on any one epoch or one problem attempts to survey all human experience, the strands are laid down one by one in separate sections of the *Grundriss* and are never woven together. But nearly all the strands are the same. They were so skillfully woven together by Schumpeter that his volume gave new force to the belief that we can learn from history the nature of the future. Marxists were already persuaded; Schumpeter's appeal, like that of Schmoller, was to intellectuals who dislike Marxian socialism. He appealed to economists more widely than Sombart because his analysis was much tighter and he had a much sounder command of fact and theory.

Especially interesting in Schumpeter's *Capitalism, Socialism, and Democracy* is the kind of theory it embodies. Schumpeter does not call it *anschauliche Theorie,* but it is something other than pure theory. He considers favorably "the idea of a theory, not merely of an indefinite number of disjointed patterns or of the logic of economic quantities in general, but of the actual sequence of those patterns or of the economic process as it goes on, under its own steam, in historic time. . . ."[59] This conception, which Marx, Sombart, and Schumpeter boldly attempted to realize, had only been hinted at by Schmoller himself, but the historical school which honored Schmoller was constantly haunted by "the idea of a theory . . . of the actual sequence . . . of patterns . . . in historic time."[60]

IV. Walter Eucken

Such an idea of theory was rejected by Walter Eucken, who was in Germany the staunchest defender of economic theory during the 1930's and whose influence on other German economists was especially strong

[59] *Capitalism, Socialism, and Democracy,* p. 43.

[60] In 1926 Schumpeter wrote that there could be found in Schmoller "ein Hinweis auf ferne grosse Linien einer bestimmten Art von Entwicklungstheorie, einer Kausaltheorie der sozialen Entwicklung die basiert auf dem, aber etwas anderes ist als das Mosaik der Teilerklärungen, aus denen die soziologische Universalgeschichte oder universalgeschichtliche Soziologie in erster Instanz besteht" (*Schmollers Jahrbuch,* L [1926], 385). The ensuing note on p. 386 foreshadows some of the ideas later elaborated in *Capitalism, Socialism, and Democracy.* In 1943, on the other hand, Schumpeter emphasized Schmoller's other trend: "A single hypothesis of the Comte-Buckle-Marx kind he did not even visualize as an ultimate goal—the very idea of a simple theory of historical evolution seemed to him a mistaken one, in fact unscientific" (*History of Economic Analysis,* p. 811).

in the years immediately after the end of World War II.[61] In 1936 Eucken launched a direct attack upon the historical school in economics, blaming it for the low esteem in which economics was held in Germany.[62] His *Grundlagen der Nationalökonomie* in 1940 continued the attack and defined the basis of his own thought.[63] His *Grundsätze der Wirtschaftspolitik,* published in 1952, after his death, completed the statement of his position and rounded out his attack on historicism by including Schumpeter with Sombart among those whose historical work he assailed.[64]

Eucken was not an enemy of historical studies—quite the contrary. He knew and valued economic history. He insisted that economic

[61] On Walter Eucken see the introductions by F. A. Lutz to Eucken's *Foundations of Economics* (Chicago: University of Chicago Press, 1951), and to Eucken's *Grundsätze der Wirtschaftspolitik* (Bern and Tübingen: Francke/Mohr, 1952). See also Alexander Rüstow, "Zu den Grundlagen der Wirtschaftswissenschaft," in *Revue de la Faculté des Sciences économiques de l'Université d'Istanbul,* II (1940–41), 105–54.

[62] The attack on historicism and on Schmoller is in the editors' introductions to the first volumes of the series "Ordnung der Wirtschaft": Friedrich Lutz, *Das Hauptproblem der Geldverfassung* (Stuttgart and Berlin: Kohlhammer, 1936), and Franz Böhm, *Ordnung der Wirtschaft als geschichtliche Aufgabe und rechtsschöpferische Leistung,* 1937. A reply by Bernhard Laum, professor of economics at Marburg, "Methodenstreit oder Zusammenarbeit," appeared in *Schmollers Jahrbuch,* LXI (1937), 257–73, followed by Eucken's "Die Überwindung des Historismus," *Schmollers Jahrbuch,* LXII (1938), 191–214, and Laum's reply, pp. 215–20.

The same volume of *Schmollers Jahrbuch* that contained this article of Eucken contained in a later issue the volume of essays in celebration of the hundredth anniversary of Schmoller's birthday. The first article therein was "Historismus" by Erich Rothacker, professor of philosophy at Bonn, a defense of Schmoller specifically, and other historicists in general, against Eucken's charge that historicism led to fatalism. But the tendency in the historical school to which Eucken was objecting is evident in the article in the same issue, pp. 733–48, by Waldemar Zimmermann, professor of economics at Hamburg, in the way in which he traces a connection between Schmoller's influence and the acceptance of National Socialism.

Although there were some currents in the historical school whose influence was favorable to fatalism and Naziism, there were strong elements in Schmoller's thought contrary to both these trends. And Laum seems to me to have been right on one point (p. 219): Eucken was following in Schmoller's footsteps in that Eucken, as is explained below, emphasized that *laissez faire* had failed and that state action was necessary to shape the economic order.

[63] Of the German editions, I have depended mainly on the first, *Die Grundlagen der Nationalökonomie* (Jena: Fischer, 1940); the English translation above cited is from the sixth German edition.

[64] *Grundsätze,* pp. 200–9. A sketch of Eucken's whole position is in his *This Unsuccessful Age or the Pains of Economic Progress* (London: William Hodge, 1951), pp. 83–96.

thinking should start with the study of particular historical situations, mainly those of the present or recent past, and that the ultimate purpose of the science was the full economic analysis of real situations. If he had lived in a different intellectual environment, he might very well have directed his attack against theorists without changing substantially his own doctrine. He probably would have done so had the prevailing fashion in his time and country been the logical elaboration of hypothetical possibilities. But Eucken lived in Germany with the shadow of the Schmollerian tradition on one side and the shadow of Naziism on the other. He attacked the historical school on the ground that the neglect of theory by Schmoller's followers had led to incompetence in economic analysis and to historicism, relativism, and fatalism.

In attacking historicism, Eucken reaffirmed the universal validity of economic theory but stressed also the inability of theoretical propositions by themselves to give economists a grasp of reality. On the one hand he insisted that there were "universally true economic laws": on the other he emphasized that what results from the operation of these laws depends on historical conditions. Although the economist cannot explain the variations in these historical conditions, it is his function, Eucken maintained, to determine what these conditions were, at least to describe those varying aspects of historical circumstance that affect economic life. Eucken explicitly rejected Menger's readiness to separate the theoretical and historical sciences. Schmoller was right on one point at least, in wanting a unified economics.[65] Thus, while Eucken attacked the methods of the historical school, he fully accepted their professed aim of bringing economics into closer touch with historical reality. But he reproached them for not asking the right questions, either about the present or the past.

His attack on their treatment of the past is illustrated by his dissection of the thesis, familiar to all readers of Sombart, that man's economic motives have changed so much that no one body of economic theory can be applied to all ages, for under capitalism the search for profits replaced the earlier and contrary principle of seeking enough to meet one's needs. The illustration deserves serious attention not only because it shows Eucken's concern with delimiting the task of economic analysis, but also because it is in itself a worthwhile piece of clear thinking on an important historical problem.

Eucken begins his dissection by removing the ambiguity of the word "needs." He clears the ground by defining "needs" to include the desire

---

[65] *Foundations of Economics,* pp. 56, 59.

for power and esteem, as well as sustenance, so that profits will be recognized as one means to the desired ends, not as an alternate end. "Everywhere and at all time," he says, "man finds himself in the daily situation of having to adjust his needs to the means at his disposal for satisfying them, and vice versa. In this respect nothing has altered fundamentally since the beginning of history."[66] But man's conception of his needs and how to satisfy them has varied. These variations deserve historical study, but cannot usefully be described by the tags "meeting needs" and "seeking profits." Instead, Eucken proposed two more clearly defined dichotomies or contrasts. The first dichotomy is based on the contrast between considering one's needs fixed and considering them flexible. In the former case, a rise in wages can be expected to decrease the number of hours worked; in the latter case to lead to an increase of output. The second dichotomy is based on the contrast between seeking maximum net receipts and seeking optimal output—contrasting principles which would lead monopolists to react differently to possibilities of technical innovation.[67]

This analysis illustrates a central feature of Eucken's way of thinking. Whether needs are felt to be fixed or variable is one of the historical conditions which the economist in his analysis takes as given. Accordingly, whether an increase in wages will induce laborers to work more or less cannot be determined by economic theory alone; it depends on the historical conditions. "*Why* men have flexible or fixed levels of material needs can only be answered for individual peoples, classes, and periods, and in particular historical situations."[68] Economic theory cannot explain it.

Eucken's program for economic history is the descriptive analysis of particular historical situations in such terms as to permit economic theory to be applied in explaining the course of economic events once the relevant historical situation is known and taken as "given." He affirmed the universality of economic theory by elaborating on the way in which its application depended on a knowledge of historical condi-

---

[66] *Foundations of Economics,* p. 281. Steps towards a similar analysis are taken by Spiethoff in *Schmollers Jahrbuch,* LVI (1932) , 921, n. 4.

Although Spiethoff and Eucken are opposites in their relation to the historical school and to the vocabulary it has developed, they seem to me to have many more common attitudes towards economics than Menger and Schmoller. For Spiethoff's comments on Eucken, see *Synopsis,* pp. 578–79, 584. Between Sombart and Eucken, however, there is little in common.

[67] *Ibid.,* pp. 281–90.

[68] *Foundations of Economics,* p. 288; *cf.* p. 213.

tions. The latter he called *Daten,* that which economic analysis takes as given and is incapable of explaining. He listed such variable conditions under six headings: (1) human needs, (2) natural resources and conditions, (3) labor power, (4) goods on hand from previous production, (5) technical knowledge, and (6) legal and social organization. "This last 'datum' must," he wrote, "be conceived in a broad sense so as to include not only the laws, morals, and customs, but also the spirit (Geist) with which we live and observe the rules of the game."[69]

In taking account especially of the sixth category of historical conditions—in analyzing their effects on the economic process—Eucken believed the first essential was to discover the extent of the existence of various "forms of economic organization." He gave much attention to the definition of these essential forms of economic organization, distinguishing two basic forms, centrally directed and exchange economy, and many subdivisions, as—under exchange economy—monopoly, oligopoly, perfect competition, etc. His definition of these concepts is an example of pure theory, he considers them "ideal types," although not precisely in Weber's sense. No real historical organization (past or present) ever corresponds exactly to one of these pure forms. Even the Soviet Union has some elements of exchange economy. The task of the economist is to find out in regard to each branch of the economic life of a people how much of each of these forms is present, and, using that knowledge, to explain the course of economic events. He criticized Spiethoff's construction of economic "styles," as well as the construction of "stages" by Schmoller and Bücher, and of the "economic systems" by Sombart. All were condemned on the grounds that they did not assist the understanding of economic reality.[70]

His "forms of economic organization" enable Eucken to analyze the effects of many historical variations which had received attention from the historical school. Closed household economy, for example, is recognized as a simple, centrally directed economy. The late stage of "capitalism" is analyzed as a mixture of centrally administered economy and various forms of exchange economy, with oligopoly and monopoly prominent among them. Eucken called the mixture of forms existing in

[69] *Grundsätze der Wirtschaftspolitik,* p. 377. Cf. *Foundations of Economics,* pp. 179–92, 213–20.

[70] *Ibid.,* Part II. Eucken noted that "style" was used in a different, broader sense by Alfred Müller-Armack in his *Genealogie der Wirtschaftsstile,* (Stuttgart: Kohlhammer, 1944). This work of Müller-Armack is deserving of attention as a much improved statement of what is commonly called the Weber thesis concerning the relation of capitalism and protestantism.

a given historical society its economic order (*Ordnung*), or organization.[71] How it came to exist at a given moment of history can be explained only by historical circumstances. The function of economic analysis is to show the effects of a given economic organization on the everyday course of economic events within the society being studied.

It might be said that Eucken urged economic historians to study *Ordnungen* instead of Schmollerian stages, Spiethoffian styles, and Sombartian systems. But the concepts are not fully comparable. An economic *Ordnung* is always a mixture of forms and it is a very specific historical situation. It is a combination of particulars lacking the kind of organic unity or inner causal connection that would make it a "whole." Eucken's method does not meet the requirements of *anschauliche Theorie*.[72] But his way of describing *Ordnungen*, his belief that the forms of market and monetary organization are the essentials, gives expression to Eucken's "vision."

V

Eucken's formulation sharpens some conceptual tools, but obviously it excludes from economics precisely those questions in which the historical school generally and Schmoller in particular were most interested, namely, the causes of the growth of various forms of social organization. Eucken excluded from economics all that Schumpeter welcomed under the name of economic sociology.

There is more at stake here than a choice of labels. Eucken believed that the economist, as economist, should study the historical conditions. It was an essential part of his task to do so; the task could not be left to sociologists, for they were not equipped to determine which

[71] In the *Grundlagen*, Eucken used *Wirtschaftsordnung* for that which I have translated as "economic order or organization." He used *Wirtschaftssystem* for that which I have translated "form of economic organization." This created difficulty for the translator, who found himself forced to translate *Wirtschaftsordnung* as "economic system." See *Foundations of Economics*, pp. 13–14. In his *Grundsätze*, Eucken avoided speaking of *Systemen*, perhaps because of the associations given the word by Sombart, and succeeds in using *Formen* instead, e.g., "Die Wirtschaftsordnung eines Landes besteht in der Gesamtheit der jeweils realisierten Formen . . ." (*Grundsätze*, p. 23). On *Ordnung*, see *ibid.*, p. 372.

[72] Salin, *Geschichte der Volkswirtschaftslehre* (1951), pp. 193–6, where Eucken's *Formen* are characterized as models, not ideal types, and the adequacy of his method criticized from the point of view of *anschauliche Theorie*. For Eucken's comment on "forms" and "ideal types" see *Foundations of Economics*, pp. 116, 310, 347–49.

parts of the historical conditions were of influence on economic life, or in what way. Starting from economic facts, such as a rise in prices, the economist should apply economic theory to determine the cause of the fact to be explained, and trace the causal connections from one fact to another until he arrived at facts which were no longer purely economic but part of the historical conditions determined, at least in large measure, by non-economic factors which economic theory could not explain.[73]

An illustration may make clear the distinction. The cause of a fall in coal prices might be traced by the economist to the decline in demand that resulted from an unusually mild winter. The economist must stop there; he cannot, as economist, explain why the weather was unusually warm. Another causal factor which would have to be considered in explaining a change in price would be the economic system, e.g., whether distribution of coal was through allocation by a central administration or through competitive markets. That in turn would depend on the political and social system. Economic theory cannot explain why the social system is as it is, just as it cannot explain the warm weather.

Evidently, economic theory is concerned with explaining results of changes in economic organization, but it cannot explain why the changes in economic organization occur. Economics cannot, for example, explain the Russian Revolution of 1917.

Excluding such questions from economics does not remove the need of seeking answers to them. Anyone advising concerning economic policy must seek answers, although in doing so he will be using other methods than those in which the economist has special training. In his *Foundations of Economics,* Eucken seems to place the burden of such questions on the backs of the general historians.[74] In reality the burden is too heavy to be borne by any one group of specialists; it is shared by all who study society. And in Eucken's last work, *The Principles of Economic Policy,* published shortly after his death, he showed how in his teaching he had manfully been carrying his share of the burden.

Does history show that changes in social institutions proceed according to natural laws, comparable to those that in biology govern the

---

[73] "The task of theory is to follow out the necessary relationships as far as the particular set of data, and in the other direction to show how the course of economic events depends on the data. Economic theory cannot show how these data come to exist" (*ibid.,* p. 213) .

[74] *Foundations of Economics,* p. 220.

evolution of species? This is the kind of question that arises when one turns from the narrow field of economics as defined by Eucken and attempts to explain why "historical situations" change. He definitely rejects any deterministic view. At any point of time the future is not determined, Eucken maintained, except by the ideas which men at that point of time freely choose and act upon. Accordingly he wrote and taught the "principles of economic policy" as a part of historical action. It was his effort to shape the undetermined future.

In taking this view of history, Eucken was following in the footsteps of the young Schmoller. Eucken recognized this and praised unreservedly the action of Schmoller in 1872 in forming the Verein für Sozialpolitik with the aim of shaping government policy towards the industrial workers.[75] Eucken and Schmoller both felt that it was part of their professional duty to point out the social and economic policy which was fitted to the needs of the time and based on the teachings of history. Both called on the state to take the necessary action, although they advocated very different kinds of state action.

Eucken accused the historical school in general, however, of pursuing a trend towards determinism the roots of which he traced back to the attitude Schmoller had taken after 1878 in acquiescing in the basic policy decisions of those in power and advising only in regard to details. The historical school's concern with finding an irreversible sequence of stages, systems, or styles seemed to Eucken to lead to belief that the next stage is determined and will come inevitably. The most influential expressions of this manner of viewing history were the studies of capitalism by Sombart and Schumpeter. To Eucken, "capitalism" was a mental construct—a useless one for the economist, since "the concept capitalism says nothing definite about the structure of the economy"[76]—which was then reified, personified, treated as a self-determining force, and made the center of a deterministic philosophy of history. Those who accepted this philosophy gave up trying to control the future by shaping wise economic policies; instead they surrendered to the inevitable.[77]

Can we then learn nothing from history except that men are free to choose, but unable to predict, what will happen next? Eucken did not go from one extreme to the other. If we cannot find laws in history, we

[75] Walter Eucken, "Überwindung des Historismus," *Schmollers Jahrbuch*, LXII (1938) , 207.

[76] *Foundations of Economics*, p. 97.

[77] *Foundations of Economics*, p. 330; *Grundsätze der Wirtschaftspolitik*, pp. 206–9; *This Unsuccessful Age*, p. 90.

can find probabilities or tendencies.[78] Analyzing economic policies in light of the historical record, Eucken concluded that some economic systems have a tendency to change into other determinable forms, for example, that the monopolistic exchange system tends to turn into a centrally directed economic system. He found also a tendency for the legal and political systems to change in determinable ways as the result of changes in the economic system. Indeed his basic positive thesis was that unwise policies adopted under *laissez faire* permitted the growth of monopolies and that the concentrations of power thus created, together with the economic maladjustments resulting from monopolies (and from the monetary system) had caused a tendency towards centrally directed economy. He argued also that under a centrally directed economy freedom would be lost, the state would become tyrannical. He concluded that the state should have a social policy, not of *laissez faire*, but of intervening as necessary to create and maintain a competitive exchange economy. Although he was sometimes so carried away by the fervor of his belief in freedom and competition that he seems to consider the disappearance of freedom under a centrally directed economy as an inevitable historical law, when he was defining his methodological or scientific position most carefully, he concluded that all the relations between the changing elements in the social, political, and economic systems are relations of probability. One tendency may be defeated by an opposing tendency. Effective action is aided by knowledge of the tendencies. General changes in social systems are not inevitably determined by the tendencies; they are determined only by the acts and ideas of the men at the point in history at which they are formed. Eucken's *Grundsätze* was an act, an expression of ideas designed to have a part in determining Germany's economic system, as well as a scientific or scholarly explanation of the need for and meaning of the act.

Neither Sombart nor Schumpeter had taken an unqualified deterministic position. Sombart stated explicitly that men, not conditions, are the driving force in history. A feeling of determinism is created by his writings, however, because individual men, policies, and movements seem dominated by the spirit of their times, and because the feeling, the overtone, in Sombart's work is that of fatalism and pessimism.[79] Schumpeter carefully qualified his statement that socialism was inevitable by throwing out the following as anchor to windward: "An-

[78] *Grundsätze der Wirtschaftspolitik*, p. 215.

[79] On the one hand Sombart wrote that man and not material circumstances were the driving force in history (*Hochkapitalismus*, p. 9) and that history could be foreseen only in broad outlines, containing different possibilities between which

alysis, whether economic or other, **never** yields more than a statement about the tendencies present in an observable pattern. And these never tell us what *will* happen to the pattern but only what *would* happen if they continued to act as they have been acting in the time interval covered by our observation and if no other factors intruded. 'Inevitability' or 'necessity' can never mean more than this."[80] Concerning "the tendencies present in the observable pattern" Eucken and Schumpeter were in substantial, although not complete, agreement. But Schumpeter seems in other passages to slip his anchor, as when he wrote: "Things economic and social move by their own momentum and the ensuing situations compel individuals and groups to behave in certain ways whatever they may wish to do—not indeed by destroying their freedom of choice but by shaping the choosing mentalities and by narrowing the list of possibilities from which to choose."[81] All the theoretical analysis in *Capitalism, Socialism, and Democracy* is overshadowed by the conviction Schumpeter had expressed at the end of a sociological essay written more than twenty years earlier, "the ancient truth that the dead always rule the living."[82]

If Sombart and Schumpeter had prophesied the coming of socialism with joyous passion as Marx did in 1848, instead of regarding it with resigned disdain, they would at least have been helping to create what they desired to be, for belief in determinism can be a spur to action when that which is desired is believed to be determined.

History is "an act of faith." Or of lack of faith. It is in these terms that Eucken passes judgment and condemns the history offered by Sombart and Schumpeter. In his preface to *Capitalism, Socialism, and Democracy,* Schumpeter presented his application of theory to history as "analysis" and claimed for his facts and arguments "scientific" value regardless of whether his prophecy was true.[83] Eucken's conception of economics made him unwilling to judge it in those terms. He judged it as history; he objected that the techniques of analysis were used to give persuasiveness to a vision of history that was false.

The basic difference is that Eucken's way of thinking leaves no room

---

the future could choose (*ibid.,* p. 1009). On the other hand, Sombart maintained some possibilities were excluded (*Hochkapitalismus*) and at the end of his *Hochkapitalismus* he presented certain future developments as "sure facts" (*sichere Tatsachen*) (*ibid.,* p. 1012).

[80] *Capitalism, Socialism, and Democracy,* p. 61.

[81] *Ibid.,* pp. 129–30.

[82] Joseph A. Schumpeter, *Imperialism and Social Classes* (New York: Kelley, 1951), p. 130.

[83] *Capitalism, Socialism, and Democracy,* Preface to the second edition (1946), p. xi, and for his use of "scientific," p. 61.

for attempts to depict the historical process as a whole. At bottom, Schumpeter believed we could perceive historical realities, such as social classes, or capitalism, directly, and could do more than analyze now one aspect now another through mental constructs of our own devising.[84] Eucken believed knowledge was gained only through looking at one aspect at a time.

The limitations of Eucken's method—limitations he recognized and considered inescapable—appear if we reconsider the contrast between the rigid necessity that he ascribes to the causal relationships established by economic theory and the indeterminacy which he ascribes to the causal relationships regarding changes in the historical conditions.[85] He can ascribe necessity to the causal relations in the economic process only because he has previously defined the economic process in such a way as to exclude the indeterminate elements. By adopting a special point of view, that of "the economist" he has shoved those elements aside as "given." In reality or history, no conditions are "given" in the sense of securely remaining unchanged. Even while the effects of "given" conditions are being worked out in the economic process, those conditions are changing and thus creating new effects. To foresee what would really happen next, it would be necessary to foresee how the "given" conditions were going to change while the effects of the condition previously given were registering in economic life. The effect of a warm winter on the size of inventories, and so on, does not necessarily mean lower prices, for there may be a very cold spring, or a rumor of war.

How far can other special disciplines enable us to predict changes in those conditions which the economist must take as given? One can ask whether the other forms of social science now proliferating cannot attain a similar assurance regarding the causal relations within their field of analysis by an equally skillful definition of their special point of view. Then each of the social sciences might construct a scheme of analysis comparable to Eucken's in that, under the circumstances taken as given, it could predict the necessary interrelations within that aspect of events covered by its own theory. For any aspect of a social event, there would then be some science that could demonstrate its inevitable relation to the "given" historical circumstances. Could we then say

---

[84] At the beginning of his essay on social classes, Schumpeter distinguished between "the real social phenomenon and the scientific construct" and referred to the former as "social entities which we observe but which are not of our making" (*Imperialism and Social Classes*, p. 137 and n.) .

[85] Eucken, *Grundsätze*, p. 216.

that, from the combined point of view of all the social sciences, all aspects of events were determined? And therefore that the total course of history was determined?

No. It is nonsense to speak in this way of the "combined point of view of all the social sciences." Their points of view are destroyed when they are combined. Or at least, they do not coalesce, they do not merge into one view of historical change as a whole. The necessity achieved by economic reasoning is in a certain sense fictitious; it is a logical necessity created in the mind through the process of description adopted, not a quality of the process described.

Therefore, the explanation of changes in historical conditions cannot escape from the uncertainty in which Eucken leaves it.

Two different conceptions of economic history, one narrow, the other broad, are suggested by Eucken's distinction between "economic events" on the one hand and "historical conditions" on the other.

If the economic historian restricts himself to analyzing economic events and the historical conditions that determined them, describing in such a way as to show the necessary relations between the economic events themselves and between them and the other conditions, he is proceeding on relatively safe ground. The critical method of evaluating evidence which is taught in historical seminars will be one guide; the analytical method of economic theory will be his other guide. He may fall short of the standard demanded of him, but he will find the rules to be followed have been carefully worked out.

When he strays away from this straight and narrow path, and seeks to explain the causes of change in historical conditions, he is on the primrose path that leads towards uncertainty or a philosophy of history. So long, for example, as he describes changes in technique in such a way as to show their effect on cost curves, or on the size of the demand for labor, he is on the straight and narrow path that Eucken considers within the competence of "economics." When he tries to explain why the technical change occurred, he raises larger questions. He may as an economist establish that rising costs or rising demand created a need for the invention, but to assert that the need created the invention is something else again. A theory of invention is merely one aspect of a general theory of innovation, indeed of a general theory of history, as Abbott Payson Usher has emphasized.[86]

[86] Abbott Payson Usher, "The Significance of Modern Empiricism for History and Economics," *Journal of Economic History,* IX (1949), 163; Usher, *A History of Mechanical Inventions* (Rev. ed.; Cambridge, Mass.: Harvard University Press, 1954), chaps. i–iv.

History contains more than recurrent elements. "The essential feature of history is the emergence of novelty."[87] In efforts at explanation
in this field, economic history merges with all other aspects of history
and cannot avoid the responsibilities inherent in any attempts at
historical synthesis. It must make interpretations that depend, not on
economic analysis, not even if that is enlarged to include some sort of
economic sociology, but depend on the author's view of the nature of
the whole historical process.

VI

In opening the final section of his *Grundriss,* Schmoller stated that
the basic idea of his economic thought was this: that economic life took
place within societies differing from each other and given internal
coherence through a unity of blood and spirit expressed primarily in
political and economic institutions.[88] Except for the ambiguous over-
tones of the words "blood" and "unity," this conception has been
generally accepted. It is recognized also that the course of economic life
varies in the societies thus differentiated, and Walter Eucken has shown
most effectively, even in the process of criticizing Schmoller's historical
school, the need of analyzing these differences. The divergence of
economic systems in our contemporary world and our enlarged knowledge of the past have led to greater emphasis on determining the
significant aspects of these historical differences.

Schmoller's very next paragraph in that same section continued his
statement of purpose and enumerated the topics he had treated "in
order to explain the course of development of economic life and its
forms *as a whole*" (italics mine) . This is the part of Schmoller's
program which, two generations later, is most seriously questioned. His
list of topics, and even his way of handling them, is not the point at
issue. Rather, the question is whether there is any sense in treating the
development of economic life through all human experience, or even
through several centuries, as a distinct but meaningful theme. To do so
is to face theoretical and factual problems that can scarcely be distinguished from those of the general historian. Some concept of the nature
of history must be explicitly or implicitly assumed. If the economic
interpretation of history is accepted, there is then logical ground for
dealing mainly with economic facts. Economic life can be kept in the

---

[87] Usher, in *Journal of Economic History,* IX, 149.
[88] Schmoller, *Grundriss,* p. 1124 (II, 666) .

center of the picture if it is considered the determining factor in history. But many of us, even some who use this principle implicitly through the way they tell the story, do not believe this interpretation is true. Because of the interactions among all aspects of culture, causal connections cannot be seen fully by looking at economic activity alone. Other sides of life must be described; and the threads of economic history are no longer visible as separate threads after they have been woven into patterns of which the motif is the interaction of all aspects of culture in a sequence of historical situations.

As a school of economists, the historical school belongs to the past. The interests it expressed move on, carried forward both by those engaged in the economic analysis of historical situations, past and present, and by those who look for meaning in history as a whole or apply their vision of the whole to studies of detail.

30

Units of Economic Growth
Historically Considered*

THERE is a tendency among economists to emphasize a number of characteristics that distinguish modern economic growth from anything that occurred before 1750. For a historian, and for anyone who seeks to utilize as wide a range of human experience as possible, a different emphasis appears desirable.

As an example of the contrast in point of view let us consider the statement that before the Industrial Revolution technological advances brought increases in population but no increase in product per capita. An historian's response to such a statement might be that the evidence concerning a rise in standard of living is about as convincing as is the evidence concerning an increase in population, particularly in regard to some specific place at some specific period for which there is evidence that the historian has studied. He might for example refer to Periclean Athens. If by this comment he could start an argument over the interpretation of evidence, the historian would feel at home. He would know the rules by which he might hope to win the argument or be forced to admit that he was mistaken. But the historian may feel frustrated and perhaps a little baffled by being told that the experiences to which he refers and which he wishes to call growth are not big enough: that they do not embrace enough people, a long enough period, a sufficient area.

Such a reply is in part an appeal by the economist to concepts well defined within the discipline of economics, but in part it involves

* *Kyklos,* XV (1962) , 95–104. (By permission.)

presuppositions which need to be illuminated. It is an appeal to well-defined concepts in so far as it relates to the span of time, but in so far as it relates to the minimum size of the unit, to its geographical extent or its population, the concepts being used are less clear. Studies of variations in output compiled from year to year have led economists to develop both theories of cycles and theories of economic growth. From raw data, some figures were extracted which showed secular trends and others that showed periodic variations. Since the concept of growth developed by contrasting long-term trends with various shorter swings, it is well understood even by historians that growth must last longer than what we call "a generation" (about thirty years) in order to be worthy of the name.

The restriction of the name economic growth to large economic units lacks a similar justification, and as far as I know lacks any explicit formulation. It does not seem to be the result of a systematic comparison, either in theory or in history, of the development of economic units of various size. Neither is it the result of studies of distribution over space of variations in output comparable to the studies of the distribution of these variations over time. Many analyses of spatial distribution have been made by geographers, to be sure. Using these studies some economists have proposed to analyze economic growth in terms, not of regional units which contain measurable amounts of economic growth, but in terms of centers which radiate influences like magnetic poles and create economic growth. Still, most discussions refer to the growth of an economy and do so in ways which seem to assume that an economy occupies an area. An example is a sentence selected almost at random from a recent symposium: "An economy which tries to emerge from a quagmire of poverty and hopelessness finds itself handicapped by the fact that it must operate in a society which finds the very notion of change alien."

The vagueness in such discussions leaves room for considerable difference and even confusion concerning what size an area must have in order to furnish an example of economic growth. In some discussions economists speak as if a period should not be called one of economic growth unless it witnessed an increase in aggregate population and average product per capita over this globe as a whole. Seldom is that asserted as a matter of dogma, however. Generally it is assumed that any unit which is conventionally called a nation is big enough.

Practically speaking, the nation is taken as the unit of observation in the study of growth because it creates the statistics. This practical reason has made "the nation," or "the national economy," concepts

used in theories of economic growth. Reasons more satisfying theoretically are that the nation has been in recent times the social unit making
many important decisions affecting growth and that nations have had
sufficient cultural unity so that attitudes or propensities influential in
economic growth differ more from one nation to another than within a
single nation, at least in many cases. Neither of these theoretical reasons tells us anything about the size of the nation (whether size be
measured in square miles or in population) and neither is applicable
to more than a small portion of the earth during more than a few
centuries. For other periods, and for areas other than western Europe,
the social units that made decisions significant for growth were either
cities and small principalities or military rulers of empires embracing
several nationalities. Cultural homogeneity followed mainly religious
lines. For studying these times and places the nation is not a satisfactory
unit either of observation or of explanation.

There were considerable increases and decreases in wealth, including
long swings up and down, during the many centuries when cities and
empires were more important than nations. Whoever is interested in
describing, comparing, and explaining these secular movements needs
to consider as units of observation and explanation the social and
cultural divisions then existing, both large and small. Observing and
explaining the changes in small units is especially important if, as may
well be the case, the institutions and policies which most affected
economic growth were those of the city, tribe, or province rather than
those of empires. To say that none of the changes in wealth in the small
units constituted economic growth seems arbitrarily narrow.

Since there is an arbitrary element in all clear definitions there might
be no objection to this narrow use of the word growth if it did not
inculcate a lack of interest in most of human history. The study of
economic growth has become one of the main themes of economic
history. This is due in large measure to the political situation since the
end of World War II; the great powers boast of their growth and the
underdeveloped pant for it. Historians accordingly look at the past
with these contemporary preoccupations in mind. If the concept "economic growth" in narrowly defined, the economic historian is encouraged to consider irrelevant all economic expansion that was not world-
wide in implications or at least national in scope. It seems, on the
contrary, well worth while to find a point of view which makes more of
the past meaningful. For this purpose it would be desirable to elaborate a concept of growth such that the size of the area in which growth
is said to occur, or the minimal population favorably affected, is not

treated as a criterion used in selecting the cases which are considered examples of growth but is treated as one of the ways in which examples of growth differ one from another. Size is to be viewed as one of several characteristics worth examining and relating to others. Of course decline as well as growth will then be studied in small units as well as in large. Such a flexible concept of growth will serve to bring men's earlier experiences and problems into relation with our own.

To elaborate this point of view let us reconsider in more specific form the question whether there were increases in product per capita before the nineteenth century. An historian, carefully defining his proposition geographically as I have argued should be done, may assert that within the boundaries of the Venetian *dogado* or the *contado* of Florence there was a substantial increase during the thirteenth century A.D. not only in population but in the standard of living, reflecting a larger average product per capita. Perhaps the student of modern economic growth will try to dismiss these examples with a two-pronged gibe, saying: Those are areas too small to count, and anyhow they were growing at the expense of somebody else. At the risk of some repetition, I will attempt to dull each prong separately.

If they are too small, what size is required? If a city of one hundred thousand is too small, is a province containing one million large enough? There were probably about that many in the Isle de France or southern England when those areas began growing vigorously in the twelfth century. If one million is not enough, and one province is not enough, presumably ten million suffices, even if in a relatively small area such as Great Britain about 1800.

Phrasing these hypothetical questions so crudely makes clear that they need not be answered unless one wishes to include the number of zeros in a definition of economic growth. The worthwhile question is: How does the process of growth differ in these cases? How does it differ when the unit that is growing is in the range of fifty to one hundred and fifty thousand people, or in the range of five to fifteen million? When it is in the range of one hundred square miles, or ten thousand, or one million? The differences are many and important. I can discuss only a few which are relevant to considering whether the undeniable growth in the standard of living in small units such as Venice or Florence was achieved at the expense of somebody else.

The comparisons that have been made between large and small nations in modern times suggest some propositions about the relation between the processes of growth and the size of the growing unit.

Shaken loose from exclusive association with national economies they may perhaps apply to other social units that were once more important.

When a new technique such as printing with movable type leads to more efficient production, its use is generally spread by imitation. This imitation occurs first where culture is relatively homogeneous with that of the place in which the use of the new technique originated. How long it will take for the innovation to be diffused through all that area depends on many conditions, but, other things being equal, the larger the cultural area the longer the period of diffusion. While this diffusion is going on, the area thus culturally defined experiences the growth based on the technique that has been newly discovered, or perhaps, although discovered long before, is now being applied because the necessary social adjustments are being made. The growth is multiplied and prolonged by the extent to which one improvement provokes others. The upshot is that the new technique produces a longer period of growth in a large area of cultural homogeneity than in a small cultural area.

While many new techniques spread by a process of imitation which is the cumulative expression of separate decisions by many individuals, some other expressions of technological progress, such as the Roman roads, require decisions by a central authority and the existence of a social organization which gives that authority power to make and execute decisions. This political unit may or may not have the same boundaries as a cultural unit. Whether growth is likely to be of longer duration when it occurs in a large political unit than when it occurs in a small one is therefore a separate question. There are probably many answers for different historical circumstances.

In a large area having cultural homogeneity and a favorable social organization, whether or not organized under one government, it is quite conceivable that sustained economic growth should occur because of indigenous changes in population, technology, and social organization without being much influenced by relations with other areas. But inter-area flows have usually had a crucial influence on economic growth. In the history of the world, first one area and then another—Mesopotamia or Egypt or Italy or England—have led in developing and applying techniques that increased output per capita. In every century of human history most areas have been "underdeveloped" compared to the country which was at that time the furthest advanced economically. Their relations to that most advanced area played an essential role in their growth or in their failure to grow. The general economic growth in medieval western Europe from the tenth century through the thirteenth owed its start, according to the great Belgian historian, Henri Pirenne, to the reopening of trade with the more advanced Moslem and Byzantine areas. The thesis is debatable: there are reasons to attribute importance also to political stabilization, increasing population, and agricultural progress within western Europe. In the earliest example of economic growth of which we have any record, namely in the development of farming and irrigation in south-western Asia, it seems that there must have been some section, some river valley or oasis, which led the others and in which the indigenous innovations exceeded in importance anything learned from abroad. But it is hard to say which area played this original role. In eighteenth-century Britain, the innovations which inaugurated a new period of growth were indigenous, and yet the high development at that time of Britain's foreign trade constituted one of the conditions which stimulated these innovations. The later initiation of growth through industrialization in other countries depended very largely on their relations with Britain. Perhaps Mesopotamia and medieval Europe are exceptions, but otherwise it would appear that in all cases external relations were of decisive importance at the beginning of economic growth.

Although crucial everywhere at the start of economic growth, external relations subsequently become less important for economies that are relatively large in area and population. Inter-area flows are less important for the United States and the Soviet Union today than they are for Britain or Norway. On the same principle and adjusting our conceptions of size to the different scale of political organization and the different technologies then involved in economic growth, we can say that inter-area flows were less important for sustaining economic growth in the Egypt of the pharaohs or of the Ptolemies than in the city states of Phoenicia or of Greece.

Even in very large areas of cultural and political unity there is a limit, however, to the extent to which growth can proceed before the external relations of the economy again become decisive. Internal opportunities for the application of the growth-producing techniques are exhausted or the invention of new techniques demand a kind of natural resource which has to be obtained abroad. For both large and small units the upper limits of growth are much affected by the nature of flows to and from other areas, but these flows are decisive in setting the upper limit sooner in small areas than in large.

Before the emergence of the modern nations the areas in Europe which had political solidity were small. Political boundaries were not clearcut and did not have as much cultural significance as they now have. Various kinds of taxes and economic regulations were imposed by several powers having overlapping jurisdictions. Often it is not easy to say which movements should be considered inter-area flows. Those between Venice and Padua in 1400? But not in 1420 after Padua had come under Venetian rule? Those between Ragusa and Venice in 1400? But not in 1350 when Ragusa was attached to Venice? Those between Venice and the remnants of the Byzantine Empire in the fourteenth century, an area different from Venice in speech, religion, and government, but not substantially different except in government from Venetian colonies such as Crete? In view of the fluctuating political situation and the shading off of cultural areas one into another, it would seem that the best view to adopt in writing an economic history of Venice, for example, would be a narrow one, which regarded the region of the lagoons as one "area" and treated as "external relations" all movements of men, commodities, money, and ideas between it and other regions (strictly speaking, between its inhabitants and those of other regions). Politically the lagoon area was defined as the *dogado*. Towns within the lagoons such as Chioggia and Murano had local governments, to be sure, and local economic regulations, so that one could make a distinction between the history of the *dogado* and that of the city of Venice in the narrowest sense, namely the settlement that was for a long time called Rialto. Such a distinction is important for the first five or eight centuries of Venetian history, but it is increasingly less important after 1000 A.D. Thereafter the *dogado* possessed notable cultural and political homogeneity and can be treated as a unit. But it would not be useful to treat as a unit for all that period all the regions subject to Venice. Beginning sometime in the seventeenth century there would be reason perhaps to view as a unit what then remained of Venetian dominions. Earlier there had been too great heterogeneity in culture and in social organization, and too much shifting of boundaries. If one wishes to compare the wealth or productivity of "Venice" at different widely separated dates, to compare comparables, and to seek explanations of changes, the most practical unit of observation and intelligible unit of analysis is the area of the lagoons, that is to say, the urban center and its immediate hinterland.

Venice is an extreme case because of the long distances and the cultural diversities within its domains. England, even medieval England, is a simpler case. But problems similar to those regarding Venice arise in choosing units for the study of economic growth, if we push the inquiry back before the nineteenth century, in all the lands of Italian and German speech and in those east and south thereof which came to be included in the Ottoman Empire. Under these conditions, small units deserve treatment separately. When there is neither cultural unity nor uniformity of social organization over a large area, the student must look for those small areas which do show considerable unity in regard to the making of social and individual decisions of the kind important for economic growth. Because these units are small the flows across boundaries will be more influential than for larger areas. That the economic growth of Venice or Florence in the thirteenth century was dependent on the relations of those city-states to other areas is but another illustration of this general finding.

To go further and say that Venice and Florence were growing at the expense of other areas raises a new question about the nature of inter-area flows. These flows include of course much more than the mere exchange of commodities. They include all the movement across boundaries of goods and money whether in trade or as investment or as tribute or as gifts, and the movement of persons and of knowledge and of services rendered. Should all these be divided into two categories: those flows that are beneficial to both parties and those that are so much more favorable to one party that the relations may be called parasitic? Venice's participation in the conquest, sack, and partition of the Byzantine Empire at the beginning of the thirteenth century is a particularly evident case of parasitic gain. But to take as the criterion of what is parasitic merely the use of force would not be satisfactory, for it is quite conceivable that a commercial agreement included in a peace treaty will prove mutually beneficial, and many a grant of commercial privileges that was more beneficial to the grantee than to the grantor has been obtained without the use of force. It hardly seems merely accidental that Britain's phenomenal growth through industrialization came in a period during which Britain had ruled the waves for a century and could trade more nearly on her own terms for that reason. Yet one hesitates to call her growth parasitic. Probably the gains brought back to England by privateers from the Spanish main or by nabobs from India were less important for the country's economic development than the booty Venetians collected at Constantinople, but in both cases loot was less important than trading privileges and the political protection given commercial enterprises. If we are to analyze inter-area flows to determine to what extent growth has been parasitic, it is a task which challenges the economic historian studying modern large units as well as the economic historian interested in the more distant past and in smaller units.

The tendency to regard growth as a uniquely modern development was once closely linked to the assumption that growth was a world-wide development. Some nations led and others followed but all were believed to be carried along by the beneficent process. Recently more attention has been focused on the enormous contrast in income per capita between the underdeveloped and the overdeveloped countries and the fact that this gap is not closing. Statistical studies have thus served to give to the concept of growth a geographical content. The elaboration of this geographical element may serve to make the concept more flexible and more useful in viewing a wider range of human experience. Growth both in population and in product per capita has occurred in various parts of the earth in various periods. In earlier epochs it was based on advances in knowledge and skill other than those which we associate with industrialism. None has yet produced a worldwide "take off." Contemplating these various examples of growth and decline in human experience will not of course supply us with a neat set of correlations which can be seized on as the lesson of history. On the contrary it is likely to make all growth, even modern growth through industrialization, seem highly contingent, occurring not by the necessary operation of a single formula but by various ways and means and special human efforts adapted to particular times and places.

31

Human History and Natural History*

I

IN discussions about the relations between history and other intellectual disciplines much confusion has arisen from comparing
history and physics. Philosophers considering whether history is a
science would have been more helpful if they had devoted more attention to comparing history with biology or geology or even engineering.
The differences between history and physics are too many. Consequences which derive from one kind of difference have been confused
with those that derive from a quite different kind.

The difference most emphasized is that we historians study human
actions whereas physicists study natural events. A second difference is
also generally made, namely, that historians are interested in individuals or unique aspects of events, physicists are interested in general
laws. It is not sufficiently recognized that these two differences are quite
independent the one of the other and that they affect the methodology
of the two disciplines in ways that are quite distinct. They raise two
distinct problems: (1) how to understand *human* action, and (2) how
to understand a particular occurrence. The two different methodological problems are confused especially in considering causal analysis in
history.[1] My purpose in this essay is to contrast the two problems and to

* "Menschliche Geschichte und Naturgeschichte," in Hugo Hantsch, Eric Voegelin,
and Franco Valsecchi, (eds.), *Historica: Studien zum Geschichtlichen Denken und
Forschen* (Vienna, 1965), pp. 19–35. (Translation by permission.)

[1] This confusion seems to me present even in Isaiah Berlin's "History and Theory:
The Concept of Scientific History," in *History and Theory: Studies in the Philosophy
of History* (1960), pp. 1 ff. Although Berlin acknowledges that a natural scientist
might be interested in particulars, he pays little attention to the consequences of a
naturalist having such an attitude, and confuses the two issues on pp. 8–19, especially in paragraph P, where he seems to attribute to the historian's concern with
particulars the uncertainties that arise in all attempts to predict or "retrodict"

show that the same logical structure of causal analysis is used in both natural science and human history. Although the student of human affairs uses processes of observation not available to the student of nature, the difficulties encountered in trying to explain particular events are the same for both.

II

To clarify my discussion I will use terms in a special sense to distinguish four fields of knowledge. The four fields are created by the two distinctions already referred to. According to whether one is studying nature or studying human thought and action he is a naturalist or a humanist. According to whether he is interested in particularizing or in generalizing he may be called a historian or a theorist. Hereafter in this discussion I will use the term "natural history" to refer to all study of nature focusing on individual events, thus including in natural history not only the emergence of new species and the rise of new volcanoes but also incidents of interest to engineers such as the collapse of a bridge. For those whose main interest, in contrast, is in discovering, refining, and verifying general laws, I adopt here the label "theorist," and will call their subject "theory." I use "theory" instead of "science" because "science" has regrettably acquired in American and English usage such a connotation as to suggest only one of many kinds of systematized knowledge, while implying that that kind alone is true knowledge. Moreover, "theory" serves better to emphasize the contrast between the search for general laws which is the mark of the "theorist" and the concern with explaining particulars which is the concern of history.

Thus these two dichotomies give us the four fields:

1. Human history
2. Natural history
3. Humanist theory (social theory)
4. Natural theory (theoretical natural science)

III

The difference between humanists and naturalists arises from their different way of perceiving data and acquiring evidence. Of course both

---

about human action and that therefore apply equally to sociology. Presumably the confusion goes back philosophically to Richert. See Ernest Nagel, "Some Issues in the Logic of Historical Analysis," in Patrick Gardiner (ed.), *Theories of History* (Glencoe, Ill., 1959), pp. 375–76.

start with sense perception. When a historian is deciphering faded handwriting he is engaged in an operation which it would be logical to call that of a naturalist, just as he is when he tests chemically the age of paper or ink. He does not begin acting as a humanist until he asks the meaning of words and why the words were used. As soon as he does ask these questions he makes the thought and feeling of other men the object of his study and thereby becomes what I am here calling a humanist.

Practically all social scientists are humanists in my sense of the word. If an anthropologist described only the sights and sounds of a native dance and stopped there, if sociologists mapped the number of people per room in a city and stopped there, they would be naturalists; but when they seek to discover and report the meaning of the dance and the emotions aroused and released or to consider the needs and resentments associated with overcrowded lodging then they too are making human thought and feeling the object of their study. I would like to say that they "perceive" excitement in the dance or resentment in replies of slum dwellers.

To perceive excitement or resentment requires the use of faculties in addition to those by which one perceives rapid motion. It requires more than eyesight. We know by experience that we have these added faculties needed to perceive the thoughts and emotions of others. They enable us to penetrate to what R. G. Collingwood calls the inside of the action or event.[2] Since our consciousness of our mental processes, of the inside of our own action, enters into our use of this kind of mental perception, it is related to intuition and it has also been called empathy, understanding or *Verstehen*. What we know about these faculties may be no more than the paleolithic hunter knew about the nature of sight. But he had very good eyes and used them with success. Similarly any successful student of human affairs, whether he is engaged in planning a political campaign, writing history, interpreting poetry or doing the day's business, uses his ability to perceive what other men are thinking and feeling and have thought and felt.

IV

In this process of observing human actions, the perceptions of the humanist, like the perceptions of the naturalist, are affected by his theories, by his preconceptions. In every man there is a constant interplay between his theories and his perceptions. He may fail to perceive

[2] R. G. Collingwood, *The Idea of History* (Oxford, 1946), p. 213.

whatever his theories have left him unprepared to perceive. The experiences of both mind and eye will come in different forms to men who enter into the experiences with different general ideas. On the other hand, men who start with the same general ideas will emerge with different ideas after having had different experiences. The humanist's perceptions, like those of the naturalist, are shaped in part by his theories, but they are not entirely so shaped. The humanist's experiences are just as genuinely the experience of realities outside himself as are the experiences of the naturalist. Knowledge of nature has advanced by walking on the two feet, theory and experience. The humanist also is a biped, not a one-footed creature.

V

There is no contradiction between understanding an action from the inside, as Collingwood says, and theorizing about it. One may even include among the theories what I will call general laws, in spite of Collingwood. It seems to me that Collingwood himself uses such laws when he solves the case of who killed John Doe. When the rector's daughter confesses to the murder she did not commit, the young constable asks himself whom she is trying to protect. The implied "law" to which Collingwood's protagonist thus implicitly appeals in the proposition that in some percentage of cases of lying the liar is trying to shield a loved one. No doubt it is logically more correct to call such a statement a probability hypothesis, but since many so-called laws are also really statements of probability, I will use the less cumbersome expression. But in using "law" I do not mean to imply any determinism, only a degree of probability.

In all humanist theories one term at least of any general proposition refers to thought, using thought in a very broad sense. For example, the general law that bad money drives out good is true only if "good" and "bad" are interpreted not by the standards of fineness of a chemist but by reference to legal tender or market value.[3] Any standard of value, even if it be unthinking custom or an emotional reaction such as a Moslem rejection of any coin bearing a human image, is in men's minds and is in that sense thought. Just because they concern human thought,

---

[3] This is especially clear in medieval monetary systems when coins were frequently converted from "good" money to "bad" money without intrinsic change by a change in value as legal tender. It is evident also in the analysis by F. A. Hayek, "The Uses of 'Gresham's Law' as an Illustration of Historical Theory," *History and Theory,* II (1962), 101–2.

the theories of the humanist differ significantly in some ways from the theories of the naturalists. I will return to that subject later, but my first and main concern here is with what humanists and naturalists have in common when both operate as historians.

VI

Whether he be naturalist or humanist, an historian's interest centers on particulars. He seeks to explain individual cases and the connections between individual events, whereas the theorist seeks to formulate and test general laws. Although this contrast is unmistakable, the separation of interests is not complete. There are many lines of thought connecting them, for particular events are conceived and described by the use of general concepts. A historian is interested in the American Revolution in its connections with contemporary conditions such as the British mercantile system. A social theorist is interested in revolutions in general and framing and testing general propositions about revolutions and their relations to economic interests, class structure, etc. But both the historian and the theorist will have occasions to use the same general concepts, such as class structure.

Moreover the extent to which either the theorist or the historian focuses on particulars is a matter of degree. "Revolution" is a more particularized concept than "social change," and "American Revolution" is a more general concept than "the signing of the Declaration of Independence." Similarly in geology one moves from the more general to the more particular according to whether one's interest is in a general explanation of why glaciation occurs, or in the glaciation of North America during the Pleistocene, or in determining when and to what extent a particular glacier filled a particular area.

VII

It is a mistake to say that the historian looks at an event in all its aspects whereas the theorist looks at it from one special point of view. The historian too has a special point of view. He looks at causal and conceptual connections which one event has with other events associated with it in time and space. The temporal and spatial relations of an event are what make it unique and the historian is interested in the uniqueness of an event in that he studies those aspects of it by which it was linked to what came before and after. These links are of various kinds and can be classified. But the linkages of every event are unique and the historian focuses attention on this uniqueness.[4] For this reason chronology and geography are the two eyes of history, as George Lincoln Burr used to say. To see a historical problem we have to locate one event with relation to others in time and place.

VIII

The similarities between human history and natural history as here defined are numerous. By illustrating some of them I hope to make clear some contrasts between history and theory, contrasts which apply to the history equally of man and of natural events. All historians, whether humanists or naturalists, are as I have pointed out elsewhere rather consumers than producers of general theory.[5]

To aid in illustrating the points of similarity and also some points of difference, I will present an historical incident. Since it involves real historical events, not an imaginary case, I must offer the reader more details than if I were dealing with such a hypothetical illustration as that of an automobile radiator's cracking on a cold night. The case I present is one with which I became acquainted incidentally, not one I investigated because of its methodological interest. If similar bits of technological history were undertaken as studies in methodology they might well increase our understanding of the relation of theory to history, in the study of both man and nature. The following summary account of some engineering failures and their investigation is presented with the intent of suggesting such possibilities and in the hope that the detail will be justified by its intrinsic interest as human history.

IX

What was being investigated was natural history, a physical event. On Sunday, January 16, 1943, at 11 P.M., a newly built tanker named the "Schenectady," while tied to its outfitting dock at the Swan Island Yard in Portland, Oregon, split across the deck and down both sides with a

---

[4] Although I do not use "uniqueness" in quite the sense in which they do, I have found very useful in this connection the discussion by Carey B. Joynt and Nicholas Rescher, "The Problem of Uniqueness in History," *History and Theory*, I (1961), 150–62.

[5] Frederic C. Lane and Jelle Riemersma (eds.), *Enterprise and Secular Change: Readings in Economic History* (Homewood, Ill., 1953), p. 529, where I say "Historical interest is thus a consumer, rather than a producer, of broad generalizations." Compare Joynt and Rescher, "The Problem of Uniqueness," p. 154: ". . . the historian is not a producer of general laws but a consumer of them."

loud bang. During the next two months there were five other somewhat comparable cases of vessels breaking in two, of what was called more scientifically "complete structural failure." At that time many shipyards that had been newly organized under the U.S. Maritime Commission were going into peak production using new methods of construction. Before the end of 1943 a total of more than eighteen million deadweight tons were to be launched to keep open the supply lines to the battle fronts of World War II. To build with the rapidity demanded, welding was substituted for riveting to an unprecedented extent. Very few all-welded vessels had seen service when the war began. In spite of slight experience with the performance of welded ships, that method was adopted for the huge shipbuilding program of the Maritime Commission. When several of these ships were reported to have split apart just as the program was getting fully under way, it was of great practical importance to know why. The search for an explanation began with analysis of the individual instances of ships that split.

Public attention focused on the "Schenectady." It made the Monday morning headlines whereas other failures, such as that of the "Esso Manhattan," which broke apart on March 29, 1943, at the entrance to New York harbor, were kept from the public by security regulations because they occurred at sea. The "Schenectady" was built in a Kaiser yard. Henry J. Kaiser had been receiving much praise for building faster than any of the old-line shipbuilders. When the "Schenectady" split some of these rivals could not refrain from saying "I told you so." It proved to them that a dam-builder could not master the art of shipbuilding. In fighting back Kaiser did not mind casting doubt on the quality of the steel supplied him. Thus the investigation began in an atmosphere of public controversy. For a student of methodology it is significant that this instance furnishes examples of what one modern school of philosophy might call the "common-sense" point of view, which was supplied by newspapermen and politicians, as well as of the "scientific" point of view, which was supplied by trained engineers and naval architects. Both points of view influenced the first official report, which was made by a committee of the appropriate technical authority, the American Bureau of Shipping.

X

This report and the public discussion give an excellent opportunity to compare the methods employed in such a case and those used in writing human history. First of all it is noteworthy that as far as possible the investigating engineers broke the event itself down into its successive stages or "subevents," just as would any historian who was called on to explain a military defeat or an economic crisis. They determined where the crack that split the "Schenectady" started, "abaft the after end of the bridge."[6] Cracking proceeded down both sides of the vessel to the bottom plates. Although it started in a bad weld, the cracking did not follow the lines of the welds. As we will see later, this analysis of stages within the event was an essential in the causal analysis of the event.

XI

Second, much attention was given to examining other events which occurred at about the same time and place, especially those immediately preceding the accident. Because of the lively public interest and because the splitting of a vessel completely in two while tied to its dock was unprecedented, a wide variety of circumstances had to be investigated. Picking out those that were relevant and finding the connections between them presented the problem familiar to every student of human affairs. This selection of a sequence or system of relevant events is what W. H. Walsh calls colligation.[7]

The Swan Island Yard is located at the mouth of the Columbia River, and silt accumulated around the center of the "Schenectady." She jackknifed after the break so that the two ends settled into the silt while the deck of the higher mid-ship section parted with a 10-foot gap. When did the silting occur? Had it contributed to the break by produc-

---

[6] Frederic C. Lane, *Ships for Victory, A History of Shipbuilding under the U.S. Maritime Commission during World War II* (Baltimore, 1951) , Chap. xvi and specifically p. 545.

[7] W. H. Walsh, *An Introduction to the Philosophy of History* (London, 1951) , p. 23. Pointing out that historians do not begin by comparing the event to be explained with similar events of other times and places, he describes their activity as "tracing the connections between that event and others with which it stands in inner relationship. . . . The underlying assumption here is that different historical events can be regarded as going together to constitute a single process, a whole of which they are all parts and in which they belong together in a special intimate way. And the first aim of the historian, when he is asked to explain some event or other, is to see it as part of such a process, to locate it in its context by mentioning other events with which it is bound up. . . ." The reference to "inner relationship" suggests, however, that Walsh regards colligation as peculiar to the humanist.

ing a straining effect at the extremities? The committee decided not. An anchor chain had broken during the trial voyage which the ship had made the previous day. That was considered irrelevant, as was an alleged shock caused by an earth tremor. But a large number of accompanying or preceding events were considered relevant. Placing ballast at both ends of the ship but not in the middle had created a hogging stress. The temperature had dropped below freezing during the preceding 8½ hours, a drop of 15 degrees, and this was thought to have contributed to the brittleness of the steel. There had been bad welding which was blamed on the lack of good workmen and good supervisors and on the use of a certain kind of welding machine. Another cause of the structural failure was declared to be the order in which different pieces of steel had been put together in sub-assemblies, and even the chronology of the welding itself, whether it proceeded outward from the center or inward from extremities. There was the more reason to investigate these matters because the "Schenectady" was the first ship built at the Swan Island Yard. The sequence of events there in the building of the vessel was the subject of suspicious analysis. Later a Senatorial committee thought that the sequence of events which went into the making of the steel might be equally relevant. The Senators discovered that there had been some falsification in the records of a company which supplied steel and that the extent to which the steel delivered to the shipyards had been up to specification could not be determined. Thus the causes of the cracking of the "Schenectady" were sought by giving the cracking its place in a complex system of events, just as the causes of World War I are generally explained by presenting the outbreak of war as the end of a closely linked sequence which includes national rivalries, the murder of the Austrian heir, mobilization plans, and so on.

XII

The first report on this engineering failure was in yet another respect similar to a monograph on human history: it was soon contradicted by later investigators. The committee of the American Bureau of Shipping (ABS) was under pressure to complete its analysis quickly so that steps might be taken to prevent such structural failures in the future. They made a tentative report in one month and their final report within two months. Four years later, in March, 1947, a more authoritative report was made by a Navy Board of Investigation. Significantly the two reports differ not in regard to the facts but in their interpretation. The

Navy Board did not contradict earlier findings about the order of events—where the crack started and where it went. Nor did they make any different findings as to what kind of welding procedures had been used. But they did evaluate very differently the causal importance of the welding procedures.

The ABS committee attributed grave consequences to the welding sequence because the expansion and contraction of the steel when heated by the welding process created "locked-in stresses." Foremost among the causes of the fracture it placed ". . . an accumulation of an abnormal amount of internal stress locked into the structure by the process used in construction. . . ." In contrast, the Navy Board found no marked correlation between fractures and the construction practices of the shipyards. It reported: "Locked-in stresses do not contribute materially to the failure of welded ships."[8]

XIII

By 1947, the Navy Board was not interested in the historical problem as such, however, nor particularly interested in the "Schenectady." They wanted to prevent failures in ships built in the future. Consequently, they formulated their conclusion more as theory than as history, as is shown by the use of the present tense in the passage quoted. The meaning of their findings might be summarized in historical terms somewhat as follows: The design of the "Schenectady" and the bad welding at one of the angles made a notch of sufficient depth in steel which was of such poor quality that it was so notch-sensitive at the low temperature reached during the night of January 16, 1943, that this combination of circumstances caused the break, even with only slight strain downward at the ends of the ship. Such a listing of a number of conditions which were together necessary and sufficient leaves still in doubt how much causal importance should be assigned to particular preceding events. Better theory can help in such an analysis but is not alone sufficient to clear up the uncertainties involved in composing a particularized historical narrative, even the narrative of a natural event.

XIV

There is general agreement that a naturalist's determination of cause depends on his general theory. The different causal importance as-

[8] Lane, *Ships for Victory.* Compare pp. 547 and 570.

signed to welding sequences in the early and later reports was not the result of new facts concerning the "Schenectady." As will be explained shortly, it was a result of facts collected from other cases and various experiments which led to new theories. These theories then threw new light on the fracture of the "Schenectady."

Does theory play the same role in the causal explanations of the humanist? As previously stated, it is only for the sake of brevity that I call the generalizations of the humanist "laws." So far as they are empirical, they are assertions of probability. But some such assertions of probability are implied in every historical narrative, by the choice of the detail which is included. Thus in describing the human reactions to the cracking of the "Schenectady," I selected as relevant some of the many circumstances of early 1943, e.g., the expanding use of welding. By my selection I implied various "general laws" such as: "When failure occurs in an artifact made by a new method, there is a tendency to ask what is wrong with the new method."

I also invoked incidentally a general law of journalism: accidents happening on Sunday generally receive more attention than those happening on other days, because other news is lacking on Monday morning.

We use such common-sense generalizations in everyday predictions and I agree with those who maintain that the logical structure of prophecy and causal explanation are the same.[9] The law that bad money drives out good fulfills the same function whether one is prophesying about the result of a change in the legal-tender value of circulating media or whether one is analyzing the reasons why a particular coin has disappeared. To that extent Popper's analysis of how historians proceed seems to me sounder than Collingwood's insistence that humanists have no use for laws or causes.

XV

Generalizations used in causal explanation are often referred to as covering laws, but it is admitted that no laws cover every aspect of the event to which it is applied.[10] Probing that point, Maurice Mandelbaum has pointed out that the law used in a causal explanation need not state "a uniform sequence concerning complex events" of the type it is used to explain. It may merely "state uniform connections between

[9] Karl Raimond Popper, *The Open Society and Its Enemies* (2 vols.; London, 1945), II, 248–51.

[10] Carl G. Hempel, "The Function of General Laws in History," reprinted in Patrick Gardner (ed.), *Theories of History* (Glencoe, Ill., 1959), par. 2.2.

two *types of* factors which are *contained within* those complex events" (italics added) .[11] The splitting of the "Schenectady" was a "complex event" which illustrates Mandelbaum's conclusion. It was not explained by a "covering law" stating a regularly recurring sequence in which the splitting of a ship was a part. True, the four-year long investigation under the Navy Board included inquiries in those terms. They examined closely all other failures that were at all comparable, such as that of the "Esso Manhattan," which split in two in New York harbor in fair weather but which was built, not in a Kaiser yard, but in the long-established Sun yard in Chester, Pennsylvania. A statistical analysis regarding all ships built by the Maritime Commission was prepared. It showed no significant correlation between the failures and the yards the ships came from or the seas they sailed except that the vessels most used in the cold North Pacific showed the most fractures.[12] The most useful information came not from records about ships as whole units, but from studies of steel. It came not from an expert in the Navy or the American Bureau of Shipping but from one in the War Metallurgy Committee. To be sure his experiments included the attaching of gauges to ships during construction, just before delivery, and after they had been in service some time. It was by this kind of close study of what might be called one factor in the event, stresses in steel, that the causal analysis was refined.

Welding makes a ship into one piece of steel. By thinking of it as such, one could think of certain design features and of some defective welds as if they were notches in a strip of steel. When a notched piece of steel is subject to strain there is a concentration of stress at the notch. How much stress will result in a cracking at that point depends on the depth of the notch and on a quality in steel called notch sensitivity. Lower temperature increases the notch sensitivity of the steel. The design of many wartime ships included sharp right angles which came at such a position in the ship's structure as to act like a notch. (This was particularly true of a cut in the top row of plates in the famous Liberty ship.) At the end of the bridge where the crack of the "Schenectady" started there was a sharp angle having the effect of a notch. A bad weld at such a point made a sharper notch. The Board summarized its analysis in general terms as follows: "The fractures in welded ships were caused by notches and by steel which was notch sensitive at

[11] Maurice Mandelbaum, "Historical Explanation: The Problem of Covering Laws," *History and Theory,* I (1961) , 234.

[12] A particular correlation explicable by the more general propositions explained below about the relation between temperature and notch sensitivity.

operating temperatures. When an adverse combination of these occurs the ship may be unable to resist the bending moments of normal service."[13]

Thus the kind of complex event in question, the cracking of a ship, was explained by reference to laws regarding notch sensitivity of steel, which was only one factor in the event. The "covering law" was not one applying specifically to ships; it was more general, applying to all structural steel.

An analogous proceeding is customarily followed by humanist historians. A war or revolution is explained not by a covering law about war or revolutions but by the application to the particular situation of a law which is in many ways more general and therefore touches only one aspect of the situation. What they have usually done, with more or less justification, is well illustrated by a brief quotation from the *Commentaries* of that celebrated fifteenth-century humanist, Aeneus Sylvius, who became Pope Pius II: "His arrival [that of a general sent by the Pope to aid King Ferrante of Naples] produced a great change in the situation. The King, who had been thought to be on the brink of ruin, was now judged superior in war and likely soon to conquer and destroy his enemies, since the Pope and the Duke of Milan were aiding him. (This is Nature's law, that men incline to favor the stronger side.) "[14]

XVI

Although humanist and naturalist historians are alike in some respects, being both consumers and not producers of theories, vital differences result from the kind of theory they use. The humanist does not have at his disposal a large body of rigorously formulated general laws which have been empirically verified, as does the naturalist. Whether the humanist will ever be able to draw on general theory of this sort is another question. My concern is the body of theory which has been accumulated up till now. Comparing it with that accumulated by naturalists (comparing what common usage calls society theory and natural science) one finds differences that seem indisputable. These differences seem to me explained by the humanist's concern with the "inside" of the event, with thought.

[13] Lane, *Ships for Victory*, p. 570.

[14] *The Commentaries of Pius II, Books IV and V*, trans. by F. A. Gragg, with notes by L. C. Gabel ("Smith College Studies in History," Vol. XXX; Northampton, Mass., 1947), p. 314.

All useful generalizations about human behavior may be analyzed into statements asserting that certain conditions will produce certain thoughts, and statements asserting that certain thoughts will lead to certain actions. These actions produce conditions which produce new thoughts, then new actions, and so on—such is the chain of historical action. But there are relatively few aspects of thought about which we can say with a high degree of probability what conditions will produce a certain thought or what action will follow from the thought. Perhaps the very nature of thought is such as to render all generalizations about it hazardous.

Seeking more dependable laws, economists and some other humanists have tried to define the circumstances in which their generalizations will always be true. In doing so they give such meanings to the terms they use that the theory is always valid. Although logically true like a proposition in geometry, it then cannot be empirically verified. The problem is to discover what measure of counterpart it has in reality. For example the law that bad money drives out good is true by definition when its terms are appropriately defined. By examining within our own thought the law of contradiction and a standard of rationality, we can find that this law is true in every case to which it applies. The difficulty is in recognizing when and how it applies in a particular case.

In order to apply it the economist has to study the evidence regarding a given situation, using the quality which in early paragraphs I called perception. It must be confessed that his perception is not always equal to the task. That the processes of observation of the humanist are different from those of the naturalist may be the reason why his general laws are either on the one hand truisms or on the other mere statements of probability and possibility.

XVII

Whatever the reason, it seems indeed to be true that most generalizations about human action, if made in terms that can be empirically verified, have a low degree of probability. The probability is so low that it might be better to call them statements of possibility. Most of the "covering laws" used in human history are of this low order of probability. Men rally to the side they think strongest, as Aeneus Sylvius said, but they do not always do so. It depends on who they are, and the circumstances. It is a possibility. But history also teaches that men sometimes fight for lost causes. Humanist history deals with an amazing range of possibilities and that is one of its chief values. Depicting possibilities is just as vital as is the weighing of probabilities or the proclamation of the inevitable.

XVIII

Whereas the purpose of the naturalist is control, the purpose of the humanist, as Dilthey said somewhere, is culture. The naturalist wishes to operate on events from the outside; the humanist aims to affect action from the inside, by giving his thought an impact on the thought of others and, through their thought, on their action. The humanist's first objective is his own culture: to cultivate his own skill in logical distinctions, his own sensitivities, his appreciation, his ability to enter into as much as possible of the range of human experience. His ultimate objective is to communicate to others some of what he has thus been able to experience. If he succeeds he changes those with whom he has been able to share his thought. In thus building up his own understanding and in communicating with others, the humanist needs both theory and history.

32

At the Roots of Republicanism*

A PROMINENT characteristic of the writing of history in the United States since 1940 has been the retreat from the economic interpretation. In American history it is sometimes expressed by attacks on Charles Beard. In the interpretation of the French Revolution and the associated group of "democratic revolutions" economic conditions now receive less attention than do political situations and political conceptions.[1] In the storm over the gentry and the Puritan Revolution in seventeenth-century England the idea of class has been thoroughly torn to pieces.[2] A somewhat similar reinterpretation of the history of such Italian city-states as Venice and Florence subordinates classes to republicanism.

My thesis here is that republicanism, not capitalism, is the most distinctive and significant aspect of these Italian city-states; that republicanism gave to the civilization of Italy from the thirteenth through the sixteenth centuries its distinctive quality and very largely explains the intensity shown in imitating classical antiquity. The attempt to revive the culture of the ancient city-states strengthened in turn the republican ideal and contributed mightily to its triumph later in modern nations and primarily in our own.

Applying to my own generation the method it has delighted to apply

* Presidential Address before the American Historical Association at San Francisco, December 29, 1965, *American Historical Review*, LXXI (January, 1966). (By permission.)

[1] R. R. Palmer, *The Age of Democratic Revolution: A Political History of Europe and America, 1760–1800*. Vol. I, *The Challenge* (Princeton, N.J., 1959), vol. II, *The Struggle* (Princeton, N.J., 1964), especially II, 572–75.

[2] Jack H. Hexter, "Storm over the Gentry," in *Reappraisals in History* (London: Longmans, 1961, Evanston, Ill., 1961); Perez Zagorin, "The Social Interpretation of the English Revolution," *Journal of Economic History*, XIX (September, 1959), 376–401.

to earlier generations of historians, I cannot fail to observe that the obvious explanation of the general retreat from economic interpretations is to be found in the changing political situation. Not only the rivalry between the United States and the Soviet Union but also the tyranny and rigidity of postwar Communism threw shadows of suspicion and disgust over Marxist history and then by association over all kinds of economic interpretation. These extraneous influences intensified a reaction of which one can find beginnings in historical studies before 1940.

Fortunately the retreat from economic interpretations has not been accompanied by any retreat from economic history. On the contrary, freed from distracting demands to supply data that might be used to serve economic interpretations of politics, art forms, and other phenomena outside its own sphere, economic history has been better able to concentrate on questions concerning the amount and distribution of production, and its methods. As a result of more knowledge about variations in economic growth, we can no longer attribute a progressive commercialization of culture in the fourteenth and fifteenth centuries to a growing volume of trade and wealth in those same centuries.[3] Economic growth has not been continuous. Between 1300 and 1500 there were severe downward movements in population and production, and the recoveries were spotty. A more vigorous, more general growth in population and trade occurred earlier, during the so-called Age of Faith in the twelfth and thirteenth centuries.[4]

For the Italian city-states the so-called Age of Faith was in fact also an age of capitalism, if we mean by capitalism a society so organized that men can make money by investing their capital.[5] Traveling merchants were beginning to be replaced by resident or sedentary merchants who were able by paper work to control transactions at a distance. The successful search for early documents regarding banking, double-entry bookkeeping, and big business partnerships has given more and more

---

[3] This is the view strongly implied by Alfred von Martin, *Sociology of the Renaissance* (New York, Harper Torchbook, 1963) , p. 1.

[4] Conflicting views are expressed in the articles of Carlo M. Cipolla, Robert S. Lopez, and Harry A. Miskimin in the *Economic History Review*, XIV, 3 (April, 1962) , 408–26, and XVI, 3 (April, 1964) , 519–29. Although Cipolla rejects Lopez's arguments for a "depression of the Renaissance," he does not dispute the rapid growth in the twelfth and thirteenth centuries.

[5] This meaning of capitalism is applied by Oliver C. Cox, *The Foundations of Capitalism* (New York: Philosophical Library, 1959) , but for Marx the essential feature was "the division of classes between propertyless wage-earners and entrepreneurs who own capital." R. H. Hilton, "Capitalism—What's in a Name?" *Past and Present,* No. 1, 1952.

reason to date their beginnings in the thirteenth century, and the more we discover of the capitalistic aspects of the economic life of that age the closer appear the links between its civilization and that of ensuing centuries.[6]

This commercialized atmosphere certainly conditioned the way republicanism developed, as did also the appearance of the new classes—merchant capitalists, shopkeepers, craftsmen, and day laborers. Without the conditions created by economic developments, the new political institutions would have been practically unthinkable. One can accept that much of the economic interpretation while rejecting the Marxist theory of the state, namely, the view that all government is essentially the dictatorship of one class over another and that class struggles are the determinants of political developments. New political programs appear in response to new economic conditions, but they were not class programs. An examination of the main stages in the development of republicanism shows that political ideas and actions pitted men of the same economic class against each other and brought men of different economic status together seeking common goals.

I use the word republicanism to summarize one set of goals: the rejection of hereditary kingship in order to devise other forms of government that their creators believed would permit and encourage more men to participate more actively in making laws and choosing leaders.

In this development, the first step toward republicanism was local independence. Only through the autonomy of small units could a substantial portion of the men in a political unit be given a share in decision-making. A feudal kingdom containing millions from whom the king summoned a few hundred notables before making any declaration of law was less republican, for example, in our sense, than a city of 20,000 to 50,000 where as many as a thousand gathered in the town square or cathedral, arguing, cursing, shouting, and perhaps also voting their approval and disapproval of laws and leaders. Unless these units of

[6] Armando Sapori, "La cultura del mercante medievale italiano," *Rivista di storia economica*, II, 2 (1937) —translation in *Enterprise and Secular Change: Readings in Economic History*, eds., Frederic C. Lane and Jella C. Riemersma (Homewood, Ill.: Irwin, 1953) ; Raymond de Roover, "The Commercial Revolution of the Thirteenth Century," *Bulletin of the Business Historical Society*, XVI (1942) , 34–39; *idem*, "The Organization of Trade," in *Cambridge Economic History of Europe*, III. On double entry, and especially of the different meanings that he and de Roover give the term, see Federigo Melis, *Aspetti della vita economica medievale (Studi nell' Archivio Datini di Prato)*, I (Siena and Florence: Olschki, 1962) , 391–403. On banking, see Roberto Sabatino Lopez, *La prima crisi della banca di Genova, 1250–1259* (Milan: Università L. Bocconi, 1956) .

10,000 to 100,000 had been insistent on their autonomy, laws and leaders would have been imposed on them from the outside. Independent, they became exponents of republicanism both in principle and in practice. They acted on the principle that rulers derived their powers from the people. Although the idea that the community was the ultimate source of political authority was carried over from antiquity in Roman law, kings and emperors, who were accustomed to using the hierarchic descending theme, showed marked reserve about embracing an ascending theme which might strengthen them against the pope but might weaken their authority over their own subjects. The Italian cities felt no such restraints.[7] Venice, the longest lived of these republics, expressed its claim to independence from the Byzantine empire through the election of its own Doge, and used that independence to turn the Doge into a republican magistrate. Later, in their fights against the Hohenstaufen emperors many Italian communes won freedom from an outside control that would have reduced the number of townsmen taking part in government and restricted the extent to which they could make their own rules.[8] Compared to all other political organizations prior to the American and French revolutions, the government of the communes was, Robert Lopez declares, the one which offered to the "greatest number a chance to make their voice heard in the conduct of public business."[9]

These communal organizations were first formed in northern Italy not mainly by merchants but by lower members of the feudal class. The association of knights as peers in a regional feudal court was one of the experiences which made joint local action seem natural and legitimate. To form a commune, various landowners joined together and pooled their rights, claiming to exercise jointly judicial and fiscal powers, fragments of which they might have asserted as individuals. They claimed in addition to speak for their bishop and exercise his temporal powers. The new kind of political organization would not have seemed practical or desirable, to be sure, without the commercial expansion of the twelfth century, but the leadership which built republics on that

[7] Francesco Calasso, *Medio evo del diritto,* I (Milan, 1954), 182–83, 198, 209; Walter Ullmann, *Principles of Government and Politics in the Middle Ages* (London, 1961), pp. 219, 222–23, 296–97; Michael J. Wilks, *The Problem of Sovereignty in the Later Middle Ages* (Cambridge: The University Press, 1963), pp. 184–85.

[8] W. F. Butler, *The Lombard Communes* (London, 1906), p. 20, emphasizes the contrast between republicanism and feudalism. Antonio Pertile, *Storia del diritto italiano* (Padua, 1880), vol. II, pt. I, *Storia del diritto pubblico e delle fonti* describes the new republican institutions.

[9] Roberto Sabatino Lopez, *Naissance de l'Europe* (Paris: Colin, 1962), p. 279.

economic base came not so much from a new class of merchants as from landowners who set their loyalty to a commune above that to any feudal superior.[10]

The success of communal republicanism depended on the readiness of its leaders to share power with others as equals. It is characteristic of a republic, as distinct from a monarchy, that when conflicts arise in its governing councils they are settled, not by deferring to the will of a superior, but by accepting the will of the majority. Where that principle prevailed, men rose to power not through the favor of an hereditary prince but by winning the confidence of men of their own rank or below.[11] In Venice, which had been largely commercial from its beginnings, republicanism was not firmly established until in 1172 a group of the wealthiest families took control of the choice of Doge and worked together, deferring among themselves to the vote of the majority and loyally taking second place when a rival was elected to the highest office. Sebastian Ziani and Enrico Dandolo are the best known of the group but even more significant were Pietro Ziani and Rainiero Dandolo, their sons, men of high ability who did not insist on succeeding their fathers. By their restraint, even more than their success in office, this group gave living effectiveness to the constitutional provisions which at the end of the twelfth century transformed the Dogeship into a republican magistracy.[12]

[10] E. Sestan, "La citta communale italiana," in International Congress of Historical Sciences, XIth, Stockholm, 1960, *Rapports, III, Moyen Age*, pp. 86–89; Luigi Simeoni, "Le origini del comune di Verona," *Nuovo archivio veneto*, n.s., XXV (1913), 74–133; Cino Franceschino, "La vita sociale e politica nel Duecento," in *Storia di Milano* (Milan: Fondazione Treccani degli Alfieri, 1954), IV, 121, illustrates this spirit by citing the Milanese statute which forbade anyone losing a fief because of failure to render service against the city, "quia contra patriam suam, pro qua pugnare iure gentium debet, pro aliquo feudo adesse non compellitur." On "patria" see Gaines Post, *Studies in Medieval Legal Thought; Public Law and the State, 1100–1322* (Princeton University Press, 1964), pp. 441–44, 449. Enrico Fiumi, "Fioritura e decadenza dell'economia fiorentina," *Archivio storico italiano*, CXVII (1959), 487–92, while admitting that nobles had a prominent part, argues that in Tuscany the lead was taken by landowning merchants.

[11] Obviously republicanism as I here use the term is more nearly equivalent to what Mosca calls liberalism and not necessarily linked with the social-political mobility which he calls democracy. Gaetano Mosca, *The Ruling Class*, trans. by H. D. Kahn, ed. G. A. Livingston (New York; McGraw-Hill, 1939), chap. XV. But mobility and liberalism were in fact linked together for some centuries, forming liberal democracies.

[12] Roberto Cessi, *et al.*, *Storia di Venezia*, II, *Dalle origini del Ducato alla quarta Crociata* (Venice: Centro Internazionale della Arti e del Costume, 1958) II, 408–17, 442–47. Giuseppe Maranini, *La costituzione di Venezia dalle origini alla serrata del Maggior Consiglio* (Venice, 1927), pp. 109–43.

Popular participation in the government of these city-states, which at first was slight or informal, was increased by a thirteenth-century movement closely connected with the rise of new classes. With deceptive simplification this movement was called the rise of the people, *il popolo*. Actually three distinct aspects of change in class structure were involved. New families were acquiring wealth through commerce and were investing it in land. At the same time families of inherited wealth invested in trade and became partially merchants. These two developments changed the character of the ruling class, but it is to be noted that they did so not through a class war but by class transformation, through absorption of new men and new methods. At the same time craftsmen and petty shopkeepers increased in numbers so as to form a distinct class ranking below the ruling class even by their own standards. While the newly rich were struggling to be accepted as equals by the old families, craftsmen and shopkeepers were demanding a share in power, although accepting a secondary social position. These contests destroyed republicanism in some places but in others they strengthened it by stimulating the formation of institutions that widened popular participation.[13]

In Venice the new rich were absorbed into the ruling class without destroying that class's extraordinary solidarity, without the fierce factions that stained republicanism in so many other Italian cities. Crucial in this process was the reform of the Great Council in 1297, a reform misnamed "the closing," because the procedure then adopted was later used to restrict membership. Its immediate purpose and effect were to enlarge the membership. Between 1295 and 1311 the membership of the Great Council was increased from about 400 to 1017. Analysis of the names of councillors shows that this was the culmination of a long process of acceptance of new men into positions of political importance.[14]

While republicanism was being more firmly rooted in Venice by the acceptance of new families into its ruling class, it was also receiving reenforcement from the formation of guilds, which gave some self-government to artisans and shopkeepers. Just as municipal particu-

---

[13] Its architectural expression in large halls is pointed out in Helene Wieruszowski, "Art and the Commune in the Time of Dante," *Speculum*, XIX (January, 1944), 14–33.

[14] Margarete Merores, "Der Grosse Rat von Venedig und die sogenannte Serrata von Jahre 1297," *Viertel jahrschrift für Sozial- und Wirtschaftsgeschichte*, XXI (1928), 33–102; Roberto Cessi, *Le origini del ducato veneziano* (Napoli, Morano, 1951), chap. XI; *idem, Storia della Repubblica di Venezia* (Milan: Messina, 1944), I, 265–270.

larism was essential to enable more men to take part directly in making the decisions which affected them all as inhabitants of the same city, so professional particularism was the means by which more men gained a part in framing the rules which regulated their activities as members of an occupational group and in choosing its officials. In both cases participation by a larger percentage of its membership was made possible by the smaller size of the rules-making group. Of course if the principle had been carried to its extreme and each guild had become as particularistic as was each Italian city-state, there would have been anarchy within the cities, just as there was a kind of anarchy in inter-city relations. In some cities the subordinate units within the city—craft guilds, trade associations, and family leagues—did destroy civic peace. But in Venice the guilds were given a strictly limited role. Their members could initiate rules governing their particular trade and could distribute among themselves the honors and duties of enforcing these rules, but in these activities they were subject to officials chosen directly or indirectly by the Great Council in which the guilds were not represented. Guildsmen as such were only second-class citizens, yet they had citizenship of a kind.[15]

Thus consolidated, the Venetian republic gained a high reputation for the success with which it solved many problems in state building that were to confront European governments during the next few centuries, namely, upholding public law over private privilege and vengeance, curbing the church's political influence, and inventing mercantilist measures to increase wealth. Byzantine traditions and the relative weakness of professional organizations in Venice made it easier to establish there a co-ordination of social life under the sovereignty of the Republic.

In Florence as in most Italian city-states, new men were not accepted so smoothly into the ruling class, the artisan-shopkeeper class was not so easily satisfied, and the co-ordination of all social life by republican means was less complete. Since old families which had established the commune were less willing to share the honors and powers of office with the newly rich, the latter had to shove their way up. They did so by

[15] This definitely inferior kind of citizenship of the guildsmen is described as a sharing in elective honors by Gasparo Contarini, *De Magistratibus & repub. Venetorum libri quinque* (Basel, 1547), pp. 196–97. But to equate guild membership, even of artists, with citizenship in a general glorification of Venetian republicanism may be going too far. Cf. H. G. Koenigsberger, "Decadence or Shift? Changes in the Civilization of Italy and Europe in the Sixteenth and Seventeenth Centuries," *Transactions of the Royal Historical Society*, X, 5, (1960), 9–10.

forming guilds of their own and allying with the artisans and shopkeepers. In Florence the crucial document in this development was the Ordinances of Justice of 1293, which the Florentines regarded as their basic constitution. Not so long ago when economic interpretation was the vogue, these ordinances were believed to represent the triumph of merchant capitalists over feudal landlords.[16] But merchants and landlords did not form separate classes in Florence at that time. Successful merchants were also landowners and most of the big landowners were either merchants themselves or had brothers and sons so engaged, and were quite ready to marry a daughter to a merchant provided he was sufficiently rich and of good repute. The wealth that enabled new families to enter the ruling class was derived mainly from trade, industry, or banking, but once arrived the newly rich bought land for economic as well as social reasons and merged their manners and political attitudes with the class to which they had attained. When that class divided on a political issue as did the Florentine upper class in 1293, it was not in accordance with any division between merchants and landlords, for there was in fact no such division.[17]

The problem that the Florentine Ordinances of Justice most obviously attempted to solve was the enforcement of law and order on members of the upper class who conducted feuds among themselves, inflicting violence heedlessly on those who got in the way. Enforcing obedience to general or civic law was a major issue in many parts of Europe in the late thirteenth century. The king was the rallying point for such efforts in France and England. In Florence it was a portion of the ruling class of the city-state, a group of the land-owning merchants, who put through a program for upholding civic law and penalizing those of their own class who held to knightly ideals of personal privilege. Their efforts at law enforcement were not notably successful,

---

[16] The classic statement of this view is the youthful work of Gaetano Salvemini, *Magnati e popolani in Firenze dal 1280 al 1295* (Florence, 1899). It appears somewhat modified in Robert Davidsohn, *Geschichte von Florenz* (4 vols.) in many parts (Florence, 1896–1927); and in Ferdinand Schevill, *History of Florence* (New York: Harper Torchbook, 1961), I, 156.

[17] N. Ottokar, *Il Commune di Firenze alla fine del Dugento* (Florence, 1926); Johan Plesner, *L'Émigration de la Campagne à la ville libre de Florence* (Copenhagen, 1939); Enrico Fiumi, "Sui rapporti economici tra città e contado nella età communale," *Archivio Storico Italiano*, CXIV (1956), 18–36; *idem*, "Fioritura e decadenza dell' economia fiorentina," *Archivio storico italiano*, CXV (1957), 395–401, 429–39, CXVI (1958), 482–96; CXVII (1959), 427–502. Marvin B. Becker, "Some Aspects of Oligarchical, Dictatorial, and Popular Signorie in Florence, 1282–1382," *Comparative Studies in Society and History*, II (1959–60), 421–24.

but in organizing for this purpose they expanded republican institutions. Guild membership was made the basis of political rights, and membership in the guilds was not hereditary. The new rich as well as the old rich were admitted to the great merchant guilds from which the rulers of the city-state were mainly chosen, and obscure parentage did not prevent the admission of either an outstanding scholar such as Leonardo Bruni or a rich businessman such as il Datini.[18] At the same time, the shopkeepers and many of the artisans were permitted to organize guilds and were empowered through their guilds to have some of their members in the highest offices of state, as well as to formulate much of the regulation governing their own line of business. The larger role given the guilds made Florentine republicanism more disorderly but also more democratic than the republicanism of Venice.

Because representation in the highest councils was distributed among the guilds, Florentine politics appeared to be dominated more than it actually was by class conflicts over economic issues. Certainly there were some clear-cut cases of class war, for example, when those who were forbidden to organize their own guilds tried in vain to gain that right—as in the proletarian Ciompi rebellion. But most political struggles were between factions within the merchant-landowning upper class. Even during the depressed decades of the fourteenth century, rich men of new families competed for power with "old families" who had achieved high office generations earlier. In each generation the "new men" were the champions of the sovereign state against special privilege.[19]

The issues agitating Florence and other turbulent Italian cities were the same as those troubling contemporary monarchies—juridical immunities, tax exemptions, and so on—but the methods of political contest in Florence were distinctively republican. They made provision for the desire of citizens to share directly in decision-making, to have

[18] Lauro Martines, *The Social World of the Florentine Humanists, 1390–1460* (Princeton, 1963), pp. 165–76; Melis, *Aspetti della vita economica medievale*, I, 55, and Iris Origo, *The Merchant of Prato, Francesco di Marco Datini* (New York, Knopf, 1957), pp. 69–70, 75, 140–48.

[19] G. A. Brucker, *Florentine Politics and Society* (Princeton, 1962), esp. pp. 390–91; Becker, in *Comparative Studies*, II, 425–30; *idem*, "An Essay on Novi Cives' and Florentine Politics, 1343–1382," *Medieval Studies*, Toronto, XXIV (1962), 35–82; *idem*, "Florentine 'Libertas,' Political Independents and 'Novi Cives.' 1372–78," *Traditio* (1962), 393–407; *idem*, "The Republican City State in Florence: an Inquiry into its Origin and Survival: 1280–1434," *Speculum*, XXXV (1960), 39–50; *idem*, "Florentine Popular Government," *Proceedings of the American Philosophical Society*, vol. 106 (1962), No. 4, pp. 360–82.

their turn in holding important offices, and in feeling the honor and responsibility. Today political liberty means to many people the protection of private individuals against arbitrary acts by government officials. This is a negative conception, perfectly compatible with a selfish lack of interest in public affairs.[20] It can lead to withdrawal in order to assert a kind of sovereignty over one's self. Florentine institutions offered a different ideal of liberty, not protection from government but a chance to be the government. Freedom was action, social and political action, and demanded virtuosity.[21]

In distributing high office among members of the guilds, extensive use was made of lots, of drawing names from a bag, since this seemed the best way of assuring a rotation in office. Practicing the craft or trade of the guild was not considered necessary in order to be admitted to its membership; the guilds became as much election districts as occupational or professional groups; corruption was easy and took many forms. Real power almost always lay with some combination of the factions dividing the landowning merchant class, either because of the large representation given their own guilds or because of the influence that their money, family connections, and personal prestige gave them in other guilds and among the people generally.[22] Florence in the fourteenth and fifteenth centuries was a corrupt republic, but it was republican all the same, just as our government is today. In the United States also chicanery, emotion, and self-interest are sometimes more important than appeals to reason in the competition of leaders for the support of their fellow citizens.

The peak of popular participation in government was reached in Italy in the thirteenth or fourteenth centuries. Thereafter it was curtailed in several ways: by the suppression of particularism to the

---

[20] This conception dominates H. A. L. Fisher, *The Republican Tradition in Europe* (New York, 1911). He dismisses the Italian cities saying, p. 18, "Liberty in the sense of political independence and class privilege was better understood than liberty in the sense of political toleration; . . ."

[21] Hannah Arendt, "What is Freedom," in *Between Past and Future* (New York, 1961), especially pp. 153–57, contrasts this virtuosity with the "free will" of Christian and philosophic traditions. "Liberté politique" is contrasted with "liberté civile" by C. L. Sismonde de Sismondi, *Histoire des républiques italiennes du moyen âge* (10 vols., Paris, 1840), vol. X, chap. VIII. The institutions which Sismondi describes as essential to "liberté politique" are the same as those Tolomeo of Lucca considered appropriate to a republic which he calls, in the work cited below, note 29, a "regimen politicum."

[22] See the studies of M. B. Becker and G. A. Brucker cited above in n. 19, and the review of Brucker's book by L. F. Marks in *Past and Present*, No. 25 (July, 1963), p. 80.

extent that the smaller cities were conquered by the larger; by a decline in social mobility; and by the spread of despotism. But the extent to which republicanism declined in Italy between 1250 and 1450 has been exaggerated. Many of the *signori*, whom we call despots following the tradition fixed by the literary brilliance of John Addington Symonds, were, in fact as well as in theory, elective monarchs bound by oath to maintain the law of the city.[23] They were the popular choice and were overthrown when they lost that support. Moreover the three leading commercial cities—Genoa, Florence, and Venice—remained republics. True, the republicanism of Genoa was expressed by deposing one would-be tyrant after another, as well as by the independence of the Bank of Saint George, but revolutions are as significant as the abuses that occasion them.[24] In Florence the Medici family finally overtopped all the others but adopted a princely style only with Lorenzo, and was driven out as soon as Lorenzo's son neglected to consider the interests and dignity of the families with whose alliance the Medici had governed.[25] Venice avoided the dominance of any single family and perfected a system of checks and balances within its ruling class. Although this class became strictly hereditary, its members were about as numerous as were the Florentines qualified for office holding.[26] Real power was concentrated in fewer hands in Florence than in Venice, because of electoral manipulation, but Florence was more democratic in admitting some of the artisan-shopkeepers to the higher offices and in keeping open avenues for the rise of new men.[27] Unskilled laborers were not, of course, eligible for office at any time, either in Florence or Venice. All my references to popular participation must be understood in a relative sense, appropriate to that age.

[23] John Addington Symonds, *The Renaissance in Italy*, vol. I, *The Age of the Despots* (London, 1875) .

[24] Jacques Heers, *Gênes au xv siècle*, École Pratique des Hautes Etudes—VIe Section, Centre de Recherches Historiques Affaires et Gens d'Affaires, XXV (Paris, S.E.V.P.E.N., 1961) , 563–611.

[25] L. F. Marks, "The Financial Oligarchy in Florence under Lorenzo," and Nicolai Rubinstein, "Politics and Constitutión in Florence at the End of the Fifteenth Century," both in *Italian Renaissance Studies: Tribute to Cecilia M. Ady*, ed. by E. F. Jacob (London, 1960) ; Rudolf von Albertini, *Das Florentinische Staatsbewusstsein im Übergang von der Republik zum Prinzipat* (Bern, 1955) , pp. 15–18.

[26] Francesco Guicciardini, "Dialogo del reggimento di Firenze," in *Opere* ed. Caprariis (La Letteratura italiana; storia e testi, vol. 30, Milan: Riccardi, 1953) , pp. 268–69, emphasized that "la plebe" was excluded in both cities and that the Venetian nobility were as numerous as qualified Florentines.

[27] Hans Baron, "The Social Background of Political Liberty in the Early Italian Renaissance," *Comparative Studies in Society and History*, II (1959–60) .

While republicanism lived on enfeebled in practice, in the fifteenth and sixteenth centuries it conquered new ground intellectually. Defenders of the principles of republicanism had not been lacking earlier. Thomas Aquinas revived many of the ideas developed by the Greeks and Romans. Basing his political theory on Aristotle as well as on the Bible, he wrote more about city-states than about feudalism or universal empire, and he opened a channel for the later flood of republican theorizing by digging out within Christian theology a respectable, even an important, place for man as a citizen. Although he declared in favor of monarchy, St. Thomas praised popularly elected, law abiding monarchies, which combined the best features of monarchy, aristocracy, and democracy.[28] One of his disciples, Tolomeo of Lucca, was more explicit. Tolomeo explained why a republican rotation of many men through public offices was the form of government which best suited men of high spirit and intelligence such as the Italians, whatever might be good for men in other climes.[29] Marsilius of Padua, building also on Aristotelean premises, asserted popular sovereignty more absolutely.[30] But these discussions, between 1250 and 1350, of the advantages and disadvantages of monarchy had a relatively detached, academic air. The form of government is a secondary matter to Thomas Aquinas; the essential for him was observance of the natural and divine law, and the burning issue of his time was the temporal power of the pope or the relations of Church and state.

These issues became secondary in Italy when republican theories attained a new and practical importance, after 1400, in conjunction with Florentine humanism. By 1400 the leading despots had abandoned all pretense of being popularly elected monarchs. The most

[28] Walter Ullmann, "The Individual in Medieval Society, Lecture III, The Humanistic Thesis: The release of the subject and his emergence as a citizen" (Lecture at Johns Hopkins University in 1965); Etienne Gilson, *Le Thomisme* (5 ed., Paris, 1948), pp. 455–59; and A. P. d'Entrèves's introduction to Thomas Aquinas, *Selected Political Writings,* trans. by J. G. Dawson (Oxford, 1918).

[29] Since Tolomeo (often called Ptolemy of Lucca) continued the "De Regimine Principum ad regem Cipri" begun by Thomas Aquinas, Tolomeo's ideas on republicanism may be found in Thomas Aquinas, *Opera Omnia secundum impressionem Petri Fiaccadori Parmae, 1852–1873,* photolithographice reimpressa (New York, 1950), vol. XVI, "De Regimine Principum," Lib. II, cap. viii–x and especially in Lib. IV.

[30] Marsilius of Padua, *The Defensor Pacis,* trans. with introduction by A. Gewirth (2 vols., New York: Records of Civilization, Columbia Univ. Press, 1956); C. W. Previté-Orton, "Marsiglio of Padua, Part II, Doctrines," *English Historical Review,* XXXVIII (1923), 1–17.

powerful among them, the Visconti of Milan, had sought and received sanction of their power from above, from the emperor, and were adding to their domains so rapidly that they seemed likely to unite Italy under a Milanese monarch; at least it seemed that way to the Florentines. Supporters of the Visconti extolled the advantages of Italian unity under efficient administration in contrast to republican anarchy. In this situation Florentine patriots presented their defense of their own particularism as a general defense of freedom and republicanism.

The intellectual reverberations of this war propaganda were magnified by the rhetoric of that generation of Florentines who trumpeted their unlimited enthusiasm for humanistic studies. The leader of these civic humanists, as Hans Baron appropriately calls them, was Leonardo Bruni.[31] Many of their specific arguments for considering republics better than monarchies—for example, the assertion that republics did more to stimulate virtue—had been suggested earlier by St. Thomas and Tolomeo.[32] The civic humanists gave the issue personal meaning, and applied it to their own historical situation. By treating monarchy as practically indistinguishable from tyranny, they identified themselves fully with republicanism. They glorified the Roman Republic to the disparagement of the Roman emperors, rescued Brutus, the tyrannicide, from the place in hell to which Dante had consigned him; and instead of reproaching Cicero for neglecting literature out of preoccupation with politics, extolled him as an exemplar of the finest manly activity, the defense of liberty and general welfare in public life. This identification of their own republicanism and their own hatred of tyranny with the sentiments recorded in Greek and Roman literature was taken up in Venice also, which finally allied with Florence against the Visconti. In Venice and Florence, men active in both the world of letters and in affairs of state applied political theories to current concerns in which the central issue was the nature and value of republican freedom.[33]

The republicanism of the Florentine humanists faded when the Visconti were crushed, and the only state that showed any possibility

[31] Hans Baron, *The Crisis of the Early Italian Renaissance: Civic Humanism and Republican Liberty in an Age of Classicism and Tyranny* (2 vols., Princeton, N.J., 1955).

[32] Thomas Aquinas, *Opera Omnia*, above cited, *De Regimine Principum*, Lib. I, cap. iii; Lib. II, cap. ix; Lib. IV, cap. viii.

[33] Baron, *Crisis*, I; C. C. Bayley, *War and Society in Renaissance Florence* (Toronto, 1961), chaps. III–V; N. Carotti, "Un politico umanista del Quattrocento," *Rivista storica italiana*, ser. S, vol. II (1937), Fasc. II, 18–28.

of dominating all Italy was the Venetian Republic. But the ideas of the civic humanists were revived vigorously in Florence at the end of the century in the republican enthusiasm which accompanied the expulsion of the Medici bosses. Guicciardini, Machiavelli, and many other Florentines, then went far beyond the humanists in systematic thinking about how their corrupt republic, or any corrupt republic, might acquire new and better institutions.[34] Machiavelli is best known for advising princes to be unscrupulous. Like a daring physician trying to cure a patient in a desperate condition, he had the courage to prescribe poison, but his standard of health was republican.[35] While the last Florentine republic was being destroyed by Spanish and papal armies, its extremist leaders exalted the will of the people in a fashion that anticipated the Jacobins of the French Revolution, and similarly turned the slogans of liberty into instruments of temporary tyranny.[36] Caustic moderates, like Guicciardini, had meanwhile perfected the analysis of ancient and modern city-states in search of norms for an ideal constitution. They could depict their standards more concretely because there was one republic of their own time in which they saw them embodied, namely Venice. Impressed by Venice's prosperity and safety in spite of the clash of powerful monarchies that destroyed freedom elsewhere in Italy, Donato Gianotti first, and then Gasparo Contarini, created in the mid-sixteenth century a picture of Venice as the perfectly organized republic.[37] This benign analysis lulled the Venetians into stagnation, but furnished inspiration to the scarce and struggling republicans of the seventeenth century.[38]

From its alliance with humanism, republicanism thus acquired the self-consciousness and sophistication which enabled it to survive as a

[34] Albertini, *Das Florentinische Staatsbewusstsein;* Felix Gilbert, *Machiavelli and Guicciardini: Politics and History in Sixteenth-Century Florence* (Princeton, 1965), esp. pp. 93–97.

[35] Leopold von Ranke, *Sämmtliche Werke*, XXXIV, 174.* On Machiavelli's republicanism, see also Hans Baron, "Machiavelli: The Republican Citizen and the Author of the Prince," *English Historical Review*, LXXVI (April, 1961); Felix Gilbert, *Machiavelli and Guicciardini*, pp. 171–79, also emphasizes his anti-aristocratic republicanism. A good review of earlier discussions is Eric W. Cochrane, "Machiavelli, 1940–1960," in *Journal of Modern History* (1961).

[36] Albertini, *Das Florentinische Staatsbewusstsein*, pp. 124–29.

[37] *Ibid.*, pp. 113–14, 146–64; Hermann Hackert, *Die Staatschrift Gasparo Contarini's und die Politischen Verhaltnisse Venedigs in Sechzehnsten Jahrhundert* (Heidelberger Abhandlingen, Heft, 69, Heidelberg: Winter, 1940).

[38] Perez Zagorin, *A History of Political Thought in the English Revolution* (London, 1954), pp. 130, 141; Z. S. Fink, "Venice and English Political Thought in the Seventeenth Century," *Modern Philology*, XXXVIII (Nov. 1940), 155–72.

fermenting element in the Western tradition even when it disappeared almost entirely from practice. The contrast between Italy and northern Europe is striking. The growth of communes out of feudalism had not been restricted to Italy. Beyond the Alps, also men had formed these local units of self-government, and in some areas they had gained considerable autonomy. But the northern communes left no republican literary tradition comparable to that of the Italians. Their embryonic republicanism did not receive the same degree of stimulus from the revival of antiquity.

The junction between republicanism and humanism in Italy was not fortuitous. Although Petrarch was more a friend of tyrants than of republics, devotees of classical literature were likely to discover sooner or later, whether because of the Visconti threat or some other incident, the similarity between their situation and that in the ancient city-states. Again men were diliberately attempting to shape institutions which would spread the powers of governing among the citizens and yet prevent a popular favorite from making himself master. Success was rare in either case. Tyranny as well as republicanism were experiences that the Italian cities shared with the ancient Greeks and Romans.

Ever since Christianity had triumphed over paganism, now one, now another aspect of classical antiquity had been studied with admiration in the West. The so-called revival of antiquity in fifteenth-century Italy was different only in being more nearly complete and in having distinctive emphases.[39] For the first time there was a revival of the ancient attitude toward political life. The passionate concern of the civic humanists with politics made them understand, better than Petrarch ever could, why such men as Cicero had placed politics first. A St. Thomas could expound Aristotle's generalizations about political organization, but a man of his principles and temper could not convey the feeling that politics was the most important thing in life, the feeling that pulsates through Machiavelli's lines as it did through those of Thucydides and Livy.

The re-evaluation of politics created more sympathetic understanding of other aspects of classical civilization. It contributed much to a kind of self-consciousness which was less self-reliant than the individualism of the feudal nobles or the pioneering merchants of earlier centuries while it was more deliberate, more intellectual, and more devoted to those skills in verbal expression and communication that enabled men to compete and co-operate simultaneously in civic

[39] R. R. Bolgar, *The Classical Heritage and Its Beneficiaries* (Cambridge, 1954).

life. The change of values which occurred in the Italian city-states is sometimes said to have emphasized the qualities esteemed by merchants and productive of success in trade. It is at least equally true that they were the qualities commanding admiration in political give-and-take, those which Whitehead has called the qualities of persuasion.[40]

To summarize this republican interpretation: From the twelfth to the sixteenth century the feature which most distinguished Italian society from that in other regions in Europe was the extent to which men were able to take part in determining, largely by persuasion, the laws and decisions governing their daily lives. This republicanism was not a class product, although commercial growth was one prerequisite for its development. This republicanism strengthened and was in turn reinforced by the efforts to revive classical antiquity and the values connected with its humanism.[41]

Acceptance of this interpretation invites a change in the usual periodization of European history. If the republicanism of the city-states was so important, it deserves to be seen as a whole instead of being split and assigned half to one period, half to another, as is now so often done, thus divorcing the period of stabilization and rationalization from that in which the cities formed their basic republican institutions. Such a division obscures the amount of republicanism existing in both the Age of Faith and the Age of the Despots, so-called. An alternative is to treat the economic growth, the elaboration of republican institutions, and the changing artistic and intellectual climate as a closely connected whole, spread over a period extending at least from 1200 to 1600, or possibly all the way from Sebastian Ziani to George Washington, an Age of Pre-Industrial Republicanism.

During those centuries European culture was being reshaped by many different movements, some of which had little connection one with the other. The antecedents explaining Europe's oceanic expansion are quite distinct from those relevant to the agitation for anti-papal religious reform. Only a very narrow conception of life will stress just

---

[40] Alfred North Whitehead, *Adventures of Ideas* (New York: Mentor Book, 1955), pp. 75–76; Hans Baron, "A Sociological Interpretation of the Early Renaissance in Florence," *South Atlantic Quarterly,* XXXVIII, 4 (Oct., 1939), and his other articles there cited.

[41] My interpretation is similar to Wallace K. Ferguson's, but his emphasis on "urban laymen" seems to me to understate the significance of the contrast between Palermo or Paris on the one hand and Venice and Florence on the other. "The Reinterpretation of the Renaissance" in *Facets of the Renaissance* (Harper Torchbook, 1963), pp. 15–16.

one aspect or consider a single cause sufficient to explain all the diversity of historical change. I am arguing only that the growth and transformation of republicanism deserves a place of honor equal to that accorded other themes.

We should not wait for Italian historians to take the lead in emphasizing this republican element in their history. Like contemporary members of the historical profession in other lands, including many members of the American Historical Association, they are largely concerned with the nationalism of their own nation. Many of them are preoccupied by the problem of national unity even in describing a period in which such unity was conspicuous by its absence, and pay less attention to the content of republican institutions than to the near-success of now one power, now another, in efforts to dominate the peninsula which was later to become their nation.[42] As Americans, we have reason to be less attracted by these repeated failures to effect Italian unity than by the success and failures of the Italians as republicans.

When Charles Homer Haskins gave his presidential address to this Association a generation ago he urged Americans not to be content with receiving European history second-hand, in packages prepared by European scholars, but to work it up for themselves first-hand from the sources. He stressed in 1922 the need of making our own evaluations of the "national psychologies" active in the First World War and its settlement.[43] Let me urge a variation on that theme and one I think particularly relevant in these times of emphasis on non-Western cultures and their histories. Although that emphasis is certainly needed to correct past neglect, our central task as a historical profession is to examine our own cultural traditions. Now one part of that tradition, now another needs re-examination as the problems of the historian's own time change. Most of our cultural traditions lead us back to Europe, but current problems take different forms in the various

[42] The not yet existing nation naturally supplies the unifying theme in any "History of Italy," e.g., Nino Valori, *Storia d'Italia* (5 vols., 1959–60) , vol. I, and his excellent, *L'Italia dell'Età dei Principati: 1343–1516* (Milan, Mondadori, 1949) . Armando Sapori, on the other hand, has emphasized the unity of the whole period 1200–1600 and the vitality of republican liberty. See his "Il Rinascimento economico" in Armando Sapori, *Studi di Storia economica, sec. XIII, XIV, XV* (3 ed., 2 vols.: Florence, Sansoni, 1955) , I, 618–52; *idem,* "Medioevo e Rinascimento," *Archivio storico italiano,* CXV (1957) , 141–64; *idem, L'Età della rinascita* (Milan: La Goliardeca, 1958) , pp. 207–21.

[43] Charles H. Haskins, "European History and American Scholarship," *American Historical Review,* XXVIII (January, 1923) , 215 and 225.

Western nations so that we have different needs in re-examining our complex common heritage. To learn what is of most value for us in European history we need to dig deep and assay the ore for ourselves.

When we look back into the growth there of our democratic ideals we of course find that the city-state was not their only source. It was only one of three main sources, although it is that to which we owe most of the language of politics, much of its machinery, and the very conception of government by the people. I can hardly do more than mention the others here but do so in order to place my theme in perspective. A second source was in the feudal parliamentary institutions which produced effective limitations on monarchy, both in theory and practice, and built the habit of government by representatives into the growth of nations of more size and power than could be embodied in any city-state. Running deepest and most varied in its manifestations have been the outpourings from the third source, namely, the idea of the rights and the worth of every human being. This conception of the dignity of human nature was cultivated by Stoic lawyers, Christian divines, and eighteenth-century rationalists and is still receiving new applications. It asks that what was attempted for only a few communities in the city-state, and for only a few classes by feudal parliamentarianism, be effected for all men. The ideal has not been realized; all three democratic traditions, even that derived from the city-state, can boast of being a tradition of failure in the sense that it embodies examples of behavior higher than were ever generally practiced.

Although Athens and Rome were the fountainheads of our republican heritage from the city-states, we received that legacy by transmission through the Italians who lived in republics from the twelfth to the sixteenth centuries. To republican practices in a pagan society worshiping local and family deities, the Italians added centuries of their own experience within a Christian society. They established Greek and Roman authors as authorities on politics, a position that these authors occupied thereafter in Western thought. They added thereto their own aspiring but critical and often bitter reflections, and formulated in terms of their experience the rules for mixing monarchic, aristocratic, and democratic elements so as to secure good government. When the upsetting of custom-established monarchy by the Puritan Revolution gave seventeenth-century Englishmen reason to speculate about the best form of government, Machiavelli's republicanism became better understood. Harrington praised him as "the sole retriever" of ancient prudence, and hailed Venice as a model republic proving that a skillful mixture of institutions could overcome human weaknesses and defy time. Although these English republicans were swept aside by the Restoration, their good name and their ideas were cultivated during the eighteenth century by writers and agitators known as the "Commonwealthmen" and it was these radicals who pulled together anti-monarchic doctrines, drawing from all three sources of the democratic tradition, and supplied the material used by the pamphleteers of the American Revolution.[44]

The founding fathers of this republic knew the republican tradition of the Italian city-states not only through the English Commonwealthmen but also by study first-hand. Seeking lessons from the city-states of Italy as well as from those of antiquity, they formulated their own judgments on that experience. John Adams, for example, completely rejected the idealization of the Venetian constitution which had found favor among the classical republicans of seventeenth-century England. He looked on all the European republics as utter failures. Their vices were evidence of the corruption of the Old World, but they were instructive failures, "full of excellent warnings," he said, for the people of America, "the young of the New World."[45]

A John Adams writing today would probably say that the warnings are particularly relevant now when our republicanism has become similarly old and corrupt. We are very different, to be sure, because industrialization has changed social structure, and political communities are now huge and bureaucratized. New technologies and new methods of production have changed the ways in which individuals can have a part in making laws and choosing leaders. Democratic ideals are being transformed in the light of these new possibilities and difficulties. At the same time the aspirations that history has built into us are themselves at work shaping new institutions to meet these conditions. If ideas were entirely determined by class interests, the aims and practices of the Italian cities would be worthy of attention only as reflections of a particular system of production. But there is a kind of life in ideas that enables them to pass from one social setting to another, changing somewhat in the process but contributing to the formation of social

[44] Z. S. Fink, *The Classical Republicans* (2 ed., Northwestern University Press, 1962), chaps. 2 and 3; Caroline Robbins, *The Eighteenth-Century Commonwealthmen* (Harvard University Press, 1959), esp. p. 386; Bernard Bailyn, *Pamphlets of the American Revolution, 1750–1776* (Harvard University Press, 1965), pp. 28–29.

[45] John Adams, "A Defense of the Constitution of the United States of America," in *The Works of John Adams*, ed. by Charles Francis Adams (Boston, 1851), V, 332, accompanied by extensive discussions of Venice, Florence, etc., in vols. IV and V.

structures, as well as receiving new meanings in new environments. Ideas born in Athens lived in Florence and are alive today.

The politics of Florence and Venice were very different from our own, certainly. In order to understand them we should start by putting aside concern with current problems and by entering into their fears and their enthusiasms for what they perceived as liberty. Not only have material conditions and social structures changed, but the kinds of lives individuals desire to live and the kinds of persons they want to be, have altered, with a corresponding change in the purposes for which political rights are sought. Men whose main concern is to prevent the government from interfering with their private lives can only by an imaginative effort sympathize with an insistence on rights that enabled individuals to be the government, that is, to be sometimes the persons responsible for giving orders. Perhaps that attitude will become more easily understandable if citizens now, instead of continuing on the defensive against bureaucracy, undertake an offensive not to limit but to infiltrate it. That is only one possibility; an appreciation of the range of differences within our republican past widens the range of action that is possible in the present as we adapt our ideas to a new situation and thereby create new elements at work in that situation.

Postscript*

WHETHER or not we find life on Mars or that the moon can be inhabited, human aspirations and relationships will continue to be influenced in the future by our conceptions of our past here on earth. Historians will lose nothing of their importance, and their central function in every country will continue to be inquiry into the formation of their own cultural traditions. But the shrinkage of space that has made all the earth's surface seem very close has also broadened the demands made on historians. By 1965 all the many cultural traditions in the world have become poignantly aware of each other to such an extent that no one of them can be fully evaluated or properly understood except in relation to the others. While examining their own cultural traditions historians have to ask how they fit into the history of the rest of humanity.

The enormous expansion of historical writing during the nineteenth century was vigorously stimulated by the nationalism of that century and was primarily concerned with national traditions. The past was examined in order to find, or to strengthen, a tradition which would give a people identity and unity as a nation. Michelet sounded the keynote in writing a history of France which told the French what it meant to be a Frenchman. Out of the feeling that they had done great things together in the past—suffered together, hated and loved together, triumphed together—was to spring the will to be a separate entity in the present and to do great things together in the future.

Of course traditions other than those of the nation also received attention. Some of these were narrower, others broader.

---

* Contribution by Frederic C. Lane to a symposium on the theme: "Do the radical changes in the modern world make all previous history irrelevant?" Published on the occasion of the Twelfth International Congress of Historical Sciences, in *Die Presse,* Vienna, August 28–29, 1965 under the subtitle: "New Perspectives."

Narrower, but sometimes more deeply embedded in familiar loyalties, were the sub-national traditions, as they might be called, of provinces or regions. In the United States, for example, in addition to the glorification of the national union, historians examined and helped to sanctify regional traditions: the self-importance of the Puritan New Englanders, the charm and burden of Southern history, or the allegedly free-wheeling "frontier" qualities of the West. Questions arose about the relation of these regional traditions to those of the nation. Did a man sufficiently identify himself by saying, "I am an American"? or was it not more meaningful to him if he said, "I am a Southerner"?

On the other hand, also competing with nationalism were broader traditions, of which the oldest were religious. Cutting across national boundaries, the Christian, Jewish, and Moslem religions were all based on distinctive answers to the question: What were the essential events in human history? Christianity and Judaism, especially, stimulated an intense awareness of the past and of the importance of interpreting it correctly. As divisions within these religions proliferated, history became essential to their explanation; indeed, many a sect or denomination is hardly explicable except as the cultivation of a separate ecclesiastical tradition.

In addition, in Europe various views of history emerged that treated all Europe and the Americas, or at least all western Europe and the Americas, as a unit. They considered Western history the equivalent of world history and saw in world history, thus narrowly conceived, broad trends affecting all nations. Among these trends may be mentioned the succession of one class after another to dominance, including the rise of capitalism and its passing. Another trend, which was stressed by the optimists who hoped to make the world safe for democracy, was the growth of free representative government. Although these two themes were sometimes in opposition they could both be combined with a belief in progress and an identification of progress with the trends of development in Western civilization.

Distinctive of the twentieth century is the discovery by the West of the possibility that it does not control the future and that consequently its own past does not reveal the whole meaning of human history. Accordingly the study of non-Western civilizations by Westerners has developed markedly and is still increasing rapidly in 1965. New professorships and fellowships, the output of books, the grants from philanthropic foundations all testify to this enlargement of historical study. At the same time the non-Western nations themselves are becoming more articulate about their own traditions. Their historical output is stimulated both by a tendency to imitate the West in taking the past seriously and by the acquisition of independent institutions and resources through which to express their own conceptions of history.

As a result of these developments it is now generally realized that traditions elaborated in the West must be re-examined as part of a larger whole. But what are the relations of the parts to the whole, if there really is a whole? Can we bring the myriad cultural traditions into a single pattern of evolution? Can we find common elements and speak with conviction of a common cultural tradition for all humanity? Answering such questions will place the national, regional, religious, and ideological traditions of the West and East in new perspectives. Finding these perspectives seems to me to be the main intellectual challenge faced by the historical profession in our rapidly changing world.

Bibliography of Frederic C. Lane

1924–66

1924

"Colbert et le commerce de Bordeaux," *Revue historique de Bordeaux,* XVII, 169–90.*

1925

"L'Église reformée de Begles de 1660 à 1670," *Revue historique de Bordeaux,* XVIII, 225–40.

1926

"L'Église reformée de Begles de 1660 à 1670," *Revue historique de Bordeaux,* XIX, 31–40, 71–80, 119–26.

1931

Review of *Der Untergang Roms im Abendlandischen Denken: ein Beitrag zur Geschichtssschreibung und zum Dekadenzproblem,* by Walter Rehm, *American Historical Review,* XXXVI, 420–21.

1932

"The Rope Factory and Hemp Trade of Venice in the Fifteenth and Sixteenth Centuries," *Journal of Economic and Business History,* IV, 830–47.*

1933

"Venetian Shipping During the Commercial Revolution," *American Historical Review,* XXXVIII, 219–39.*

1934

"Venetian Naval Architecture about 1550," *The Mariner's Mirror,* XX, 24–49.*

* Reprinted in this volume.

Venetian Ships and Shipbuilders of the Renaissance. Baltimore, The Johns Hopkins Press.

1935

Review of *Geschichte von Venedig,* Band III, Der Niedergang, by Heinrich Kretschmayr, *American Historical Review,* XL, 316–18.

Review of *Der deutsche Seehandel im Mittelmeergebiet bis zu den Napoleon-ischen Kriegen,* by Ludwig Beutin, *American Historical Review,* XL, 555–56.

1937

"Venetian Bankers, 1496–1533: A Study in the Early Stages of Deposit Banking," *Journal of Political Economy,* XLV, 187–206.*

"Why Begin at the Beginning?", An Address to the Middle States Association of History and Social Science Teachers, 1937, *Proceedings of the Middle States Association of History and Social Science Teachers,* XXV, 73–77.*

1940

"The Mediterranean Spice Trade: Further Evidence of Its Revival in the Sixteenth Century," *American Historical Review,* XLV, 581–90.*

1941

"National Wealth and Protection Costs," in *War as a Social Institution* (New York: Columbia University Press) , pp. 32–43.*

Review of *The Renaissance,* by Wallace K. Ferguson, *Journal of Modern History,* XIII, 78–80.

Review of *La Guerre dans la pensée économique du XVIe au XVIIIe siècle,* by Edmond Silberner, *Journal of Economic History,* I, 108.

1942

"The Economic Meaning of War and Protection," *Journal of Social Philosophy and Jurisprudence,* VII, 254–70.*

Review of Machiavelli, *The Prince and Other Works, Including Reform in Florence, Castruccio, Castracani, On Fortune, Letters, Ten Discourses on Livy,* by Allan H. Gilbert, *Modern Language Notes,* LVII, 478–79.

Review of *Rome and China. A Study of Correlations in Historical Events,* by Frederick J. Teggart, *American Journal of Philology,* LXIII, 355–58.

1943

"Not Inevitable: Five Foundations for Peace," *The Johns Hopkins Magazine,* XXXI, 101–5.

1944

Andrea Barbarigo, Merchant of Venice, 1418–1449 ("The Johns Hopkins University Studies in Historical and Political Science," Ser. LXII, No. 1 [Baltimore, The Johns Hopkins Press]) .

"Family Partnerships and Joint Ventures in the Venetian Republic," *Journal of Economic History*, IV, 178–96.*

1945

"Venture Accounting in Medieval Business Management," *Bulletin of the Business Historical Society*, XIX, 164–72.*

Review of *A Basic History of the United States*, by Charles A. and Mary R. Beard, *Journal of Economic History*, V, 134–35.

Review of *Leonardo da Vinci, His Life and His Pictures*, by H. Langton Douglass, *Journal of Modern History*, XVII, 368.

1946

Review of *Amerigo Vespucci, Pilot Major*, by Frederick H. Pohl, *Journal of Economic History*, VI, 102.

1947

The World's History (with Eric F. Goldman and Erling M. Hunt) . New York, Harcourt, Brace and Co.

1948

"Social Science and the Humanities," *Proceedings of the American Philosophical Society*, XCII, 356–62.*

Review of *Studi di Storia economica medievale*, by Armando Sapori, *American Historical Review*, LIII, 865–66.

Review of *Industrial Mobilization for War, History of the War Production Board and Predecessor Agencies, 1940–1945*, *Journal of Economic History*, VIII, 213–15.

1949

"Ritmo e rapidità di giro d'affari nel commercio veneziano dal quattrocento," in *Studi in Onore di Gino Luzzatto* (4 vols.; Milan, Dott. A. Giuffrè) , I, 254–73.*

Review of *Nouvelles et speculation à Venise au débût du xvi siècle*, by Pierre Sardella; *Trois essais sur histoire et culture*, by Charles Morazé, *Journal of Economic History*, IX, 72.

1950

"Oceanic Expansion: Force and Enterprise in the Creation of Oceanic Commerce," in *The Tasks of Economic History,* Suppl. to *Journal of Economic History,* X, 19–31.*

Review of *Zur Getreidenpolitik Oberitalienischer Stadte Im 13. Jahrhundert,* by Hans Conrad Peyer, *American Historical Review,* LVI, 175–76.

1951

Ships for Victory: A History of Shipbuilding Under the U.S. Maritime Commission of World War II. Baltimore, The Johns Hopkins Press.

"Building Ships for War," *The Johns Hopkins Magazine,* II (April), 9–11, 32.

1953

Enterprise and Secular Change, Readings in Economic History (with Jelle C. Riemersma, Assistant Editor). Homewood, Ill., Richard D. Irwin, Inc.

1954

The World's History (with Eric F. Goldman and Erling Hunt). Rev. ed. New York, Harcourt, Brace and Co.

1955

Discussion of "Toward a Theory of Economic Growth," by Simon Kuznets, in *National Policy for Economic Welfare at Home and Abroad.* Published material growing out of the Conference on National Policy for Economic Welfare at Home and Abroad, held at Columbia University, May 26–29, 1954. Garden City, N.Y., Doubleday & Co., pp. 89–93.

"Consumption and Economic Change," *Journal of Economic History,* XV, 107–9.

Review of *The Social Sciences in Historical Study: A Report of the Committee on Historiography, Journal of Economic History,* XV, 65–67.

Review of *Machiavelli AntiCristo,* by Giuseppe Prezzolini, *Romanic Review,* XLVI, 290–92.

1956

"Some Heirs of Gustav von Schmoller," in *Architects and Craftsmen in History, Festschrift für Abbott Payson Usher* (Tübingen: J. C. B. Mohr), pp. 9–39.*

Review of *Comasco sotto il dominio Spagnolo: Saggio di storia economica e Sociale,* by Bruno Caizzi, *American Historical Review,* LXI, 390–91.

Review of *Medieval Trade in the Mediterranean World: Illustrative Documents*, by Robert S. Lopez and Irving W. Raymond, *Journal of Economic History*, XVI, 386–87.

1957

"Fleets and Fairs: The Functions of the Venetian Muda," *Studi in Onore di Armando Sapori* (2 vols.; Milan: Cisalpino) , I, 651–63.*

Review of *Settanta anni fà: Il ritorno all'oro nell'occidente duecentesco,* by Roberto Lopez, *Journal of Economic History*, XVII, 129–30.

Review of *Nel VII Centenario della nascita di Marco Polo,* by Roberto Almagio and others; *La civiltà veneziana del secolo di Marco Polo,* by Riccardo Bacchelli and others, *Speculum*, XXXII, 530–34.

1958

"Economic Consequences of Organized Violence," *Journal of Economic History*, XVIII, 401–17.*

"Le vecchie monete di conte veneziane ed il ritorno all'oro," *Atti Dell'Istituto Veneto di Scienze, Lettere ed Arti,* 1958–1959, pp. 49–50.

Review of *Il Viceregno di Napoli nel sec. XVII,* by Giuseppe Coniglio, *Journal of Economic History*, XVIII, 124–25.

Review of *La società veneta alla fine del settocento: Richerche storiche,* by Marino Berengo, *Journal of Economic History*, XVIII, 351.

1959

The World's History (with Eric F. Goldman and Erling Hunt) . Second revision. New York: Harcourt, Brace, and Co.

Review of *The New Cambridge Modern History,* Vol. I: *The Renaissance, 1493–1520,* edited by G. R. Potter, *Journal of Economic History*, XIX, 146–48.

Review of *Theory and History,* by Ludwig von Mises; *The Poverty of Historicism,* by Karl R. Popper, *Economic History Review*, XI, 550–52.

1960

Review of *Insurance in Venice from the Origins to the End of the Serenissima: Documents published for the 125th Anniversary of the Company* [1831–1956], 2 vols., by Giuseppe Stefani, *Journal of Modern History*, XXXII, 52–53.

Review of *The Foundations of Capitalism,* by Oliver C. Cox, *Economic History Review,* XII, 517–18.

Review of *Naufrages, corsaires et assurances maritimes à Venise, 1592–1609* by Alberto Tenenti, *American Historical Review*, LXV, 218.

1961

Review of *Ambassador from Venice: Pietro Pasqualigo in Lisbon,* by Donald Weinstein, *American Historical Review,* LXVI, 806.

1962

"Units of Economic Growth Historically Considered," *Kyklos,* XV, 95–104.*

"Cargaisons de coton et réglementations médiévales contre la surcharge des navires—Venise," *Revue d'histoire économique et sociale,* XL, 21–31.*

"La marine marchande et le trafic maritime de Venise à travers les siècles," *Les Sources de l'histoire maritime en Europe, du moyen âge au xviii siècle,* Actes du Quatrième Colloque International d'Histoire Maritime, Paris, May, 1959, ed. by Michel Mollat (Paris, S.E.V.P.E.N., 1962), 7–32.*

"Venetian Maritime Law and Administration (1250–1350)," in *Studi in Onore di Amintore Fanfani.* (6 vols.; Milan: Dott. A. Giuffrè), III, 21–50.*

Review of *Venezia e i Corsari, 1480–1615,* by Alberto Tenenti, *American Historical Review,* LXVII, 786.

1963

"The Economic Meaning of the Invention of the Compass," *American Historical Review,* LXVIII, 605–17.*

"Venetian Merchant Galleys, 1300–1334: Private and Communal Operation," *Speculum,* XXXVIII, 179–203.*

"From Biremes to Triremes at Venice," *Mariner's Mirror,* XLIX, 48–50.*

"Salaires et régime alimentaire des marins au début du XIVᵉ siècle: Vie matérielle et comportements biologiques," *Annales: économies, sociétés, civilisations,* (Jan.–Feb., 1963), pp. 133–38.*

"The Cambridge Economic History: The Medieval Period," *Journal of Economic History,* XXIII, 215–23.

"Sull'ammontare del 'Monte Vecchio' di Venezia," in G. Luzzatto, *Il Debito Pubblico della Republica di Venezia* (Milan: Cisalpino), 275–92.*

"Recent Studies on the Economic History of Venice," *Journal of Economic History,* XXIII, 312–34.

Review of R. Cessi and P. Sambin, eds., *Le deliberazioni del Consiglio dei Rogati (Senato), Serie "Mixtorum."* Vol. I: Libri I–XIV, a cura di R. Cessi and R. Sambin. Vol. II: Libri XV–XVI, a cura di R. Cessi e M. Brunetti. (Monumenti Storici pubblicati della Deputazione di Storia Patria per le Venezie, n.s. xv–xvi.) Venice: A spese della Deputazione, 1960, 1961. *Speculum,* XXXVIII, 121–23.

Review of *The Ancient Mariners: Seafarers and Sea Fighters of the Mediterranean in Ancient Times,* by Lionel Casson; *Oared Fighting Ships from Classical Times to the Coming of Steam,* by R. C. Anderson, *American Journal of Philology,* LXXXIV, 309–12.

1964

"Investment and Usury in Medieval Venice," *Explorations in Entrepreneurial History,* Second Series, II, 3–15.*

"Tonnages, Medieval and Modern," *Economic History Review,* XVII, 213–33.*

Discussion of "Market Expansion: The Case of Genoa," by Robert S. Lopez, *Journal of Economic History,* XXIV, 465–67.

Review of *Gênes au XVe Siècle: Activité économique et problems sociaux,* by Jacques Heers, *Speculum,* XXXIX, 146–50.

Review of *The Rise and Decline of the Medici Bank, 1397–1494,* by Raymond de Roover, *American Historical Review,* LXIX, 732–34.

Review of *Marino Faliero. Avanti il Dogado-La Congiura. Appendici,* by Vittorio Lazzarini, *Speculum,* XXXIX, 547–48.

1965

"Menschliche Geschichte und Naturgeschichte," in *Historica: Studien zum Geschichtlichen Denken und Forschen.* Hugo Hantsch, Eric Voegelin, and Franco Valsecchi, eds. (Vienna, Herder), 19–35.*

"Gino Luzzatto's contributions to the history of Venice: an appraisal and a tribute," *Nuova Rivista Storica,* XLIX, 49–80.

Navires et Constructeurs à Venise pendant la Renaissance. École Pratique des Hautes Études—VIᵉ Section, Centre de Recherches Historiques. Oeuvres Étrangeres, V. Paris, S.E.V.P.E.N.

"Unter den neuen Perspektiven," *Die Presse,* No. 5210, Samstag-sonntag, August 28–29, Vienna.*

1966

"At the Roots of Republicanism," *American Historical Review,* LXXI (January, 1966).*

"Medieval Political Ideas and the Venetian Constitution," *Venice and History: Collected Papers of Frederic C. Lane.* Baltimore: The Johns Hopkins Press.*

Index

(Index of special terms and topics, and of Venetians named)

A

Accounting: balancing of accounts, 101, 103, 107; capital, 39*n;* double entry, 107, 521, 522*n;* exchange bought and sold, 103; expense accounts, 103–5 and *n;* Florentine, 53, 54, 99, 100, 103, 104, 107, 117; galley accounts, 47*n,* 48*n,* 103; Genoese, 107; goods in process, 106; goods in stock, 106–7; inventory, 40, 104, 107; journals, 39, 47, 275; ledgers, 39, 99, 103, 104, 106, 107, 123, 275; merchandise, 99–105, 113–115, 122*n;* of agents, 100–6; of the Tana, 275; of traveling merchants, 58–59; Ragusan, 103, 106; sales accounts, 99, 103; venture accounts, 99–106, 108, 117, 122*n;* Venetian method of, 107–8; wage accounts, 99, 103
Admirals of fleets, 202, 208, 215*n,* 216
Admiral of the Venetian Arsenal, 165, 198, 280
Advocatores communis, 219, 241, 293
Aggiunte: to anchorage tax, 154*n,* 155, 158, 162
Agostini, Matteo, 71, 72*n,* 73, 76, 77, 80
Amphore, 352
Anchorage tax, 9, 150–62
Anfora, 264*n*
Anschauliche Theorie, 460, 471, 472, 474, 476, 479, 482, 487
Apostis, 175
Arbiters, 241
Arimondo, Andrea, 71, 73, 83, 84
Armentur per Comune, 197, 203, 204, 216, 235*n; per divisum,* 197, 202, 214, 216, 235*n*
Arming of ships. *See* Artillery; Crews; meaning of, *see Armentur, disarmate*

Arms, 5*n,* 33, 62, 234, 244, 245, 250, 256, 257, 349, 366, 370
Arsenal, 8, 46, 154*n,* 155, 156, 159, 197, 224, 249
Artillery, 4–5, 16, 19, 172
Asta da prova, 182, 185
Asta de pupa, 176, 178, 182
Auctions: of anchorage tax, 153–56, 159–60; of charter contracts, 52, 194, 199; of galleys, 7*n,* 16, 45–46, 197, 198, 213, 214, 223, 224, 226, 249–50, 249*n*
Austrian school, 464, 466, 476

B

Bachalari, 178
Badoer, Jacomo, 104
Badoer, Marino, duke of Crete, 1313–15, 299
Balador, 185
Balbi, Francesco and Bernardo: bank of, 121, 125, 126
Bales: size of, 259–60
Ballast, 239, 257, 261
Banda, 173, 174, 175 and *n,* 177, 235*n*
Bank money, 81–86, 123; checks, 85
Banks: Florentine, 93; Venetian, 44*n,* 60, 62, 65, 69–86, 100–102, 121, 124, 126, 221, 237
Banzonus, 215*n,* 233, 234*n*
Barbarigo, Alvise, 105, 106
Barbarigo, Andrea: account books, 104, 106, 107; commercial affairs, 118–26; cotton trade, 116
Barbarigo, Daniele, 28*n*
Barbarigo, Nicolò, 105, 106, 259; cotton trade account, 113, 114
Barbo, Francisco, 210*n*
Barbo, Marco, 206, 207

VENICE AND HISTORY:
THE COLLECTED PAPERS OF FREDERIC C. LANE

edited by A Committee of Colleagues and Former Students

designer:	Edward D. King
typesetter:	Kingsport Press, Inc.
typefaces:	Deepdene, Baskerville
printer:	Kingsport Press, Inc.
paper:	Warren's 1854 Medium
binder:	Kingsport Press, Inc.
cover material:	Columbia Riverside Linen